50 ... lonely ... OF T...

CARIBBEAN ISLANDS

Bermuda p662

The Bahamas p126

Cuba p214

Turks & Caicos p616

Cayman Islands p197

Jamaica p382

Haiti p361

Dominican Republic p276

Puerto Rico p452

See Enlargement

British Virgin Islands p172

St-Martin/ Sint Maarten p545

Anguilla p57

US Virgin Islands p641

St Kitts & Nevis p501

Antigua & Barbuda p72

Guadeloupe p338

The ABC Islands p95

Dominica p255

Martinique p431

St Lucia p518

St Vincent & the Grenadines p564

Grenada p323

Barbados p153

Trinidad & Tobago p587

Alex Egerton, Ray Bartlett, Tenille Clarke, Bailey Freeman, John Garry, Jackie Gutierrez-Jones, Anna Kaminski, Mirva Lempiainen, Noelle Nicolls, Kira Paulemon, Joe Sills, Nasha Smith, Mara Vorhees, Wendy Yanagihara

CONTENTS

Plan Your Trip

The Journey Begins Here....4
Caribbean Islands Map....8
Our Picks....10
Islands at a Glance....28
Itineraries....34
When to Go....42
Get Prepared....44
The Food Scene....46
The Outdoors....50

The Guide

Anguilla....57
The Valley....62
West End Village....68

Antigua & Barbuda....72
English Harbour....78
Eastern Antigua....85
Codrington....89

The ABC Islands....95
Aruba....100
Bonaire....108
Curaçao....116

The Bahamas....126
Northern Bahamas....132
Central Bahamas....138
Southern Bahamas....147

Barbados....153
Bridgetown & the South Coast....158
The West Coast....164
The Atlantic Coast....169

British Virgin Islands....172
Tortola....178
Virgin Gorda....183
Anegada....188
Jost Van Dyke....192

Cayman Islands....197
Grand Cayman....202
Cayman Brac....206
Little Cayman....209

Cuba....214
Havana....220
Viñales....226
Trinidad....232
Cayo Guillermo....237
Santa Clara....242
Santiago de Cuba....247

Dominica....255
Roseau....260
Northeastern Coast....265
Morne Trois Pitons National Park....269
Soufrière Bay....271
Portsmouth....273

Dominican Republic....276
Santo Domingo....282
Southwest Coast....289
Jarabacoa....294
North Coast....301
Peninsula de Samaná....307
Punta Cana....314

Oranjestad (p102)

Fort-de-France (p436)

Grenada....323
Grenada Island....328
Carriacou....334

Guadeloupe....338
Basse-Terre....344
Grande-Terre....349
Offshore Islands....354

Haiti....361
Jacmel....366
Cap-Haïtien....376

Jamaica....382
Kingston....388
Treasure Beach....397
Negril....404
Montego Bay....411
Ocho Rios....417
Port Antonio....422

Martinique....431
Fort-de-France....436
Northern Martinique....443
Southern Martinique....447

Puerto Rico....452
San Juan....458
Río Grande....465
Vieques....470
Ponce....476
Jayuya....484
Utuado....488
Rincón....493

St Kitts & Nevis 501
- Basseterre & Frigate Bay 506
- Charlestown 512

St Lucia 518
- Soufrière 524
- Castries 530
- Rodney Bay 534
- South Coast 539

St-Martin & Sint Maarten 545
- Philipsburg 550
- Grand Case 555

St Vincent & the Grenadines 564
- St Vincent 570
- Bequia 576
- Mayreau & Tobago Cays 579
- Union Island 581

Trinidad & Tobago 587
- Central & South Trinidad 592
- Port of Spain 597
- Northeast Coast 601
- Crown Point 605
- Castara 610

Turks & Caicos Islands 616
- Providenciales 622
- Twin Islands 629
- Grand Turk 635

US Virgin Islands 641
- St Croix 646
- St John 651
- St Thomas 655

Bermuda 662
- Hamilton & Central Bermuda 668
- St George's & East End 673
- South Shore & West End 676

Wild pig, the Exumas (p148)

Toolkit

Accommodations 684
Family Travel 685
Health & Safe Travel 686
How to Travel during Hurricane Season 687
Food, Drink & Nightlife 688
Responsible Travel 690
LGBTIQ+ Travelers 692
Accessible Travel 693
How to Dive in the Caribbean 694
Nuts & Bolts 695

Storybook

A History of the Caribbean Islands in 15 Places 698
Music: Pride & Purpose 702
Sustainability in the Caribbean 704
Saltwater Bliss: the Caribbean's Best Beaches 706
Caribbean Wildlife 710
Spend Wisely, Travel Fully 712

Tobago Cays (p579)

CARIBBEAN ISLANDS

THE JOURNEY BEGINS HERE

Like many visitors to the Caribbean, I was first lured here by the promise of sunshine, white sands and brilliant blue waters full of marine life. And on my initial trips through the Greater Antilles and the Windward Islands, I did indeed find paradisiacal beaches unlike any I had seen before.

But having arrived home and washed the sand out of my backpack, it wasn't the images of seaside utopia that fueled the irresistible urge to return but rather the fascinating cultures of the islands, each markedly different but sharing an infectious easygoing approach to life.

The longer I spend away, the stronger the pull of the region's music, spice-filled Creole cuisine and the engrossing stories of its larger-than-life residents. The only way to scratch the itch is to set off island-hopping once again.

Alex Egerton

@alexetravel

Alex is a journalist based in central Colombia writing about travel, culture and history in Latin America and the Caribbean.

My favourite experience is skipping across the glowing waters of the southern Grenadines in a tiny boat to swim among sea turtles in the Tobago Cays Marine Park (p580).

WHO GOES WHERE

Our writers and experts choose the places which, for them, define the Caribbean Islands.

FROM LEFT: WIRESTOCK CREATORS/SHUTTERSTOCK ©, CHRISTINE NORTON PHOTO/SHUTTERSTOCK ©, DAMSEA/SHUTTERSTOCK ©

I could keep returning to **Cuba** (p214) for decades and still have more to explore. My best moments are always the unexpected ones: getting help from random strangers when my car wouldn't start or chatting for hours with a new friend I've met on a corner somewhere.

Ray Bartlett

@kaisoradotcom; kaisora.com

Ray is an acclaimed travel writer, photographer and novelist.

With a sprawling 250 acres of greenery, the historical **Queen's Park Savannah** (p598) is a cultural amalgamation of the very best that Trinidad and Tobago has to offer.

Tenille Clarke

Instagram @tenilleclarke1

Tenille is an avid diaspora story-teller from Trinidad and Tobago who covers global topics in travel, culture, entertainment and business through a Caribbean lens.

The underwater marvels surrounding **Bermuda** (p662) and the **ABC Islands** (p95) remind us all how spectacularly beautiful our planet is – protecting this treasure is of the highest importance.

Bailey Freeman

Instagram @the_traveling_b

Bailey is a travel and culture writer who loves learning from the world and all the people in it. When she's not on the road, she works as an aerial acrobat (really!).

LEFT: CAVAN IMAGES/GETTY IMAGES © RIGHT: MATYAS REHAK/SHUTTERSTOCK ©

Cañón Blanco (p490), located in Utuado, delivers a bit of everything: secret swimming holes, mountain views and, if you know where to look, Taíno petroglyphs. It's the best of karst country rolled into one destination.

John Garry

Instagram @garryjohnfrancis

John is a writer and teacher based in Brooklyn, New York.

Coming from the sun-drenched arid coasts, **Jarabacoa** (p294) was like a cool drink of water, and a pure joy to explore on horseback, through hiking trails or floating down a river.

Jackie Gutierrez-Jones

Instagram @jaxwriteswords

Jackie is a Cuban-American writer and editor living in Nashville who covers travel, food and drink for various lifestyle publications.

Little Cayman (p209) is infinitely appealing. It's pretty quiet, since most visitors are scuba divers like myself – early to bed, early to rise. It's also not a place where you can remain anonymous for long, since some of the 135 residents will want to trade life stories with you at the island's three hangouts. At night, when you're walking back to your lodgings, the stars overhead are the brightest you'll ever see.

Anna Kaminski

Twitter @ACkaminski

Anna is a travel writer who has lived in Jamaica and Puerto Rico, majored in the history of the Caribbean, and who specialized in adventure travel.

I'm partial to tropical beaches like those in The **Bahamas** (p126) and the **Turks and Caicos Islands** (p616). It's the simplicity and absolute beauty of their shared natural landscapes, beneath and above the water, that evokes a profound sense of peace, awe and serenity whenever I unplug from everyday concerns and connect with the natural world.

Noelle Nicolls

Instagram @thedomestictourist

Noelle, a Bahamian writer, human rights activist and globetrotter, finds utmost joy in being a domestic tourist, island-hopping through her native country. She owns a squash and social club in Nassau.

Guadeloupe (p338) is one of the most diverse destinations in the Lesser Antilles, being an archipelago of six inhabited islands that are geographically all very different from each other. Since it's a French overseas department, the infrastructure here is pretty much up to par with the European Union. That makes 'Gwada' an exceptionally good choice for families and those considering a longer stay in the Caribbean.

Mirva Lempiäinen

Instagram @guadeloupeguide

Mirva is a globetrotting Finnish travel writer living in the Caribbean.

Haiti (p361) offers a level of peace and perspective, unique to its people, food, customs and sounds. Even in the face of recurring crises, its hospitality and lightheartedness coupled with an impressive history will leave you yearning for more time on the island. Bring your sense of adventure, as unlike in most other countries, things aren't always done 'by the book' (or by Google!) over here.

Kira Paulemon

Kira is a Haitian humanitarian worker who loves to write about Haiti when given the opportunity. She especially tries to highlight the ongoing crisis in Haiti while showcasing its beauty and humanity.

'Steve Howes is Josiah's Bay.' I heard those words at **Nigel's Boom Boom Beach Bar** (p179). Howes built his surf school on a spit of sand beside a Tortola surf break only to see it all blown away by hurricanes a year later. Then, he did what many non-islanders didn't do after the storms – he stayed. Surf School BVI welcomes all people, so long as they bring good vibes. To me, that feels like the welcoming spirit of the BVIs more than anywhere else I found.

Joe Sills

Instagram/Twitter @joesills

Joe is a travel writer, photographer and host of the award-winning adventure show, The Get Lost Podcast.

When flying into St Lucia, I prefer to sit on the plane's left side to watch the iconic Pitons descend into view. **Soufrière** (p524) is breathtakingly beautiful, and its peaks are only a sliver of the town's many natural attractions. Healing mud baths and restorative hot springs await at the Sulphur Springs, a Têt Paul hike is steps away from heaven, and unwinding on Sugar Beach's powdery sand unveils yet another vantage point of the skyline-dominating peaks.

Nasha Smith

Twitter @nashasmith Instagram @naturallynasha

Nasha is a travel, food and sports writer from St Lucia who advocates for Caribbean travel and study abroad.

Surrounded by a posh resort on one of the Caribbean's most exclusive islands, you wouldn't expect to see the ramshackle **Dune Preserve** (p70). Bankie Banx' legendary music club, built out of driftwood and recycled boats, welcomes all comers to get their groove on, against a beguiling backdrop of sea and sky. Here is the true appeal of Anguilla – not its exclusivity, but rather, its rich culture, spectacular nature and warm welcome that are free for all.

Mara Vorhees

havetwinswilltravel.com

Mara is a travel writer and coauthor of the narrative nonfiction book, The Tsarina's Lost Treasure.

Barbuda's northeast coast (p92) remains one of those wild places that spark wonder, from its shell-pink beaches to its mangroves and wheeling frigate birds. Hike the arid trail to a sinkhole cave where you'll look down at the tops of the palm trees within. Then climb down, watching hermit crabs trundle off your path, into the cool shade of a completely incongruous oasis.

Wendy Yanagihara

Instagram @wendyyanagihara

Wendy is a writer and artist who has contributed to more than 50 Lonely Planet guidebooks since 2003.

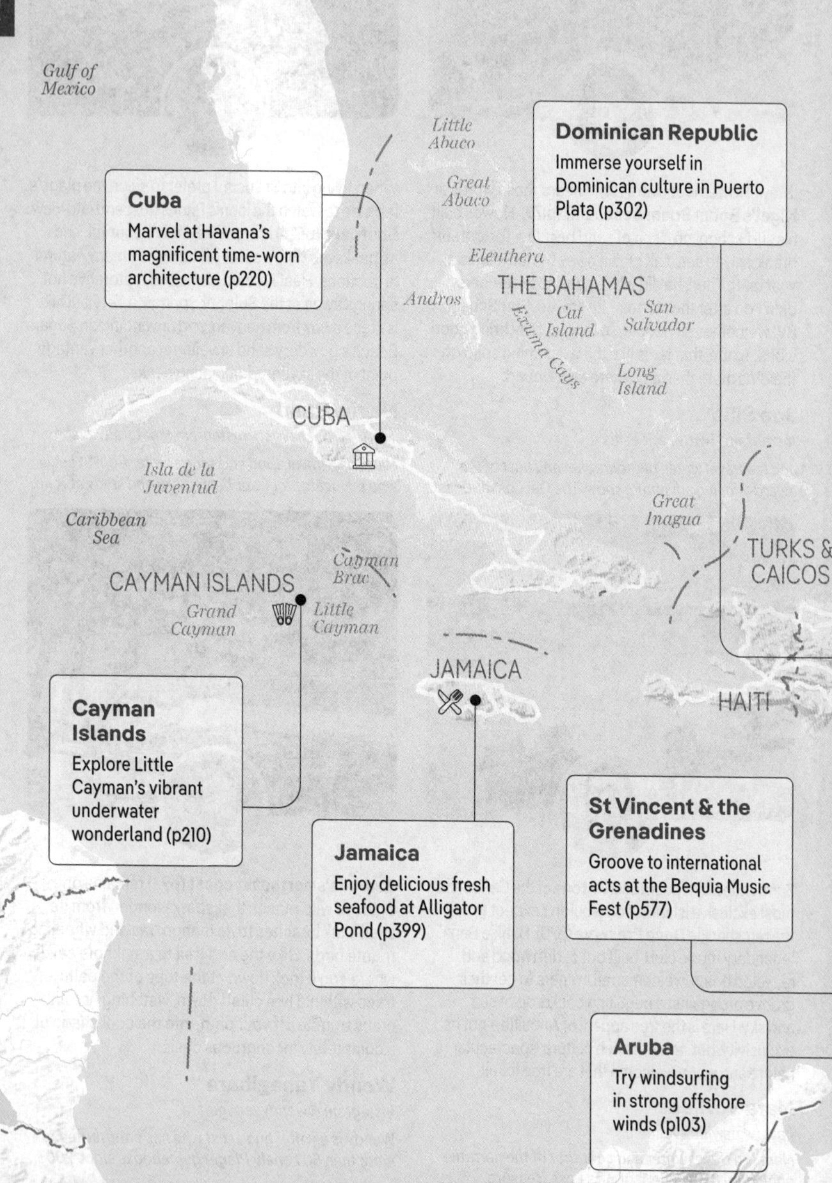

Cuba
Marvel at Havana's magnificent time-worn architecture (p220)

Dominican Republic
Immerse yourself in Dominican culture in Puerto Plata (p302)

Cayman Islands
Explore Little Cayman's vibrant underwater wonderland (p210)

Jamaica
Enjoy delicious fresh seafood at Alligator Pond (p399)

St Vincent & the Grenadines
Groove to international acts at the Bequia Music Fest (p577)

Aruba
Try windsurfing in strong offshore winds (p103)

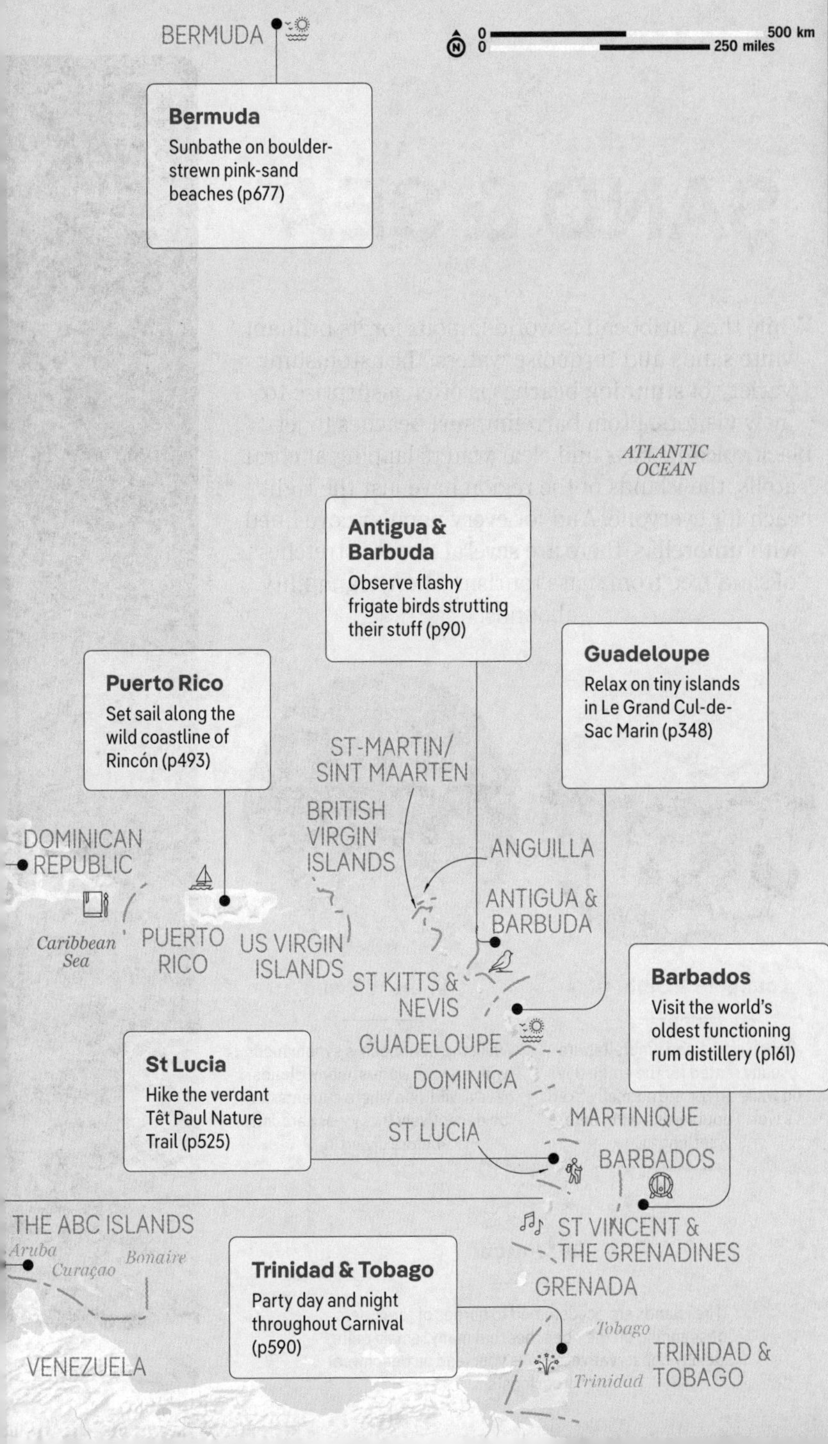

BERMUDA
0 500 km
0 250 miles
N
Bermuda
Sunbathe on boulder-strewn pink-sand beaches (p677)
ATLANTIC OCEAN
Antigua & Barbuda
Observe flashy frigate birds strutting their stuff (p90)
Guadeloupe
Relax on tiny islands in Le Grand Cul-de-Sac Marin (p348)
Puerto Rico
Set sail along the wild coastline of Rincón (p493)
ST-MARTIN/ SINT MAARTEN
BRITISH VIRGIN ISLANDS
ANGUILLA
DOMINICAN REPUBLIC
ANTIGUA & BARBUDA
Caribbean Sea
PUERTO RICO
US VIRGIN ISLANDS
ST KITTS & NEVIS
Barbados
Visit the world's oldest functioning rum distillery (p161)
GUADELOUPE
DOMINICA
St Lucia
Hike the verdant Têt Paul Nature Trail (p525)
MARTINIQUE
ST LUCIA
BARBADOS
THE ABC ISLANDS
Aruba
Curaçao
Bonaire
ST VINCENT & THE GRENADINES
Trinidad & Tobago
Party day and night throughout Carnival (p590)
GRENADA
Tobago
TRINIDAD & TOBAGO
Trinidad
VENEZUELA

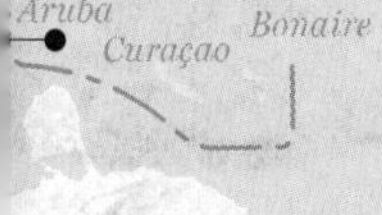

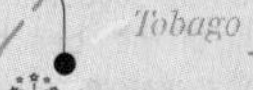

SAND & SEA

While the Caribbean is world-famous for its brilliant white sands and turquoise waters, the astonishing variety of stunning beaches is often a surprise to new visitors. From barreling surf beaches to jet-black volcanic bays and clear waters lapping at coral atolls, the islands of the region have just the right beach for everyone. And for every popular cove lined with umbrellas, there are several remote stretches of sand free from mass tourism where tranquility abounds.

Loungers & Umbrellas

Beach chairs and umbrellas are usually rented for the entire day and while prices are normally fixed, it's worth double-checking before settling in.

Where to Swim

While the Caribbean is synonymous with tranquil waters, many islands have a wild side where currents can be deceptively tricky – ask around before diving in.

Beachwear

The islands are accustomed to hordes of foreigners descending on their beaches, but many remain quite socially conservative, so take your lead on beachwear from locals.

FROM LEFT: SEAN ASHFORD/SHUTTERSTOCK ©, TRAVELLING JACK/SHUTTERSTOCK ©, SEAN ASHFORD/SHUTTERSTOCK ©

Horsehoe Bay, Bermuda (p677)

BEST BEACH EXPERIENCES

Soak up the sun, sip rum drinks and dance away the afternoon on gorgeous ❶ **Shoal Bay East** in Anguilla. (p66)

Bare it all for an even tan on the clothing-optional beaches of ❷ **St-Martin**. (p561)

Stake your claim to a swathe of soft white sand all for yourself on uncrowded ❸ **Brownes Beach** in Barbados. (p160)

Wade into the glowing turquoise waters in front of breathtaking boulder-strewn pink beaches in ❹ **Bermuda**. (p677)

Hit the sugar-white sands of Jamaica's ❺ **Seven Mile Beach** for water sports during the day and live music at night. (p406)

Carnival, Kralendijk (p109)

PARTY TIME

Booming bass shakes the ground as colorful feathers fly through the air and glistening oil-covered limbs move together in one rhythmical mass. Carnival in the Caribbean is the most intense expression of the vibrant culture, history and joie de vivre of the region. Choose from enormous capital-city events or more intimate small-island bashes.

Catchy Tunes

The soundtrack to the biggest Carnivals in the region includes lively soca and zouk music, with artists releasing their best new songs in the lead-up to the events.

Taking Part

Many Caribbean Carnivals are more than spectator events, with visitors able to take part in parades – contact local dance groups well in advance to sign up.

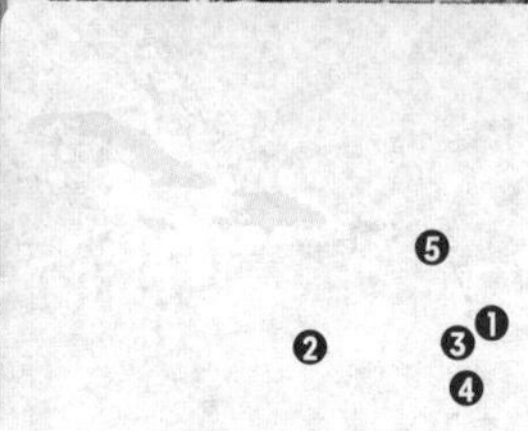

BEST CARNIVAL EXPERIENCES

Join a band, don the uniform and dance your way through Bridgetown, Barbados, at the end of ❶ **Crop Over**. (p163)

Hit three Carnivals in quick succession in ❷ **Aruba**, **Bonaire** and **Curaçao**. (p140)

Watch costumed men trade Shakespearean quotes during the wonderfully wacky ❸ **Carriacou Carnival** in Grenada. (p336)

Dance for days on end at ❹ **Trinidad Carnival**, the region's loudest and most colorful celebration. (p590)

Down delicious rum cocktails while watching the parades at ❺ **Sugar Mas** on St Kitts. (p505)

SENSATIONAL STRUCTURES

From the colorful facades of Curaçao to the baroque residences of Habana Vieja, the architecture of the Caribbean is the result of a medley of influences being tailored to challenging local conditions. Whether exploring tunnels beneath old forts or climbing a stone windmill for a panoramic view, the region's buildings are a window onto its fascinating history.

Colorful Cottages

Trinidad and Tobago and Barbados are located outside the storm belt and retain many traditional wooden homes that were once commonplace across the Caribbean.

Popular Plazas

One feature that sets Latin American nations in the Caribbean apart from their neighbors is the presence of ornate town squares that are at the center of daily life.

Muscular Monuments

The hilltop forts of the Caribbean were once overcrowded and unsanitary dumps but these days are some of the most tranquil places with stunning views.

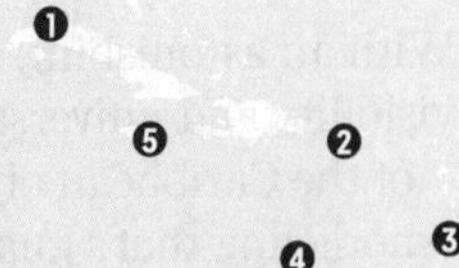

BEST ARCHITECTURE EXPERIENCES

Gaze at the handsome, time-worn facades lining the streets of ❶ **Habana Vieja**. (p221)

Stroll around Ponce's ❷ **Plaza Las Delicias** to observe the fine neoclassical mansions, baroque beauties and striking Moorish former fire station. (p478)

Hike up to ❸ **Fort Charlotte** for expansive views from behind rusted cannons over Kingstown and to the northern Grenadines. (p572)

Take a guided walking tour of historic ❹ **Willemstad** to check out nearly 800 historical monuments in Curaçao's capital. (p118)

Roam around ❺ **Fort Charles**, the British fortification that survived the mighty earthquake which destroyed Jamaica's Port Royal. (p396)

UNDERWATER ADVENTURES

With an astonishing range of marine sites, superb visibility and universally warm waters, the islands of the Caribbean offer phenomenal diving and snorkeling that's guaranteed to thrill novice and experienced underwater enthusiasts alike. From shallow shore reefs to wall dives, coral-encrusted wrecks and underwater art galleries, there's so much to see that many visitors spend a big chunk of their vacation underwater with an amazing array of marine life for company.

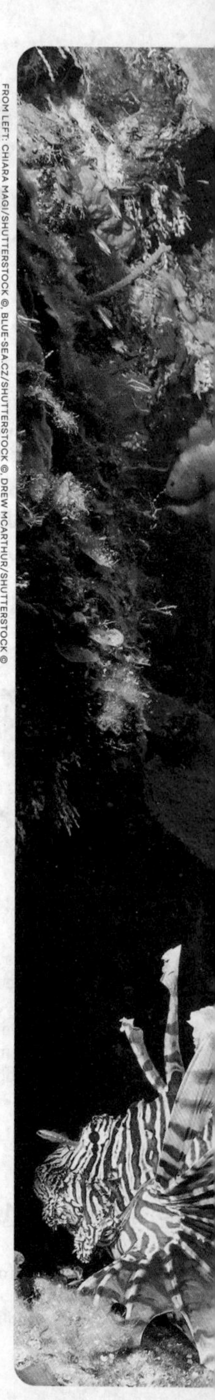

FROM LEFT: CHIARA MAGI/SHUTTERSTOCK ©, BLUE-SEA.CZ/SHUTTERSTOCK ©, DREW MCARTHUR/SHUTTERSTOCK ©

Off-Peak Immersions

When cruise ships are in dock, many snorkeling sites can get busy; try to visit early in the morning or in the evening to beat the crowds.

A Captivating Cast

The waters of the Caribbean are awash with marine life, including a staggering variety of colorful tropical fish and many species of shark, stingray and sea turtle.

Bring Your Own

Bringing your own snorkel and mask not only saves on rental fees – it means you can be sure of a good fit, maximizing time in the water.

Lionfish, Bloody Bay (p210)

BEST DIVING & SNORKELING EXPERIENCES

Marvel at sunken figures covered with coral at Molinere Bay's Underwater ❶ **Sculpture Park** off the coast of Grenada. (p332)

Explore half a dozen shipwrecks that were purposefully sunk in the waters around ❷ **Anguilla**. (p67)

Descend to ❸ **The Wall** near La Parguera in Puerto Rico where triggerfish and turtles swim through a coral forest. (p481)

Snorkel through the clearest waters in the Eastern Caribbean at the ❹ **Tobago Cays Marine Park** in St Vincent and the Grenadines. (p580)

Discover Little Cayman's extraordinary underwater topography at ❺ **Bloody Bay**, where walls plummet into the blue abyss. (p210)

Steel pans, Trinidad & Tobago (p587)

INFECTIOUS RHYTHMS

Music is as synonymous with the Caribbean as white sand and coconut palms, with many of the world's most loved genres emerging from the cultural melting pots on these islands. Every itinerary through the region comes with its unique soundtrack, as heard in taxis, beach bars, dancehalls, block parties and barbecues, that will echo long after you've returned home.

Cradle of Latin Beats

Many types of music popular throughout the Latin world have their roots in the Antilles, with merengue, bachata, reggaeton and the precursors of salsa all originating here.

Recycled Melodies

The Caribbean's most distinctive musical instrument is the steel pan, which hails from Trinidad and is made from the bottom of a 55-gallon oil drum.

BEST MUSIC EXPERIENCES

Jam with reggae legend Bankie Banx at the ❶ **Dune Preserve** bar or at his annual Moonsplash festival in Anguilla. (p70)

Join Fèt a Kabrit in ❷ **La Désirade**, Guadeloupe, where the tunes are hot and the goats are well dressed. (p358)

Groove to blues, jazz and more at the ❸ **Bequia Music Fest** in the Grenadines, where artists from around the globe play intimate concerts. (p577)

Hear traditional Caribbean folk music at the lively ❹ **Maroon and String Band Festival** in Carriacou, Grenada. (p327)

See dozens of reggae and dancehall stars at ❺ **Reggae Sumfest** in Jamaica's Montego Bay. (p412)

AN ISLAND TIPPLE

Since the first drops were distilled in Barbados in the 17th century, rum has held onto its place as the undisputed drink of choice across the region. Long maligned as the unsophisticated beverage of scurvy pirates and the working class, the spirit is finally getting some overdue love with boutique distilleries and gourmet pairings.

Rhum Agricole

Most rum is made from molasses but *rhum agricole*, produced throughout the French Caribbean, is distilled from fresh sugarcane, giving it a bright, grassy flavor.

Savor the Flavor

While sugary rum punch and fruity cocktails are a huge hit among travelers, locals in many Caribbean nations prefer their rum neat or on the rocks.

Off the Scale

Some island distilleries produce potent overproof rums with up to 80% alcohol, but be aware that anything over 70% can't be taken aboard your flight home.

BEST RUM EXPERIENCES

Watch rum be made the age-old way at the charming ❶ **River Antoine Rum Distillery** in rural Grenada. (p331)

Tour the oldest working rum distillery in the world at ❷ **Mount Gay Rum Distillery** in Barbados. (p161)

Explore the facility, taste the rum and bottle your own at ❸ **Topper's Rhum Distillery** in Sint Maarten. (p553)

Order a rum swizzle – Bermuda's national drink – at the famous ❹ **Swizzle Inn**, the country's oldest pub. (p674)

Follow the journey from fresh cane to rum barrels at ❺ **Appleton Estate**, Jamaica's oldest rum distillery. (p402)

DOWNTOWN DISCOVERY

Break away from the beach and walk narrow cobblestone alleyways that have barely changed for centuries, or take on bustling metropolitan marketplaces stacked to the rafters with a rainbow of fresh produce in towns and cities across the Caribbean Islands. Far from sanitized resort life, the urban centers of the region are not all stunners, but they're universally fascinating. Meet the locals, try typical grub and get to know another side of island life.

FROM LEFT: JASON WELLS/SHUTTERSTOCK ©, TUPUNGATO/SHUTTERSTOCK ©, DARRYL BROOKS/SHUTTERSTOCK ©

Big City, Low Budget

The larger cities in the Caribbean offer surprisingly good value to travelers, with a range of accommodations and economic street food.

Leave the Car

Narrow hilly roads, unmarked one-way streets and a distinct lack of parking mean the best way to explore many Caribbean urban centers is on foot.

Delve into the Interior

From Cuba to Trinidad, many of the region's most charming villages are found in agricultural heartlands spared from the coastal development boom.

Basseterre (p506)

4
5
2
3
1

BEST URBAN EXPERIENCES

Take in the massive murals that cover the walls of ❶ **San Nicolas**, Aruba's former refinery town turned culture hub. (p106)

Discover the historic sights and contemporary life of bustling ❷ **Basseterre**, the capital of St Kitts. (p507)

Snap envy-inducing vacation pictures in the colorful narrow streets of ❸ **Deshaies**, Guadeloupe's most enchanting village. (p348)

Wander through the timeless pastel-painted streets of Cuba's ❹ **Trinidad**, stopping for a drink in one of the lively plazas. (p232)

Immerse yourself in the Dominican Republic's history and culture in the ultra-colorful town of ❺ **Puerto Plata**. (p302)

Mayreau (p579)

CRUISING THE COAST

Looking in on a tropical island from the sea gives a whole new perspective on a destination, with every island seen at its best from a comfy deck with a cocktail in your hand. Sailing cruises give visitors access to hidden bays, but top snorkeling spots are often more about the ride than the sightseeing stops.

A Floating Feast

Most sightseeing cruises include a meal on deck, snacks and beverages; watch out for the rum punch, which can have quite a kick when quaffed in the sun.

Size Matters

Boats used for sailing trips vary greatly even within a country; small monohulls are usually more intimate while large catamarans often give a smoother ride.

BEST SAILING EXPERIENCES

Cruise the magical west coast of ❶ **Barbados**, stopping to snorkel with turtles and explore sunken wrecks. (p165)

Board a handsome old schooner and sail to ❷ **Mustique**, the ultra-exclusive private retreat of the rich and famous in the Grenadines. (p578)

Help hoist one of the seven hefty sails to propel a 137ft schooner through the waters off ❸ **Christiansted**. (p648)

Drop anchor off ❹ **Mayreau** in the Grenadines and swap tales with fellow mariners over rum cocktails beneath the coconut palms. (p579)

Sail the wild coastline of ❺ **Rincón** in Puerto Rico to get up close to sea birds and magnificent marine animals. (p493)

INCREDIBLE CREATURES

While the most high-profile wildlife-watching in the Caribbean goes on beneath the waves, the islands are also home to some fascinating fauna. The rainforest-covered volcanic islands are particularly fruitful terrain for spotting rare birds, monkeys and other small mammals, but even on more developed islands there are curious endemic species to delight nature aficionados.

Stowaway Monkeys

The mischievous monkeys that can be seen on many islands are not native to the Caribbean but were introduced from Africa early in the colonial era.

Precious Parrots

The rainforest-clad Windward Islands of Dominica, St Lucia and St Vincent are home to four beautifully plumed endemic parrot species that are critically endangered.

Nesting Turtles

You don't need to get wet for close encounters with sea turtles – green, hawksbill and leatherback turtles all lay their eggs on beaches across the region.

BEST WILDLIFE EXPERIENCES

Peek at showy frigate birds strutting their stuff during mating season in the mangroves of Barbuda's ❶ **Codrington Lagoon**. (p90)

Try to spot the rare St Vincent parrot on a hike into the rainforest-filled interior of the island along the ❷ **Vermont Nature Trail**. (p574)

Watch magnificent sea turtles come ashore to lay their eggs at remote ❸ **Levera Beach** in northern Grenada. (p331)

Take a boat tour from ❹ **Black River** into Jamaica's biggest wetlands to spot American crocodiles and a wealth of birdlife. (p403)

Admire the brilliant plumage of scores of Caribbean flamingos from the ❺ **Flamingo Pond Lookout** on Anegada. (p189)

INTO THE WILD

While it may surprise those who have never visited, the Caribbean is a wonderful hiking destination, with a multitude of adventurous treks through diverse landscapes that afford spectacular views and close encounters with nature. Many islands have towering volcanic peaks shrouded in mist where temperatures are refreshingly cool and the foliage is lush, while coastal walks around secluded bays and across cliff-tops can be followed with a celebratory dip in refreshing aquamarine waters.

FROM LEFT: FOKKE BAARSSEN/SHUTTERSTOCK ©, DESIGN PICS INC/ALAMY ©, TOM MADGE-WYLD/GETTY IMAGES ©

Short & Sweet

Many of the best hikes in the region can be completed in one day, meaning you can get muddy without giving up the comfort of your resort bed.

Gonna Make You Sweat

While distances may be generally short, hiking near the equator can be extra tiring due to the high humidity which reaches boss levels during the wet season.

Local Insights

While many trails can be self-guided, it's well worth contracting a 'bushman' guide who can point out flora and fauna many outsiders would otherwise miss.

Waitukubuli National Trail (p272)

BEST HIKING EXPERIENCES

Scramble your way to the top of the menacing ❶ **La Soufrière Volcano** on St Vincent to reach the otherworldly crater. (p348)

Trek through lush landscapes with magnificent mountain views on the ❷ **Têt Paul Nature Trail** in St Lucia. (p525)

Test your endurance on the challenging ❸ **Waitukubuli National Trail** across Dominica, taking in Boiling Lake and Emerald Pool along the way. (p272)

Hike to the summit of ❹ **Pic Paradis** for sweeping views of St-Martin and beyond. (p560)

Take on the ❺ **Troy-Windsor Trail**, Jamaica's toughest day hike, which traverses an overgrown 17th-century military track. (p403)

Klein Curaçao (p120)

PINT-SIZED PARADISES

Even in this age of mass travel, in the Caribbean it's still possible to have an entire desert island for yourself – at least for a couple of hours. Numerous tiny offshore cays with requisite white-sand beaches and lonely swaying coconut palms dot the region and can be visited by water taxi or even by kayak.

Yacht Anchorages

Many small pristine islands are popular anchorages for cruising yachts but once storm season arrives, independent travelers have them to themselves.

Water-Taxi Pickups

Many water taxis will drop off and return at an agreed time rather than wait. Set a realistic return – time can pass very slowly in total isolation.

BEST TINY ISLAND EXPERIENCES

Make a day trip to ❶ **Klein Curaçao**, an uninhabited island with crystalline waters and lots of history to explore. (p120)

Hire a water taxi to reach postage-stamp-sized ❷ **Mopian** islet in the Grenadines, with its solitary thatched umbrella. (p584)

Paddle out to tropical beach perfection on ❸ **Sandy Island**, just offshore from Carriacou in Grenada. (p335)

Spend a day at one of ❹ **Anguilla's** diminutive offshore islands for a decadent lunch and utter relaxation. (p66)

Visit one of the pristine islets wihin ❺ **Le Grand Cul-de-Sac Marin**, a 15,000-hectare biosphere reserve in Guadeloupe. (p348)

ADVENTURE ON THE WATER

Adrenaline-pumping water sports are not only for the resort crowds – there are many excellent independent operators found on beaches across the region. Whether it's learning to kite-surf, finding your feet on a longboard or heading off on a kayak adventure, the Caribbean has an island where conditions are just perfect for your chosen pursuit.

Trade Winds

The best months to enjoy wind sports across much of the Caribbean are November to June, when the trade winds blow without pause across the region.

Surf's Up

While most imagine the Caribbean as an endless sea of perfectly still waters, the region actually has some epic waves that inspire even pro surfers.

Exclusive Rooms

Many surf and kite schools have houses and apartments for rent just steps from the action, which means learners get to spend more time in the water.

BEST WATER SPORTS EXPERIENCES

Test your mettle on the legendary ❶ **Soup Bowl**, Barbados' biggest and most powerful break. (p170)

Glide over the brilliant blue waters off ❷ **Union Island**, the southern Grenadines premier kitesurfing spot. (p584)

Take a wing-foiling lesson in front of the wild white sands of Antigua's ❸ **Jabberwock Beach**. (p88)

Try your hand at windsurfing on the strong winds offshore from ❹ **Aruba**. (p100)

Kayak to the stunning hidden cove of Anguilla's ❺ **Little Bay** to explore sea caves and try cliff jumping. (p64)

TASTE-BUD TINGLING

Reflecting the rich history of the region, Caribbean cuisine is incredibly diverse, yet there remain many commonalities across the islands. Whether indulging in a gourmet seafood meal or grabbing a snack at a roadside shack, the rich spice mixes and sensational sauces will get your taste buds tingling. And in recent times, a new generation of chefs have brought an innovative approach to traditional cooking, taking island cuisine to the next level.

Some Like it Hot

Hot sauce is standard on tables across the Caribbean and every island has its own particular recipe, but they're all fantastically fiery.

Farm Fresh

Weekend farmers markets and roadside stalls in the countryside are the best places to try locally grown fruit and vegetables while supporting the rural economy.

Seafood Festivals

Seasonal festivals dedicated to fish and other seafood can be found across the region and usually involve plenty of partying once the plates are cleared away.

FROM LEFT: BRANDON ROSENBLUM/GETTY IMAGES ©, MATYAS REHAK/SHUTTERSTOCK ©, ERIKA CRISTINA MANNO/SHUTTERSTOCK ©

Belmont Estate chocolate (p332)

BEST GOURMET EXPERIENCES

Follow the chocolate-making process from the cocoa plantation to the finished bar on the organic estates of ❶ **Grenada**. (p332)

Join world-renowned chefs on Grand Cayman for some stellar dining and drinking as part of the annual ❷ **Cayman Cookout**. (p200)

Feast on succulent slabs of slow-cooked spit-roasted pork along ❸ **La Ruta del Lechón** in Guavate, Puerto Rico. (p464)

Tuck into the freshest possible conch prepared every which way at the ❹ **Union Island Conch Festival** in the Grenadines. (p577)

Gorge yourself on jerk fish at ❺ **Alligator Pond**, a fishing village that has become Jamaica's top seafood destination. (p399)

ISLANDS AT A GLANCE

Find the places that tick all your boxes.

Greater Antilles

Incorporating the largest islands in the Caribbean, the nations of the Greater Antilles are the region's cultural powerhouses. From Jamaica to Cuba, Puerto Rico, Haiti and the Dominican Republic, these islands have put Caribbean music, food and arts on the world map; each is fascinating and spectacular in equal measure.

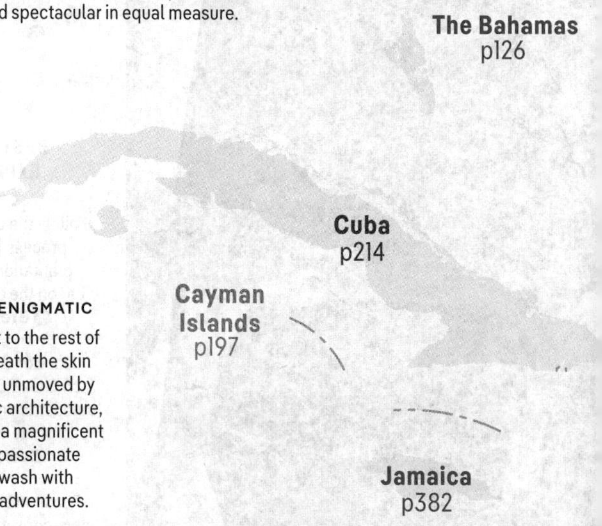

The Bahamas
p126

Cuba
p214

Cayman Islands
p197

Jamaica
p382

Cuba

BEAUTIFUL, HISTORIC, ENIGMATIC

Grooving to a different beat to the rest of the region, Cuba gets beneath the skin of travelers and leaves few unmoved by the experience. With classic architecture, evocative traditional music, a magnificent unspoiled coastline and passionate residents, each visit is awash with extraordinary, unscripted adventures.

p214

Jamaica

MUSIC, BEACHES, FOOD, CULTURE AND NATURE

Whether you're lying back on one of its spectacular beaches, dancing till dawn outside a Kingston bar, rafting down a jungle river or hiking through the mountains, in Jamaica your adventures will be fueled by delectable spice-infused traditional food and accompanied by the hippest soundtrack in the Caribbean.

p382

Bermuda
p662

Atlantic Islands

Technically not part of the Caribbean at all, but with stunning white sands and glowing waters that rival any of those found in the eponymous sea, the North Atlantic nations of Bermuda, The Bahamas, and Turks and Caicos epitomize the idyllic island getaway; they are paradise for beach bums and divers alike.

Dominican Republic

BREATHTAKING BEACHES, MOUNTAINS AND HERITAGE SITES

It's easy to get trapped by the charms of Santo Domingo, home to the Caribbean's largest and oldest colonial quarter and some of its best nightlife. But look beyond the capital to discover biodiverse national parks, adrenaline-pumping water sports, refreshing mountain hikes and stunning beaches throughout the country.

p276

Puerto Rico

NATURAL WONDERS, SLOW-ROASTED IN SUNSHINE

From the history-filled streets of San Juan to the sensual tropical rhythms, there's no doubting Puerto Rico's Latin credentials. But this is a quintessentially Caribbean country, too, with brilliant beaches, rainforest and pristine reefs. The gourmet trends and craft-beer scene reflect the island's position as a cultural crossroads.

p452

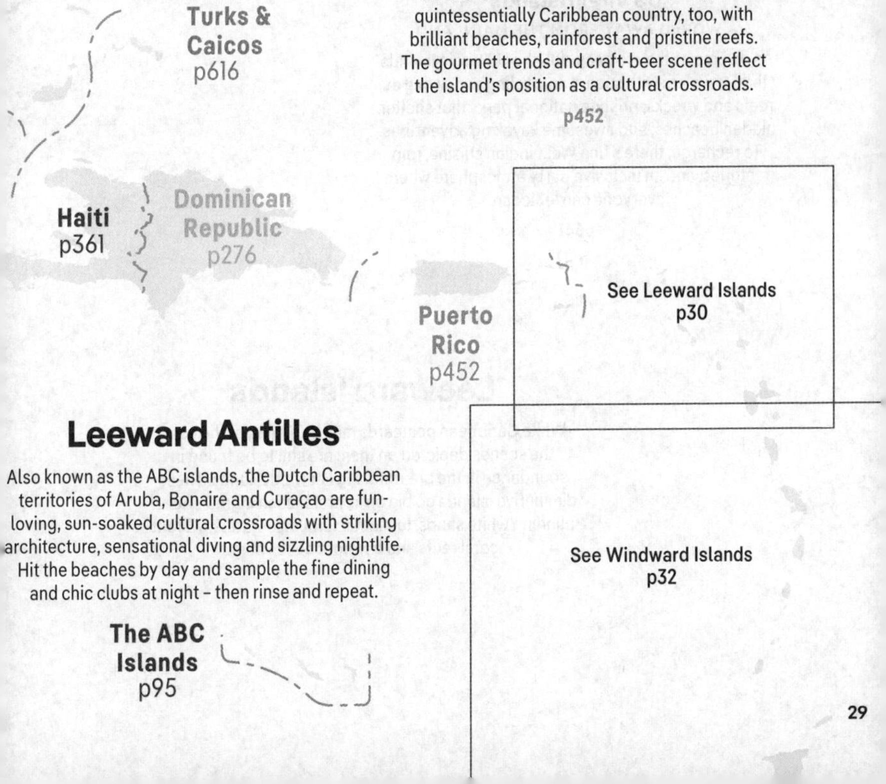

Turks & Caicos
p616

Haiti
p361

Dominican Republic
p276

Puerto Rico
p452

See Leeward Islands
p30

Leeward Antilles

Also known as the ABC islands, the Dutch Caribbean territories of Aruba, Bonaire and Curaçao are fun-loving, sun-soaked cultural crossroads with striking architecture, sensational diving and sizzling nightlife. Hit the beaches by day and sample the fine dining and chic clubs at night – then rinse and repeat.

See Windward Islands
p32

The ABC Islands
p95

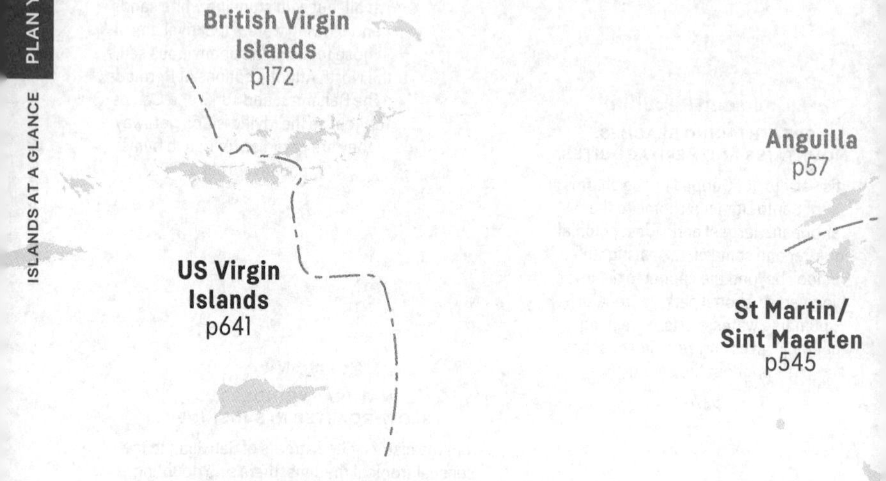

British Virgin Islands
p172

Anguilla
p57

US Virgin Islands
p641

St Martin/ Sint Maarten
p545

US Virgin Islands

A WORLD AWAY FROM THE MAINLAND

As diverse as they're beautiful, the US Virgin Islands thrill travelers with superb snorkeling and diving at reefs and wrecks, pristine national parks that shelter hidden beaches, and awesome kayaking adventures. To recharge, there's fine West Indian cuisine, rum factories, and an inclusive party atmosphere where everyone can let loose.

p641

Leeward Islands

While Caribbean postcards may be a thing of the past, the scenes depicted on them are still to be found in abundance in the breathtaking Leeward Islands. These diminutive islands go big on key relaxation ingredients of blinding white sands, luminous turquoise waters, vibrant coral reefs and barefoot beach bars.

St Kitts & Nevis

TWO ISLANDS, ONE COUNTRY

Ultra laid-back and welcoming, the two islands of this small nation are united by a common culture and rich history, but offer quite different experiences. The larger island, St Kitts, is a bustling good-time vacation hub, while unhurried Nevis with its quiet beaches oozes rustic charm.

p501

Antigua & Barbuda

EASY, BREEZY LEEWARD ISLES

Two very different islands make a visit to Antigua and Barbuda like two vacations in one. Antigua offers the best of pampered resort relaxation with fine dining, great golf and historic settlements, while Barbuda is an unspoiled wonderland awash with wildlife. Needless to say, both have phenomenal beaches.

p72

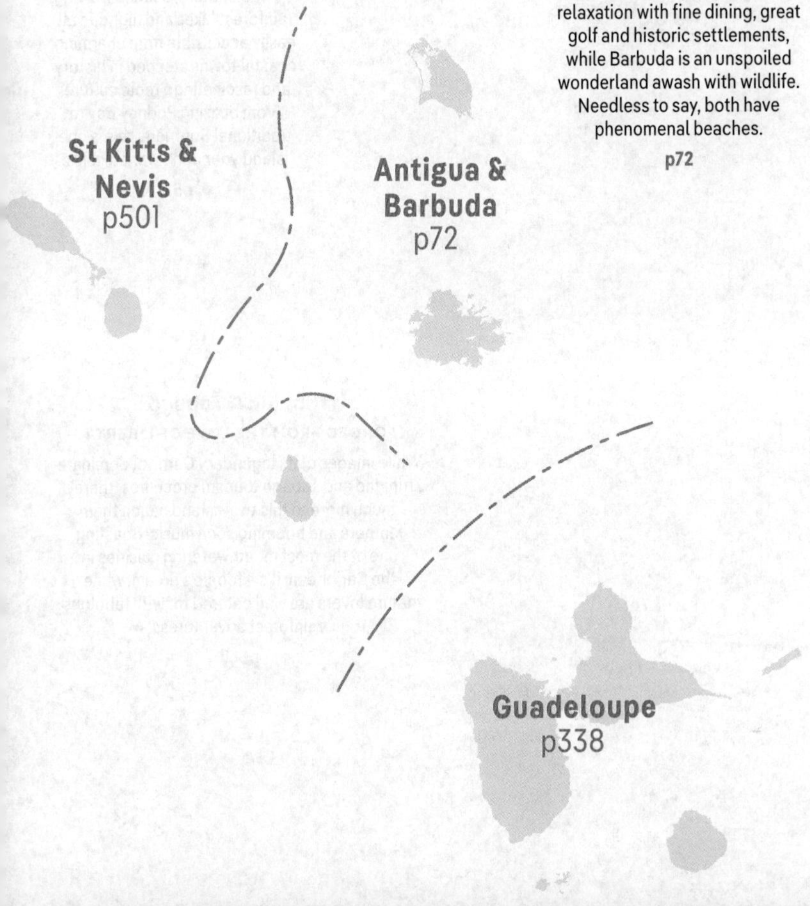

St Kitts & Nevis
p501

Antigua & Barbuda
p72

Guadeloupe
p338

Windward Islands

Picture rainforest-covered mountains sloping down to pristine beaches, then add artisanal rum distilleries, mouthwatering cuisine and terminally laid-back locals, and you've got the Windward Islands. Big enough to escape the crowds, but small enough to always be a short drive from home, these are some of the region's premier vacation destinations.

St Lucia

ICONIC LANDMARKS AND BEAUTIFUL BEACHES

Many islands claim to have the lot, but St Lucia backs it up with top-shelf nature, beaches, diving, rainforest hikes and nightlife all easily accessible from charming coastal towns steeped in history and fascinating Creole culture. From buzzing Rodney Bay to traditional Soufrière, this is one island your don't want to miss.

p518

Trinidad & Tobago

FORGED FROM THE LOVE OF LIBERTY

While images of its legendary Carnival dominate Trinidad and Tobago tourism brochures, there's much more to this twin-island nation than feathers and booming soca music. Boasting one of the most mouthwatering cuisines in the Caribbean, it's a foodie's dream, while nature lovers are well catered for with fabulous rainforest adventures.

p587

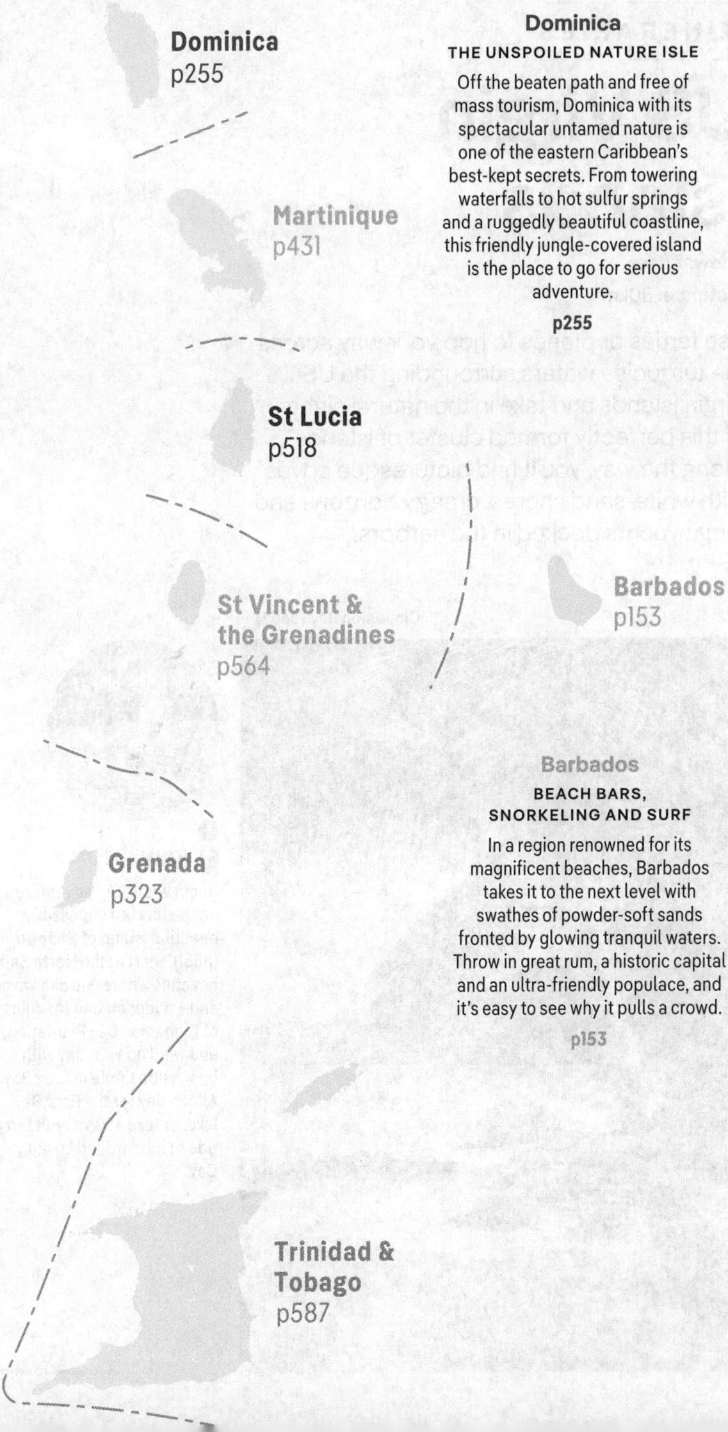

Dominica
p255

Martinique
p431

St Lucia
p518

St Vincent & the Grenadines
p564

Grenada
p323

Trinidad & Tobago
p587

Barbados
p153

Dominica

THE UNSPOILED NATURE ISLE

Off the beaten path and free of mass tourism, Dominica with its spectacular untamed nature is one of the eastern Caribbean's best-kept secrets. From towering waterfalls to hot sulfur springs and a ruggedly beautiful coastline, this friendly jungle-covered island is the place to go for serious adventure.

p255

Barbados

BEACH BARS, SNORKELING AND SURF

In a region renowned for its magnificent beaches, Barbados takes it to the next level with swathes of powder-soft sands fronted by glowing tranquil waters. Throw in great rum, a historic capital and an ultra-friendly populace, and it's easy to see why it pulls a crowd.

p153

ITINERARIES

US Virgin Islands

Allow: 7 days

Distance: 80km

Use ferries or planes to hop your way across the turquoise waters surrounding the US Virgin Islands and take in the natural sights of this perfectly formed cluster of islands. Along the way, you'll find picturesque coves with white-sand shores, craggy horizons and mega yachts docked in the harbors.

Cinnamon Bay (p652)

SASHA BUZKO/SHUTTERSTOCK ©

❶

ST JOHN ⏱ 2 DAYS

Begin your USVI adventure on the tiny but impossibly beautiful island of **St John** (p651). Start at the North Shore beaches where you can kayak and wander among the ruins of Cinnamon Bay Plantation, and wind up your day with a beachside tipple in Cruz Bay. Allot a day for the Reef Bay hike, or take a 10-minute ferry ride to hike around Lovango Cay.

CHUCK W WALKERSHUTTERSTOCK ©

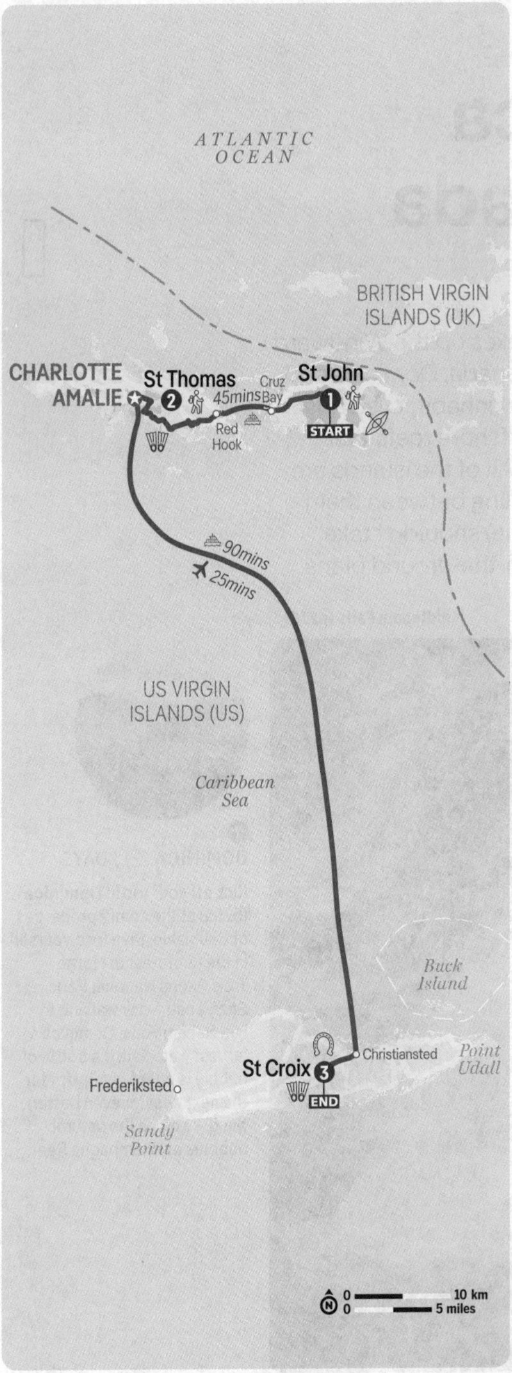

ATLANTIC OCEAN
BRITISH VIRGIN ISLANDS (UK)
CHARLOTTE AMALIE
St Thomas
2
45mins
Cruz Bay
St John
1
START
Red Hook
90mins
25mins
US VIRGIN ISLANDS (US)
Caribbean Sea
Buck Island
Christiansted
Point Udall
St Croix
3
END
Frederiksted
Sandy Point
0 10 km
0 5 miles

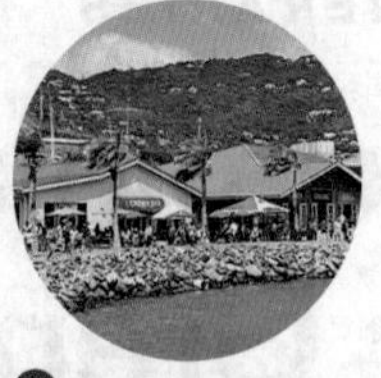

2

ST THOMAS ⏱ 2 DAYS

Hop on a ferry to check out **St Thomas** (p655). Browse the galleries and sample the local cuisine in Charlotte Amalie. Beach lovers can try snorkeling in the crystal-clear waters, while adventure seekers can hike to legend-shrouded John Brewer's Cave. In the evening, wander over to the quirky bars of **Red Hook** (p656) for a taste of Caribbean nightlife. .

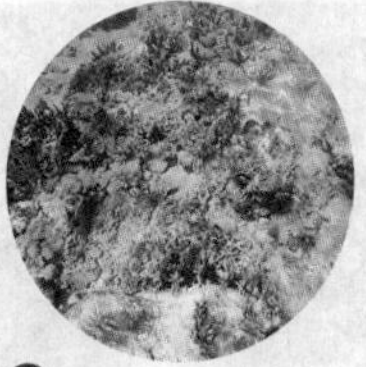

3

ST CROIX ⏱ 2 DAYS

Take a seaplane or ferry from St Thomas to Christiansted on **St Croix** (p646). Spend the remaining two days horse-back riding on Cowboy Beach, hiking to tide pools along the Trumball Trail, diving the Buck Island Reef and paddling through the glowing waters of Salt Bay. You can also tour former plantations and mill ruins for some historical insight.

TOP: PAUL MCKINNON/SHUTTERSTOCK ©, BOTTOM: VLAD ISPAS/SHUTTERSTOCK ©

ITINERARIES

Dominica to Grenada

Allow: 2 weeks
Distance: 646km

The archipelago that makes up the Windward Islands – St Vincent, Grenada, Dominica and St Lucia – offers sparsely inhabited islands and bays with thriving offshore reefs that are ripe for exploration. All of the islands are relatively close, so traveling between them (whether by ferry or plane) shouldn't take much time away from on-the-ground plans.

Middleham Falls (p270)

1
DOMINICA ⏱ 3 DAYS

Kick off your trip in **Dominica** (p255) at the comfy properties of Calibishie, then lose yourself in the rainforest at Morne Trois Pitons National Park. Spend half a day walking to Middleham Falls, Dominica's largest waterfall. If a bottle of bubbly is out of reach, opt for the next best (or even better) thing – a dip in the natural bubbles at Champagne Reef.

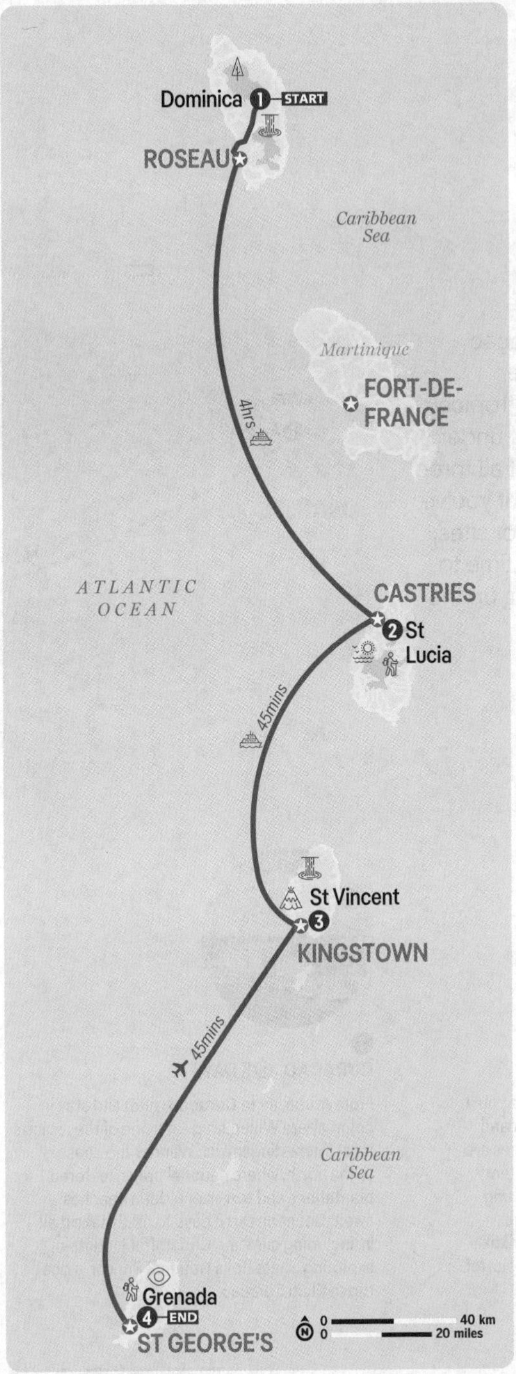

Dominica 1 START
ROSEAU
Caribbean Sea
Martinique
FORT-DE-FRANCE
4hrs
ATLANTIC OCEAN
CASTRIES
2 St Lucia
45mins
St Vincent
3
KINGSTOWN
45mins
Caribbean Sea
Grenada
4 END
ST GEORGE'S
0 40 km
0 20 miles

2

ST LUCIA 3 DAYS

Take the scenic ferry to **St Lucia** (p518) and cruise gently through some of the most emerald waters of the Caribbean. Stay in Soufrière, a town on the island's west coast that's shadowed by the iconic peaks of the Pitons – you can hike these in the morning and dive in the afternoon. Check out the small beach at Marigot Bay.

3

ST VINCENT 3 DAYS

St Vincent (p564) is a cultural and environmental hub of energy. This volcanic island's diminutive capital, Kingstown, has a colorful market buzzing with activity. Dedicate some time to hiking through tropical rainforests or to Dark View Falls, lazing on the charming beaches, exploring the lush unspoiled countryside, or simply taking in the spectacle that is La Soufrière Volcano.

4

GRENADA 3 DAYS

Hop on a flight from St Vincent to the pint-size island of **Grenada** (p323). There, explore one of the Caribbean's most charming capitals – St George. See the sunken structures covered in coral at the Underwater Sculpture Park in Molinere Bay, then head to the Grand Etang National Park where you can hike past several cascades to Concord Falls.

ITINERARIES

ABC Islands

Allow: 10 days
Distance: 193km

Aruba, Bonaire and Curaçao may be tiny, but they offer ample opportunities for tropical adventuring and relaxing under the sun. The small size of all three islands means that even if you've penciled in all of the major sites, you'll still have plenty of time to relax on the sand soaking up the rays.

1 ARUBA 3 DAYS

Aruba's (p100) north coast is where you'll find a majority of places to stay, eat and play. The island's sugar-sand beaches are its real draw, so plan on spending plenty of time beach-hopping. If you're itching for something different, spend some time exploring the hiking trails at Arikok National Park or checking out the colorful port at Oranjestad.

2 CURAÇAO 3 DAYS

From Aruba, fly to **Curaçao** (p116) and stay in colonial-era Willemstad – it's one of the region's most interesting towns. Wander the coast to the north, where national parks, restored plantations and troves of hidden beaches await. Count on three days to really take it all in, including climbing Christoffel Mountain, exploring Shete Boka National Park or, a boat trip to Klein Curaçao.

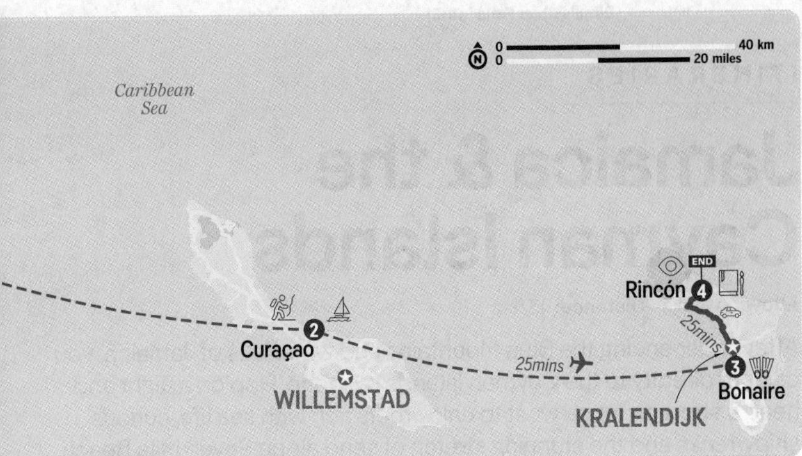

3 KRALENDIJK, BONAIRE 2 DAYS

Hop on a plane from Curaçao to Bonaire, one of the best diving locations in the world. In fact, there are 100 named dive sites that will keep you busy, including the coral reef at Bonaire Marine Park. It's located near the capital of **Kralendijk** (p109), a cute little town that offers opportunities for eating, sleeping and fun.

4 RINCÓN, BONAIRE 1 DAY

Spend your last day leisurely exploring bucolic **Rincón** (p493), the island's second city. Things move at a slow and inviting pace here, while at the horizon-spanning salt flats in the south you can see the evidence of slavery and colonial trade. There's also plenty of flamingo-spotting and turtle-watching to be had along the coast.

Dunn's River Falls (p418)

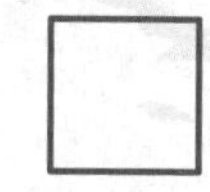

ITINERARIES

Jamaica & the Cayman Islands

Allow: 3 weeks **Distance:** 437km

After experiencing the Blue Mountains and waterfalls of Jamaica, you can get directly to the Cayman Islands by plane. Hop on a flight and head a short distance west to enjoy reefs rich with sea life, curious shipwrecks and the stunning stretch of sand along Seven Mile Beach.

1

OCHO RIOS, JAMAICA

3 DAYS

Kick off your three-week exploration in **Ocho Rios** (p417), situated on the north coast of the island. A cruise-ship haven, the city is also close to lush rainforests, stunning waterfalls and adventure activities. Make your way up Dunn's River Falls, a cascading waterfall that you can climb, and check out Mystic Mountain, a rainforest adventure park.

2

NEGRIL, JAMAICA

3 DAYS

Next, drive to **Negril** (p404) on the western tip of the island. With its stunning sunsets and laid-back vibe, you can unplug and recharge. Explore the shore of Seven Mile Beach and grab a drink at Rick's Cafe, where you can also watch cliff divers perform daring stunts. The Negril Lighthouse offers stunning views of the coastline.

3

MONTEGO BAY, JAMAICA

3 DAYS

After Negril, head east to Jamaica's second-largest city, **Montego Bay** (p411). Spend some time enjoying Doctor's Cave Beach with its sugary white sands and floating dive platforms. Just east of Montego Bay is Rose Hall, a restored plantation house with a fascinating (and haunted) history.

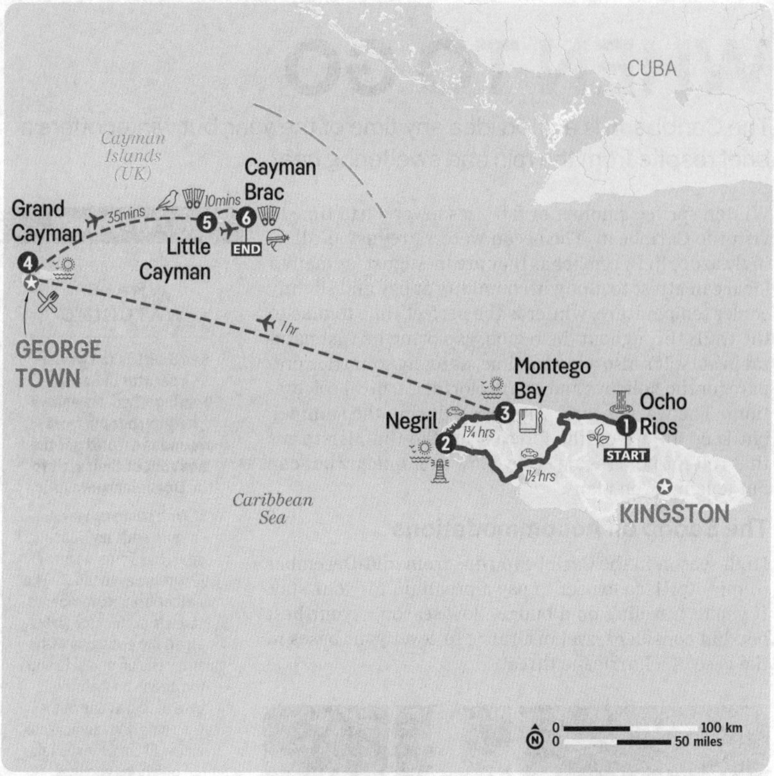

CUBA
Cayman Islands (UK)
Grand Cayman
35mins
10mins
Cayman Brac
Little Cayman
END
GEORGE TOWN
1hr
Montego Bay
Negril
1¾ hrs
Ocho Rios
START
1½ hrs
KINGSTON
Caribbean Sea
0 100 km
0 50 miles

❹
GEORGE TOWN, GRAND CAYMAN ⏱3 DAYS

Hop on a direct flight from Montego Bay to your next stop, **George Town** (p203). The cosmopolitan capital of the Cayman Islands is located on the western side of the island. Carve out a few days to lounge on the postcard-worthy Seven Mile Beach and explore Grand Cayman's sophisticated dining scene. Snorkel among the resident fish in Smith's Cove.

❺
LITTLE CAYMAN ⏱3 DAYS

Your next stop is **Little Cayman** (p209), the smallest of the Cayman Islands. What it lacks in size it makes up for in birdlife, marine life and glorious natural scenery. Dive the crystal-clear, warm waters of Bloody Bay Marine Park and channel your inner pirate on Owen Island. Stop by Booby Pond Nature Reserve, home to one of the hemisphere's largest breeding populations of red-footed boobies.

❻
CAYMAN BRAC ⏱3 DAYS

End the trip in **Cayman Brac** (p206), a wedge of an island that's also the most authentically Caymanian. You can experience some world-class diving at one of the 70-plus sites. Hike the limestone bluff on the west end of the island and stop by the Great Cave, the largest cave on Cayman Brac with resident bats.

WHEN TO GO

The Caribbean is a good idea any time of the year, but winter offers a brief respite from the rain and sweltering heat.

Winter, spring, summer or fall – it's never a bad time to visit the Caribbean. The ocean waters are just as alluringly azure in December as they are in August, as many a local can attest to. But with humidity at bay and slightly cooler temperature, winter is the perfect time to take to the trails throughout the region, exploring its vast natural beauty. It's also a festive time, as many countries prepare for the holidays and their colorful Carnival celebrations. The warm ocean waters call during the summer, but keep an eye on the forecast for the thunderstorms that roll into the region. They blow over quickly but can put a damper on plans.

The Scoop on Accommodations

High season in the Caribbean runs from mid-December to mid-April, so expect to pay a premium for your stay. If you're traveling on a budget, low season is your best bet, but consider travel insurance to cover your bases in the case of a hurricane threat.

I LIVE HERE

WHALE-WATCHING

Ken Smith is the owner-operator of Santo Domingo Taxi. He enjoys helping people from around the world get the most out of their visit to the Dominican Republic.

"With stunning views, nature and lazy beach days, Las Terrenas is my go-to getaway location. The weather from November to March is perfect for walks along the coastline with palm trees on one side and the ocean on the other. I love dining at one of the town's amazing restaurants, visiting El Limón waterfall, or witnessing the humpback-whale migration in Samana Bay."

Las Terrenas (p312)

RAINY ROADS

Rain is fair game pretty much throughout the year, but storm activity really picks up during the summer. Intense thunderstorms rumble through the region, leaving flooded roads and soggy grounds in their wake. The good news: the Caribbean's storms usually blow over quickly.

Weather through the year

JANUARY
Avg max: **82°F (28°C)**
Avg rainfall: **34mm**

FEBRUARY
Avg max: **86°F (30°C)**
Avg rainfall: **37mm**

MARCH
Avg max: **87°F (31°C)**
Avg rainfall: **36mm**

APRIL
Avg max: **89°F (32°C)**
Avg rainfall: **89mm**

MAY
Avg max: **89°F (32°C)**
Avg rainfall: **214mm**

JUNE
Avg max: **91°F (33°C)**
Avg rainfall: **166mm**

THE SNOW BIRDS HAVE LANDED

Winter is the Caribbean's driest and most temperate season. Northerners looking to flee harsh winters flock down to the region in droves, so expect crowds. Mountain regions in Cuba, the Dominican Republic, Jamaica and The Bahamas can get surprisingly chilly.

Carnival in the Caribbean

Carnival is one of the most vibrant and exciting celebrations throughout the Caribbean. Each island has its unique version of the event, featuring colorful costumes, dancing, music and street parades. The season typically lasts for several weeks, with festivities culminating in a grand finale on the last day before the Christian observance of Lent. However, the exact timing of the celebrations varies from island to island.

In Trinidad and Tobago, Carnival season kicks off in February, with events and parties taking place throughout the month. The main parade, known as 'The Greatest Show on Earth', takes place on the Monday and Tuesday before Ash Wednesday. In Jamaica, Carnival is celebrated in April and is known as 'Bacchanal Jamaica', while in The Bahamas, festivities kick off in late April or early May. In various other islands like Antigua, Barbuda, Barbados, Grenada and St Lucia, Carnival is celebrated in July or August.

HIKING

Tabiah Regis is a photographer who captures striking images of the people and landscape in and around St Vincent and the Grenadines. @nthusedphoto

"My favorite seasons are fall and winter. In the fall, the surroundings are still lush and green; also, the moon is at its most gorgeous and the night sky is a sight to behold, so I make every effort to go full-moon hiking. During winter, the temperature is usually at its best during the day, people are more jovial, and pigeon peas and sorrel come in for the harvest."

Sporting Events

The Caribbean is home to a number of major sporting events that attract athletes, fans and tourists from around the world.

Cricket is one of the most popular sports, with several international events including the **Caribbean Premier League**, which features six teams from across the region competing in a T20 format in the late summer months.

In Puerto Rico, Cuba and the Dominican Republic, baseball plays a large role in the cultural landscape, with the **Caribbean Series** playoffs dominating national calendars beginning in February.

Soccer is also played widely, with the **Concacaf Gold Cup** being the biggest international tournament – the official draw typically kicks off in April. The Caribbean also hosts several domestic football leagues.

Horse racing receives quite a bit of attention, with several major events throughout the year including the **Barbados Gold Cup**, the **Trinidad and Tobago Derby** and the **Jamaica Derby**.

Trinidad Carnival (p590)

HURRICANE WATCH

Hurricane season is from June to November. Expect watches and warnings several days before an event, but closures – from airports and ports to hotels and restaurants – are common in the days leading up to landfall.

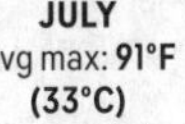

JULY	AUGUST	SEPTEMBER	OCTOBER	NOVEMBER	DECEMBER
Avg max: **91°F (33°C)**	Avg max: **93°F (34°C)**	Avg max: **91°F (33°C)**	Avg max: **87°F (31°C)**	Avg max: **84°F (29°C)**	Avg max: **84°F (29°C)**
Avg rainfall: **176mm**	Avg rainfall: **174mm**	Avg rainfall: **231mm**	Avg rainfall: **170mm**	Avg rainfall: **79mm**	Avg rainfall: **34mm**

Beach hats, Montego Bay (p411)

GET PREPARED FOR THE CARIBBEAN

Useful things to load in your bag, your ears and your brain

Clothes

Light clothing Even in the winter, it's warm in the Caribbean. Temperatures during the summer can soar way past 30°C/86°F, so you'll want articles of clothing that can breathe and repel the sweat off your skin. Lightweight shorts, pants, and breezy T-shirts or button-ups made from natural fabrics (like linen or cotton) or a moisture-wicking polyester are your best bet. Leave the heavy jeans and sweaters at home.

Reef shoes Water shoes or sandals will be your best friend and the item of clothing you'll turn to the most. A sturdy pair can traverse rocky streams, help you climb the boulders in and around waterfalls, and comfortably carry you through a walking city tour.

Hats and sunglasses Both are crucial gear for protecting your face from the sun's rays.

Manners

Island time is a real phenomenon. From restaurant service to transportation, the Caribbean moves at its own meandering pace.

Greetings are important. Always greet people properly, and treat elders with extra respect. After the introductions, don't be surprised at the directness of many conversations.

Haggling isn't unheard of. Almost everything – beach vendors, market stalls, accommodations – can be negotiated. Large stores/duty-free malls are the exception.

READ

How to Love a Jamaican (Alexia Arthurs; 2019) Collection of short stories about Jamaican immigrants and their families back home.

Love After Love (Ingrid Persaud; 2021) A story of family and love, teeming with insights on Trinidadian life.

Land of Love and Drowning (Tiphanie Yanique; 2015) Epic family saga set against rhythms/cultural influences of the Virgin Islands.

Everything Inside (Edwidge Dandicat; 2020) Eight stories of wisdom and humanity taking place in Miami and the Caribbean.

Words

You'll find several languages spoken throughout the Caribbean, including Spanish, French, Dutch, and Creole. Here are some key phrases to keep in mind.

Spanish

Hola (o-la) is 'hello'.
Adios (a-dyos) is 'goodbye'.
Por favor (por fa-vor) means 'please'.
Gracias (gra-syas) is 'thank you'.
¿Habla/Hablas inglés? (a-bla/a-blas een-gles) is 'Do you speak English?' (pol/inf)
No entiendo (no en-tyen-do) means 'I don't understand'.

French

Bonjour (bon-zhoor) is 'hello'.
Au revoir (o-rer-vwa) is 'goodbye'.
S'il vous plaît (seel voo play) means 'please'.
Merci (mair-see) is 'thank you'.
Parlez-vous anglais? (par-lay-voo ong-glay) is 'Do you speak English?'
Je ne comprends pas (zher ner kom-pron pa) means 'I don't understand'.

Dutch

While it isn't necessary to speak Dutch in Saba, Sint Eustatius and Sint Maarten, these phrases may help you get by.

Goedendag (khoo-duh-dakh) means 'hello'.
Tot ziens (tot zee-ens) is the formal way to say 'goodbye'; **Dag** (dakh) is more informal.
Pardon (par-don) is 'excuse me'.
Alstublieft (al-stew-bleeft) or **alsjeblieft** (a-shuh-bleeft) are both used to say 'please' (pol/inf).
Dank u/je (pol/inf) (dangk ew/yuh) means 'thank you'.

Haitian Creole

Bonjou means 'good day'; typically used before noon.
Bonswa is 'good evening'; used after 11am.
Silvouple, **tanpri** and **souple** all mean 'please'.
Mèsi anpil means 'thank you'.

WATCH

Better Mus' Come (Storm Saulter; 2010) A love story that unfolds within the political backdrop of turmoil in Jamaica.

Boleto al Paraíso (Gerardo Chijona; 2011) In early '90s Cuba, a couple run from their home in search of paradise.

Cristo Rey (Leticia Tonos; 2013) A Caribbean take on *Romeo and Juliet* that examines tensions between Dominicans and Haitians.

Rain (Maria Govan; 2008) Young girl leaves her sheltered life on Ragged Island and comes to Nassau with overwhelming results.

Chasing Coral (Jeff Orlowski; 2017) A team of divers, photographers and scientists set out to discover why corals are vanishing.

LISTEN

We Are Crayons Podcast (Dhano Mc Nicol and Dionne Mc Nicol Stephenson; 2019) Stories from Trinidad and Tobago's creative thinkers/makers.

The Style & Vibes Podcast (Mikelah Rose; 2018) A discussion of Caribbean style, culture, and music with tastemakers from the region.

Caribbean Connection Radio Show (Mike Andrews; 1987) Caribbean news, entertainment, cultural tidbits, and music for listeners around the Caribbean diaspora.

Mi Tierra (Gloria Estefan; 1993) Spanish-language album paying homage to Estefan's roots, featuring Cuban musical genres bolero, *danzón* and *son*.

Drinks kiosk, Ocho Rios (p417)

THE FOOD SCENE

The Caribbean pulls culinary inspiration from the abundance of the ocean and the tropical plants that thrive among its islands.

Caribbean cuisine knows how to find the sublime in simplicity. Fresh-caught fish thrown over a flame, steamed rice punctuated by savory beans, and starchy plantains ready to sop up all of the citrusy sauces and juices pooling up on your plate – the islands understand how to harness the fruits of the sea, with each country adding its own unique dishes, flavors, and cooking techniques to the proverbial pot.

It's a vibrant mix of Indigenous, African, European and Asian influences, some of which are more prominent in certain regions – like the South Asian–inspired roti in Trinidad and Tobago, the Jamaican jerk seasoning pulled from African spice blends, or the Spanish-introduced plantains, sour oranges, and pork that dominate Dominican, Cuban, and Puerto Rican cuisine.

Food is nourishment, but it's also celebratory – and nothing helps get the party started like rum, with each Caribbean country claiming its version is superior to the rest. Instead of igniting a heated debate, order a mojito and toast your drinking companions.

Regional Seafood Specialties

There's no shortage of seafood throughout the Caribbean, but specialties vary from country to country. Conch – whether it's in a fritter or citrusy salad – is prevalent in The Bahamas, while fried snapper sings in Jamaica's popular *escovitch*. *Pulpo* (octopus) gets its proper due in the Dominican Republic with a tender, flavorful preparation in a chopped garlic sauce. Over in St Lucia, lobster is the main attraction, while in Trinidad and Tobago, you'll find 'bake and shark',

Best Caribbean Islands dishes

PULPO AL AJILLO
Octopus in aromatic garlic sauce. (Dominican Republic)

FRIED FISH SANDWICH
Raisin bread with fried fish, coleslaw, tartar sauce, cheese. (Bermuda)

KESHI YENA
Cheese rind filled with spiced meat, then baked. (Aruba, Bonaire, Curacao)

LECHÓN ASADO
Suckling pig with crispy skin, roasted over coals. (Puerto Rico)

a popular street-food dish with marinated or seasoned pieces of shark meat, sauces, chutneys, and vegetables in a flatbread.

Beyond the Sea

Aside from seafood, you'll find other proteins stealing the culinary spotlight on menus across the Caribbean. Poultry is a popular option, popping up in the Spanish-speaking islands' *arroz con pollo* (rice with chicken that closely resembles a paella), Jamaica's jerk chicken, and Bahamian chicken souse. *Chivo* or *cabrito* (goat) is often found braised or marinated in the central highlands of the Domincan Republic, fried in Haiti's *tassot cabrit,* or cooked in a rich curry stew in several Caribbean islands. Another island favorite is pork – especially in Cuba and Puerto Rico, where you'll find a tender, mouth-melting version of the protein packed into sandwiches, or fried up and served in crunchy, savory hunks called *chicharron.*

What's in Your Glass?

With the abundance of tropical fruit found throughout the Caribbean, fresh-squeezed and pressed juices are a popular option for breakfast, lunch, or a refreshing afternoon sip. Papaya, sugar apple, passionfruit, pineapple, mango, guava, and tamarind are popular throughout the region, as are 'coco frio' stands selling chilled coconuts with their tops expertly hacked off, so you can slurp up the juice inside.

The region is also known for its exceptional coffee. Look no further than the volcanic soil of Puerto Rico, the Blue Mountains of Jamaica, or the beans grown in the Cordillera Central of the Dominican Republic for rich and flavorful expressions of this aromatic brew.

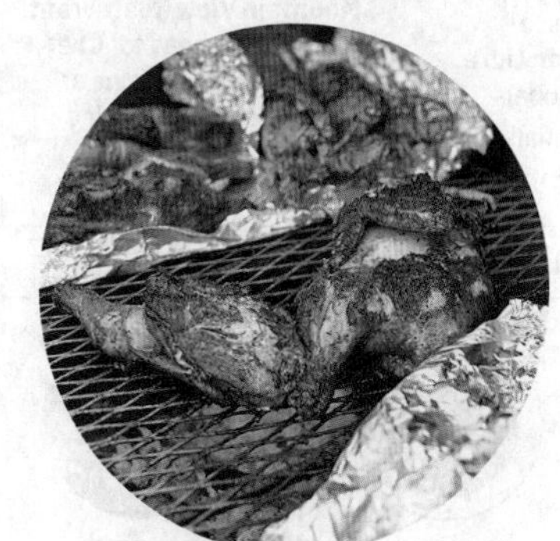

ALCHEMIST CHRONICLES 876/SHUTTERSTOCK ©

Jerk chicken, Jamaica (p382)

Grilled conch

NIGEL NICHOLAS/SHUTTERSTOCK ©

FOOD & WINE FESTIVALS

Union Island Conch Festival (p577) Dedicated to the staple shellfish of the southern Grenadines, this February festival is a must for seafood lovers, as conch gets grilled, barbecued, and sautéed all over the island.

Fête des Cuisinières (p343) Taking place in Guadeloupe in August, this event has honored female chefs and Creole culinary traditions for over a century.

BVI Emancipation Festival Food Fair (p177) This biggest cultural celebration in the BVIs happens in July, with pageants, a food fair, musical shows, horse races, and a parade.

Jamaica Coffee Festival (p387) Coffee enthusiasts flock to Kingston in October to indulge in Blue Mountain Coffee.

Barbados Food and Rum Festival (p162) Come October, chefs from all around the island prepare traditional dishes, and the island's distilleries bring out special reserve rums.

FLYING FISH & COU COU	BREADFRUIT & JACKFISH	GOAT WATER	JERK CHICKEN	SALTFISH AND BAKE
Steamed fish in mild gravy served over okra and cornmeal mash. (Barbados)	Fluffy, roasted breadfruit and crispy, fried fish. (St. Vincent & the Grenadines)	Goat stew with breadfruit and green papaya. (St Kitts & Nevis)	Slow-cooked/ grilled chicken coated in sweet and fiery spices. (Jamaica)	Seasoned saltfish with onion and veg, and a side of baked or fried bread. (Grenada)

Local Specialties

Seafood Staples

Cracked conch Sliced, battered, and fried bits of conch. (Bahamas)

Pescado con coco Fresh fish stewed in coconut milk, tomato, and onions. (DR)

Ackee and saltfish Salted codfish served with the ackee fruit. (Jamaica)

Bajan flying fish Breaded flying fish doused with lime juice. (Barbados)

Fish and fungi Okra and cornmeal boiled together with butter and served with saltfish. (BVI)

Kallaloo Caribbean seafood gumbo using a base of leafy greens. (Various Caribbean islands)

Sweet Treats

Dulce de coco con leche Thick, fudgy sweet made from young coconut, evaporated and condensed milk. (DR)

Tembleque Creamy coconut dessert that wiggles like Jell-O. (Puerto Rico)

Duff Pinwheel-style dessert lined with fruit, typically using guava. (Bahamas)

Cassava pone Yuca root cake made with coconut milk and spices. (Jamaica)

Cracked conch
ALLMYROOTS/SHUTTERSTOCK ©

Red grout Decadent tapioca and guava concoction topped with vanilla cream. (USVI)

Beverages

Coco frío Chilled coconut juice. (Various Caribbean islands)

Irish moss Mild flavored seaweed combined with milk and spices. (Jamaica)

Switcha Tangy, lemon-lime flavored beverage. (Bahamas)

Akasan Porridge-style drink made with corn flour, evaporated milk, and spices. (Haiti)

Café Cubano Espresso sweetened with sugar with a light foam on top. (Cuba)

Rum The quintessential Caribbean booze.

MEALS OF A LIFETIME

Aromas de la Montaña (p295) Dominican classics at this mountaintop restaurant with aerial views of the Central Highlands.

Zeerover (p106) Anglers catch and clean seafood the same day it makes it onto your plate before the chef cooks it to order.

Bacoa Finca + Fogón (p464) Hearth-to-table restaurant located on 3.5 rural acres, using seasonal ingredients from rural farms.

Champers (p161) Enjoy succulent grilled seafood overlooking the translucent waters of Rockley Beach.

Le Pressoir (p556) Exquisite French-Caribbean fare, prepared with seasonal local ingredients.

Mountain View Restaurant (p179) Book ahead for Chef Jim Cullimore's cuisine at this homey mountainside cafe.

THE YEAR IN FOOD

SPRING

Pineapple and ackee come into focus around the Caribbean during spring. Late April ushers in mango season in the DR; the best mangoes come from the town of Baní.

SUMMER

Blistering temperatures bring a bounty of crops around the Caribbean. While bananas, coconut, sugarcane and guava are omnipresent on menus throughout the year, they thrive during this time.

AUTUMN

Starchy fruits and veggies shine during the fall and winter months, with pumpkin, squash, and sweet potatoes taking center stage in dishes like kallaloo, pumpkin soup, and fish and chicken curries.

WINTER

The holidays bring roast pork, black cake, and creamy cocktails *ponche* and *coquito*. February welcomes Carnival dishes like *oil down* in Grenada, *pelau* in Trinidad and Tobago, and fried *escovitch* in Jamaica.

KONSTANTIN KOPACHINSKY/SHUTTERSTOCK ©, AISHA SYLVESTER/SHUTTERSTOCK ©, CONTENT ZILLA/SHUTTERSTOCK ©, BRENT HOFACKER/SHUTTERSTOCK ©

THOMASLENNE/SHUTTERSTOCK ©

Punch bottles, Guadeloupe (p338)

A. EMSON/SHUTTERSTOCK ©

Dunn's River Falls (p418)

THE OUTDOORS

With consistently balmy temperatures and the ocean as its playground, the Caribbean offers ample opportunity for outdoor adventuring all year-round.

Miles of breathtaking coastline and azure beaches are certainly one of the Caribbean's calling cards, but the island nations that make up the region offer a fascinating variety of ecosystems that go beyond the ocean and are ripe for exploration.

Lush rainforests with cascades, volcanoes with billowing smoke, mountainous peaks that run off into roaring rivers, and arid sand dunes that mimic the Sahara are just some of the environs that offer an exhilarating backdrop for outdoor adventures.

Snorkeling & Diving

The Caribbean has access to some of the world's best beaches and abundant opportunities to discover the reefs and sea life that surround its shores. Several marine reserves throughout the island nations offer pristine snorkeling and diving conditions for viewing the reefs and the parrotfish, angelfish, grouper, and barracuda that inhabit its warm waters.

Anegada's Horseshoe Reef, the largest barrier reef in the Caribbean, has been the demise of many ships, all of which make for interesting environments to explore on a dive.

For families, the calm waters of Doctor's Cave Beach in Jamaica allow visitors of all ages to view the marine life in the waters. You can swim out from shore or, older kids can jump from the pier into deeper waters.

At Starfish Point in Grand Cayman, you're pretty much guaranteed to see dozens of the eponymous invertebrates in the shallows of the beach.

Adrenaline Sports

KITEBOARDING

Skim the water in **Orient Bay** (p561) in St-Martin or in St Vincent & the Grenadines' **Union Island** (p581).

PARAGLIDING

Drift through the air with the help of a parachute from the mountaintops of **Jarabacoa** (p294) in the Dominican Republic.

WHITE-WATER RIVER RAFTING

Barrel down Class-II rapids on the Dominican Republic's longest river: **Yaque del Norte** (p296).

FAMILY ADVENTURES

Watch jockeys race their goats to victory in Tobago's **Buccoo (p609)** – an 80-year-old cultural tradition.

Grab a tube and drift down the crystal-clear water of the **Rio Yasica (p304)** in the Dominican Republic.

Strap on a snorkel and explore the sea life at **Horseshoe Reef (p189)**, the Caribbean's largest barrier reef, in Anegada.

Climb your way up a series of limestone rocks that step down 180m into a series of beautiful cascades and pools at **Dunn's River Falls (p418).**

Saddle up and gently meander along a beachside trail on horseback at **Cowboy Beach (p647)** in St Croix.

Zip line through a verdant canopy at the family-friendly **Akro Park (p345)** in Petit-Bourg in Guadeloupe.

Hiking

Hiking in the Caribbean offers a unique opportunity to explore the region's diverse landscapes, from its leafy rainforests to its rugged mountain peaks.

Popular hiking trails in the Caribbean include the Waitukubuli National Trail in Dominica, the Caribbean's longest walking trail spanning 115 miles across the island and featuring volcanic landscapes and stunning ocean views. The Gros Piton Trail in St. Lucia offers breathtaking views of the island's famous twin peaks, while the El Yunque National Forest in Puerto Rico houses an extensive network of trails through tropical foliage and picturesque waterfalls.

For a more adventurous hike, look to Jamaica's Blue Mountains or consider summiting DR's Pico Duarte – the Caribbean's highest peak.

BEST SPOTS

For the best outdoor spots and routes, see the map on p44.

Surfing & Kiteboarding

The thrill of riding the waves and catching some serious air in the Caribbean's waters is a draw for adrenaline fiends all across the globe. Several of the islands around the region are well-known to surfers and kiteboarders for their magnificent swells and whipping winds.

The northern coast of the Dominican Republic is known as the water-sports capital of the Caribbean, with three beaches along Cabarete dedicated to a different sport. The winds on Kite Beach are known to take kitesurfers to heart-stopping heights, while the waves on Encuentro Beach suit the surfers. The third beach, Cabarete Beach, sees its fair share of kitesurfers.

In the British Virgin Islands, Josiah's Bay beckons with its white-sand beach and A-frame peaks – it's known for helping surfers get their sea legs, as the waves aren't as tumultuous and imposing as in other areas.

Over in Puerto Rico, Rincón's balmy weather and consistent swells make it a favorite for recreational surfers.

Snorkeling, Grand Cayman (p202)

SURFING

Catch a wave at Barbados' the Soup Bowl, as it rolls in off the Atlantic in front of (p170).

CASCADING

Scramble up to boulder-topped **Mt Qua Qua** (p333) in Grenada for fine coastal views.

CANYONING

Test your endurance hiking, climbing, swimming, and cliff jumping in Puerto Rico's **Cañón de San Cristóbal** (p483).

FIERY HIKES

Hike to the top of **Soufrière Volcano** (p348) in St Vincent from either the windward or leeward side of the island.

ACTION AREAS

Where to find the Caribbean Islands' best outdoor activities

Horseback Riding

1. Buccoo, Tobago (p608)
2. Cowboy Beach, USVI (p647)
3. Gold Mine Ranch, Aruba (p100)
4. Jarabacoa, Dominican Republic (p294)
5. Cove Bay, Anguilla (p70)

Snorkeling/Diving

1. Buck Island, USVI (p649)
2. Doctor's Cave Beach, Jamaica (p413)
3. Horseshoe Reef, Anegada (p189)
4. La Parguera, Puerto Rico (p482)
5. Starfish Point, Grand Cayman (p202)

Canyoning

1. Basse-Terre's waterfalls, Guadeloupe (p345)
2. Cañón de San Cristóbal, Puerto Rico (p483)
3. Jarabacoa, Dominican Republic (p295)
4. Les Gorges de la Falaise, Martinique (p444)
5. Trafalgar Falls, Dominica (p264)

Walking/Hiking

1. Bubbly Pool, Jost Van Dyke (p193)
2. Mount Qua Qua, Grenada (p333)
3. La Soufrière Volcano, St Vincent & the Grenadines (p572)
4. The Baths National Park, Virgin Gorda (p184)
5. Virgin Islands National Park, St John (p652)

Surfing/Kiteboarding

1. Josiah's Bay, Tortola (p179)
2. Kite Beach, Dominican Republic (p304)
3. Orient Bay, St Martin (p561)
4. The Soup Bowl, Barbados (p170)
5. Tres Palmas, Rincón, Puerto Rico (p495)

CARIBBEAN ISLANDS

THE GUIDE

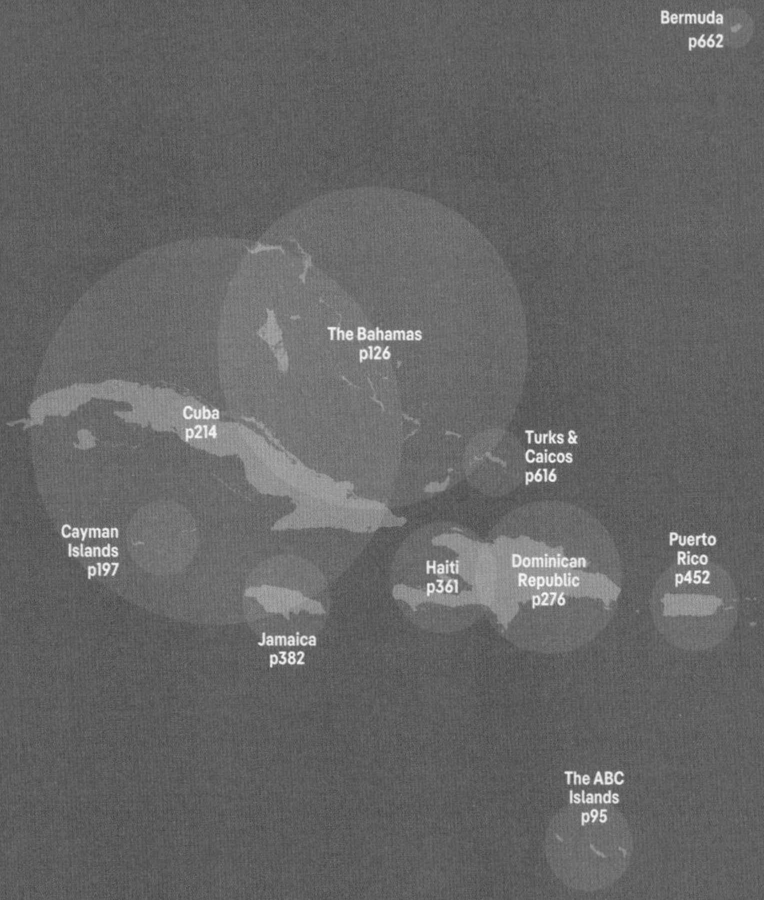

Bermuda p662

The Bahamas p126

Cuba p214

Turks & Caicos p616

Cayman Islands p197

Haiti p361

Dominican Republic p276

Puerto Rico p452

Jamaica p382

The ABC Islands p95

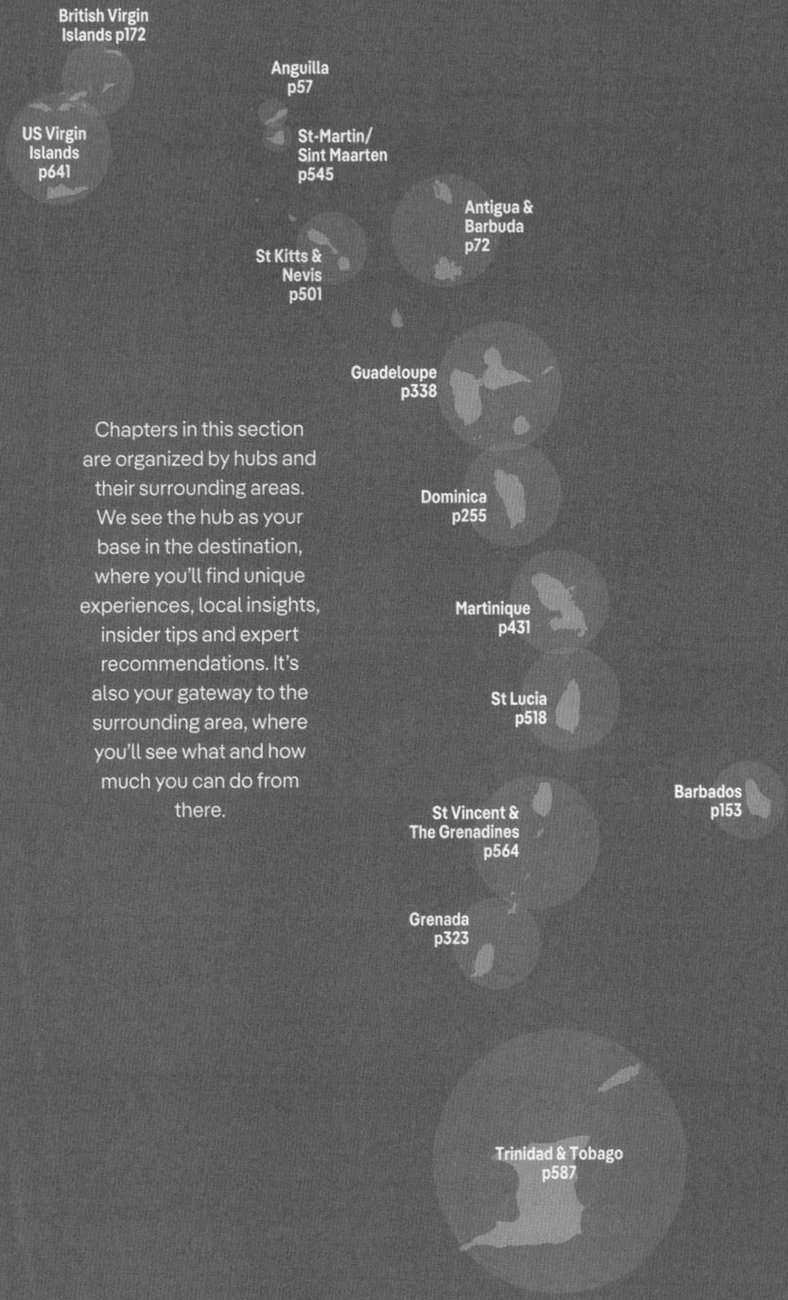

British Virgin Islands p172
Anguilla p57
US Virgin Islands p641
St-Martin/Sint Maarten p545
Antigua & Barbuda p72
St Kitts & Nevis p501
Guadeloupe p338
Dominica p255
Martinique p431
St Lucia p518
Barbados p153
St Vincent & The Grenadines p564
Grenada p323
Trinidad & Tobago p587

Chapters in this section are organized by hubs and their surrounding areas. We see the hub as your base in the destination, where you'll find unique experiences, local insights, insider tips and expert recommendations. It's also your gateway to the surrounding area, where you'll see what and how much you can do from there.

Above: The Valley (p62); Right: Barnes Bay (p68)

ANGUILLA

SAND, SEA AND SUN

Kick back and relax on one of 33 glorious beaches, indulging in cooling dips in turquoise waters, decadent barbecue lunches and soulful island tunes.

If you are dreaming of the ultimate Caribbean vacation, lounging on endless shimmering beaches with tropical cocktail in hand and waves lapping at your toes, you've come to the right place – an island that has deservedly earned the nickname 'Tranquility Wrapped in Blue.' Anguilla is tiny – barely over 100 sq km – with a disproportionate share of delicious sandy shorelines. Take your pick from the south side, with views of the rolling mountains of St-Martin, or the north side, with views out to sea. You can also decide if you prefer to lounge in a shaded beach chair with a steady supply of drinks and snacks from a nearby beach bar, or if you would rather have the company of pelicans and tropicbirds on your own secluded stretch of sand. It is this perfect balance of pampering and privacy that makes Anguilla the chosen playground of the rich and famous (and other discerning travelers).

DIEGOMARIOTTINI/SHUTTERSTOCK ©

When you're ready to pick yourself up off the sand, the sea beckons. Take yourself snorkeling with sea turtles and colorful fish, scuba diving on historic shipwrecks, or sea kayaking to hidden coves. Sate your appetite with spicy barbecue ribs and succulent grilled lobster. Dance barefoot to reggae beats. And don't miss the fireworks, every night, when the sun sets into the sea and turns the sky to magic.

THE MAIN AREAS

THE VALLEY
Small city on a small island. p62

WEST END VILLAGE
Luxurious beachy bliss. p68

Find Your Way

Anguilla is 25km long and 5km wide, drivable from end to end in 30 to 40 minutes. The Valley – the capital – sits dead center, while beaches beckon from all around, especially the western end of the island.

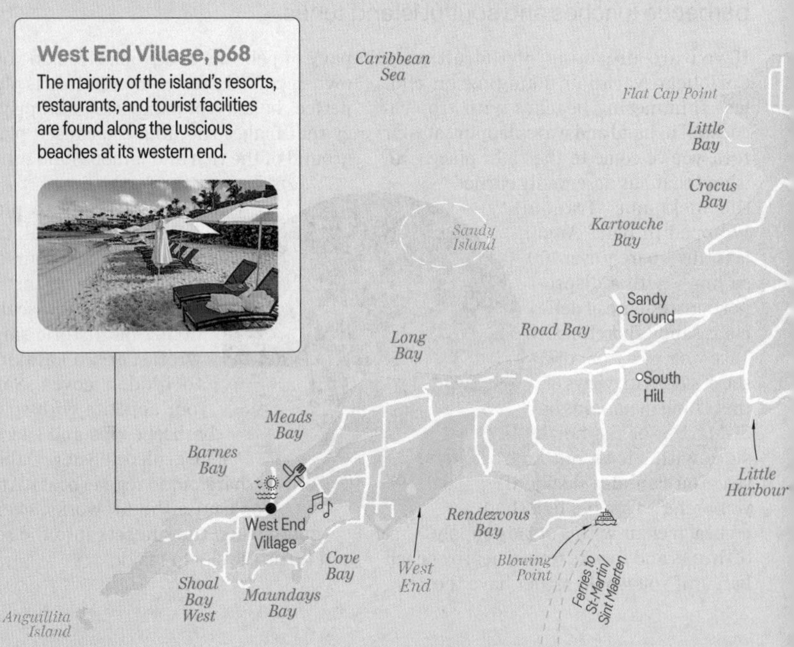

West End Village, p68

The majority of the island's resorts, restaurants, and tourist facilities are found along the luscious beaches at its western end.

The Valley, p62
The capital of Anguilla is a laid-back little city, with a few historic sites, several surprisingly pristine beaches, and some of the best barbecue on the island.

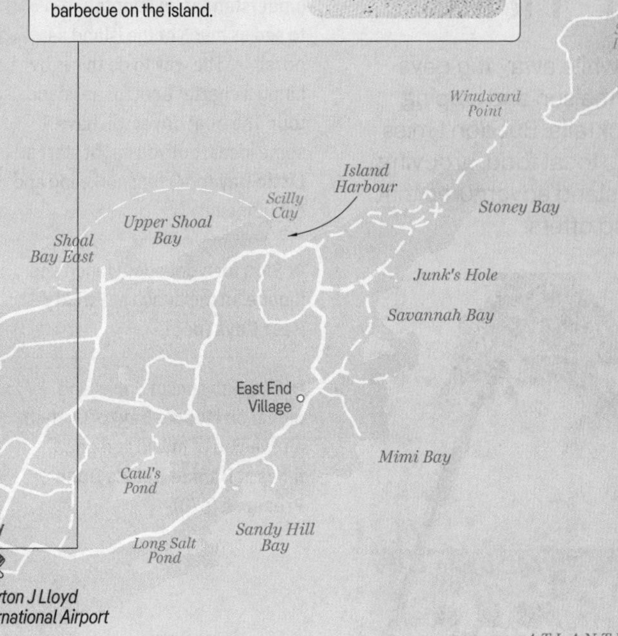

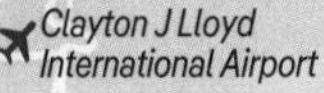

DRIVING

Discover secluded beaches, backyard barbecues and out-of-the-way places without worrying about how to get to or fro. The rental-car company will provide a temporary drivers' license for a fee. Don't forget to drive on the left!

TAXI

Many taxi services cater to guests who don't want to drive themselves. Fares range from US$10 to US$36 for two people, depending on distance. Resorts, restaurants and tour operators can help book a taxi when needed.

BIKE

There are no bike lanes on these twisting, turning (and often potholed) roads. But Anguilla's relatively short distances and mostly flat landscape make cycling feasible. Rent bikes from AXA Bicycles (264-35-7736) or Junie Fleming's Bike Shop (264-35-702).

Plan Your Time

It's easy to while away the days soaking up the sun and sipping tropical cocktails. But don't miss the fantastic local food, grooving music and island adventures that Anguilla also offers.

MARCO BICCI/SHUTTERSTOCK ©

Mead's Bay (p70)

If You Only Have One Day

- With one day on Anguilla, the (understandable) temptation is to see as much of the island as possible. The way to do this is by hiring a charter boat for an island tour. The boat driver will have some ideas, but you might start at **Little Bay** (p64) for snorkeling and cliff jumping.

- Stop for a decadent lunch and lounge on the beach at **Prickly Pear Cays** (p66).

- End with sunset drinks and dinner on **Mead's Bay** (p70), then an evening of music and good times at **Bankie Banx's Dune Preserve** (p70).

Seasonal Highlights

Anguilla is dreamy all year round – except maybe during hurricane season (mid-August through mid-November), when many resorts and restaurants close.

JANUARY

The high tourist season (through April) is characterized by warm temperatures and sunny skies.

MARCH

Bankie Banx's Dune Preserve hosts **Moonsplash** (p69), a fantastic music festival that draws great talent to the club on Rendezvous Bay.

APRIL

In Island Harbor, the two-day **Festival del Mar** celebrates the sea, with live music, boat races and (of course) seafood.

DIEGOMARIOTTINI/SHUTTERSTOCK ©, SLIM PLANTAGENATE/ALAMY ©, DAVIX3X/SHUTTERSTOCK ©

Three Days of Island Exploration

- With more time, the itinerary doesn't change much; it just adopts a more leisurely pace. Go to **Little Bay** (p64) by kayak instead of boat.

- Enjoy an afternoon relaxing on **Crocus Bay** (p64) and catch the sunset from **Mead's Bay** (p70) or from the iconic **Anguillan Arch** (p70).

- On day two, you might spend all day at **Prickly Pear Cays** (p66), exploring the islands and snorkeling the reef, followed by an evening at **'the Dune'** (p70).

- Swing by **Shoal Bay East** (p66) for swimming and snorkeling, a decadent beach massage or even a beach party!

A Week on the Island

- If you have a week on Anguilla, time begins to lose its meaning, as you might spend full days lounging around on various beaches, relaxing in the sun, sipping cocktails and entirely dedicating yourself to soaking up the island vibe.

- Explore **Cove Bay** (p70) on horseback and **Island Harbor** (p67) by glass-bottom kayak. Dive down through crystalline waters to explore a **shipwreck** (p67). Feast on scrumptious island **barbecue** (p63). And don't miss the chance to learn a thing or two about the **history** (p64) of this special place.

MAY

The tourist season brings fun local events such as the **Anguilla Regatta** and the island's independence day, aka **Anguilla Day**.

AUGUST

The island's biggest event is the **Anguilla Summer Festival**, a 10-day Carnivalesque street festival with parades, boat races and music.

SEPTEMBER

Help the National Trust protect nesting sea turtles and hatchlings on **Turtle Patrol tours** during September and October.

DECEMBER

From mid-December through early January, **Festive Season** celebrates Christmas and New Year with special events and sky-high prices.

THE VALLEY

The capital of Anguilla, The Valley is the island's largest town and its center of government and commerce, with crowded streets and bustling shopping centers (except on Sundays, when the place is a ghost town). Amid the workaday world, there are a few delightful surprises. Driving through mundane residential areas, you'll stumble on spectacular coastal views. You can forget your notions of 'city beach': here are several nearly deserted stretches of soft white sand, flanked by dramatic limestone cliffs, just a kilometer or two from the city center. Some modest but interesting historic buildings are along the way, including preserved plantation houses, the island's oldest church, and the recently restored courthouse (now containing the national museum). And of course, there's some excellent eating around here, especially along 'the Strip' (on Landsome St in the city center), where roadside food stands serve up tasty barbecue and other tempting local specialties.

TOP TIP

The Anguilla National Trust shows off an intriguing but oft-overlooked side of the island. Heritage tours cover the island's historic sites, including an Arawak ceremonial site at Big Spring with hundreds of ancient petroglyphs. It also offers a variety of nature hikes, traversing beaches, tide pools, dry coastal forest and limestone cliffs.

Little Bay (p64)

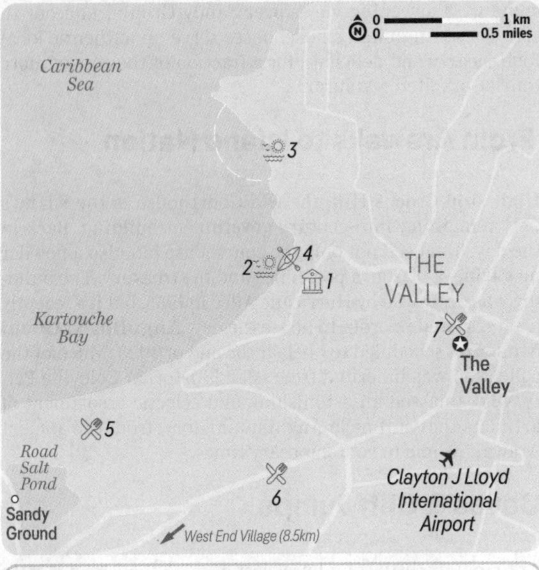

SIGHTS
1 Anguilla National Museum (Old Courthouse)
2 Crocus Bay
3 Little Bay

ACTIVITIES, COURSES & TOURS
4 Da'Vida

EATING
5 Eat Slow Feed Long
6 Jelly BBQ
7 Ken's Pork BBQ

Barbecue, Baby

SAMPLE THE BEST LOCAL EATS

When it comes to food, the island specialty is Anguillan-style barbecue: chicken, ribs and seafood that have been cooked up on a smoking-hot grill. **Ken's Pork BBQ** is an island institution located in The Valley right on the Strip. Tourists and locals alike flock to Ken's for grilled ribs and pork chops, served up with his famous homemade barbecue sauce. Ken cooks up the good stuff from Wednesday to Saturday. The price is right at **Jelly BBQ**, an unassuming roadside grill in George Hill. From Thursday to Sunday, this is the place to sample local favorites such as conch soup, tender oxtail, and curry goat, as well as chicken and ribs. **Eat Slow Feed Long** is tucked into the residential area on North Hill. At this backyard barbecue operation (open on Saturday and sometimes Friday night), you'll devour cracked conch sandwiches and saltfish cakes, in addition to the regular fare. All meals

BOAT RACE

Jessica Davis, moderator of *The Pulse: Anguilla* (@thepulseanguilla), shares her love of Anguilla's national sport, boat race.

J'ouvert means more than just 'daybreak' in the Caribbean. Here, it is an early-morning street party. On the first Monday in August – aka August Monday – Anguilla does it with style! Infectious rhythms entice thousands to jam from the capital to Sandy Ground for one of the island's biggest beach parties. Approaching the beach, you are greeted by majestic white sails dancing in the wind in anticipation of the day's boat race. Rooted in the island's rich maritime history, boat race is definitely one of my favorite pastimes!

WHERE TO EAT IN THE VALLEY

Good Korma
Excellent curries, samosas and other Indian food in an unexpected location on the Strip. $

Hungry's
Unassuming Hungry's serves next-level soups, including unusual choices like lobster and corn, conch and bullfoot. $

Da'Vida
An enticing beachfront restaurant on Crocus Bay serving seafood and grills. $$

WHY I LOVE ANGUILLA

Mara Vorhees, writer

On my last day in Anguilla, I decided to check out the 'local' beach near my cottage in North Hill (a somewhat innocuous residential area wedged in between The Valley and Sandy Ground). I strolled down a quiet lane and cut through the scrubby forest, then emerged onto a perfect semicircle of sand, backed by greenery, with impossibly blue waters lapping at the shore. And there was not another soul in sight. I climbed over the rocks at one end to discover a tiny, gorgeous, secret cove surrounded by limestone cliffs. My own private paradise, a seven-minute walk from my cottage. What's not to love about that?

come with sweeping views over Sandy Ground and out to sea. These Anguillan smokehouses serve up authentic local food, hearty and delicious, for a fraction of the cost of more tourist-oriented restaurants.

From Arawaks to Island Nation

DISCOVER THE ISLAND'S RICH HISTORY

High atop Crocus Hill, the Old Courthouse is the island's only remaining 18th-century government building. Back in the day, it housed not only the courthouse but also a powder magazine, a prison, a post office and the treasury. The building was destroyed by Hurricane Alice in 1955, but it's recently been restored in order to house the new **Anguilla National Museum**, scheduled to open at the end of 2023. Much of the collection was inherited from island historian Coleville Petty, who amassed an astonishing and eclectic assortment of artifacts that chronicle Anguillan history, from the ancient Arawak people to contemporary times.

Caves & Cliff Jumps

KAYAK TO A HIDDEN COVE

Arguably the littlest and prettiest cove on the island, **Little Bay** is a tiny crescent of sand, surrounded by tawny limestone cliffs, intriguing sea caves and the beautiful Caribbean blue. Best of all, this spot is inaccessible from land. Rent a kayak and snorkel gear from **Da'Vida** on Crocus Bay and paddle east for about 15 minutes along a stunning stretch off cliff-lined coast. On arrival, you can leave your kayak on the beach and make Little Bay your playground! Snorkel along the cliffs on the north side and explore the sea caves. Look out for the massive freestanding limestone rock – the ultimate cliff-jumping spot. (Wear water shoes for the climb up.) From the top, take in magnificent views of sea and coast before making the terrific 6m jump into the welcoming waters below.

If you don't want to paddle to Little Bay, you can catch a lift with a local fisher named Calvin; inquire at Da'Vida. Tour boats and charters also drop anchor here.

Upon your return, a fresh and fabulous lunch at Da'Vida caps your adventure. Incidentally, gorgeous **Crocus Bay** is a lovely destination in itself, if you like the idea of spending the afternoon lounging on a luscious beach and sipping cocktails. Again, the good folks at Da'Vida will set you up.

GETTING AROUND

Distances aren't great in The Valley, so walking can be a reasonable way to get from one place to another. But depending on where you're staying, you'll probably need a car or taxi to get here – and once you're here, there's not much reason to wander, especially considering the lack of sidewalks (and shade). Driving and parking are fairly straightforward: follow the arrows when making a right-hand turn to/from The Valley Rd.

Beyond the Valley

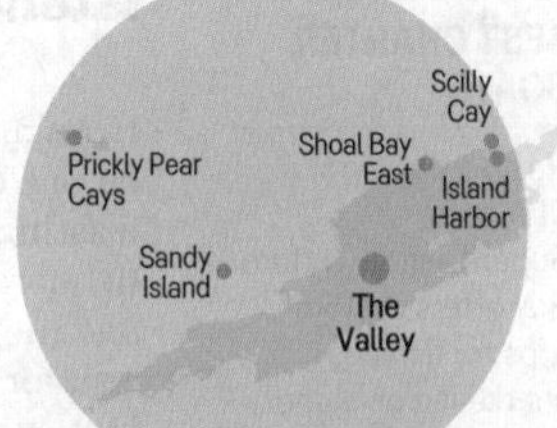

From long, luscious beaches to tiny offshore islands, the region beyond The Valley offers myriad opportunities to swim, snorkel, scuba dive and eat seafood.

Just 5km west of the capital, wedged in between Road Bay and the eponymous salt pond, Sandy Ground is a busy strip, thanks in part to the commercial port at its southern end. It is the jumping-off point for scuba-diving trips and boat journeys out to some offshore islands, such as Sandy Island and Prickly Pear Cays. Sandy Ground is also a destination in its own right, thanks to the string of lively bars and restaurants on the beach. Heading in the other direction, the lovely long beach at Shoal Bay East and the charming village of Island Harbor draw travelers to the island's eastern end for snorkeling, kayaking, good food and good times.

TOP TIP

Catch a boat to the offshore islands from the small dock at Sandy Ground. Otherwise, you'll need a car to reach beaches and activities outside The Valley. Any taxi service can also transport you.

Shoal Bay East (p66)

Island Getaways

TAKE A VACATION FROM YOUR VACATION

If Anguilla is just too big of an island for you, spend a day on one of the tiny offshore islets – lounging, snorkeling and feasting on grilled lobster, fish and ribs. **Sandy Island** is little more than a sandbar surrounded by crystal-clear waters and life-filled reefs. It is the quintessential desert island, except for the restaurant serving tasty Caribbean food and potent rum punch. Shuttles leave hourly from the small dock in Sandy Ground to make the 15-minute trip.

Further asea, **Prickly Pear Cays** are a pair of islands covered with scrubby greenery and a salt marsh. There are beach chairs for lounging on the sparkling sand, a reef for snorkeling in the turquoise sea, and a rocky coastline for exploring. Lunch is served family-style, so you can sample a bit of everything. (Prices are somewhat fluid, so beware.) Most folks come to Prickly Pear Cays by tour or charter boat, but you can also take the 'shuttle' with the staff, departing around 11am and returning around 3pm (island time). Inquire at the dock in Sandy Ground.

At Anguilla's eastern end, in the village of Island Harbor, there really is an island in the harbor. This is what's locally known as 'gorgeous' **Scilly Cay**, a scenic spot bedecked with conch shells and a restaurant under a thatch-roof palapa. A party atmosphere prevails, as a band plays reggae music and the bar turns out a steady stream of rum punch, alongside lobster, crayfish and delectable brown-sugar ribs. Most of the seating is at the water's edge, under the shade of palms and other greenery. It's open on Wednesday and Sunday (Thursday by reservation). Catch a boat from the Island Harbor jetty, next to the Falcon Nest restaurant.

Tip: Charter boats usually provide snorkeling gear for their guests. If you're exploring independently, rent gear from Da'Vida (Crocus Bay, p63) or Scuba Shack (Sandy Ground). There's none available to hire at Sandy Island or Prickly Pear Cays.

BEST CHARTER BOATS

Nature Boy Boat Charters
Super-friendly Nature Boy offers custom trips for fishing, snorkeling or island hopping on his boat *Summer Wind*.

Rum & Reel
Fishing outings, sunset cruises and trips to the offshore islands on the luxurious party boat *Striker*.

Gotcha! Garfield Sea Charters
Gotcha! takes guests fishing and beach-hopping around Anguilla, as well as on cruises to St-Martin/Sint Maarten and St-Barth.

Tradition Sailing
Stunning wooden sailboat that provides first-rate service on trips to Little Cove and Prickly Pear Cays.

SUNDAY FUN DAY

Sunday *is* fun day on Anguilla, and not only at Gwen's Reggae Bar. For more music and good vibes, you can crash the island party at 'gorgeous' **Scilly Cay** or attend 'Sunday School' at **Bankie Banx's Dune Preserve** (p70).

Rum & Reggae All Day

BLISS OUT AT THE BEACH

The best-known beach at the eastern end of the island is **Shoal Bay East**, about 6km northeast of The Valley. It's a long stretch of crushed-shell sand that reflects pinkish hues in the right light. There's no big development – just small-scale resorts and beach bars – which lends this shoreline an easy-going charm. Bring

WHERE TO EAT AND DRINK IN SANDY GROUND

Elvis & Roy's
Expat favorites anchoring Sandy Ground beach. Hit Elvis for tacos and Roy's for burgers or brunch. **$$**

Tasty's Restaurant
Sophisticated Caribbean cuisine, including seafood salad and coconut-encrusted fish in banana-rum sauce. **$$$**

Veya Restaurant
This 'cuisine of the sun' features Indian, North African, Southeast Asian and Caribbean flavors. **$$$**

snorkel gear to explore the crystal-clear waters and offshore reef. (You can also hire a boat to take you out to beautiful **Fan Coral Reef**, which is just around the corner.) For the ultimate in relaxation, book a beach massage at **Malakh Day Spa**, where you can hear the waves crash and feel the ocean breeze as the therapists work their magic.

The energy level at Shoal Bay kicks up a few notches on Sunday afternoons, when the beloved Scratch Band plays calypso and reggae music at **Gwen's Reggae Bar** (from 2pm). Folks come from around the island to feast on tasty grills, suck down powerful rum punch and dance barefoot in the sand.

Sea Life at Night

KAYAK IN A GLASS-BOTTOM BOAT

A 10km drive northeast of The Valley, the bay at **Island Harbor** has a sandy bottom with lots of vegetation, which makes it a favorite territory for sea turtles, as well as stingrays and eagle rays. By day, you can see them coming up for air (turtles) or bellyflopping out of the water (rays). But what are these creatures up to at night? Find out on a kayak tour with **Liquid Glow**, a paddling outfit that has transparent kayaks fitted with LED lights, to illuminate the sea below. In addition to turtles and rays, you might also see giant tarpon, spiny lobsters and other critters. It's a fascinating peek into the underwater world.

Underwater Archeology

DISCOVER THE STORIES OF THE SEA

Anguilla is surrounded by seven marine parks, protecting coral reef and offshore islands, as well as a slew of shipwrecks that were deliberately sunk for divers to explore. The island's largest wreck, at 70m, is **Sarah**, sitting upright in the sand at 10m to 25m. For fantastic sea life, there's **Commerce**, home to some huge lobsters and plenty of reef fish, and **Oosterdiep**, a great night-diving destination, with garden eels, southern stingrays and more than a few sea turtles. The wreck with the most interesting history is **Meppel**. Formerly known as *Hilda*, this WWII vessel rescued nearly 3000 troops during Operation Dynamo, the heroic 1940 evacuation of Dunkirk. Later, the ship was recommissioned as an inter-island ferry in the Caribbean, which is how she found her final resting place off the coast of Anguilla. Book your dive outing with the **Scuba Shack** in Sandy Ground, 5km west of The Valley.

BIG SPRING

Farah Mukhida, Executive Director of the Anguilla National Trust (@axatrust), recommends a visit to an ancient Amerindian site.

Big Spring Heritage Site is one of Anguilla's little gems. Tucked away at the eastern end of the island within the Island Harbour community, it was used by the Amerindian Taínos between 600CE and 1200CE as a place of celebration. Here you can find stone art speckled across the site's ragged limestone walls, with each carving representing the faces of the first peoples who called Anguilla home. Named after a spring that once gushed freshwater from the underground aquifer, Big Spring sits on a half-acre of land, sheltered by native trees and dotted by cacti. It's a truly special place.

WHERE TO EAT AT THE EASTERN END

Palm Grove Grill (aka Nat's Place)
Serves killer ribs, lobster and crayfish on remote Junks Hole beach. **$**

Artisan
Thin-crust pizza, straight from the wood-burning oven, followed by house-made gelato. **$**

Falcon Nest
Sit at a picnic table on the beach and feast on well-priced grilled lobster. Next to the Island Harbor jetty. **$$**

WEST END VILLAGE

West End Village is less a 'village' and more a string of luxuriant beaches lining both the north and the south sides of Anguilla, each more stunning than the last. High-end resorts, gourmet restaurants, and friendly beach bars occupy these sandy shores, promising the ultimate in luxury and service, in addition to the magnificent setting and technicolor sunsets. About 3km of beaches stretch along the north side: Mead's Bay, with restaurants and resorts scattered along its shore, and nearby Barnes Bay, lined with private villas. The south side is an even longer series of gorgeous beaches, stretching at least 6km from vast Rendezvous Bay to windswept Cove Bay to exclusive Maunday's Bay to nearly deserted Shoal Bay West. So whether you like a private patch of sand on a deserted shore or a busy beach bar with umbrella-topped cocktails, you'll find it around West End Village. Welcome to your dream beach-vacation destination.

TOP TIP

If you prefer less lounging and more moving on the beach, get in touch with Anguilla Watersports to rent kayaks or SUPs. This outfit will deliver them to any hotel or beach on the island. It also offers kiteboarding lessons for aspiring wind-riders.

Cap Juluca

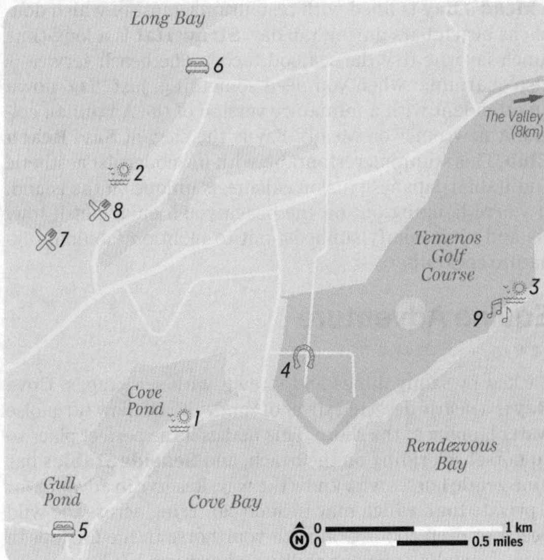

SIGHTS	ACTIVITIES, COURSES & TOURS	EATING
1 Cove Bay	**4** Seaside Stables	**7** Savi Beach Club
2 Meads Bay	**SLEEPING**	**8** Straw Hat
3 Rendezvous Bay	**5** Cap Juluca	**ENTERTAINMENT**
	6 Malliouhana	**9** Bankie Banx's Dune Preserve

MOONSPLASH MUSIC FESTIVAL

This little island attracts some big names in music every March, when the **Moonsplash Music Festival** takes place at Bankie Banx's Dune Preserve. Going strong since 1991, this is the oldest independent music festival in the Caribbean. The wonderful, feel-good weekend takes place over three days around the last full moon before Easter. The lineup always features Bankie Banx and his son Omari Banks and other local performers, as well as musicians from around the region and around the world. Past special guests have included Steel Pulse, Nas, John Mayer and Jimmy Buffett. But it's always a great lineup of excellent reggae and diverse international acts, playing under the full moon on Rendezvous Bay.

Luxe Living

TAKE PARADISE TO A NEW LEVEL

At the western end of the island, several five-star resorts outdo themselves with their exquisite design, luxurious amenities and super-attentive service. Even if you don't spend the night at one of these swanky spots, you might indulge in a decadent meal or an afternoon at a classy beach club. Discerning travelers stay at **Cap Juluca**, overlooking gorgeous Maunday's Bay on the south side of the island. Each of the suites has direct access to the sand, where beach attendants cater to every whim. Across the island on Mead's Bay, **Malliouhana** is the island's 'original' luxury resort, with grand architecture and flower-filled grounds. If you can drag yourself away from the dreamy two-tier infinity pool, it's a short stroll down to the beach.

WHERE TO EAT AND DRINK IN WEST END VILLAGE

B&D's Barbecue
Pull up a lawn chair and devour chicken, ribs and lobster straight off the grill. Open Thursday to Saturday. **$**

Picante
Mexican dishes with Caribbean highlights, eg spicy tuna tacos. Wash it down with a jalapeño margarita. **$$**

Jacala
Romantic restaurant on Mead's Bay serving Caribbean fare with French flair. **$$$**

SUNSET MAGIC

Looking for a memorable setting to watch the fiery orb drop into the sea? Just drive west – pretty much as far as you can without trespassing on private property. At this far end of Anguilla, the coastline is marked by dramatic limestone cliffs that reflect hues of yellow and red at sundown. Far below, waves crash against the rocks – and jutting out from the shoreline, the sea has cut an arch out of the coastal cliff. The **Anguillan Arch** is beautiful at any time of day, but its colors come alive in the late-afternoon light. And, of course, the sky turns a million shades of orange and pink and gold as the sun disappears below the horizon.

Mead's Bay is lined with restaurants, most of which double as beach bars during the day. **Straw Hat** is a long-time lunch favorite (try the seafood tacos). The beach service is also charming: when you need something, just 'flag' down an attendant with a miniature version of the Anguillan colors. A newcomer on Mead's Bay is the elegant **Savi Beach Club**. This stunning restaurant, with its modernist aesthetic and Italian-Japanese fusion cuisine, is unique on the island. If you're hanging out on the beach you'll enjoy plush towels and ultra-comfy sunbeds, not to mention fabulous signature cocktails.

Equine Adventure

RIDE O'ER SAND AND SEA

Backed by sandy dunes and strewn with sea grapes, **Cove Bay** is a nearly deserted sliver of sand with shallow turquoise water lapping at the shore. This makes it the perfect place to go horseback riding on the beach, and **Seaside Stables** has nine gentle horses who know the way. Reserve in advance for a private tour, which may include cantering across the wild beach or even cooling off with your horse in the Caribbean blue, depending on your ability and comfort level.

Island Icon

SEASIDE TUNES AT 'THE DUNE'

Set on the long, sandy stretch of **Rendezvous Bay**, **Bankie Banx's Dune Preserve** is a ramshackle music club and beach bar, crafted from driftwood, recycled boats and other island scraps, and decked out with funky artwork and old photographs. The bar itself is made from the hull of an old wooden boat named *It Ain't Easy*. The stage has seen some huge names in music, such as The Wailers and Jimmy Buffett. It all takes place against the backdrop of sea and sky, with the hills of St-Martin in the distance. This one-of-a-kind music club is owned by island legend Bankie Banx, the singer and songwriter who is often called the 'Anguillan Dylan' for his soulful music, poetic lyrics and rebellious spirit. An evening at the Dune Preserve is a chance to hear music by Bankie Banx himself, as well as his son Omari Banks and other special guests (Wednesday, Friday and Saturday). On Sunday the club hosts 'Sunday School,' with various artists playing from noon until late in the evening, and music ranging from classic rock to reggae to heartfelt blues. The music is solid, the breeze is salty and the vibe can't be beat.

MUSIC LOVERS

Bankie Banx's Dune Preserve is the only dedicated music club on the island, but several restaurants offer live music, including **Veya** (p66) in Sandy Ground and **Savi Beach Club** (p70) on Mead's Bay.

GETTING AROUND

The beaches of West End Village are perfect for long strolls in the sand, stopping off for a snack here, a drink there, and perhaps some live tunes or a spectacular sunset. You'll need wheels for longer distances, although a taxi can get the job done as well as a rental car.

Arriving

Regional and international flights go in and out of Anguilla's little airport just outside The Valley. But more often than not, the easiest way to get here is to fly into Princess Juliana Airport (SXM; pictured) in Sint Maarten, and then take a pleasant boat ride across the channel to Anguilla.

By Air

Tiny Clayton J Lloyd International Airport is on the north side of the island, just off The Valley Rd. Anguilla Air flies several times daily to/from Sint Maarten and St-Barth, while Trans Anguilla Airways has flights to seven islands around the region. TradeWind Aviation and Seaborne Airlines have flights to/from San Juan, Puerto Rico. Sky High Aviation and SAP go to/from the Dominican Republic. There are also daily direct flights to/from Miami, USA, on American Airlines. Outgoing passengers must pay US$28 in departure tax (cash only).

By Boat

Busy Blowing Point Ferry Terminal has eight daily ferries to Marigot, St-Martin (US$30, plus US$28 departure tax), and charter boats to Simpson Bay, Sint Maarten (run by Calypso Charters and FunTime Charters; US$75, plus US$36 departure tax). Both trips take 20 to 30 minutes.

Money

Currency: Eastern Caribbean dollar (EC$)

CASH

Eastern Caribbean dollars (usually called ECs) are pegged to US dollars (EC$2.7 equals US$1). US dollars are widely accepted, and dispensed at local ATMs.

DIGITAL PAYMENTS

Some local businesses – especially charter-boat and tour operators and other self-employed people – may accept payment by Apple Pay, Venmo or some other digital service.

CREDIT CARDS

You can pay with Visa or MasterCard at most hotels, restaurants, stores and car-rental companies, but American Express is not always accepted.

ANTIGUA & BARBUDA

EASY, BREEZY LEEWARD ISLES

Hikes and overgrown forts, kitesurfing winds, beauteous diving and a dry, breezy climate complement the stellar fantasy-island beaches of Antigua and Barbuda.

Antigua's corrugated coasts cradle hundreds of perfect little coves lapped by beguiling jewel-toned water, while the sheltered bays have provided refuge for everyone from Admiral Nelson to buccaneers and yachties. If you can tear yourself away from your beach chaise, you'll discover a distinct English accent to this island. You'll find it in the busy capital of St John's, in salty-aristocratic English Harbour, and in the historical forts and other vestiges of the colonial past. Antigua is also classic Caribbean: full of pastel houses and churches, a rum-infused mellowness and engaging locals who will generously point you to their favorite spots and trust you to respect them as your own.

Barbuda, Antigua's captivating sister island 30 miles north, walks on the wilder side. Besides its history of communal land ownership and responsible caretaking of its arid natural beauty, Barbuda also retains its unique cultural flavor in contrast to that of Antigua. Its resilient population of around 1300 is still recovering from Hurricane Irma in 2017, which flattened most of the delicate, low-lying island and necessitated the complete evacuation of its human inhabitants. Its extraordinary beaches were unaffected, so travelers wishing to lounge on white sand, snorkel around pristine reefs and watch the famous frigate birds should not hesitate to journey here while this fragile ecosystem remains in balance.

ROBERTO MOIOLA/GETTY IMAGES ©

THE MAIN AREAS

ENGLISH HARBOUR
Maritime and historical hub. p78

EASTERN ANTIGUA
Atlantic beaches and offshore islands. p85

CODRINGTON
Wild, natural beauty. p89

SIMON DANNHAUER/SHUTTERSTOCK ©

Above: Galleon Beach (p80); Left: Frigate birds

Find Your Way

At only 14 miles across and 11 miles long, everything in Antigua lies within 45 minutes' drive. Thirty miles north, petite and wild Barbuda has one main road connecting the ferry dock with the sole town of Codrington.

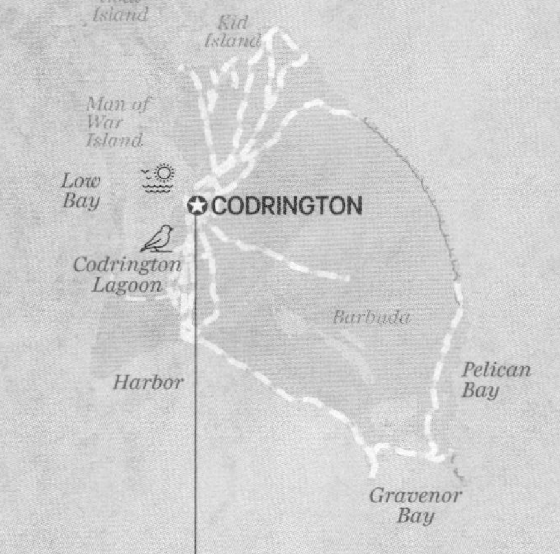

Codrington, p89
On Barbuda's west coast, the island's only town is the launch point for tours of the frigate bird sanctuary, Codrington Lagoon and a pink-sand beach.

CAR

Renting a car is the most convenient way to get around the islands and make the most of your time. Alternatively, taxis have set rates and can be hired by the day for multiple stops.

BUS

Local minibuses serve most of the island and run hourly to English Harbour from St John's. Bus license plate numbers begin with 'BUS.' The main bus station in St John's is just south of the public market.

BOAT

Ferries typically run daily from Antigua to Barbuda in the morning, and back to Antigua in the afternoon. On both islands, some beaches that have been developed by resorts are more easily accessed by boat than on foot.

English Harbour, p78

Hub of Antiguan history and lively contemporaneous activity, this southern harbour village has sites of interest, beaches, hikes and dining options.

Eastern Antigua, p85

Windswept kitesurfing waters and Atlantic-side beaches attract sunbathers, snorkelers and wing foilers. Interior roads lead to ruins of sugar mills, a donkey sanctuary and sunny parish towns.

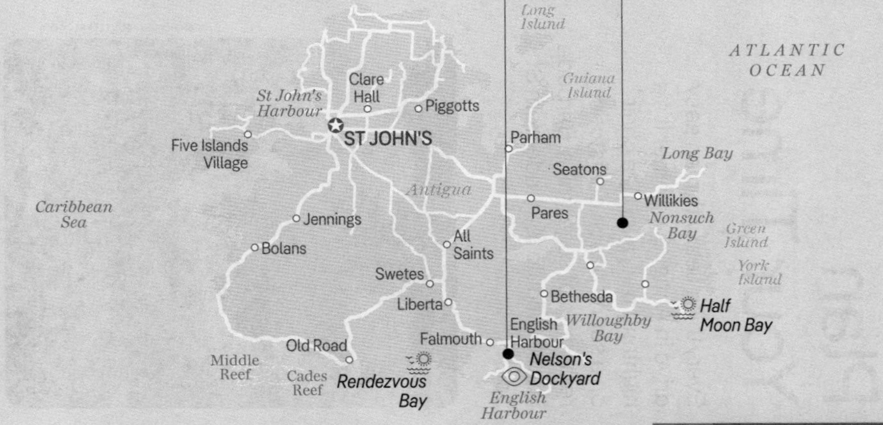

Long Island
ATLANTIC OCEAN
Guiana Island
Clare Hall
St John's Harbour
Piggotts
ST JOHN'S
Parham
Five Islands Village
Seatons
Long Bay
Antigua
Willikies
Caribbean Sea
Pares
Nonsuch Bay
Green Island
Jennings
All Saints
Bolans
York Island
Swetes
Bethesda
Liberta
Half Moon Bay
English Harbour
Willoughby Bay
Falmouth
Old Road
Middle Reef
Nelson's Dockyard
Cades Reef
Rendezvous Bay
English Harbour

Plan Your Time

Everything lies within an easy drive in Antigua, whether it's a highland trail, a lounge chair on a sunny beach or historic remnants of sugar mills. Barbuda is a 90-minute ferry ride from St John's.

SEAN PAVONE/SHUTTERSTOCK ©

View from Shirley Heights (p80)

If You Only Have One Day

- Visit the museum at **Nelson's Dockyard** (p79) in English Harbour for a primer on Antigua's maritime and sugarcane-growing history. Wander around the restored marina buildings and admire the yachts, and pair the visit with a drive up to **Shirley Heights** (p80) for a classic view of English Harbour below.

- Retreat down the hill to **Galleon Beach** (p80) and rent snorkel gear, have lunch and soak up some Antiguan sunshine with a rum cocktail in hand. Alternatively, drive out to the beautiful west coast and set yourself up for a spectacular Caribbean sunset on the terrace at **Dennis Restaurant** (p84) at **Ffryes Beach** (p83).

Seasonal Highlights

Beach weather rules from December through April, with daytime highs averaging 84°F/29°C. Hurricane season peaks September to November.

JANUARY

Cricket season begins – Antigua's favorite sport season runs through July, with matches held at Sir Vivian Richards Stadium.

APRIL

Gorgeously maintained yachts swan about the waters off English and Falmouth Harbours during the **Antigua Classic Yacht Regatta**.

MAY

Antigua Sailing Week culminates with the Dockyard Day celebration in early May, symbolically marking the end of the yachting season.

MYSTIC STOCK PHOTOGRAPHY/SHUTTERSTOCK ©, PAUL D SMITH/SHUTTERSTOCK ©, SOUTH FLORIDA AERIALS/SHUTTERSTOCK ©

Three Days to Travel Around

- Explore teeming reefs on a snorkeling or diving boat trip to **Cades Reef** (p84) or take a kitesurfing lesson at **Jabberwock Beach** (p88).

- Learn about the flora and fauna on the lush highlands with a guided hike at the **Wallings Reservoir** (p82). Walk the old sugar-estate grounds of **Betty's Hope** (p86) and brush a docile new friend at the **Donkey Sanctuary** (p86).

- Discover the contrast of Barbuda's natural beauty by catching the morning ferry from St John's to visit the **frigate bird sanctuary** (p90) and pink-sand beach, lunching on lobster and sunning on **Princess Diana Beach** (p92) before returning to Antigua.

More Than a Week

- Combine your Nelson's Dockyard visit with a hike along the **Middle Ground Trail** (p80) to **Pigeon Point Beach** (p80) for dramatic views from the bluff. Enjoy lunch and an afternoon at the beach before walking back to English Harbour. Don't miss the live reggae on Thursdays, or Sunday evening barbecue parties at **Shirley Heights** (p80).

- Stay the night on Barbuda to check out its limestone caves, including the sinkhole **Darby Cave** (p92), and remote beaches at **Two Foot Bay** (p92). On your return to Antigua, walk the ruins of **Fort James** (p88), have a quiet beach afternoon along **Runaway Bay** (p88) and take a sunset dinner at **Casa Roots** (p86).

JULY

Preceded by weekend festivities all summer, Antiguan **Carnival** kicks off in July and ends the first week of August.

AUGUST

Sample Antiguan flavors at the **Urlings Seafood Festival**, where local restaurants and vendors offer fish, conch and lobster specialities.

OCTOBER

Weeklong run-up to **Independence Day** on November 1, with parades, performances and steel-pan music competition.

DECEMBER

On December 9, the country commemorates Vere Cornwall Bird, Antigua and Barbuda's first Prime Minister, with **VC Bird Day**.

ENGLISH HARBOUR

Named for the Royal Navy base the British established here in the 17th century, English Harbour made an excellent strategic location with its deepwater bays protected by high coastal hillsides. Remnants of its forts and cannons still stand in varying states of preservation along the high points overlooking the camera-ready English Harbour and adjacent Falmouth Harbour, with hiking trails to most.

Modern-day English Harbour has an unmistakably international flavor, with a lively dining and drinking scene, marinas and beautifully restored historic sites now housing restaurants and boatyard services. The town hits 'peak yachtie' around the many sailing events centered in this southern hub, most notably during Antigua Sailing Week. If traveling independently, it makes a superb base, with everything from rare budget accommodations, groceries and fruit stands, and car-rental offices. English Harbour is central to weekly Shirley Heights festivities, dive trips, well-catered beaches and a variety of cuisines.

Barbuda

Antigua

ST JOHN'S

English Harbour

TOP TIP

When you purchase your admission ticket to Nelson's Dockyard, Dow's Hill Interpretation Centre or Shirley Heights, ask the staffer to endorse your admission ticket for the duration of your stay. This allows you to visit on multiple days without paying admission each time you pass through the dockyard.

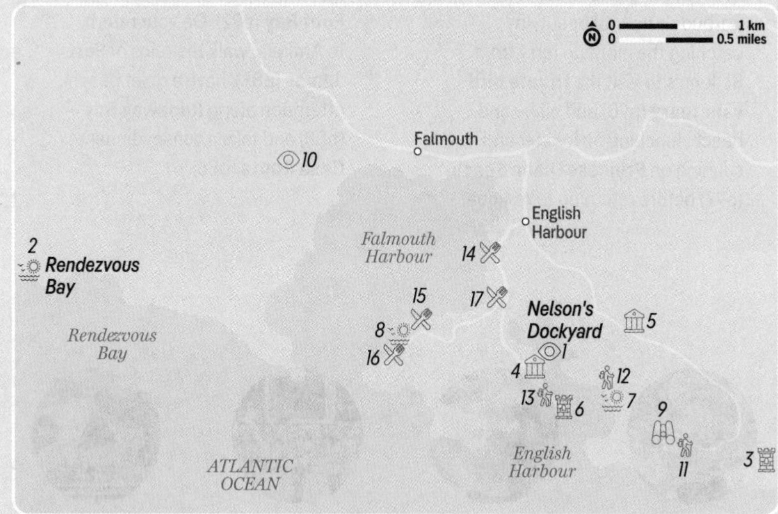

TOP SIGHTS
1 Nelson's Dockyard
2 Rendezvous Bay

SIGHTS
3 Blockhouse
4 Dockyard Museum
5 Dow's Hill Interpretation Centre
6 Fort Berkeley
7 Galleon Beach
8 Pigeon Point Beach
9 Shirley Heights
10 Springhill Riding Stables

ACTIVITIES, COURSES & TOURS
11 Carpenter Rock Trail
12 Lookout Trail
13 Middle Ground Trail

EATING
14 5 Senses
15 Bumpkins
16 Catherine's Café Plage
17 Colibri
(see 4) Dockyard Bakery

CHIARA MAGI/SHUTTERSTOCK ©

Nelson's Dockyard

Antigua's Maritime History

MUSEUMS AND LIVING MARITIME CULTURE

Walking between the brick wall and conch-bejeweled limestone hillside into **Nelson's Dockyard** illustrates the logic of its locale as a strategic harbor. Efforts to preserve and restore its Georgian-era colonial structures in the 1950s resulted in its designation as a Unesco World Heritage Site in 2016. The attractive brick buildings now house inns, restaurants and boatyard businesses in this working marina, where modern-day yachts float in contrast with stout 19th-century British fortifications.

The best starting point – after picking up a pineapple turnover at **Dockyard Bakery** – is the **Dockyard Museum**, which occupies a former naval officer's residence. The various rooms cover the site's natural history, early Arawak settlers, European development of the dockyard and the work that happened here. It also includes an exhibit on the ongoing 8th of March Project that examines the lives of eight enslaved men who perished in a dockyard explosion on March 8, 1744. The historical background gives excellent context for your nearby next stops that are part of **Antigua and Barbuda National**

THE 8TH OF MARCH PROJECT

Desley Gardner, Heritage Resources Officer at National Parks Authority, on crucial oral histories:

This initiative tries to highlight who these African laborers were and what they did for us, how they really shaped our culture today.

We have a lot of centenarians in Antigua, many of whom would've known somebody who was born before emancipation in 1834, and could pass down their stories. We wanted to record those oral histories, so we could try and cross-reference them with existing records. Oftentimes, as Black people, our oral traditions are not seen as valuable in academia, but when there's no written record of the people, we need these oral histories to help cement the British Navy's documentation.

LOCAL EATS IN ENGLISH HARBOUR

Roti Sue's
Made-to-order roti paired with a fresh juice like pineapple-turmeric – perfection. Open lunch hours only. $

Caribbean Taste
Sample delicious, real-deal local specialties like *fungee*, *ducana* and roti made by an Antiguan granny. $

Flatties Flame Grill
Barbecued ribs, peri peri chicken and other grilled delights on Dockyard Dr. $$

Park. Your admission ticket to Nelson's Dockyard entitles you to entry at **Dow's Hill Interpretation Centre**, where you can experience the retro multimedia intro to Antigua (narrated by the sun, who has a charming Antiguan accent!), and up the hill to the **Blockhouse** and Shirley Heights, offering the classic view down on the boats in English Harbour.

Take a few sunset snaps before heading back down the hill for dinner at **5 Senses** for Mexican-inflected French cuisine or French Creole **Colibri** in the center of town.

NIGHTS AT SHIRLEY HEIGHTS

If you hadn't heard it from us, some friendly Antiguan would clue you in to **Sunday night barbecue parties at Shirley Heights** (US$10 cover). Most visitors show up before sunset to take in the spectacular views of English Harbour at magic hour, set to a joyous soundtrack of live steel-pan music. Local vendors offer the usual trinkets and colorful maracas, and the indoor and outdoor bars keep the drinks flowing and the barbecue going. Later in the evening the steel-pan orchestra packs up to make way for live reggae – this is when the real party starts. If this sounds like your jam, don't miss the **Thursday night reggae parties** here.

Southern Hikes & Beaches

HIKES ENDING WITH BEACH TIME

The most accessible hike from English Harbour starts near the water-taxi dock at Nelson's Dockyard. The **Middle Ground Trail** (aka the Goat Track) begins from the paved path zigzagging uphill toward **Fort Berkeley**, a spur from the main trail that juts into the harbor. The one-mile trail climbs up a peninsular cliff, offering dramatic views of the sea below and revealing fort ruins as you pass barrel cacti and roaming goats. The trails drops you at **Pigeon Point Beach**, a lovely spot for a post-hike dip and lunch at **Catherine's Cafe Plage** or the more casual **Bumpkins** at the other end.

To walk up to the remarkable **Shirley Heights** view, start east of English Harbour at Galleon Beach. The steep **Lookout Trail** is the fastest route to Shirley Heights. From the top, connect with **Carpenter Rock Trail** for beautiful harbor views on the descent, which leads down to the beautiful **Mermaid Gardens** rock pool – mermaid sightings not guaranteed – and a spur trail further west that drops down to the coastal rock formations known as the **Pillars of Hercules**. From here you can scramble over boulders along the beach if the tide is low enough and reward yourself with a cocktail and a snorkeling session back at Galleon Beach.

If your dream for the day is for solitude, leave English Harbour behind and drive west toward Springhill Riding Stables. Follow the road until it turns into a dirt track; park and follow the track about a mile down to the rock-and-sand beaches of remote **Rendezvous Bay**. You're often likely to have the entire beach to yourself.

GETTING AROUND

The town of English Harbour is best navigated on foot. Park in the wedge-shaped lot leading to Nelson's Dockyard, or in the lot at the corner of Dockyard Dr and the road to Antigua Yacht Club Marina. Pigeon Point Beach, Dow's Hill and Shirley Heights are accessible via hiking trails, car or taxi. Water taxis provide a little maritime adventure, shuttling between Nelson's Dockyard and nearby Galleon Beach.

Beyond English Harbour

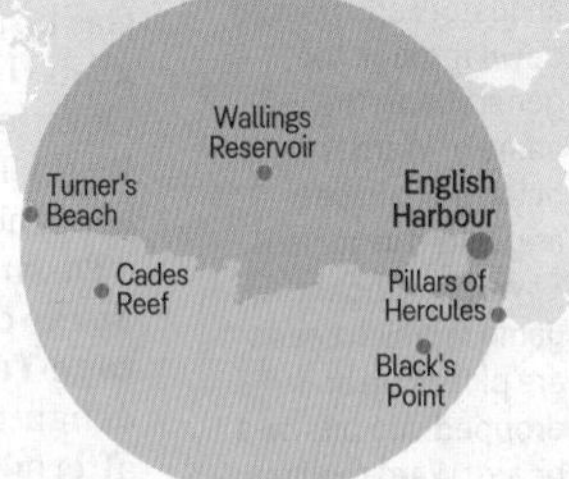

Antigua's west coast is some people's best coast, while Fig Tree Drive gives lush, tropical vibes in contrast to the rest of this dry leeward isle.

Heading north along Matthews Rd leaves yacht culture behind and into the parish villages where authentic Antigua resides. Graceful stone churches on hilltops, roadside fruit stands and primary schools cluster along the road as it climbs into the more humid, tropical sector of the island. Following Fig Tree Drive will take you to the Wallings Reservoir and tree-shaded hiking trails, as well as a zip-line park, a British-Caribbean teahouse and an art gallery nestled into a forest glade.

Continuing west along Fig Tree Drive drops you onto the southwest coast to some of Antigua's loveliest Caribbean-side beaches. The southern coast also shelters some of the island's top dive spots.

TOP TIP

West-coast beaches can get inundated with cruise-ship crowds midday, but the masses usually clear out around 3pm, leaving the beaches gloriously emptier.

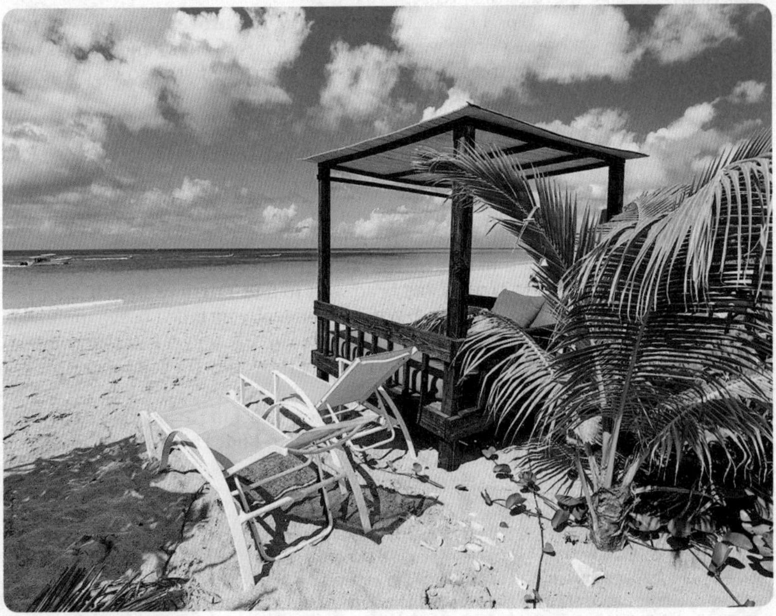

Turners Beach (p82)

WARRI

Brought with African ancestors and passed down through the generations, the game of Warri is believed to have originated in ancient Egypt. A mancala game in which seeds are picked up and dropped into pits on a board, Warri requires strategic thinking (and ideally a poker face) to succeed at winning more than half the seeds on the board. Warri is still a popular pastime in Antigua, played in public spaces with onlookers offering commentary. While Barbados is the other Caribbean nation retaining a Warri tradition, Antigua's more widespread, passionate Warri community continues sparking the love of the game in the next generations of Warri masters.

Interior Island Heights & Delights

ANTIGUA'S FORESTED HIGHLANDS

Gas up the rental car and head 20 minutes northwest from English Harbour into Antigua's green highlands. Though these elevations may be modest – **Mt Obama**, formerly known as Boggy Peak, hits 1319ft – they are about as lush as the island gets and a fresh contrast to the dry, sunny beaches.

Passing westward through the village of John Hughes, keep an eye out for the sign on the right pointing to **Antigua Vintage Tea House** on the grounds of Mt Tabor Retreat. This delightful, open-air British-Caribbean spot to take brunch or afternoon tea is open four days a week.

Continuing less than half a mile west, stop by the lovely **Fig Tree Studio Art Gallery**, ensconced in a forest glade, to peruse the prints of artist Sallie Harker and the paintings, sculptures and work of other local artists.

The **Wallings Forest** turnoff lies at the top of the next rise. This reserve comprises the largest remaining forest on the island, composed of secondary-growth evergreen and deciduous trees, including mahoe, ironwood and locust. The trail system no longer retains the signage from its brief lifespan as a community-run nature reserve, so it's best to hike with a guide.

The trails begin at **Wallings Reservoir**, completed in 1900 with attractive, Victorian-style stone and brickwork, and drained in 1912 following a drought. Picnic tables along the edge of the old reservoir make a great lunch stop after hiking – silent but for birdsong, the occasional donkey bray and the breeze.

For a bigger thrill, **Antigua Rainforest Zipline** – a minute's drive west of Wallings Forest – runs canopy tours over the trees, with professionally trained staff to assure a safe adrenaline rush.

White Sands of Western Antigua

POWDERY BEACHES, PRISTINE CARIBBEAN WATERS

Antigua famously touts its 365 beaches, but the handful of perennial favorites remain that way for a reason.

From English Harbour, drive yourself to the south coast via Fig Tree Dr and head west to find **Turners Beach**, about 35 minutes' drive. With permanently installed beach umbrellas and easy access from the road, it's convenient and comfortable for families, with all of the white sand and sparkling sea you could desire.

Five minutes north, Valley Rd begins to hug the coast, making **Darkwood Beach** easy to find. This stretch of beach is

HIKING GUIDES

Footsteps Rainforest Hiking Tours
Over 30 years' experience and forest knowledge; based at Fig Tree Studio Art Gallery.

Happy Heights Hiking Tours
Owned and run by a born-and-raised Antiguan with insight into the environment and culture.

Trek Tours Antigua
Tailors trips to ability level and desired experience, and arranges transport with local guides.

SOLARISYS/SHUTTERSTOCK ©

Antigua Rainforest Zipline

beloved by Antiguans, with umbrella and chair rentals, several eating options nearby and a shallow reef for snorkeling the crystal-clear water.

Continue several minutes north up Valley Rd to quiet **Ffryes Beach**, another favorite with locals and visitors alike. With plenty of space, both southern and northern ends offer umbrella and chair rental, as well as a bar and cafe bookending this chill zone.

On the other side of Ffryes' northern point lies the popular **Valley Church Beach**, with services at the north end including **Nest** for a lobster lunch, changing rooms, and umbrella and chair rental. Come here morning or late afternoon to avoid midday cruise-ship crowds. Note that the beach drops off a bit suddenly at the shore, so watch little ones extra carefully. Find the turnoff a few minutes north up Valley Rd, across from a small church, with a surfboard marking the correct road.

Snorkeling & Diving Antigua

REEFS, WRECKS AND BEACHSIDE SNORKELING

Antigua and Barbuda's inviting beaches may be their prime draw, but their underwater allure cruises somewhat under the radar. Even if you're not a strong swimmer, nearshore shallow reefs allow you to float around in calm waters to see sponges, colorful darting reef fish and maybe a moray swaying amid the eel grass. Dive sites noted below are accessed on boat dives, lying 10 to 20 minutes' boat ride from Falmouth or English Harbours.

UNINHABITED OFFSHORE ISLANDS

Off the northeastern coast of Antigua, the **North Sound Marine Park** is dotted with about two dozen uninhabited islands. Boat tours to **Great Bird Island** and **Hells Gate Island** offer the fantastic opportunity to snorkel and climb up limestone cliffs to phenomenal panoramic views. Catch a glimpse of a red-billed tropic bird or an Antiguan racer, one of the rarest snakes in the world.

If you can arrange a morning charter to **Green Island**, the beaches and snorkeling will be vastly more serene before more boat excursions arrive before noon. Kitesurfers will find their stoke off the north shore of Green Island; kitesurfing school **40knots** picks up from various points around **Nonsuch Bay**.

BOAT TOUR OPERATORS

Creole Antigua Tours
Established in 2005, this outfit offers group or private charters on a 55ft catamaran.

Adventure Antigua
Explores Great Bird and Hells Gate Islands, a turtle conservation area and mangroves.

Wadadli Cats
Circumnavigate Antigua by catamaran; or take snorkeling trips to Great Bird Island and Cades Reef.

BEST PLACES TO STAY & EAT IN THE WEST

Dennis Restaurant
After sunning at Ffryes, take in the sunset with a seafood dinner and rum cocktail. $$

Fox House
Fresh local ingredients feature in flavorful Antiguan and Caribbean cuisine, paired with stellar cocktails. $$

Wild Lotus Glamping
Sleep right on Valley Church Beach in a luxury tent, off-grid with solar power. $$$

ANNA HOYCHUK/SHUTTERSTOCK ©

Cades Reef

If you're a diver, find reliable, long-running local operators **Dive Carib** at the **National Sailing Academy** in English Harbour. In Jolly Harbour, about 45 minutes' drive from English Harbour, look up **Indigo Divers** (indigo-divers.com). Dive guides usually decide on specific sites on the day, based on conditions and with guest preferences in mind. Among the thriving hard and soft corals, you might see showy species of damselfish, parrotfish, puffer fish, blue tangs, reef sharks and rays, as well as lobsters, pipefish and sea turtles.

Off the south side of Antigua, the several-miles-long **Cades Reef** is popular for its many dive sites, ranging in difficulty for beginners to experts. The **Pillars of Hercules**, just outside English Harbour, are bristling with reef life and also easily accessed by walking about 15 minutes beyond the south end of Galleon Beach (p80). **Black's Point** near Falmouth Harbour is another nearby reef with superb diversity and is accessible to all levels. Advanced divers might want to check out the **Montserrat wreck**, a bit further outside Falmouth Harbour, at a depth of over 110ft.

BEACH SNORKELING

Check out **Long Bay** (p86) or **Galleon Beach** (p80) for consistently calm swimming conditions with shallow reefs right off the beach, where you can also rent snorkeling gear.

GETTING AROUND

Buses (around EC$3) run regularly during the day from St John's down Valley Rd, from where you may have a walk to the nearest beach. It's easiest to drive, which also gives you flexibility to stop at several beaches if one looks too crowded or not quite the scene you're seeking.

Boat tour operators usually offer a few options for pickup points, but check with specific companies to find out how to get to your vessel.

EASTERN ANTIGUA

The wilder, windswept eastern side of Antigua beckons those who chase windy seas and seek more solitude on its Atlantic coast. The flatlands in the east are home to the sunny villages of Willikies, Newfield and FreeTown, gateways to gorgeous beaches, coastal national park lands and historical sites. As the sign into Willikies enthuses: 'Welcome to Paradise!!!'. The east coast beaches do exemplify archetypal visions of paradise, with perfect crescents of sand and every hue of turquoise and aquamarine shimmering in the reef-rife waters beyond. Sandy beaches lie in contrast to the exhilarating sea spray of the Devil's Bridge National Park headlands.

Antigua's sugarcane history mirrors that of other Caribbean islands, and an understanding this era of the island's past is made more accessible in places like Betty's Hope and its thoughtfully curated interpretive layout. This side of Antigua is for active (and inactive) recreation, but also invites deeper contemplation.

Barbuda
Antigua
ST JOHN'S
Eastern Antigua

TOP TIP

If you'll be in eastern Antigua on a Sunday, Betty's Hope is closed that day. However, Sunday evenings after 5pm or 6pm are prime time for contemporary culture: live reggae, local food and dancing with an Antiguan crowd at Road House in Newfield.

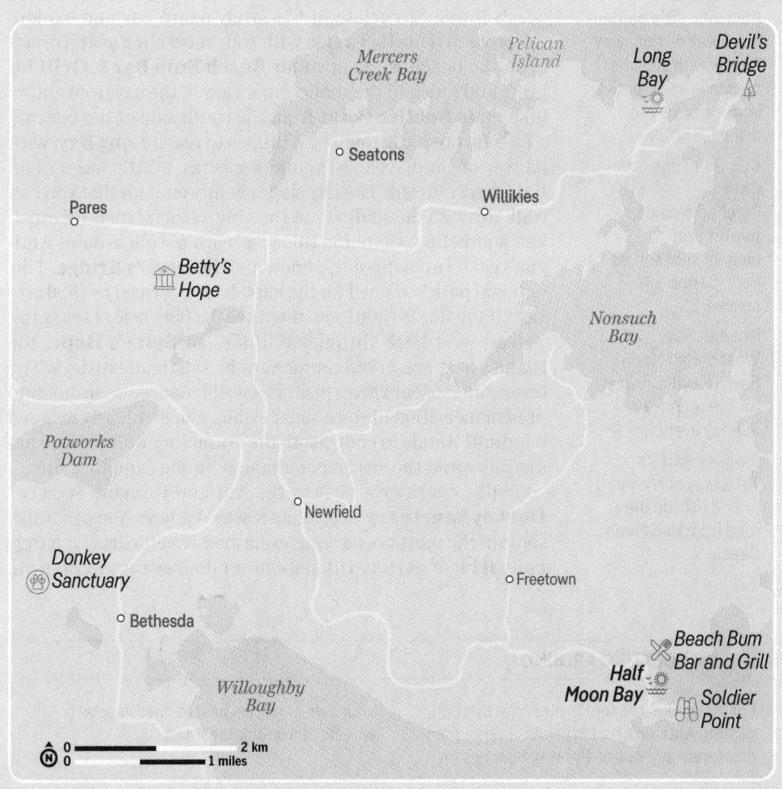

CATHYRL/SHUTTERSTOCK ©

Devil's Bridge

BEST NORTHEAST DINING

Beachlimerz
Enjoy a curry on the terrace at the south end of Fort James Beach. $

Casa Roots
Romantic little garden hideaway on Runaway Beach, with sublime cocktails and creative, ingredient-driven dishes. $$$

Cecilia's High Point Café
Perched seaside, this breezily elegant spot serves Euro-Caribbean cuisine. $$

Road House
West of Half Moon Bay in Newfield, best for live reggae on Sunday evenings. $

Smiling Harry's
Takeaway curry and grilled fish, up the road from Half Moon Beach. $

Beaches, Bluffs & Bricks

ATLANTIC-SIDE BEACHES, SUGAR-INDUSTRY RUINS, DONKEYS

In the southeast, east of FreeTown, you'll find famously picture-perfect **Half Moon Bay**. This gorgeous crescent of white-sand beach makes a perfectly serene locale for laying down your beach towel. Luxuriate in the lovely azure bay and explore the protected northern side with your snorkeling gear. Directly on the beach is the open-air **Beach Bum Bar & Grill** for beers and lunch in the shade. For a view of the bay from above, hike up to **Soldier Point** from the south side of the beach.

Pass through the town of Willikies to reach **Long Bay**, with its row of candy-colored vendors' casitas, a little bar and an Italian restaurant. The bay slopes gently enough that you can walk through the shallows to thriving, colorful reefs for excellent snorkeling. Combine this visit with a walk around Antigua's easternmost point, punctuated by **Devil's Bridge**. This national park is named for the karst bridge formed by tidal erosion; if the tide is right, you might see the blowhole of sea spray.

Head west back through Willikies to **Betty's Hope**, the island's best preserved remnant of its sugarcane history. The one-room museum gives visitors a well-balanced snapshot into pre-emancipation life on a sugar estate. A meticulously restored windmill stands in contrast to the crumbling walls of the rum distillery and the rusting equipment on the rambling site.

Finally, consider a visit to the Antigua Humane Society's **Donkey Sanctuary** to meet its rescue donkeys. You can brush some of the most docile, long-eyelashed sweethearts for a free, mutual hit of oxytocin (donations for donkey care welcomed).

GETTING AROUND

For maximum freedom to meander through eastern Antigua's parish towns, interior points of interest and out-of-the-way beaches on your own clock, it's best to have your own wheels or a dedicated driver.

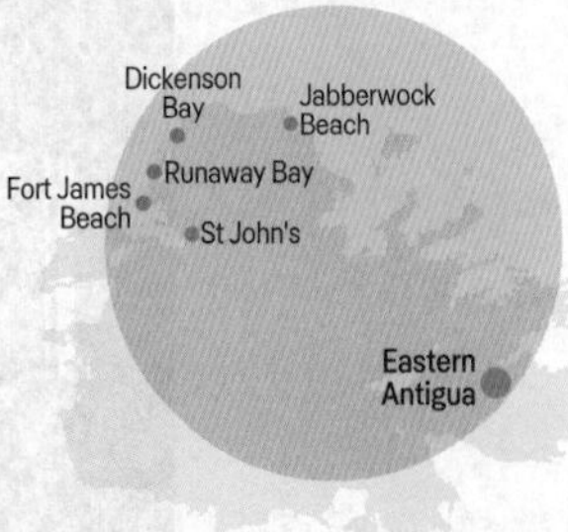

Beyond Eastern Antigua

North Antigua has world-class kitesurfing conditions, fort ruins and worthwhile beachfront dining. Uninhabited offshore islands offer much to explore.

The northern sector of Antigua is central in many ways. On the west side is St John's, port of call for massive cruise ships and the island's only big city. On the east side is VC Bird International Airport and introduction to the island for many.

Go forth and find your quiet bit of beach near St John's – be catered to at the resorts at Dickenson Bay, or poke around Fort James and then relax at the nearby locals' beach.

You can polish your wing-foil skills at Jabberwock Beach, or book a dive trip or offshore-island exploration from a dedicated boat. Or take an excursion to the intriguing, uninhabited islands offshore.

TOP TIP

The only ATMs on Antigua that dispense US$ are located inside King's Casino at Heritage Quay in St John's.

NAPA/SHUTTERSTOCK ©

St John's (p88)

M.J BULICH/SHUTTERSTOCK ©

Fort James

ANTIGUA'S CRICKET OBSESSION

The sport of cricket is akin to a religion in Antigua. The island has produced some of the world's best cricketers, including homegrown legend Sir Vivian Richards – nicknamed 'King Viv' and the 'Master Blaster' for his aggressive batting style. The national cricket stadium is named in his honor, and a life-sized statue of him takes pride of place by the front door of the Museum of Antigua and Barbuda in St John's.

Cricket season runs from January to July, with official matches usually played on Thursday, Saturday and Sunday. If you want to see this local passion in action, check windiescricket.com for the schedule.

Port, Forts & Board Shorts

KITESURFING AND ST JOHN'S' ATTRACTIONS

At some point, you'll likely transit through **St John's** to catch a Barbuda ferry, withdraw cash or get from A to B. From Willikies, the 30-minute drive to St John's follows Sir Sydney Wallings Hwy across the island.

While in town, it's worth wandering down to the **public market** to pick up snacks, cooling off with some ice cream or a cocktail at **Redcliffe Quay**, admiring the stately **Anglican Church** and making a circuit through the **Museum of Antigua and Barbuda** for a one-room intro to the country's history.

Then off to the beach; the ones nearest St John's are quite lovely, though their proximity to town means you may share space with loads of cruise-ship visitors. **Dickenson Bay** has a lively beach party kind of scene, with all the amenities and service you could desire. A quieter alternative lies further south along **Runaway Bay** and **Fort James Beach**, with more local flavor and fewer facilities. Take the time to ramble around the ruins of **Fort James**, which are usually deserted. It's strangely peaceful to wander up to the fortification walls, where you can look down at the busy, modern port alongside the silent, decommissioned British cannons.

At the northeastern reach of the island, the long, east-facing **Jabberwock Beach** catches the prevailing winds, creating world-class conditions for water sports. At the same time, it's a great place for beginners to take a kitesurfing or wing-foiling lesson. Or simply lay out your beach towel to enjoy this wilder stretch of white beach backed with sea-grape trees.

GETTING AROUND

It's easiest to get around north Antigua in a rental car or taxi. Negotiate a price with a driver to keep one on retainer for the day.

It's possible to take buses from St John's, but you'll lose a lot of time and flexibility as schedules can be unpredictable.

CODRINGTON

Named for the sugar baron brothers to whom Britain granted a 50-year lease in 1685, Codrington is Barbuda's main town – where horses are turned out to graze and feral donkeys roam. The village of Codrington fans out from the fisheries dock on Codrington Lagoon, with the south end of downtown defined by the island's airstrip. Following the main River Rd about 3½ miles due south from the village takes you to the River Wharf, where passenger and cargo ferries from Antigua arrive and depart.

Barbuda has struggled to bounce back after Hurricane Irma in 2017, but there is a thriving community here, with small businesses serving food, guiding tours, fishing, and otherwise keeping the island's economy afloat. The tourism office says it best: 'We live it, you'll love it.' Take the time to live it, watching frigate birds in flight and noticing the grains of sand, shell and coral of its rose-colored shores.

TOP TIP

If self-catering, consider stocking up in Antigua. Food prices are higher on Barbuda, as supplies are ferried over from Antigua after being imported from abroad. That said, the tiny main grocery store near the Codrington fisheries dock is crammed with a surprising variety of goods.

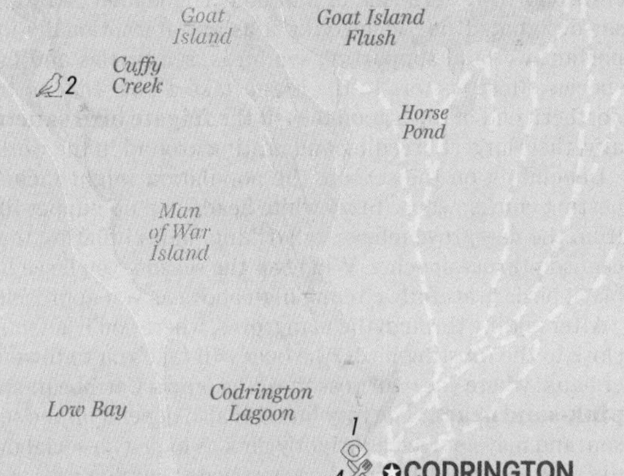

SIGHTS
1 Codrington Lagoon
2 Frigate Bird Sanctuary
3 Pink Sand Beach

EATING
4 CD's Café
5 Wa'Omoni's Best Burgers

Pink Sand beach

Frigate bird sanctuary

NURSERY IN THE LAGOON

George Jeffery, tour guide:

Codrington Lagoon is one of the largest natural lagoons in the Caribbean chain, and it's a nursery for marine life. Strong populations of mangrove and yellowtail snapper and a lot of little reef fish all hatch in the lagoon. The current brings eggs from various species into the lagoon, and the eggs get hidden among the mangroves. After hatching, those little creatures stay there until they get big enough to move out along the ocean floor.

Some of the lobsters initially tagged in Codrington Lagoon have been caught as far as Anguilla, St-Martin, Nevis, St Kitts. So, we know it's a really important nursery for marine life beyond just Barbuda.

Pristine Marine Wildlife Refuge

FRIGATE BIRDS AND PINK SANDS

Separated from the Caribbean Sea by a miles-long, narrow strip of beach, the saltwater **Codrington Lagoon** buffers the entire northwestern side of Barbuda. The lagoon is a Ramsar-designated site, identifying it as an internationally important wetland supporting sea birds, sea turtles and fish species. Most visitors to the island take a boat tour to the northern end of the lagoon to visit the **frigate bird sanctuary**, their largest breeding and nesting ground in the world.

Depending on the season, the population might include nesting chicks, whose fuzzy white heads pop up puppet-like from the mangrove foliage, or striking males inflating their crimson throat pouches. Whatever the season, you'll see the black birds gracefully circling high above as you approach.

After gliding through the mangroves, where you'll get quite close to the roosting birds, the boat will take you to the outer bank, where you can cross the dune onto a Caribbean-side **pink-sand beach**. The rosy hue will also depend on the season, and may not look as brightly pink as hyped on social media. But as you walk with the warm water lapping over your feet, you'll see for yourself the thousands of tiny pink seashells mesmerizingly swishing back and forth with the tide. Take a dip and requisite photos at the pink-sand beach before motoring back across the lagoon to Codrington town.

Walk into the village for a local lunch at **Wa'Omoni's Best Burgers** or **CD's Café**, or stop when you see a roadside barbecue grill for a jerk chicken takeaway lunch.

GETTING AROUND

Codrington village is very walkable, centering on the fisheries dock. Leaving from the road on the north side, find the tourism office on the left and grocery store on the right. This road takes you to the main River Rd leading north and south; at this intersection and southbound, you will encounter a roadside grill or two if you follow your nose.

Beyond Codrington

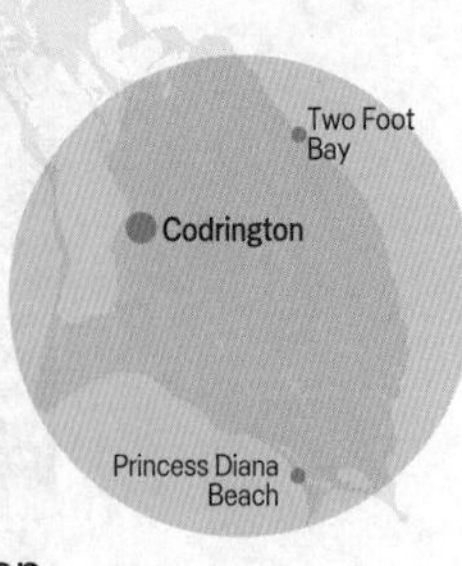

One of the least-developed inhabited Caribbean islands, Barbuda brings solitude and natural beauty in its pristine waters, pink beaches and limestone caves.

Barbuda's wild nature – embodied in its mangroves and reefs, isolated white- and pink-sand beaches and silently soaring frigate birds – has always been its allure. The Caribs called the island Wa'omoni, believed to mean 'Island of Herons,' possibly referring to its frigate bird population. The main River Rd runs south from the River Wharf along the southwestern coastline and its soft, sandy beaches to Coco Point in the south. Northward from Codrington, the road crosses the island to its wild, austere northwestern coast and limestone caves, and its 'highlands' that top out at a modest 125ft. Barbuda's isolated, windswept beaches and clear, pristine water make it a spectacular visit-now island, as it teeters on the razor's edge of ecosystem-crashing development.

TOP TIP

Locally run website barbudaful.net has excellent general information and tips on where to eat and places to stay for independent travelers.

Two Foot Bay (p92)

OLIVIERO GODI/GETTY IMAGES ©

Princess Diana Beach

BEST PLACES TO STAY & EAT

Frangipani Glamping
Get off the grid, catching fish for dinner and reading in a hammock near your sweet cabana on the northeastern coast. $$

ArtCafe
Stop by for lunch, browse the art gallery, and book well ahead for the room available here, outside of the village with garden space. $$

Barbuda Cottages & Uncle Roddy's
Cottages south of the River Wharf, where horses trot down the beach at day's end. Dine at Uncle Roddy's for a guaranteed lovely/lively eve. $$$

Naturally Barbuda-Ful

FRAGILE WILDERNESS, MAGICAL NATURAL BEAUTY

The main road from Codrington heads north before arcing east across the island to the highlands – about a 15-minute drive by car – where the British-colonial Codrington family based their homestead in the 1720s. The estate ruins afford the highest panoramic views to the coast, and are worth a look, even if that's as far as you venture – it's possible to drive within a 100-yard uphill walk to the **Highland House** site.

But the real stunner here is **Darby Cave**, a limestone sinkhole about a half-mile hike from Highland House. The cave first appears in view when the trail discernibly ends with the tops of palm trees swaying before you below eye level. Climbing down the karst wall, the coolness (both temperature-wise and awesomeness factor) becomes obvious. At the bottom of the cave, walk around the left side to look up from beneath the overhang and inhabit another world entirely.

To explore Darby Cave and the **limestone caves** at **Two Foot Bay** a few minutes further east up the road, it's best to find a guide, as there are **petroglyphs** and other fascinating features you'd be hard-pressed to find on your own.

South of Codrington village, carve out time to laze on magical, white-sand **Princess Diana Beach**, at its best in late afternoon after Barbuda day-trippers have departed and the light begins to cast its spell on the seascape. Feast on a Barbudan lobster lunch at **Shack-a-Kai** as you marvel at your good fortune to enjoy the same beach as its eponymous princess who escaped here for solitude.

GETTING AROUND

Arrange a car rental through Barbuda Rentals. The owner can also arrange tours and taxis by the day. Private transportation is a must, as the outlying attractions aren't regularly served by public transport.

Arriving

Most visitors arrive in Antigua by plane or cruise ship, with a healthy sailing community navigating themselves by private boat during yachting season. VC Bird International Airport (ANU; pictured) is located in the northeast of Antigua, with plenty of restaurants, shops and rental-car agencies. There are fixed rates for taxis, which helps keep your airport exit straightforward and stress-free.

By Air

International flights arrive and depart from VC Bird International Airport, with arrivals greeted by live steel-pan music in the terminal. It's possible to fly to Barbuda from Antigua via scheduled or chartered flights in the high season.

By Boat

Cruising season coincides with the driest weather: from November through April. Cruise ships dock in St John's, where the daily ferries to Barbuda also depart and arrive. The best equipped harbors for independent sailors are English Harbour in the south and Jolly Harbour in the west.

Money

Currency: Eastern Caribbean dollar (EC$), US dollar (US$)

CASH

Cash is generally the preferred payment in grocery stores, gas stations and local restaurants. The EC$ is pegged to the US$ (EC$2.70 = US$1). Both currencies can be used; however, you will usually receive change back in EC$. You can also expect that any torn or damaged US$ bills will not be accepted.

ATMS

Find ATMs in the main towns, though some may not accept your debit card, even when part of your banking network. The ATMs inside King's Casino in St John's dispense US$; elsewhere across the island and in Barbuda, ATMs dispense EC$ only.

CREDIT CARDS

Businesses catering to tourists, including car-rental agencies, tour operators, restaurants and bars, widely accept credit-card payments. Smaller businesses are usually able to take credit-card payments, but it's worth carrying a little stash of cash as a backup.

SCHOENFELDER/SHUTTERSTOCK ©

Above: Lighthouse, Klein Curaçao (p121); Right: Malmok Beach (p103)

THE ABC ISLANDS

SUN, SNORKELING AND HISTORIC SIGHTS

Dynamic culture, thriving underwater worlds and reliably paradisiacal weather: welcome to the ABC islands.

Aruba, Bonaire and Curaçao comprise a dainty trio of islands hovering at the southern edge of the Caribbean. Colloquially known as the ABC islands, they can only be described as terrestrial explosions of culture and nature. Here you'll find cactus-studded deserts just a few kilometers from street-art-splashed neighborhoods, and dynamic reefs just off the coast from cutting-edge restaurants and historic monuments. And while these islands may share cultural similarities, they offer three distinct travel experiences that merit both time and dedication.

Aruba, the smallest of the ABCs, entices visitors with pearly stretches of sand, varied coastal landscapes and a solid tourism infrastructure. Its established resort area caters to creature comforts before giving way to a windswept north, while its laid-back southern half celebrates local arts and an invitingly slow way of living.

Unpretentious Bonaire delights travelers with amiable small-town vibes onshore and spectacular waterscapes offshore. This island is home to the healthiest reefs in the Caribbean and is regarded as one of the best snorkel and dive spots in the world.

Meanwhile, Curaçao walks a successful balance between being a metropolitan country and a rugged, nature-oriented getaway. Its capital, Willemstad, unites past and present, encompassing Unesco World Heritage sites, contemporary restaurants and vibrant nightlife. Outside the city, the island stuns with cliff-lined beaches, colorful reefs and wonderfully wild national parks.

THE MAIN AREAS

ARUBA
Exciting water adventures and luxurious living. **p100**

BONAIRE
Underwater treasures. **p108**

CURAÇAO
City living and rugged coasts. **p116**

Find Your Way

The ABC islands are easy to navigate due to their size and solid infrastructure. Both Aruba and Bonaire can be circumnavigated in a day if you move fast, but traversing larger Curaçao takes more time.

Aruba, p100

Aruba combines the best of opposing worlds: take to the coast with sports like diving and sailing, or dig into the ruggedness of the desert interior.

VENEZUELA

FROM LEFT: FOKKE BAARSSEN/SHUTTESTOCK ©, BIRDIEGAL/SHUTTESTOCK ©, JMJ PHOTOS/SHUTTESTOCK ©

PLANE
If you plan to hop around the islands, book a flight with the local airlines, as the islands aren't connected by ferry. Most folks use Divi Divi Air or EZ Air for their inter-island flights.

CAR
If you want to maximize your time and determine your own schedule, rent a car. The airports on all three islands have robust rental offerings from local and international companies, but make sure you reserve in advance.

TAXI
Taxi services are available across all three islands, with fixed fares determined by the local governments. Note that most taxi drivers do not accept card payments, so make sure you have cash on hand.

Curaçao, p116
This island has it all, from a dynamic capital city and beautiful cliff-lined beaches to a rugged, rural Westpunt for those looking for adventure.

Bonaire, p108
This tiny island is ringed with the healthiest coral reef in the Caribbean – mind-blowing dive and snorkel sites are just a wade-in away.

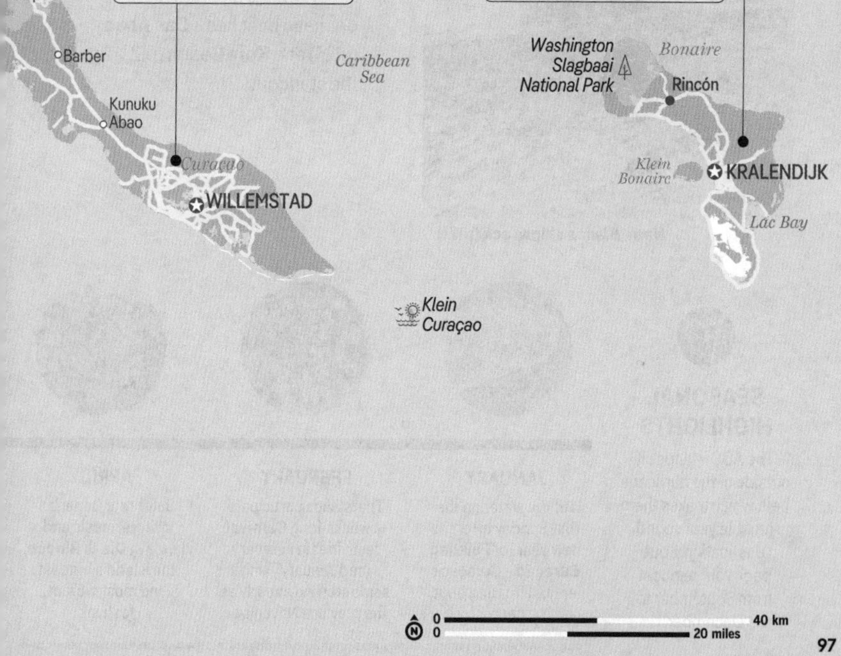

Westpunt
Barber
Kunuku Abao
Curaçao
WILLEMSTAD
Caribbean Sea
Klein Curaçao
Washington Slagbaai National Park
Bonaire
Rincón
Klein Bonaire
KRALENDIJK
Lac Bay
0 — 40 km
0 — 20 miles

Plan Your Time

The ABC islands wear their hearts on their sleeves, so you'll get a good taste of them, even on a short trip. However, if you've got more time, they also offer plenty of opportunities to dig deep.

MASTERPHOTO/SHUTTERSTOCK ©

***Maria Bianca* shipwreck (p121)**

If You Only Do One Thing

- If Aruba's your island, hit the pristine sands of **Eagle Beach** (p103) or make your way south to snorkel near **Mangel Halto** (p102); if you've got a little extra time, book a diving tour of the **Antilla** (p103), a WWII-era ship sunk off Aruba's coast.

- In Bonaire, grab a snorkel and jump in pretty much anywhere along the leeward coast for mind-blowing underwater views. If you want to explore deeper reefs, consider completing your diving certification here.

- If you're in Curaçao, snag a set of wheels and hit Westpunt's dramatic beaches – **Cas Abao** (p123) and **Knip Beach** (p123) are the standouts.

SEASONAL HIGHLIGHTS

The ABC islands sit outside of the hurricane belt, which makes them reliable year-round destinations, but pack your raincoat from September to December.

JANUARY

Hit the water on the first Sunday after the new year for **Fuikdag Curaçao** – Curaçao's annual floating boat party.

FEBRUARY

The islands participate in weeks-long **Carnival** festivities in February (and January), with some starting as early as the previous November.

APRIL

Celebrate Bonarian culture, music and dance at **Dia di Rincón**, the island's biggest (and most vibrant) festival.

GAIL JOHNSON/SHUTTERSTOCK ©, ANNA KRASNOPEEVA/SHUTTERSTOCK ©, STEPHANKOGELMAN/SHUTTERSTOCK ©

Three Days to Travel Around

- Three days in Aruba deliver a solid highlight reel; in addition to the stops above, spend a morning in **Arikok National Park** (p104) and use the afternoon to tour the murals in **San Nicolas** (p106).

- With three days, you can enjoy the beauty of Bonaire's north and south ends. Take a day to explore the north, starting from **Kralendijk** (p109) and circling up to the *salinas* of **Gotomeer** (p111). From there, visit historic **Rincón** (p111) and wander **Washington Slagbaai National Park** (p112). Use another day to drive south – windsurf in **Lac Bay** (p115) and hit the southern snorkel sites across from the island's saltworks.

More Than a Week

- As the largest island, Curaçao deserves at least four or five days. Take a couple of days to explore the beaches and national parks of **Westpunt** (p119) before diving into **Willemstad's** (p118) candy-colored streets. There, spend an afternoon marveling at the historic architecture and street art, and don't miss the **Kura Hulanda Museum** (p118) and **Landhuis Bloemhof** (p118).

- Take a day trip out to uninhabited **Klein Curaçao** (p120) for an afternoon of relaxation, and finish up with a lazy day in southern Curaçao's **beach clubs** (p123).

- Do some island hopping! With a little over a week, you can easily link trips to the islands without rushing.

MAY
Watch some of the world's best water sport athletes compete at the Aruba's annual **Hi-Winds World Challenge** (p106) competition.

JUNE
Curaçao holds the biggest **Pride** celebration of the three islands, with rainbow-clad venues throughout Willemstad.

SEPTEMBER
The **Aruba Art Fair** takes over San Nicolas, and Curaçao's **Kaya Kaya Festival** (p118) brings additional art and theater to Willemstad.

OCTOBER
Boats hit the water for Bonaire's **International Sailing Regatta**, and the streets of Kralendijk, Bonaire's capital, come alive with parties.

ARUBA

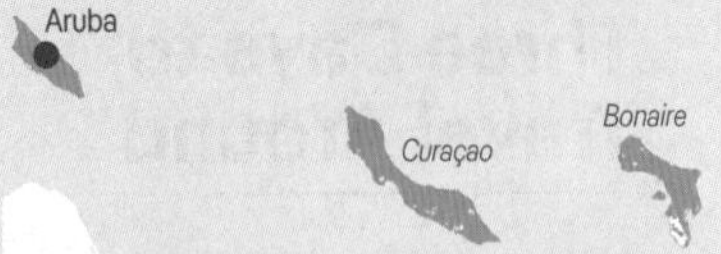

Aruba features large on itineraries of North Americans looking for a tropical escape, making it the most visited island in the ABC chain. Lying only 25km off the coast of Venezuela, Aruba is a distinctly international place, with its culture drawing from South American, African, Dutch and North American influences, evidenced by the multilingual, multiethnic folks who live here.

More so than any of its neighbors, Aruba caters to the cruise and resort crowd, with areas like downtown Oranjestad, Palm Beach and Noord making up Tourism Central. You'll find plenty of restaurants, bars and shops, making it an ideal base for families.

If the resort life just ain't your style, Aruba's north and south ends embrace the wild, arid landscape that makes the island a true paradise – giant cacti reach for the sky, songbirds whistle from mangrove trees, water laps at remote beaches and gnarled fofoti trees bend in the trade winds.

TOP TIP

Some of Aruba's roads can get rough once you leave the main thoroughfares. If you plan on doing any adventuring on the eastern side of the island, we recommend renting a high clearance vehicle just to be safe. Some parts of the national park are only accessible in a 4WD.

JUNIOR BRAZ/SHUTTERSTOCK ©

Mangel Halto (p102)

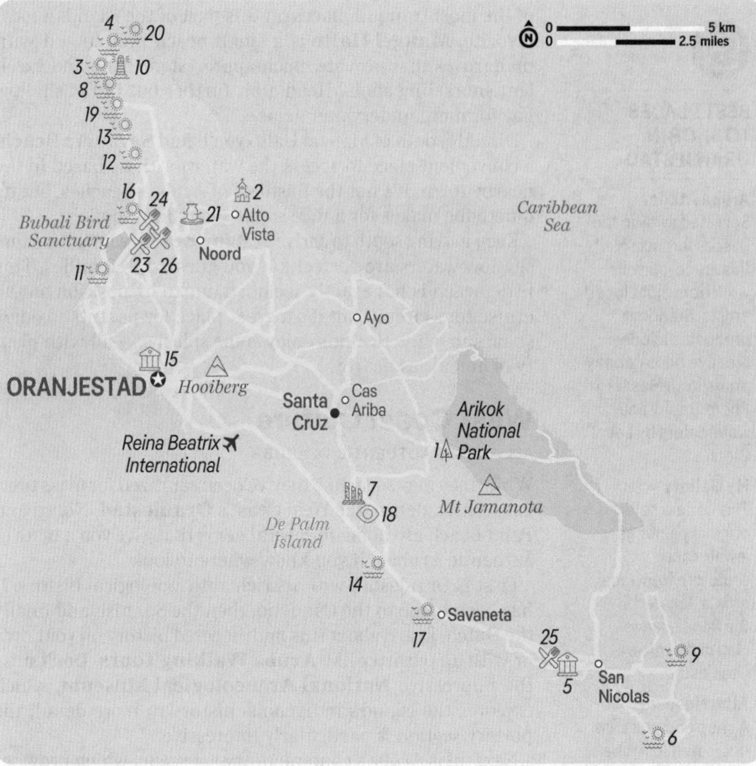

TOP SIGHTS
1 Arikok National Park

SIGHTS
2 Alto Vista Chapel
3 Arashi Beach
4 Arashi Dunes
5 Artisa Gallery
6 Baby Beach
7 Balashi Gold Mills
8 Boca Catalina
9 Boca Grandi
10 California Lighthouse
11 Eagle Beach
12 Hadicurari Beach
13 Malmok Beach
14 Mangel Halto
15 National Archeological Museum
16 Palm Beach
17 Savaneta Beach
18 Spanish Lagoon
19 Tres Trapi
20 Westpunt Beach

ACTIVITIES, COURSES & TOURS
21 Terrafuse
(see 3) Westpunt Loop

EATING
23 Gasparito
24 Local Store
25 Neighba
26 Papamientu

DRINKING & NIGHTLIFE
(see 5) Kulture Café

Slow Down in the Southwest

ARUBA AT ITS MOST RELAXED

If southwestern Aruba's outdoor experience can be summed up in a word, it's serene. Do yourself a favor and take it slow through these sweet spots – they're to be relished.

Start with a walk around **Spanish Lagoon**, a peaceful, mangrove-lined wetland that's the only one of its kind on the island. Enjoy the bird's-eye-view of the lagoon from the nearby ruins of the **Balashi Gold Mills** – relics from Aruba's 19th-century gold rush – or head into the mangrove forest itself via a short but lovely trail for excellent bird-watching.

For your next mangrove adventure, add a dash of sand: **Mangel Halto** sits just south of Spanish Lagoon and is one

OUTFITTERS IN THE SOUTHWEST

Aruba Atelier
Book a pedal kayak and explore the mangroves of Spanish Lagoon and the coast.

Aruba Bob
Outstanding snorkeling/diving outfit offers 'snorkel scooters', among other things.

BEST PLACES TO SHOP IN ORANJESTAD

Aruba Atelier
Secreted away in the Paseo Herencia Mall, this art co-op sells work from eight local artists. Standout products include creative photography prints from MesArt Photography and watercolors by Laura Clots.

My Gallery
This gallery sells original paintings, jewelry and sculpture from local artists; located in the Renaissance Mall in downtown Oranjestad.

Aloe Museum
A shop and museum dedicated to Aruba's most valued export: aloe. Check out the numerous bath products; the hand cream is especially indulgent.

of the most tranquil places on this part of the island. A local favorite, **Mangel Halto** is a small beach punctuated with mangroves that provide much-appreciated shade and excellent snorkeling spots. Head a bit further out in the shallow bay for more underwater gems.

Directly south of Mangel Halto you'll find **Savaneta Beach**, a convenient place to access the water for those based in the nearby town. It's not the flashiest of Aruba's beaches, but its quiet vibe makes for a nice sunset-watching spot.

Keep moving south to arrive at **Baby Beach**, where the calm, shallow waters are perfect for, you guessed it, families. This little beach is not exactly secluded due to its position on the cruise tour circuit, but it's a great place for parents to enjoy some sun while the kids enjoy some splashes – all with plenty of amenities nearby.

West Coast Culture

ALL THINGS AUTHENTIC IN ARUBA

While they may seem like they've been sanitized for mass tourism at first glance, the West Coast's **Oranjestad**, Noord and Palm Beach are home to several gems that give you a taste of authentic Aruba – if you know where to look.

First is Oranjestad with its rich anthropological history. It has been home to the Caquetio, then the Spanish and finally the Dutch. Learn about this multifaceted history on your own or with an outfitter like **Aruba Walking Tours**. Don't miss the impressive **National Archeological Museum**, which explores the island's indigenous history in more detail; the pottery section is particularly impressive.

Next up is Aruba's contemporary art scene, which provides a unique insight into the culture of the area. So pop into **Terrafuse**, a studio/artist compound that acts as Oranjestad's artistic oasis. It's run by two local artists – Ciro and Marian Abath. Here, students attend glass-bead-making workshops and visitors can chat with Ciro and Marian about their latest works or wander the thoughtfully curated garden, which doubles as a creative space for sculptors and writers.

At this point, you're bound to have worked up an appetite. Most Arubans will advise you to check out **Local Store** at least once for excellent chicken wings and the laid-back energy the island is known for; be sure to grab a seat on the cheery patio. If you're looking for an elevated eating experience, head to **Gasparito** or **Papamientu** for authentic Aruban dishes like *keshi yena* (Gouda rind stuffed with spiced meat) and *keri keri* (shredded spiced fish).

WHERE TO STAY ON THE WEST COAST

Brisas
A cool, tropical and bohemian property that specializes in self-catered studios and apartments. $

Costa Esmeralda Village
Modern apartments and cottages, complete with two spotless pools and a hot tub. Perfect for relaxing. $

MVC Eagle Beach
A budget-friendly hotel right across the street from Aruba's most famous beach. $$

FOKKE BAARSSEN/SHUTTERSTOCK ©

Eagle Beach

The Beaches of Aruba's West Coast

ARUBA'S BEST SANDY STRIPS

Aruba's western coast is a gorgeous assemblage of beaches, each one with its own personality. Beach-hop up the shore to catch 'em all, or pick a favorite and settle in for the vibes.

Eagle Beach is Aruba's most famous swath of sand, and for good reason. The beach is long and wide, giving people plenty of space to spread out, even on the busiest of days, and the sand is clean and pearly, brightly contrasting with the cerulean waves that lap at its edges.

Just north of Eagle Beach, you'll find **Palm Beach**, Aruba's party center with a high-rise backdrop. This is the place for you if you're looking for plenty of food options and lots of camaraderie with fellow vacationers.

Just 3.5km up L. G. Smith Blvd sits a hat trick of magnificent stops. This is Aruba's west-coast snorkeling hub: **Malmok**, **Tres Trapi** and **Boca Catalina**. Malmok's craggy walls and Boca Catalina's rocky sea floor are havens for a myriad of tropical fish, while sea turtles are a common sight at Tres Trapi. Pro tip: go in the morning to avoid the cruise-ship crowds.

Aruba's northernmost beaches are **Arashi Beach** and **Hadicurari** (aka Fisherman's Huts) – windsurfing central, and

ARUBA HIGH AND LOW

The Hooiberg
This cone-shaped mountain seems like a geological anomaly, given the overwhelming flatness of its surrounds, but the **Hooiberg** (a Dutch moniker that means 'haystack') is a volcanic structure made of quartz diorite left over from Aruba's geological creation. If you're feeling adventurous, climb the 600 steps (164m) up to the top for unparalleled island views.

The SS Antilla
Germany's WWII-era ship is one of the Caribbean's largest wrecks. It's a piece of war history that has become a thriving reef and one of Aruba's most famous dive spots.

The vessel was in Aruban waters when the Germans invaded the Netherlands in 1940 and was scuttled after the Dutch government responded by ordering the seizure of all German ships in the Dutch Antilles.

BEACH BARS ON ARUBA'S WEST COAST

MooMba Beach Bar
A Palm Beach staple that's a relaxed lunch stop during the day and a lively beach party at night.

Arashi Beach Shack
Busy (but convenient) beach bar serving a substantial menu of sandwiches, seafood baskets, burgers and more.

Surfside Beach Bar
Off-the-beaten-track bar on a sandy crescent near the airport – sun loungers, frozen daiquiris and landing 737s included.

SERGE YATUNIN/SHUTTERSTOCK ©

PRACTICALITIES
Scan this QR code for entry prices and opening hours.

TOP SIGHT

Arikok National Park

Aruba's terrestrial offerings are resplendent. Arikok National Park represents Aruba's wild side, and no trip is complete without spending an afternoon marveling at its treasures, large and small. Grab a set of wheels and make your way inland to see some of the most fascinating elements of Aruba's natural and human history.

DON'T MISS

- Cunucu Arikok Trail
- Sero Arikok Trail
- Conchi
- Boca Prins Dunes
- Fontein Cave
- Quadirikiri Cave
- Dos Playa

Explore the Caribbean Desert

Arikok National Park encompasses 20 percent of Aruba's total landmass, and within its bounds is the island's largest swath of uninterrupted desert. The landscape is dominated by candelabra cactus (better known on the island as cadushi cactus), aloe vera, agave, prickly pear cactus and the golden kibrahacha tree, which blooms after the rainy season. Arikok features several walking trails that wind through this spectacular ecosystem, all accessible from the visitor center.

Cunucu Arikok Trail

The preferred trail of bird-watchers, the Cunucu Arikok Trail offers visitors the chance to glimpse much of the park's birdlife. Spot orange-and-black troupials, bright yellow orioles and tropical mockingbirds as they flit around the cacti, and if you're lucky, you may even spot a ruby topaz hummingbird among the flowers. This trail also leads to the largest and most detailed collection of indigenous petroglyphs (rock carvings) in the park.

Sero Arikok Trail

This trail winds up the side of the second-largest hill in Aruba (at 185m elevation) and offers panoramic views of the park and the island beyond. Views from here reveal Aruba's unique tapestry of desert and dunes as the trail runs into the rocky coast, illustrating the wide diversity of ecological zones in a relatively small place.

Go Subterranean in Arikok's Caves

The park is home to a fascinating combination of geological formations ranging from volcanic tuff to uplifted coral stone, with the latter having eroded away to form two major caves that are well worth exploring.

Fontein Cave

This cave is most recognized for its pre-Columbian cave drawings, a testament to the island's original residents. Follow the designated path into this low-ceilinged cave to admire the limestone columns throughout the space and see the drawings up close.

Quadirikiri Cave

Just down the road from Fontein lies Quadirikiri (pictured), a series of domed chambers with distinct skylights that let in rays of Caribbean sun to magical effect. Look at the walls closely to spot the fossilized coral.

Travel to Arikok's Wild Coast

Arikok's easternmost border runs directly into the ocean and comprises a mesmerizing combination of cliffs, sandy inlets and pounding waves.

Conchi

Perhaps one of the most popular stops in Arikok, Conchi (aka Natural Pool) offers visitors the only chance to safely enter the ocean from the park. A ring of lava stone breaks the force of the waves, protecting a circular pool of enticing turquoise water. You won't have it to yourself, but it's one of the most unique swimming spots on the island.

Boca Prins Dunes

Sandwiched between the desert and Aruba's rocky shores are the Boca Prins Dunes: glistening waves of white sand anchored in place by small but resilient shrubs. Wander the dunes at will, but be careful not to get disoriented while you're walking around – there are no trails here.

Dos Playa

Accessible from the gravel road at Boca Prins, Dos Playa consists of two coves that form a secluded heart-shaped beach. Swimming isn't advised here due to the strength of the waves, but Dos Playa offers a gorgeous spot to sit back and appreciate the sun and sand. The area is also a known nesting area for four different species of sea turtle.

A QUICK TOUR

If your schedule only allows for a short visit, opt for one of the short hiking trails that veer off from the visitor center to get an idea of Arikok's landscape. Then make a beeline for the caves at the southern point of the park before heading toward the wind farm at Vader Piet, right outside the park's border.

TOP TIPS

- While you technically don't need a 4WD to make it down the main road of the park, proceed with caution if you have a low-clearance car; the road has several deep ruts to guide rainwater, and they can be a challenge for sedans and small hatchbacks.
- Visit the park early in the morning to avoid the intense sun and heat that comes with midday visits. Always bring more water than you think you need.
- If you're going to hike, wear adequate footwear – shoes without tread will slip on the fine gravel.

WHERE TO EXPERIENCE ARUBAN CULTURE

Tito Bolivar – founder of Artisa Gallery, the Aruba Art Fair and Aruba Mural Tours – shares his recommendations for the best places to find the soul of Aruba's culture scene.

Hardgrooves Jazz Cafe
If you're a jazz fan, Hardgrooves hosts weekly performances by local and international jazz musicians.

Space21.art
This San Nicolas gallery showcases the works of 21 local artists, with driftwood art, jewelry, painting and sculptures.

Chaos Cafe
This cafe is the perfect place to unwind on a Friday, hosting live band performances that showcase Aruba's vibrant rock-music scene.

home to the **Hi-Winds World Challenge** competition. Arashi has a busy southern end thanks to the beach restaurant there, but the northern area provides a bit more peace and quiet. When you don a snorkel, watch out for the pelicans that dive into the waves to scoop up scores of little silver fish.

Go Remote on the North & East Coasts

A JOURNEY INTO ARUBA'S WILDERNESS

Wild and windswept, Aruba's north and east coasts are a world away from the hubbub of the resorts – and great destinations for hikers and shutterbugs.

The **Westpunt Loop** starts north of Arashi Beach (p103) and winds around Aruba's northern tip, featuring a network of barely-there trails and a car-friendly path. From the trailhead, head north for views of weather-worn limestone and wind-charged ocean; then turn east for a dramatic shoreline replete with hidden caves, 'fields' of rosy succulents and trees twisted by the trade winds. This is also where you'll find the sweeping **Arashi Dunes** and **Westpunt Beach**, a stretch of beach peppered with large black boulders.

Circle back toward your starting point and you'll come upon the area's primary constructed landmark – **California Lighthouse**. Built in 1910, this lighthouse is open to climb, and you can even book a dinner inside. If you're ready for more, drive to the photogenic **Alto Vista Chapel**. The original chapel was built in 1750, but the area was originally home to a Caquetio community, meaning the chapel fell into disrepair. It was rebuilt in 1952, and today you can light a candle at the chapel or walk one of the trails behind it.

Continue south and you'll run into Arikok National Park (p104), which encompasses a whopping 20 percent of the island's total landmass. A haven for hikers, historians and bird-watchers, Arikok enchants with its biodiversity.

Once you exit the park, loop south to land at **Boca Grandi** – park yourself under one of the driftwood shelters and watch the kitesurfers perform acrobatics from the waves. Don't try swimming here though, as the currents are strong.

The Arty Side of San Nicolas

ARUBA'S BIGGEST OPEN-AIR GALLERY

San Nicolas was home to Aruba's oil refinery, one of the island's biggest sources of capital, until it shut its doors in 1985. The once-booming town then entered a slumber as workers departed in search of other opportunities, but recent years have seen a resurgence of energy, powered by motivated and creative Arubans.

WHERE TO EAT NEAR SAN NICOLAS

Zeerover
If you only eat at one place in Aruba, eat here. Their fresh fish and shrimp are caught daily. $

O'Neil Caribbean Kitchen
Jamaican-inflected Caribbean dishes served in generous quantities. Don't miss the goat stew. $$

Mauchi Smoothies
Fresh, health-focused and delicious smoothies, juices and shakes, including DIY mix options. $

KHAIRIL AZHAR JUNOS/SHUTTERSTOCK ©

Alto Vista Chapel

Start your cultural tour of San Nicolas with the lovely folks at **Aruba Mural Tour**, headquartered out of **Artisa Gallery**. Tito Bolivar and his team of artists have turned the town into an outdoor gallery, with huge street-art pieces splashed across nearly every wall and sculptures dotting the sidewalks. And these aren't regular murals – they are towering tableaus that shift with 3D glasses, cutting-edge works that come alive with AI and large-scale portraits done with an almost photographic level of detail. Bolivar hosts the annual **Aruba Art Fair** every November, adding new art from local and international artists, ten pieces at a time.

Once you've learned about San Nicolas' hidden corners on the tour, head to the Nicolaas Store – aka the **Kulture Cafe** – for some coffee and sandwiches in atmospheric digs. The cafe is the town's cultural hub, so if you hit it at the right time, you may find a party in the square outside the shop.

And San Nicolas doesn't go to sleep when it gets dark – head over to **Neighba**, a hip open-air lounge serving up good food and inventive cocktails. Stick around late(ish) for the live music.

PROTECTING THE MANGROVES

Aruba is home to 420 acres of **mangroves** – largely located in the southwest – and these wetland and tidal areas are essential to the island's ecosystems. Not only do they provide homes to countless animal species – Spanish Lagoon harbors 190 species alone – but they also play an essential role in preventing erosion in the low-lying coastal areas. On top of that, they function as carbon sinks and natural air conditioners, with the ability to regulate microclimates and ward off the effects of global warming.

STREET ART IN THE ABC ISLANDS

Neighboring Curaçao has similar initiatives that center art in their urban renewal projects – check out the **Kaya Kaya Festival** (p118) for a taster.

GETTING AROUND

When it comes to getting around, your options in Aruba depend on your itinerary. If you plan to stay along the densely populated West Coast, a car rental may not be necessary; taxis abound (though they aren't exactly cheap), and the Arubus makes stops from San Nicolas all the way to Arashi Beach. Oranjestad, San Nicolas and the resort areas are walkable, but anything outside of that requires a set of wheels – your own or someone else's. If you want to make the most of your time in the more rugged north and east, rent a high-clearance vehicle.

BONAIRE

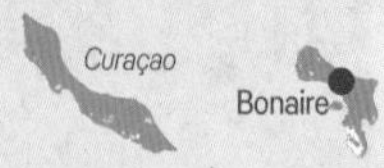

Laid-back Bonaire may not have large, sandy beaches, but it does have some of the most spectacular waters in the Caribbean. Ringed by reefs protected by Bonaire Marine Park, the island is a wildlife enthusiast's dream, specifically if you're interested in finned fauna. And the best part? Most of the dive and snorkel spots can be reached right from the shore, no boat required.

On land, Bonaire's relaxed vibe manifests in low-key hotels and resorts, many of which partner with local dive shops to get their guests safely in the water. The majority of the island's restaurants and bars cluster in Kralendijk, Bonaire's mellow nexus and capital city. Culturally, Bonaire differs a bit from its neighbors, as it remains a special municipality of the Netherlands rather than an independent country. That said, Bonarian traditions are alive and well in Rincón, the island's oldest town and cultural center.

TOP TIP

Use a map app before you head out to make sure you know what your return route looks like – some parts of Bonaire's main roads (such as Queen's Hwy) are one-way, so you won't be able to simply backtrack.

STEPHAN KOGELMAN/GETTY IMAGES ©

Above: Flamingos; Right: Kralendijk

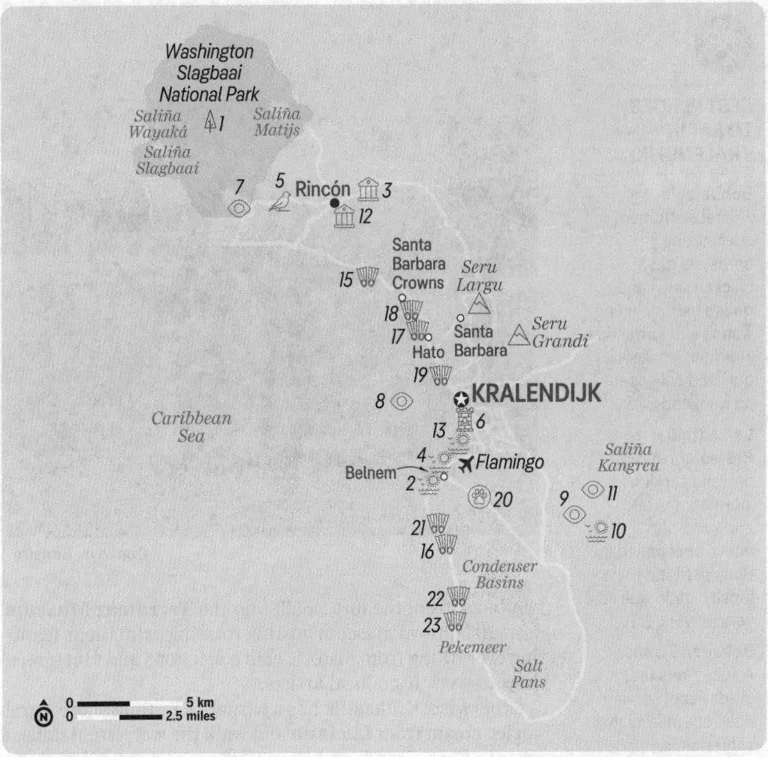

Washington Slagbaai National Park
Saliña Wayaká
1
Saliña Matijs
Saliña Slagbaai
7
5
Rincón
3
12
Santa Barbara Crowns
Seru Largu
15
18
17
Hato
Santa Barbara
Seru Grandi
19
8
KRALENDIJK
6
Caribbean Sea
13
4
Flamingo
Belnem
2
Saliña Kangreu
20
9
11
10
21
16
Condenser Basins
22
23
Pekemeer
Salt Pans
0 5 km
0 2.5 miles

TOP SIGHTS
1 Washington Slagbaai National Park

SIGHTS
2 Bachelor's Beach
3 Cultural Park Mangazina di Rei
4 Donkey Beach
5 Echo Dos Pos Conservation Center
6 Fort Oranje
7 Gotomeer Lake
8 Klein Bonaire
9 Lac Bay
10 Lac Cai Beach
11 Mangrove Center
12 Museo Chich'i Tan
13 Te Amo Beach
(see 6) Terramar Museum

ACTIVITIES, COURSES & TOURS
15 1000 Steps
16 Alice in Wonderland
17 Andrea I
18 Andrea II
19 Bari Reef
20 Donkey Sanctuary
21 Hilma Hooker
22 Invisibles
23 Pink Beach

EATING
(see 6) Luciano
(see 4) The Beach

DRINKING & NIGHTLIFE
(see 12) Cadushy Distillery

SHOPPING
(see 6) Jungle Concept Store
(see 6) Salt Shop

Chilling in Kralendijk

TAKE IT SLOW IN KRALENDIJK

Of the ABC capital cities, Kralendijk – locally known as Playa – is by far the smallest in population, giving it a genial small-town feel. All roads begin here, and it's likely the city will be your hub for your stay, unless you're searching for a truly remote experience.

Like many island nations colonized by foreign powers, the first thing built in the town following the Dutch acquisition of Bonaire from the Spanish was a fort, **Fort Oranje**. Restored in the late 1990s, the fort still greets cruise passengers and functions as a small open-air museum.

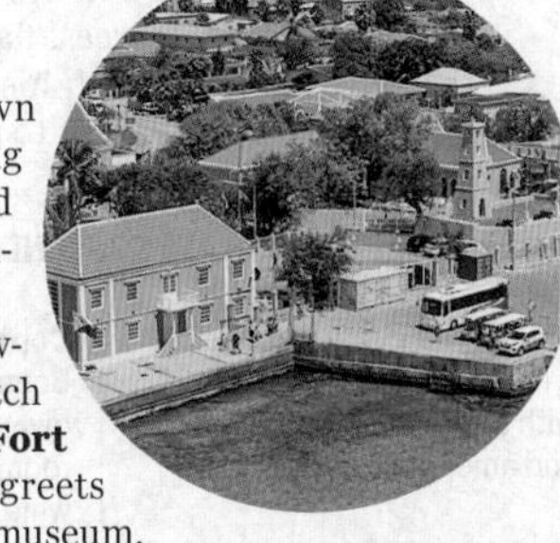

EWY MEDIA/SHUTTERSTOCK ©

BEST PLACES TO EAT IN KRALENDIJK

Bobbejan's
A local institution specializing in barbecue ribs, chicken satay and grilled fish, including wahoo and barracuda. This joint is takeaway only and only opens on weekends. $$

La Cantina
Restaurant and brewery serving international fare and suds, plus a house beer called the Bonaire Blond that's locally made with aloe vera flowers. $$

Between 2 Buns
A sunny, relaxed, all-day spot serving delicious mile-high sandwiches, salads and desserts – passion fruit cheesecake, anyone? $$

BEN SCHONEWILLE/SHUTTERSTOCK ©

Donkeys, Bonaire

A block from the fort, you'll find the **Terramar Museum**, a small cultural museum hosting rotating exhibitions featuring everything from historic coin collections and film screenings to work from local artists.

Otherwise, Kralendijk has a casual DIY atmosphere – grab an ice cream from **Luciano** and walk the waterfront or head over to Kaya Grandi and Kaya Gerhart to peruse downtown shops like **Jungle Concept Store** and the **Salt Shop**.

Head south to the neighborhood of Sabal Palm to drink in ocean views (and a margarita or two) at **The Beach**, a waterfront bar/restaurant complete with sun loungers. If you're looking for a more hands-on activity, drive out to Bonaire's **Donkey Sanctuary**, which cares for an amazing 800 rescued donkeys ranging in age from five months to 46 years.

Find the Soul of Bonaire in North End

WHERE CULTURE MEETS NATURE

Bonaire's North End is a tapestry of all the things that make Bonaire more than just a dive hub – parrots flit between the trees, flamingos preen in the setting sun and Rincón hums with history while krioyo bands play cheerful tunes. If you want to get to know Bonaire, this is your stop.

WHERE TO STAY IN KRALENDIJK

Bellefonte Luxury Resort
A high-end hotel on the water with a variety of room options and amenities for divers. **$$**

Captain Don's Habitat
Bonaire's original haunt for divers; features cottages, rooms and a newly constructed wing of apartments. **$$**

Bamboo Bonaire
Luxe cottages complete with plunge pools; the resort is also home to one of Bonaire's most exclusive restaurants. **$$**

Boka Slagbaai (p113)

Head north from Kralendijk via Kaya Gobernador N. Debrot and onto the scenic Queen's Hwy. Hang a hard right to arrive at the scenic lookout over the blue-hued lake of **Gotomeer**, encircled by green hills. This body of water is home to thousands of flamingos – go at golden hour for a gorgeous panorama.

Further down the road you'll run into **Echo Dos Pos Conservation Center**, which protects and rehabilitates Bonaire's yellow-shouldered Amazon parrots and runs a restoration project for Bonaire's trees – book a tour to learn more.

Keep driving east from the conservation center, and the verdant Rincón Valley will open up before you. It's home to the island's oldest town and neighbor to the expansive Washington Slagbaai National Park (p112). In Rincón proper, head to the **Cadushy Distillery** to taste spirits distilled from the island's favorite cactus, and pop into the small-but-charming **Museo Chich'i Tan**, where you'll learn about Rincón's past residents and the town's musical history.

Slightly further afield you'll find **Cultural Park Mangazina di Rei**. Enslaved people used to make the 10-hour walk back to Rincón from the salt pans in the south to get their provisions from the storehouse that the cultural park now occupies. Today, Mangazina di Rei contains a museum, hosts cultural events, and runs a monthly food and art market.

THE SOUNDS OF RINCÓN

The small town of Rincón is the epicenter to Bonaire's big **musical tradition**. Krioyo, the island's folk music, features prominently in Bonaire events throughout the year. It's a genre flavored with hints of traditional African rhythms, European waltzes and polkas, American jazz, and distinctly Bonairian Barí and Simadan (both of which have their own specific accompanying dances).

Krioyo bands sing largely in Papamientu and incorporate local instruments like the *barí* (drum), *wiri* (a metal version of a *güiro*, a Spanish percussion instrument) and the *kwarta* (a small, four-stringed guitar), alongside international staples like the accordion, mandolin and piano.

WHERE TO EAT IN NORTH END

Posada Para Mira
A treehouse-like hilltop restaurant that serves up local fare, fresh juices and stunning views. **$$**

Cactus Fence Supreme
A spacious restaurant serving classic stews and *tutu* (mashed cornmeal and black-eyed peas). **$**

Kos Bon So
Rincón's main barbecue joint, serving ribs, pork chops, fish, shrimp and ice-cold beer. **$**

GAIL JOHNSON/SHUTTERSTOCK ©

PRACTICALITIES

Scan this QR code for entry prices and opening hours.

TOP SIGHT

Washington Slagbaai National Park

Washington Slagbaai covers one-fifth of Bonaire. Formerly two plantations, these 14,000 acres were ceded to the government in 1969 and now stand as testament to the island's varied natural landscapes. Drive the park loops to take in mountains of coral stone, giant boulders delivered to the island's shore by an ancient tsunami, *salinas,* home to local bird life, and pristine diving sites.

DON'T MISS

- Lagadishi Trail
- Boka Kokolishi
- Malmok
- Pos Mangel
- Brandaris
- Put Bronswinkel
- Wayaka
- Boka and Salina Slagbaai

Long Loop

Indicated by yellow markers along the park's main road, this loop takes two and a half hours if you drive straight through, but it will easily take up a whole day if you stop at the sights along the way. Take this route for the full Washington Slagbaai experience.

Lagadishi Trail

Start your morning off with the short hike up Lagadishi Trail, one of the only major walkable routes in the park. You'll spy tons of giant cadushi cacti, historic walls, a dramatic coastal blowhole and views of Playa Chikitu. You'll also get the chance to peer out over Salina Matius and its resident flamingos.

Boka Kokolishi

One of the rare sandy 'beaches' on Bonaire, Boka Kokolishi offers the chance to get your feet wet in the inviting tide pools hidden among the beach's boulders. This cove is quiet and remote, and you'll likely have it all to yourself.

Malmok

Malmok (pictured) is thought to be one of the island's earliest inhabited places – archaeologists have found evidence of humans dating back to 800 BCE. It was also used as a residential area for the plantation's enslaved people. Today, the main ruins on display are an unfinished lighthouse and lightkeeper's house from 1906.

Pos Mangel

Bird-watchers shouldn't miss Pos Mangel, one of the park's two main watering holes, and a natural home for several bird species, including the tropical mockingbird and the eared dove. Come early in the morning for the best chance of spotting wildlife.

Short Loop

Indicated by green markers, this loop shares some stops with the long loop, but it omits the park's northernmost sights. Instead, this loop cuts straight west across the park and is the way to access Brandaris, Bonaire's highest point.

Brandaris

The hike to the top of Brandaris takes about 45 minutes and is considered one of the more challenging hikes in the park, but the payoff is bird's-eye views of Washington Slagbaai's forests, *salinas,* plains and coasts. On clear days, you might spot neighboring Curaçao. The park requires that anyone completing this hike enter the park by noon.

Put Bronswinkel

Another must-see for bird enthusiasts, Put Bronswinkel is the park's other watering hole, and a reforestation project that's really starting to take root. Originally home to the Amerindians who tended fruit trees here, and later the location of one of the plantation's wells, it's now an excellent place to spot scaly-naped pigeons, bananaquits, yellow warblers, yellow-shouldered parrots and crested caracaras.

Underwater Wayaka

Dive sites at Wayaka offer a respite from the daytime heat and subaquatic views of Bonarian fish life – spot French angelfish, colorful sea snails and stingrays. This is a particularly easy in-and-out for divers.

Boka & Salina Slagbaai

Formerly one of Bonaire's main ports, Boka Slagbaai is the park's southernmost dive site and a popular stop for picnicking, bird-watching, cliff jumping and snorkeling. See if you can find remnants of the bay's past life: anchors, ballasts, cannons and more, all underwater. The adjacent *salina* used to be a salt pan, but today it's home to happy flamingos and other waterfowl.

A QUICK TOUR

If you've only got time for a brief visit, opt for the short loop (which takes roughly an hour and a half) or stay close to the park entrance. Tour the small museum at the visitor center to learn about the ecology, geology and human history of the park, or hike one of the two trails near the visitor center: Lagadashi or Kasikunda.

TOP TIPS

- All visitors must enter the park by 2:30pm; if you arrive after that, you won't be admitted.
- The loops generally require a high-clearance vehicle, though periodic maintenance is done on the roads after the rainy season ends, making them accessible to other cars. Ask a park official at the visitor center.
- The park loops are one-way, so only begin the drive if you plan to see it through to the end.
- If you're visiting the park to dive, you need to be in the water prior to 2:30pm.
- Always call ahead after heavy rain to check park conditions.

THE SIGHTS OF WASHINGTON SLAGBAAI

Ovier Maduro, a park ranger at Washington Slagbaai National Park, shares his favorite things to look out for when visiting the park.

Kibrahacha Tree
This tree is so strong, it's strength is even described in its name – *kibrahacha* means 'break axe' in Papamientu. But the main reason I love this tree is its flowers. When it rains for two or three days after a drought, bright yellow blooms cover the tree. It really lights up the park!

Flamingos
People come from all over to see the park's flamingos.

BYVALET/SHUTTERSTOCK ©

Windsurfing, Lac Bay

Underwater Treasures of Bonaire's Marine Park

EXPLORE THE CARIBBEAN'S HEALTHIEST REEF

Bonaire is considered one of the best snorkeling and diving destinations in the world due to the health and accessibility of its reefs. Even if you're a novice snorkeler, you'll easily be able to spot the abundant marine life here.

Established in 1979, **Bonaire Marine Park** encompasses 2700 hectares of reef, seagrass beds and mangrove forest. Within these ecosystems you'll find 350 species of reef fish and 50 varieties of stony coral. The park features nearly 100 different diving and snorkeling sites (marked by yellow rocks along the roadside), the majority of which are located along the west coast.

The sites in the southern half of the park are sandier and experience stronger currents – **Pink Beach**, the **Invisibles** and **Salt Pier** are home to rays, eels and turtles.

Slightly further north you'll find **Alice in Wonderland** and **Hilma Hooker**, two sites defined by a unique double reef – divers will also be treated to a shipwreck at the latter, a freighter busted for transporting marijuana that was later scuttled.

Bari Reef is an epic dive if fish are your fave. Five minutes up the road you'll find **Andrea I** and **II** dive spots, great

WHERE TO HIT THE SURF IN SOUTH END

Jibe City
A well-established outfitter offering windsurfing, SUP and windfoiling lessons on picturesque Lac Bay.

Kiteboarding Bonaire
Trade windsurfing for kiteboarding at this outfitter, just south of the Red Beryl dive site.

FX Kiteschool
Located at the same beach as Kiteboarding Bonaire. Also offers windfoiling and SUP.

locations for beginner divers and snorkelers, with tons of soft coral and anemones.

Along the Queen's Hwy, **1000 Steps** is worth a visit due to its abundance of star and stag coral; whale sharks also pass through.

The marine park also includes **Klein Bonaire** – an uninhabited island and turtle nesting site – and Lac Bay.

Bonaire's South End Loop

PERFECT BAYS, RUGGED COASTLINES AND VIBRANT DIVE SITES

While the southern end of Bonaire's interior largely consists of active salt pans, a drive around the coastal highway reveals lots of treasures.

Start by cutting east from Kralendijk (p109) on Kaminda Sorobon, which will take you toward stunning **Lac Bay**, where you'll find expansive seagrass beds, a fringe reef and the largest mangrove forest of the ABC islands. It's the preferred hangout of the Bonairian windsurfing community.

Hang left on Kaminda Lac to observe flamingos in their *salinas* and connect with the excellent **Mangrove Center** for their sustainability-oriented kayak/snorkel tours. Continue down the road to affable **Lac Cai Beach**, a family-friendly spot with shallow water and a peppy beach bar.

Stay the course on Kaminda Sorobon to arrive at its namesake beach, a bustling peninsula that's a favorite for locals and visitors. You'll find a few buzzing restaurants, convivial beach clubs and windsurfing outfitters – if you've ever wanted to learn how to ride a wave, this is the place.

Keep heading south as the road wraps around Bonaire's southern end. Most of the eastern side is inaccessible coastline, but you'll see several sculptures made of natural elements and plastic along the way – commentary on the Caribbean's battle against the waterborne trash that washes up on its shores.

As you arrive back on the western side of Bonaire, you'll pass a series of local beaches – Pink Beach (p114), **Bachelor's Beach**, **Donkey Beach**, and our personal favorite, **Te Amo Beach**. Grab your cooler and settle in for a stunning sunset – speakers bump everything from reggaeton to house to Afrobeat, and the vibe is nigh unbeatable.

THE HISTORY BEHIND BONAIRE'S SALT

Visible from the plane, the **Cargill Salt Flats** and their adjacent salt pyramids cover much of southern Bonaire. The Spanish were the first to harvest salt from Bonaire in the early 1500s, but upon acquiring the island, the Dutch turned salt into a verifiable industry. Enslaved people were forced to mine salt in the hot sun without any form of eye or body protection and then make the hours-long walk back to Rincón on Fridays to reunite with their families.

The Dutch eventually built small huts for the enslaved people; these tiny structures were supposed to house two people, but often housed many more. The huts are now a historical site and are easily spotted along EEG Boulevard.

GETTING AROUND

If you want to really get to know Bonaire, you'll need a car – public transport is not common. However, if you're staying at a resort or working closely with a local dive shop, they'll often provide transportation or rent out their own vehicles. Downtown Kralendijk is really the only walkable area, as the rest of its restaurants, hotels, etc. sit more or less single-file along the roads ringing the island. Bonaire also has a taxi system, but this won't be practical in the island's more rural areas.

CURAÇAO

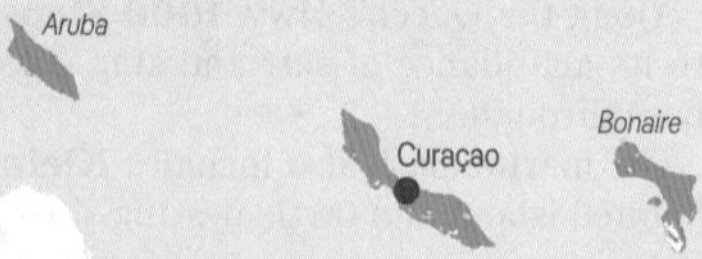

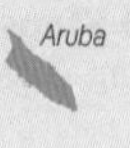

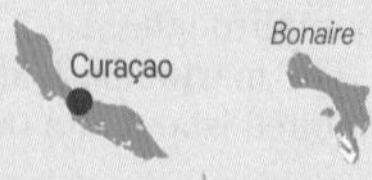

The largest of the ABC island chain, Curaçao delivers the whole package: a bustling capital city with a flourishing art and culture scene, a striking coastline peppered with sandy inlet beaches, and spectacular underwater excursions.

Willemstad, the island's beating heart, melds the old and the new – contemporary street-art sprawls across the walls of 17th- and 18th-century Dutch buildings, while a distinctly hip energy manifests in creative bars and restaurants. While ships do dock here, the town deftly avoids the artifice that sometimes plagues cruise towns.

Though a large part of the island feels distinctly metropolitan, Curaçao's wild side delivers a big dose of adventure for those that want to see the Caribbean at its most magnificent. Whether you're climbing Christoffel Mountain, enjoying the sea spray at Shete Boka or diving among the reefs encircling the island, you'll arrive at the same conclusion – there's no place quite like Curaçao.

TOP TIP

While Aruba is the main travel hub in the ABC islands for visitors from North America, Curaçao tends to be the primary point of entry for European travelers. If you're island-hopping the ABCs, inter-island flights from Aruba to Bonaire stop to connect in Curaçao.

SIMON DANNHAUER/SHUTTERSTOCK ©

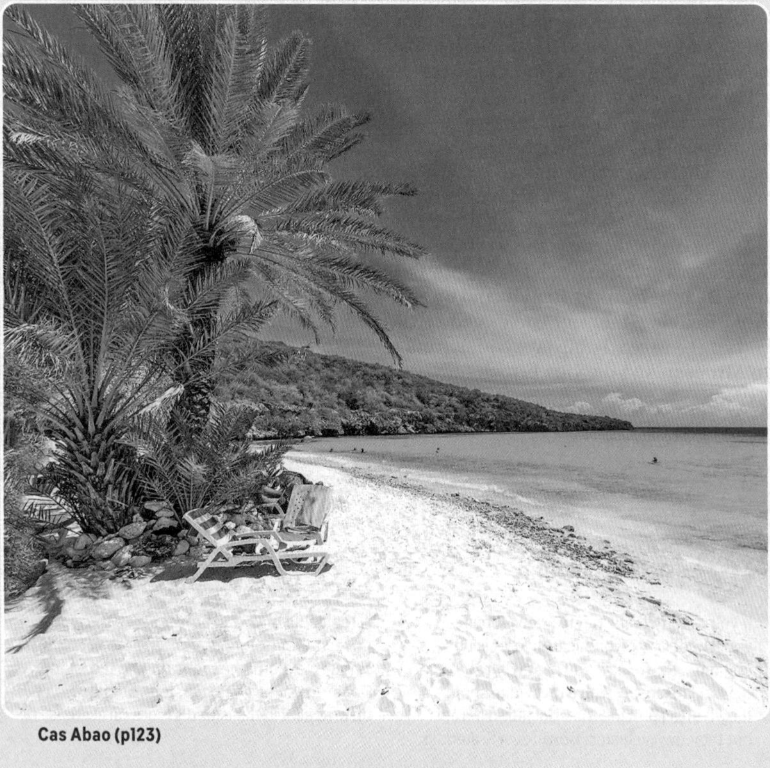

Cas Abao (p123)

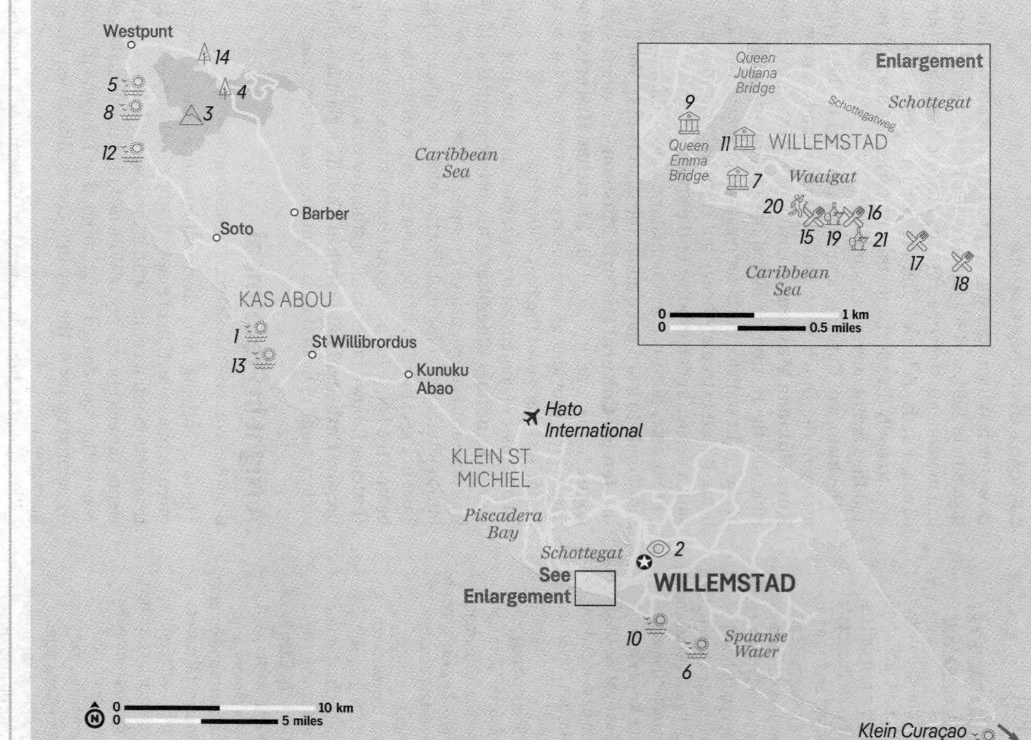

SIGHTS
1 Cas Abao
2 Cathedral Labyrinth of Thorns
3 Christoffel Mountain
4 Christoffel National Park
5 Grote Knip
6 Jan Thiel Beach
7 Jewish Cultural Historic Museum
8 Klein Knip
9 Kura Hulanda Museum
(see 2) Landhuis Bloemhof
10 Mambo Beach
11 Maritime History Museum
(see 7) Mikve Israel-Emanuel Synagogue
12 Playa Lagún
13 Playa Porto Mari
14 Shete Boka National Park

EATING
(see 10) Bonita Beach Club
15 Ginger
16 Kome
(see 10) Madero Ocean Club
17 Rozendaels
18 Soi95

DRINKING & NIGHTLIFE
19 Mr. Porter
20 Mundo Bizarro
(see 6) Papagayo Beach Club
(see 10) Riléks Beach Bar
21 Saint Tropez Ocean Club

ENTERTAINMENT
(see 10) Wet & Wild

CURAÇAO'S ART RENAISSANCE

Like neighboring Aruba, Curaçao has fully embraced the positive impact that street art has on a city – large-scale murals can be found all over Willemstad, but you'll find the highest concentration of them in Otrabanda, largely thanks to the **Kaya Kaya Festival**. Headed up by Kurt Schoop, Raygen Zuiverloon and Clayton Lasten (Schoop and Lasten also run Bario Hotel and its restaurants), Kaya Kaya focuses on creating economic opportunities for the residents of Otrobanda through art, music and community projects. Each Kaya Kaya, artists paint new murals, and concerts and outdoor theater take over the streets, with community members also implementing new neighborhood amenities like steps and playgrounds. Follow @kayakayafestival on Instagram for more details.

The History & Culture of Willemstad

CURAÇAO'S LIVING TIME CAPSULE

Downtown Willemstad was deemed a Unesco World Heritage Site in 1997, and it's home to nearly 800 official historical monuments strewn across the historic districts of Otrobanda, Punda, Scharloo and Pietermaai. Spend some time here to really dive deep into the intricacies of Curaçao's past and the vibrant energy of its present.

The history of Curaçao is inextricably tied to the terrible legacy of the Dutch West India Company and slavery; the **Kura Hulanda Museum** in Otrobanda delves into the terrible role the institution played in Curaçao, which was one of the main transfer ports for enslaved people in the Caribbean. It's an extremely heavy but essential visit in order to gain a deeper understanding of the area.

From here, head across the historic Queen Emma Bridge into Punda to learn more about the island's past. You'll find the **Jewish Cultural Historic Museum**, the oldest **synagogue** in the Americas, and the **Maritime History Museum**, which provides an exhaustive treatment of Curaçao's seafaring legacy over the past 500 years.

For a taste of contemporary Curaçao, make the quick drive over to **Landhuis Bloemhof**. This former plantation house was once worked by enslaved people. It has been converted into a cultural center highlighting the talent of Curaçao artists. Take in the exhibition in the main gallery, wander the trails behind the house for pop-up art installations, meet sculptor Hortence Brouwn in her outdoor studio or walk over to the impressive **Cathedral Labyrinth of Thorns**, a giant labyrinth/gallery made of bush thorns from the *Acacia tortuosa*.

A Night in Pietermaai

DINING IN WILLEMSTAD'S LIVELIEST NEIGHBORHOOD

The most enticing thing about Willemstad is that it's so much more than a collection of empty historic buildings – this is a true metropolitan capital with a thriving nightlife. To experience the eclectic energy of Willemstad at night, make your way to the rejuvenated neighborhood of Pietermaai, a candy-colored sector of the city that comes alive when the sun goes down.

Pietermaai is home to several of Willemstad's more contemporary eateries that represent a forward-thinking wave of Caribbean tastemakers. Try the best of Asian-Caribbean fusion cuisine at **Ginger**, or elevated international fare with a Curaçao twist at **Kome** (which means 'eat' in Papamientu).

WHERE TO EAT IN WILLEMSTAD

Plasa Bieu
A food hall serving up Curaçao specialties like red snapper, goat stew and *moro* (brown rice and beans). **$**

Maira's Kitchen
A darling (and pink!) breakfast spot with wraparound patio seating and crowd-pleasing morning favorites. **$$**

Bario Urban Street Food
A lively food-hall-esque patio that features several local eateries. Don't miss the excellent cocktails. **$$**

SERGE YATUNIN/SHUTTERSTOCK ©

***Big Mama* sculpture by Hortense Brouwn, Kura Hulanda Museum**

Venture further down Penstraat for Dutch-Caribbean dishes like *keshi yena* (pulled chicken with gouda cheese) and coconut fish at **Rozendaels**. Or try out some modern Asian food at **Soi95**.

Once you've eaten your fill and are ready for some evening festivities, you've got a few options. Those looking for a place to see and be seen should head to the posh **Saint Tropez Ocean Club** and sip cocktails on the pool deck. If you're ready to grab a partner and dance, head to the Cuba-inspired **Mundo Bizarro** for live music and a dance party that spills onto the street. Down the road, **Mr. Porter** shares a jovial party atmosphere with a few other bars in its immediate vicinity.

While weekends are an obvious choice for nights on the town, Punda and Pietermaai also party on Thursdays.

Wander Westpunt's National Parks

CURAÇAO'S WILD WEST

Looking northwest, the Willemstad sprawl gives way to Curaçao's wilderness, a hilly, green expanse rimmed by rocky cliff lines, pocket inlets and great beaches. A large section of Westpunt is occupied by the island's two national parks, each delivering a unique outdoor experience.

WHY I LOVE CURAÇAO

Bailey Freeman, writer

Simply put, Curaçao is a grab bag of awesome. This is a Caribbean island that truly has it all – a vibrant multicultural community, energetic creatives and plenty of natural beauty to go around. Wandering Willemstad feels like a treasure hunt thanks to kaleidoscopic street art around every corner, and its neighborhoods each project their own unique personalities. Further afield, Curaçao's cultural beauty gives way to a natural one, distinct from all its neighbors, which continues into the underwater world off its shores. The best part, in my opinion? Curaçao has something new to show you every time you visit.

WHERE TO STAY IN WILLEMSTAD

Pietermaai Boutique Hotel
A labyrinthine historical property with 37 earthy-chic rooms and an inviting central garden area. **$$**

Scuba Lodge & Ocean Suites
A family-friendly property with ocean views and connections to the dive shop down the road. **$$**

Elements
Willemstad's newest independent hotel, with modern rooms, and an excellent rooftop pool and bar/restaurant. **$$**

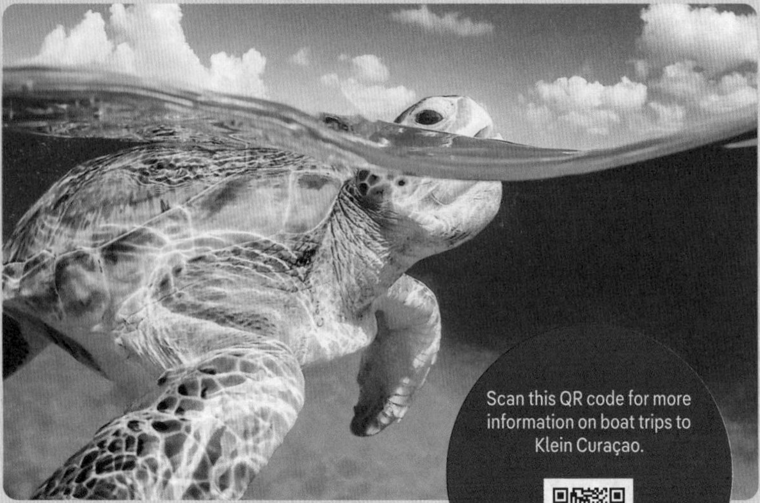

GAIL JOHNSON/SHUTTERSTOCK ©

Scan this QR code for more information on boat trips to Klein Curaçao.

TOP SIGHT

Klein Curaçao

Klein Curaçao is a place shaped by its past – the island was scraped clean due to phosphate mining in the 19th century, but it's on the mend. Reforestation efforts have brought back the seabirds that have historically roosted here (including some rare species), and the waters teem with fish and sea turtles. A trip here reveals the regenerative power of nature.

DON'T MISS

- Lighthouse views
- Shipwrecks
- Snorkeling
- Bird-watching

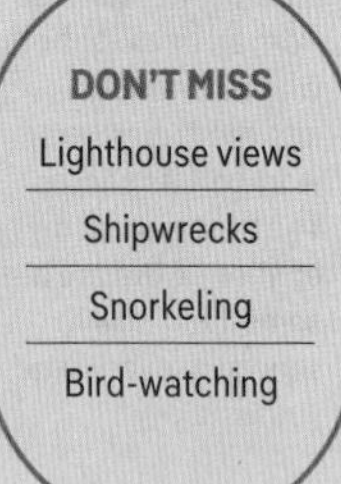

History

Klein Curaçao wasn't always uninhabited. It was first occupied as a lookout to protect Curaçao from pirates (really!), and became a phosphate mine in the 19th century – the island's flatness is a direct result of this activity. Klein Curaçao also has a tragic history as a quarantine site for enslaved people arriving to Curaçao; those who did not survive were buried on the southern tip of the island.

Exploring Klein Curaçao

The trip to Klein Curaçao is the most popular daytrip from Curaçao – this uninhabited island evokes the feeling of a true tropical paradise. Make the trip to experience astoundingly clear Caribbean waters, sparkling sand and numerous nautical landmarks. The biggest attraction, though? The chance to unplug and simply relax. The island is only 1.7 sq kms in size, meaning you can wander most of it via a short network of trails. We recommend exploring when you first arrive to avoid the afternoon sun.

Lighthouse

Klein Curaçao's photogenic lighthouse was built in 1885. Made of coral stone, lime and steel, the structure housed two lighthouse keepers and performed the essential task of making sure boats didn't run aground on the island, which is practically invisible on the horizon due to its flatness. The lighthouse is still functional thanks to a solar-powered LED light. Visitors can enter and climb the shaft for views of the island.

Maria Bianca

Despite the lighthouse's best efforts, boats have still wrecked here, their skeletons making interesting stops for the curious hiker. The most famous of these is the *Maria Bianca* (sometimes referred to as the inverse, *Bianca Maria*), a tanker built in 1964 that met its fate on the shores of Klein Curaçao in 1984. A victim of strong Caribbean currents and trade winds, the tanker ran aground and continues to weather the ocean's force; the ship has disintegrated over the years.

Tchao

Klein Curaçao's other accessible shipwreck is the *Tchao*, a French sailing yacht that crash landed in 2007. All four people aboard lived to tell the tale, but the unsalvageable boat was left on the sand.

Snorkeling

You can't visit Klein Curaçao without taking a dip in its spectacular water, the clarity and color of which can't be overstated. Spot lots of small schooling fish beneath the waves, and lucky folks will also see some sea turtles – Klein Curaçao is a nesting ground for green and hawksbill turtles, and conservationists actively monitor the nesting activity here. Reminder: if you see a turtle, don't touch or chase it! These guys are endangered.

Bird Life

Interesting fact: prior to the construction of the lighthouse, Klein Curaçao's warning system to passing ships was actually its bird colonies – birds would fly out to approaching boats to protect their breeding grounds. This was such an essential indicator that authorities prohibited people on the island from eating bird eggs. While these colonies no longer exist due to the impact of the mining industry, migratory birds still use Klein Curaçao as an essential stopover. Spot herons, sandpipers, least terns, blue winged teals and ospreys.

TOUR DETAILS

Klein Curaçao sits 10km from Curaçao and is only accessible by boat. No public water taxis make the trip, only private tour companies. The most well-known providers are Mermaid and Miss Ann Boat Trips, though several other outfitters offer trips on smaller boats; it's worth noting that these two are the only ones with permanent structures and shade palapas for guests, a very useful amenity when the mid-afternoon sun hits its peak. Most tours arrive after 8am and leave around 3 or 4pm.

TOP TIPS

- These trips fill up quickly, so book well in advance.
- The boat ride to Klein Curaçao is very choppy. If you're even the least bit prone to seasickness, make sure you take anti-nausea pills before your trip. Sit on the bottom deck, too.
- Be serious about sunscreen. The sun's rays are magnified by the white sand and super reflective water.
- There is no cell service on Klein Curaçao – enjoy the peace and quiet.

STAY SAFE IN THE SUN

Curaçao's national parks should feature prominently on any itinerary, but come prepared. The sun gets very hot here, and natural water sources are not common, so heat-related issues are very possible.

The national park system advises that visitors bring two liters of water per person, as well as snacks for the trail. The UV index in Curaçao is extremely high, so good sunscreen, a hat and sunglasses are all essential gear as well; if you plan on hiking the mountain, wear good hiking shoes (not sandals).

Centered around **Christoffel Mountain**, **Christoffel National Park** encompasses the Savonet Plantation – formerly a large-scale agricultural and livestock plantation worked by hundreds of enslaved people – which has returned to a mostly untouched landscape teeming with wildlife: white-tailed deer, barn owls, hummingbirds, blaublau lizards and iguanas. One of the most unique features of the park is its mountainside plant life, a florid mix of bromeliads, orchids and hanging lichen.

Accessing Christoffel takes a bit of planning, as the park closes at 2pm, with last admittance at 1:30pm (a measure taken to avoid heat-related injuries). If you plan on making the hike up Christoffel Mountain or driving the mountainside loop, the rangers require that you arrive prior to 10am. Entry is US$15.

Shete Boka National Park is the yang to Christoffel's yin, a dazzling stretch of coastline that puts the power of Curaçao's sea on full display. The name means 'Seven Mouths,' a reference to the park's yawning pocket inlets that funnel the waves into thunderous explosions of water; in reality, there are actually 10 inlets, all accessible by rustic trails across the rocky terrain. The area is a protected nesting site for hawksbill, loggerhead and green turtles, with local researchers monitoring the area year-round.

Shete Boka's hours are 9am–5pm, with last admittance at 4pm, and entry is US$10.

Discover Westpunt's Most Beautiful Beaches

BEACH-HOP CURAÇAO'S DYNAMIC COAST

Chances are that you're heading to Westpunt for one main reason: breathtaking beaches. Hemmed in by dramatic coralstone cliffs, Curaçao's beaches are refreshing tropical getaways with cozy, intimate atmospheres; each one feels like its own secret.

The beaches vary in size and amenities, ranging from rustic to fully kitted out. Most are within a 20-minute drive of each other, making beach-hopping a fun way to experience Curaçao's coast.

Starting up north you'll find **Grote Knip** and **Klein Knip**. 'Big' Knip is a family-friendly pie slice of sand and incandescent water with bathrooms, sun loungers and occasionally a food truck in the parking lot serving snacks and smoothies. 'Little' Knip doesn't have any facilities, but it does have some of the best snorkeling in Curaçao thanks to the colorful reefs

MORE AMAZING WESTPUNT BEACHES

Playa Grandi
A top favorite for visitors, especially families, thanks to its numerous resident turtles.

Playa Forti
A small rocky beach best known as a good place for cliff jumping into the water.

Playa Jeremi
A quiet, local favorite, cosily tucked away from the bustle of the busier beaches.

Z. JACOBS/SHUTTERSTOCK ©

Shete Boka National Park

wrapped around the base of its cliffs. Sometimes you'll find folks whipping up snacks at a food stand right on the beach.

South of the Knips sits **Playa Lagún**, a local favorite and another good spot to break out the snorkel gear. The beach itself is small but characterful thanks to a few wooden boats that have taken up permanent residence on the sand. The only facilities here are pay-to-use bathrooms.

The two beaches located closest to Willemstad are **Cas Abao** and **Playa Porto Mari**. The former is the Goldilocks of Curaçao beaches – not too big and not to small, home to a sparkling sand/water combo and a restaurant to sustain you during your visit. Playa Porto Mari takes amenities up a notch with a beach shop, showers, lockers and a more robust restaurant.

REVOLUTIONARY HISTORY IN GROTE AND KLEIN KNIP

The Knip beaches are located on land that used to be part of the Kenepa Plantation, the site of Curaçao's largest uprising of enslaved people. Inspired by the Haitian Revolution, an enslaved man named **Tula Rigaud** amassed a resistance numbering 2000 – the total enslaved population on Curaçao at the time was 12,000 – and organized a month-long revolt against the island's slaveowners in August 1795. The uprising was ultimately quelled and Tula was executed two months later.

The event represents an important moment in Curaçao's history. August 17, the first day of the revolt, is recognized as a historic day in the long struggle for liberation.

Sun in Style in Southern Curaçao

LOUNGE AT CURAÇAO'S BEACH CLUBS

Curaçao's south coast exists in opposition to its large and nature-oriented north – its main attractions are the curated beach clubs just south of Willemstad, with the most southern region largely inaccessible to visitors. These clubs offer a beach experience with all the amenities while still largely

WHERE TO EAT IN SOUTHERN CURAÇAO

Zest Restaurant & Beach Cafe
Choose the restaurant for more elevated fare and the beach bar for fairy lights and Caribbean stars. **$$**

The Pier
A cozy, marina-side eatery in Caracasbaai with fish stew, Caribbean sea bass and wahoo. **$$**

Bliss the Berry
A Mambo Beach lunch spot serving beautifully presented smoothies, açaí bowls, paninis and sandwiches. **$**

BEST DIVE OUTFITTERS IN CURAÇAO

Dive Center Peitermaai
Part of Scuba Lodge, this laid-back outfit offers dive courses, snorkeling tours and 'fun dives' for folks who already have their certs.

Fun Diving Curaçao
Organized dive center that offers courses, guided dives, boat trips, and PADI Bubble Maker classes for kids aged eight and up.

Jan Thiel Diving
Dive company offering standard dive courses as well as interesting PADI specialties like night diving, underwater naturalist and deep diver courses.

Jan Thiel Beach

avoiding the pitfalls of high-rise coastal developments, and they are a good choice for families or for those who want a luxe day on the sand.

Upon heading south from Willemstad, **Mambo Beach** will be the first beach area you'll encounter. Here you'll find a small mall 'boulevard' full of shops and restaurants overlooking the beach itself. Access the sands via the area's beach clubs: **Bonita Beach Club**, **Madero Ocean Club**, **Riléks Beach Bar** and **Wet & Wild** (Mambo's biggest nightlife spot). Loungers and cabanas are available for rent, and each club features its own restaurant/bar.

A quick 15-minute drive down the road will take you to **Jan Thiel Beach** and **Papagayo Beach Club**. The set-up is similar to Mambo in that the beach is paid access, but this area feels a bit more low-key, trading shops and foot traffic for a smattering of restaurants.

If you're looking to leave the resort area behind, keep heading south to Caracasbaai, a distinctly nautical sliver of land near the small towns of Spaanse Water and Santa Barbara. Here you'll find an active marina, from which the boats to Klein Curaçao (p120) depart, a charming little pier, and a quiet, pebbly beach with good snorkeling and fascinating views of the *Balder*, a *Star Wars*-esque deep-water construction vessel.

GETTING AROUND

Like Aruba and Bonaire, Curaçao is best explored by car – roads are in good condition and well marked, so driving really is a breeze. Willemstad itself is quite walkable, so find a place to park (there's a surprising amount of lots and street parking) and get your steps in to see the city.

SF PHOTO/SHUTTERSTOCK ©

Arriving

Getting to the ABC islands is relatively straightforward: most travelers will pass through either Reina Beatrix Airport in Aruba or Hato International Airport (CUR; pictured above) in Curaçao. Those moving on to Bonaire will connect on a small regional airline to arrive at Flamingo International Airport. A few international flights go directly to Bonaire, but prices are high.

By Air

No ferries operate between the ABCs, so air travel is the only way to go. Divi Divi Air and EZ Air operate multiple daily flights, but make sure you book ahead, especially if traveling on the weekends, as planes fill up fast.

By Boat

Cruise ships are the only boats moving between the ABCs, with major ports in the capital cities of each island. The only other water transport is through day trips – Klein Curaçao is accessible by tour; Klein Bonaire is accessible via water taxi.

Money

Currency:
Aruba: Aruban Guilder (AWG)

Bonaire: US$

Curaçao: Antillean Guilder (ANG)

DOLLAR OR GUILDER?
The US dollar is accepted alongside the local guilders (which are also referred to as florins) in Aruba and Curaçao – US$1 comes out as ƒ1.80. Menus and activity prices vary in the currency they use, so double check ahead of time if you're not sure. Note that you'll often get guilders back in change, even if you pay with dollars.

CASH
Credit cards are widely accepted across the islands, except when it comes to paying for transport, so make sure you have cash to pay for taxis and the like. ATMs are fairly easy to find, but international cards may be charged a decently steep fee. The super local joints in more rural areas can be cash only, so it helps to have cash on hand when venturing outside of the cities.

CREDIT CARDS
Most major credit cards are accepted throughout the islands, with the front-runners being Visa and Mastercard.

THE BAHAMAS

RETREAT INTO PURE BEACH BLISS

The Bahamas is a geographic outlier with over 700 alluring islands of unique cultural charm and breathtaking natural beauty for relaxation and adventure.

The Bahamas has been a sought-after destination for centuries, coveted by the British colonial empire as a retreat for the wealthy and influential to divvy up and frolic about. Independent since 1973, the country's secluded coves and bays and protected harbors have also historically served as safe havens for pirates, privateers and rum runners, adding to its mystique and allure as a destination for beach lovers seeking relaxation.

This Caribbean nation is a geographic outlier. Located just off the coast of Florida, the country is a land of contrasts from the bustling island of New Providence to the more tranquil and rustic Family Islands. These smaller, more remote retreats offer a welcome respite from the more populated, urbanized political and cultural epicenter that is Nassau.

An archipelago of exceptional beauty, The Bahamas has over 700 islands and cays. It's riddled with river-like saltwater creeks that form hundreds of marine estuaries. Choosing a base is important to shape the experience of your trip. The northern Bahamas is a haven for fishing and diving enthusiasts, while the central Bahamas features islands of pure beach bliss and the capital Nassau. The southern Bahamas' untouched eco-islands offer a true retreat into nature. No matter which region you plan your itinerary around, each island has its distinct charm, along with a vibrant food and festival scene, serene beaches and crystal-clear waters.

MATT A. CLAIBORNE/SHUTTERSTOCK ©

THE MAIN AREAS

NORTHERN BAHAMAS
A boating, diving and fishing playground. **p132**

CENTRAL BAHAMAS
Cultured islands of pure beach bliss. **p138**

SOUTHERN BAHAMAS
The wildest, untouched eco-islands. **p147**

GASTON PICCINETTI/SHUTTERSTOCK ©

Above: French Leave Beach (p143); Left: The Abacos (p134)

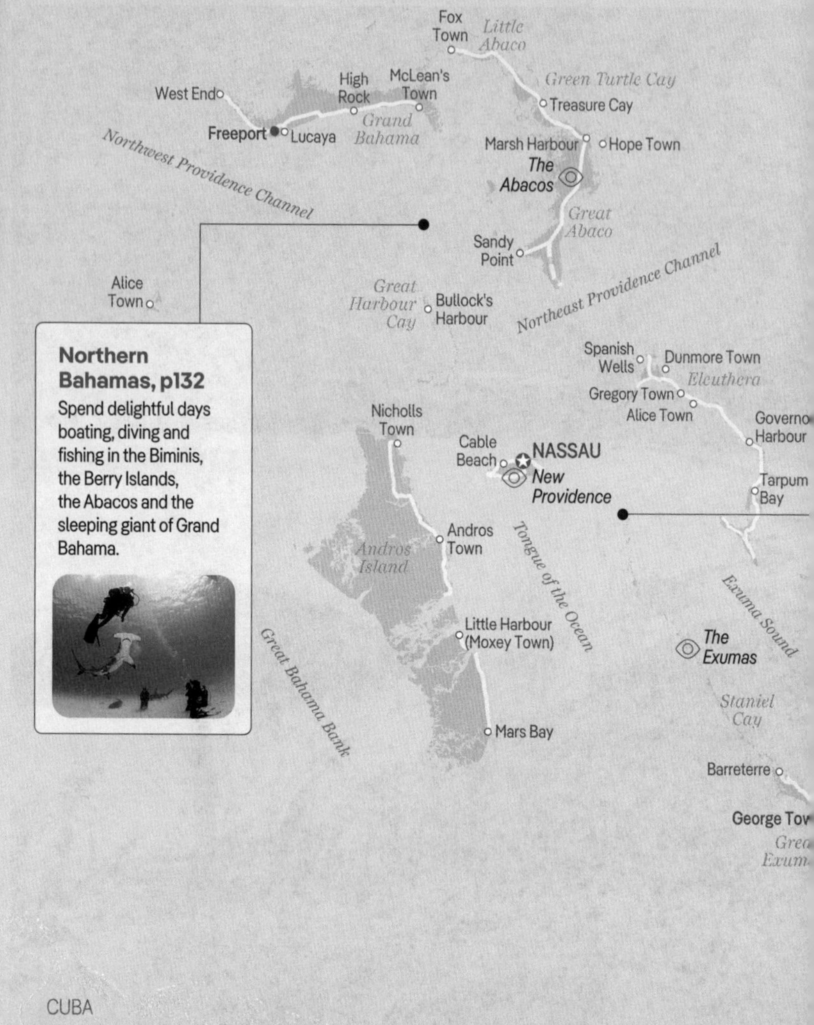

Fox Town
Little Abaco
Green Turtle Cay
Treasure Cay
West End
High Rock
McLean's Town
Grand Bahama
Freeport
Lucaya
Marsh Harbour
Hope Town
The Abacos
Northwest Providence Channel
Great Abaco
Sandy Point
Alice Town
Great Harbour Cay
Bullock's Harbour
Northeast Providence Channel
Spanish Wells
Dunmore Town
Eleuthera
Gregory Town
Alice Town
Governo[r's] Harbour
Nicholls Town
Cable Beach
NASSAU
New Providence
Tarpum Bay
Andros Town
Andros Island
Tongue of the Ocean
Exuma Sound
Little Harbour (Moxey Town)
The Exumas
Great Bahama Bank
Staniel Cay
Mars Bay
Barreterre
George Tow[n]
Grea[t] Exum[a]
CUBA

Northern Bahamas, p132

Spend delightful days boating, diving and fishing in the Biminis, the Berry Islands, the Abacos and the sleeping giant of Grand Bahama.

AIRPLANE

Domestic airlines have regularly scheduled flights from Nassau to 20 airports in the Family Islands. Not all of them have daily flights, and most small airports can't accommodate night flights, so schedules are often limited to daylight hours. Private air charters are available, including seaplanes.

CAR, TAXI & GOLF CART

To explore beyond the tourist district, rent a car for your vacation and road trips. Book golf carts in advance for smaller islands. Find taxis at airports, mega-resorts and major attractions. Use them sparingly as they're expensive.

FERRY

Public transportation vessels include modern passenger ships and slow-moving mail boats, which are passenger and cargo ships that take supplies to restock the Family Islands. Some island groups also use smaller passenger ferries to connect the mainland with their offshore cays.

Find Your Way

The Islands of The Bahamas start as far north as West Palm Beach, USA and as far south as Guardalavaca, Cuba. The capital Nassau is where most visit, but the allure of the archipelago goes far beyond.

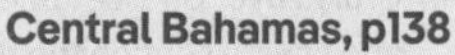

Central Bahamas, p138

Beach lovers go off the beaten path in Andros and Cat Island, and experience nightlife and culture in New Providence, Paradise Island, Eleuthera and its cays.

Southern Bahamas, p147

The most tranquil islands for nature lovers including the beach oasis, Exumas, plus the tiny towns of Long Island, San Salvador, Inagua, Acklins and Crooked Island.

rthur's Town
Cat Island
New Bight
Cockburn Town
onception Island
Rum Cay
San Salvador
Seymours
Port Nelson
lliam's wn
Stella Maris
Long Island
ittle xuma
Deadman's Cay
Clarence Town
Samana Cay
Gordons
Crooked Island Passage
Colonel Hill
Crooked Island
Chesters
Albert Town
Acklins Island
Mayaguana Passage
Spring Point
Mayaguana
Abraham Bay
Caicos Passage
TURKS AND CAICOS (UK)
Little Inagua
Great Inagua
Matthew Town
0 100 km
0 50 miles

Plan Your Time

To narrow your choice between so many islands, consider how remote, rustic and connected to nature you wish to be, and whether your focus is the beach, the active outdoors or culture and nightlife.

PAULHARDING00/SHUTTERSTOCK ©

West Hill St, Nassau (p141)

If You Only Do One Thing

● Enjoy conch salad at **Arawak Cay** (p141) before heading to **Rose Island** (p141), the closest, most spectacular beach enclave off the coast of Nassau. Charter a private boat for a day trip, which you can customize with a turtle encounter. Cruise over on a catamaran and snag a seat on the mesh trampolines to ride suspended over the turquoise waters. A luxury boat charter has the added attraction of a private chef. However you get there, enjoy a beach day on the sandy sanctuary and get a seaside view of the famous **Paradise Island** (p141) on your way there and back.

Seasonal Highlights

The Bahamas has year-round tourism that peaks between the US Thanksgiving weekend and mid-April. March gets particularly busy with spring break. In the winter, you may need a sweater due to cold fronts.

MARCH

The **Nassau Paradise Island Wine & Food Festival** is a week-long celebration of food with the best of Bahamian and celebrity chefs.

MAY

The **Long Island Regatta** in Salt Pond is a festive event for indigenous sloop sailing, local music, food and island revelry.

JUNE

The Cat Island **Rake & Scrape Festival** starts the month. Summer rains kick off **crab season**; try Bahamian land crab, a Father's Day staple.

PORNPRAPA KORPRASERT/SHUTTERSTOCK ©, SAATON/SHUTTERSTOCK ©, JVP PHOTOGRAPHY/GETTY IMAGES ©

Three Days to Travel Around

- Stay in **Nassau** (p141) and visit West Hill St, stopping at the **Graycliff Heritage Village** (p141) and the **National Art Gallery of The Bahamas** (p141). Move on to the **Educulture Junkanoo Museum** (p140); book ahead for the 20-minute immersive musical experience. Across the road on Delancy St are the manicured grounds of **John Watling's Distillery** (p141). Exploring this culturally rich part of town and its many historic buildings will take a half day.

- For a Bahamian meal, dine at **Arawak Cay** (p141).

- An island-hopping excursion to the **Exumas** (p148), **Harbour Island** (p146) or **Spanish Wells** (p146) is a must.

If You Have More Time

- With more time, ditch the capital and plan your stay around the remote Family Islands, where the lack of development is the appeal. If you're a newcomer, explore the **Exumas** (p148) on a wildlife safari, starting in Staniel Cay, Black Point or Great Exuma; or take a road trip across **Eleuthera** (p142) combined with a day trip to **Harbour Island** (p146). If you've visited before, try the serene and untouched **Cat Island** (p144), where you can eat authentic Bahamian food.

- You'll likely have to overnight in **Nassau** (p141) on your return. During the stopover, visit the immersive **Atlantis Marine Habitat** (p141).

JULY
The **Bahamian Independence** holiday on July 10 is a time of cultural celebration. It's also high season for **Bahamas Boating Flings**.

OCTOBER
The **Bahamas Culinary & Arts Festival** at Baha Mar is a weekend event. Party with celebrity chefs while enjoying tastings, private dinners and exhibitions.

NOVEMBER
Watch **Junkanoo** groups practice weekly from September to December for a lesser-known but more immersive music and dance experience.

DECEMBER
The public service enters vacation mode, culminating with the grand spectacle of Boxing Day and **New Year's Day Junkanoo**.

NORTHERN BAHAMAS

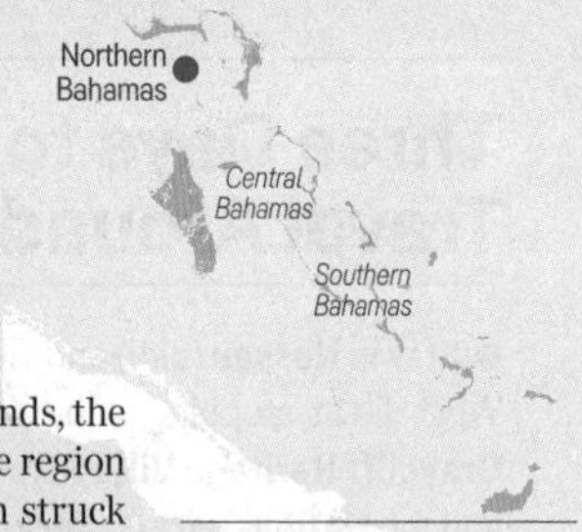

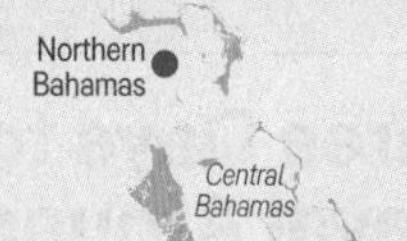

The northern Bahamas comprises the Biminis, Berry Islands, the Abacos, and Grand Bahama, the area's largest island. The region gained global attention in 2019 when Hurricane Dorian struck the latter two, causing catastrophic damage. But these islands are known for their resilience and have since bounced back. The cays in the Abacos, in particular, were rebuilt remarkably fast thanks to the influx of resources from wealthy Bahamians and the relatively large community of foreign second-home owners in the Abacos.

The northern region is particularly famous for its annual boat flings, where flotillas from Florida gather to make the crossing over the Gulf Stream. These flings allow novice and seasoned boaters alike to learn about crossing the Gulf Stream safely and enjoyably.

Watch the winter weather for cold fronts, especially when traveling in the north – you may find yourself missing the customary tropical sun during this time.

TOP TIP

There's no better way to immerse yourself in the culture of The Bahamas than through its music. Check out Phil Stubbs' 'West End Move' or 'Bonefish Folley', an homage to a bonefishing guide in West End on Grand Bahama, or 'Lay Low in Bimini' by Stevie S, capturing the Biminis' laid-back style.

The Abacos (p134)

TOP SIGHTS
1 The Abacos

SIGHTS
2 Gold Rock Beach
3 Hoffman's Cay Blue Hole
4 Paradise Cove Beach
5 Shark Creek Beach
6 Smith's Point
7 Taino Beach
12 Sugar Beach Caves
13 Turtle Creek

ACTIVITIES, COURSES & TOURS
8 Chub Cay Resort & Marina
9 CocoNutz Cruisers
10 Lucayan National Park
11 Old Bahama Bay Resort and Yacht Harbour

EATING
14 Agave
15 Candy Captain's Popcorn Factory
16 Cappucino's Fine Italian Restaurant
17 Flo's Conch Bar
18 Zorba

DRINKING & NIGHTLIFE
19 Bahamian Brewery

ENTERTAINMENT
20 Great Harbour Cay Marina

SHOPPING
21 Port Lucaya Marketplace

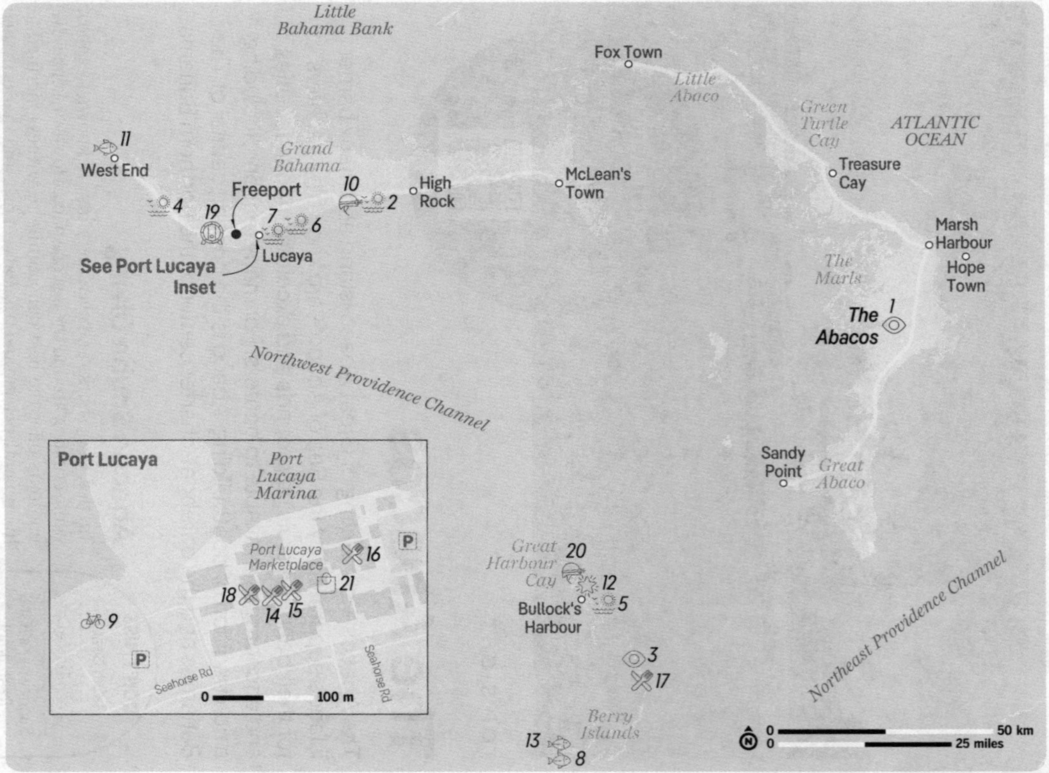

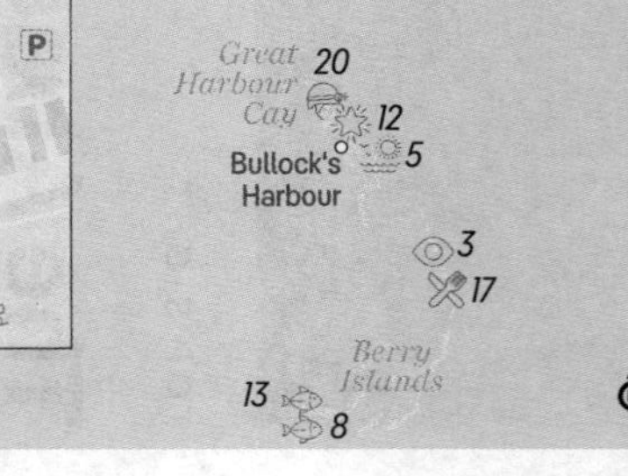

Taino Beach (p137)
LUKAS WALTER/SHUTTERSTOCK ©

SINN P. PHOTOGRAPHY/SHUTTERSTOCK ©

PRACTICALITIES
Use this QR code to view a list of attractions and places to stay in the Abacos.

TOP SIGHT

The Abacos

The Abacos – consisting of Great Abaco Island and many barrier islands separated by the Sea of Abaco – are known by yachters for their beautiful cruising grounds and excellent marine facilities and anchorages available to boaters. For many reasons, including a rich tradition of boatbuilding, Abaco is the boating capital of The Bahamas and the bareboat-charter center of the northern Bahamas.

DON'T MISS

- Tahiti Beach
- Green Turtle Cay
- Sundowner's Bar & Restaurant
- Elbow Reef Lighthouse
- Pete's Pub & Gallery
- Treasure Cay Beach
- Grabbers Bed, Bar and Grill
- Cherokee Sound

Abacos Scuba Diving

Turtles, rays, sharks and even dolphins are known to appear while cruising around the Sea of Abaco. However, scuba-diving tours offer the best opportunity to witness marine life, living coral, pelagic and tropical reef fish, and sharks in their deep-water habitats. Most of the dive sites are located on the Atlantic side of the barrier islands. **Brendal's Dive Center & Water Sports** is run by dive instructors who lead expert trips to top dive sites, including **Tarpon Dive** (a massive wall with schooling tarpon) and **Coral Cavern** (a submerged network of miniature caves and naturally sculpted tunnels). At **Grouper Alley**, best visited when grouper season is closed, you'll find a rare congregation of critically endangered groupers engaged in mating rituals. Wreck dives, reef dives and shark dives round out the mix.

Abacos Beach Bar Crawl

Bar-hopping in the Abacos is a boating affair, where you pull up directly to a dock or anchor on the beach. If you only visit one spot, make it **Thirsty Cuda Bar & Grill**, a floating beach bar on Tahiti Beach. At this phenomenal location, the beach protrudes into the sea like a horn; wade in waist-deep water from the shoreline to the floating bar. **Big O's Restaurant and Bar** on No Name Cay is home to swimming pigs. The signature rum punches at the **Tranquil Turtle Beach Bar** in the Bluff House Beach Resort and Marina are potent concoctions. Find beach volleyball, cornhole games and a beach swing at this stop. **Pete's Pub & Gallery** in Little Harbour is a fun and lively beach bar with a funky and artistic style. Great Guana Cay is known for the party vibes at **Nipper's Beach Bar and Grill** and the sunsets at **Grabbers Bed, Bar and Grill**. Both have private docks. **Firefly Bar and Grill** on Elbow Cay has an elevated menu with gourmet island favorites.

Marsh Harbour, Great Abaco

Located on Great Abaco, Marsh Harbour (pictured) serves as a hub for visitors entering and leaving the archipelago and ferrying about the cays. Although predominantly a residential area for locals, the town provides access to numerous amenities for visitors such as marinas, dining and shopping – especially at **Abaco Ceramics** – and places to stock up on provisions. The phenomenal **Treasure Cay Beach** with its vacation-rental community is also on Great Abaco.

Green Turtle Cay

Golf carts are the preferred way of exploring the quaint town of New Plymouth on Green Turtle Cay, featuring colorful houses and charming watering holes like **Miss Emily's Blue Bee Bar**, originators of the famous Goombay Smash cocktail, and the fun nightspot of **Sundowner's Bar & Restaurant**. Beyond Green Turtle Cay is an attraction with stingrays, turtles and sharks at **Manjack Cay**.

The grand sandbar on Fiddle Cay is party central each July for **Cheese Burger in Paradise**, a massive party and fundraiser for the Green Turtle Cay Foundation, with countless boats encircling the disappearing beach.

Hope Town, Elbow Cay

This picturesque village on Elbow Cay is known for its historic red-and-white striped lighthouse, charming waterfront cottages and iconic harbor, which hosts a regular congregation of sailboats. Beyond Elbow Cay is a snorkeling site in the **Pelican Cays Land and Sea Park**.

QUICK TOUR

Sandy Point's Homecoming Conch Fest enlivens the usually sleepy town in South Abaco every first Friday in June. The proud and scenic **Cherokee Sound** community is home to the longest wooden dock in The Bahamas (770ft), built in 1942.

TOP TIPS

- Ferries are essential for exploring the Abacos. The daily passenger service is dependable, affordable and largely cash-based.
- The 20-minute ferry to Hope Town leaves from the Ferry Dock at Crossing Beach in Marsh Harbour. It stops on Elbow Cay at the Lower, Upper and Lodge Dock, so clarify your final destination. Ask for the Fuel Dock for the Elbow Reef Lighthouse.
- The Treasure Cay Ferry Dock, 40km outside Marsh Harbour, has daily service to Green Turtle Cay with stops in White Sound, Black Sound and the New Plymouth Public Dock.
- Ferries to Great Guana Cay leave from the G&L Dock on Front St, and the Red Bay Marina (10 minutes outside Marsh Harbour).

SHARK DIVING IN THE BIMINIS

The Biminis are a world-renowned shark-diving destination. The islands' shallow waters, warm climate and nutrient-rich currents create an ideal habitat for tiger and bull sharks, lemon sharks and the great hammerhead, which has a season from December through April, peaking in January and February.

Dive shops such as **Bimini Big Game Club Resort & Marina**, **Neal Watson's Bimini Scuba Center** and **Stuart Cove's Dive Bahamas** offer epic shark-diving experiences at the **Victory Reef**, **Tuna Alley**, **Triangle Rocks** and **Bull Run**. Between North and South Bimini – actually two islands – there are other attractions, including the **Resort World Bimini** casino hotel and cruise port, **Tiki Hut Beach** in South Bimini, and the famous shipwreck where divers can jump off and explore.

Unwind on Great Harbour Cay

LAID-BACK VIBES IN THE BERRY ISLANDS

The Berry Islands are relatively undeveloped, with small laid-back settlements scattered throughout. Great Harbour Cay is the largest and most populated, and the hub of activity for fishing and relaxation. It's also a launch pad for many cruise-ship tours.

The liveliest place is the **Great Harbour Cay Marina** on Friday nights for a rum-punch-fueled grill with live music and an open mic in high season. Otherwise, Great Harbour Cay is best suited for idle time, trekking to **Sugar Beach Caves** or **Shark Creek Beach** in solitary bliss. Offshore attractions include **Hoffman's Cay Blue Hole**, a natural swimming pool in the middle of an uninhabited, forested island, and the ultra-secluded **Flo's Conch Bar** in Little Harbor for conch fritters and rum punch with the owner and one-man band, Chester Darville.

Fishing Thrills on Chub Cay

THE BILLFISH CAPITAL OF THE BAHAMAS

The Berry Islands are located on the eastern edge of the Tongue of the Ocean, a deep oceanic trench providing some of the best fishing and diving in The Bahamas. Chub Cay, the most southwestern in the group, is known as the 'billfish capital of The Bahamas' and has a long history of fishing, hosting many big-game fishing tournaments. It's where hardcore anglers go to reel in big catches. The island revolves around the **Chub Cay Resort & Marina**, which provides luxury accommodations, boat rentals, fishing gear and guides for seeking out pelagic billfish, tuna, wahoo and king mackerel plus snapper, grouper and other reef fish. There's also excellent bonefishing and fly fishing, including in **Turtle Creek**.

Grand Bahama's Chill & Wild Sides

FIND YOUR INNER EXPLORER

The **Port Lucaya Marketplace** remains a highlight of Freeport, on Grand Bahama, despite businesses still recovering from Hurricane Dorian in 2019. This open-air facility houses restaurants and bars, along with a few colorful storefronts for jewelry and souvenirs. Located by the Port Lucaya Marina and cruise port, dining options are diverse. **Cappucino's Fine Italian Restaurant** serves freshly made pasta; **Zorba** specializes in Greek cuisine; **Agave**, a favorite for lunch

WHERE TO STAY ON THE BERRY ISLANDS

Chub Cay Resort and Marina
A luxury marina resort for hardcore anglers in the remote and lovely south. $

Soul Fly Lodge
Peaceful, all-inclusive, ocean-front fishing lodge in Great Harbour Cay. Cozy rooms, stunning views and expert guides. $$

Great Harbour Cay Yacht Club and Marina
Resort with comfortable canal-side rooms, on-site dining and beach access. $$

KRISTEN LOPEZ/SHUTTERSTOCK ©

Hammerhead shark, Biminis

and dinner, delivers a fusion menu of Caribbean and Mexican cuisine. To satisfy your sweet tooth, sample treats from **Candy Captain's Popcorn Factory**.

Grand Bahama has a vast expanse of unexplored pine forests and untouched beaches, notably in isolated East End. West End has residential communities and bountiful bonefishing flats, with **Old Bahama Bay Resort and Yacht Harbour** – a haven for serious anglers – at the solitary tip of the island. Freeport is the best gateway to explore the island, especially with an e-bike tour of landmarks and beaches by **CocoNutz Cruisers**. Go on a **Bahamian Brewery** tour, especially on a rainy day, for a quick glimpse of the factory underbelly and sampling of six local brews. Spot sea turtles at **Paradise Cove Beach**, or visit the **Lucayan National Park** with its intricate cave and mangrove creek systems, explorable on a kayaking tour, and the magnificent **Gold Rock Beach**. **Taino Beach** and **Smith's Point** are both great spots for sunbathing, swimming and beach games. On Thursday nights, Smith's Point is best known for its **Fish Fry**, a local hangout with laid-back party vibes, food, music and drinks.

BEST PLACES TO STAY ON GRAND BAHAMA

Pelican Bay Hotel
Harbor-view boutique hotel within walking distance of the Port Lucaya Marketplace. $

Lighthouse Point
All-inclusive, beachfront resort with spacious and stylish rooms, a private beach and pools. $$

Taino Beach Resort & Clubs
Family-friendly resort in Freeport with condo-style accommodations, pools and a restaurant. $

Viva Wyndham Fortuna Beach
All-inclusive resort on the south shore of Grand Bahama with water sports and nightlife. $$

Island Seas Resort
Condo-style marina resort on Silver Point Beach, a sunset-viewing gallery. $

GETTING AROUND

The northern Bahamas has several walkable towns, most notably Hope Town and New Plymouth, settlements in the Abacos cays, and North Bimini. Regardless, most people opt to rent a golf cart. Beyond Freeport in Grand Bahama and Marsh Harbour in Great Abaco, you'll need to cover long distances to get around. It's best to travel with a tour company in a rented car. Water taxis and boat rentals are widely available in the Abacos.

CENTRAL BAHAMAS

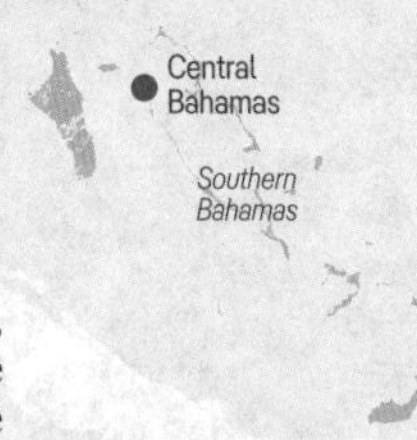

The Central Bahamas includes New Providence, Cat Island, Eleuthera and Andros. The Bahamas' rich musical heritage provides a window into everyday life and traditions of the people who call these islands home. Eric Minnis' song 'Fox Hill Gal' toasts the beauty, strength and resilience of the women from Fox Hill, a historic neighborhood in Nassau. Tony McKay's 'Gone to Cat Island' is a folk song celebrating the simplicity and peacefulness of island life.

Roachy's 'Boom Pineapple Wine' refers to a dance move that resembles stirring a pot of pineapple wine on Eleuthera, which honors its pineapple farming traditions annually at Pineapple Fest. 'Party in the Backyard' by The Brilanders reflects the welcoming culture of Harbour Island, where the food and drinks flow freely as people gather to have a good time.

Elon Moxey's lighthearted 'Catch Da Crab Crawling' is about the crabbing tradition on Andros and the joy of cooking and eating the native land crabs with loved ones.

TOP TIP

Bahamians use the names Nassau and New Providence interchangeably; however, Nassau is the capital city, located on the island of New Providence. For itinerary-planning purposes, they're essentially one and the same, as Nassau is commonly used to refer to both the island and the capital.

Above: Nassau (p140); Right: Diving with sharks off Cat Island (p144)

TOP SIGHTS
1 New Providence

SIGHTS
2 Blue Holes National Park
3 Dunmore Town
4 Joe Sound Creek
5 Pink Sands Beach
6 West Side National Park
13 Hawk's Nest Creek
14 Mermaid Hole
15 Mt Alvernia
16 Orange Creek
17 Royal Island
18 South Andros Barrier Reef Marine Park
(see 8) Winding Bay

ACTIVITIES, COURSES & TOURS
7 Alligator Creek
8 Bat Hole
9 Bennet's Harbour Creek
10 Bottom Harbour
11 Current Cut
12 Fernandez Bay Creek

EATING
19 Acquapazza Wine Bar & Ristorante
20 Cocoa Coffee House
21 Queen Conch
22 Rock House
23 Sandbar Bar & Grill
24 Wrecker's Restaurant and Bar

LUKAS WALTER/SHUTTERSTOCK ©

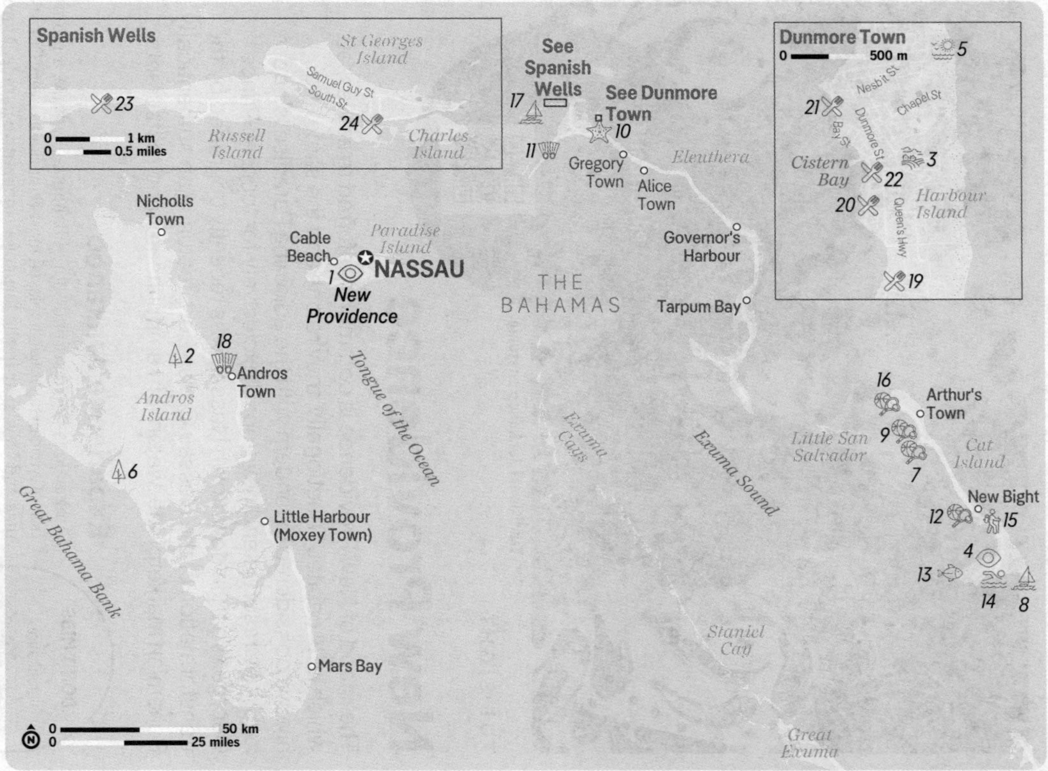

Spanish Wells
St Georges Island
Samuel Guy St
South St
Russell Island
Charles Island
23
24
0 1 km
0 0.5 miles

See Spanish Wells
See Dunmore Town
17
10
11
Gregory Town
Alice Town
Eleuthera
Governor's Harbour
Tarpum Bay
Nicholls Town
Cable Beach
Paradise Island
NASSAU
1
New Providence
THE BAHAMAS
2
18
Andros Town
Andros Island
Tongue of the Ocean
Exuma Cays
Exuma Sound
6
Great Bahama Bank
Little Harbour (Moxey Town)
Mars Bay
Staniel Cay
Great Exuma
16
Arthur's Town
9
7
Little San Salvador
Cat Island
New Bight
12
15
4
13
14
8
0 50 km
0 25 miles

Dunmore Town
0 500 m
5
Nesbit St
Chapel St
21
Bay St
Dunmore St
Cistern Bay
3
22
20
Queen's Hwy
Harbour Island
19

Traditional Junkanoo costume

WIRESTOCK CREATORS/SHUTTERSTOCK ©

PRACTICALITIES
Scan this QR code to search for accommodations and for island maps.

TOP SIGHT

New Providence

The island of New Providence is commonly referred to as Nassau, which is its capital. Functionally, they're one and the same and always considered in tandem with the adjoining Paradise Island, a luxurious resort island developed exclusively for tourism. Prince George Wharf in downtown Nassau was recently upgraded by the transformation of the Nassau Cruise Port, featuring an authentically Bahamian marketplace, waterfront amphitheater and restaurants.

DON'T MISS

- Junkanoo
- Arawak Cay
- Atlantis Marine Habitat
- Exuma Cays
- Rose Island
- National Art Gallery of The Bahamas
- Clifton Heritage National Park

Experience Junkanoo

Junkanoo is the heart and soul of Bahamian culture, a retention of African heritage displayed most remarkably every Christmas and New Year in the form of a competitive parade. More than just a Christmas festival, it's a creative lifestyle anchored in community and ritual celebrations. One of the best ways to sample the energy is via an immersive tour of the **Educulture Junkanoo Museum**. You'll learn that Junkanoo is also a trade with skilled builders, musicians and choreographers. They take over the streets with drums, cowbells and conch horns, while dancing in massive costumes handcrafted from cardboard and brightly colored crêpe paper. While the annual Boxing Day and New Year's Day parades are the ultimate showcase of Bahamian creativity, many hotels have weekly Junkanoo rush-outs (mini parades). Junkanoo season peaks between September and December – this is the time to get up close to the action.

Cable Beach Strip

The Cable Beach strip has been a tourism epicenter since the 1950s. Always anchored by a mega hotel, this resort district is densely populated with restaurants, attractions and residential communities. Within its resort complex, **Baha Mar** has a casino, waterpark and the Royal Blue Golf Club. Live bands at the **Jazz Bar** inside Grand Hyatt Baha Mar are exceptional. **Social House Sushi & Grill** is a reliably good place to eat, and **Daiquiri Shack** is a refreshing pit stop where you'll also meet residents. **Goldwynn Resort & Residences** is the latest addition to this strip.

Paradise Island

The iconic Nassau Harbour is framed by Paradise Island, an inhabited barrier island connected to the mainland by two cantilever-style bridges. The enchanting **Atlantis Resort** is the most recognizable mega property in The Bahamas. Its massive aquarium, the **Atlantis Marine Habitat**, overlaps with multiple touch points across the property. The eastern end of **Cabbage Beach** is a hidden treasure along with the **Versailles Gardens and Cloisters** and the Junkanoo rush-out at **Marina Village**.

Island Tours

For a nontraditional walking tour of the historic downtown Nassau district, join the food and cultural tour by **Tru Bahamian Food Tours** or the rum tour by Islandz, which stops at **John Watling's Distillery**. Self-guided, stroll through **Arawak Cay**, an epicurean haven of Bahamian food with dozens of causal eateries and bars, or the picturesque **Graycliff's Heritage Village**, home to an interactive chocolate factory, and artist studios. The flamingo parade at the **Ardastra Gardens & Wildlife Conservation Centre** is a fun activity for families. The plantation tour at the **Clifton Heritage National Park** is for history buffs. Inside the park, there's also a statue garden honoring African ancestral mothers, and an underwater sculpture garden.

Boating Excursions

Nassau is a hub for domestic air travel and island-hopping by boat. Consider boating excursions to the nearest offshore islands, especially **Rose Island**, where any beach is the best beach in proximity to Nassau. Choose a solitary spot or anchor by **Sandy Toes Beach Bar** or **Footprints Beach Bar and Grill**. To experience a Family Island with a personality and landscape totally different from the capital, go on a day trip to the **Exuma Cays** by speedboat or **Harbour Island** (p146) by passenger ferry.

AUTHENTIC SOUVENIR FINDS

Shop for authentic keepsakes at **Craft Cottage Bahamas** on Village Rd, **Bahama Art & Handicraft** on Shirley St, and **Down Home Bahamas** on Parliament St. The Craft Cottage is located on the same property as **Doongalik Studios Art Gallery**, which hosts a lovely Saturday farmers market.

TOP TIPS

- Extend beyond the island's sun, sand and sea offerings with an expertly curated dose of Bahamian art, culture and history at the National Art Gallery of The Bahamas and the Pompey Museum of Slavery and Emancipation.
- Cable Beach, Sea Beach Estates, The Grove, Village Road and Paradise Island are considered safe areas. They have vacation rentals that are within walking distance of the beach, with access to a nearby convenience store, bar or restaurant. The north coast is generally best. If you want somewhere very remote, look to the southeast or southwest in areas such as Yamacraw or Coral Harbour.

ROAD TRIP

From Jeans Bay to Tarpum Bay

With settlements scattered across 177km, choosing your primary location is important. Staying on Harbour Island or Spanish Wells (the northern offshore islands) and taking a mainland road trip allows you to experience the luxurious amenities, pink-sand beaches and natural wonders of the north, the liveliness and beauty of central Eleuthera (the most populated area), and the privacy of the rural south.

1 Jeans Bay

Head off the beaten path to family-run Bahamas Paradise Farms, with luscious vegetation and juicy mangoes, and meet the resident pigs, goats and donkeys on the beach. This detour (book ahead) entails a conversation with the passionate host, a beach picnic with kayaking and a feast of seasonal local fruits. On Jeans Bay Rd, you can take a daring plunge at Sapphire Hole – the only way out is to scale the 9m cliff on a rope ladder. Also stop at Preacher's Cave, a safe haven for shipwrecked Puritans in the 1700s.

The Drive: Continue south on Queen's Hwy until you cross the Glass Window Bridge and see the Gregory Town welcome sign. Immediately after, the Queen's Bath sign is on the left. Park by the road and follow the trail.

2 Queen's Bath

On approach to Queen's Bath, the Glass Window Bridge has an impressive view of the island's narrowest point. From here, you can see Gaulding Cay, a beach cove perfect for swimming. Minutes away, Queen's Bath has rock formations that create a patchwork of tidal pools. Waves batter the cliffs,

GUS GARCIA/SHUTTERSTOCK ©

Spanish Wells (p146)

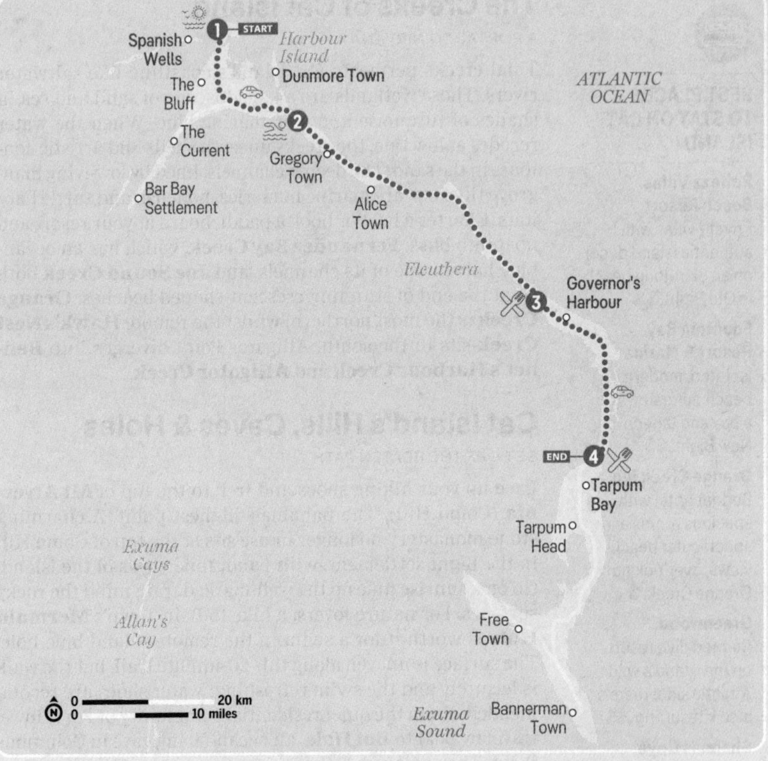

cascading down to a low-lying platform in front of a cave. The waves fill the shallow pools, slowly heating in the sun. Wear hard-bottom shoes for a short, rocky hike. Enter the sandy trail through a pine forest and follow the rocks toward the ocean.

The Drive: Back on Queen's Hwy, past the turn-off for Surfers Beach and before entering Governor's Harbour, turn left onto Haynes Ave. Turn right onto Banks Rd at the crossroads. There are many stops along this 10km coastal road.

3 Banks Road

Along Banks Rd, you'll find French Leave Beach, a secluded pink-sand beach; Tippy's Restaurant and Beachside Bar, a staple of the island; and the Leon Levy Native Plant Preserve, a nature lover's wonderland. Closer to North Palmetto Point, you can stop to eat and drink poolside at La Bougainvillea, a boutique beach hotel and restaurant.

The Drive: Drive through the North Palmetto Point settlement until you reach Queen's Hwy. Head south for 24km, until you see signs for Tarpum Bay. Continue until the road meets the coast.

4 Tarpum Bay

Tarpum Bay is a small but vibrant residential settlement in southern Eleuthera. Stop here for a fun and relaxing time at Seaside Breeze Restaurant and Coffee House, a charming outdoor rest stop with tropical decor. Order conch salad while you play on the beach swing, or simply submit yourself to the calm energy of this tranquil bay area. A little further afoot, with more time, visit the turtle-breeding ground at Winding Bay Beach and take the One Eleuthera Foundation farm tour with a fresh lunch in Rock Sound.

BEST PLACES TO STAY ON CAT ISLAND

Rollezz Villas Beach Resort
Private villas with authentic island decor on an 8km-long beach in Old Bight. $$

Fountain Bay Resort & Marina
Isolated, modern beach bungalows on a bay and lagoon in New Bight. $$

Orange Creek Inn
Budget hotel with spacious rooms and spectacular beach views, overlooking Orange Creek. $

Greenwood
Rugged dive resort on the island's wild Atlantic side; there's also kitesurfing. $$

Shannas Cove
Secluded resort in the island's north, with hillside bungalows and private beach. $

The Creeks of Cat Island

A PORTAL TO NIRVANA

Tidal creeks permeate Cat Island's coastline like saltwater rivers. These wetlands are a kaleidoscope of sand and sea in shades of turquoise and aquamarine blue. When the water recedes at low tide, the creeks unearth shells and artistic contours in the sand. The deeper channels, lined by low-lying mangrove thickets, are marine nurseries, bonefish and turtle habitats. Charter a boat or book a paddleboard at your resort and float into bliss. **Fernandez Bay Creek**, which has an ocean-blue hole in one of its channels, and **Joe Sound Creek** both sit at the end of stunning crescent-shaped beaches. **Orange Creek** is the most northern, whilst the remote **Hawk's Nest Creek** sits in the south. Alligator Point diverges into **Bennet's Harbour Creek** and **Alligator Creek**.

Cat Island's Hills, Caves & Holes

GET OFF THE BEATEN PATH

Lace up your hiking shoes and trek to the top of **Mt Alvernia** (Como Hill), The Bahamas' highest point. A charming stone monastery no longer in use sits at the top of Como Hill in the Bight settlement, with panoramic views of the island. Go on a sunrise hike up the well-marked trail; mind the rocky surfaces. For nature lovers, a hike to Bain Town's **Mermaid Hole** is worth it for a swim in the remote inland blue hole. The surface is uneven along this 20-minute trail, but the walk is leisurely and the swim refreshing; water shoes are recommended. From the quiet residential community of Port Howe, travel by boat to **Bat Hole**, an ocean-facing cave in Columbus Point. Then enjoy a beach picnic at the pristine **Winding Bay**.

Meet Two Remarkable Ecosystems in Andros

ECOTOURISM CAPITAL WITH DIVERSE PARKS

The Bahamas has some of the world's deepest waters beneath the Tongue of the Ocean, but also one of the largest shallow tidal flats within the Great Bahama Bank. Andros is sandwiched between these two remarkable ecosystems. This rustic island has a porous texture, with the world's highest concentration of blue holes. You can swim, cliff-jump and hike on nature trails within the **Blue Holes National Park**, with 50-plus recorded holes surrounded by pine and coppice forests. The **West Side National Park** is a remote, untouched coastal reserve on the Great Bahama Bank. It's a productive

WHERE TO EAT ON CAT ISLAND

New Bight Fish Fry
Multiple local food stalls on Regatta Beach, open daily for breakfast, lunch and dinner. **$**

Smith's Bay Dock
The public dock, where the weekly mailboat restocks the island, is a local hangout to eat and drink on weekends. **$**

Tingum Dem Beach Bar
Newer restaurant in New Bight with Bahamian specialties and bar food. Launchpad for water sports and island excursions. **$**

Cat Island

PICS721/SHUTTERSTOCK ©

marine nursery and habitat for flamingoes, butterflies and iguanas. The best snorkeling and diving is within the **South Andros Barrier Reef Marine Park**. There's limited infrastructure within the parks; arrange a Bahamas National Trust guide through your hotel.

Catching Crabs under Cover of Darkness

TRADITION, DRAMA AND EXCITEMENT AWAIT

Crabbin' is a Bahamian way of life, with Andros and Cat Island leading the tradition. Hunting for this Bahamian delicacy begins under the cover of darkness with flashlights and burlap sacks. The timid land crab may freeze on sight, but its mighty claws pack a punch. Proper techniques are necessary to catch them, whether plucked from the brush or deep in their holes. Book a guide for a night of crabbing on Andros. It will likely be your local hotelier or someone they recommend. In June, summer rain triggers the annual migration to lay eggs in the sea for mating season. The crabs emerge from their nesting holes and start walking, everywhere.

BEST PLACES TO STAY ON ANDROS

Kamalame Cay
All-inclusive luxury resort near Staniard Creek with chic beach bungalows along the coast of a private cay. $$$

Small Hope Bay Lodge
All-inclusive dive resort offering daily excursions, with rustic beachside cabins and delicious meals. $$

Andros Island Beach Resort
Dreamy beach locale for families or solo travelers with comfortable accommodations, beach access and water sports. $

Dream Villas
Quaint beachside property with one- and two-bedroom villas in Fresh Creek Andros. Connected to the overwater Brigadier's Restaurant. $

WHERE TO STAY ON ANDROS

Andros Island Bonefish Club
North Andros lodge on Cargill Creek, with easy access to the West Side National Park. **$$**

Swain's Cay Lodge
Mangrove Cay lodge with laid-back beachside rooms and the option of daily prepared meals. **$**

Nathan's Lodge
South Andros lodge with rustic charm, guided fishing trips and delicious meals. **$**

BEST PLACES TO EAT IN ELEUTHERA

Buccaneers
Excellent local cuisine, especially boiled or stewed fish, in Governor's Harbour. $$

Fish Fry
Casual food shack and bar with a simple menu at the entrance of Cupid's Cay. $

Leorose Sunset Beach Bar & Grill
Eclectic waterfront spot in James Cistern with tasty food and a jovial atmosphere. $

Front Porch
Gorgeous sunset view from a deck overlooking Hatchet Bay; order the seafood platter. $$

Daddy Joe's Restaurant & Inn
A mellow place to eat, with an outdoor tiki bar, in Gregory Town. $$

Romance & Relaxation on Harbour Island

SMALL ISLAND, GRAND SPIRIT

Rise early on Harbour Island to watch the sunrise on its famed **Pink Sands Beach**. Boutique resorts, private estates and vacation rentals blend seamlessly into the peaceful surroundings. **Dunmore Town**, the historic seaside village, is recognizable by its colorful wooden homes with front porches and picket fences along the main street. Walk the harborside strip or ride a golf cart to **Queen Conch** and other local food shacks and bars. The tiny island is known worldwide for its exceptional food. The cozy yet refined **Rock House** makes for a romantic dinner date with gourmet food and sunset views. **Acquapazza Wine Bar & Ristorante** has classic Italian flair in a casual setting. A morning pit stop at **Cocoa Coffee House** will perk you up.

An Intriguing Wallflower off Eleuthera's Coast

THE LOBSTER CAPITAL OF SPANISH WELLS

Spanish Wells, off the north coast of Eleuthera, comprises two islands linked by a tiny truss bridge. The island has a distinct Cigillian dialect and is still populated by descendants of European settlers from the 1600s and Haitian migrants. For many years, Spanish Wells was a dry island, serving no alcohol. Although no longer dry, it's still known for its Puritan lifestyle. Commercial lobster fishing is a way of life, but the local dining scene is comparatively modest. There are notable restaurants, such as **Wrecker's Restaurant and Bar** on St George's Cay and **Sandbar Bar & Grill** on Russell Island, but ocean-to-table dining with a private chef is the way to go. Spend time out to sea on a boating excursion to the **Royal Island** sandbar, **Bottom Harbour** for turtles and stingrays, or **Current Cut** for a drift dive or snorkel.

GETTING AROUND

There are daily flights to the Lynden Pindling International Airport in Nassau from major cities around the world. Connecting to Andros is a 15-minute hop, often on a Cessna aircraft. There are no daily flights to Cat Island, so plan for longer stays. The North Eleuthera International Airport is the second busiest in the entire Bahamas.

There are two ferry docks in north Eleuthera that provide convenient transportation between the three adjacent islands. From Nassau, passenger ships visit these islands daily.

To cover the long distances in Eleuthera, rent a car. Taxis are pricey. Move around Spanish Wells and Harbour Island on a golf cart.

SOUTHERN BAHAMAS

There's no shortage of sand and surf along the southern Bahamas coastline. Exclusive beaches are yours for the picking in the Exumas, Long Island, San Salvador, Inagua, Acklins and Crooked Island, making these idyllic islands perfect for travelers seeking serenity, solitude and water-based adventures.

In the Exumas, hundreds of islands and cays form a long linear sequence like stepping stones across a vast seascape. The northern cays and the Exuma Cays Land & Sea Park form one grouping. The southern cays and Great Exuma, where the capital George Town sits, form another. Inagua is a bird lover's paradise, San Salvador has endless beaches rich in history, and Long Island holds peaceful retreats and gems for adventure-seekers.

In truth, the region's most tranquil islands aren't major tourist destinations. They include Rum Cay, Mayaguana and the completely solarized Ragged Island. Collectively, these islands have a population of less than 500 people.

TOP TIP

The West Indian flamingo was on the verge of extinction, but conservation efforts around the Inagua National Park helped revive the species. Head to Great Inagua, a bird-watching hot spot, to marvel at The Bahamas' national bird, now living in healthy breeding colonies across the island's extensive salt marshes.

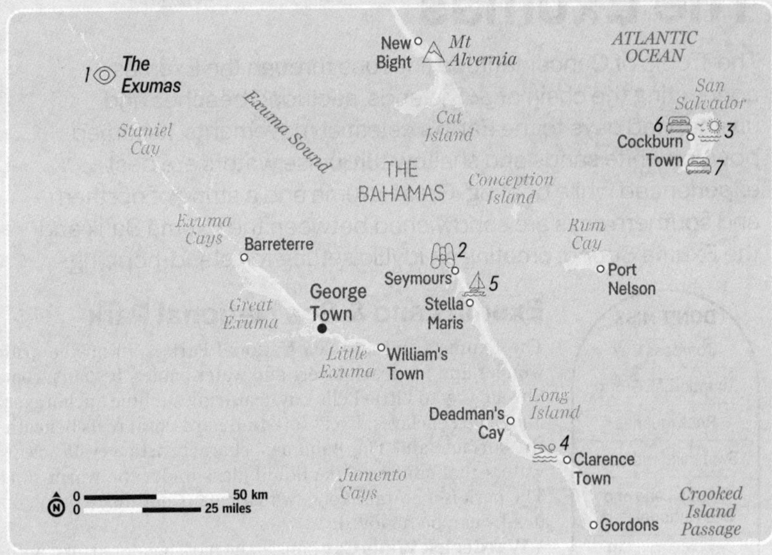

TOP SIGHTS
1 The Exumas

SIGHTS
2 Columbus Point
3 San Salvador

ACTIVITIES, COURSES & TOURS
4 Dean's Blue Hole
5 Stella Maris

SLEEPING
6 Club Med Columbus
7 Guanahani Beach Club
(see 6) Riding Rock Inn Resort & Marina
(see 6) The Sands Hotel

BLUEORANGE STUDIO/SHUTTERSTOCK ©

PRACTICALITIES

Use this QR code to find travel specials and discover Exumas' top attractions.

TOP SIGHT

The Exumas

The Tropic of Cancer latitude line runs through the Exumas, connecting the chain of 365 islands, secluded beaches and uninhabited cays to the Earth's celestial movements. Its famed powder-white sands and shallow turquoise waters are best experienced while boating. Great Exuma and a string of northern and southern cays are sandwiched between the Exuma Bank and the Exuma Sound, creating an idyllic setting for island-hopping.

DON'T MISS

- Compass Cay
- Thunderball Grotto
- Rock iguanas
- Swimming with pigs
- Exuma Land and Sea National Park
- Stocking Island
- Man-o-War Cay sandbar
- Hoopers Bay Beach
- Great Exuma

Exuma Land & Sea National Park

The Exuma Land and Sea National Park is an off-the-grid wonderland for beach lovers and water babies. It spans from Shroud Cay to Little Bells Cay, featuring sublime anchorages and beach enclaves; lively soft- and hard-coral reefs beneath the surface; and The Bahamas' characteristic crystal-clear waters that shimmer like liquid glass under the warm sun. The park is a no-take zone, which means nothing – living or dead – can be removed.

Warderick Wells Cay houses the park headquarters, with hiking trails leading to dramatic blowholes along the iron shore rocks. On the beach is the preserved skeleton of a 16m-long sperm whale. This anchorage has 360-degree panoramic sand and sea views and nearby snorkeling. **Shroud Cay** is mostly covered by salt marshes, mangrove creeks and endless beaches. Park rules only allow motorized vessels to enter the north tidal creek, one of several saltwater, river-like channels on the island. You can explore other creeks with paddle craft. The **Washing Machine** is a natural wonder of Shroud Cay, where tidal currents create an oceanic vortex in a small cut, perfect for drift diving or floating on the lazy river above.

Marine Caves

Explore the mysterious world of the Exuma Cays' hidden marine caves, including **Thunderball Grotto** near Staniel Cay and **Rocky Dundas** in the national park. Drive into the open chamber of the breathtaking **Cave Cay** near Barraterre for stunning pictures of the beach hidden inside.

Swimming with Pigs

In The Bahamas, plump and well-fed pigs live a life of leisure and indulgence on pristine beaches. The fascinating contrast means the Exumas' frisky and photogenic swimming pigs (pictured) have a spellbinding appeal. On land, some of the pigs are aggressive during feeding; it's best to capture adorable photos from the safety of your boat.

Wildlife Safaris

Boating safaris around the southern cays start in Barraterre, Great Exuma, or around Staniel Cay and Black Point. They are certain to deliver the Exumas' big five animals: sharks, turtles, iguanas, stingrays and swimming pigs. Critically endangered rock iguanas have large habitats on **Allan's Cay**, **Big Major Cay** and **Leaf Cay**. **Compass Cay** is known for its habituated nurse sharks, while **Hoopers Bay Beach** on Great Exuma is home to habituated young sea turtles. Stingrays love the beach on **Stocking Island** by Chat 'N' Chill Beach Bar & Grill, as they can reliably find conch scraps and other food. On rare occasions, there are dolphin sightings in **Elizabeth Harbour** and other cays, but it's a lucky occurrence. On snorkeling and diving trips, a diversity of tropical fish is a guarantee.

The Northern Cays

Speedboats from New Providence frequent the northern cays, largely for day trips – **Ship Channel Cay**, in particular. **Norman's Cay** and **Highbourne Cay** are luxury islands with private mega-yacht marinas and high-end restaurants.

Elizabeth Harbour, Great Exuma

Elizabeth Harbour is a well-protected anchorage and remarkably picturesque harbor used as a key location for commerce and trade on Great Exuma, and is a main destination for sightseeing by boat. The barrier islands and cays have many attractions, including **Starfish Beach** and **Stocking Island**.

QUICK TOUR

Make the most of the disappearing beaches that emerge at low tide. Be sure to provision your boat for a happy-hour beach picnic on a sandbar near **Mush Cay**, **Pipe Creek**, **Man-o-War Cay**, **Moriah Harbour Cay National Park** or **O'Brien's Cay**. These sandy, submarine plateaus stretching for miles are hallmarks of the Exumas' beauty.

TOP TIPS

- Because of the archipelago's size, an Exumas itinerary is shaped by two critical choices: where you start and your mode of transportation.
- Start in the south on Great Exuma to include cultural and historical experiences. Land at a minor airport or private airstrip in the northern cays of Black Point, Staniel Cay or Norman's Cay for a more exclusive experience.
- When you stay in George Town, charter a private boat for excursions in Elizabeth Harbour and the southern cays.
- A catamaran cruise, ideally for a week, will cover the greatest distance at an even pace.

BONEFISHING IN ACKLINS & CROOKED ISLAND

Nestled in the warm waters of the southern Bahamas, **Acklins** and **Crooked Island** – plus the nearby **Long Cay** – share familial, economic and social connections. They offer a great vacation experience for bonefishing enthusiasts, who prefer to visit in the coldest months when big bones are most active.

Residents on these sparsely populated islands make their living through fishing and small-scale farming. The world-renowned bonefishing draws anglers from all over to the shallow Bight of Acklins. Even 8km from shore, the water is knee-height or shallower on this massive wilderness wetland. Beyond bonefishing, visitors can enjoy other forms of fishing, snorkeling, caving, bird-watching, island-hopping and exploring the natural beauty of the region.

Endless Beaches & Calming Waters

A SERENE OASIS IN SAN SALVADOR

The stress of daily life fades away in San Salvador, a tiny outlying island in The Bahamas floating atop an Atlantic Ocean ridge. The endless beaches slip off a ledge and plunge deep to the ocean floor, providing the conditions for windsurfing, fishing and diving. Water sports are readily available at the all-inclusive **Club Med Columbus**. The family-owned **Riding Rock Inn Resort & Marina** especially caters to divers and boaters. However, it's the island's serenity that draws most visitors. At **The Sands Hotel**, customer service is so personalized, you'll feel like part of the family. Experience tranquility on the beach there and at the elegant **Guanahani Beach Club**. The island's history is intertwined with Christopher Columbus; historic landmarks in Long Bay include an underwater monument marking where the famous explorer apparently dropped anchor in 1492.

The Best of Long Island's Attractions

UNFORGETTABLE SIGHTSEEING ADVENTURES

Dean's Blue Hole is a natural wonder that draws visitors from around the world to Long Island. Tucked away in a protected nook, surrounded by towering cliffs, it sits at the curve of a pristine cove. Avoid the setting sun, when mosquitoes emerge, and come for a swim, free dive or cliff jumping. Beyond this famous attraction, other incredible places on Long Island include **Hamilton's Cave**, a former archaeological site (tours go from the Cartwright Homestead), and **Columbus Point**, a cliffside lookout over the captivating Blue Sound with a monument honoring the island's indigenous people. **Stella Maris**, the northern settlement, is an excellent base for boating excursions, vacation rentals and resort stays.

Dean's Blue Hole
SVEN HANSCHE/SHUTTERSTOCK ©

GETTING AROUND

Small planes and charter flights are popular for inter-island travel. They emanate from Nassau and fly to all islands in the south. Domestic airlines travel to all of the islands; however, not all southern islands have daily service.

In Great Exuma, water taxis serve multiple destinations in Elizabeth Harbour. You can walk the entire coastline of San Salvador in a day, although a bicycle ride is a great way to get around. Car rental is the best way to travel in Long Island and Acklins and Crooked Island – it gives you the convenience to explore freely and access the major attractions.

Arriving

All international flights arrive at the same terminal, but US departures have a separate terminal from the one for domestic and other international flights. Departing to the US from The Bahamas presents the advantage of US Customs and Border Protection Preclearance. Bahamian dollars and US dollars are interchangeable at a 1:1 rate, so there's no need to exchange money on arrival.

By Air

Dozens of nonstop commercial flights connect to The Bahamas daily from major cities in the USA and Canada. The busiest international airports are in New Providence and North Eleuthera; however, flights arrive at over 20 airports and private airstrips across the islands.

By Boat

On arrival to The Bahamas, boaters must clear Customs and Immigration at the nearest port of entry. No one except the captain is permitted to leave the vessel until it has been cleared. Over 12 major islands have official ports of entry.

Money

Currency: Bahamian dollar (BS$)

CASH

The remote Family Islands have many cash-based businesses. Some islands also have extremely limited banking services including ATMs. Plan to conduct business mostly in cash, especially for ground transportation services, ferries and boat charters.

CREDIT CARDS

Credit card use is prevalent in major hotels, established hospitality businesses and throughout New Providence, but it's not guaranteed. The gap between cash and credit card use remains wide, even though there are a handful of cashless businesses. More and more, businesses that accept credit cards can also accept various forms of digital payments such as Apple Pay.

TAXES & TIPPING

VAT of 10% is added to all checks for registered businesses in The Bahamas. Hospitality services typically attract an automatic gratuity ranging from 15% to 20%. Charges can climb to 25% due to service fees.

NELSTUDIO/SHUTTERSTOCK ©

Above: Sea turtle; Right: Bathsheba Beach, which is too dangerous to swim on (p170)

BARBADOS

BEACH BARS, SNORKELING AND SURF

Relax with white sand between your toes and rum punch in your glass on this most fun-loving of islands.

From the moment your flight begins to line up for its final approach into Bridgetown, it becomes apparent that you've made the right decision for your vacation as beach after beach of dazzling white sands fronted by the most brilliant blue waters spread out before you.

Barbados is famed throughout the world for its beaches and it really does live up to the hype, with fine powdery white sands in the southeast, golden bays with mirror-like waters in the west and rugged windswept wilderness on the Atlantic side. Meanwhile, in the interior of the island, flower-filled gardens, spectacular caves and brightly painted village rum shops await.

One thing you can't see from the plane window, but soon becomes clear after touching down, is the magical atmosphere that makes Barbados so much more than a beach destination. With a history dating back nearly 400 years, this is an island rich in legend, where sugarcane was first turned into rum, gentlemen were turned into pirates and where a mixing of cultures has led to a very Caribbean take on classic British idiosyncrasies.

Which leads us to the Bajans themselves. In a region of outgoing and friendly folk, Barbados takes it to the next level with a patient, kind and incredibly relaxed people that go out of their way to ensure visitors enjoy this charming island as much as they do.

THE MAIN AREAS

BRIDGETOWN & THE SOUTH COAST
History, nightlife and turquoise waters. p158

THE WEST COAST
Glamorous golden sands. p164

THE ATLANTIC COAST
Wild, windswept beaches with big surf. p169

Find Your Way

While we have listed the main accommodations hubs around the island, Barbados is a flat country and therefore it's relatively quick to get between districts regardless of where you set up base.

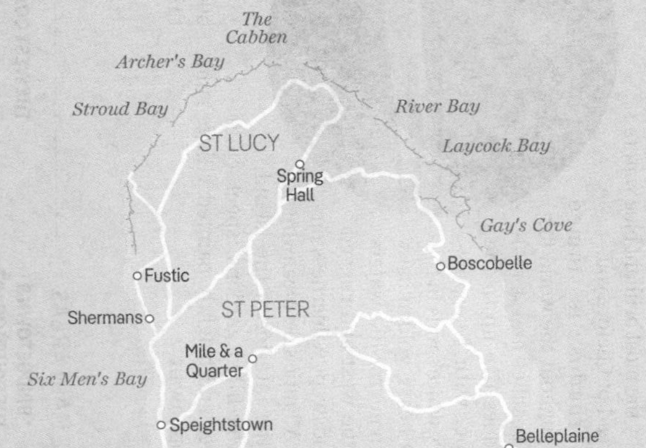

The Atlantic Coast, p169
Lightly populated, with long wild beaches ideal for walks accompanied by the sound of crashing waves, the Atlantic coast is Barbados' best place to disconnect.

TAXI

Taxis are not cheap in Barbados but are the most stress-free way to explore the country. There are no meters so agree on a fare before getting in. Many taxis are spacious vans so getting a group together can make trips more viable.

BUS

Barbados has one of the best public transportation networks in the Eastern Caribbean, with government-run electric buses equipped with air-conditioning and wi-fi, noisy yellow private buses and unnervingly fast minivans reaching even the most remote corners of the island.

CAR

While car hire is fairly expensive in Barbados, it's the best way to ditch the crowds and see more of the island. Bajan drivers tend to be very patient with hire vehicles, which are clearly identifiable with 'H' number plates.

The West Coast, p164
With golden sands and tranquil waters, the west coast is the most glamorous part of the island yet it remains unpretentious and easily accessible.

Bridgetown & the South Coast, p158
The Bridgetown area is rich in history and culture, while just south of the capital lie some of the island's most alluring white-sand beaches.

FOTOLUMINATE LLC/SHUTTERSTOCK ©

Plan Your Time

While any trip to Barbados is sure to involve plenty of beach time, make sure you leave a couple of days to explore the wild Atlantic coast and the garden-filled interior.

BARBARA ASH/SHUTTERSTOCK ©

Lobster Claw (Heliconia)

A Short Beach Break

- If you plan on spending most of your vacation bathing in the sun, choose a hotel on the **south coast** (p160) within walking distance of one of the many white-sand beaches and from where you can explore downtown **Bridgetown** (p161) and the historic **Garrison Savannah** (p161).

- Any of Rockley, Worthing or Dover Beaches offer white sands and beautiful clear waters as well as a good choice of nearby restaurants and nightlife options. Make sure you keep Friday night free for the **Oistins Fish Fry** (p162) and also spend an afternoon snorkeling with sea turtles at **Carlisle Bay** (p160).

Seasonal Highlights

Slightly hotter and drier than its neighbors, Barbados has good beach weather year-round. However, the very best conditions are found during the dry, balmy months from December to March.

FEBRUARY

Perfect weather at the height of the dry season means maximum hours on the beach.

APRIL

Crowds are down across the island and surf's up on the island's Atlantic coast where the **Soup Bowl** gets popping.

JUNE

Many of Barbados' exotic **tropical fruits** come into season, including acidic gooseberries and the wonderfully named Fat Pork.

BYVALET/SHUTTERSTOCK ©, ND JOHNSTON/SHUTTERSTOCK ©, NAHHANA/SHUTTERSTOCK ©

A Week on the Island

For your first couple of nights in Barbados settle in to a hotel on the glitzy **west coast** (p165) to enjoy the magnificent golden beaches with tranquil warm waters that the region is famed for. After a day or two of sunbathing, head to the **Folkestone Marine Park** (p165) to check out the colorful underwater world before hitting **Speightstown** (p165) for a traditional Bajan meal and sunset drinks in a busy waterside bar.

For your last couple of days, pack up and drive or take a bus over to **Bathsheba** (p170) and check into accommodations just meters from the crashing waves of the Atlantic.

More Than a Week

After getting your fill of sun, sea and sand on either the south or west coasts, take a day trip into the interior of the island to check out the rock formations deep in **Harrison's Cave** (p168) and the magnificent heliconias at **Flower Forest** (p168) and **Hunte's Gardens** (p168).

Next, head to the remote north of the island to take a tour of the oldest working rum distillery in the world at **Mount Gay Rum Distillery** (p161). Spend another day exploring secluded **Bottom Bay** (p163) and the other pink-sand beaches of the southeast before finishing your trip with a sailing cruise up the coast from Bridgetown.

JULY

Baby **hawksbill turtles** begin to hatch in numbers at beaches on the south and west coasts.

AUGUST

The biggest party on the island, the **Crop-Over Festival** (p163), reaches a spectacular finale with concerts and the Grand Kadooment parade.

OCTOBER

Low season brings good accommodations deals and the taste-bud tingling **Barbados Food and Rum Festival**.

NOVEMBER

Rains ease as Barbados celebrates its **Independence** at the end of the month with a number of cultural events.

BRIDGETOWN & THE SOUTH COAST

Blessed with white-sand beaches fronted by impossibly brilliant blue waters, the southern coast of Barbados is the most developed part of the island and its tourism epicenter.

The southern beaches are generally wider and with softer sand than their quieter west-coast counterparts (although often with slightly rougher waters). While many are backed by large resort developments, the sheer number of world-class beaches means it's fairly easy to escape the crowds.

But there's more to the region than beaches. Bridgetown remains the cultural heart of the country, with vibrant streets that radiate history and a fascinating waterfront from where old-world traders and pirates once set forth on incredible adventures. Just south of the river, the historic Garrison Savannah district houses some of the islands most elegant buildings, which are linked by mysterious underground tunnels.

Bridgetown & the South Coast

TOP TIP

Beaches in front of the large resorts around Rockley, Dover and Hastings can get very crowded but at the northern and southern end of the hotel strip there are stretches of sand that seldom get overrun and can be reached by a short, cheap van ride.

ANDMIR/SHUTTERSTOCK ©

Dover Beach (p160)

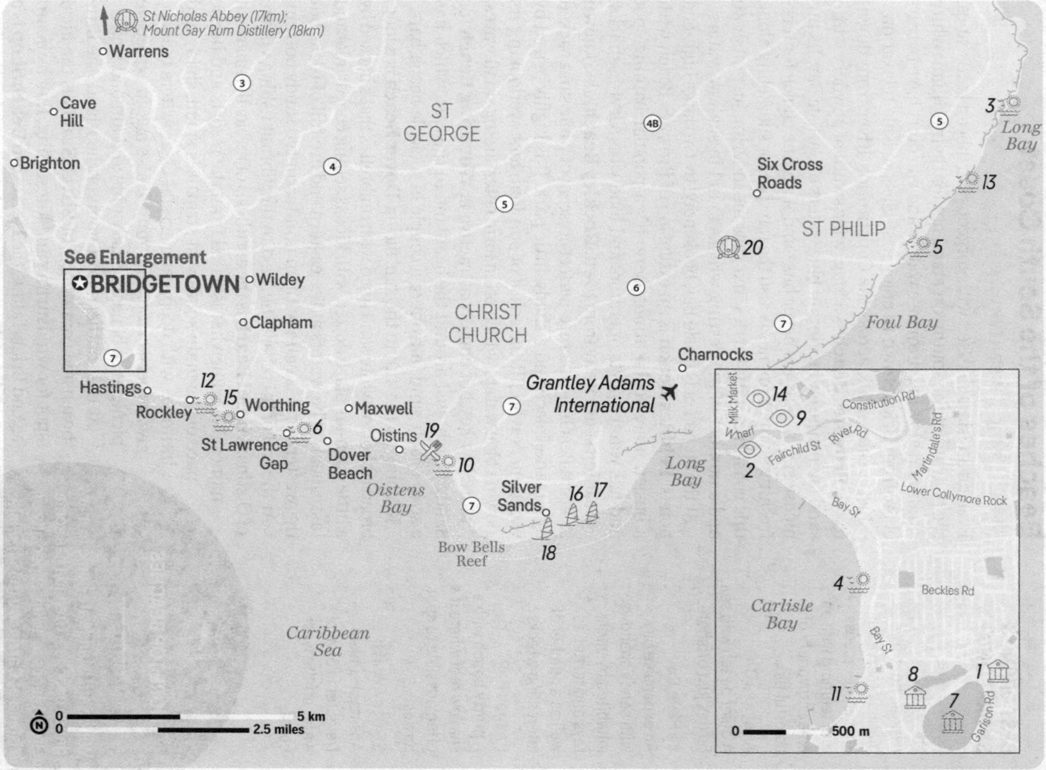

SIGHTS
1 Barbados Museum
2 Blackwoods Screw Dock
3 Bottom Bay
4 Brownes Beach
5 Crane Beach
6 Dover Beach
7 Garrison Savannah
8 George Washington House
9 Houses of Parliament
10 Miami Beach
11 Pebbles Beach
12 Rockley Beach
13 Shark Hole
14 Swan St
15 Worthing Beach

ACTIVITIES & TOURS
16 De Action Beach Shop
17 Endless Kiteboarding
18 Silver Sands

EATING
19 Oistins Fish Fry

DRINKING & NIGHTLIFE
20 Foursquare Distillery

Blackwoods Screw Dock (p161)

St Nicholas Abbey (17km); Mount Gay Rum Distillery (18km)
Warrens
Cave Hill
Brighton
ST GEORGE
See Enlargement
BRIDGETOWN
Wildey
Clapham
CHRIST CHURCH
Six Cross Roads
ST PHILIP
Long Bay
Foul Bay
Charnocks
Grantley Adams International
Hastings
Rockley
Worthing
St Lawrence Gap
Maxwell
Dover Beach
Oistins
Oistens Bay
Silver Sands
Bow Bells Reef
Long Bay
Caribbean Sea
0 5 km
0 2.5 miles
Milk Market
Wharf
Constitution Rd
River Rd
Fairchild St
Martindale's Rd
Lower Collymore Rock
Bay St
Carlisle Bay
Beckles Rd
Bay St
Garison Rd
0 500 m

BEST DIVING & SNORKELING

Folkestone Marine Park
A large, boat-free marine reserve with an easy-to-access reef teeming with an amazing variety of colorful fish.

Alleynes Bay
A quiet beach with sea turtles just offshore.

Carlisle Bay
An expansive bay with sandy shallows inhabited by eagle rays and turtles as well as a number of interesting wrecks.

Paynes Bay
A pretty beach with a shallow reef where it's often possible to spot turtles.

SS Stavronikita
An intact sunken freighter in 36m of water off the west coast.

Beaches of the South Coast

WHITEST SANDS, BRIGHTEST WATERS

Even on an island blessed with gorgeous Caribbean landscapes, the beaches of the southwest stand out for their brilliant white sands and glowing turquoise waters and you don't have to travel far from Bridgetown to enjoy first-class seaside relaxation.

Just a short walk across the Constitution River from downtown, **Brownes Beach** is a long, wide swath of powdery white sand facing the calm, vibrant blue waters of Carlisle Bay. Its immense size means it's never busy and it's a fine choice for a refreshing swim. Brownes is also the top spot for snorkeling along this coastline, with turtles and rays meandering just offshore and a number of interesting wrecks found in shallow waters.

At the far end of Carlisle Bay, bookended by two large high-end hotels, **Pebbles Beach** is an extension of Brownes Beach with a busier, more social atmosphere. It's a popular bathing spot and has water-sports operators and food vans serving snacks.

Heading south away from town, **Rockley Beach**, also known as Accra Beach, is a picture-perfect crescent of white sand backed by a marketplace and a shady, little park. It is highly prized by vacationers who fill the mass of sun loungers overlooking its glowing blue waters, which often form entertaining small waves.

More low-key but equally attractive is **Worthing Beach** (or Sandy Beach) just around the headland to the east, which has a strip of soft sand in front of a couple of sociable beach bars.

Keeping up the 'fun in the sun' flavor, **Dover Beach** is a long, broad ribbon of white sand lined with umbrellas that's backed by a little open-air plaza dotted with kiosks selling cool drinks and tasty meals. The waters at the eastern end are full of rocks but the western end is calm with an uninterrupted sandy bottom.

At the end of this coastline, next to the vibrant fishing village of Oistins, **Miami Beach** is the antithesis of its North American namesake. Somewhat isolated from the resorts and hectic pace of the main southwest strip, it is small, shady and intimate, with deep, calm crystal-clear waters that are always perfect for swimming. It also has an expansive picnic area beneath shady pine and almond trees.

At the southernmost point of the island, the little beachside community of **Silver Sands** is the ideal spot for windsurfing and kitesurfing. Run by board legend Brian Talma, the **De Action Beach Shop** is a colorful wooden compound right on the beach where you can take classes with seasoned pros or just settle in with a cold drink at the cafe and watch the kites twirl overhead. Nearby, **Endless Kiteboarding** is run by an enthusiastic young Bajan and offers lessons with good equipment and patient, certified instructors.

MORE TOP BEACHES

The Windward Islands are home to many gorgeous beaches. Grenada has some excellent places to swim, especially on the island of **Carriacou** (p334), while in St Vincent and the Grenadines **Union Island** (p581) and **Bequia** (p576) also boast fine waters.

WHERE TO STAY AROUND BRIDGETOWN

Southern Palms Beach Club
A cheery resort with plenty of character fronted by a fine stretch of sand. $$$

Little Arches Hotel
A Mediterranean-style boutique hotel with Caribbean flair that offers maximum privacy and luxury. $$$

Yellow Bird
Excellent modern studios with all the mod cons and sunset views from the balconies. $$

Historic Bridgetown

MUSEUMS, TUNNELS AND A WATERFRONT

Barbados' oft overlooked capital is the cultural heart of the country and offers a fascinating window onto the island's complex history. The best way to get to know Bridgetown is to walk its compact center, trying delicious local specialties and stopping to chat with its many colorful characters.

The city's most iconic landmark is the neo-Gothic **Houses of Parliament**, which were built in 1871 and feature a striking clock tower and stained-glass windows.

But perhaps the place to best feel Bridgetown's rich history is down on the waterfront, where several 18th- and 19th-century buildings still stand. Make sure you check out the ingenious, Victorian-era **Blackwoods Screw Dock**, the only dry dock of its kind in the world.

For a taste of modern Bridgetown, pedestrian-only **Swan St** is the city's main shopping district. Lined with street vendors, it's a riot of color and island sounds that bustles with energy from morning to dusk.

Around 2km south of downtown, on the other side of the river, the **Garrison Savannah** was once the British military command on the island and still clings to airs of another era. At the heart of the district is an oval-shaped park strewn with 17th-century cannons that is home to the island's horse-racing track.

Overlooking the Savannah, the **Barbados Museum** is housed in a former military prison and has engaging displays on all aspects of the island's history, while nearby **George Washington House** is a meticulously restored 18th-century estate where visitors can descend into one of the many tunnels that run beneath the garrison.

The Birthplace of Rum

PEAK INSIDE LEGENDARY DISTILLERIES

While rum is the tipple of choice across the Caribbean, Barbados is the original home of the spirit, with the very first drops of the cane-based beverage said to have been distilled on the island sometime in the 17th century. At present, there are four distilleries on the island, three of which welcome visitors.

The oldest working rum distillery in the world and maker of the island's most prestigious rums, **Mount Gay Rum Distillery** has been producing flavorful spirits at its St Lucy facility on the north of the island since 1703. Rum is still produced with water drawn from the original well and visitors can take a tour

THE GENTLEMAN PIRATE

Long before Rihanna stole the mantle, Barbados' most famous superstar was an unusual pirate by the name of Stede Bonnet. Born into a plantation-owning family, well-educated Bonnet grew bored of his comfortable lifestyle and decided to try pillaging on the high seas. Despite never having been a sailor, in 1717 he went out and bought himself a sloop, which he named *Revenge*, and hired a crew from the rum shops of Bridgetown who were paid wages out of his savings. After a slow start, Bonnet went on to have significant success, but his adventures didn't end well – he was hanged in South Carolina in late 1718.

WHERE TO EAT AROUND BRIDGETOWN

Mustor's Restaurant
An old-school, unpretentious Bridgetown diner serving a small menu of traditional Bajan plates. **$**

Brown Sugar
Awesome ambience and even better food at this local institution serving outstanding Bajan cuisine. **$$**

Champers
Fine dining overlooking lovely Rockley Beach with great grilled seafood and pasta dishes. **$$$**

FOOD FOR CHAMPIONS

Brian Talma (@briantalma), water-sports legend and sustainable development advocate, shares his favorite places to refuel.

I spend most of my time on the beach but when I do go out I love **Ericanna Bakery**, which not only has amazing Barbadian pastries (salt bread, lead pipes, rock cakes, horseshoes and jam puffs) and yummy cakes, it also has rotis and fish cutters.

Another great choice is **Buffy Mini-Market & Restaurant**, a community hub run by a local personality and his family, where an amazing blend of visitors and locals congregate to eat and drink.

And I buy all my fresh supplies at **H & R Fruit & Vegetables**, a family-run business where everything on the shelves is fresh from the fields.

DAXUS/GETTY IMAGES ©

Oistins Fish Fry

of the distillery to check out the process up close before retiring to the tasting room to try samples from across the Mount Gay range – make sure you come with a designated driver!

A smaller, more low-key distillery, the **Foursquare Distillery** is located on a former sugar plantation south of Bridgetown and produces the popular Old Brigand brand. Visitors are welcome to wander through the facility unaccompanied, join a tour or just head to the on-site bar to try the many varieties.

For an insight into how rum was produced in the early days visit the artisanal distillery at **St Nicholas Abbey**, on the remote east side of the island, which totally shuns modern machinery.

And if you're in Barbados in October, you can try the country's best rums together with dishes from the island's most talented chefs at the lively **Barbados Food and Rum Festival**.

Friday Night at the Fish Fry

FISH, BEER AND DANCING

It feels like half of Barbados and almost every visitor on the island descends on the little fishing village of Oistins on a Friday night for the country's most popular party: the **Oistins Fish Fry**.

A particularly Bajan concept that is part seafood barbecue, part boisterous block party, the Fish Fry takes place in a purpose-built maze of more than 30 small restaurant kiosks right next to a busy fish market that overlooks a little beach.

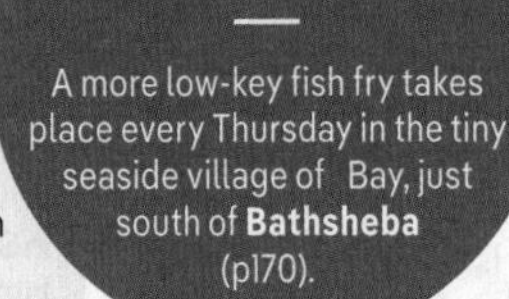

MARTIN'S BAY FISH FRY

A more low-key fish fry takes place every Thursday in the tiny seaside village of Bay, just south of **Bathsheba** (p170).

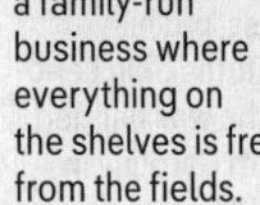

WHERE TO DRINK AROUND BRIDGETOWN

Mojo
A sociable bar in a big old house with a wide open veranda and great tunes.

The Cove
A hip indoor/outdoor club with split levels and plenty of space to sit.

Boatyard
A lively multicolored beach bar on Carlisle Bay with inflatables and giant swings in the water.

Most of the stalls offer a similar menu: a variety of grilled fish and shellfish served with macaroni pie, chips, plantain, grilled breadfruit, garlic bread and more. Unless you specify, you'll get a bit of each side with your main.

There are also a number of bars with muscular sound systems and a stage with live music that keeps the party going well after the plates are cleared.

A Southeast Sojourn

EXPLORE SECLUDED PINK SANDS

The quiet parish of St Phillip is home to a number of gorgeous beaches with soft sands that take on a pink hue in the late afternoon light. Tricky currents mean many are only suitable for expert swimmers but even if you're not going in, the peaceful surrounds are great for a picnic or just to read a book.

Backed by steep cliffs below which lies a strand of coconut palms, **Bottom Bay** is one of the most attractive beaches on the island, while nearby **Crane Beach** has two magnificent long stretches of soft sand divided by a headland. And don't miss **Shark Hole**, a tiny hidden cove protected by rocks that form a deep, inviting pool.

Cut Loose at Crop-Over

DANCE THROUGH BARBADOS' BIGGEST CARNIVAL

Stretching over several months but really ramping up in mid-July, the **Crop-Over Festival** is Barbados' biggest bash and an unmissable event for those that love to party.

Originating in colonial times as a celebration to mark the end of the sugar harvest, these days Crop-Over has morphed into a multifaceted carnival with soca and calypso competitions, art exhibitions and concerts.

The festival reaches a crescendo in August on **Grand Kadooment Day**, a national holiday that sees upwards of 15,000 costumed revelers dance their way through the streets of Bridgetown behind trucks weighed down with speakers as the bass shakes the ground and feathers fly through the air. At the conclusion, those still conscious gather for a swim at Brighton Beach and a fireworks display.

Crop-Over is not only a magnificent spectacle: visitors can join the celebrations by registering with one of the more than a dozen bands and by purchasing a matching costume to book a spot in the parade.

BAJAN SPECIALTIES

Fish Cutters
The Bajan version of a fish sandwich, with a grilled fillet served in a bread roll; best with a slice of cheese and a dollop of hot sauce.

Pudding and Souse
A favorite weekend breakfast of pickled pork with spiced sweet potato; if you don't fancy ears and feet ask for it 'lean.'

Fish Cakes
Delicious deep-fried balls of fish and seasoned flour, often eaten for breakfast.

Flying Fish and Cou-Cou
Barbados' national dish features steamed flying fish in a mild gravy served over a cornmeal and okra mash.

MORE CARNIVAL FUN

For more fantastic carnival mayhem check out **Vincy Mas** (p574) on the island of St Vincent and the **Carriacou Carnival** (p336) in Grenada, both of which are authentic and colorful affairs that receive few visitors.

GETTING AROUND

The best way to get around downtown Bridgetown is on foot – the narrow roads and traffic make a vehicle a hindrance.

Bridgetown is the nation's transportation hub, with bus and van services departing to even the most remote corners of the island from the two main terminals: Princess Alice for destinations to the north and Fairchild St for locations to the south and east.

The south coast is Barbados' busiest transport corridor, with buses and vans running every couple of minutes along Hwy 7, which hugs the coast from Bridgetown to Oistins, passing close to all the main beaches.

THE WEST COAST

With endless tranquil, narrow beaches lined with tropical greenery tucked away behind discreet luxury hotels and immense private villas, Barbados' west coast is the most exclusive part of the island, yet it's also one of the most traditional.

Also known as the Platinum Coast, it has a slower pace than the south and is set around two contrasting main towns: chic Holetown, with its designer shops, and its working-class neighbor Speightstown.

In colonial times the area was a popular holiday retreat for the upper crust of British society and it remains a popular playground for the rich and famous. But it's not all glitz and glamour; for every ostentatious villa with faux-Roman columns there is a tiny wooden rum shop overlooking the sea or a group of old-timers playing dominoes under an almond tree.

As with elsewhere on the island, all of the beaches here are public so day-trippers are free to share the sands with those paying a fortune for the pleasure.

The West Coast
Bridgetown

TOP TIP

Avoid touching poisonous manchineel trees, which are usually marked with red paint. The sap and the fruit are highly toxic and can cause painful blisters. Don't stand beneath the trees when it's raining.

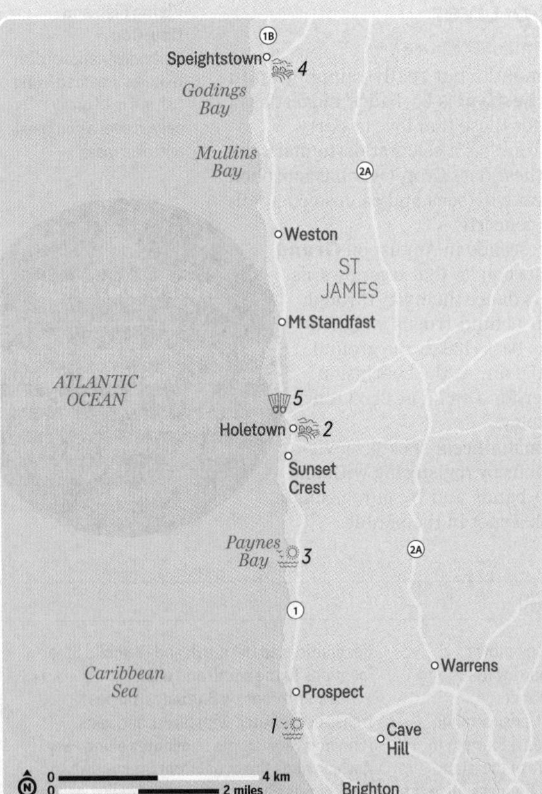

SIGHTS
1 Batts Rock Beach
2 Holetown
3 Paynes Bay Beach
4 Speightstown

ACTIVITIES, COURSES & TOURS
5 Folkestone Marine Park

Fishing, Speightstown

Beaches, Snorkeling & Sunsets

THE BEST OF THE WEST

The best way to get a taste of the west coast is to travel up scenic Hwy 1, which begins just north of Bridgetown. While it's convenient with your own wheels, limited car parking makes the local buses a good option too, and services come by every couple of minutes.

Right at the beginning of the highway, **Batts Rock Beach** is one of prettiest on the island. Tucked away off the road at the bottom of a forested bluff, it's backed by a pretty park where green monkeys like to hang out, while out front the gentle waters are perfect for even the youngest swimmers and offer good snorkeling too.

Jump off at the fish market 2km up the road to visit **Paynes Bay Beach**, a popular, long, tree-lined bay with calm waters where sea turtles can often be spotted.

Heading north, the highway passes the exclusive Sandy Lane development, where Barbados' most famous export Rihanna has a home, before reaching **Holetown**, the place where the first English settlers arrived in 1627. These days it's posh without being pretentious, with visitors browsing designer shops and dining in high-end restaurants with the sand still stuck to their legs.

There's good snorkeling off the beaches around the town, especially at **Folkestone Marine Park** just to the north, where a vibrant coral reef with next to no current is just steps from the sand.

Hwy 1 continues north through Alleyne's Bay, a quiet, calm beach with great swimming, to reach **Speightstown**, a down-to-earth fishing town with excellent restaurants and some vibrant beach bars from which to enjoy the famous western Barbados sunsets.

MORE TOP SNORKELING

Barbados has many other fantastic snorkeling spots that are easily accessible by car or bus. **Brownes Beach** (p160) on immense Carlisle Bay has a number of shallow wrecks and is home to turtles and manta rays, while nearby **Pebbles Beach** (p160) also has varied marine life.

BEST BEACH BARS

Little Bristol
Right on the water in the heart of Speightstown, this sociable bar has regular live music and good fish plates.

La Cabane
Enjoy gourmet meals and great cocktails under shady trees with soft sand beneath your feet at this hip bar/restaurant on quiet Batts Rock Beach.

Carib Beach Bar
A great place to watch the action on Worthing Beach, either from the breezy deck or at tables under coconut palms.

Braddy's Bar
An old-school family-run bar perfectly situated for superb St Peter sunsets.

Cruising the Platinum Coast

RUM PUNCH, TURTLES AND SUNSETS

Without doubt the most relaxed way to see the west coast is sitting back on the deck with a rum punch in hand while sailing north from Bridgetown.

Looking back on the coastline from the sea gives a very different perspective on this most ravishing part of the island, with serene hidden bays, tiny golden beaches and forested headlands that are otherwise hidden by hotel walls when traveling by road.

WHERE TO STAY ON THE WEST COAST

Coral Beach Club
A charming luxury hotel with a gingerbread main building set on gorgeous landscaped grounds. **$$$**

Tropical Sunset Hotel
Good-value spacious rooms overlooking the sea right in the heart of Holetown. **$$**

Tamarind Hotel
A discreet luxury hotel with a hacienda motif right on the beach at beautiful Paynes Bay. **$$$**

WHY I LOVE THE WEST COAST

Alex Egerton, writer

If I find myself with a couple of free days on Barbados, I always head straight to the west coast, which for me encapsulates the very best of the island. While the spectacular coastline with golden beaches fronted by inviting placid waters has made it the destination of choice for the ultra-wealthy, the west coast really does belong to everyone. I love wandering along the coastal road, checking out the movement at the fish markets and brightly painted bars before choosing an appealing spot to wade into the warm sea for a spot of snorkeling.

ELEANOR SCRIVEN/SHUTTERSTOCK ©

Paynes Bay Beach (p165)

You don't need your own boat- or yacht-club connections to experience the magnificent seascapes. A number of operators run cruises up the coastline on all kinds of vessels, ranging from spacious modern catamarans that are essentially rum-fueled floating parties to much more intimate smaller boats.

Half-day morning and sunset cruises are popular but there are also full-day options that travel further up the coast. Most trips make a couple of snorkeling stops at wrecks and reefs full of colorful fish or in quiet bays to swim among turtles. Even non-swimmers can get involved with most boats carrying life jackets and other flotation aids.

In general cruises include snacks, a buffet meal and free-flowing booze. If you're drinking, watch out for the rum punch, which can creep up on you, especially when you're outside in the baking sun.

Among the companies to look out for are **Calabaza**, which has professional yet extremely friendly staff and runs regular morning and afternoon excursions with a maximum of 13 guests, and **El Tigre**, a long-running operator offering a variety of larger group trips on two catamarans.

GETTING AROUND

With most attractions, hotels and eating spots found within a few blocks of shoreline-hugging Hwy 1, getting around the west coast is very straightforward. Buses and vans pass by on the highway every couple of minutes while taxis can be found at ranks in the main towns of the region. Note that parking is limited at many beaches so it's often easier to leave the car behind and grab a bus.

Beyond the West Coast

The west coast is the ideal base from which to explore the hilly rural interior of the island.

Heading east from Holetown and Speightstown a pair of 'highways' – in reality little more than narrow country roads – lead up into the hilly interior of the island where some of the last tracts of native forest can be found alongside lush gardens, deep caves, lookout points and nature reserves. It's perfect territory for a leisurely drive, with glorious lush landscapes, almost no traffic and plenty of interesting attractions within a fairly short distance of one another.

Even more remote are the series of backroads leading north into St Lucy parish on the northern tip of the island, a sparsely populated rural area of imposing cliffs, hidden bays and seaside grottoes.

TOP TIP

Once you leave the coastal plain, restaurants and cafes are few and far between; it's a good idea to bring a picnic here.

Cherry Tree Hill (p168)

CENTRAL BARBADOS ROAD TRIP

From **1 Holetown** Hwy 1A immediately climbs into the hills to reach the expansive **2 Harrison's Cave**, which is filled with stalactites, stalagmites and pools of water deep within the limestone heart of the island.

Back in the light, join Hwy 2 for the short drive north to **3 Welchman Hall Gully**, one the island's best tracts of remnant forest and, according to local legend, the birthplace of the grapefruit. A short stroller-friendly path runs the length of the gully, which is inhabited by loads of green monkeys.

For a more landscaped experience, take Bloomsbury Rd through the forested hills dotted with towering palm trees to reach **4 Flower Forest**, with its spectacular collection of flowering gingers and heliconias.

Keep the garden theme going by heading south and then taking Hwy E to **5 Hunte's Gardens**, a riot of colorful blooms backed by tropical greenery in a collapsed cave. Make sure you have a rum punch with the eccentric host on the balcony (but drivers should stick to just one – it's potent stuff).

Heading north from the gardens, the longest drive of the circuit follows Hwy 3A to the Atlantic coastal flatlands at Belleplaine before climbing on Hwy B to the handsome **6 Morgan Lewis Windmill**, the largest functioning mill left in the Caribbean. Climb to the top before continuing via the **7 Cherry Tree Hill** lookout point to **8 St Nicholas Abbey**, to walk through the ornate Jacobean mansion and check out the old-style distillery.

Continue on Hwy B before heading to **9 Farley Hill National Park**, to finish the tour with sweeping views of the Atlantic coastline before turning around and taking Hwy 2A then Hwy 1 back to the west coast.

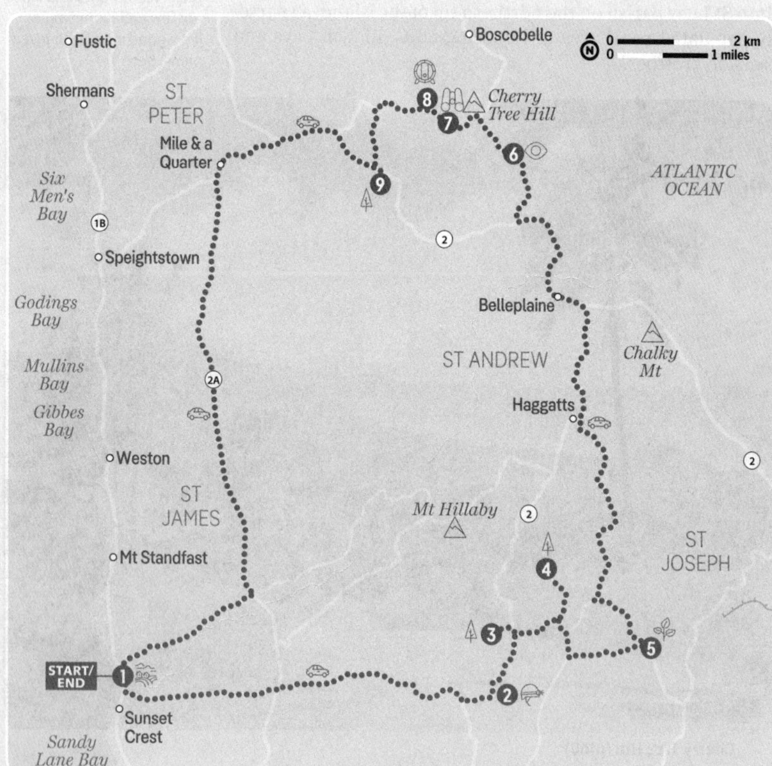

THE ATLANTIC COAST

The Atlantic Coast

Bridgetown

Wild and undeveloped, with miles of empty beaches buffeted by rolling waves, the Atlantic side of Barbados couldn't be more different from the Caribbean-facing coast. In fact it often feels like another island altogether. With empty roads linking tiny villages and rolling green hills rising from the boulder-strewn coastal plain, this is a place for quiet contemplation and for getting lost among nature.

With the exception of the sheltered waters of Bath Beach, the beaches here are rough, often covered in seaweed and generally not suitable for swimming. However, the powerful waves are perfect for surfing, with the island's best break found right in front of Bathsheba, the largest town on the coast.

The Atlantic is a top destination for hikers too. To the north of Bathsheba, long windswept stretches of sand are great for solitary walks accompanied by seabirds, while to the south an old railway line runs down to timeless fishing villages.

TOP TIP

While it is very remote, the Atlantic region is generally safe even for solo hikers, and with most trails hugging the coast, it's hard to get lost. Just make sure you bring plenty of snacks and water as shops are few and far between.

Bathsheba Beach (p170)

SURFING BARBADOS

Riding epic waves might not be the first activity visitors imagine when planning a Caribbean vacation, but Barbados actually has an excellent variety of breaks.

Soup Bowl
Barbados' legendary break is a full-on gnarly slab of a wave suitable for experienced riders only.

Duppies
A challenging powerful right point break on the northwest tip of the island.

Freights Bay
The longest left break on the island is perfect for beginners.

South Point
A hollow and fast reef break that splits into a number of sections.

Brandon's
A long, slow learner-friendly left just south of Bridgetown.

THE ATLANTIC COAST

Soup Bowl
Bathsheba
ATLANTIC OCEAN
Andromeda Botanic Gardens
3
Martin's Bay
Ocean Echo Stables
Conset Bay
Bath Beach
0 — 1 km
0 — 0.5 miles

Bewitching Bathsheba

SMALL TOWN, BIG WAVES

Blink and you'd drive right on through **Bathsheba**, the exotically named largest town on the east coast. Here an attractive seaside park leads to a beautiful craggy beach where foamy waters whipped up by the Atlantic swell flow in all directions around massive coral boulders. Its tranquil, old-fashioned fishing-town ambience is hard to beat, unless you're a surfer in which case you'll want to check out the legendary **Soup Bowl**, which breaks over the reef and forms a beautiful barrel. Even non-surfers will enjoy sitting with a drink and watching others brave the wave.

While Bathsheba Beach is too dangerous for swimming there are some sheltered pools among the rock formations that are good for a dip, or you can head south to **Bath Beach** where a long barrier reef takes the sting out of the waves.

On your way back stop in at **Andromeda Botanic Gardens**, a flower-filled wonderland alive with birds and monkeys.

Atlantic Horseback Adventures

A RIDE ON THE WILD SIDE

A wonderful way to explore the rugged coastline of Barbados' Atlantic region without breaking a sweat is on horseback, with a number of adventurous rides on offer taking in bush, farmland and the beach. **Ocean Echo Stables** in Newcastle just south of Bathsheba has fit and healthy mounts and offers guided rides down to Bath Beach early in the morning and in the evenings.

GETTING AROUND

Regular buses travel between Bathsheba and Bridgetown and the west coast. However, transport up and down the Atlantic coast is extremely limited and even taxis are hard to come by. If you plan to explore, a rental vehicle is the way forward.

Arriving

The vast majority of visitors to Barbados fly in to Bridgetown's airport or arrive on a cruise. With many direct flights to Europe and North America, the country is one of the most important gateways to the region.

In general, entry formalities are quick and streamlined and immigration staff are some of the most friendly in the Caribbean.

By Air

Barbados has only one airport, Grantley Adams International (pictured), located on the south coast around a half-hour drive from Bridgetown. Taxis right outside Arrivals are plentiful but if you're traveling light you can walk across the car park to the road and take a city-bound bus or van.

By Boat

While there are no passenger-boat services between Barbados and the neighboring Windward Islands, cruise ships stop here on Eastern Caribbean itineraries and provide a significant proportion of the island's visitors. Ships dock at Bridgetown Port, a 1km walk along the water to/from the city center.

Money

Currency: Barbadian dollar (B$)

CASH & CREDIT CARDS

Cash is still the norm for most transactions in Barbados. Due to the fixed and easy-to-calculate exchange rate, US banknotes are also widely accepted.

Both credit and debit cards are widely accepted in hotels, restaurants and larger stores, but not so commonly in smaller shops, rural areas and for most transportation.

ATMS

You'll find ATMs in all major towns around Barbados but note that local fees vary widely, so it's often worth going a bit further for one that will only apply minimum charges to your card.

TIPPING

Most Bajan restaurants add a service tax to the bill. If it's not included a tip of 10% to 15% is the norm; if it is, a small additional tip is up to you.

A small tip on top of taxi fares is also recommended.

BRITISH VIRGIN ISLANDS

AN AQUATIC PARADISE

Four main islands and some 50 islets and cays inspire travelers searching for a rest in the BVIs.

Paradise awaits in the British Virgin Islands (BVIs), a global sailing hot spot with a lofty reputation for luxury and fame. Some 50 islands comprise this archipelago, where the smooth, granite remnants of prehistoric volcanic activity crisscross peaks bristling with tyre palm and tamarind trees. These islands may come with cachet, but little pretense adorns the main hubs of Tortola, Virgin Gorda, Jost Van Dyke and, the lonesome outlier, Anegada.

Outside self-contained resort ecosystems, the BVIs still offer travelers going it alone access to sparsely populated beaches that often rest alongside vibrant coral reefs whose primary inhabitants are straight from the pages of a nature magazine. Acclaimed as a snorkeling and diving destination, the BVIs are also an excellent outlet for topside activities like hiking, bouldering and beachcombing.

Mighty Tortola entices travelers hankering to spend long days in secluded surf spots. Luxurious Virgin Gorda is a beacon for photographers and food lovers. Tiny Jost Van Dyke, 'the barefoot island,' is lined with beach bars and pirate tales. And far from the rest, the seagrape hammocks along Anegada's outstretched sandy beaches await adventurers in search of one of the Caribbean's biggest reefs.

While you're never far from a mooring, the BVIs serve up more than yacht culture. They're a collection of colorful islands with a Caribbean spirit waiting to be heard.

THE MAIN AREAS

TORTOLA
The largest island of the group. p178

VIRGIN GORDA
Acclaimed for its famous national parks. p183

ANEGADA
Expansive, far-flung reef system and beaches. p188

JOST VAN DYKE
Beach bars and pirate lore. p192

KARL WEATHERLY/GETTY IMAGES ©

Above: The Baths National Park (p184); Left: Snorkeling, Anegada (p188)

Find Your Way

Whether you arrive in the BVIs by air or by sea from the US Virgin Islands (USVIs), you'll be relying on ferries, rental cars and cabs to navigate between islands, settlements and beaches.

TAXI SERVICES

The most convenient way to get around is also the most expensive. Cab drivers on the islands know their worth, and while they are almost always friendly and responsive on WhatsApp, they also charge a premium for their services.

RENTAL CARS

Once on land, rental cars offer relatively good value. A car is really only needed on Tortola and Virgin Gorda. Fortunately, rates are usually cheaper than if you were to take a handful of cab rides per day.

FERRIES

Ferry services Speedy's, Native Son and Road Town Fast Ferry are the dominant means of island-hopping in the BVIs. Rates have doubled in recent years and competition is lite. Factor this into your plans.

Anegada, p188

The outlier of the group, Anegada offers a flat, forested landscape that holds the key to the most snorkeling and the largest beaches.

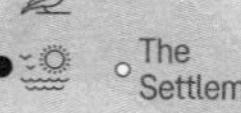

Jost Van Dyke, p192
A day trip for most, Jost Van Dyke is best known for some famous beach bars and a short hike to the Bubbly Pool.

Tortola, p178
Road Town is more commercial than quaint. Look toward the north shore and interior for outdoor adventure. Tempting restaurants are scattered in all directions.

Virgin Gorda, p183
More relaxed than Tortola, Virgin Gorda is famous for the Baths National Park and luxury resorts. Look to Spanish Town for charming local restaurants.

BLUEORANGE STUDIO/SHUTTERSTOCK ©

Plan Your Time

With landscapes and vibes that vary from island to island, the BVIs are accommodating of itineraries that ebb and flow with the activities you prioritize the most.

Catamaran, Great Harbour (p193)

Pressed for Time

- Make a quick trip to **Tortola** (p178), by far the most easily accessible island, whether you're flying into Terrance B Lettsome International Airport or arriving via ferry to Road Town or West End.

- Grab a rental car and hit the highways to enjoy surfing, snorkeling and sunbathing at **Josiah's Bay** (p179) and hiking at **Sage Mountain** (p180). Cap a day of play with an evening meal at **D'CoalPot** (p179) or **Pusser's** (p179).

- Arrange a day trip from Road Town or Beef Island to **The Baths National Park** (p184) on Virgin Gorda. These transfixing caverns are the cream of the crop.

Seasonal Highlights

Warm temperatures year-round means the BVIs never completely slow down. Peak season runs from November to March.

MARCH

The **Spring Regatta and Sailing Festival** takes center stage in Sir Francis Drake Channel.

MAY

The spring **Charter Yacht Show** garners a spotlight on Tortola before returning in November.

JUNE

Wreck Week celebrates the island nation's sunken treasures and dive sites.

Five Days to Explore

● A little more time opens up a door to exploring the BVIs' blend of varied cultures. Make your way to **Tortola** (p178) where you can choose to kick-start your Caribbean campaign with a plunge in **Josiah's Bay** (p179) or a sunset stroll at Smuggler's Cove. The island's numerous short-term rentals, villas and resorts offer a variety of base camps for both exploring this island and nearby **Jost Van Dyke** (p192).

● Spend two nights on Tortola before ferrying over to **Virgin Gorda** (p183) for another pair of evenings spent in its laid-back atmosphere and boulder-strewn natural beauty.

Two Weeks to Travel Around

● Get lost on **Anegada** (p188). If you're hankering for a trip to the outlier of the BVIs, a longer journey holds the key, as ferries to Anegada from Road Town are infrequent, especially on weekends. Start your trip on **Tortola** (p178) before ferrying over to Anegada for at least three more nights. Bonus points for a rare overnight on **Jost Van Dyke** (p192), where **Foxy's Taboo** (p193) and the **Soggy Dollar Bar** (p193) beckon night owls.

● Carve out time for several nights on **Virgin Gorda** (p183) to enjoy sunsets at the top of North Sound Rd, isolated snorkel spots and quiet mornings in the tidal caverns of **The Baths National Park** (p184).

JULY
Full-moon parties offer a break from the heat, while the **Emancipation Festival** kicks off at the end of the month.

AUGUST
Live music and parades continue during Emancipation Festival and the stage is set for the **Scrub Island Billfish Invitational**.

OCTOBER
Foxy's Taboo throws a legendary **Halloween** party on Jost Van Dyke. **Fishing** is at its peak.

NOVEMBER
Culture & Tourism Months begins across the islands, while Anegada celebrates the **Lobster Festival**.

Anegada

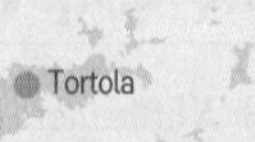

TORTOLA

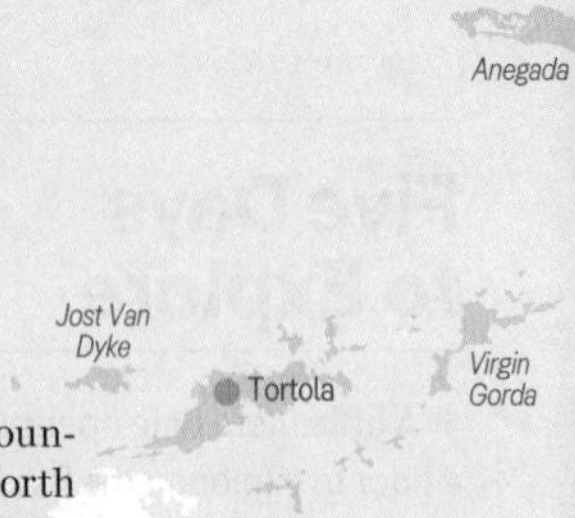

The pockmarked, winding roads of Tortola circle this mountainous island from the West End to Road Town and the North Shore. This jungle-covered island is the most populous among the BVIs and the most likely to be your hub of adventure in the country. A combination of surreal surf spots melds with a busy cruise port and a population of about 24,000 inhabitants, ranging from lifelong islanders to European and Caribbean transplants, making this a destination percolating with accents and cuisines from across the globe.

Those in search of nightlife can find a party in vibrant Road Town or Frenchman's Cay. However, a home for the casual at heart resides here as well: the quiet streets of the North Shore hide a bounty of secluded getaways for travelers who want to feel like they've reached a beach bar at the edge of the world. And hidden guesthouses abound.

TOP TIP

If you can afford it, a rental car is a lifesaver. Tortola taxi drivers know their market and take advantage of supply-and-demand economics on the island. It's easy to spend several times more per day on cabs than it would cost to simply rent a vehicle for your visit.

ERIC RUBENS/SHUTTERSTOCK ©

Tortola

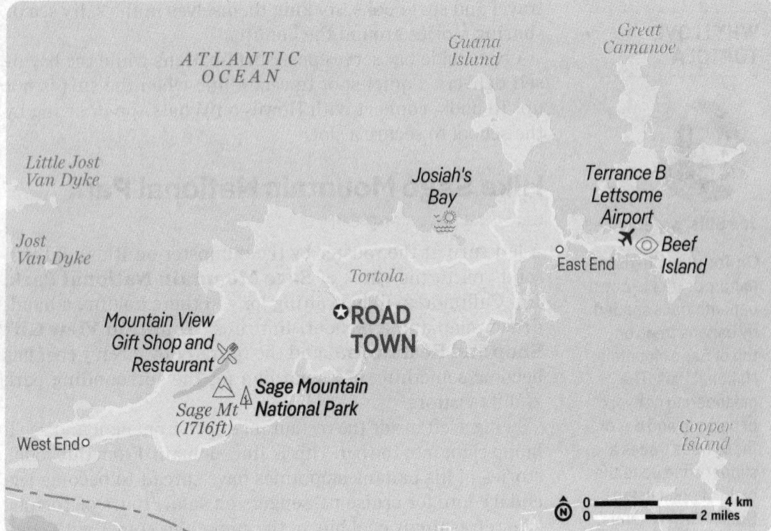

Surf Josiah's Bay

GOOD VIBES AND GREAT COMPANY

A skateboard ramp and crashing waves greet visitors to **Josiah's Bay**, where Surf School BVI has set up shop in a pair of shipping containers. The school has a prime position along Tortola's northern coastline, which catches swells year-round. Tucked beneath the rocky point at Josiah's, South African transplant Steve Howes, Jamaican pro surfer Icah Wilmot and local Alex Dick-Read spend their days teaching surfers how to stick the rolling reef break a few feet from their school.

When hurricanes Irma and Maria destroyed the school in 2017, Howes and company stayed behind to rebuild their broken dream. The project earned them island-wide respect, and it brought the surf school back better than ever. A topside viewing deck, complete with an old lifeguard chair, serves up views of the swirling sets below.

Howes and company work with surfers of all skill levels. Students have the chance to snag a board and stroll to their pick of breaks. A shallower, beginner-friendly break is just right for novices taking tutelage from the experienced team. More advanced surfers have plenty of swell to carve up further out near the point. On any given day, folks of all ages can be found either shuffling through the school's library of

TORTOLA EATS

Nigel's Boom Boom Beach Bar
A cash-only Smuggler's Cove stand serving barbecue classics. $

Pusser's
Live music and casual seafood. Locations in Road Town and the West End. $$

Omar's
Authentic Mexican fusion in multiple locations. $

Mountain View Restaurant
Two tables only. Served by a former Royal Navy chef. $$$

D'CoalPot
Romantic restaurant with sunset views. $$$

WHERE TO STAY ON TORTOLA

Sayula's Shack
East End tiny home in the trees with panoramic views of Beef Island. **$**

Seascape Villas
West End condos with included rental car; designed for work-from-home travelers. **$$**

Sugar Mill Hotel
Apple Bay luxury with amenities galore and adjacent popular surf spots. **$$$**

travel and surf books, soaking themselves in the salty sea or sharing stories around the bonfire.

A beachside bar serves post-surf libations while the bay itself delivers a quiet spot to cast a line when the surf is not up. To book, connect with Howes on WhatsApp or swing by the school to secure a slot.

Hike Sage Mountain National Park

BANANA LEAVES AND GUM TREES

A left turn at the rooster by the dumpster on Ridge Rd will send you to the gates of **Sage Mountain National Park**. Jim Cullimore will be waiting for you there holding a hand-drawn map and a blender. Jim runs **Mountain View Gift Shop and Restaurant**, and the retired Royal Navy chef has become something of a guardian for the surrounding park and its visitors.

Swing a left inside the restaurant's open front door and you'll bump right into the bar. This is Jim's domain. From this room, stories of his banana smoothies have spread to become legendary lore for cruise passengers on safari tours of Tortola. The refreshingly cool bite of the smoothies comes with commanding views of Sir Francis Drake Passage and the crashing Caribbean Sea some 1700ft below.

The mercurial, muddy paths of Sage Mountain National Park hold an abundance of secrets, illuminated by the rays piercing its lush canopy of banana leaves. Jim knows this. And he knows that the trails here are not particularly well-marked. To solve this riddle, Jim dispenses free maps of the meandering trail system inside of the adjacent park. His hand-drawn directions may be the best way to navigate to sights like the **Highest Point in the British Virgin Islands** and the majestic, ancient gum tree dominating a slice of path deep inside the canopy.

Return the pages of the maps intact, and Jim might just invite you in for a home-cooked dinner if he takes an interest in your journey.

WHY I LOVE TORTOLA

Joe Sills, writer

On Tortola, sun-kissed raindrops trickle down beneath trails shaded by banana trees on top of Sage Mountain National Park. The meandering network of paths in and out of these trees traces a slippery line up to the highest point in the British Virgin Islands. Up here, a quick leap over worn, wooden stairs delivers sweeping views of Road Town below.

Plenty of other travelers make the trip to Sage Mountain. It's likely that you'll be stuck behind at least one safari bus on the 1700-ft drive up, but it's unlikely that they'll linger with you deep in the forest. This is a place to jot in your journal and savor the lofty Caribbean breeze.

GETTING AROUND

Getting around Tortola can feel overwhelming at first. Taxis and walking are an option for those staying in Road Town or transiting from the airport; however, the best way to make the most of this island is to grab a rental car. Be advised, the roads here may be unlike any you've encountered before. Traffic can be heavy around Road Town during early morning rush hour, and a labyrinth of steep, narrow highways with frequent potholes can make driving intense. There is no easy way around this, so be prepared to steel your nerves when crisscrossing the island.

North shore highlights and the idyllic harbor at Frenchman's Cay make the extra headache and cost of your own wheels worth it.

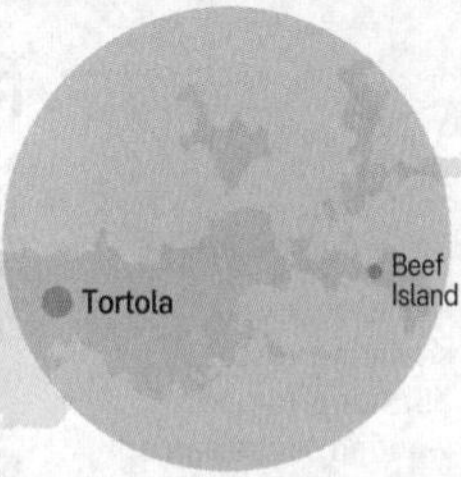

Beyond Tortola

Beef Island beckons travelers past the far eastern end of Tortola, where another micro-community awaits.

The private jets form a flock on the tarmac at Terrance B Lettsome International Airport. Throughout the year, dozens of Gulfstreams and Citations –the multimillion-dollar play toys of the rich and famous –can be spotted here, just across the chain link fence from a renegade patch of cotton trees leftover from the island's colonial past.

This spit of runway within a short walk of Tortola's peaks is the gateway to Beef Island, a community clinging to the edge of its neighbor like a press-on nail to a thumb. But the glossy doorstep of Beef Island belies its nature. This is a place with down-to-earth hideouts for those who know where to look.

TOP TIP

Don't judge a book by its cover. The folks on Beef Island can be as laid-back as they come.

Beef Island (p182)

THE CARIB CANOE

A one-of-a-kind seafaring vessel, 35ft-long, dugout wooden canoe named *Gli Gli* was built to retrace the paths of ancient Carib people across the Caribbean. The canoe is the brainchild of artist and painter Jacob Fredericks of Dominica. In 1996, Fredericks set sail from Dominica with a crew, including Tortola-born artist Aragorn Dick-Read.

The crew sailed all the way to Venezuela in the canoe – made from two large gommier trees, in order to symbolically link Carib and Arawak people dispersed by colonialism. Visitors to Beef Island can stop by Aragorn's studio and pay their respects to *Gli Gli*, which is rumored to be gearing up for an eventual trip back out to sea.

Paddle the Mangroves

AN INTIMATE VIEW OF NATURE'S NURSERY

Alex Dick-Read has a love affair with Beef Island, but not for its lofty social status. Alex, who co-manages BVI Surf School, spends much of his time gently gliding beneath the silhouette of the airport's control tower in the mangrove forest of **Beef Island Lagoon** on a paddleboard. Thanks to a philanthropic investor, the mangroves here are protected from most developers, offering the area a natural barrier to hurricanes and a way to mitigate the effects of climate change.

Connected to Tortola via a short bridge, the Beef Island mangroves are a nursery for the BVIs' marine life. They provide a sanctuary for juvenile lemon sharks, a home for sensitive single-cell organisms and a haven for crustaceans, jellyfish and the mangrove shoots themselves. Alex says the mangroves here saved the airport from major destruction during back-to-back hurricanes Irma and Maria, and the former reporter and surf magazine editor works with scientists to help restore the delicate ecosystem in between bouts with Mother Nature. His work doesn't take place in a vacuum, though. Alex hosts guided kayak and paddleboard tours of the mangroves through **Ground Sea Adventures BVI**, using his firsthand experience to show travelers Beef Island's less-heralded natural side.

A short drive from the lagoon, travelers can belly up to the bar at the **Loose Mongoose** for famous daiquiris, wood-fired pizza and local beer before walking over to **Aragorn's Studio**, where Alex's brother Aragorn hosts legendary full-moon parties set amid handmade metalwork and a pottery studio.

GETTING AROUND

Beef Island is connected to Tortola via the 230ft Queen Elizabeth II Bridge. A long walk from Parham Town is possible, but most travelers opt for their own transport or a taxi. Once on Beef Island, most destinations are within walking distance.

If you've arrived on Tortola via ferry from the USVI, it's easy to miss Beef Island, far off on the island's East End. However, ferry passengers from Virgin Gorda will most likely be deposited at a ferry terminal adjacent to Terrance B Lettsome Airport. A gathering of taxi drivers can usually be found lingering around either the airport or the ferry dock. It's advisable to save a phone number for your driver of choice in the highly likely need of additional services.

VIRGIN GORDA

The scene can be dizzying at first. Arriving on Virgin Gorda by ferry, you're greeted by a terminal typically teeming with European and American travelers, rapidly racing around the docks with roller bags and backpacks. At first glance, this island seems packed. But spend a little time on Virgin Gorda and your mind may change.

Many travelers here seem to head straight for resorts and villas, skipping over Spanish Town and generally keeping inside guarded gates at night. There's little need to. Spanish Town is a beautiful hodgepodge of shops and restaurants, from kitchens dishing out Caribbean staples to a blend of flavors from Dominica to India. And the island's signature feature is best explored on your own: for many, a trip to Virgin Gorda is a photo op at The Baths National Park and little else. However, adventurers may find this to be their favorite of the BVIs.

TOP TIP

You don't need a room in a five-star resort to enjoy Virgin Gorda. Though ultra-luxury properties abound, the helpful folks at places like Fischer's Cove Beach Hotel in Spanish Town can set you up with a locally run beachside cottage for a fraction of the price.

The Baths National Park (p184)

VOLCANIC BEGINNINGS

The story of The Baths National Park did not begin with Instagram. Rather, it began about 70 million years ago when molten rock began seeping up into existing rock layers before ultimately eroding and forming the enchanting labyrinth of secret pools and caverns that draws so many to the island today.

In 1990, the government declared the area encompassing these geologic formations a national park, and their already widespread allure grew even stronger.

Hiking to The Baths involves negotiating a mostly downhill stretch of sand, roots and rocks for less than a mile.

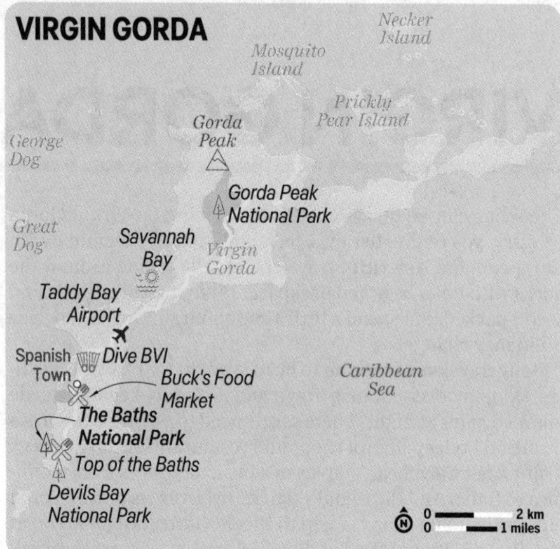

Scramble Through the Baths

THE REASON YOU CAME HERE

Rise with the sun and make your way to **The Baths National Park** by opening time at 9am. You want to climb through these caves. You want to feel your hands slide along the smooth, granite boulders. You want that shot of sunlight scattering into a surf-strewn, turquoise cave while you bask in its golden glow. And so does every traveler at every resort on the island.

Prepare for your visit to this epochal national park by first ensuring you have cash for the entry fee of just US$3. An ATM behind **Buck's Food Market** is located in Spanish Town, conveniently en route to the parking lot. From the parking lot alongside **Top of the Baths**, trail signs pointing down toward the baths themselves are easy to follow.

For the first few hours of the morning, the gift shops and cafes located near the bottom of the trail will be closed. Look for a narrow opening between the rocks that opens almost immediately into a pyramid-shaped cavern full of glowing morning light and foaming, aquamarine waves. From the cavern, the trail continues upward in a roundabout fashion before depositing adventurers on a rocky shore adjacent to **Devil's Bay National Park**.

WHERE TO EAT ON VIRGIN GORDA

Hog Heaven
Barbecue and a full bar with panoramic views of Leverick Bay and Necker Island. **$**

Island Pot Restaurant
Caribbean fusion and foiled parrot fish on the main drag in Spanish Town. **$$$**

Chez Bamboo
Garden fresh salads with an Asian twist on the road to Savannah Bay. **$$**

By 10am, expect to see truckloads of fellow travelers fresh out of resorts and cruise ships piling into the caverns at The Baths and the beaches of Devil's Bay. This is your cue to make a decision: join in the party or hit the highway for a quieter slice of paradise.

Savor Savannah Bay

SECLUDED SANDS AND SERENITY

The island's longest white sand beach has few facilities beyond trash bins, but **Savannah Bay Beach** is simply stunning. And more often than not, it's also sparsely occupied.

Locals come here, of course. It's a rare, free, public hangout on an island renowned for exclusivity, but it's also because Savannah Bay is home to crystalline waters lapping over a dazzling coral reef with an underwater snorkeling trail. It's a favorite of Spanish Town's **Dive BVI**, whose instructors use the trail brimming with blue tangs and sea turtles to teach beginners about the marine ecosystem just steps away from the sun-soaked, alabaster sand.

Bushwhack to Gorda Peak

ROCKY SWITCHBACKS AND BASKING REPTILES

The Baths and Devil's Bay may be the signature national parks of Virgin Gorda, but looming **Gorda Peak National Park** in the island's north offers an immersion into its lesser-publicized natural side. Here, a rambling, 7.9-mile hiking trail from North Sound Rd leads into one of the Caribbean's last remaining dry forests. Bananaquits, anoles, iguanas, worm lizards, skinks and even occasional goats can be seen in this scraggly, verdant labyrinth of roots, shrubs and foliage.

The remnants of shattered picnic tables and information signs allude to brighter times for this park in days gone by; however, the trail itself is typically in good condition. Eventually, the dusty single track leads to 1370ft Gorda Peak, though you'll need to scramble up a boulder and hope for a glimpse of the sea between the leaves to fully appreciate the view.

Plan to park on the side of the highway here, and be sure to bring plenty of water. Cap the hike with a visit to the north end's **Hog Heaven**, where epic views and affordable brews await.

THE LIFE AFFLUENT

Whether you're staying at a resort or not, these properties are landmarks and major employers on the island.

Oil Nut Bay
Multimillion-dollar boutique villas with restaurants and rentals. $$$

Rosewood Little Dix Bay
Acclaimed getaway for global celebrities. $$$

Bitter End Yacht Club
Eco-chic nautical village with water sports. $$$

Mango Bay
Seaside studios and beachside stand-up paddleboard rentals. $$$

GETTING AROUND

Access to Virgin Gorda generally comes via two ferry services from Road Town: Native Son Ferry and Speedy's. These companies also offer irregular service from Beef Island. Getting around Virgin Gorda is best done via rental car.

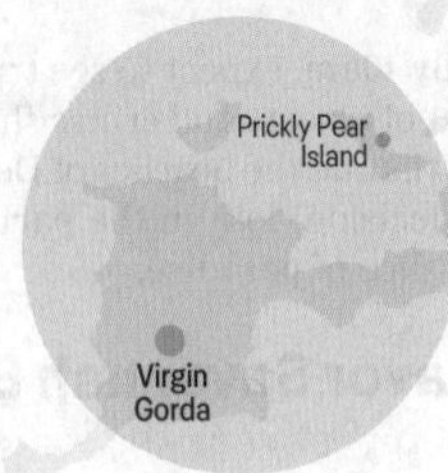

Beyond Virgin Gorda

An uninhabited island with a lesser-known national park sits offshore.

Resting on the north sound of Virgin Gorda and beneath the shadow of Necker Island, uninhabited Prickly Pear Island is only accessible by boat. Secluded beaches brimming with wildlife await those willing to make the journey. An active scene at The Sandbox bar and grill and a hiking trail to Vixen Point give visitors places to relax by the beach or stretch their legs. Bring a mask and fins, as Prickly Pear is surrounded by a barrier reef teeming with marine life and dotted with red, black and white mangrove forests.

Declared a national park in 1988, this remote island remains a favorite for Virgin Gorda regulars, but little-known to first-time visitors.

TOP TIP

Contact local dive shops for a scouting report on sea conditions in layperson's terms before heading out.

Sandbox, Prickly Pear Island

Brown Booby

MINTIMAGES/SHUTTERSTOCK ©

Peruse Prickly Pear Island

A NEARLY UNINHABITED ISLAND

Prickly Pear Island is a great place to relax, unwind, and enjoy the natural beauty of the BVIs. Grab your flip-flops and set out to forge your own path. The island's clear waters offer an opportunity for swimming and snorkeling among the area's signature granite boulder formations. If you didn't manage to avoid crowds at The Baths National Park, a visit to Prickly Pear could provide another opportunity for seaside solitude.

Protected from the island's typical winds, the eastern shore has plenty of places to stretch out, picnic or delve into the trails system leading through the island's interior. Prickly Pear Island's southern beach is particularly known for its coral reefs and colorful marine life, but keep an eye out for nesting sea turtles from March to July. Undersea exploration is stellar, and Spanish Town's Dive BVI can also organize scuba trips here.

Hiking across the island, covered with organ-pipe cacti and Turks cacti, is well worth the effort for wildlife lovers. Birds like blue-winged teals, black-necked stilts and white-cheeked pintails can be spotted flitting about as you walk. If that trek works up an appetite, sandwiches, conch fritters and local rum libations are available nearby at the **Sandbox**.

The best way to reach the island is to rent a dinghy at **Leverick Bay** or kayak over from **Bitter End Yacht Club**. Dinghys and kayaks are free to beach at any reasonable opportunity, giving you an extra degree of freedom not often found on organized group outings.

THE BIRDS OF PRICKLY PEAR ISLAND

This isolated enclave of wildlife is a perfect place to bring a long camera lens or a pair of binoculars to catch a glimpse of some of the Caribbean's most charismatic avian wildlife. Brown boobies, greater flamingos, snowy egrets, yellow-crowned night herons and gray kingbirds can all be spotted on and around Prickly Pear Island.

Prickly Pear National Park encompasses 180 acres of this island and it is frequently used for scientific research. Stroll along the white-sand beaches of Vixen Point to spot shorebirds, moorhens, gulls and pintails.

Don't forget the dry bag if your transit over is via kayak or dinghy from Virgin Gorda proper.

GETTING AROUND

Getting around Prickly Pear Island couldn't be easier. Dock your kayak or dinghy on the island's western beach, just across the water from Leverick Bay. The beach offers a natural path to walk around the island to its eastern shore.

Anegada
Jost Van Dyke
Tortola
Virgin Gorda

ANEGADA

You thought you were away from it all until you arrived on Anegada. Now, you're completely gone. Home to one of the largest barrier reefs in the world, the outlier of the BVIs takes an hour to reach by ferry from Road Town. But that timestamp might as well be light speed. This island feels like another galaxy. Gone are the mountains and the dramatic, volcanic rocks of Tortola and its neighbors. They've been traded in for flat swaths of forests of sea grape interspersed by paths of limestone and coral, along with shipwrecks and rock iguanas.

With barely 300 residents and no elevation higher than 30ft above sea level, Anegada feels like finding another nation tucked inside of the BVIs. Donkeys, cattle and horses ply the land from Cow Wreck Beach to Conch Island, providing a plodding backdrop to this peaceful place.

TOP TIP

Ferries depart irregularly for Anegada. Monday, Wednesday and Friday are the only opportunities to get on or off the island. Be sure to plan your trip to grab the morning or afternoon ferry to and from Setting Point.

Paddleboarding, Anegada

Hover Over Horseshoe Reef

SHIPWRECKS AND CORAL CONVERGE

Hundreds of shipwrecks litter the record books of Horseshoe Reef, an 18-mile-long barrier reef that has been harvesting hulls since the 1600s: HMS *Astraea*, 1808; MS *Rocus*, 1929; The *Parametta*, 1829. All told, more than 300 frigates, galleons, sailboats and steamers have collided with the fringing coral reef encircling Anegada. From encrusted piles of ballast stones to rusting metal husks, they now form a cauldron of captivating destinations for divers. Mazes of staghorn, elkhorn, and fire and brain coral form a refuge for snapper, grouper, barracuda and butterfly fish. Hawksbill and green sea turtles can be seen soaring over a lush seascape that forms one of the largest barrier reefs on the planet. **Anegada Beach Club** has an in-house dive center on the island, though dive trips from Tortola and Virgin Gorda can also be booked.

Kitesurf at Anegada Beach Club

FLY ABOVE THE WAVES

Widely considered one of the premier destinations on the planet for kitesurfing, Anegada is home to steady cross-shore winds and calm waters that make for a world-class laboratory for learning. Professional kitesurfer Tommy Gaunt founded a **kiting school** on the island in 2014. Today, the school offers lessons, gear rentals and – on days when the conditions just aren't right for shredding the waves – paddleboard tours of the island's south side.

WHAT THE FLOCK?

Thousands of Caribbean flamingos once lived on Anegada before being hunted to local extinction in the 1800s. In 1992, the birds were reintroduced to the island and established a recovering colony.

Today, several hundred of these flamboyant birds once again call Anegada home. Spot them from the **Flamingo Pond Lookout**, midway between Setting Point and The Settlement.

WHERE TO EAT ON ANEGADA

Cow Beach Bar
Full-service bar on an unforgettable, white-sand beach with turquoise seas. **$$**

Potters by the Sea
Dockside snapper and lobster with complimentary beach shuttle located near Horseshoe Reef. **$$$**

Anegada Reef Hotel Restaurant
A swordfish, mahi mahi and grouper spot for yachties. Also houses the island's preeminent dive school. **$$$**

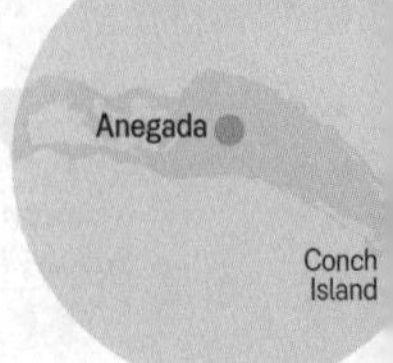

Beyond Anegada

For hundreds of years, humans have been building bizarre conch pyramids off the Anegada coast.

A bizarre spectacle lies in wait just off the Anegada Coast – dunes of prickly pink pyramids reaching up from a cerulean sea. For 800 years, the pyramids have steadily grown, as generations of conch harvesters have picked, popped and plopped the supple, savory meat of giant sea snails from the water.

This is Conch Island, a conch graveyard that boggles the mind. This is where conch shells meet their eternal rest after the snail inside has been collected for crispy fritters, savory ceviches and mouthwatering salads. A tradition that began with indigenous hunters migrated to British settlers and, eventually, to the modern inhabitants of Anegada: when a conch is harvested, its shell goes here.

TOP TIP

Skip the cab fare and splurge with a scooter rental. It's the best way to explore Anegada's nooks and crannies with flexibility.

Conch Island

Kodiak Queen shipwreck

Investigate Conch Island

MYSTERIOUS SHELLS SHROUDED IN LEGEND

Sail to a maze of bewildering conch heaps, just offshore of Anegada. Averse to the presence of their fallen comrades, living conch seem to migrate away from these perplexing, biodegradable garbage piles reaching 12ft into the air. Conch can travel great distances when motivated. But with the shells clustered in a small area, rather than strewn across the entire fishing ground, a healthy population of conch has remained around Anegada, even as the species has dissipated elsewhere.

Scientists speculate that conch's natural aversion to dead snails stems from a survival instinct to avoid predators. Either way, while overfishing has negatively affected conch populations around other Caribbean islands, the snails near Anegada appear to be thriving.

While visitors can't really walk on **Conch Island** (ouch), they can spot an abundance of marine life in the gin-clear water surrounding the shells. Stingrays, sea turtles and nurse sharks are frequently found around the island.

Though the mounds appeared on charts as early as the 1600s, until recent times Conch Island remained a secret of local anglers, stored in their memories as a trivia question at the beach bar. These days, **Kelly's Land & Sea Tours** will take you out to the piles for a few hours in the sun. A half-day tour includes sightseeing, flamingo watching, snorkeling, lobster hunting and a trip to Conch Island itself. There, you can gaze in wonder at what is truly an ancient monument to generations of seafaring people around Anegada before swimming off into the blue.

THE BEST SHIPWRECKS ON ANEGADA

Some 300 shipwrecks fill the seabed around Anegada. These are some of the most eye-catching.

RMS Rhone

A majestic 19th-century steamship that met its demise during a hurricane in 1867. This 310ft vessel is now home to colorful corals and teeming marine life.

Chikuzen

A Japanese fishing vessel intentionally sunk in 1981 to create an artificial reef. The 246ft-long ship is home to tropical fish, eagle rays and turtles.

Kodiak Queen

A former naval fuel barge, this wreck was transformed into the 'BVI Art Reef,' with vibrant sculptures and coral colonies forming an enchanting habitat for divers.

GETTING AROUND

You'll find no need for a map on Conch Island. In fact, you won't even need your phone. Navigating this miniature maze is as simple as splashing into the water and taking off. A pair of flippers might speed up exploration; but swimming gear and sunscreen are probably the only essentials here. Kelly's Land & Sea Tours is the go-to outfitter around these parts. The locally owned business specializes in sightseeing around Anegada, spotting wildlife and safely ferrying visitors to and from Conch Island.

Anegada
Jost Van Dyke
Tortola
Virgin Gorda

JOST VAN DYKE

Named for a Dutch privateer who allegedly hid from the Spanish Navy on this tiny island in the 1600s, Jost Van Dyke comes with legitimate 'Pirates of the Caribbean' credentials. The population of this four-mile-long island officially numbers fewer than 300 individuals; however, far greater numbers can often be found offshore residing in catamarans, yachts and cruise ships.

A visit to Jost Van Dyke has become a feather in the cap of any sailor worth their salt in the BVIs. Its bars are the stuff of engine-room stories and wheelhouse legends. Stunning White Bay welcomes visitors making a day trip from Tortola, St John and St Thomas. Bubbly Pool beckons outdoor lovers interested in exploring the island's natural beauty. And a handful of overnight accomodations, like The Hideout, are available for travelers who don't want to catch the last ferry home at night.

TOP TIP

Cash is king on Jost Van Dyke. Befitting an island wrapped in pirate lore, keeping a few dollars on hand, whether dry or soggy, is the best way to secure transportation on the fleet of pickup trucks playing double duty as the island's public transportation.

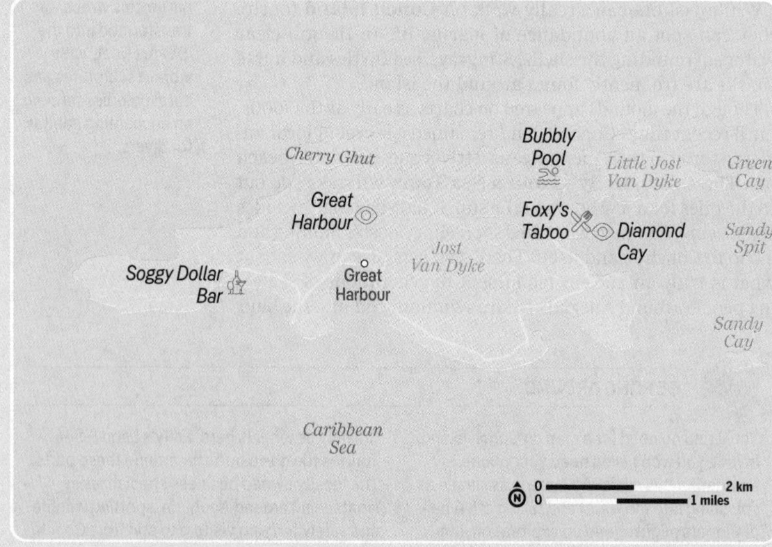

Bubbly Pool

FOXY WHO?

Rivaling Jost Van Dyke himself as the island's most recognizable name, Philicianno 'Foxy' Callwood is credited with popularizing the BVI's yacht touring industry by setting up a beach bar beneath a Great Harbour tamarind tree in 1968. Beneath its outstretched branches, Callwood entertained passing sailors with salty stories, calypso songs and jokes – as he still does today.

Foxy's legend spread so far that it reached Queen Elizabeth II, who awarded him an MBE (Member of the British Empire).

Foxy's Taboo became the island command center during catastrophic hurricanes in 2017 and is still a focal point of the community today.

Bask in the Bubbly Pool

A FAMOUS FOAM BATH

Cab drivers know where to go. Ask for the **Bubbly Pool** and you'll be whisked away in the back of a pickup truck, past aisles of beachside bars in **Great Harbour** and around the island to a drop-off point near **Foxy's Taboo**, a bar with views of tiny Diamond Cay. From there, a 20-minute hike will take you over pebbly paths spritzed with cacti and coral fragments to the most famous natural attraction on Jost Van Dyke. At the Bubbly Pool, waves from the oncoming tide crash violently over a rocky outcrop and into a tide pool that laps leisurely at the feet of hikers. Adrenaline junkies can wade into the pool for a foamy bath, while those who wish to remain dry can hike up top for a bird's-eye view of the action.

Swim to the Soggy Dollar Bar

BVI TRADITION OF GETTING WET

A beloved staple of BVI yachting culture awaits at Jost Van Dyke's **Soggy Dollar Bar** (pictured right). It's so named for the dripping wet currency cashed in by yacht passengers swimming to its stools from moors along White Bay.

The joint has expanded from the humble, wooden shack that once housed its liquor cabinet decades ago. Today, it's possible to walk to the busy beachside bar without soaking your currency; however, plenty of patrons still anchor offshore and make the traditional swim inside for a 'Painkiller' cocktail that uses its in-house Soggy Dollar Rum.

GETTING AROUND

Unless you're cruising in on a dinghy, there's only one ferry dock on Jost Van Dyke. Cab drivers know when the ferries run, and they're eager to charge a cash fee to transport passengers from the dock to nearby beaches and bars. You can technically walk to most places on Jost Van Dyke, though the hilly terrain means you could spend valuable time doing so. The local cab drivers are the best bet here.

SERGEY KELIN/SHUTTERSTOCK ©

Arriving

Some sail, some fly and some cruise over on a ferry from the US side. Either way, the majority of travelers to the British Virgin Islands arrive on Tortola, the hub of these scattered islands. Road Town, West End and Beef Island all operate regular ferry services, though the country's only international airport is located on the latter.

By Air

Terrance B Lettsome International Airport operates regular flights to/from the USA and Europe. Fly in and hop on a ferry or charter to Virgin Gorda, or take a taxi via the bridge that connects Tortola to Beef Island.

By Boat

Road Town hosts the BVIs' most-used cruise port (pictured). There's a modern outdoor mall of global brands dockside, though the town is within walking distance. Moorings for private vessels abound, giving those with a sailing spirit nearly limitless places to land.

Money

Currency: US dollar (US$)

CASH

Leave your British pounds at home. The BVIs' economy runs on the US dollar, and you'll be using it frequently here. Taxis and many tour operators prefer greenbacks. If you're running short, a handful of banks in Road Town and Spanish Town operate ATMs. Be warned: there are no ATMs on Anegada.

DIGITAL PAYMENTS

In general, digital payments are not widely adopted yet. The BVIs were dealt a devastating blow by the 2017 hurricanes, forcing locals to make bank runs and relearn the lesson that cash is sometimes still king. Don't rely on a digital wallet in these parts either, though short-term rental hosts may accept payments for add-ons via apps.

CREDIT CARDS

Most retail stores, hotels and restaurants accept credit-card payments. Visa and Mastercard are widely accepted. Amex vendors are less common. Many charge a surcharge for credit-card usage – another reason to keep cash on hand.

Getting Around

Unless you have a sailboat, island-hopping is...not really a thing most people attempt here. That doesn't mean you can't do it, though. In fact, it's not that difficult to get around the BVIs once you figure out the system in play.

PUBLIC TRANSPORT

Rail service does not exist here. Safari buses can sometimes be seen picking people up from 'bus stops,' but these are frequently commandeered by cruise passengers paying a substantially higher markup than commuters. Don't rely on public transport at all.

BLIDEKPANDA/SHUTTERSTOCK ©

CAR

Renting a car makes a lot of sense on both Tortola and Virgin Gorda. Rates offer good value when compared to cab fares, and the vehicles are generally well-suited to taking a bashing on the bumpy island roads.

BOAT

Daily ferries run from Tortola to Jost Van Dyke and Virgin Gorda. Every few days, a ferry heads off for Anegada, too. Private charters can get you from place to place on your own time for a premium fee.

TAXI/RIDESHARE

The best alternative to rideshare is to grab the WhatsApp number of a respected taxi driver and stick with their recommendations for the duration. This will burn through your dollar bills, but can pay off with local knowledge and insights.

AIR

You can charter private planes or helicopters around the BVIs. This is a surprisingly popular mode of transport for some; however, expect to pay mightily for the privilege. In general, air travel between the islands is not necessary.

DRIVING ESSENTIALS

Drive on the left side.

Tortola's (largely ignored) speed limits are 20mph in town and 35mph out of towns.

Scooters suffice on Anegada.

Above: Diving, Cayman Brac (p206); Right: Grand Cayman (p202)

CAYMAN ISLANDS

DIVING, BEACHES, SHOPPING & STELLAR DINING

Welcome to the Cayman Islands, home to a cosmopolitan cruise-ship town, uncrowded beaches, superb dive sites, excellent bird-watching and vibrant communities.

Comprising three specks of land in the western Caribbean, the Cayman Islands are more diverse than they first appear. Granted, clichés abound in Grand Cayman: George Town, the capital, is the quaint mix of clapboard fisherfolk's houses, fort ruins, duty-free diamond boutiques and banking establishments that you'd expect of a tax haven. Cruise ships disgorge thousands of day trippers, who descend on the port's duty-free shops and the white-sand sweep of Seven Mile Beach, while well-heeled yachties and vacationers dine on sumptuous, wallet-emptying fare at international restaurants in Camana Bay. But head to the east of the island, and you'll find low-key communities, deserted sandy coves, colorful fish-fry joints and a wealth of natural attractions, including caves and a swampland wilderness trail.

In contrast to their glitzy big sister, Little Cayman and Cayman Brac have small, close-knit populations, and their respective underwater worlds are as spectacular as their communities are laid-back. On Little Cayman, which you can easily circle in a day, iguanas greatly outnumber people, and most visitors tend to be scuba divers drawn by the world-class wall and reef dives. While dives are a great part of the Brac's draw, it also has much to offer on dry land: superb rock-climbing and spelunking, nature trails, local artists, and numerous craftspeople who work with the island's endemic semi-precious stone, caymanite.

THE MAIN AREAS

GRAND CAYMAN
Superb dining, shopping and sandy beaches. p202

CAYMAN BRAC
Diving, hiking and local crafts. p206

LITTLE CAYMAN
Excellent diving and bird-watching. p209

Find Your Way

The only way to get between the three Cayman Islands is by daily twin-propeller plane. Little Cayman is walkable and cyclable; Cayman Brac is best explored by bicycle and car; and Grand Cayman is covered by minibuses.

Little Cayman, p209

Stunning wall and reef dives, superb bird-watching and iguana-spotting, and a warm welcome from a close-knit community await on this tiny sliver of land.

Cayman Brac, p206

Nature trails on the limestone bluff, quirky local characters, superb diving and a laid-back vibe are some of the draws of Cayman's second-largest island.

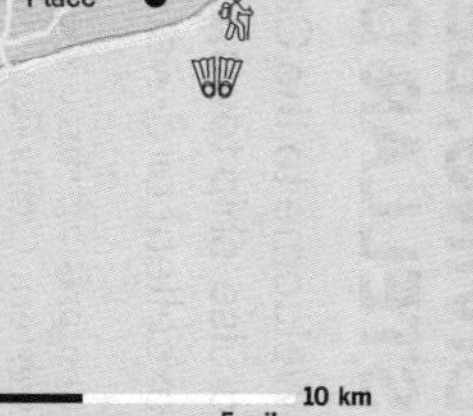

Big Channel
Blossom Village
Charles Bight
The Narrows
Caribbean Sea
Channel Bay
WEST END
South East Bay
Stake Bay
The Bight
Watering Place
Spot Bay
THE BLUFF
0 10 km
0 5 miles

BUS

Grand Cayman has a comprehensive network of color-coded minibuses that run to most corners of the island from the George Town bus depot; services are sporadic on Sunday. There are no bus services on Little Cayman or Cayman Brac.

CAR

Self-driving offers maximum flexibility, and the roads are in good condition, though on Grand Cayman, driving also means sitting in traffic jams. Car rental on Grand Cayman is priciest.

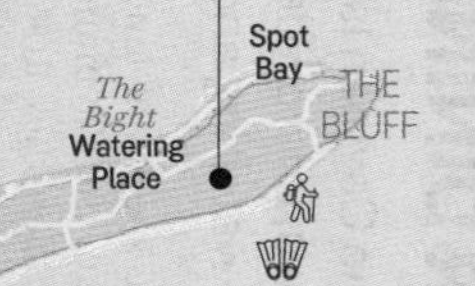

BIKE

Resorts on Little Cayman and Cayman Brac rent bicycles to guests, and cycling is a good way of getting around. However, there are few bicycle-hire options on Grand Cayman, and cycling on the busy roads can be scary.

Grand Cayman, **p202**

Brash and glitzy, 'the Grand' entices with its chichi boutiques, restaurants and beaches, while its natural treasures – dive sites, caves, coves and gardens – are many.

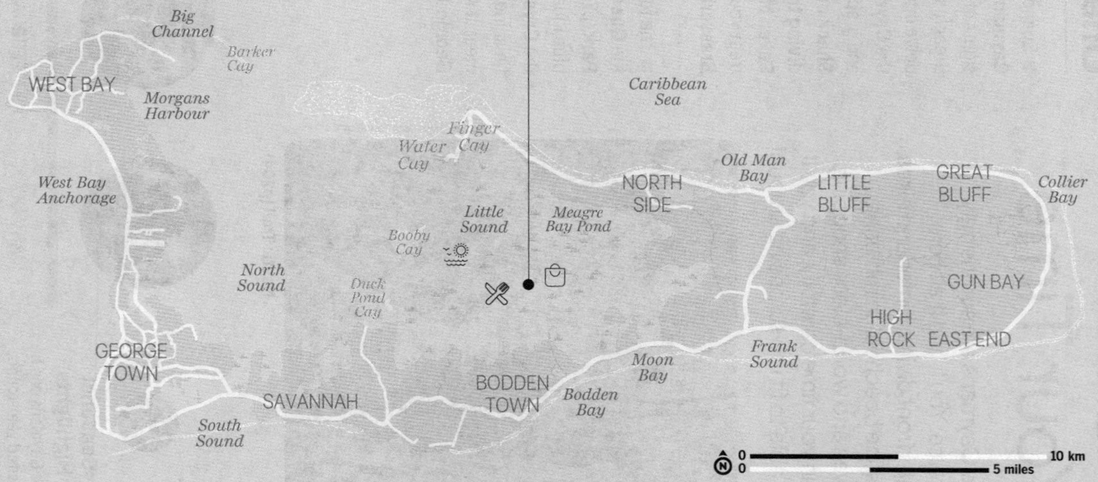

Plan Your Time

The Caymans are surprisingly diverse. You'll find it all here: waterfront diving, hinterland hikes, pristine beaches, shimmering caves and world-class shopping. Plan your time carefully, and you'll be able to fit in a surprising amount.

JOYCAYM/SHUTTERSTOCK ©

Mastic Trail (p204)

If You Only Visit One Place

- Spend a weekend in **Grand Cayman** (p202), taking in the sights of **George Town** (p203). Breakfast at the **Daily Grind Cafe**, delve into Cayman's history at the **Cayman National Museum**, and grab fish tacos at **Da Fish Shack** before opting for a half-day **diving trip** (p203) or a spell on **Seven Mile Beach** (p205). Then, treat yourself to dinner at **The Brasserie** (p203).

- The following day, drive to the **Queen Elizabeth II Botanic Park** (p204) to commune with blue iguanas, and venture into the **Crystal Caves** (p204) before finishing the day with a blowout meal at **Abacus** (p205) back in George Town.

Seasonal Highlights

The Caymans can be visited year-round. Hurricane season lasts from June to November, with some resorts and businesses closing.

JANUARY

Beachside barbecues meet fine dining at the **Cayman Cookout**, hosted by celebrity chef Eric Ripert at the Ritz-Carlton. Nights are pleasantly cool.

FEBRUARY

Cayfest's extravaganza showcases performances from musicians, dancers, actors and storytellers. **Taste of Cayman** is the Grand's biggest food festival.

MARCH

Excellent visibility for divers, relatively cool weather in the evenings, and few tourists make this an excellent month to visit.

TONY QUINN/SHUTTERSTOCK ©, NIYAZZ/SHUTTERSTOCK ©, DREW MCARTHUR/SHUTTERSTOCK ©

A Week's Travel

- Take a couple days to explore **North Side** (p204), chilling at **Cayman Kai** (p204), hiking the **Mastic Trail** and circumnavigating **East End** before stopping to check out the beaches at **Old Man Bay** and **Colliers** (p204). Then, marvel at the **blowholes** (p204) before stopping at the **Czech Inn Grill** (p205) for beer and jerk chicken.

- Peruse the great house of **Pedro St James** (p205) in Bodden Town before heading out to **Little Cayman** (p209) for three days to go diving in **Bloody Bay** (p210), bird-watching at **Booby Pond** (p212) and dining with locals at the **Hungry Iguana** (p211).

If You Have More Time

- Set aside 10 days or even two weeks to make the most of the Cayman Islands and their underwater world. After giving yourself a day on dry land in **Little Cayman** (p209), head over to **Cayman Brac** (p206) and spend several days checking out their **wreck** and **wall dives** (p207), plus Cayman's own version of the **Lost City of Atlantis** (p208).

- When not in the ocean, hike the **Lighthouse Footpath** (p208), explore the **caves** (p207) and chat about the Great Hurricane of 1932 with Tenson Scott of **NIM Things** (p207) before joining locals for Mudslides at the **Tipsy Turtle Pub** (p208).

MAY

Locals and visitors rock out to ***soca*** and parade around, scantily-clad, as part of the exuberant **Batabano** street carnival.

JULY

Days are decidedly sultry and sweaty as Grand Cayman celebrates **Constitution Day** with extravagant fireworks displays over Camana Bay.

OCTOBER

Wellness buffs flock to the **Cayman Rejuvenate** festival, while locals dress up as buccaneers for **Pirates Week** – a food- and firework-filled carnival.

DECEMBER

Nights are cool, and boats draped in colorful lights float along Camana Bay harbor as part of the **Parade of Lights**.

GRAND CAYMAN

Cruise ships, glitzy restaurants, white-sand beaches dotted with sun worshippers – Grand Cayman has it all in spades. To many, Grand Cayman *is* the Cayman Islands, an Americanized global financial center where the fabulously wealthy come to play (and hide their millions), with luxe resorts lining Seven Mile Beach; and some of the Caribbean's best restaurants welcoming visitors in historic George Town. And yet, there's an intimate, small-town feel to the pastel-colored houses and coffee shops, with chickens seen pecking between the chic boutiques.

There's also as much to 'the Grand' below the waves as there is above, with superb wreck and reef diving. If you head to the east of the island, the scenery and vibe changes: here, you can hike through wooded hinterland, meet endemic blue iguanas, kayak in a bioluminescent bay, explore subterranean caves and sun yourself in unpeopled coves.

TOP TIP

Grand Cayman is *not* a budget destination. To save money, travel outside peak season; book accommodations far in advance; self-cater as much as possible (supermarkets are closed on Sunday); eat at small, family-run restaurants; and use public transportation or cycle where possible. The cheapest air fares to the Sister Islands sell out fast.

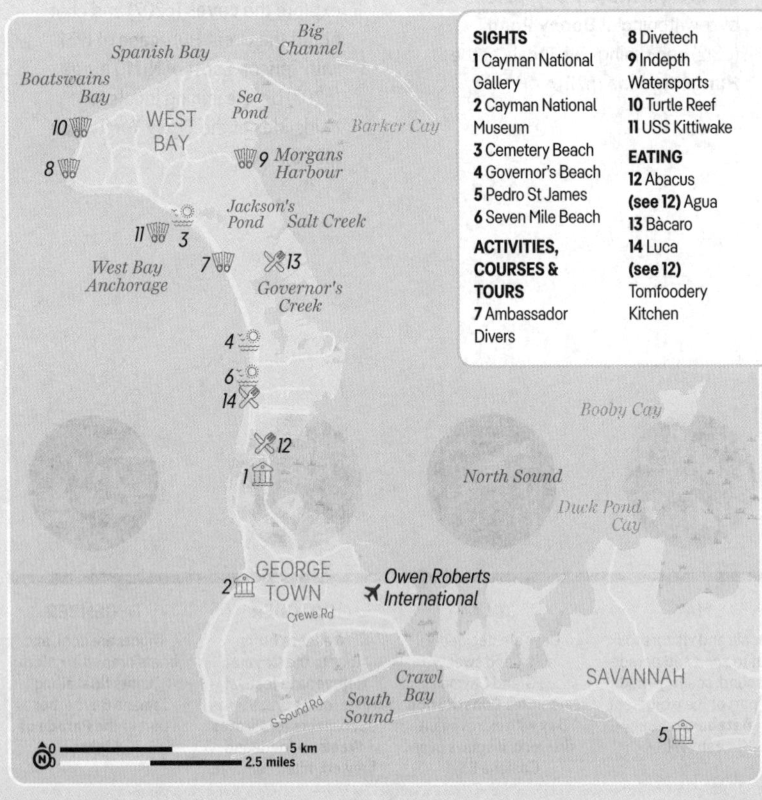

BYVALET/SHUTTERSTOCK ©

Cayman National Museum

Exploring Grand Cayman's History & Art

A NATIONAL MUSEUM AND GALLERY

For a taste of Cayman's culture, swing by George Town's oldest building (1833), which houses the **Cayman National Museum** – a jolly stampede through the island's ecosystems and wildlife, past and present. History exhibits upstairs include displays on turtling and shipbuilding, as well as moderately creepy animatronic figures of notable citizens. Rotating Caymanian art exhibits, an engaging introductory video and graffitied Old Gaol rooms complete the experience.

Next, head to the **Cayman National Gallery**, where bold modernist paintings by Cayman's artists compete for your attention alongside landscape and realist prints, a sculpture garden, and traditional and contemporary crafts, including decorative items made from the endemic silver thatch palm. Expertly curated temporary exhibitions are held on the ground floor.

The Grand Beneath the Waves

GRAND CAYMAN'S BEST DIVE SITES

The Grand's underwater topography offers some excellent shore and off-shore dives. Standout sites include **North Wall** – a magnificent underwater wall that drops off some 6000ft into the abyss and attracts reef sharks, sea turtles and eagle rays; the hugely popular **USS Kittiwake** – a 251ft US Navy

BEST PLACES TO EAT IN GEORGE TOWN

Da Fish Shack
Perch on the deck outside this clapboard gem, savor the harbor views and munch on superlative fish tacos. $

Singh's Roti Shop
Avoid drifting into insolvency by chowing roti filled with chicken or potato curry at this cheerful cheapie. $

The Brasserie
Rub shoulders with local power-brokers over eclectic sea- and farm-to-table dishes, and innovative cocktails and tapas. $$$

Daily Grind Cafe
Grand Cayman's best cup of coffee, with a supporting cast of delicious muffins, bagels and sandwiches. $

WHERE TO STAY IN GRAND CAYMAN

The Locale
Boutique hotel with king-sized beds, kitchenettes, Alexa-powered personal concierges and a 'lobby' for digital nomads. **$$$**

Kimpton Seafire Resort & Spa
Huge windows drink in beach views, plus an award-winning spa and a lobby decorated with local art. **$$$**

Caribbean Club
Boutique hotel with luxurious apartments overlooking Seven Mile Beach, with infinity pool and on-site trattoria. **$$$**

NORTH SIDE & EAST END DRIVING TOUR

If you imagine Grand Cayman to be whale-shaped, this scenic driving route takes in the whale's head, belly and dorsal fin. From **1 George Town** (p203), take the main highway east, through historic Bodden Town, and turn north up Frank Sound Rd to reach **2 Queen Elizabeth II Botanic Park**. Check out endemic plants and the orchid collection in the landscaped gardens, then take the woodland trail through the park to the Blue Iguana Recovery Center to commune with these striking, critically endangered reptiles. Just beyond the turnoff to the North Shore Rd, stop by the **3 Crystal Caves** for a 90-minute tour of the three caves. The underground lake and wealth of stalactites and stalagmites are spectacular. Detour to the **4 Mastic Trail** to stretch your legs through old-growth forest and marshland. A short drive west, stop by the regulars' haunt **5 Over the Edge** for wallet-friendly curried conch and grilled fish, or else press on to Cayman Kai for wahoo crudo and callaloo fritters at **6 Kaibo Beach Restaurant**. Get your snorkeling gear to check out the red starfish in the water off **7 Starfish Point**, with its pine-fringed, white-sand coves. Then proceed to nearby **8 Rum Point** for a wander along the mangroves, and sample the potent Mudslide cocktail at the beachside **9 Wreck Bar**, which allegedly invented them. Head back east, continue on past the scenic Old Man Bay, and spend some quality beach time on **10 Colliers Public Beach**. Stop by the memorial for the **11 Wreck of the Ten Sails**, and then for a sunset dinner enjoy **12 Eastern Star Fish Fry** for superb pan-grilled snapper and conch fritters. On your way back to George Town, spot geysers shooting up through the ironshore at **13 Blowholes**.

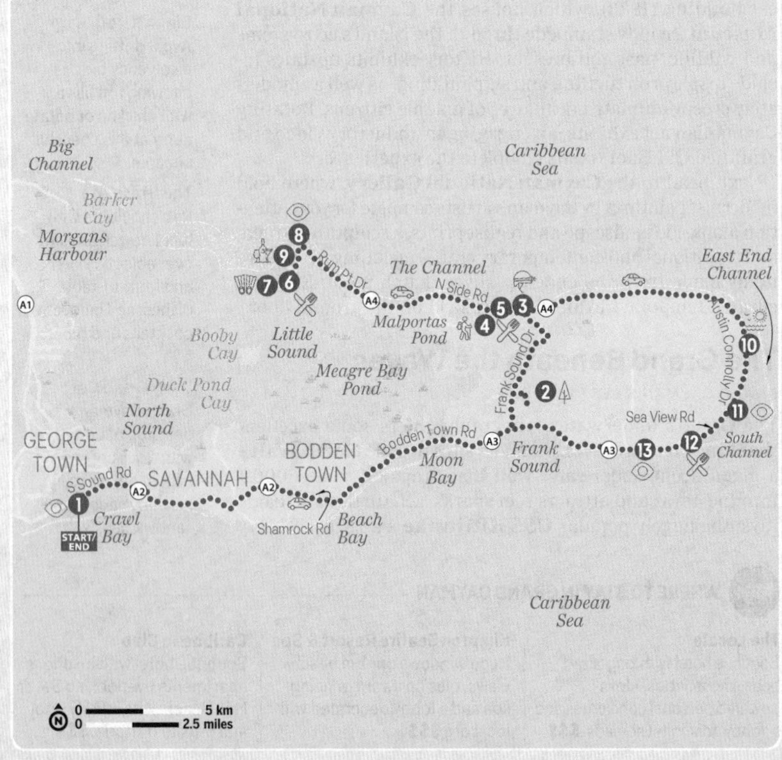

submarine rescue ship that was deliberately sunk off Cemetery Beach, and which now rests between 35ft and 84ft beneath the waves; and West Bay's **Turtle Reef**, which begins in the shallows and descends to a 60ft mini wall, with its kaleidoscopic sponges alive with darting reef fish.

The standout diving operators here include **DiveTech**, **Indepth Watersports** and **Ambassador Divers**.

Grand Cayman's Best Beach

THE EPIC SEVEN MILE BEACH

Teal waters lap at the picture-perfect strand of white sand that is **Seven Mile Beach** (5.5 miles long, actually). With luxury resorts peeking out of the greenery beyond, the beach is at the heart of the Grand's cultural life, with the sandy shores playing host to numerous festivals, and its restaurants and bars hopping till the wee hours. It's also at the epicenter of Grand Cayman's sophisticated dining scene. Camana Bay – a gorgeous open-air shopping mall – is home to **Abacus**, renowned for its farm-to-table contemporary Caribbean cuisine. Another swish option is **Agua**, with its emphasis on seafood, be it Peruvian or Italian. Also Italian, **Bàcaro** at the yacht club is renowned for its Venetian-style *cichetti* (tapas), while **Luca** has an incredible wine list and serves the island's best pastas. For jerk brisket burgers, saltfish fritters and Jamaican curry chicken, head to **Tomfoodery Kitchen**.

For less swanky beach options, further north, **Governor's Beach** is good for snorkeling and sunbathing beneath the seagrape trees. By West Bay, resort-free **Cemetery Beach** is consistently uncrowded.

Facing History at Pedro St James

GRAND CAYMAN'S OLDEST BUILDING

Rain hammers on the tin roof and a misty spray dampens your face during the multimedia introduction to Grand Cayman's oldest building of **Pedro St James**, near the former capital of Bodden Town. Constructed in 1780, the antique-filled great house with breezy dark-wood verandas built by enslaved people has worn many hats: jail, courthouse and parliament building, which saw both the birth of Caymanian democracy with the formation of the first elected parliament in 1831, and the end of slavery with the Slavery Abolition Act in 1835. Daily entry only by guided tour.

BEST RESTAURANTS IN BODDEN TOWN & EAST END

Czech Inn Grill
A graffiti-scrawled roadside bar known for its awesome jerk chicken, craft beer and American oldies on the stereo. $

Rankin's Jerk
Consume superlative jerk pork, curry goat and steamed snapper at colorful picnic tables. $

Vivine's Kitchen
East End's Miss Vivine serves up home-style goat curry, fish and fritters, and sweet-potato cakes, with sides of ocean views. $

Tukka
Enjoy delicious fish tacos made from lion fish at this breezy seafront Aussie joint. $$

GETTING AROUND

Owen Roberts International Airport has international flights to the US, Canada, the UK and Jamaica, plus daily local hops to Cayman Brac and Little Cayman. The airport is walkable from George Town, which is very congested. From the George Town bus depot on Edward St, color-coded minibuses (fares C$2 to C$5; small change essential) serve destinations around the island (roughly every 15 minutes, 6am–11pm Mon–Sat; sporadic service on Sunday). Flag buses down anywhere along their routes.

Car-rental fees average US$100 per day, and two-wheeled transportation includes Cayman Auto scooter rental, rented bicycles at many hotels and Bird electric scooters.

Cayman Brac
Little Cayman
Grand Cayman

CAYMAN BRAC

Dominated by the limestone bluff after which it was named when Scottish Highland fisherfolk settled the island in the 1830s, the Brac is the most easterly of the Cayman Islands. Riddled with caves and sinkholes rumored to be hiding pirate treasure, the Brac consists of a sliver of land 12 miles long and features the most rugged topography in the Caymans, ending in a sheer 196ft cliff at its eastern end. The island's cactus-studded semi-desert and woodlands are crisscrossed by hiking trails, and it shelters more than 200 bird species, while its sponge-encrusted wrecks and healthy coral reefs draw scuba divers from all over the world. A pit stop for Columbus in 1503, and for marauding pirates for a couple of centuries after, the Brac currently has around 2000 laid-back residents who are happy to strike up a conversation and engage in storytelling about the Great Hurricane of 1932.

TOP TIP

The Brac is easy to navigate: Charles Kirkconnell International Airport at the Brac's western end is served by a few daily flights from Grand Cayman and Little Cayman. Resorts lend or rent bicycles, and a complete lack of crime makes hitchhiking safe and easy. Alternatively, rent a car from CB Rent-A-Car.

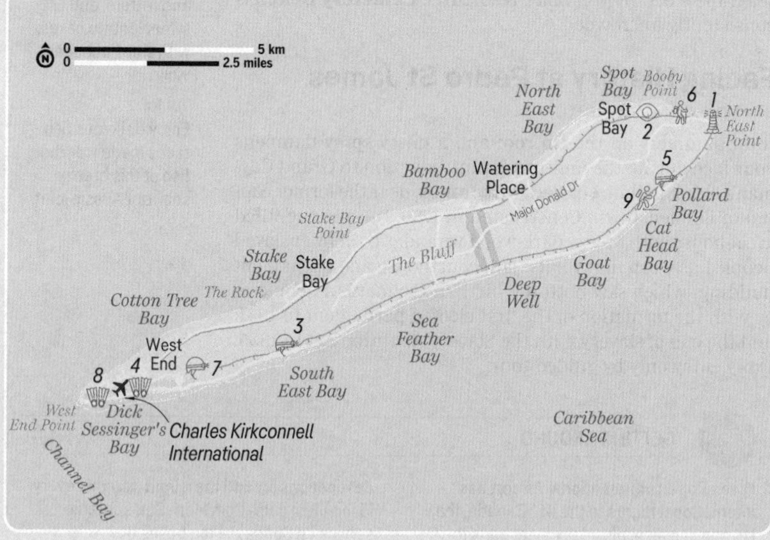

SIGHTS
1 Cayman Brac East End Lighthouse
2 Lighthouse Steps

ACTIVITIES & TOURS
3 Bat Cave
4 Brac Scuba Shack
5 Great Cave
6 Lighthouse Footpath
(see 2) Peter's Cave
7 Rebecca's Cave
8 Reef Divers
9 Rock Iguana Ltd

DELVIT/SHUTTERSTOCK ©

Cayman Brac

In Search of Blackbeard's Treasure

CAYMAN BRAC'S SUBTERRANEAN WONDERS

The bluff is defined by (mostly off-limits) caves that are a whopping 25 million years old, and many are said to hide the legendary Blackbeard's treasure. The odds of you finding Blackbeard's gold are not great – you're far likelier to come across bat guano here. In **Rebecca's Cave**, used as a shelter in the Great Hurricane of 1932, and reachable via the Saltwater Pond Path, a plaque commemorates the infant who perished here during the hurricane.

You'll smell **Bat Cave** before you enter it, thanks to its pungent population of Jamaican fruit bats and barn owls. At the far end of the south coast road, **Great Cave** is a scramble up rickety ladders, while the short yet spectacular **Southern Shore Trail** leads along the jetsam-strewn beach. Finally, north coast's **Peter's Cave** was also used as a shelter during the hurricane, and there are superb views of **Spot Bay** from its lofty perch.

CARVING CAYMANITE & LAYING ROPE

With its earth-toned color reminiscent of vibrant sunsets, caymanite is a semi-precious stone found only in crevices on the Brac and around Grand Cayman's East End. An amalgam of metals and minerals, it's a hard material to work with, requiring diamond-tipped cutting tools. At **NIM Things** in Spot Bay, artist Tenson Scott – who used to scale the cliffs without ropes to chisel the stone – creates exquisite jewelry from caymanite, with no two pieces the same. Also at NIM Things, you can buy Annelee Ebanks' baskets, purses and hats made from the dried leaves of the endemic silver thatch palm. 'Laying rope' (drying the thatch palm leaves and twisting them into hemp-like rope) is a Cayman tradition.

WHERE TO STAY IN CAYMAN BRAC

Cayman Brac Resort
Diving packages, fine dining, nature trails past hammock-hung trees and rooms overlooking the pool await. **$$$**

Le Soleil d'Or
This creeper-clad hotel on the south coast features bright, spacious rooms overlooking the ocean. **$$$**

Carib Sands
A pink beachfront condo complex featuring comfortably furnished apartments near the Brac's West End. **$$$**

THE LOST CITY OF ATLANTIS

In the seafront yard of Cayman Brac sculptor Ronald 'Foots' Kynes, a miasma of objects greets you, from fake missiles and a giant pair of sculpted feet to portraits of Che Guevara and female vampires. Inside the cheerful yellow house, you're likely to meet the man himself. 'Foots' is responsible for the hugely ambitious art-meets-engineering underwater project that is Cayman Brac's **Lost City of Atlantis**, aka the Brac's artificial reef and unique dive site. The 'city' is complete with sculptures and pyramids below the waves off the north shore, at the **Radar Reef** dive site. The impressive 'Atlantis' is constructed using specially made barges, cranes and drag floats, and has to be seen to be believed.

The Brac Below the Waves

WORLD-CLASS SCUBA DIVING AND SNORKELING

With its underwater landscapes of plunging walls, barnacle-encrusted wrecks and multicolored coral reefs, and a marine life ranging from hammerheads to sea horses, Cayman Brac is a world-class diving destination. It boasts 70 diving sites, including **West Chute**, with its barrel sponges and roaming stingrays; the **Cemetery Wall**, with its cleaning stations, eagle rays, turtles and a drop-off into the abyss; **South Wall** (aka Cayman's Grand Canyon), with its swim-throughs, tunnels and arches; and Cayman's own version of the **Lost City of Atlantis**. The most accessible of the wrecks is MV *Captain Keith Tibbetts*, a Russian frigate resting 40ft underwater. Playgrounds for snorkelers include **Snapper Reef**, **Greenhouse Reef** and **Lighthouse Reef**.

Brac Scuba Shack specializes in small-group dives and night, wreck and nitrox diving, while **Reef Divers** at Cayman Brac Beach Resort arranges dive and snorkel packages for guests and non-guests.

The Brac's Great Outdoors

HIKING AND ROCK-CLIMBING ADVENTURES

The Brac has a lot to offer outdoor enthusiasts. For a gentle hike, take the **Lighthouse Footpath**, which starts at the now-defunct **Cayman Brac East End Lighthouse** (1937) at the highest point of the bluff (140ft). The Brac's dramatic hiking trail skirts the top of the cliffs all the way to Peter's Cave (p207) and the steep, scenic **lighthouse steps**, once used by lighthouse keepers to carry gas tanks to the lighthouse, and by farmers to carry produce from their bluff-top plots of land. The trail snakes its way across an arid, sun-bleached landscape, past endemic silver thatch palms, 'maypole' cacti and numerous sheer drops, with frigate birds gliding in the updrafts and brown boobies nesting in the cliff crevices below.

And for the adrenaline junkies, know that experienced climbers have been coming to the Brac for years to dangle from limestone overhangs high above the churning waves. The bluff has over 70 routes, with difficulty levels ranging from the easy 5.8 to the heart-stopping 5.14, many accessed via private property (though local Brackers are likely to welcome you in for a cold one). **Rock Iguana Ltd**, led by rescue-trained mountaineer Angel who used to climb in the Himalayas, offers instructions and adventures for rookie climbers and aficionados.

WHERE TO EAT IN CAYMAN BRAC

Barry's Golden Jerk
Barry cooks jerk chicken and pork in an oil-drum grill on Wednesday, Friday and Saturday. $

Star Island
The highlight here is the old-school Caymanian cooking, from fish stew to curried conch. $

Tipsy Turtle Pub
Split-level, alfresco bar where everyone ends up, renowned for its excellent pub grub and killer Mudslides. $

LITTLE CAYMAN

Little Cayman is tiny indeed, but its marine offerings are larger than life: the island's plummeting walls and healthy reefs rank it among the world's top scuba-diving destinations and, helpfully, diving is excellent year-round. On dry land, you'll spot signs by local artists imploring you to give way to the rock iguanas – Little Cayman's endemic (and endangered) reptiles. The island (human population 135 at last count) is so quiet that these prehistoric-looking lizards outnumber vehicles on the main road. Brackish wetlands, mangrove swamps, lagoons that teem with birdlife, and splendid, unpeopled beaches form the topography. One airstrip connects Little Cayman to the outside world, and a visit is not cheap here, since the majority of accommodations comprise all-inclusive resorts. However, Little Cayman is unforgettable, both because of it's underwater world and its close-knit communities, the members of which you'll likely know by name by the time you leave.

TOP TIP

Cycling is a fantastic way to tour the island, giving plenty of flexibility to stop and swim, snorkel and spy on birds along the way. From the airport it's 8 miles to Point of Sand (one way) and 22 miles to make a complete circle around the island. Bicycles are available at all the resorts.

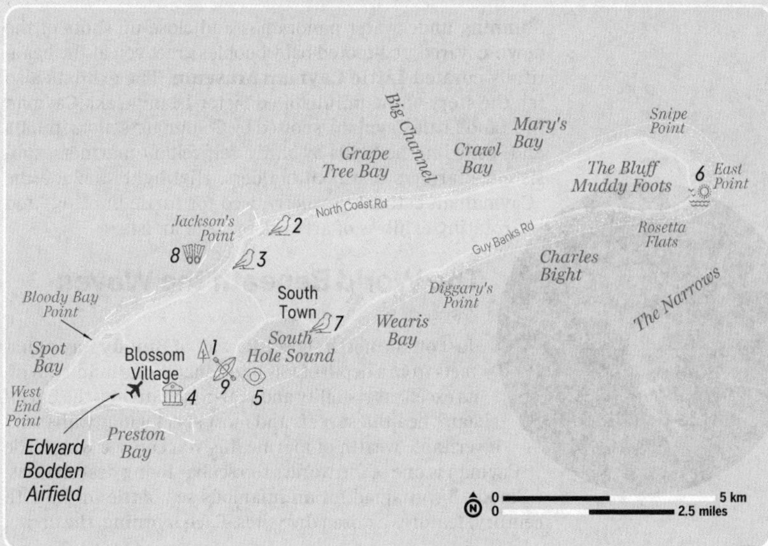

SIGHTS
1 Booby Pond Nature Reserve
2 Grape Tree Pond
3 Jackson Pond
4 Little Cayman Museum
(see 4) National Trust Visitors' Centre
5 Owen Island
6 Point of Sand
7 Tarpon Lake

ACTIVITIES, COURSES & TOURS
8 Bloody Bay

SLEEPING
9 Southern Cross Club

Above: Rock iguana; Below: Hawksbill turtle

Glimpse the Island's Past

A FASCINATING LOCAL MUSEUM

Stunning underwater panoramas and close-up shots of the down-covered, red-footed baby boobies greet you at the beautifully curated **Little Cayman Museum**. The exhibits also tell the story of the uninhabited Sister Islands (aka Cayman Brac and Little Cayman), spotted by Columbus' sailors in 1503 and settled in the 1830s by hardy, self-reliant mariners, subsistence farmers and boat builders. Highlights include the Caymanian catboat (formerly used for turtle hunting) and rotating exhibits of artwork by local artists.

The World Beneath the Waves

A SCUBA-DIVING HAVEN

Just off the north shore, the wall of **Bloody Bay** plummets from a depth of 18ft into aquamarine infinity. With its excellent visibility and year-round diving, the Caribbean's healthiest reefs and most spectacular walls, and a veritable wealth of marine life, you can see why Little Cayman is one of the world's top scuba-diving destinations. Bloody Bay (named for an infamous sea battle in the 17th century) features a dozen dive sites. Each morning, the diving

WHERE TO STAY ON LITTLE CAYMAN

Little Cayman Beach Resort
A diving-focused resort with tropical rooms surrounding the pool, ocean-facing balconies, hammocks and beach bar. **$$$**

Just Chillin'
Gorgeous two-bedroom house with pool near the airstrip; commune with the owner's cats and beagles next door. **$$**

Southern Cross Club
Pastel-colored bungalows with outdoor showers cater to divers and deep-sea fishers. Outstanding food and service. **$$$**

RLS PHOTO/SHUTTERSTOCK ©

Diving, Little Cayman

outfits attached to the resorts decide where to take underwater enthusiasts, dependent on wind conditions. Commune with sea turtles, reef sharks and eagle rays at Bloody Bay Wall, admire the 6000ft drop-off and swim through shimmering silver clouds of jacks and minnows. Where Jackson's Bay meets Bloody Bay, explore the sloping reefs, sandy flats and kaleidoscopic sponges of **Mixing Bowl**, with its great macro life, including seahorses, stingrays, yellow-headed jawfish and schools of groupers. Moray eels, sea turtles and barracuda haunt the aptly named **Barracuda Bight**, while **Randy's Gazebo** is a chimney that lets you descend into the abyss, past huge barrel sponges with cleaning stations full of shrimp.

The independent **Conch Club Divers** offers top-notch valet service to anyone on the island, while Gay Morse is a divemaster who caters to special interests, such as macro diving. Most dive sites are best accessed by boat.

Little Cayman's Best Beaches

CASTAWAY FOR A DAY

Forested **Owen Island** sits a quarter-mile offshore from the **Southern Cross Club** resort. Rent a sea kayak or paddleboard (per hour US$20) from the resort to stroll barefoot on pristine beaches that'll never be developed, and explore the

WHERE TO DIVE, DRINK & SNORKEL

Dianne Fite, divemaster and chef at Seahorse Boutique, and **Gay Morse**, divemaster and owner of Seahorse Boutique

Bloody Bay Wall
That's the dive site that we are world-famous for – a beautiful drop-off that plunges down to 6000ft. (Gay)

Point of Sand
It's a gorgeous beach, and you'll see the channel where you can snorkel with the current. Lots of eagle rays, but ask a local about sea conditions, since the current is strong on some days. (Gay)

Owen Island
Great for snorkeling: you'll always spot conch. (Gay)

McCoy's
It's a shack on the north shore of Little Cayman – the best place on the island to watch the sunset and have a drink with the locals. (Dianne)

WHERE TO EAT ON LITTLE CAYMAN

Hungry Iguana
Oceanside 'Iggy' serves lunchtime burgers and sandwiches, and steak and seafood dishes for dinner. **$$**

Seahorse Boutique
Munch on Dianne's breakfasts, lunchtime quesadillas and brownies while trading diving stories with Gay. **$**

Pirates' Point
Owner Susan hosts sushi nights on Friday; popular with locals and visitors for their fresh fish. **$$**

WHY I LOVE LITTLE CAYMAN

Anna Kaminski, writer

Little Cayman is not for everyone. For starters, it's pretty quiet, since most visitors are divers – early to bed, early to rise. It's also not the sort of place where I could remain anonymous for long, since on an island of 135 people, many want to get to know you. I soon found myself trading life stories with locals at the island's three hangouts: the restaurant, the cafe/boutique and the bar, and when I made my way to my lodgings at night, the stars overhead were among the brightest I've ever seen.

SANDARINA/SHUTTERSTOCK ©

Owen Island (p211)

bustling underwater world with snorkeling gear. Another place to play at being a castaway is the powder-white **Point of Sand** at the island's easternmost point, with a tiny pier, limited shade and great snorkeling (but strong currents at the reef mouth).

Little Cayman's Feathered Friends

SPYING ON BOOBIES AND HERONS

Pull up at the **National Trust Visitors' Centre** in Blossom Village, overlooking the **Booby Pond Nature Reserve**, and peer through the telescopes on the deck to see the magnificent frigate birds wheeling overhead and the fluffy baby boobies in the trees beyond the wetlands.

Little Cayman's wetlands and elevated viewing platforms provide access to the island's more than 200 endemic and migrant bird species. Booby Pond Nature Reserve is home to the Western Hemisphere's largest colony of red-footed boobies (20,000 in total). The visitors' center (with erratic opening hours) features info on local birdlife, including the West Indian whistling duck at the **Grape Tree Pond**; the herons, plovers and sandpipers at the mangrove-fringed **Jackson Pond**; and the fishing ospreys at **Tarpon Lake**.

GETTING AROUND

Two daily Cayman Airways flights connect Little Cayman to Cayman Brac and Grand Cayman. The resorts offer free transfers from the airstrip and have free bicycles for guests.

Rent a scooter from **Scooten Scooters** or a car from **Little Cayman Car Rental** to explore far-flung parts of the island.

BLUE SKY IMAGERY/SHUTTERSTOCK ©

Arriving

There are three ways to arrive to the Cayman Islands: by flying into Owen Roberts International Airport (GCM; pictured) on Grand Cayman (from where you can walk to George Town), by international cruise ship to George Town, or by yacht to West End. Car rental outlets are across the street from the airport terminal, and there are some rental facilities in the arrivals hall.

By Air

The only international airport on the Cayman Islands is Owen Roberts, on Grand Cayman. International flights from the US, Canada, the UK and Jamaica to Little Cayman and Cayman Brac require passing immigration controls and changing planes at Grand Cayman.

By Boat

Grand Cayman is a popular cruise-ship destination, with George Town seeing all the action. There's a yachting marina at West End. Unfortunately, there are no boat services to Little Cayman or Cayman Brac.

Money

Currency: Cayman dollar (C$), US dollar (US$)

CASH

Cash is still used on the Cayman Islands, particularly by small businesses and hole-in-the-wall restaurants. The Cayman dollar is tied to the US dollar, and they are used interchangeably. Save small bills to pay the bus fares on Grand Cayman, as bus drivers often find it difficult to break up large bills.

DIGITAL PAYMENTS

All hotels, resorts, big-name businesses as well as most restaurants, cafes, attractions and gift shops accept digital payments. Bear in mind that some local museums, craft markets, food stands and other small businesses aren't able to process digital payments, so always try to have cash on you, just in case.

CREDIT CARDS

Credit and debit cards are widely used across the Cayman Islands, by both locals and foreigners. Visa and MasterCard are more common than Amex and can generally be used on all three islands. Some businesses add a surcharge for credit-card purchases.

CUBA

BEAUTIFUL, HISTORIC, ENIGMATIC

The Caribbean's largest island has a wealth of unspoiled rural beauty, historic monuments, Unesco-listed cities, spectacular beaches and underwater wonderworlds.

Few islands in the Caribbean carry more mystique than incredible, delightful Cuba. Yes, political issues will be front and center, and yes, you'll be reminded by billboard after billboard of whom to thank for *La Revolucíon,* but the country is a wonderful place for travelers, full of deep paradoxes, incredible discoveries and sweet friendships to be made. After all, where else can you drive with the top down in a 1957 convertible, next to a fleet of super-modern electric scooters and horse-drawn buggies that hearken back to a century ago?

The country is rich, indeed overflowing, with hospitality, and Cubans delight in taking good care of their guests, whether you're staying in an all-inclusive resort on the beach or in a different town and different *casa particular* (guesthouse) each night. Gas shortages cause problems, but one thing you won't find (at least for the time being) is clogged highways: roads are open and wide, and getting from place to place is easy. When you do arrive at your chosen destination, expect incredible food and good conversations with people who are longing to share their stories with the world.

THE MAIN AREAS

HAVANA
The unmissable capital. **p220**

VIÑALES
Rural beauty and limestone caves. **p226**

TRINIDAD
Spectacularly historic city and beaches. **p232**

BECA GONZALEZ/SHUTTERSTOCK ©

Above: Cayo Guillermo (p237); Left: Havana (p220)

CAYO GUILLERMO
Stunning sands and shorelines.
p237

SANTA CLARA
The heart of *La Revolucíon.*
p242

SANTIAGO DE CUBA
The east's historic port city.
p247

Find Your Way

Cuba is the Caribbean's largest island and is approximately 160km south of Key West, Florida. It's also near Haiti, to the east, Jamaica to the south, and The Bahamas to the northeast.

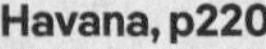

Havana, p220

The bustling, stunning capital city feels like a veritable time machine, with its 1950s-era vehicles and gasp-inducing architecture.

Santa Clara, p242

This city claims Che Guevara as its own, with monuments aplenty lionizing the revolutionary hero, but there's a vibrant art and culture scene here, too.

Viñales, p226

A rural paradise and the country's main tobacco-growing area, with delightful hills, waterfalls and beaches.

Trinidad, p232

A historic city, rich with museums and traditions, and also a thriving, modern hub, just a few minutes away from great beaches.

CAR

Hiring a rental car or using local taxis is the best way to explore certain parts of Cuba, especially the west. This way, you can discover its secluded mountain retreats, beaches, wildlife spots and tobacco farms.

BUS

A reliable bus system runs mostly east to west across the country, but there are far fewer connections on the north–south passage. It's best to make reservations online, as the buses fill up days or weeks in advance.

TRAIN

Train travel is scenic and should be a delightful way to get around. However, a number of 'we're in Cuba' problems have meant it's unreliable, due to fuel shortages, the embargo and poor maintenance. But if you don't mind delays, it's a whimsical option.

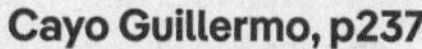

Cayo Guillermo, p237

Ernest Hemingway's favorite beach in the world is now a great all-inclusive destination, with postcard-perfect azure water and pillow-soft sand.

Santiago de Cuba, p247

The gem of the east, Cuba's second-largest city is famous for its music and its Carnaval, as well as its role in the Cuban Revolution.

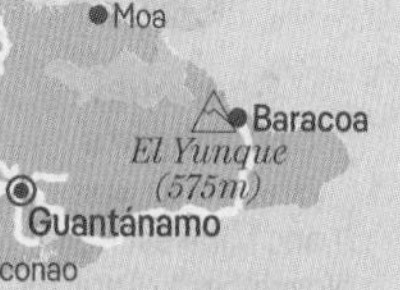

Plan Your Time

Visiting Cuba depends more on the state of supplies than the seasons, so always come prepared with a Plan B...or Plan C...or Plan D. You get the picture.

JEROME LABOUYRIE/SHUTTERSTOCK ©

Plaza de la Revolución Che Guevara (p243)

If You Only Do One Thing

- If you're only going to do one thing, you'll arrive in **Havana** (p220) and stay there, exploring the **Plaza Vieja** (p221) and the stunning, imposing **Fortaleza de San Carlos de la Cabaña** (p222), which guards the mouth of the harbor.

- At night, you'll want to finish up with the **Cañonazo** (p222), a drama-filled reenactment of the gate-closing ceremony. As you wander the streets marveling at the architecture, be wary – not of crime, but of pieces of stone falling off the buildings above you. Oh, and be sure to take a ride in one of those incredible classic cars.

Seasonal Highlights

Cuba is busiest and balmiest from November to April. By April's end, it's hot and rainy, meaning fewer tourists and cheaper prices.

JANUARY

Havana's **Jazz Festival** brings in both big-name foreign talent and cherished names from home.

FEBRUARY

Light up a cigar at Havana's fancy and glittering **Habanos Festival** for all things Cuban-cigar related.

JUNE

The blustery, fickle and sometimes dangerous hurricane season officially begins, lating until the end of November.

KAMIRA/SHUTTERSTOCK ©, MATYAS REHAK/SHUTTERSTOCK ©, MANJA/SHUTTERSTOCK ©

Three Days to Travel Around

- Three days gives you time to do everything in **Havana** (p220) and then take a day trip to **Varadero** (p224) and hit the beaches for some relaxation and Vitamin-D replenishment.

- You can overnight or, if beaching isn't your style, head the other direction and check out the pastoral landscapes of **Viñales** (p226). Be sure to see the *mirador* (lookout) at the **Hotel Los Jazmines** (p227) for bird's-eye views of the valley.

- If you have a plane to catch, make sure you head back with plenty of time, as gasoline supplies were low at the time of writing, and shortages make for interesting travel.

More Than a Week

- If you have more than a week, then you're in for a treat. Start by luxuriating in **Havana** (p220), spending at least a few days sightseeing.

- Head to **Viñales** (p226). Smoke a cigar if you're a smoker, then hop on over to **Trinidad** (p232), where you'll be able to see an entirely different kind of Cuba. Enjoy the vivaciousness here, then move to **Santiago de Cuba** (p247) and sightsee there.

- Be sure to also check out **Santa Clara** (p242) and all things 'Che,' and if there's time, zip up for a night (or at least a swim) in **Cayo Guillermo** (p237).

JULY

The conga, Caribbean dancing and numerous rituals fill Santiago's streets for the **Fiesta del Caribe** and **Carnaval**.

OCTOBER

The Cuban National Ballet hosts the **Festival Internacional de Ballet**. Watch Cuban performers and stellar foreign dancers at work.

NOVEMBER

Put away that umbrella: hurricane season is over by the end of the month, and the **high season** begins.

DECEMBER

Pilgrims crawl (yes, crawl) to the sanctuary of **El Rincón** on the Día de San Lázaro to pray for health and prosperity.

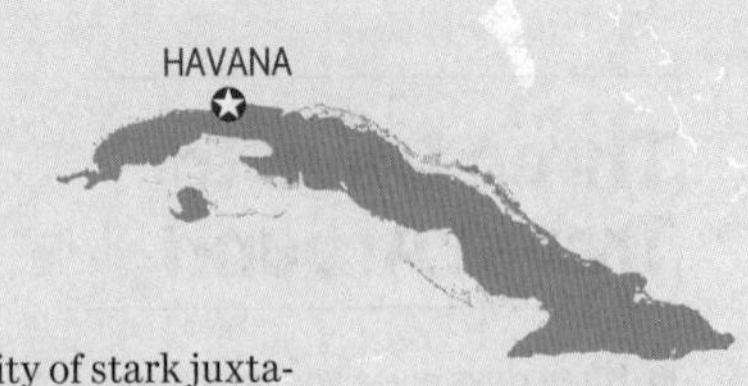

HAVANA

Cuba's impossible-to-pigeonhole capital is a city of stark juxtapositions and jarring contradictions, where doctors moonlight as hotel porters and *socialismo* dances to a syncopated tropical beat. If it's your first visit, suspend your judgment. With its baffling bureaucracy and visibly shabby buildings, initial impressions can be deceptive. Instead, prepare for a long, slow seduction that involves the aroma of pungent Cohiba cigars and the fiery essence of Havana Club rum, the rattle of a 1952 Plymouth careering around Parque Central and the sight of massive waves exploding against the Malecón sea wall.

Geographically, the city can be broken into three main parts: Havana Vieja, with its restored historical monuments; the animated street life of Centro Havana; and the clubs, hotels and restaurants of Vedado. Added together, Havana never fails to impress with its art, music, bars, historic old town and gritty authenticity.

TOP TIP

'Es Cuba!' bureaucracy and the stifling embargo mean at any one time, roughly half a dozen of Havana Vieja's hotels and museums could be undergoing lengthy *reparaciones* (repairs) or subject to erratic closures during your visit. To cover this eventuality, always come prepared with a back-up plan.

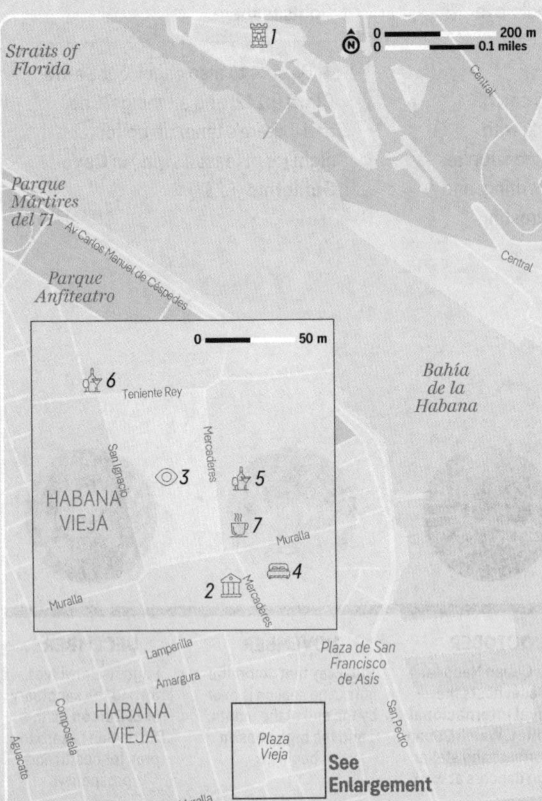

SIGHTS
1 Fortaleza de San Carlos de la Cabaña
2 Museo de Naipes
3 Plaza Vieja

SLEEPING
4 Palacio Cueto

DRINKING & NIGHTLIFE
5 Azúcar
6 Café Bohemio
7 Café El Escorial

DAMIAN CHIAPPE/SHUTTERSTOCK ©

Plaza Vieja

VINTAGE FOOD

La Vitrola, on the southwestern corner of Plaza Vieja, is a perennially busy restaurant crammed with pre-revolutionary memorabilia, and its gregarious waitstaff stand like ushers on the street outside. It might not be Havana's most gourmet eating option, but it's a fun spot to flop down and absorb the energy of the square, with live music throughout the day and fortifying breakfasts, which arrive at your table with your country's national flag attached to a toothpick. If you're hungry come evening time, there's also an affiliated pizza place, **Pizza Retro**, right next door.

Plaza Vieja's History & Haunts

AN ARCHITECTURALLY ECLECTIC SQUARE

Originally called 'New Square,' Plaza Vieja (which translates as the 'Old Square') has gone through numerous name changes and functions to reach its current incarnation. Markets, executions and bullfights all provided questionable 'diversions' in days of yore.

It was first laid out in 1559 as a residential plaza for rich colonial merchants. Over time, it steadily evolved to incorporate a broad range of epoch-spanning architecture, from Spanish Mudéjar to art nouveau. The brick-paved square was rescued from unsightly development in the 1990s when an underground car park that had been installed in the 1950s was removed. Today, it stands as one of the finest restoration projects of the Office of the Historian of the City, and is known for its splendid *vitrales* (arched stained-glass windows). The square is ringed by salubrious bars and cafes, and the presence of a local school adds authenticity and charm, as children use the square as their unofficial playground during break-times.

Plaza Vieja curiosities include a small planetarium, a camera obscura and a photo gallery connected to the city's main archive. The esoteric **Museo de Naipes**, in the square's oldest

WHERE TO STAY IN HAVANA

Hostal Chacón 160
Arty antiques and thoughtful design create glamorous boutique accommodations in the Loma del Ángel. **$$**

Loft Habana
Chic apartment-style rooms in a handsome old building overlooking the harbor, with a rooftop restaurant. **$$**

Gardens
Gardens is a beautifully decorated boutique hotel with handmade furniture and a rooftop pool. **$$$**

THE CAÑONAZO

Long established as one of Havana's essential nocturnal experiences, the **Cañonazo** replicates a centuries-old tradition that used to mark the closing of the city's gates every night at 9pm. To this day, actors dressed in full 18th-century military regalia reenact the cannon firing over the harbor from the ramparts of La Cabaña. It's a powerfully evocative event, with fire torches, showy marching and the deafening explosion of the cannon over the sturdy walls as the lights of Havana twinkle in the background.

building, is dedicated to playing cards, while the **Palacio Cueto** in the southeast corner was once an erstwhile hat factory that stood empty for over two decades before reopening as a hotel in 2019. The square also harbors a rare-for-Cuba micro-business, with **Café El Escorial** roasting its own coffee. Newer drinking holes include the chic **Azúcar** and the delightful **Café Bohemio**, named after a Cuban arts magazine.

An Impressive Fortress

LARGEST SPANISH FORT IN THE AMERICAS

Immense, foreboding and impenetrable, **Fortaleza de San Carlos de La Cabaña** is Cuba's military masterpiece. It comprises a giant fort built between 1763 and 1774 on an exposed ridge overlooking Havana harbor that the British had exploited when they captured the city in 1762.

After regaining Cuba in 1763, the Spanish resolved to eradicate any remaining weaknesses in Havana's intricate defense system to repel future invaders. The fort, named for the contemporaneous Spanish king, Carlos III, was the answer, and it served its purpose well, as the city was never captured again. Measuring 700m from end to end and covering 10 hectares, the bastion formed the final link in a chain of over six forts that protected the city from attack. Aside from defense, the fort has served numerous other purposes over the years, not all of them pleasant. During the 19th century, Cuban patriots faced the firing squad here, while 20th-century presidents Gerardo Machado and Fulgencio Batista used it as a military prison. The firing squads returned in January 1959 when Che Guevara set up his headquarters inside the ramparts and meted out 'revolutionary justice' with barely a lawyer in sight.

Since becoming a Unesco World Heritage site in 1982, the fort has embraced more benign functions, which include hosting Havana's annual book fair and a nightly cannon-firing ceremony (see left). Contemporary visitors can while away half a day perusing the bars, restaurants, souvenir stalls, cigar shop (containing the world's longest cigar) and two **museums** – one relating to armaments, the other an engrossing examination of Che Guevara.

GETTING AROUND

You'll find that a vehicle is by far the best way to get around the city, and most visitors find it best to take a taxi. The cheaper rides won't be in a classic car, but you'll get where you need to go. Some visitors find that hiring a driver for a half or whole day makes sense, as often the driver can act as a resource for suggestions about what to see and do, and some will try to include a city tour for a bit of extra money. The traffic is often terrible, so leave plenty of time, and remember that gas shortages often affect the city. For short rides, consider zipping around on a CocoTaxi – otherwise known as those yellow coconut-shaped tuk-tuks.

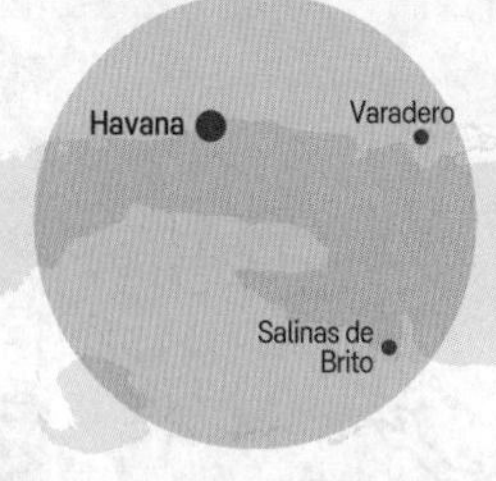

Beyond Havana

There are some great spots beyond Havana that are possible to day-trip to, but the longer spent in these places, the better.

The region around Havana is so diverse, especially from north to south, that it almost feels like you're visiting a completely different country. The luxury all-inclusive experience on the beaches of Varadero is vastly different from the quiet, laid-back surroundings in Playa Larga, where some of the best shore diving lies just a short and easy swim away. The country's largest national park, the Ciénaga de Zapata, hosts unparalleled birdlife and wildlife spotting, with some parts of the park easily accessible by car. Ideally, that car will be one of the uniquely Cuban 'Frankencars' that *look* classic but have actually been put together with a vibrant assortment of odds and ends – Cuban ingenuity at its best.

TOP TIP

Avoid during the peak vacation months (December to February), when it gets crazy crowded. Other times of year are more relaxed.

ONDREJ BUCEK/SHUTTERSTOCK ©

Playa Larga

THE CLASSIC CUBAN FRANKENCAR

Yes, sure, you're here in Cuba and dying to ride in a classic car, preferably one of those 1950s-era beauties you see in the photographs. Well, it turns out there's a good chance that you'll actually end up in a classic Cuban 'Frankencar' – something that looks old but is actually a mish-mash of different makes, models and eras. You might hop into a 1957 Chevy and see that it's been tricked out with a USB charger and satellite radio. Or you'll kick the tires of a 1954 Pontiac and be told it's actually using the suspension of a 2000s-era Toyota imported from Japan. In fact, creative Cubans have even been known to retrofit boat engines into their supposedly 'classic' cars.

Varadero

Beachgoer Bliss

VARADERO'S SLICE OF HEAVEN

Imagine water so turquoise it seems to be illuminated, with powder-white sand that stretches as far as the eye can see. Imagine rows of immaculate chaise longues waiting beneath shade umbrellas. Imagine the occasional curious pelican or chirping tern. 'Welcome,' they might be saying. Yes. Welcome to **Varadero**, just an hour's drive from Havana.

There's simply nothing that's not perfect about this beach: the water is shallow, the color is dazzling and the waves are gentle. It's a spot where even non-swimmers can safely splash around or wade, as there's little in the way of current or undertow. The balmy temperatures make – at times – the waves seem as warm as bathwater, and while sunburn is a risk, that's about the only serious thing you'll need to think about. Just bring your beach towel, slather on the sunscreen and prepare to dose up on a year's worth of vitamin D. If you get too hot on the sand, cool off in the gentle waters or don a snorkel and mask and see what cool critters you can find below the surface. Though not as varied as the snorkel spots on the island's south side, there's still a lot to see here while you swim, including a variety of fish, rays and crustaceans.

Depending on where you stay, your section of the beach may be more (or less) developed, with amenities like restrooms and showers a quick walk back to the nearest hotel. Some spots have rental chairs, towels and umbrellas; with others, you'll have to bring your own.

WHERE TO STAY IN VARADERO'S CASAS PARTICULARES

Casa Amelia
Enjoy two quiet rooms in a house at the end of a cul-de-sac with a friendly family. **$**

Beny House B&B
Right next to the park, this *casa* has good beach access and tasty food. **$$**

Casa Leyla
The friendly Leyla makes you feel at home in this small *casa* right on the beach. **$**

SLEPOY/SHUTTERSTOCK ©

Reddish egrets, Ciénaga de Zapata

Flamingo Forays in the Salinas de Brito

A BIRD-WATCHING PARADISE

You don't even have to be a bird-watcher to enjoy a morning, afternoon or whole-day excursion to the **Salinas de Brito** – whatever your views of our feathered friends, there's something universally cool about spotting your first wild flamingo, then seeing dozens or even hundreds more as you continue about the preserve, located on the shores of the vast **Ciénaga de Zapata**, about a three-hour drive from Havana. The experience begins at the park gate in thick woodland, where you'll spot thrushes, catbirds and woodpeckers. As you drive along what was once the area's only train track, the trees begin to vanish, giving way to reddish-colored lagoons. Waterfowl of all kinds come here to enjoy the shallow, mangrove-dotted flats, where vibrantly orange (and super tiny) krill and brine shrimp are seen thriving – they also make easy prey for the larger birds. In fact, the color of flamingos and several other species comes not from their DNA but from the pigments that are present in what they eat. Immature birds are white, and they gradually gain their adult color over years of exposure to their colored food sources.

Look for tri-colored herons, flamingos, roseate spoonbills, ibis, cormorants, ducks and egrets. In the bushes you'll likely see many species of warblers, as well as the endangered Cuban bullfinch, which is quickly vanishing due to its beautiful song – this attracts some individuals to trap it and keep it in tiny cages. Note that what you will see depends a bit on the water levels. At times there's mostly dry mudflats; in the rainy season, things are more lush.

THE PRECIOUS BIRDS OF ZAPATA SWAMP

Yoandys 'Kiko' Garcia, bird-watching guide (+53-5-353-6958):

Zapata Swamp National Park is the largest wetland in the west Caribbean area and has enchanted me with great bird sightings my entire 10 years here as a bird-watching guide.

The three birds I love seeing the most are these endemic species: the Zapata wren, the Zapata sparrow and the Zapata rail.

The Zapata wren is stunning because of its beautiful call and how rare it is; the Zapata rail also because of its rarity – unfortunately, the last record we have of it in this park is from the 1930s; and the Zapata sparrow is an intrepid, fearless bird, and easy to approach. These three species are why the Zapata swamp is worthy of protection!

GETTING AROUND

Getting to many of these sights is easiest with a car, assuming there's gasoline and an available rental. But buses, taxis or the Cuban Frankencar and driver are all alternatives.

VIÑALES

The Viñales Valley is a beauty. The base of domed, craggy limestone hills draped in jungle plants grace the valley floor. The neighboring valleys – Ancón, Silencio and Palmarito – are also studded with clusters of these limestone *mogotes* (monoliths). It's a Jurassic wonderland formed by the erosion of karstic landscape; the oldest rocks date back 199 million years, and they form the backdrop to valley life: fields are tilled by oxen, and tobacco and food crops flourish. New *secaderos* (leaf-drying huts) are being erected after 2022's Hurricane Ian, and royal palms, their fronds bristling in the breeze, stand tall over the idyllic scene. At the heart of the Viñales Valley is the 19th-century village, consisting of one-story homes and a main road lined with Caribbean pine.

Explore caves, horse-ride into the valleys, visit farms and soak up the atmosphere in the bars, music venues and outstanding *casas particulares*.

TOP TIP

To get around, the hop-on hop-off Viñales Bus Tour drives around the valley. However, it's not regular, so you'll need to rely on local taxis, your feet, and the odd horse and cart. The National Park's Centro de Visitantes offers guided walks, as do many private guides.

Tobacco plantation, Viñales Valley

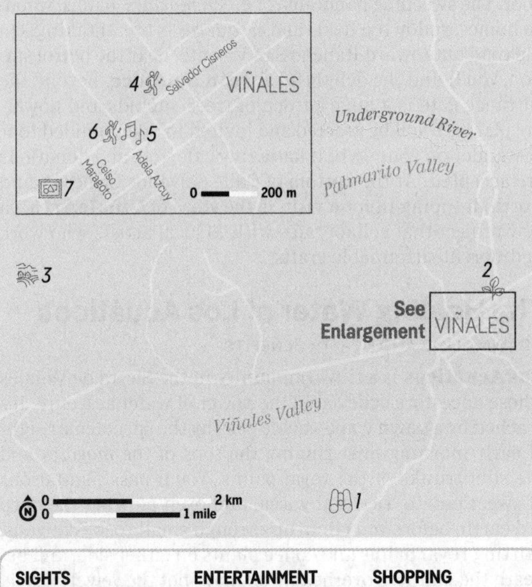

SIGHTS	ENTERTAINMENT	SHOPPING
1 Hotel Los Jazmines	4 Centro Cultural Polo Montañez	7 ViñaleArte
2 Jardín Botánico	5 Jardin del Arte Sano	
3 Los Acuáticos	6 Patio del Decimista	

The Quaint & Lovely Viñales Village

MUSIC, CRAFTS AND A BOTANICAL GARDEN

Viñales village was officially founded in 1875 by European colonists and developed by cattle farmers and tobacco growers. Low-slung homes radiate out along roads that stretch into the valley; most have a porch shaded by a roof, under which a couple of rocking chairs provide time for contemplation (and homemade mojitos). Whiling away the time with your hosts and watching the bustle of daily life is one of the most appealing things about Viñales. Village life centers on the main plaza with its small church. In one corner is the **Centro Cultural Polo Moñtanez**, with regular nights of dancing. Just down the road is the **Patio del Decimista** with its roster of live music. **Jardin del Arte Sano**, off the main street, also offers live music into the early hours in its pretty garden.

It's obligatory at some point in your stay to stop by the *mirador* (lookout) at the **Hotel Los Jazmines** above the valley

BEST BARS IN VIÑALES

Mogote Café
Overlooking the valley, Mogote is all hammocks and rocking chairs, and serves up all the classics. Make sure you try the *canchánchara* cocktail!

Tarecos
Cool vibes and cooler drinks at this bar with a rooftop terrace that's perfect for valley sunsets. Its daiquiri is a winner, as is the Tarequeando, ramped up by Guayabita liquor.

Tres Jotas
A great tapas bar with a clubby vibe and an extensive drinks menu, featuring the best Cuban rums and some stonking mojitos.

WHERE TO STAY IN VIÑALES

Casa Haydée Chiroles
A fine *casa* with six rooms and a lush patio run by the friendly Haydée. **$**

Cabaña Mía
A special private *cabaña* overlooking a *mogote* in an untouristy spot in the valley. **$$**

Casa Deborah
Two quiet rooms set around a small patio in a lovely home behind the plaza. **$**

A UNESCO WORLD HERITAGE SITE

In November 2021, Cuba declared the **Viñales Valley** the country's first geopark, highlighting 57 geosites, 10 of which have international importance. In addition to dinosaur fossils, rocks related to the meteorite impact that wiped out the dinosaurs 66 million years ago have been located in the area. But 22 years before that, Unesco declared the valley a World Heritage site. When you drill down, you learn that part of the Unesco protection relates to the 'living landscape' of the unusual karst setting. Unesco declared that the valley's traditional agricultural practices of growing tobacco are of significant cultural value, as they avoid mechanical cultivation and harvesting practices (as this degrades tobacco quality), instead using time-honored traditions of animal traction.

floor. The sweeping panorama of green *mogotes*, palms, wooden homes, ruddy red fields and *secaderos* is breathtaking. On the road out toward Rancho San Vicente, near the petrol station, you'll find the delightful **Jardín Botánico**. Beyond the entrance gate is a huge garden of trees, orchids and flowering plants. You'll be greeted and invited to take a guided tour or wander on your own; it has a tiny cafe, too, and donations are accepted. At the bottom of Calle Salvador Cisneros, and worth dropping in for a visit, is the store of **ViñaleArte** – a new project that collaborates with 15 local artists who work in different sustainable crafts.

The Healing Water of Los Acuáticos

A DAWN CLIMB AND HEALTH BENEFITS

Los Acuáticos is a tiny community in the Sierra de Viñales whose ancestors believed in the power of water as a cure. It's reached by a dawn walk – made easy by the spectacular sight of early morning mist ringing the tops of the *mogotes* and the slim trunks of the royal palms. You'll pass plantations of sweet potato, rice and yucca, and oxen plowing the deep red earth, before you climb up through small rocky canyons, skirting royal palms and coffee plants on either side, and beneath the vultures overhead. You may spot the velvety black, smooth-billed ani, the Cuban tody, the tocororo, and egrets attending the oxen to look for insects. After reaching one of the first wooden houses in the community, you can sip coffee or fruit juice while waiting for the sun to break through behind the *mogotes*.

In 1936, Antoñica Izquierdo, without resources to pay for a doctor, claimed she heard the Virgin Mary tell her how to cure her ill son with water. Her son recovered, and the pilgrimages began. The community of Los Acuáticos was established using Antoñica's guiding principles. Go guided with Sergio Enrique Luis Nodarse (sergioluis.vinales@gmail.com); at the end of the guided walk, you'll breakfast with a local farmer (with unrivalled views of the sierra), whose farm crops were wiped out by Hurricane Ian. Learn how to order the oxen to plough the fields, collect coffee and feed the farm animals.

GETTING AROUND

Víazul is the only public coach service leaving Havana, with stops in Pinar del Río and Viñales. You'll need a hire car or taxis to get around. *Casa particular* owners can help you arrange this. Both Pinar del Río and Viñales are small enough to walk around, and the daily hop-on hop-off bus tour gets around the furthest highlights of the valley. Yellow Cubataxis line up on Calle Ceferino Fernández in Viñales. Shared taxis run up to Cayo Jutías.

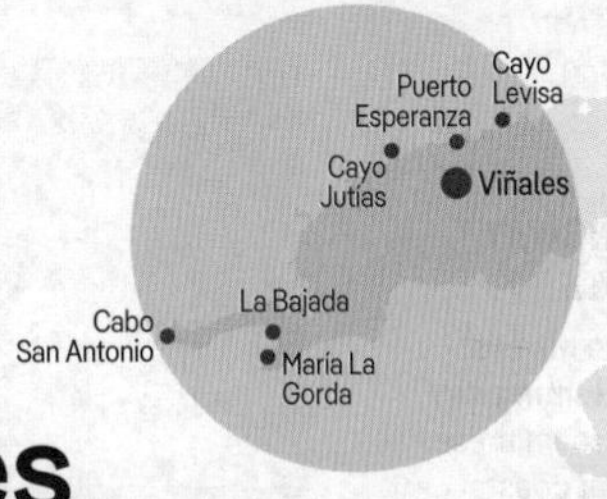

Beyond Viñales

Beyond the Viñales Valley, you'll find glorious white-sand beaches, dive spots, wildlife, sleepy towns and top tobacco *terroir*.

Exploring beyond the Viñales Valley is difficult without your own set of wheels. But heading deeper into western Cuba is worth it, as it opens up a whole new world steeped in tobacco farming: this is the country's most important tobacco-growing region. Further west, and reached by a rutted road, are the remote coastal spots of María La Gorda, known for its diving; La Bajada, with homestays and an alluring sea pool; and Cabo San Antonio, enveloped in the wildlife-rich, unusual landscapes of the Unesco-protected Peninsula de Guanahacabibes. Spurred off the heavily potholed coast road is beach paradise Cayo Jutías; time-warped and pretty Puerto Esperanza; and idyllic Cayo Levisa.

TOP TIP

You'll need plenty of mosquito repellent and sun block for the remote corners of western Cuba. Bring both. Use both.

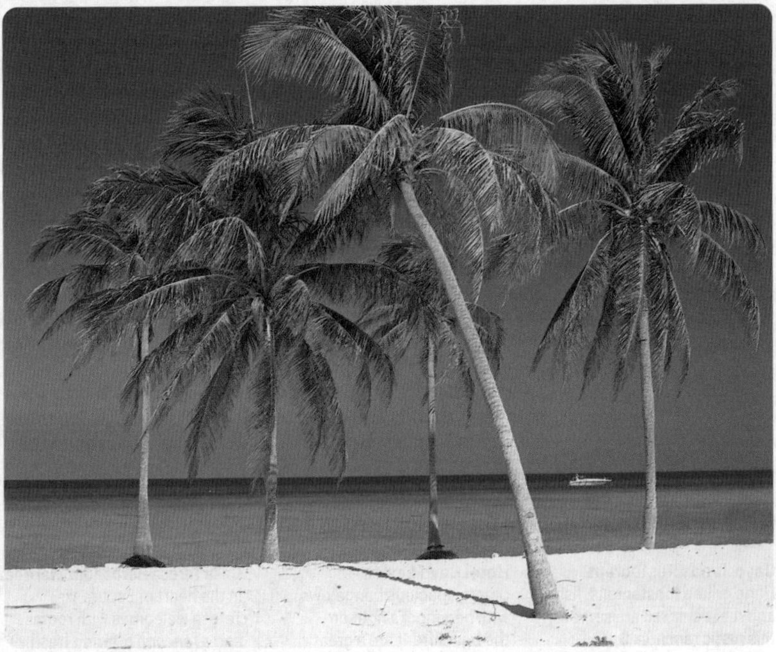

RICHARD SEMIK/SHUTTERSTOCK ©

María La Gorda Beach (p231)

A HEMINGWAY FAVORITE

American novelist **Ernest Hemingway** loved to roam these northwest coastal waters. Spend some time exploring, and you'll soon see why: at the tip of Cayo Jutías is a colony of large orange starfish, protected by the hooked tip of the peninsula. Walk 90 minutes along the beach, passing fantastical driftwood sculptures; go inland via the mangroves and casuarina trees; or hire a boat. The colony of red cushion sea stars *(Oreaster reticulatus)* is long-standing (please don't touch them), and easily visible in the shallow water. Your chances of spotting endangered green marine turtles *(Chelonia mydas)* might not be easy, as illegal poaching along the northwest coast is rife, with divers taking fishing nets on boats to capture them.

Puerto Esperanza

Explore the Northwest Coast

SANDY BEACHES, STARFISH AND SEAFOOD

The northwest coast of Cuba is remote, infrequently visited and reached through roads gouged by some serious potholes and hopelessly fractured tarmac. But one achingly beautiful cinematic stretch of road winding its way through the San Vicente Valley on its way north has been renovated: it emerges close to **Puerto Esperanza**, a faded Viñales-by-the-Sea that's a 45-minute drive north of Viñales. This is a fishing port of columned homes with pretty boats bobbing in the water; come for an off-the-tourist-trail stay.

East is **Cayo Levisa** island, a slice of sugar-soft sandy paradise reached by a 30-minute boat ride from Palma Rubia, northeast of Viñales. Swing in a hammock, snorkel and dive. The island's only hotel was closed post 2022's Hurricane Ian but should have reopened to visitors by the time you read this. Boats leave Palma Rubia (where there are a handful of *casas*) twice a day.

Cayo Jutías, roughly two hours from Viñales by car on a potholed road, is the preferred sliver of soft sand for those staying in Viñales. Reached by a causeway, a dazzling white

WHERE TO STAY AND EAT ON THE NORTHWEST COAST

Cayo Jutías Restaurant
Huge grilled lobster tails, fish and roast chicken are served in this rustic *ranchón*. **$**

Hotel Cayo Levisa
Smart, spacious bungalows with hammocks right on the beachfront are a great choice. **$$**

Casa Teresa Hernández Martínez
In the heart of Esperanza, Teresa welcomes with rooms and a *ranchón* offering fresh seafood. **$**

beach drops into the bluest, warmest sea. Jutías was rattled by Hurricane Ian, so the languid coconut palms that once framed the pretty beach are gone. Hire sun loungers and umbrellas, as well as kayaks, stand-up paddleboards (SUPs) and pedal boats from the water sports center. Walk or hire a boat to take you to the tip of the peninsula – which resembles a scene from a 1990s Bounty chocolate ad – where you'll find starfish in the shallows. Snorkel trips and a visit to offshore **Cayo Mégano** can be arranged, too.

Beachy Bliss in the Península de Guanahacabibes

DIVING, WILDLIFE AND SEA POOLS

Peppered with coconut palms, **María La Gorda Beach** is postcard-perfect. A three-hour drive from Viñales, the beach shelves into luminescent turquoise sea with a coral reef just offshore. Thatched *palapas* (palm shelters) and sun loungers dot the sand. Behind the dive hotel is a wooded patch with *cabañas,* a favorite with enormous iguanas. Most visitors come for the diving, as 32 dive spots curve around the Bahía de Corrientes. The **María La Gorda Hotel** is named after María the 'Fat Lady,' who serviced passing pirates, and it fringes some of the most beautiful sea in all of Cuba – pristine sapphire, indigo and turquoise waters. The 6km **Sendero El Tesoro de María** walk, replete with beautiful views, leaves from the hotel.

Kick back in off-piste **La Bajada**, a tiny community of around 150 people, with five *casas particulares* offering rooms facing the sea. Its gorgeous attraction is a beautiful sea pool, **Pozo de Juan Claro**. Find it in front of the military post. Snorkel in crystal-clear waters and spot colorful tropical fish, the odd barracuda and a cavern. Be sure to wear water shoes and be careful of those spiky black urchins.

At the **Estación Ecológica La Bajada**, compulsory guides can be arranged for walks into the Guanahacabibes Biosphere Reserve and a trip to Cuba's westernmost tip – **Cabo San Antonio**. Osmany is the most experienced guide, and it's best to get to the *estación* the day before to book a walk or tour, as the office closes at 3pm.

THE WILDLIFE OF GUANAHACABIBES

Unesco-protected **Guanahacabibes Biosphere Reserve** is home to unusual creatures great and small. In April, you'll witness the massive migration of red crabs from the forest to the sea (where they lay their eggs). In doing so, the crabs need to cross the park's main road. If you're driving during this spectacle, you have no option but to drive fast and commit a massacre. A slow crawl will mean the crab pincers, reared in fear, could puncture your tires.

You'll find endemic birds, Cuban rock iguanas, white-tailed deer, wild pigs and crocodiles here, and it's also an important area for honey production, with the bees collecting nectar from the local yellow mastics, copperwoods, palms and mangroves.

GETTING AROUND

If you don't have a car already, your best bet for transport to the more remote spots of the northwest coast is to ask at your hotel or *casa particular* for suggestions. Often someone knows (or is!) a driver, and they can get you where you need to go.

TRINIDAD

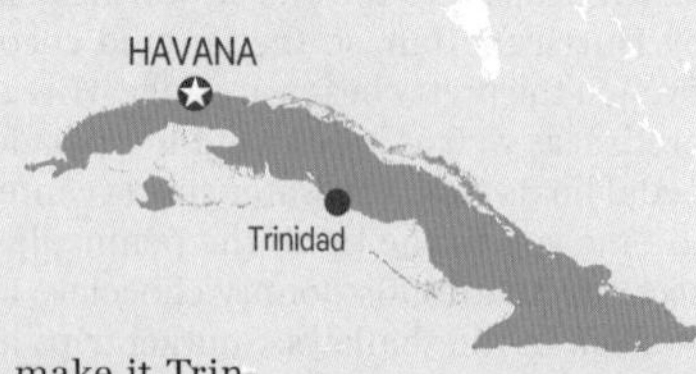

If you stop in just one town in central Cuba, make it Trinidad. It will charm, delight, surprise and leave you understanding a bit more about Cuba than you did before. One of the country's oldest towns, it depended on the sugarcane industry for much of its early history, and, interestingly, it was moved several times (from earlier locations near the ocean) to protect it from pirates. Today, its historical tapestry makes the town one of the most vibrant and diverse, rich in offerings for all who come here. The pubs and bars are full of an engaging mix of locals, Cuban tourists and foreigners, and you'll find music everywhere. In a way, it can be thought of as Cuba's New Orleans. Its food, historic architecture, cultural events and cobblestone streets are too beautiful to be believed. It's all here. Enjoy.

TOP TIP

Drivers will find that the maze of cobblestone alleys and one-way streets makes for challenging driving, and parking is tricky in the town center, so choose a hotel on the outskirts if you can, and then walk or take a tuk-tuk around the town to avoid hassle.

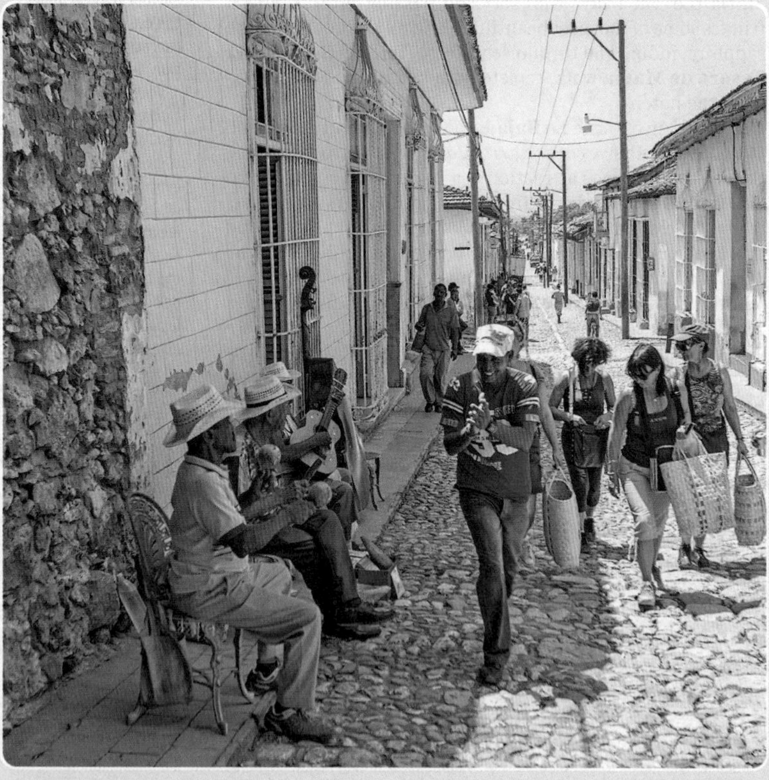

ROSTISLAV AGEEV/SHUTTERSTOCK ©

Street musicians, Trinidad

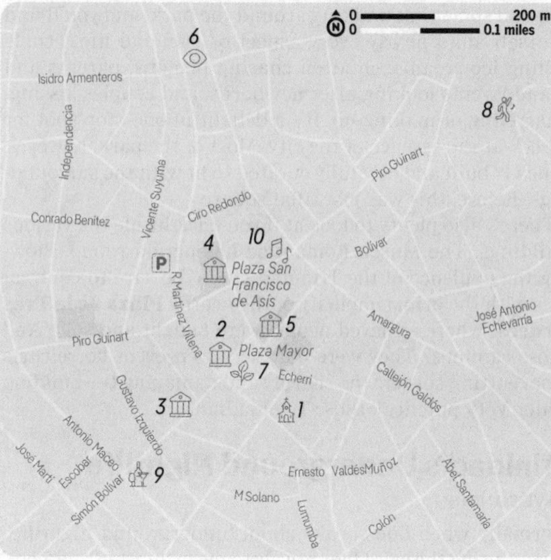

SIGHTS
1 Iglesia Parroquial de la Santísima Trinidad
2 Museo de Arqueología
3 Museo de Historia de Trinidad
4 Museo Nacional de la Lucha Contra Bandidos
5 Museo Romántico
6 Plaza de las Trés Cruces
7 Plaza Mayor

DRINKING & NIGHTLIFE
8 Disco Ayala
9 Muñoz Tapas

ENTERTAINMENT
10 La Botija

The Marvelous Plaza Mayor

HISTORY AND BEAUTY COMBINED

Trinidad's **Plaza Mayor** is the center of the town in more than just the geographic sense: this park used to be the main market, where everything was bought and sold. Look at a map and you'll see it sitting there like the hinge on a spread-out fan, with roads like vanes leading out to the town's fringes. There's beautiful historic buildings, paved stone streets and curiously upended cannons on street corners. (There's a reason for this!)

Stop for shade outside the humble **Iglesia Parroquial de la Santísima Trinidad** and you'll notice that it's rather plain – which is surprising for a church in a central plaza such as this one. Look closely and you'll see the twin towers on either side that were never finished. Other things to look out for are the ceramic upturned vases on the fenceposts that match those atop the nearby **Museo Romántico**.

BEST MUSEUMS IN TRINIDAD

Museo de Historia de Trinidad
A must-see stop with period carriages, furniture, decorations and photographs.

Museo de Archeología
Explore pottery, brass items and vases, and learn about the country's ancient cultures here.

Museo Nacional de la Lucha Contra Bandidos
The military and bandit history is underwhelming, but getting to climb the tower is the main reason to come here.

Museo Romántico
Once the private home of a wealthy merchant, this museum features 19th-century furniture, chandeliers, vases and tableware.

WHERE TO STAY IN TRINIDAD

Las Cuevas
A midrange option on a hill, with easy access to the plaza and Disco Ayala. **$$**

Iberostar
An all-inclusive, government-run spot with the usual amenities and decor. (Plastic money only, please!) **$$$**

Hostal Romero
A no-frills *casa particular* that's full of heart and will make you feel like family. **$**

Spend some time walking around the park, and you'll find yourself amid nearly every aspect of Trinidad life. People selling ice creams, children chasing pigeons, parents and grandparents looking after newborns, and couples kissing, quarreling or making up. It's a delightful one-stop spot for a peek at the essence of the city. Most of the park, however, is newly built and carefully curated to fit with the surroundings. Before, this was just a flat square.

There's also plenty to look at if you duck inside the various buildings. The Museo Romantico has period rooms showing the opulence of the Trinidad elite – be sure to contrast this with the grim simplicity of the nearby **Plaza de la Trés Cruces**, where enslaved people were bought and sold. And those cannons? They were put there to prevent horse carts from cutting corners too sharply and damaging the building walls. Very practical, those Trinidadians.

THE TASTY CANCHÁNCHARA

The *canchánchara* is both a drink and the vessel it's served in, which consists of a simple earthenware pot with smooth sides, usually only glazed on the inside. You can find these cups sold as souvenirs in shops throughout the city, but be wary of those that only use wax instead of glaze – if you want to drink from it, make sure it's the real thing. The drink comes as part of the country's legacy of slavery: alcohol, usually something landowners thought undrinkable, was given to the enslaved workers, who sweetened it to drinkability with honey, and added tartness with lime. Over time, the drink was recognized and assimilated into Cuban cuisine.

Trinidad's Underground Nightlife

CAVE DANCING

Normally when one speaks about 'underground nightlife,' they're using the word figuratively to mean 'hipster' and 'cool.' But here in Trinidad, you are literally underground: one of the town's biggest and best clubs is in a vast underground cavern known as the **Discoteca Ayala**. It's located up on a hill, away from the main plaza. A rather narrow doorway leads to a cave with numerous levels and chambers; some of them, like the main dance area, can fit hundreds of people. There's quieter sections, too, but this place mostly rocks to hip-hop and Latin pop tunes, with cheap drinks and beers sloshed around. With great DJs, performers and lightshows, it's about as surreal a party spot as it gets. Definitely go late, as it's only crickets chirping before midnight, but in the wee hours, it's packed.

A disturbing side note: the cave's name, 'Ayala,' comes from a gruesome series of serial killings committed by Trinidad resident Carlos Ayala at the end of the 19th century. Ayala used the cave to torture and kill his victims. Thankfully, there's plenty of other spots to drink and dance in Trinidad, so if you're claustrophobic, or just don't like dancing where a serial killer once lived, then try the beautiful terrace of **Muñoz Tapas** for cocktails, or catch live music at **La Botija**.

GETTING AROUND

Trinidad is well-served by buses from Havana and other parts of the country. You can get around best by foot, as it's a small town. But hop on a tuk-tuk if you need something with wheels. When it's running (which is hit or miss), a sightseeing train makes the route from Trinidad into the Valle de los Ingenios and back.

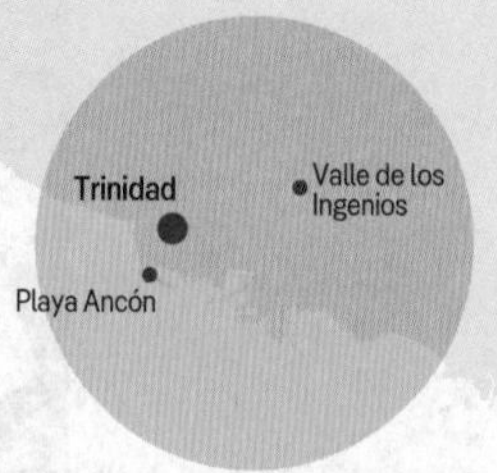

Beyond Trinidad

Beautiful beaches, intriguing historical valleys and some truly delightful national parks lie outside the bounds of Trinidad.

It doesn't really matter which direction you go from Trinidad: just spin the compass and you'll end up somewhere fun, beautiful or fascinating. There's nearby spots like the gorgeous Playa Ancón to the south, or the historic, pastoral beauty of the Valle de los Ingenios to the north, where you can learn about sugar and the haciendas that produced it, and see countless ruins and relics. Then there's the Gran Parque Natural Topes de Collante, to the west, where hikers, trekkers and waterfall-seekers will find plenty to occupy themselves. It's a region as rich as the town of Trinidad itself, and you'll want to be sure to give yourself time to explore it.

TOP TIP

Hikers should plan their routes well, especially if doing overnight trips. Count on *not* having reliable cell service on the trails.

Playa Ancón (p236)

CHRISTOPHES/SHUTTERSTOCK ©

Playa María Aguilar

BE AWESTRUCK AT THE MIRADOR

You don't even have to be in the Valle de los Ingenios to be amazed by it: just outside Trinidad, as the road climbs up in preparation for its plunge down into the valley, is a rest stop called **Mirador del Valle de los Ingenios**. Sure, it's a bit hokey, and there's everything from a pool table to a restaurant, and even a zip line there, so it's a bit of a tourist trap. But it's undeniably the best view you'll get of the valley as a whole, with its wide patchwork quilt of farms and fields, and the river snaking through. If you're really lucky, you might even see the tourist train chugging along down there somewhere.

Bask on the Beaches

SUN AND SAND SUBLIME

Trinidad is so close to **Playa Ancón** and its neighbor, **Playa María Aguilar**, that you can cycle to both beaches if you fancy some exercise. Both sandy shores sit on the south side of a long peninsula that is currently being developed, with lots of large hotels and more surely on the way. Of the two beaches, Playa Ancón is the more developed and has the looming Hotel Ancón behind it. It's thus less natural, but the facilities are better here, and it's easier to make a day of things, with good restaurants such as the **Ranchón Ancón**, and even a dive shop you can rely on, the **Cayo Blanco International Dive Center**. The smaller, less developed Playa María Aguilar will be the better choice for those who like their beach to be mostly beach, with a few palm-thatch umbrellas and a shack selling snacks, food and beverages. There aren't any dive shops or places to rent diving and snorkeling equipment, so you'll need to bring your own.

Both beaches offer sublime views of the Caribbean, with crystal-clear turquoise water and delightful crushed-coral sand. Look closely and you'll spot shells, pieces of gemstones and larger pieces of coral. Don a snorkeling mask and you'll be surrounded by an underwater wonderland of fish, corals and other marine life, with blessedly warm water and relatively mild currents. Be wary, however, of the conditions of the currents, as the weather may change quickly, especially in the rainy season. But a trip to these beaches will hit the spot just about any time of year.

GETTING AROUND

Bicycles make good sense if you're staying in the beach areas of Playa Ancón and Playa María Aguilar. Otherwise, you'll likely want to have private transportation for the Gran Parque Natural Topes de Collante to get the most out of being there. If you need a taxi, try bargaining for a decent full-day rate rather than a one-way or wait-and-return fare.

HAVANA
Cayo Guillermo

CAYO GUILLERMO

Ernest Hemingway believed the island of Cayo Guillermo to have the best beaches on the planet, and you might nod in agreement when you get here. Part of a long string of islands called the Jardines del Rey ('King's Garden'), they are certainly second to none in Cuba. There's just nothing that matches the vibrancy and beauty of the sea here, and its dappled shades run from minty milk all the way to bluish ebony. You'll see windsurfers and foils skimming over the surface and hear grackles and orioles chirping in the coconut palms. The powdery white sand beckons – no, insists! – that you take off your shoes and let your bare feet stay for a while. The all-inclusive resorts offer just about anything a visitor could need, but even if you only zip up for a peek from the mainland, you'll be wowed and want to stay.

TOP TIP

Watch out for thieves while you're on the beaches or eating a meal – and no, not the human kind. Grackles and orioles will audaciously head for anything you leave unattended, so try to make sure your smaller items are in zippered pockets. And if you're eating food, don't leave it unattended or the birds will get it.

TUPUNGATO/SHUTTERSTOCK ©

Cayo Guillermo

A LOST CAUSE...WAY

Those flying into Jardines del Rey Airport on nearby Cayo Coco may not ever see the causeway that connects the keys to the mainland, as most visitors park themselves on the beach and stay there until they fly home. The causeway was built in 1986, at great cost and environmental expense: unsurprisingly, putting a long dam across a tidal plain resulted in a change to its drainage patterns and salinity. This has caused some changes in the birdlife here, especially the flamingos – experts say aren't coming in the same numbers that they used to. To mitigate this to some degree, tunnels were added after the dam's construction, allowing more water to flow beneath the structure.

Beachy Keen

HEMINGWAY'S BEACH

The beaches of **Cayo Guillermo** are so sublime they're almost mythical. This is the place Ernest Hemingway loved and vacationed to so often that the entrance bridge there has not one, not two, but three life-sized statues of the man. The water here almost defies description. At times it's bathwater temperature, almost hot; other times, it's warm but refreshing. You can wade out for a long time and not get deeper than your waist, but for many the magic lies in the pillow-soft sand. If you get bored, or a cloud passes by, you can get just about everything your heart desires at whichever all-inclusive you have chosen: massages, cocktails, beach gear, clothing...it's all mere steps away.

If you come here on a visit from the mainland, you won't have access to the all-inclusive sections, but **Playa Pilar** is just as good. It's at the westernmost tip and has wooden walkways that lead over the barrier dune to the beach. **Playa Pilar Restaurant** serves mostly fried fish platters and other seafood, as brazen flocks of grackles wait to pounce on leftovers. There's a bar where you can get mojitos or a scooped-out pineapple filled with your favorite liquor-laden beverage. Hemingway may have had his faults, but you'll agree he was right about this place.

GETTING AROUND

Cayo Coco (the island next door) has its own airport – Jardines del Rey – so folks often just fly here directly and then use a taxi service to get to Cayo Guillermo and travel round the island. If you decide to drive, there's not much parking that's for non-all-inclusive customers, so be aware of this. However, access from the mainland is easy thanks to the causeway.

Beyond Cayo Guillermo

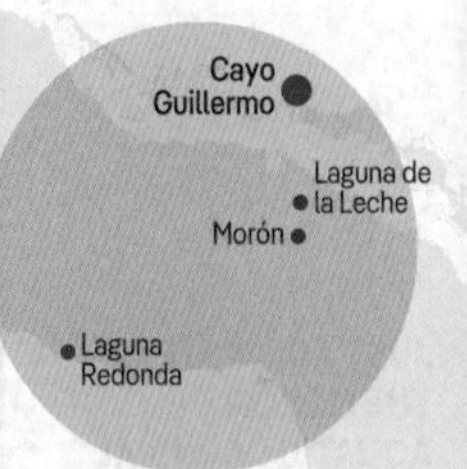

Beautiful lagoons, vast shallow bays and scruffy mainland all make this a fun place to daytrip, overnight or enjoy a long explore.

Whether you're staying in one of the all-inclusives or coming up from cities like Ciego de Ávila, the region around the 'Cayos' is a fun place to check out. Bird-watchers will be in heaven, as the diversity of habitats means you'll potentially see dozens, possibly even hundreds, of different species. But there's also small-town life, beautiful vistas and interesting natural wonders, all within a relatively small radius. Check out festivals, stop in at ranches where it seems like time stopped a century ago, or just road-trip around and see part of the real Cuba that's starkly different from life on the keys. It really can seem like a different world once you leave the all-inclusives behind.

TOP TIP

Rather than slather on the bug cream or sprays, pack some repellent-infused clothing and never look back.

Ciego de Ávila

JUST ADD WATER: THE MORÓN AQUATIC CARNIVAL

If you want to see floats that are actually floating, come to the **Morón Aquatic Carnival**, held each year in September. It's a gala affair, with all the usual fun of a Cuban fiesta, held on, in and around the beautiful Laguna de la Leche. There's less of the showiness and grandeur of the carnivals on land (in truth, some of the floats look a bit rickety), but it's lots of fun nonetheless, with food, dancing, costumes, contests and of course, lots of *musica en vivo* (live music) and dancing. The event usually ends the summer, closing out events that are often sponsored (as are many of the floats) by the biggie hotels across on the keys.

Neoclassical architecture, Morón

Get Festive in Teeny Morón

A TRAVEL STOP AND MORE

Also known by the 'cocky' name 'Ciudad del Gallo' (City of the Rooster), the railway-stop city of **Morón**, about an hour's drive from Cayo Guillermo, has a lot of beautiful architecture that, if you've been in Cuba long enough, you may be yawning at. But for those coming from the Cayos to the north, it's your first and possibly only chance to really see the colonial architecture of these beautiful towns. Unmissable is the massive – and beautiful – **Terminal de Ferrocarriles**, Morón's train station. The exterior has the look and feel of a historic European train depot, with large balconies and an iron awning. Inside, the simple wooden benches and multiple murals (one of a rooster, reflecting the town's nickname) make for a fun visit. There's also beautiful stained glass, if you look up. Sure to vanish at some time, you can even still find, in a small nook, a dusty, forlorn pay phone, aptly named 'Telefono.'

Other city delights are the history museum – the **Museo Caonabo** – a beautiful neoclassical building built in 1919 that

PLACES TO STAY AND EAT IN MORÓN

La Casona de Morón
An historic yellow and white hotel with simple rooms and a nice shaded pool. **$$**

Alojamiento Vista al Parque
A sweet *casa particular* with three rooms in a colorful house. Breakfast is across the street. **$**

Restaurante Maité La Qbana
Definitely the spot to come if you're in Morón, with great cocktails, appetizers and paella. **$$**

was once a bank. Inside, you'll find excellent exhibits on archaeology not just from the local area but also from as far away as Mexico and Peru. There's also a Cuban history exhibits of swords, machinery, farm equipment and more. The explanations are in Spanish but often they are short, and many items are easy to understand on their own – no language needed.

Also unmissable is the **Central Azucarero Patria**, a vast and decaying sugar hacienda that's just a few kilometers outside the town. Here, you can learn about the lives of the many enslaved workers who worked here and learn about the process of milling sugar. There's also a train ride you can take, which makes this a fun detour for those with kids.

Not Just Spilled Milk

AS IF SPILLED FROM SPACE

The **Laguna de la Leche**, an hour by car from Cayo Guillermo, translates to 'Milk Lagoon,' and the moment you see it, you'll know why: instead of the turquoise of the surrounding waters, this one lagoon has an opaque, milky color to it. It's as if someone spilled a vast quantity of cow juice into the sea. The lagoon is a Cuban national park, and the color comes not from anything human-made, but from the water mixing with the white limestone sediments of the lake floor. Its uniqueness doesn't end there, however: it's also the largest of Cuba's natural lakes (the bigger ones are all human-made reservoirs). And it's a brackish lake, meaning the water is a mixture of salt and *agua dulce* (freshwater).

The lake is a key fishing destination, where anglers come from around the world to try catch some of Cuba's prize species, including tarpon, tilapia and perch. These trips can be organized from nearby Morón, or sometimes at the park entrance. Most fishing is catch-and-release, but depending on the species and the facilities of the guide, you may be able to have it for dinner. Not far from the lake's marshy southeastern side is a crocodile breeding station, where the reptiles can be viewed. This may also be your only chance to get up and close to a *hutia,* the adorable Cuban 'tree rat.'

TOUR & FISH IN LAGUNA REDONDA

Believe it or not, the tiny **Laguna Redonda**, at only 4 sq km, is Cuba's premier bass and trout destination. So if you're an angler, plan on bringing that rod. You can do four-hour fishing trips (or longer, if you like) and take boats through the narrow, mangrove-lined canals that connect up (in places) with the nearby Laguna de la Leche. It's an almost jungle-like journey, and exciting catches await if you drop a lure. Even if you're not into fishing, there's a decent bar and restaurant where you can hang out...and one could do worse than have a beer with such a pretty view.

GETTING AROUND

The closest airport to fly into is Jardines del Rey, back on Cayo Coco. Morón and Laguna de la Leche can be reached either by tour from the keys or from the mainland by bus. There's even train service into Morón from other mainland destinations. If you're based in the Cayos, you'll access these places via the causeway. Sometimes there's a toll to pass; sometimes it's out of order and you can just drive through.

SANTA CLARA

Santa Clara is at once stately and gritty, grandiose and humble, lofty and practical. It's always been a key hub of Cuba, but it gained increasing importance and stature in 1958 when Che Guevara and his small band of revolutionaries liberated the city from Batista control. The event was akin to pouring gasoline on a fire. It gave hope that the Fidel Castro movement would – as it indeed did –succeed. Today, many parts of the city pay homage to Che and *La Revolucíon,* and some buildings still show the battle scars. But there's more here than just history: it's also a vibrant arty place and has an established LGBTIQ+ community, and many of its restaurants and cafes are top-notch, rivaling anything in Havana. It's also got a grittier side: touts here are more aggressive than in some places, and tourist vehicles may be damaged if left unattended.

TOP TIP

If you're driving, be wary of parking in the main plaza (or anywhere not in a privately owned lot). Santa Clara is famous for its 'helpful' locals who point out a punctured tire (that they've just punctured) and then try to extort money from the unsuspecting victim to fix it.

GIOIA PHOTO/SHUTTERSTOCK ©

Plaza de la Revolución Che Guevara

AN EAGLE'S VIEW FROM CAPIRO'S HILL

Often included in a city 'Che' tour, **El Mirador** (also known as Loma de Capiro) is a delightful lookout point over the city, but definitely not ideal for those who haven't been on the treadmill in a while: the spot has over 300 steps to climb before you reach the top. Once there, enjoy the monument that looks a bit like an alien spaceship radio – look closely and you'll see Che's face there – and gorgeous 360-degree views of the city. This was a vital, strategic spot for the revolution, as it offered a clear vantage point of every spot in the city. The trenches used by Che and his guerrillas are still visible.

Ernesto 'Che' Guevara is Alive & Well

AN ENIGMATIC REVOLUTIONARY ICON

The Che Guevara–Santa Clara connection runs deep. Some feel the taking of Santa Clara was the single most decisive victory in the entire revolution. Once the city had been liberated from Batista, he fled the country and the war was essentially won. So it's little wonder that the city takes great pride in celebrating its place in Cuban history. If you need convincing, head to the impressive **Plaza de la Revolución Che Guevara**. The square contains a massive monument topped with an imposing statue of the man in his later years, dressed in his beret and fatigues, rifle in hand, and a thick, grizzled beard covering his face.

Be sure to cross behind the statue to the somber mausoleum, with its 38 niches carved to honor valiant guerrillas who lost their lives fighting in Bolivia's failed revolution (where Che was killed). In 1997, his remains and those of 16 others were repatriated here from a secret Bolivian mass grave. Fidel Castro himself lit the eternal flame that burns here in their memory.

From here, duck into the small museum. There are photos, memorabilia and much propaganda to see, but most visitors will find it a bit underwhelming. You're not allowed to take photos, and all backpacks and even cell phones have to be left in a guarded area outside while you tour the modest museum.

GETTING AROUND

Santa Clara is a major stop for most cross-country bus routes, so getting here by bus (or, when it's running, by train) is relatively easy. In town, numerous tuk-tuks and horse-and-carts can get you around the sights. Drivers, be sure to use paid parking instead of street parking, especially around the Plaza Vidal area, as deliberate tire punctures are a common scam.

Beyond Santa Clara

Sagua La Grande
Remedios
Santa Clara
Embalse Hanabanilla

This rich region has a lot to offer those who choose to explore it, including hikes, waterfalls, trails, lakes and villages.

Beyond Santa Clara is the province of Villa Clara, which has all kinds of things to do and see, many of them unique to the region. Find hidden waterfalls, catch bucket-list fish, hike to the top of mountains and survey the world below...the possible day trips and overnights are almost limitless. Further afield, myriad mangrove hammocks and keys make for spectacular wildlife and bird spotting. You can also settle down in a quiet village and experience Cuban life with a luxury that only comes from being away from it all. As is the case everywhere in Cuba, the people are welcoming and excited to share their part of the country.

TOP TIP

There's a lot to see here, and the best way to take it all in is by having a private vehicle, either self-driven or with a driver.

Embalse Hanabanilla

ALEXANDRE LAPRISE/SHUTTERSTOCK ©

Waterfall, Hanabanilla

The Enchanting Embalse Hanabanilla

WATER FUN FOR EVERYONE

The **Embalse Hanabanilla**, a 90-minute drive from Santa Clara, is a top fishing destination, with record-setting bass lurking in the myriad roots, shelves, submerged trees, stumps and other watery hideouts that fish – and fisherfolk – so dearly love. It's a pretty spot, even if you're not goin' fishing: the water is a pleasant green, matching the verdant hills that surround it, and there's rocky outcrops and cliffs that make for scenic backdrops, and even a few uninhabited islands as well. One of the biggest attractions is the *salto* (waterfall), where you can strip and dip in the refreshing spray as it tumbles over the rocks. Look for turtles, pelicans and other critters as you tour around.

You can hire boats for a variety of excursions from the **Hotel Hanabanilla**, which is on the northwestern shore, and there's a good chance you'll be the only tourist on the 'pond,' as somehow, this beautiful spot still remains mostly untouristed. There aren't a lot of hotel options here, and if noise isn't your thing, you may want to avoid staying at the Hanabanilla, which caters more to those looking to have a pool party than those looking for calm and tranquility. But *casas particulares* can offer quieter accommodations, or you can visit the Embalse Hanabanilla as a day trip, even from Santa Clara if you leave early enough in the morning.

The really intrepid may want to hire a guide (ask at the Hotel Hanabanilla) and hike from here across the mountains of the **Sierra del Escambray**, arriving in a few days at **El Nicho**, a lovely series of waterfalls surrounded by lush greenery.

GO WILD IN REMEDIOS

Remedios is a calm, tranquil spot that is off the tourist map for most of the year, and (we'll be honest) pretty boring. But come Christmas, all the stops are pulled out for a festival that's one of the area's most spectacular: **Las Parrandas**, which features a mock 'battle' of competing floats, a massive fireworks display and multiple events and parades. You'll need to plan ahead if you want accommodations, as options fill up months in advance.

In addition to the festival, the town is noted for the two churches on its main plaza – the only city in all of Cuba to have more than one.

WHERE TO STAY IN SANTA CLARA

Hotel Hanabanilla
Noisy for some, but a perfect one-stop-shop for anyone wanting to stay lakeside. **$$**

Hotel America
A Santa Clara option with inexpensive rooms and excellent access to the town square. **$**

Villa Las Brujas
A smaller government-run spot directly overlooking the water, with a white-sand beach just steps away. **$$$**

POSSOHH/SHUTTERSTOCK ©

Sagua La Grande

BEST SPOTS IN SAGUA LA GRANDE

Iglesia de Purisima
The church predates the town's incorporation, though it's been rebuilt four times.

Hotel Sagua
A beautiful four-story structure with restored grandeur and loads of elegance. If you can't stay here, at least take a peek inside.

Puente El Triunfo
A lovely, photogenic iron truss bridge that spans the Sagua River on the northeast side of town.

Café Real
One of the town's few nexus points for chatting over a good cup of coffee.

Stop Over in Sagua La Grande

A SLEEPY, GLORIOUS SUGAR TOWN

You can't get much further off the mainstream map than a visit to **Sagua La Grande**, a languid sugar town that really hasn't seen much action since the 1930s, when the sugar industry here began to slow down. An eponymous river winds through it, making for some pretty vistas and photo ops, but it's remote enough that you can't even get here by bus, it's that far off the regular beaten path.

But what this means for the discriminating traveler is a real chance to spend time in a spot where you'll get to know the place, enjoy the people and perhaps not want to leave. It's also possible that as the northern keys are developed, this quietude may fade as the focus moves northward and the town becomes a stopping point along the way. But for now, it's a treasure: tall buildings with beautiful decorated facades, ornate towers on the churches and a relaxed pace that makes it seem as if time itself has slowed. You can stay in the **Hotel Sagua** and be wowed by restored marble, beautiful velvet curtains and an elegance that gives you a sense of a different Cuba, long ago. Atmospheric street lamps line the avenues, illuminating the excitement (or lack thereof) that's happening in the streets below. If you're this far, it's worth continuing on (or taking a day trip) to **Isabela de Sagua**, known as the 'Venice of Cuba' for its docks and waterways that extend into the vast lagoon of Cuba's north coast.

GETTING AROUND

If you're coming from Havana or Santa Clara, you'll likely already have a car and will need it if you want to fully explore this region. If you fly into Cayo Las Brujas Airport, both CubaCar and Via Rentacar have offices on the nearby keys.

SANTIAGO DE CUBA

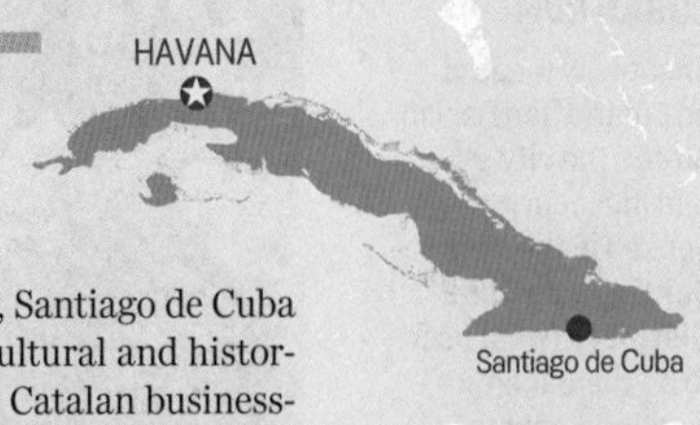

Cuba's former capital, and now its second city, Santiago de Cuba is where many of the nation's most defining cultural and historical movements exploded into action. In 1862, Catalan businessman Facundo Bacardí purchased a small, bat-infested distillery in the city and began to develop a pioneering, high-quality rum that changed the industry forever. On July 26, 1953, a young Fidel and Raúl Castro led a surprise attack on Santiago's Moncada Barracks, an event widely regarded as the turning point of the Cuban Revolution. Although the attack failed, Fidel's famous speech, 'History Will Absolve Me,' which he delivered during his trial, became the revolution's manifesto and had a transformative impact on the Cuban people. Musically, Santiago de Cuba is the birthplace of many of Cuba's most important genres: *son*, *trova* and even Cuban reggaeton. It's a fiery furnace of history, music and culture, with an entirely different vibe from the current capital, Havana.

TOP TIP

It pays to be streetwise in Santiago. The city has a dodgy reputation, especially during big events like Carnaval in July. Keep your possessions out of sight and be careful of pickpockets.

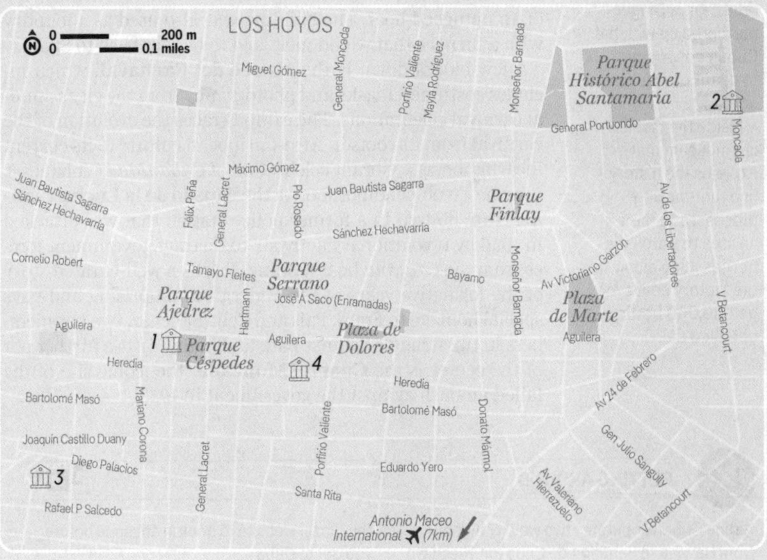

SIGHTS
1 Casa de Diego Velazquez
2 Cuartel Moncada
3 Museo de la Lucha Clandestina
4 Museo del Carnaval

THE POLEMIC HISTORY OF CUBAN RUM

Previously located on centric San Basilio Street, the city's rum museum is now housed in the **Ron Santiago de Cuba Distillery** (what used to be the Bacardí distillery) next to the Hatuey Brewery (also formerly owned by Bacardí). After 1959, the Castro government nationalized the Bacardí company, forcing the family to leave and establish a new HQ in Bermuda. The state controversially renamed the brand Ron Santiago de Cuba. In 2019, the drinks giant Diageo partnered up with the Cuban government to distribute the rum abroad.

Inside the distillery is a museum that explains the history and rum-making process, and there's an area to watch the bottles glide along the factory conveyor belt (10,000 bottles get filled daily).

HEMIS/ALAMY ©

Carnaval preparations, Santiago de Cuba

The Cradle of Revolution

SANTIAGO'S HISTORICAL SITES

From its early days as the capital to its vital role in the revolution, Santiago is rich with history. Just off Parque Céspedes, the beautiful **Casa de Diego Velazquez** is the oldest house in Cuba. Belonging to the Spanish conquistador who founded the city in 1515, the house is a classic example of Spanish colonial architecture with two floors, high ceilings and a wooden roof in the shape of an upturned boat. The building was also used as a foundry with a furnace that would melt gold to be sent back to Spain.

A few blocks down is the **Museo del Carnaval**, which includes costumes, masks and photography from the city's annual carnival celebrations. The exhibit traces the evolution of the carnival from its roots in Afro-Caribbean culture to its current incarnation as a vibrant celebration of *Cubanidad* (Cubaness).

In the Tívoli neighborhood is the **Museo de la Lucha Clandestina**, housed in a former police station that was attacked in 1956 by revolutionary activists to distract government forces from the *Granma* boat landing. It tells a well-curated story of the formative years of the underground uprising and pays special homage to Frank País and Celia Sánchez, two key members in the struggle against Batista. Finally, a little further out of the center is the **Cuartel Moncada**, the iconic site of the failed ambush against the government in 1953.

GETTING AROUND

Airline Cubana operates two weekly flights from Havana to Santiago de Cuba (on Tuesdays and Fridays) for around US$150 each way. Alternatively, get the Viazul bus, which starts in Havana and makes its way down past each central and eastern province. There are three daily buses that take between 15 and 20 hours, depending on the number of stops, and they cost approximately US$58 one way. Head to the Viazul website to book in advance before you get to Cuba.

Known as the city of motorbikes, hundreds can be seen zipping through Santiago's colonial streets. If you stand on a street corner and put your hand out, a moto-taxi is sure to offer you a lift. Be aware that this is not the most formal way of getting around – pay a few dollars maximum to anywhere in and around the city center.

Beyond Santiago de Cuba

Take a rest from the intensity of the city and delve deeper into Cuba's most Caribbean province.

While the city of Santiago de Cuba has more than enough to keep you occupied when it comes to bars, restaurants, museums and music, the heat and hustle can get a little stifling. Beyond the city limits, there are several day trips and excursions that showcase the religious, historical and geographical richness of the wider province of Santiago de Cuba. Visit strange rock formations at La Gran Piedra, or explore other parts of the beautiful Bacanao Biosphere Reserve. On the way, stop at a beautiful botanical garden, the aptly named Jardín Ave del Paraíso. Alternatively, make a pilgrimage up to Cuba's most venerated church, El Cobre, and marvel at its bizarre offerings, including stethoscopes and military badges.

TOP TIP

To organize these excursions, seek assistance from the host at your accommodations, or head to the Cubatur office in Santiago de Cuba.

La Gran Piedra (p251)

THE STORY OF CACHITA

In 1612, three young fishermen were caught in a fierce sea storm and miraculously survived after praying to the Virgin Mary. When the storm passed, they found floating in the water a small statue attached to a board that read 'I am the Virgin of Charity.' The statue was brought back to shore and the Virgin, affectionately known as **Cachita**, has become a defining Cuban symbol of salvation in times of turbulence. It is common practice to take a stone with flecks of copper from the Basilica of El Cobre grounds, as it's said to protect you.

Our Lady of Charity is also linked to the Afro-Cuban deity Oshún, who is represented by the color yellow and sunflowers.

MOVIEPRO.NL/SHUTTERSTOCK ©

La Basílica del Cobre

Cuba's Greatest Pilgrimage

SUNFLOWERS AND STATUES

Driving toward the copper mining town of **El Cobre**, about 30 minutes from Santiago de Cuba, a church perched atop a hill appears on the horizon like an enchanting fairy-tale castle. This is **La Basílica del Cobre**, one of the most significant sites in Cuba, and a place of pilgrimage for Cubans from far and wide. The church is dedicated to the Virgin of Charity, the patron saint of the nation. Coming into the town, the sidewalks are lined with ornate religious trinkets and giant bunches of bright yellow sunflowers for pilgrims to purchase and give as offerings. The church's exterior is a beautiful example of neobaroque architecture, and its interior is full of religious decorations, artifacts and curiosities.

In one corner lies an eccentric assortment of crutches, tangled stethoscopes, piles of university diplomas and army badges. These are offerings left by churchgoers over the years, believing that the Virgin helped cure their ailments, pass their exams or keep them safe in times of danger. The main attraction is the small-yet-striking statue of the Virgin of Charity,

WHERE TO EAT IN SANTIAGO DE CUBA

Roy's Terrace Inn
This *casa* welcomes guests to come and dine on their romantic terrace. **$**

St. Pauli
A bar, restaurant and nightclub just off Plaza Marte that attracts a young Cuban crowd. **$**

El Madrileño
An outdoor restaurant in Vista Alegre with Spanish-themed décor; order the *tostones rellenos*. **$**

who floats high up in her golden glory in a glass case at the front of the church. Cubans wearing yellow T-shirts and dresses with sunflower designs (symbols associated with the saint) sit solemnly in front of the statue, praying for miracles or giving thanks to the Virgin for prayers that were answered. Whether you are religious or not, it is impossible to deny the church's magnetism and spine-tingling energy – a feeling that you are indeed on hallowed ground.

The Rock at the Top

SANTIAGO'S BEST VIEW

With the pretty self-explanatory name of 'the Big Rock,' **La Gran Piedra** is a curious natural landmark an hour from Santiago de Cuba (p247), in the **Bacanao Biosphere Reserve**. For some, this is just another rock, but for anyone with an interest in geology, it may be the highlight of a visit to this area of Cuba. And the reserve itself is worthy of exploration, with birds, butterflies, insects and reptiles waiting to be spotted. So bring those binoculars!

The site is home to a colossal volcanic boulder that is over 50m long and weighs around 63,000 tons. It is said to have been formed millions of years ago, most likely from the eruption of magma from an underground volcano that rose to the surface and cooled into granite. To get to the rock, you must first drive on a series of very steep and windy mountain roads. Around halfway up, the climate becomes instantly cooler and fresher, a welcome respite from the cruel Santiago sun felt all too keenly below. Once at the base, climb 459 steps through prehistoric-like ferns (of which there are over 200 species) to the top of the rock. At 1214m above sea level, the view is quite spectacular, as mountains, valleys, countryside, city and sea are all laid out in front of you, though some will roll their eyes and quibble at the rather unattractive lookout tower with radio antennas poking off it. At nighttime, you can even see the lights of Jamaica glowing in the distance.

THE GARDEN OF PARADISE

On the way up or down from La Gran Piedra, take a detour to the **Jardín Ave del Paraíso**, which is built on top of the ruins of an old coffee plantation, 'La Siberia.' This botanical garden is filled with highly fragrant flowers, such as the colonia plant, which smells like cologne, and the gardenia's sweet and creamy aroma not dissimilar to jasmine.

While the garden has many plants you would expect to find in tropical Cuba, the former French owners introduced species from around the world – including peach trees, forget-me-nots and fennel – that thrive in the cool climate.

The gardeners also tell of the black roses that grew here before Hurricane Sandy wiped them out.

GETTING AROUND

The regions beyond Santiago de Cuba are marked by roads that can vary from pretty good to pretty damn terrible, with driving often the easiest and most convenient way to access remote sites. Buses – especially now, with gas shortages – are infrequent and often unreliable, so use your own judgment about which transportation methods will give you the most value.

YANDORY FERNANDEZ/GETTY IMAGES ©

Arriving

Most travelers arrive by air, but cruise ships may – depending on the politics – be another way to enter the country. There are currently 10 international airports sprinkled throughout the country. Expect waits if you come in high season (from November to February). Weather conditions also change frequently and can affect flights.

By Air

Cuba's international airports are distributed around the country. José Marti (pictured) is the busiest, so consider an alternative if you're not spending time in Havana. If your budget allows, enter through one airport and leave from another, allowing you to travel one-way through the country.

By Boat

At the time of research, cruise ships are not coming to Cuba because the American embargo prohibits American citizens from entering Cuba as tourists (with a few exceptions). If the embargo lifts or the political mood changes, they may start running again.

Money

Currency: Cuban peso (CUP$, MN$)

CASH

Cash is king in Cuba, and you may find yourself walking around with shopping bags of it. It's common (and comical, and also a shame) to have lunch and spend as much time counting out the bills to pay for your sandwich as it took to eat the meal. In many places, credit cards don't work, so plan on always having plenty of cash on hand. However, though cash is king most of the time, some government-owned establishments do not accept it.

DIGITAL PAYMENTS

Very few places in Cuba accept digital payments. Don't plan on using them.

CREDIT CARDS

American-issued credit cards will not work in Cuba for any kind of purchases; however, if you're not American, the resort areas, tourist bars, good hotels and high-end restaurants will accept them. In some government-run places, cash is not accepted at all, so you must pay with a credit card...making things very inconvenient for Americans.

Getting Around

Getting around Cuba is relatively easy, as a good long-distance bus system can mostly get you where you want to go, and if you're driving, the roads are decent. Currently, flying in is the best option, as cruise ships are not allowed to stop here for now. Fuel shortages have made travel within the country a bit tricky, so be prepared for hiccups.

PUBLIC TRANSPORT

Excellent, comfy, cost-effective, long-distance bus services can get you around the island's major cities. Buses may be full, and some may not run, but on the whole, they're reliable – especially if you've made an advance reservation online. The biggest issue, however, is scheduling.

KAMIRA/SHUTTERSTOCK ©

CAR

Cuba boasts wide highways, little traffic, no speed bumps and generally courteous, polite drivers – all which makes renting attractive, if expensive. The trickiest part is actually getting a rental car, as they are hard to book and reservations are often canceled.

TAXI/RIDESHARE

Taxis are plentiful, as are tuk-tuks, which in Havana are known as Cocotaxis due to their yellow, round shape that resembles a – you guessed it – coconut. As always, it's good to agree on the fare before heading off to avoid misunderstandings.

BOAT

Cubans are not allowed to have private boats, except under very special circumstances, so there's very little boat traffic in and out of the country. And at the moment, cruise ships are (yet again) prohibited from stopping in Cuba.

AIR

Air travel means you can zip quickly from one side of the island to the other, but it's not always reliable and can be very dependent on weather conditions. Especially during the hurricane season, expect long delays and cancellations.

DRIVING ESSENTIALS

Drive on the right side.

You do not need an international driver's license to rent a vehicle in Cuba.

Because of fuel shortages, always stop for gas, even if the tank is nearly full.

WESTEND61/GETTY IMAGES ©

Above: Trafalgar Falls (p264); Right: Portsmouth (p273)

DOMINICA

THE UNSPOILED NATURE ISLE

Natural hot springs, crisp air, volcanic landscapes and green-blanketed mountains make the Caribbean's 'Nature Isle' the ultimate destination to unwind.

If you're looking for archetypal idyllic Caribbean beaches with long strands of golden sand caressing cerulean seas, Dominica will surprise you. The 'Nature Isle' is a mélange of untamed tropical rainforests, imposing mountains, black-sand beaches and geothermal phenomena.

Boiling Lake is a volcanic crater with bubbling hot water cradled inside Morne Trois Pitons National Park and is among Dominica's most distinctive features. A trip to the island wouldn't be complete without witnessing this geological marvel – the world's second-largest hot spring and a reminder of the island's volcanic origins. Dominica is loaded with exhilarating activities and tranquil spots to soak up some sun, including countless cascading waterfalls, natural pools and hot springs.

The heavily forested island features an absurd number of rivers – one for every day of the year. The Indian River is the widest and flows through the *Pirates of the Caribbean* films. Another showstopper is the 115-mile-long Waitukubuli National Trail, which winds through coastal towns, mountain ranges and dense rainforest along Dominica's entire length. The island also shelters many endangered species, including the Sisserou parrot, its national bird.

Dominica has an intoxicatingly easygoing atmosphere, making it the ideal destination for unplugging and unwinding. While you won't find infinite white-sand beaches, it's the dramatic gorges, seemingly endless rivers, gushing waterfalls and shockingly verdant foliage that will take your breath away.

THE MAIN AREAS

ROSEAU
The picturesque and verdant capital. **p260**

NORTHEASTERN COAST
A rugged yet idyllic wilderness. **p265**

MORNE TROIS PITONS NATIONAL PARK
An adventurer's wonderland. **p269**

SOUFRIÈRE BAY
A charming coastal village. **p271**

PORTSMOUTH
A serene and charismatic town. **p273**

Find Your Way

Dominica's coastline is fringed with dramatic cliffs, an overflow of vegetation and deep gorges, characterized by winding, steep roads that necessitate cautious driving.

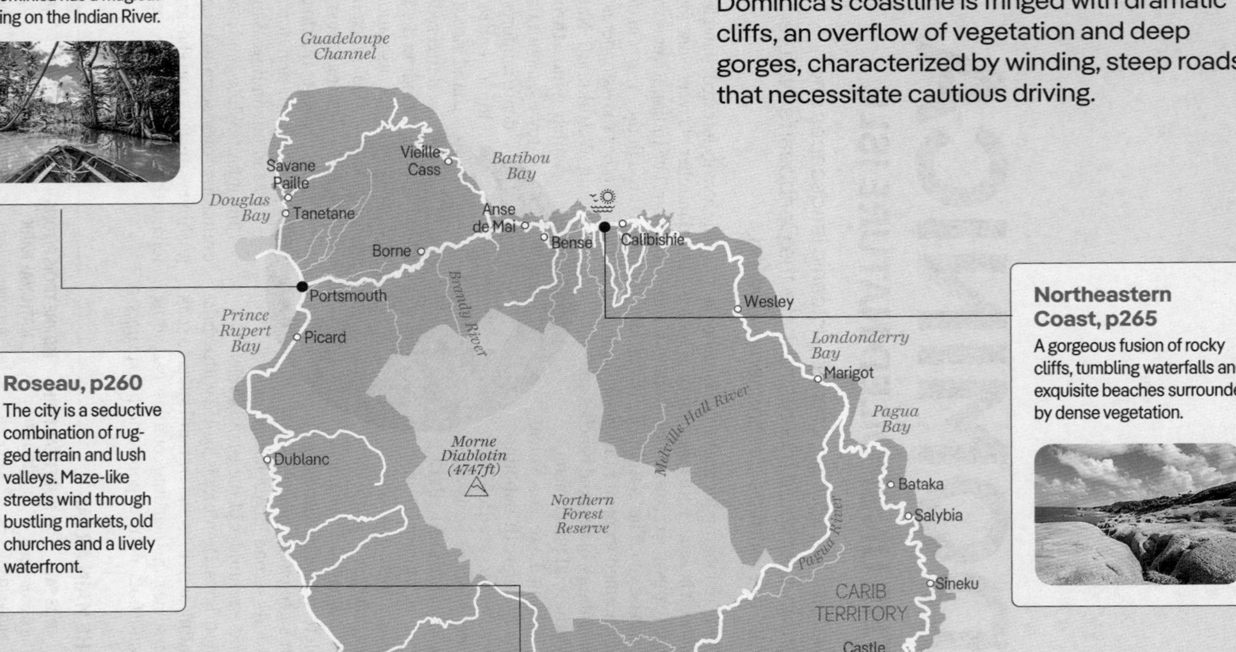

CAR

Numerous car rental agencies are on the island but you must obtain a local driver's license, which costs EC$30 (US$12). You must be between 25 and 65 years old, with two years of driving experience, to qualify for a permit.

TAXI

Taxis are available from the airport and Roseau to all over the island. They're identified by H, HA or HB before registration numbers on license plates. Call ahead to book past sunset, as taxis can be difficult to find at night.

BUS

Dominica's public transportation system consists of private minibus drivers. All routes originate in Roseau, with bus stops at specific locations throughout the city. Look for the H or HA license plate. The standard bus fares range from EC$1.50 to EC$10.25.

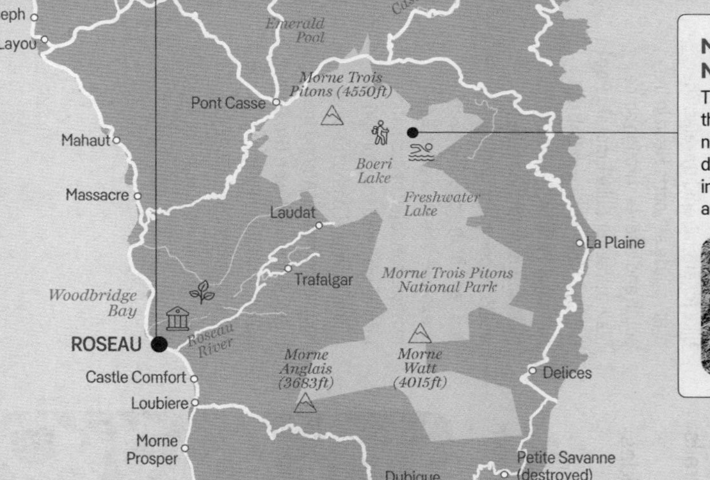

Morne Trois Pitons National Park, p269

p269

The volcano dominates the jagged landscape, and numerous hiking trails take daring travelers through an incredible tapestry of flora and fauna.

Soufrière Bay, p271

The village's untamed vista, dotted with volcanic hot springs and gurgling mud pools, provides a glimpse into the island's geologic past.

FROM TOP LEFT: DEREK D. GALON/SHUTTERSTOCK ©, DAVE PRIMOV/SHUTTERSTOCK ©, RAFAL MICHAL GADOMSKI/SHUTTERSTOCK ©, TRAVELOSKOP/SHUTTERSTOCK ©

Plan Your Time

From hiking on demanding trails to snorkeling in translucent waters, this pure jewel provides an array of exhilarating experiences for daring visitors. Relax in secluded bays and savor the peace of this Caribbean gem.

GAIL JOHNSON/SHUTTERSTOCK ©

Fort Shirley (p274)

If You Only Do One Thing

● The iconic 114-mile **Waitukubuli National Trail** (p272) is a must-hike for any intrepid traveler. The route starts at Scotts Head in the south and weaves through some main attractions like **Emerald Pool** (p270) before ending in **Cabrits National Park** (p274). Hiking all 14 segments would take two weeks to complete; fortunately, you can choose specific sections to explore. The Roseau Valley features a medley of dramatic terrain, waterfalls, sulfur springs and hot mineral baths for those hoping to unwind. Among the highlights are **Ti Kwen Glo Cho** (p264), **Trafalgar Falls** (p264) and **Tia's Sulphur Spa** (p264).

Seasonal Highlights

As the rainy season winds down from October to mid-December, the temperature is cooler and perfect for hiking the seemingly infinite trails on the island.

JANUARY

Mas Dominik celebrates the traditional roots of 'The Real Mas', including dancing to the drumming of ***lapeau kabwit*** bands.

APRIL

Jazz 'n Creole is a blend of jazz, Creole music, local food and cultural traditions, set against the picturesque Portsmouth backdrop.

MAY

The **Dominica Festival of Arts** features theatre and dance, concerts and creative workshops encouraging regional artistic expression.

DAVID POU/SHUTTERSTOCK ©, DEREK GALON/ISTOCK EDITORIAL/GETTY IMAGES ©, DEREK GALON/ISTOCK EDITORIAL/GETTY IMAGES ©

Three Days to Travel Around

- Linger around **Roseau Valley** (p263) for a couple of days, using it as a base to explore the neighboring communities' natural attractions. Spend some time at the **Morne Trois Pitons National Park** (p269), where you can take in some of Dominica's signature sights like the **Boiling Lake** (p270), **Middleham Falls** (p270), **Emerald Pool** (p270) and **Ti Tou Gorge** (p270).

- Return to the natural treasures of **Trafalgar village** (p263) and **Wotten Waven** (p264), or spend a day immersed in the culture of the indigenous **Kalinago people** (p268).

- If time permits, visit the effervescent **Bubble Beach** (p272) in the southwest.

More Than a Week

- **Roseau** (p260) is the quaint capital city. Visit its historic structures and relax in the lovely **Dominica Botanic Gardens** (p261) or climb **Morne Bruce** (p261) for a picturesque view.

- Head east to Roseau Valley for some thermal healing at **Ti Kwen Glo Cho** (p264) and **Tia's Sulphur Spa** (p264), or take a cool dip at the base of **Trafalgar Falls** (p264).

- Hike part of the **Waitukubuli National Trail** (p272) from Soufrière's Scotts Head and go snorkeling at **Champagne Reef** (p272). Stop to admire Dominica's **Batibou Beach** (p266), the prettiest in Calibishie.

- Visit **Fort Shirley** (p274) and take a boat tour along the Indian River to finish in **Portsmouth** (p273).

JULY
Dominica's **Dive Fest**, the longest-running scuba diving and water sports festival in the Caribbean, unites lovers of aquatic life.

SEPTEMBER
Kalinago Week has been observed since 1930 and honors the cultural heritage and traditions of the indigenous community.

OCTOBER
Dominica's **World Creole Music Festival** showcases the diverse styles and rhythms of the culture, including ***bouyon***, zouk and ***compas***.

NOVEMBER
Every year, the island celebrates **Independence Day** on November 3 with a month of cultural festivities.

ROSEAU

The island's capital, located on its southeastern coast, is a fantastic home base for seeing as much of this beautiful Caribbean island as possible. Still, Roseau is intriguing enough on its own to warrant a trip. One of the island's best and most convenient viewing spots is Morne Bruce, a small mountaintop outside Roseau. Old Roseau Market has shed its troubled past to emerge as a vital hub for arts and crafts. Hurricanes severely damaged the Botanic Gardens, but the resilient park still thrives. The city museum presents an intriguing collection of cultural exhibits that trace the island's indigenous history; Lennox Honychurch, a historian and author, essentially maintains it by himself. Dominica's capital also hosts the island's largest music festival and Carnival. And when you're feeling hungry, there are plenty of places to try delicious, authentic Creole food without breaking the bank.

TOP TIP

Take a sip of the unofficial national beer, Kubuli. The pale golden lager gets its name from the indigenous Kalinago name for the island, *Wai'tu kubuli,* meaning 'Tall is her body'. Kubuli is made with local bottled spring water, Loubière, and is light and refreshing on a hot day.

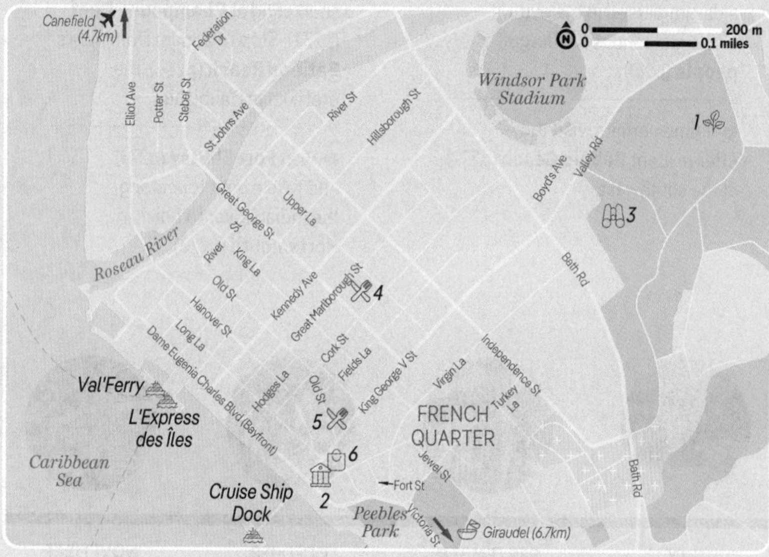

SIGHTS
1 Dominica Botanic Gardens
2 Dominica Museum
3 Morne Bruce

EATING
4 Pearl's Cuisine
5 Tropical Blendz Cafe

SHOPPING
6 Old Market Square

Dominica Museum

BEST BREAKFAST SPOTS IN ROSEAU

Tropical Blendz Cafe
Fill up on fresh-pressed juices, all-natural healthy smoothies and breakfast staples like omelettes and pancakes. Add some fried plantains and saltfish *accras* (fritters) to your order for a truly local experience. $

Pearl's Cuisine
This Great Marlborough St institution has been churning out a mouth-watering menu for 30 years. You will devour their souse, saltfish *accras*, bakes, stuffed pies and local cocoa tea. $

The Resilient Botanic Gardens

FLOURISHING AMID TRAGEDY

The **Dominica Botanic Gardens** used to be a tropical flower paradise before damage from Hurricane David in 1979 and Hurricane Maria in 2017. But more than 50 indigenous plant species including the Bwa Kwaib (Carib wood), as well as Dominica's national bird, the Sisserou parrot, are still found here. The iconic baobab tree, which fell during Hurricane David, is a testament to the nation's fortitude.

For gorgeous panoramas of the city, don't skip the hike to **Morne Bruce** that takes about 20 minutes on a trail from the Botanical Gardens and is a five-minute drive from the city center.

Roseau from a Historical Perspective

RETRACING THE ISLAND'S PAST

The small **Dominica Museum** has a wealth of historical and cultural artifacts collected by the island's foremost historian, Lennox Honychurch. The exhibits include prints, vintage maps and musical instruments used by early settlers. There's even a *pwi pwi*, a raft constructed by the native Kalinago

Purple Allamanda, Dominica Botanic Gardens

WHERE TO STAY IN ROSEAU

Fort Young Hotel
A luxurious, all-inclusive property with an infinity pool, a cocktail-ready hot tub and restorative spa services. **$$$**

Potter's Place
Rooms are spacious and modern, and it's just a couple of blocks from the Roseau River. **$$**

Ma Bass Guest House
Guests can expect a warm welcome at this simple, centrally located guesthouse with old-school furnishings. **$**

people from tree trunks. The museum, converted from an old post office on Roseau's quayside, has been around since 1810.

Behind the museum, Dominica's **Old Market Square** is a significant historical site in itself. In the past, enslaved people were auctioned off and even put to death on this cobblestoned square bordering the seafront. The area was renovated in 1988, and it's now a lively market where artisans sell handcrafted goods like woven baskets, jewelry, essential oils and soaps. You can buy fresh produce right by the water after pondering the square's tragic past.

WHY I LOVE ROSEAU

Nasha Smith, writer

The World Creole Music Festival reflects the diversity and cultural fusion of the Creole-speaking world. It brings together several Creole music genres, from zouk and soca to reggae, *bouyon* and *compas*. I'm a big fan of *bouyon*, a Dominican genre that emerged in the late 1980s by blending soca and zouk with indigenous Dominican styles like *cadence-lypso* and the more familiar *jing ping, chanté mas* and *lapeau kabwit* rhythms. And among the many bands that have popularized bouyon, WCK are the pioneers with tunes like 'Met Veye', 'Balance Batty' and my favorite, 'Band Wagon Train'. If you ever have an opportunity to see them perform at the festival, don't miss the masters.

A Celebration of Dominican Artistry

DISCOVER THE ISLAND'S CULTURAL HERITAGE

Roseau's Carnival, **Mas Dominik**, is known as 'The Real Mas' for its adherence to Carnival traditions. It takes place before Ash Wednesday, in February or early March. Calypso contests and Carnival queen pageants precede the main street jump-up. Ole Mas, a post-slavery emancipation tradition, begins on Monday after J'ouvert, the dawn street fête signaling the start of the parade. Bwa Bwa (stilt walkers) and Negre Mawon (the runaway enslaved) chip away in the streets to the beat of *lapeau kabwit* bands. The Tuesday parade features elaborate costumes, free-flowing drinks and exuberant dancing.

Another major event, **World Creole Music Festival** was conceived to provide a global stage for Dominica's traditional music. Every year, starting on the last Friday in October, a slew of international superstars from the Caribbean, the French Antilles, Africa and North America treat festival attendees to three electrifying evenings of performances. Some of the most recognizable names in Creole, African and Caribbean music, such as WCK Band, Burna Boy, Kassav, Buju Banton, Sean Paul and Wyclef Jean, have performed here.

A Culinary Feast with Daria

LEARN TO COOK LOCAL

If you're a fan of Caribbean food, **Daria Eugene** (cookingwithdaria.com) can teach you how to make *titiwi accras* (codfish fritters), spice-battered plantains and other delectable local dishes. Eugene, a local cuisine expert, has been featured on *Ainsley's Caribbean Kitchen*. She advocates using fresh local produce, herbs and spices to create flavorful meals. The Dominica native is also fond of incorporating rum infusions into her mouthwatering dishes. It's a personalized cooking experience at Eugene's hilltop home in **Giraudel**, where guests are treated like family during the 3½-hour class. Pick up a copy of the *Cooking Caribbean with Daria* recipe cookbook, which delves into Dominica's gastronomic delights, to replicate the tasty meals at home.

GETTING AROUND

Roseau is small enough to navigate on foot. Stay alert, as walking through the city is an exercise in dodging traffic with parked cars on either side of the already narrow roads.

Beyond Roseau

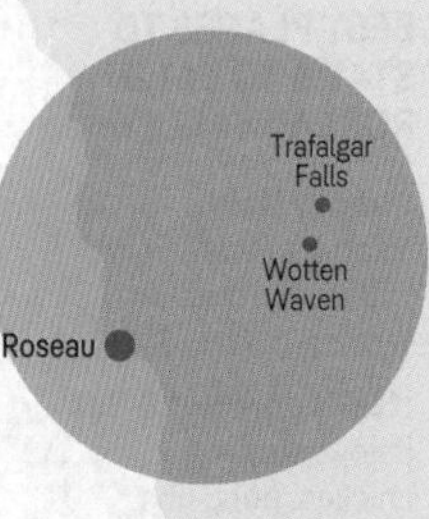

Stunning natural scenery awaits just outside the city limits, featuring lush tropical forest and cascading waterfalls.

Only a short drive to the east from Dominica's capital, the Roseau Valley harbors some of the island's most stunning and frequented attractions. Trafalgar village and its namesake twin waterfalls are dispersed amid the impressive landscapes in the gorgeously green valley. Wotten Waven is a small, sloping village famous for its purportedly therapeutic sulfur hot springs and lovely natural surroundings.

Experience tranquility listening to the chirping of birds, the gurgling of streams and the rustling of leaves in a tropical rainforest. Take advantage of the valley's constant cool, pure, fresh mountain breezes. The Roseau Valley is a prime example of why Dominica is best enjoyed outdoors.

TOP TIP

Consult the online schedule of cruise ships arriving in Dominica to avoid the busier days at these popular natural attractions.

Trafalgar Falls **(p264)**

BEST PLACES TO STAY & TO EAT IN ROSEAU VALLEY

Strictly Itals
Hearty and delicious vegetarian meals in Wotten Waven. $

M&G's Jerk Hut & Bar
Enjoy spicy jerk chicken, pork, ribs, steamed fish and other local fare. $

Water Bar
Stop by to sample locally grown fruits like coconuts, oranges and watermelons. $

Cocoa Cottage
A guesthouse in the Roseau Valley mountains, close to all the area has to offer. $$

D'Auchamps Cottages
Reasonably priced cottages in a picturesque garden with a panorama of the nearby mountains. $

STEVE TAYLOR ARPS/ALAMY ©

Ti Kwen Glo Cho

The Dynamic Trafalgar Falls Duo

DOUBLE THE EXCITEMENT

A 30-minute bus ride from Roseau takes you to Dominica's **Trafalgar Falls**. A pair of towering waterfalls flowing parallel to one another is an unusual occurrence. You can take in the spectacle from a viewing platform after a cool 15-minute stroll through the rainforest. 'Papa' (on the left) and 'Mama' (on the right) each have their unique characteristics. At 125ft tall, Papa dominates the dramatic scenery, while Mama's slighter 75ft generates a powerful gush of water. Plunge into the pool at Mama falls' base. Hiking Papa falls is dangerous without a guide because of the trail's slippery boulders.

The Restorative Powers of Hot Water

A NATURAL SAUNA

The name **Ti Kwen Glo Cho** means 'little corner of hot water' in Creole, and this spa sanctuary in Wotten Waven village, a 20-minute drive from Roseau, lives up to its name. Large stone pools of healing thermal waters are wrapped in a lush garden with cool springs nearby. The water is 'comfortably' hot – just what you need to soothe your aches. Since the spa is open until late, visitors can enjoy a relaxing moonlight soak. Home-cooked meals, refreshing drinks and bush rum are available on site.

You can also relax at **Tia's Sulphur Spa**, choosing from one of three sizable outdoor pools or retreating to one of two private pools enclosed in bamboo huts. After a day of hiking, you'll appreciate a soak in the hot tub. There's a restaurant and bar for post-spa food and drinks, and charming bamboo guest cottages set in a floral garden. It's a 10-minute walk from Ti Kwen Glo Cho.

GETTING AROUND

Minibuses frequently run between King George V St (near Astaphans supermarket) in Roseau and Trafalgar and Wotten Waven.

NORTHEASTERN COAST

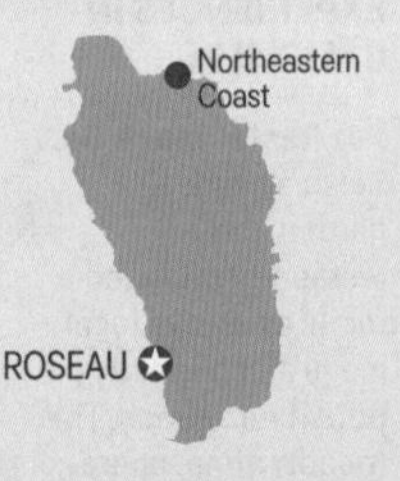

Upon arrival, most first-time visitors to Dominica will quickly become acquainted with the northeastern region – the larger of the island's two airports, Douglas-Charles Airport, is located here. This part of Dominica is characterized by red cliffs, compelling reefs, and rivers that wind their way through mangrove swamps and coconut groves. It is easy to see why many key *Pirates of the Caribbean* scenes were shot in this area. Dominica's finest beaches are found here, whether you are looking for isolated white-sand coves or palm-fringed bays. Batibou Bay is great for swimming, and there are many estates such as Hampstead, or large historic farms, where fruit trees have been planted.

Calibishie is the largest of many small fishing villages in the northeast. The charming coastal village stands out against a backdrop of rainforest-covered mountains, while mellow bars and restaurants dot the landscape.

TOP TIP

Pointe Baptiste is one of the rare golden-sand beaches in Dominica. It's close to the Red Rocks formation and the ideal place to unwind after some sightseeing. It's usually quiet, and the water is shallow. Enjoy some time with family or fly solo.

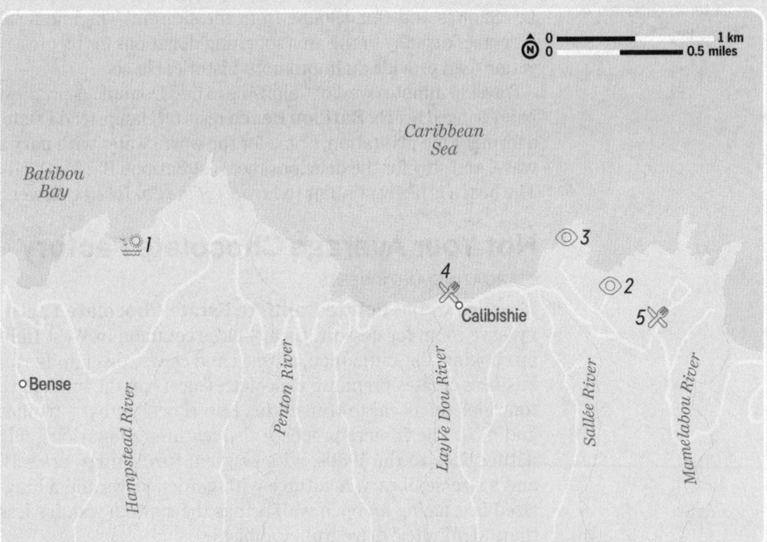

SIGHTS
1 Batibou Beach
2 Pointe Baptiste Estate Chocolate Factory
3 Red Rocks

EATING
4 Coral Reef Restaurant
5 Poz Restaurant & Bar

BEST DINING EXPERIENCES IN CALIBISHIE

Poz Restaurant & Bar
Set in a magical garden, this restaurant is lauded for its extensive local menu and perfectly potent rum punch. The friendly atmosphere reflects the warm personality of the proprietor Poz. $$

Coral Reef Restaurant
This ocean-view restaurant is a literal revelation; it's behind a grocery store. The menu is packed with authentic Creole cuisine and the most tender ribs in Calibishie. $$

DAVID SVESTKA/SHUTTERSTOCK ©

Red Rocks

Explore the Windswept Coast

THE EXTRAORDINARY OUTDOORS

The unusual rusty hue of the **Red Rocks**, which extend into the Atlantic Ocean a 10-minute drive east of Calibishie, is the result of mineral oxidization from constant exposure to sun and seawater. The large rock formations appear to have been occupied at some point. Small caves are wedged between the smooth surfaces, and there are petroglyphs and stairs carved into the rock. On a clear day, you can see the nearby islands of Marie-Galante, Les Saintes and Guadeloupe from the summit. The unofficial caretaker (usually in the area soliciting donations for its preservation) can provide an impromptu historical lesson.

Travel 15 minutes west of Calibishie to find Dominica's prettiest palm-fringed beach. **Batibou Beach** rests on Hampstead Estate, a former lime plantation. Come for the warm water with nary a wave, and stay for the delicious meals at Batibou Bar and Grill. The beach is likely familiar to *Pirates of the Caribbean* viewers.

Not Your Average Chocolate Factory

STARGAZING AND SWEETS

If you go to the **Pointe Baptiste Estate Chocolate Factory**, save room for dessert. Using spices common in West Indian cooking, like cinnamon, nutmeg and cloves, this family-run business creates premium chocolate. Guests on the immersive tour look on as cacao transforms into chocolate bars, truffles and nibs. The 25-acre property also features a luxurious villa dating back to the 1930s, with original furnishings, artwork and a sizable library. A cottage with garden views and a king-sized bed facing an open wall brings the stars to you. It's less than 10 minutes' drive from Calibishie.

GETTING AROUND

From Roseau, catch a bus near the New Market on River Bank Rd. Minibuses traveling from Portsmouth to Marigot and Castle Bruce pass through Calibishie and can be flagged down along the route.

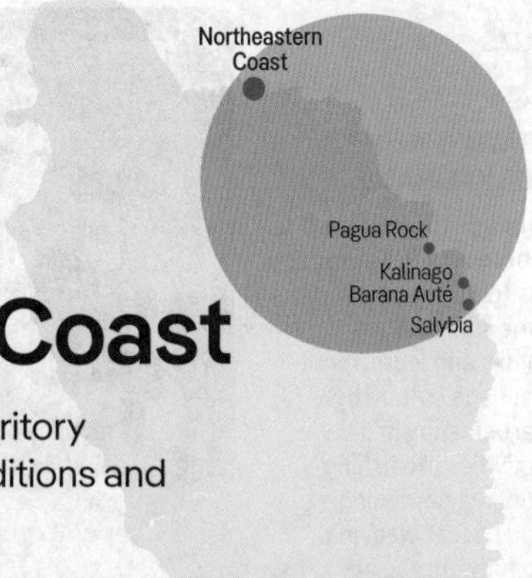

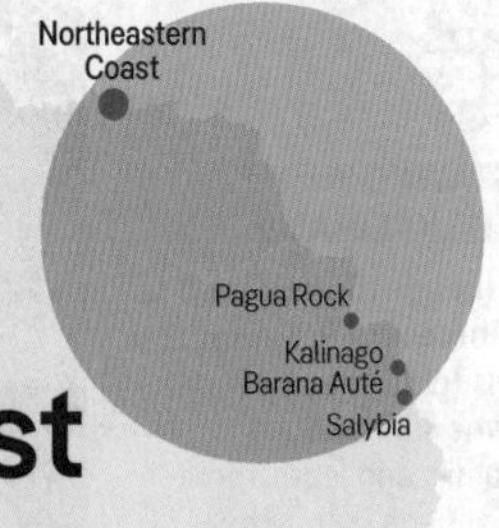

Beyond Northeastern Coast

The inhabitants of the Kalinago Territory showcase their unique culture, traditions and way of life.

The Kalinago, originally known as the Carib, are an indigenous people of the Lesser Antilles. They are the descendants of the first people to settle in the Caribbean and reside primarily in the northeastern region of Dominica. Approximately 3000 people live in the Kalinago Territory. A council of six people, headed by a chief, manages the collectively owned area. British colonial authorities formally established this 3700-acre territory in 1903. Tours devoted to forging genuine connections with the Kalinago culture allow visitors to fully immerse themselves in the experiences of the original settlers. These activities also generate revenue for the community in one of Dominica's most socioeconomically disadvantaged regions.

TOP TIP

Cassava has been a crucial part of the Kalinago culture in Dominica. Try *ouicou* juice extracted from grated cassava.

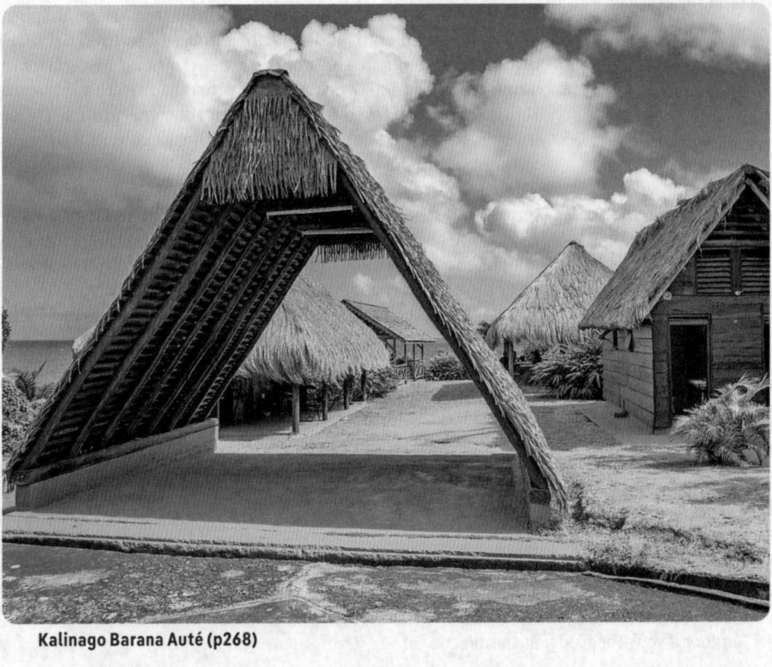

Kalinago Barana Auté (p268)

STAYING WITH THE KALINAGO

Through the **Kalinago Homestay Program**, visitors can spend time with a native family and learn about Kalinago culture by participating in daily activities like fishing, hunting, gardening and basket-weaving. To fully appreciate the Kalinago way of life, stay with a local family in more conventional housing for at least one night and participate in daily activities. Although some Kalingo live in modern houses, finding a traditional hut *(ajoupa)* is not uncommon. While staying in an *ajoupa*, visitors will also share the meals and household facilities with the family. Otherwise, **Aywasi Kalinago Retreat** is a stunning natural haven in the heart of the Kalinago Territory. The eco-friendly villa is just a five-minute walk from Barana Auté.

Kalinago Barana Auté

Pay Homage to Kalinago Culture

LEARN ABOUT THE ISLAND'S FIRST INHABITANTS

Barana Auté translates as 'village by the sea' – the Crayfish River swirls its way through the village before plunging into the Atlantic Ocean over the Isulukati Falls. The cliff-top location of **Kalinago Barana Auté** affords breathtaking views of the Atlantic below. An outdoor museum recreates a traditional Kalinago community, depicting life before the European colonization. *Ajoupas,* or clusters of smaller wooden dwellings, surround a communal *karbet,* which only houses male Kalinago. Canoes fashioned from the gommier tree are on display, and visitors can enjoy daily performances of Kalinago dance, drama and songs at the main *karbet.* You can also observe a master artisan at work and gain insight into the intricate Kalinago craft passed down through the generations. Those interested in the island's indigenous heritage will find it an authentic and educational experience.

South of Crayfish River, Salybia is the administrative center of the Kalinago Territory. **Sainte Marie de Caraïbes** is a Catholic church featuring a colorful mural of the Kalinago people encountering Columbus' fleet. The ruins of the previous church and a cemetery are nearby.

Just outside the northern border of the Kalinago Territory, **Pagua Rock** overlooks the Pagua River valley. According to Kalinago folklore, the 60ft rock houses a mythical spirit, and if you followed the stairs leading to the summit, you would find good fortune. But the most intriguing tale is that of a small white flower that only blooms once a year and has mind-control powers.

GETTING AROUND

Buses making their way from Portsmouth or Marigot in the north to Castle Bruce in the south typically cut through the Kalinago Territory. If you're coming from the direction of the capital, take a bus on River Bank Rd.

The sites are within a 20-minute drive – and in some cases a short walk – of each other.

MORNE TROIS PITONS NATIONAL PARK

Morne Trois Pitons National Park
ROSEAU

The government of Dominica designated the 17,000-acre Morne Trois Pitons National Park as a protected area in 1975. It was named a Unesco World Heritage site in 1997 for its exceptional universal value and distinctive natural features. Morne Trois Pitons is the most dominant (dormant) volcano within the park's green-blanketed confines, topping out at an imposing 4403ft. There are amazing views of the surrounding luxuriant rainforest from the summit, including the peaks of Morne Micotrin, Morne Watt and Morne Anglais to the south.

The park is also home to the Valley of Desolation, a barren patch of land with an otherworldly assemblage of fumaroles, hot springs and steaming vents. The Boiling Lake, formed by the collapse of a volcanic crater, is one of the largest of its kind in the world. Along the way, you'll encounter the surreal beauty of Ti Tou Gorge, a narrow gorge with crystal-clear waters.

TOP TIP

Daily passes to Dominica's ecotourism sites cost US$5, while weekly passes are US$12. During that time, pass holders can visit any participating locations as often as they like. Boeri Lake, Boiling Lake, Morne Trois Pitons, Middleham Falls, Freshwater Lake and Emerald Pool are all eligible.

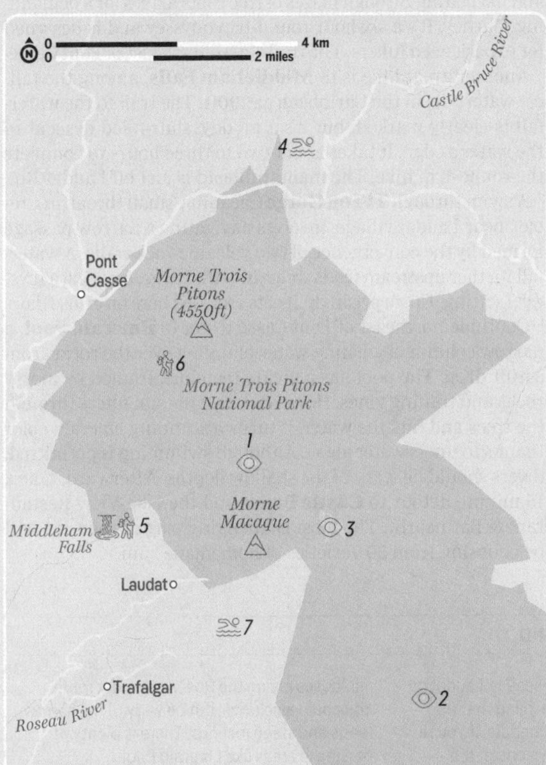

SIGHTS
1 Boeri Lake
2 Boiling Lake
3 Freshwater Lake

ACTIVITIES, COURSES & TOURS
4 Emerald Pool
5 Middleham Falls
6 Morne Trois Pitons
7 Ti Tou Gorge

Ti Tou Gorge (p270)

DOMINICA'S GREAT LAKES

Boiling Lake
This flooded fumarole is 200ft wide and represents the hottest such lake in the world, with reportedly recorded temperatures as high as 197°F (91°C).

Boeri Lake
Dominica's highest lake is sandwiched between the mountains of Morne Micotrin (Macaque) and Morne Trois Pitons at an elevation of 2800ft.

Freshwater Lake
The largest of Dominica's four lakes serves as the Roseau River's natural source and is situated just over 2500ft above sea level.

Emerald Pool

An Abundance of Natural Wonders

AN ORGANIC OUTDOOR PLAYGROUND

Dominica's second-highest peak, **Morne Trois Pitons** is worth the challenging and, at times, chaotic ascent for the unobstructed views to the north and west. Climbing up slippery, steep rocks and navigating through mazes of tree roots makes for a demanding journey. It's a six-hour round-trip odyssey and is designed for experienced hikers. The trail starts northeast of Pont Cassé.

Another great hike is to **Middleham Falls**, among the tallest waterfalls in the Caribbean at 200ft. The trail to the waterfall is clearly marked, but it's a muddy, stair-filled descent to the water's edge. It takes about two to three hours to complete the round-trip hike. The main trailhead is just off Laudat Rd.

A swim through **Ti Tou Gorge** (meaning 'small throat' in Creole), near Laudat village, involves navigating a narrow passage formed by the convergence of two volcanic-rock walls. A waterfall further upstream feeds water into the gorge, creating a mystical setting. Unsurprisingly, it gets crowded here on cruise days.

Continue northeast of Pont Cassé to get to **Emerald Pool**, a narrow column of gushing water plunging over the rocks from a 40ft drop. The pool has a vivid green hue, framed by mossy rocks and trailing vines. However, when the sun filters through the trees and hits the water, it turns a stunning emerald color thanks to underwater algae. Although swimming is permitted, divers should be wary of the shallow depths. Afterward, take a 15-minute detour to **Castle Bruce** and the Islet View Restaurant & Bar nearby. The most challenging part of your day will be choosing from 50 varieties of homemade rum.

GETTING AROUND

You can catch a bus from Roseau to Laudat on King George V St, but keep in mind that they don't operate on a regular schedule. If you're staying in Trafalgar, flag down one of the minibuses plying the Roseau–Laudat route. You could also drive, but be wary of the narrow roads and steep inclines. There is plenty of parking in areas like Emerald Pool.

SOUFRIÈRE BAY

ROSEAU
Soufrière Bay

Southwest Dominica isn't exactly a hive of activity, but that doesn't make it any less fascinating. The Scotts Head peninsula is a sliver of land on the summit of a dormant volcano that protrudes from the ocean floor. This geographic phenomenon allows you to stand between the Caribbean Sea and the Atlantic Ocean. From Scotts Head village, hikers can follow the route through tropical forests, across sparkling rivers and into the heart of Dominica's stunning scenery on the Waitukubuli National Trail.

Soufrière Bay, located near the southernmost point of Dominica, is the island's most popular dive site and is widely considered to be among the best in the Caribbean. Divers and snorkelers agree that Champagne Reef is one of the Caribbean's most fascinating and distinctive reefs. The presence of geothermal activity produces a genuinely unforgettable underwater adventure.

TOP TIP

You can snorkel at Champagne Reef on your own or rent equipment from Donny's Beach Bar, conveniently located right on the beach. The guides are extremely well informed and offer helpful advice for snorkelers. Of course, you can stop by the bar later for a celebratory drink.

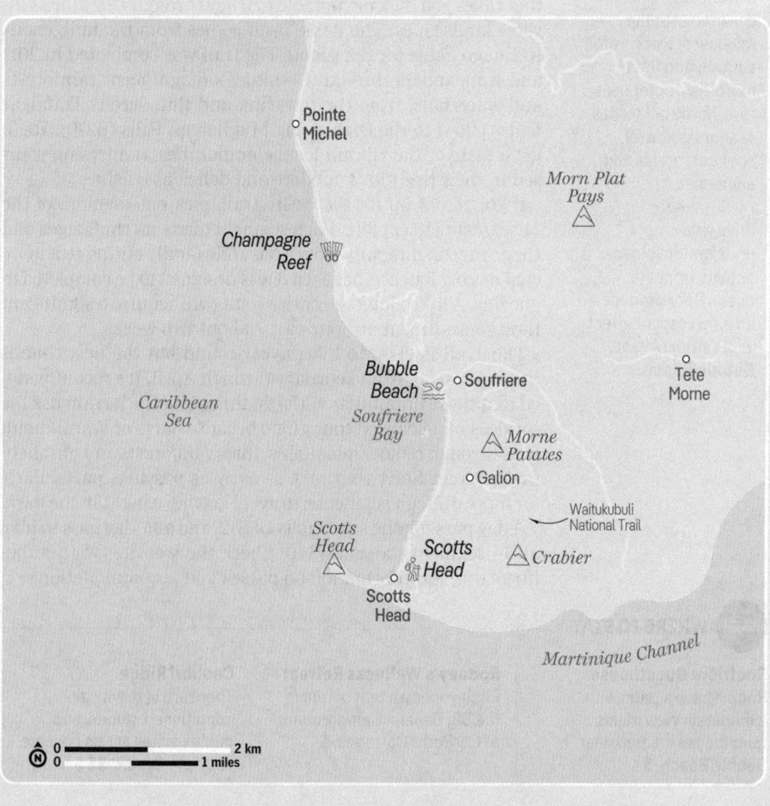

THE EFFERVESCENT SOUTH

Soufrière is known for its diving, and some of the island's most popular and well-known dive sites are found in the **Scotts Head Marine Reserve**. The volcanic thermal springs on the seabed release tiny bubbles at **Champagne Reef** that make it feel like you're swimming in a giant glass of the fizzy drink. The golden tones of the reef complete the illusion. Snorkelers can marvel at the rainbow of marine life surrounding them: parrotfish, octopuses, rays, hawksbill turtles, seahorses, barrel sponges, corals and anemones.

A 10-minute drive away, more underwater volcanic activity from the ocean floor produces an effervescent effect while swimming at **Bubble Beach**.

Waitukubuli National Trail

The Caribbean's Longest Hiking Trail

WALK THE WAITUKUBULI NATIONAL TRAIL

Extending an extraordinary 114 miles from the southern village of Scotts Head to the northernmost point of Capuchin, the **Waitukubuli National Trail** is a long-distance hiking trail that takes you on a memorable journey through Dominica's diverse landscapes. The name itself comes from the indigenous Kalinago name for the island. The trail was completed in 2011 and it meanders through Dominica's magnificent rainforests and waterfalls, from the towering and thunderous Trafalgar Falls (p264) to the enchanting Middleham Falls (p270). You'll get a taste of the vibrant local communities, immersing yourself in their traditions, folklore and delicious cuisine.

If you're not up for the entire trail, pick one or more of the 14 segments to explore. Each segment offers its challenges and they range in difficulty from a leisurely family outing to a more challenging journey, but each one is designed to be completed in one day. A hike along the entire route will require a significant time commitment on your part – about two weeks.

The Trail is open to hikers year-round but the best time is the dry season, from February through April. It's recommended that those unfamiliar with Dominica and the terrain use the services of a licensed tour guide because parts of Waitukubuli pass through remote mountains, thick rainforests and uninhabited regions. Start your hike as early as possible, particularly for more difficult segments, to avoid getting caught in the dark.

A day pass for one segment is US$12, and a 15-day pass to hike all 14 segments costs US$40. Check the website (waitukubulitrail.dm) for information on passes and accommodations.

WHERE TO STAY

Soufrière Guesthouse
Rooms have a patio with a mountain view at this guesthouse located near Bubble Beach. **$**

Rodney's Wellness Retreat
Pitch your own tent or rent in the Big Banana Campground or CarRod's Cottages. **$**

Coulibri Ridge
There are 14 roomy air-conditioned studios and duplex suites at this upscale, cozy eco-resort. **$$$**

PORTSMOUTH

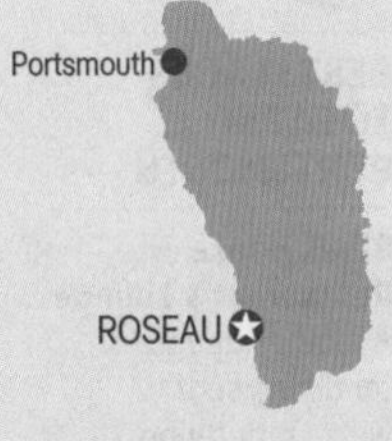

The second-largest town in Dominica, Portsmouth is situated on the Indian River in Prince Rupert Bay, on the northwestern coast. The town was initially intended to serve as the island's capital, but due to a malaria outbreak, the capital was moved to Roseau where it remains today. Hurricane Maria's fierce winds and torrential rains devastated Portsmouth in 2017, destroying buildings, infrastructure and homes and leaving a stark and somber landscape behind.

Portsmouth is still in a phase of rebuilding and revitalization. Nonetheless, many activities are available, whether an adventure seeker, history enthusiast, nature lover or you're just looking to relax. Cabrits National Park is a delightful nature reserve. It's also home to the historic Fort Shirley, a restored 18th-century British garrison. The Indian River is shaded by towering mangrove trees and enveloped by lush vegetation, perfect for gliding on the water in serene silence.

TOP TIP

You'll quickly learn that people in the West Indies often go by an alias. Ask for tour favorites 'Cobra', 'James Bond' and 'Lawrence of Arabia' on the Indian River excursion. James Bond was a guide during the filming of *Pirates of the Caribbean*.

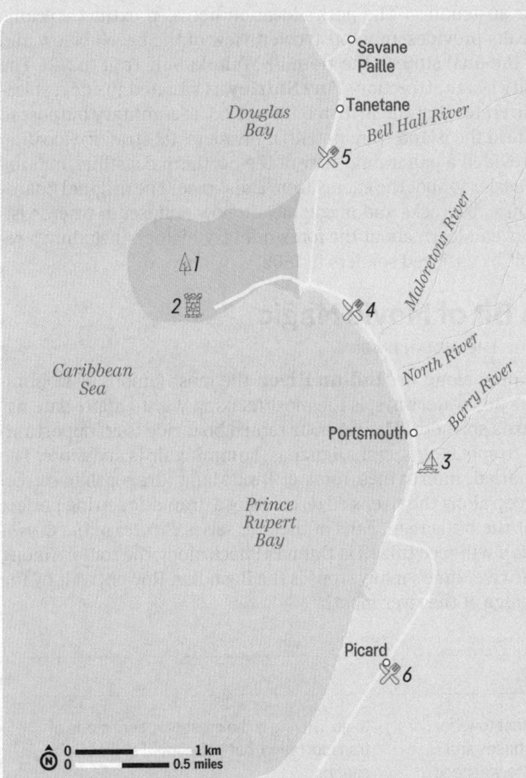

SIGHTS
1 Cabrits National Park
2 Fort Shirley

ACTIVITIES, COURSES & TOURS
3 Indian River

EATING
4 Madiba Beach Café
5 Roots Rock Bar & Grill
6 Steak House Restaurant & Lounge

Egret, Indian River (p274)

PHILIP DUMAS/GETTY IMAGES ©

BEST PLACES TO EAT IN PORTSMOUTH

Steak House Restaurant & Lounge
A mother-daughter dining spot with a reputation for exceptional customer service and mouth-watering meals. $

Roots Rock Bar & Grill
Watch the setting sun disappear while downing a few shots of the local bush rum from a breezy wooden deck. $

Madiba Beach Cafe
Fresh seafood is served in this unpretentious open-air cafe on the beach. The soothing sound of the waves accompanies your meal. $

WIRESTOCK CREATORS/SHUTTERSTOCK ©

Cabrits National Park

History, Hiking & Panoramic Views

A JEWEL ON THE PENINSULA

Cabrits National Park is a beautiful peninsula spanning over 1300 acres of land. Its name comes from *cabri* ('young goat' in French) – supposedly, sailors once brought goats to the island for sustenance. The park's location between extinct volcanic peaks provides an unobstructed view of the beach below and is the final stop on the 114-mile Waitukubuli Trail (p272). The park's star attraction, **Fort Shirley**, is situated inside a volcanic crater that the British built in 1765 as a military outpost to guard the island from potential invaders. Its strategic location provided a panoramic view of the northern coastline, making it easier to spot the enemy from a distance. The original guardhouse, barracks and magazine are now a museum where visitors can learn about the fort's military history, including a revolt by enslaved soldiers in 1802.

A Bit of Movie Magic

SAIL THE INDIAN RIVER

Sailing along the **Indian River**, the most famous of Dominica's 365 waterways, is the most relaxing way to appreciate nature's splendor. The 1½-hour return boat ride is an opportunity to spot egrets, crabs, iguanas, hummingbirds and more. The gnarled, intertwined roots of Bwa Mang (dragonsblood tree) creep along the river's edge, creating a dramatic setting perfect for the big screen. Fans of the film series *Pirates of the Caribbean* will recognize Tia Dalma's Shack along the route. Among the river lime's many stops is the Bush Bar. Rowers wait by the bridge at the river mouth.

GETTING AROUND

Portsmouth is the second-largest town in Dominica, so there are always buses and taxis available to take you where you need to go. Driving is the most practical mode of transportation, but you should still exercise caution.

Arriving

When arriving by air, visitors will likely touch down at Douglas-Charles Airport, which welcomes flights from North America and Europe. Canefield is an additional option for some regional airlines and small private aircraft. Cruise ships regularly berth on the island, giving passengers a day to explore. There is also a ferry service from nearby islands to Dominica.

By Air

Most flights arrive at Douglas-Charles Airport. Dominica's main airport is near Marigot in the island's northeast, over an hour's drive from Roseau. The smaller Canefield Airport is 15 minutes from the capital. American Airlines provides direct service from Miami; there are also flights from Europe and the Caribbean.

By Boat

You can take a ferry to Dominica with L'Express des Îles from Guadeloupe, Martinique and St Lucia year-round, but more frequently during the summer. Val Ferry offers a service from Guadeloupe via Marie Galante to Portsmouth in the north. Cruises, sailboats and yachts also go to the island's ports.

Money

Currency: Eastern Caribbean dollar (EC$)

CASH

While Dominica's official currency is the Eastern Caribbean dollar, businesses and vendors typically accept US dollars, euros and British pounds. However, any change will be given in Eastern Caribbean dollars.

DIGITAL PAYMENTS

Dominica, like other Eastern Caribbean islands, uses the Eastern Caribbean Central Bank–backed DCash Wallet as a cashless payment option.

CREDIT CARDS

Most companies, with the exception of small vendors, accept major credit cards. However, it is wise to keep some cash handy at all times. In Roseau, the nation's capital, numerous ATMs are connected to banks that dispense Eastern Caribbean dollars.

DOMINICAN REPUBLIC

BREATHTAKING BEACHES, MOUNTAINS AND HERITAGE SITES

Underneath the sheath of a colonial past lies an island of ecological wonders intertwined with African, indigenous and Iberian cultural influences. Welcome to the Dominican Republic.

In 1492, Christopher Columbus reached the shores of Hispaniola, precipitating a brutal colonization effort that all but decimated the indigenous and peaceful Taíno tribe, a subculture of the Arawak people. Today, two-thirds of that verdant and fertile island is known as the Dominican Republic, an independent nation and the second-largest island of the Greater Antilles. But its history continues to unfold in the unique melding of indigenous, Spanish and African cultural touch points that can be found throughout the country's food, music and art.

The country's tourism slogan – 'Dominican Republic has it all' – is no exaggeration. Along with hundreds of kilometers of enviable coastline that includes both the Atlantic Ocean and the Caribbean Sea, it's also home to four of the five highest peaks in the Caribbean, a fact reflected in its nickname: the Caribbean Alps. Interspersed within its pine-studded mountains and sugary shores are arid desert climes, raging rivers, precipitous waterfalls, underground caverns and humid rainforests teeming with all manner of flora, fauna and wildlife.

Bachata (a traditional dance set to a syncopated rhythm) and baseball are universally beloved here; you should throw yourself into both with reckless abandon. And for your palate: rich pours of rum, aromatic cups of coffee and seafood so fresh it'd be a crime to eat anything else. Except for *pasteles* – you definitely don't want to miss out on those.

THE MAIN AREAS

SANTO DOMINGO
The island's historic capital. p282

SOUTHWEST COAST
Country roads and desolate beaches. p289

JARABACOA
The 'Dominican Alps' mountain range. p294

Above: Punta Cana (p314); Left: Parque Nacional Los Tres Ojos (p288)

NORTH COAST
Water sports and waterfalls. p301

PENÍNSULA DE SAMANÁ
Whale-watching and beach towns. p307

PUNTA CANA
Luxury resorts and ancient caves. p314

Find Your Way

While you'll find walkable areas in some of the major cities like Santo Domingo or Puerto Plata, you'll need a car or one of the ubiquitous *motoconchos* (motorcycle taxis) to get you around various regions.

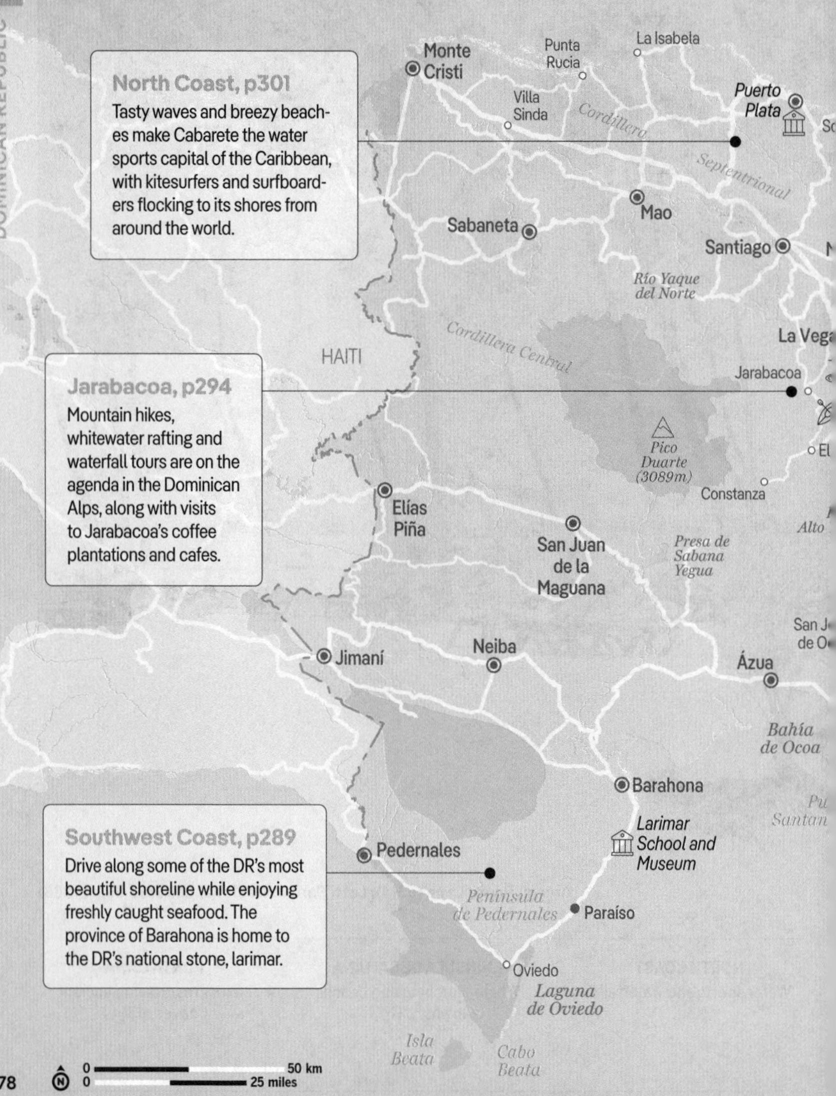

North Coast, p301

Tasty waves and breezy beaches make Cabarete the water sports capital of the Caribbean, with kitesurfers and surfboarders flocking to its shores from around the world.

Jarabacoa, p294

Mountain hikes, whitewater rafting and waterfall tours are on the agenda in the Dominican Alps, along with visits to Jarabacoa's coffee plantations and cafes.

Southwest Coast, p289

Drive along some of the DR's most beautiful shoreline while enjoying freshly caught seafood. The province of Barahona is home to the DR's national stone, larimar.

CAR

Renting a car is the best way to see the Dominican Republic. Rideshare companies aren't widely available but can be found in most of the major cities. Using one is highly recommended in the capital, where driving can be extremely hazardous.

BUS

The DR has a fairly reliable stable of large coach buses offering frequent service to a network of major cities and towns. The three most popular companies – Caribe Tours, Expreso Bávaro and Metro – provide comfortable rides along their routes with air-conditioning and wi-fi.

GUAGUAS

Guaguas are smaller, privately owned buses or minivans that can take you to small or large destinations all around the DR. They're more affordable than the large coach buses, but also not as comfortable. They're often the only available public transport.

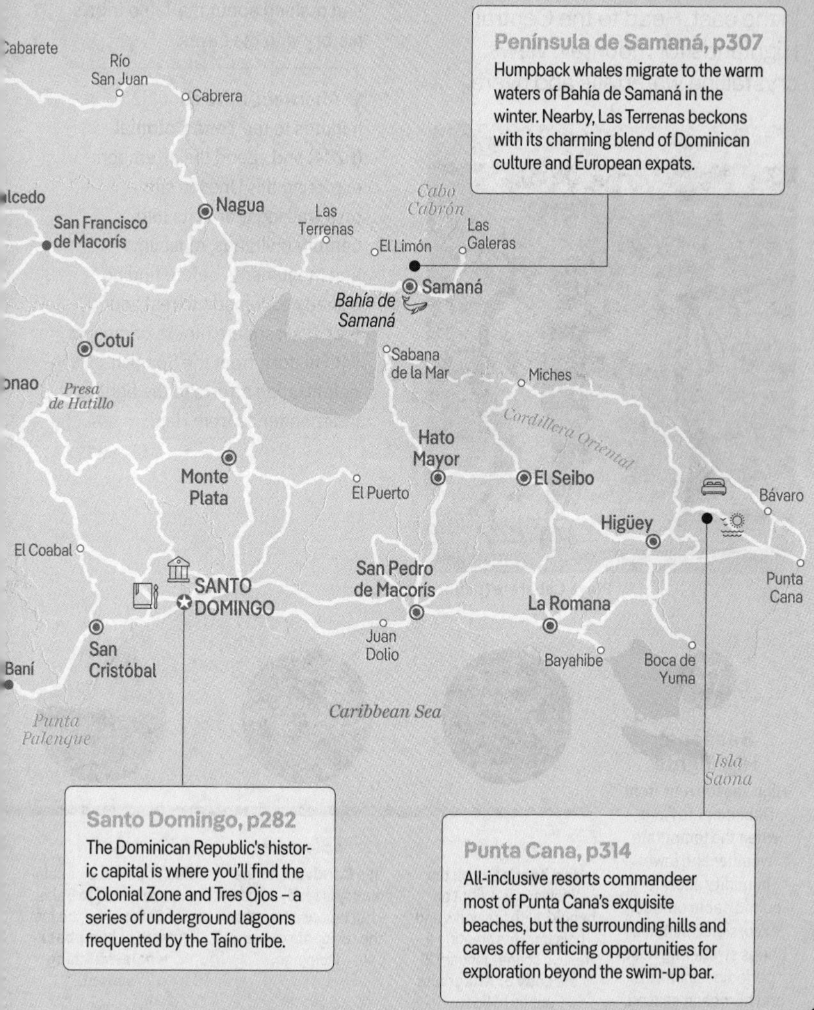

Península de Samaná, p307
Humpback whales migrate to the warm waters of Bahía de Samaná in the winter. Nearby, Las Terrenas beckons with its charming blend of Dominican culture and European expats.

Santo Domingo, p282
The Dominican Republic's historic capital is where you'll find the Colonial Zone and Tres Ojos – a series of underground lagoons frequented by the Taíno tribe.

Punta Cana, p314
All-inclusive resorts commandeer most of Punta Cana's exquisite beaches, but the surrounding hills and caves offer enticing opportunities for exploration beyond the swim-up bar.

Plan Your Time

Beaches in the DR are a must, with a different flavor in each region – ecological parks in the south, water sports to the north, glitzy resorts in the east. Head to the Central Highlands for mountain views, crystalline waterfalls and rivers.

CHRISTOPHER V JONES/SHUTTERSTOCK ©

Playa Cabarete (p304)

Pressed for Time

- Beat the crowds with an early morning start at **Parque Nacional Los Tres Ojos** (p288) in Santo Domingo. You can easily spend two hours exploring the three different underground lagoons and reading about the Taíno tribe's history with the caves.

- Afterward, drive about 12 minutes to the **Zona Colonial** (p284) and spend the afternoon exploring this Unesco site on a walking tour of its 16th-century buildings, museums and monuments before finding a shady esplanade to rest your feet. It's 11 square blocks brimming with history, from the Spanish colonization efforts to the fight for independence from Haiti.

Seasonal Highlights

High season runs from December to April, when the temperate weather and lower humidity allow for comfortable outdoor excursions. Summer brings sweltering heat, periodic rainstorms and hurricane season, but lower travel costs.

JANUARY

New Year's Eve on the Malecón is a sight to behold, with fireworks and noisemakers creating a festive scene. January 21 is the **Lady of Altagracia** public holiday.

FEBRUARY

It's **Carnival** and the country is ready to party – but no one more than the residents of Santo Domingo.

MARCH

Pack a pair of binoculars as you head to Bahía de Samaná for the last month of **humpback-whale-watching** season.

ANDRES ANIBAL NUNEZ CUELL/SHUTTERSTOCK ©, ALEKSANDR RYBALKO/SHUTTERSTOCK ©, JUDITH LIENERT/SHUTTERSTOCK ©

Four Days to Travel Around

- Hit the Central Highlands and tackle the hike up to **Pico Duarte** (p298), a fairly advanced multiday summit to the highest peak in the Dominican Republic; make sure you have a guide and a pack mule for the trip.

- After a taxing two or three days getting to the peak, use your last day to visit **Akasha Spa** (p295) for muscle-soothing massages by the pool and a home-cooked meal by Chef Andres. If time allows, pop into **Café Monte Alto** (p298) in Jarabacoa before your treatment for a quick primer on their beans and a cup of organic coffee.

If You Have More Time

- Dedicate a day to sightseeing around **Puerto Plata** (p302) before heading into **Cabarete** (p304). From there, spend about three days discovering its three main beaches, **Cabarete**, **Kite** and **Encuentro** (p304), sliding your way down the **27 waterfalls of Damajagua** (p305), floating down the **Río Yasica** (p305) and sampling fried fish at **Wilson's at La Boca** (p305).

- If you're in season, add two more days to trek out to **Bahía de Samaná** (p308) and watch the humpback whales in their native winter home. Outside the whale-watching season, spend those last couple of days taking in the sights of **Las Terrenas** and **Las Galeras** (p312).

APRIL

Holy Week, or **Semana Santa**, is a big celebration in the DR. Prepare for island-wide pageants, parties and burning effigies of Judas Iscariot.

JUNE

The DR wakes from its Semana Santa slumber for **Espíritu Santo**, celebrating the country's African heritage with drumming rituals, colorful costumes and masks.

JULY

The **Festival de Merengue** transforms Santo Domingo's Malecón into a raucous beachfront party with live bands, colorful dresses and day-long dancing.

NOVEMBER

Baseball season kicks off. Pick up tickets to a game and get ready to cheer – loudly.

SANTO DOMINGO

To truly understand the Dominican Republic, spend a few days in its cultural heart: Santo Domingo. Flanked by Río Ozama to the east and the Caribbean Sea to the west, this vibrant city served as the first capital of the Spanish colony, the crumbling remnants of which can still be found in its historic center – the Zona Colonial.

Among the remains of these 16th-century buildings are colorful homes, cobblestone streets, vendors hawking *pasteles en hoja* (plantain masa wrapped in leaves) or *coco frío* (chilled coconut water), and throngs of locals gathered in Parque Colón or Plaza de España to play music, swap stories or simply soak up the boisterous scene.

At night, the city lets loose with throngs of chaotic revelers partying late into the night on the shores of Santo Domingo Este or flocking to one of the many nightclubs pulsating with fast-paced *bachata* and merengue rhythms.

TOP TIP

Sundays are a popular festival day, with live music performances on city squares. The biggest festival happens in February for Santo Domingo Carnival, where the best of Dominican music, dance, art and street food converge in a costumed spectacle that outshines the Carnival festivities elsewhere in the country.

CARLOS NIN GOMEZ/SHUTTERSTOCK ©

Carnival, Santo Domingo

Coconut water vendor, Zona Colonial

TOP PLACES TO EAT

Sabor Criolla
Santo Domingo Este hut serving *mofongo*, *sancocho*, frozen drinks and beer. $

Barra Payán
Dishing up late-night pork sandwiches and juices since the 1950s. $

Time
Known for classed-up vegetarian fare and tropical cocktails. $$

Mesón de Barí
Sunlit dining room and traditional fare. $$

El Mesón de la Cava
Romantic cave restaurant serving wood-fired Spanish fusion. $$$

Pat'e Palo
Creative dishes in a 500-year-old tavern. $$$

Exploring the Fight for Independence

ZONA COLONIAL WALKING TOUR

Declared a Unesco World Heritage site in 1990, Zona Colonial is a tale of Spanish conquest, Haitian rule and a strong undercurrent of rebellious independence told through 11 square blocks of historic buildings, museums and monuments. Sprinkled throughout these often decaying remnants are charming streets and alleys, modern hotels and trendy restaurants – a paradoxical marriage of an often brutal past with a present-day *joie de vivre*.

Start your tour at **1 Parque Colón**, a picturesque park located at the heart of Zona Colonial, where musicians often play and a statue of Christopher Columbus permanently listens. The park is surrounded by several historic buildings, including the **2 Catedral Primada de América**, a Gothic-style cathedral built in the early 16th century where a construction worker found the alleged remains of Christopher Columbus. There's plenty of controversy over where Columbus' body actually lies, but ask any local and there's no question – at least half of his remains now rest within the Faro a Colón (Columbus Lighthouse) in Santo Domingo Este.

Directly to the west of Parque Colón is **3 Calle El Conde**, one of the oldest streets in Santo Domingo and a lively thoroughfare with string lights, rustic lamp posts, musicians, and

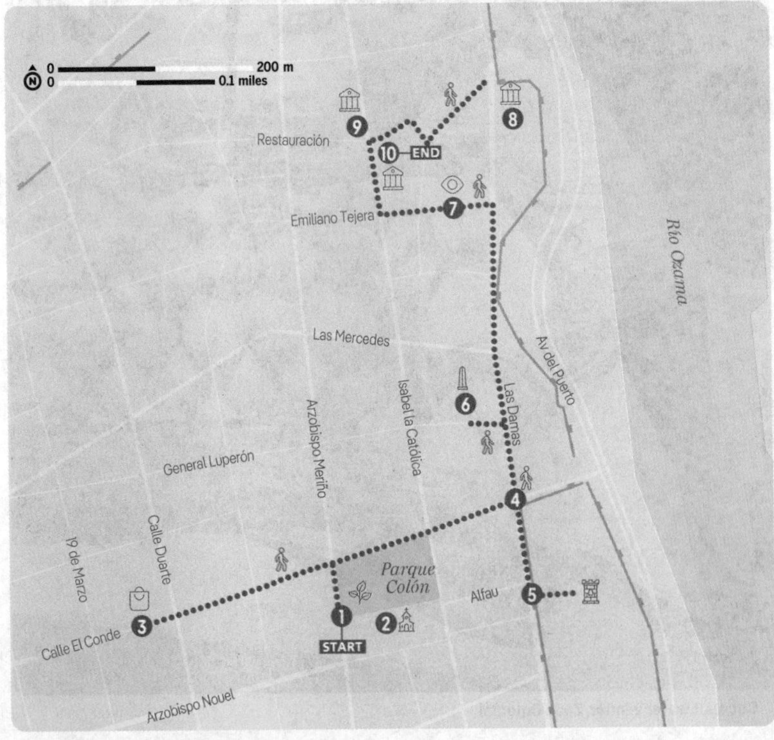

plenty of small shops for picking up a few cigars, souvenirs and Dominican crafts.

After exploring El Conde, walk back east past Parque Colón toward **4 Calle Las Damas**, a cobblestone street once used by the wives of dignitaries for their nightly strolls, including María de Toledo (Diego Columbus' wife) and her ladies. Along this street, you'll find the **5 Fortaleza Ozama**, a Spanish fortress built in 1502; and the **6 Panteón Nacional**, a resting place for the Dominican Republic's national heroes.

Continue north on Calle Las Damas to **7 Plaza España**, an expansive square often filled with tourists and visitors listening to musicians from the chic restaurants and cafes housed in historic buildings. In Plaza España, you'll also find the **8 Alcázar de Colón**, a former palace built in the 16th century by Christopher Columbus' son, Diego. Today, it's a museum that showcases life during the Spanish colonial period in the Dominican Republic.

Just west of Plaza España is the **9 Instituto Duartiano**, a wax museum that commemorates the life of Juan Pablo Duarte, widely considered the father of Dominican independence and one of its most integral activists and thinkers. Inside, wax figures tell the story of the Dominican fight for independence from Haiti through the eyes of the Duarte family.

Finally, wind down your walking tour with a sip of the DR's favorite spirit: rum. Directly south of the Instituto Duartiano, you'll find the **10 Museo del Ron y la Caña**. Housed in a 16th-century building, the museum is an ode to the storied history of rum in the Dominican Republic and has some of the tools and equipment used to produce rum in the 1500s on display. There's a small area for sampling and purchasing some of their flavored rums, along with a sizeable bar that opens up at night for thirsty revelers.

Calle Las Damas

BASEBALL TIPS

Nati, a national tour guide, shares his recommendations for one of the Dominican Republic's favorite pastimes: baseball.

When to watch The baseball season runs from October to February.

Where to watch The Estadio Quisqueya – home to the Tigres del Licey and the Leones del Escogido – is on Av Tiradentes, easily accessible from most Santo Domingo hotels.

Who to root for There are six teams: Tigres de Licey, Leones del Escogido, Los Toros de Este, Águilas Cibaeñas, Estrellas Orientales and Gigantes del Cibao. There's an intense rivalry between Los Escogidos and the Tigres because they're both from Santo Domingo. Like the Yankees and the Mets, people are very passionate about those teams.

GETTING AROUND

Driving isn't for the faint of heart in Santo Domingo. Street lights and stop signs are a rarity and are rarely heeded. Horns are often substitutes for turn signals and cars create lanes where there aren't any, making fender benders a common sight. Essentially, driving in Santo Domingo is a free-for-all – there are no rules. Best let someone else take the wheel.

In terms of public transportation, use the metro (Santo Domingo's commuter train), *públicos* (old buses and minivans that travel the same route, but stop whenever someone flags them down) or *guaguas* (old buses and minivans that cram in commuters by the dozen) to move around the city.

Ultimately, the most convenient and safest way to maneuver around the capital is to use Uber or call Santo Domingo Taxi (1-305-204-6504) for reliable transportation.

Beyond Santo Domingo

Parque Nacional Los Tres Ojos
Santo Domingo
Dunas de Baní

From arid deserts to ancient underground lakes, Santo Domingo's surroundings offer surprising vistas worthy of a day trip.

Beyond the busy and cacophonous capital lies a treasure trove of natural wonders that seem at odds with the frenetic pace of the city. At Parque Nacional Los Tres Ojos, crystalline lakes in underground caverns reveal a history beyond Spanish colonial rule – one that places the Taíno tribe at the center of a sacred site known for its lush foliage and tranquil beauty.

Just west of the city center, the land becomes arid and sparse, hinting at the Saharan-like desert clime that awaits past Baní. There, the results of the Pleistocene epoch's effects are on full, glorious display alongside the area's resident goats, iguanas cacti, plus the errant sandboarder cresting its sandy dunes.

TOP TIP

Look for roadside stands selling fresh mangoes as soon as you leave the capital – some of the tastiest versions are grown in Baní.

Dunas de Baní

TODD AARON SANCHEZ/SHUTTERSTOCK ©

Roadside fruit stall, Baní

Dreamy Desert Dunes

A SAHARAN OASIS BY THE SEA

Although it's a 1½-hour drive from Santo Domingo, the **Dunas de Baní** feels like a world away. Head west out of the city and through the small town of Baní until you hit the military base guarding the Dunas de las Calderas National Monument. Wind your way past sleepy goats and sunbathing iguanas until you reach the nondescript entrance to the dunes on your left.

The dunes have a considerable history. They date back to the Pleistocene epoch, when the sand deposited by nearby rivers was magnificently sculpted into subtle waves by the region's harsh winds. And it's a startling scene – a vast expanse of sloping sand dunes cresting up to 35m high, dotted with olive trees and prickly pears that provide just enough shade for the resident goats.

The sand is hot (wear sneakers, not flip-flops) and the whipping winds are fierce, but your reward comes at the end of a 10-minute trek that leads to the rough currents of **Bahía de Las Calderas**. Desolate and wild, the beach here feels private and untamed as the dunes aren't heavily touristed. Colorful, glossy stones and pieces of quartz tumble over each other on the shore as the rollicking waves break in pounding succession. Swimming in the surf isn't advised.

Sandboarding is also a popular activity in the dunes. Bring your own board or use one of the planks or pieces of driftwood left behind by other surfers and cruise your way downhill.

DULCES & PASTELERÍAS

No trip to the Dunas de Baní is complete without a stop at one of the area's *dulcerías* (sweets shops) and *pastelerías* (pastry shops). The town of Baní is well known for its sugar handiwork, the most popular of which are on display at **Dulcería Las Marías** and **Dulcería Las Tres Rosas**. Glass cases carefully shield *polvorones* (Spanish shortbread), *churumbeles* (candy-coated coconut pops), *deditos de novia* (sugar-coated guava biscuits) and *bolas de tamarindo* (sweet tamarind bonbons) from overeager hands. But the real treasure is found in the refrigerated cases behind the counter: chilled tubs of *dulce de leche con coco* – a cool, creamy concoction akin to ordering a soft-serve cone after a long, hot day on the beach.

WHERE TO STAY IN SANTO DOMINGO

Whala Boca Chica
A simple, no-fuss all-inclusive resort within walking distance of the popular Boca Chica beach. **$**

Hodelpa Nicolás de Ovando
Set up base camp at the entrance of the Zona Colonial in the historical home of DR's first governor. **$$**

Casas del XVI
Escape to one of seven opulently restored colonial houses boasting private plunge pools. **$$$**

A WORD ON MAMAJUANA

Walk around Santo Domingo long enough and you'll eventually run across a glass bottle filled with what looks like soggy wood chips, herbs and a mysterious dark liquid. It's mamajuana – a drink native to the Dominican Republic and a legend in its own right. Invented in the 1950s by Jesús Rodríguez, it was touted as an aphrodisiac that could knock out the flu, aid in digestion, and even cleanse the blood, liver and kidneys. Recipes are often passed down within families from generation to generation, but almost always include some combination of rum, red wine and honey. The resulting concoction then steeps with pieces of tree bark and a blend of herbs for up to 20 years.

UHRYN LARYSA/SHUTTERSTOCK ©

Parque Nacional Los Tres Ojos

An Underground Taíno Treasure

SUBTERRANEAN LAKES IMBUED WITH MAGIC

In the midst of Santo Domingo's frenzied hustle lies **Parque Nacional Los Tres Ojos**, a lush, open-air limestone cavern that was created centuries ago when underground caves collapsed in on themselves and filled with water.

Consisting of three humid caverns (the *tres ojos* or 'three eyes') with dark-blue lagoons connected by stalactite-filled passages, Los Tres Ojos was once a sacred site for the indigenous Taíno tribe who would come here to worship and observe fertility rites. The lakes are continually fed by an underground river, bringing a diverse array of minerals, bacteria and animals to the site. And if you believe local lore, touching the water is said to bring good fortune.

The three eyes, 'discovered' in 1916, are Aguas Azufradas, La Nevera (named for its cooler temperature) and Las Damas (named after the women who would bathe here). In addition to the three lagoons, a fourth called Los Zaramagullones can be seen from above if you walk toward the end of the park.

Upon entrance, a long stairway will take you down a narrow tunnel in the rock, and a concrete path at the bottom leads through the caves. At the third *ojo,* a small boat can be hired to visit the fourth *ojo*. Awaiting you is a gorgeous lake beneath open sky, filled with fish and peckish birds skimming the water for their next meal. And if deja vu kicks in, it's not entirely out of place – *Jurassic Park III* and *Tarzan* were both filmed here.

GETTING AROUND

If you're driving to the Dunas de Baní, expect several cash-only toll roads along the way and intense traffic congestion when making your way through the town of Baní itself.

SOUTHWEST COAST

Bucolic and untamed, the southwest coast of the Dominican Republic is one of the country's best-kept secrets. Most tourists flock to heavy-hitters like Punta Cana and Puerto Plata, leaving the provinces of Barahona and Pedernales quiet and flush with secrets worth exploring. This is where you can hike a mountain (the Bahoruco range), splash around in the falls of a cool river (San Rafael), visit the largest lake in the Caribbean (Lake Enriquillo) and admire the frothy waves of the Caribbean Sea relentlessly striking the shore – all in one day. It's why ecotourism is quickly on the rise here.

The southwest coast, especially Pedernales, feels undiscovered and raw – a place where life has a meandering pace and people take their time. But this is all on the verge of changing. Several large-scale resorts have set their sights on the region, so appreciate this unspoiled paradise before mass development drastically changes its way of life.

Southwest Coast

SANTO DOMINGO

TOP TIP

Don't count on rideshare or public transportation in the southwest – they're sparse or unavailable. It's best to rent a car or opt for a tour company. Driving at night is inadvisable – the desolate terrain means a lack of street lamps. Spotting speed bumps (and the errant livestock) becomes nearly impossible.

Barahona

ROAD TRIP

Country Road, Take Me Home

The southwest coast is where country living meets the sea, and the best way to experience it is to wind your way along the coastline of the Barahona province into the arid plains of Pedernales. The route connects small seaside towns that have their own secrets to share – from exquisite larimar jewelry to fresh cow's-milk cheese. The route can be easily driven in one day but is best spread over two or three.

1 Lake Enriquillo

Begin at Lake Enriquillo, located off DR-48. Clocking in at 352 sq km, this saline lake is the largest in the Caribbean and home to American crocodiles, iguanas and flamingos. You can take a boat trip to a small island in the middle of the lake, called **Isla Cabritos** – it was formed from the remnants of an ancient seabed, so sightings of fossilized coral and seashells are quite common.

The Drive: Get back on DR-48 and wind your way through DR-535, crossing through wide expanses of dry brush and undeveloped land.

2 Barahona

The busy beachside town of Barahona is where local students learn the art of refining larimar stones and crafting one-of-a-kind jewelry (p293). Make it a point to stop at **Delicias Mariscos** for a plate of tender *pulpo al ajillo* (octopus in garlic sauce) and fresh *chinola* (passion fruit) juice – the outdoor terrace catches a nice breeze from the neighboring sea.

The Drive: The coastline along Av Enriquillo is one of the country's most scenic drives. Larimar School & Museum (p293) is also on the way to San Rafael.

ROSTASEDLACEK/SHUTTERSTOCK ©

Iguana, Isla Cabritos

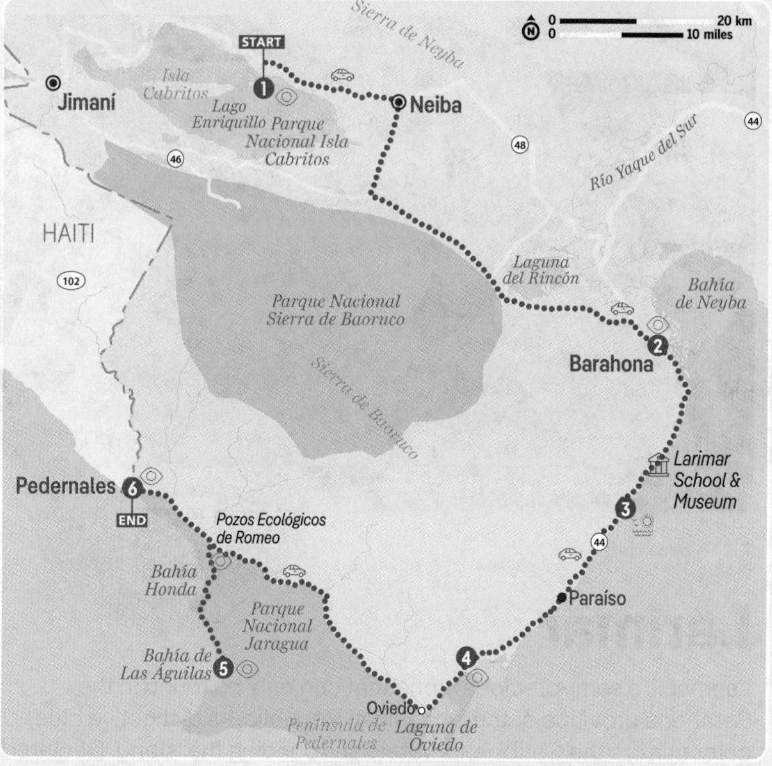

3 San Rafael

Here, locals have built small pools where the Río San Rafael flows into Playa San Rafael; several shacks sell fried fish and cold beer. The water is clean and cool. Don't miss the pools at **Villa Miriam**. It's a private residence, but open to the public on most days.

The Drive: Continue south on Av Bahia for about 27km, stopping at Parque Eólico Los Cocos to observe the largest wind park in the Caribbean.

4 Colonia Juancho

Colonia Juancho is a small town where cows, horses, goats and the ubiquitous strays roam free. Pop into **JF El Sofoke** to sample some of the town's salty white cheese paired with savory garlic crackers. Then stop by **Arroyo Salado**, a small, mangrove-shrouded lagoon where locals hang out and swim.

The Drive: From Arroyo Salado, drive 44km west on roads dusted with red clay before turning into the Parque Nacional Jaragua. Stop at the Pozos Ecológicos de Romeo, three cenotes filled with crystal-clear water and tiny fish.

5 Bahía de las Águilas

Within **Parque Nacional Jaragua** lies one of the DR's most pristine beaches: **Bahía de las Águilas**. You have to take a boat from the Cueva de las Águilas glamping site to access it, but once you're there, you'll have full run of an unspoiled stretch of shore. When your boat returns, enjoy an oceanfront feast of chargrilled lobster, paella and octopus-stuffed *mofongo* at **Cueva de las Águilas**.

The Drive: Double back to the entrance of Parque Nacional Jaragua and drive 30km north through winding barren roads. There are no street lights along the way, so take caution driving at night or avoid it altogether.

6 Pedernales

Right on the border with Haiti, the city of Pedernales is a great place to overnight (try Vista de Águilas Ecolodge) while enjoying some fresh-from-the-sea delicacies at *comedores* (small dining rooms) or restaurants like **Pengamo** and **Bocanye**.

MARINA KRYUCHINA/SHUTTERSTOCK ©

Scan this QR code for more insight into Taller Artesanal de Larimar Vanessa.

TOP SIGHT

Larimar

Larimar is a semi-precious stone that can only be found in the Barahona province of the Dominican Republic. Its distinctive blue color mirrors the Caribbean waters surrounding the island. Declared the DR's official stone in 2011, it even has its own national holiday (November 22). Larimar is a patriotic symbol for Dominicans, and some believe the stone imparts peace, clarity and good energy.

DID YOU KNOW?

Larimar isn't the only stone that can be found in the Dominican Republic. Blue amber, a rare variety of amber resin, is most commonly found in the mines located around Santiago. The greenish-blue hue is actually fluorescence stimulated by ultraviolet light.

A Brief History

Larimar – a rare, blue variety of the mineral pectolite – has only been found in the Dominican Republic. The stone is the result of hydrothermal fluids flowing into cavities in volcanic rock that's collected a certain mix of minerals. This gemstone was discovered in 1916 by Father Miguel Domingo Fuertes de Loren, a Spanish priest from the Barahona parish, as he was exploring the island's mountainous region. But it wasn't until 1974, when Miguel Méndez and Peace Corps volunteer Norman Rilling rediscovered it on a beach at the foot of the Bahoruco mountain range, that the stone's popularity took off. It was named after Méndez' daughter, Larissa, and the Spanish word for sea *(mar)* due to its oceanic-blue color.

Larimar Jewelry

Larimar is prized for its beauty and rarity. Its light-blue color is reminiscent of the Caribbean Sea and its swirling patterns are said to resemble the waves of the ocean. There are different grades of larimar – the highest-quality stones are a pure blue, turquoise color. Generally, the more white quartz and red clay that are present in the stone, the lower the quality.

Local artisans in the Dominican Republic have honed their skills in cutting, polishing and setting larimar stones to create unique and beautiful pieces of jewelry. Many of them use traditional techniques and tools, such as hand-held grinders and polishers, to create intricate designs in the stone. Since the pandemic, a new generation of young local artists have rediscovered their national stone as a way to express their Dominican pride through unique and thoughtfully crafted pieces of jewelry.

A Note on Mining

Extracting larimar is difficult, dangerous and can be deadly. The stone is found in the rugged and remote mountainous region of Bahoruco, and miners must traverse steep terrain and work in cramped and dark tunnels to extract the stone. The mining process is also hazardous due to the use of explosives to blast open the rock formations where the larimar is located. These explosions can cause cave-ins, and miners have been injured and killed in the process.

Additionally, the mining of larimar has had a negative impact on the environment. The use of heavy machinery and explosives can damage the surrounding ecosystem, and the runoff from the mining process can pollute nearby rivers and streams.

In recent years, efforts have been made to regulate the mining of larimar. The government has imposed restrictions on mining operations to prevent over-extraction of the stone and to ensure that the industry operates in an environmentally sustainable manner. Recently, some mining companies have implemented programs to improve the safety and well-being of their workers.

While you can find tours and excursions that will offer to take you directly to the mines, the ethics are often questionable and border on poverty tourism. The best way you can help support local small businesses is by learning about larimar through the area's museums and artisan shops and then buying a beautiful piece of jewelry from them to take home and enjoy.

SEE & DO

While watching the students at the Larimar School and Museum is special, it's not a hands-on experience. For a better shot at that, stop by **Taller Artesanal de Larimar Vanessa**. There, you can watch César and Mari Féliz crafting one-of-a-kind pieces. Depending on their schedule, you might just get the chance to work on refining and polishing a piece of your very own larimar.

TOP TIPS

- The best time to watch the students at the Larimar School and Museum work is during the evening or on Saturdays when they're not at work.
- You can also visit smaller roadside artisan workshops in Bahoruco, where the stone is mined.
- Most of the southwest – including the Larimar School and Museum in Barahona – is not wheelchair-accessible. Something to keep in mind during planning.
- Larimar prices vary depending on the region of the DR you're in. The best prices are generally found in Barahona.

JARABACOA

Jarabacoa
SANTO DOMINGO

Perhaps because the Dominican Republic's coastline and resorts have made it synonymous with sun and beach, its central range comes as a bit of a surprise. From the dry brush of the southwest coast emerges a lush, forested escape in the foothills of the Cordillera Central, where caoba trees form a cool canopy through winding mountainous roads punctuated by bright orchids and coconut palms.

Along the way, bleating goats and grazing cows crowd its verdant hills, which are also a repository of crystalline waterfalls cascading from jagged rocks and cliffs – not to mention some of the country's premier coffee plantations. Pico Duarte, the DR's highest mountain peak 3098m, summons adventurous hikers for multiday camping excursions. Fortunately, the area – nicknamed the Dominican Alps – is also well known for its spas, a welcome respite from hours spent on the various trails and rocky terrain in and around Jarabacoa.

TOP TIP

While driving into the Jarabacoa area, stop at Jacaranda, an elevated truck stop hawking Dominican sweets, pastries and fresh-pressed juices. There's even a small cocktail stand pouring up piña coladas and coco locos using freshly cut pineapples and coconuts – just make sure you're not the one behind the wheel.

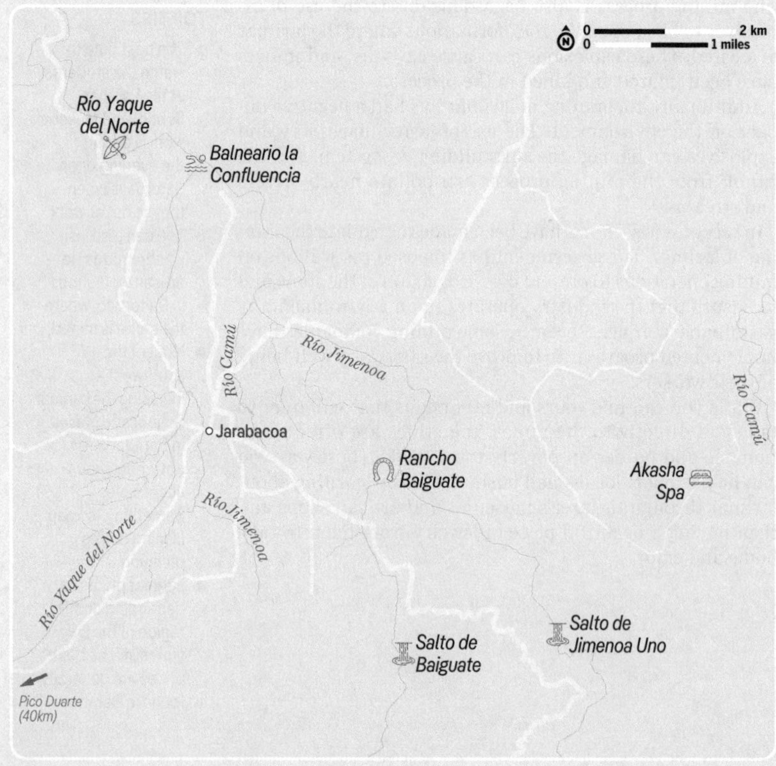

Salto de Jimenoa Uno

Chasing Waterfalls

COOLING OFF ON SCENIC HIKES

Jarabacoa and its surrounding areas are home to some of the DR's most beautiful waterfalls, so making the town your base camp is a wise idea. You can easily make a day of hiking to several of these scenic sights, and the journey to the area's waterfalls is typically a more approachable alternative to the strenuous and more advanced hikes required for locations like Pico Duarte.

If you don't have a rental car, the best way to get to the falls is with a local taxi or a tour operator. Fortunately, most are only 15 to 20 minutes from Jarabacoa.

About 9km from Jarabacoa's city center is **Salto de Jimenoa Uno**, a 60m cascade pouring from a gaping hole in an otherwise solid rock cliff. There's a sandy beach and an appealing swimming hole, but the water is ice-cold and potentially dangerous; if you do swim, stay far away from the swirling currents. Before reaching the falls (which were used in the opening scene of *Jurassic Park*), you'll pass a bean plantation and catch a glimpse of local life in the mountains.

Salto de Baiguate, about a 15km drive from Salto de Jimenoa Uno, may not have the impressive height and power of

JUST SAY SPAAAH

After a day of hiking, rafting and paragliding, your body might have a few things to say. Heed the call of your achy muscles and book a day pass at **Akasha Spa** in Jarabacoa. The pass guarantees that the entire property is yours from 11am to 5pm (no other guests will be allowed on the premises), and includes your choice of treatments, access to the sauna, use of the pool, and a barbecue feast prepared by Chef Andrés Pirela. Treatments are performed in an outdoor tent where the sound of birds, rushing waters and wind lull you into a deeply restorative state of peace. Bookings must be 48 hours in advance; contact Chef Dre via WhatsApp (829-423-9377).

WHERE TO STAY AND EAT IN JARABACOA

Sonido del Yaque Eco-Lodge
Community-tourism project consisting of six cabins set amid lush jungle above the Río Yaque del Norte. **$$**

Hotel Gran El Jimenoa
Tropical hotel situated right next to the Río Jimenoa with a pool, hot tub, spa service and in-house restaurant. **$$$**

Aromas de la Montaña
Festive mountaintop restaurant inside Jamaca de Dios with sweeping views, serving steak and Dominican favorites. **$$$**

WHY I LOVE JARABACOA

Jackie Gutierrez-Jones, Writer

For a country primarily known for its sun, sand and surf, Jarabacoa is a marvelous surprise. It's the cool compress to the DR's fevered beach scene, a verdant balm in the midst of its arid landscapes and scorching sand. Driving into Jarabacoa is a bit like entering Narnia – all of a sudden you're transported into a completely different universe. Mahogany trees, orchids and mountain peaks are woven together by rushing rivers and waterfalls. But the one-off palm tree reminds you the tropics aren't too far off.

It's the perfect mix of adventure (paragliding, anyone?) and glorious lazing about – just try to stay stressed during an hour-long massage in an outdoor mountain spa. It's impossible, I promise.

Jimenoa, but it has its own rocky allure. Plus, its smaller stature makes it ideal for kids – or those looking for a more tame waterfall experience. One of the best ways to access it is on horseback (you can book a tour with **Rancho Baiguate**), where you'll meander through local farms and see the occasional donkey loaded with satchels of chayote (choko). The waterfall itself is 25m high and spills out onto a shallow pool in the dry season. During the wet season, the water levels rise substantially, allowing for a refreshing swim.

Canyoning is also a popular activity at Salto de Baiguate – you'll likely encounter a few groups making their way down the edge of the rocky cliffs via rope. If you're interested, you can hire an experienced guide to help you descend the canyons encroaching the falls until your feet touch down in the Río Baiguate.

Note: Salto de Jimenoa Dos is a smaller waterfall that also extends from the Río Jimenoa – however, in 2018 a storm caused a suspension bridge that connected visitors to the falls to collapse. At the time of writing, it has yet to be repaired and cannot be accessed by pedestrians.

While you're wet (or maybe before you set off on a waterfall journey), tap into some of the action on the river. Locals and visitors frequently swim in areas of the Río Jimenoa – the **Balneario la Confluencia**, about 4km north of Jarabacoa, is a popular spot. For thrill-seekers, whitewater rafting excursions can be had on the **Río Yaque del Norte**. At 296km, it's the longest river in the DR and the second-largest in Hispaniola. The waters of the Yaque del Norte are classified as Class II rapids – accessible enough for novices but with just enough drops and thrills to keep an advanced rafter's attention. You can find organized whitewater rafting tours through the area's resorts or by contacting Rancho Baiguate.

GETTING AROUND

Walking to and from different experiences isn't an option here. However, the Central Highlands are fairly easy to navigate by car – the asphalt roads on most of the major routes have made this scenic drive a breeze as far as your car's shock absorbers are concerned; dozens of switchbacks, however, will test your driving skills.

If you don't have your own vehicle, taxis are your next option in terms of convenient transportation around the area. *Públicos* and *guaguas* are also available but operate on reduced hours and can be difficult to find in later hours.

Beyond Jarabacoa

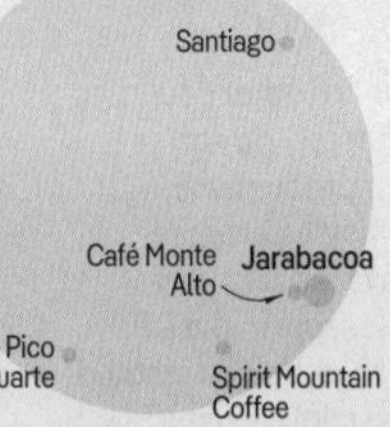

Whether you're hiking a mountain, sampling coffee cherries or exploring a museum, the areas around Jarabacoa offer both outdoor and cultural adventures.

The Cordillera Central is the highest mountain range not only in the Dominican Republic but in all of the Caribbean. It extends through the heart of the country for hundreds of miles, boasting crests between 1500m and 2400m, with several isolated higher peaks throughout – an ideal cooler clime for growing coffee and for physically taxing hikes.

While you're up in the mountains (and if time allows), dedicating a few days to summit the Pico Duarte or visit the coffee plantations in the region are excellent ways to experience a different side of the Dominican Republic's sun-and-surf reputation.

Itching to explore a more metropolitan scene? The city of Santiago beckons with museums, shopping and beautiful baubles made of amber.

TOP TIP

While driving through the area, stop at one of the many roadside stands selling slices of *arepa* (a cornmeal and coconut cake).

Hiking, Pico Duarte (p298)

BEAN THERE, DONE THAT

Unlike other countries that rely on coffee for productivity, enjoying a cup of java is a leisurely pleasure in the DR. The preferred method is simple – just a few dashes of cinnamon or nutmeg thrown into the grounds before brewing, and then a spoonful of sugar. And that's by design – you don't want too many tastes muddling the flavor of the brew. That's because the predominant variety grown in the Dominican Republic is arabica, a bean famous for its delicate flavors and natural sweetness. And while the country's coffee farms are small in size (most top out at about 3 hectares), their yield is relatively high, producing 350,000 to 500,000 bags per year.

Hit the Coffee Trail

CRUISING FOR CAFFEINE

Coffee aficionados, take heed: the brew made in the DR is a deliciously well-kept secret. It's a way of life here, but not through major chains selling syrupy concoctions. Depending on which site you plan to visit, you won't have to go very far to experience the art of Dominican coffee production – several of the region's coffee plantations can be found within 15 to 45 minutes' drive from Jarabacoa.

Spirit Mountain Coffee, an organic coffee plantation about 25km southwest of Jarabacoa, grows six varieties of coffee beans that are collected, washed, sorted and fermented before being laid out to dry in African drying beds. Most of its raw beans are delivered to local and international roasters, but Spirit Mountain roasts a few of its own batches to keep on hand for brewing and on-site sales. To access the plantation, prepare for a 4km drive through unpaved rocky terrain, creeks and farmland – a 4WD is highly recommended. After you arrive, a short, moderate hike will take you through an informational tour of the plantation – you can opt for a self-guided experience or enlist the expertise of their staff.

Closer to home, **Café Monte Alto** is a short five-minute drive from Jarabacoa's center. Owned by a local family that's been in the coffee business since the 1940s, Monte Alto's organic beans are grown in the Valle de Cibao but processed in Jarabacoa. Getting to their factory is considerably smoother than the rough path to Spirit Mountain. Once you're there, you can tour the facilities, learn about production methods, and sample a few cups at their on-site cafe.

Tackling Pico Duarte

HIKE THROUGH THE DOMINICAN ALPS

The one thing that Hispaniola has in spades is mountains. Primary among mountain ranges is the Cordillera Central that runs from Santo Domingo into Haiti, encompassing a third of the island's landmass. The Cordillera Central is home to **Pico Duarte**, the Caribbean's highest mountain at 3098m, which is so big it causes a rain shadow that makes much of southwest DR very arid. It's protected within the **Armando Bermudez National Park**.

Getting to the top of Pico Duarte is a source of pride for most Dominicans; fewer than 200 tourists complete the hike every year. It's a tough, multiday excursion that's not for the faint of heart – you'll need guides and support mules to finish the trek.

You'll start at base camp in **Manabao**, hike along streams in Los Tablones and gain a fair bit of altitude at Alto la Cottora

WAYS TO TOUR PICO DUARTE

Rancho Baiguate
Local tour outfitter offering waterfall, horseback and three-day Pico Duarte excursions from Jarabacoa.

Iguana Mama
One of the DR's first licensed adventure tour operators. Multiday treks include equipment, guides and mules.

Explora EcoTour
Sustainable company offering tours from Santo Domingo (transportation, guides, meals, snacks and mules included).

Coffee beans, Jarabacoa

before stopping at a wooden pavilion in **La Laguna** for a breather and a few snacks. From there, you'll cross the valley of Aguita Fría with its pine trees, green pastures and cold river that leads to some of the best views of your hike at **Descanso Alto de la Vela**.

At **Compartición**, you'll find a camping site with cabins, fire pits and a nearby river for bathing. It's a good spot to stop for the night before embarking on the final ascent. The next day, the temperature will drop considerably as you cross the **Valle de Lilis**, with vegetation often found in chillier climates. From there, it's about 1.8km to Pico Duarte, and then the descent back to Compartición for the night and, finally, Manabao.

HOW TO PREPARE FOR YOUR HIKE

Before you tackle a hike to Pico Duarte, it's wise to properly prep for the days ahead. It's a challenging trail, so be sure you're well rested, hydrated and properly warmed up for the climb ahead. As far as gear goes, you'll need a sturdy pair of hiking boots, wool socks, a hiking pole, a light backpack for water and snacks, a jacket, gloves (it gets chilly up in the mountains), a sleeping bag, blanket and a basic first aid kit. Most tour outfitters provide tents and tarps as part of their package, as well as mules – a must for transporting most of the cargo up the mountain.

Sightseeing in Santiago

MUSEUMS, BREWERIES AND BOTANICAL GARDENS

Whether you're interested in history, culture or nature, Santiago has a little bit of everything. A little over an hour's drive north of Jarabacoa, the DR's second-largest city is the capital of a vast tobacco- and sugarcane-growing region. Obviously, a visit here requires sipping rum and puffing a local cigar, but not before soaking up its many museums, galleries and gardens.

CULTURAL STOPS IN SANTIAGO

Casa del Arte
Studio and gallery space located in a renovated Victorian home exhibiting local artists.

Museo Rosita Fadul
Santiago museum honoring the accomplishments of Dominican women born in the Valle de Cibao region.

Theatron Stgo
Performing arts venue with a bar showcasing live music, plays and stand-up comedy shows by Dominican artists.

FOSSILIZED GOLD

Larimar isn't the only semi-precious stone mined from the Dominican Republic. The country also has sizeable reserves of amber, honey-hued resin from the extinct tree *Hymenaea protera* that can hold preserved insects and pieces of plants. Most of the DR's amber is mined in the Santiago province, an often dangerous endeavor for those extracting it from tight bell pits that are prone to collapsing.

The amber found here is considered some of the highest quality in the world due to its transparency and the frequency with which fossilized particles are found, making it appealing to jewelers and collectors. While yellow is the most frequently found color of amber, the DR also produces red, green and a rare blue amber.

Monumento de los Héroes de la Restauración

Start at the **Centro León**, home to exhibits and installations that showcase the art and history of the Dominican Republic. From stunning pre-Columbian artifacts to fascinating displays of contemporary art, it's a great place to gain a deeper understanding of the local culture.

The **Monumento de los Héroes de la Restauración** was originally constructed for the late dictator Rafael Trujillo, but after his death this iconic monument was given new life as a tribute to those who fought to liberate the country from foreign rule in the late 19th century. Climb to the top for breathtaking views of the city and the surrounding mountains. The **Jardín Botánico de Santiago** is perfect for a picnic lunch. This botanical garden features exotic plants that speak to the biodiversity of the Valle de Cibao, plus an arboretum, walking and cycling trails and a butterfly farm.

Santiago is also home to quite a few breweries focusing on local craft beer. **Cibao Brewing Co** and **Gallo Pelón** both serve various styles of brew along with light bites. For souvenirs, stop at the busy **Mercado Modelo** on Calle El Sol to sample some Dominican food while picking up a few pieces of jewelry or a *muñeca sin rostro* (doll without a face) to take home.

GETTING AROUND

Like in most regions of the Dominican Republic, a car is crucial for exploring the areas around Jarabacoa. The mountainous curves and the twists and turns can be mildly alarming – especially when guard rails are unnervingly absent. A 4WD will come in handy for traversing gravelly roads and crossing small streams.

NORTH COAST

North Coast
SANTO DOMINGO

Surfing hamlets, bohemian villages and rollicking beachfront bar scenes set the vibe for the Dominican Republic's picturesque north coast. Hugging the tumultuous waves of the Atlantic, the region is widely considered the water sports capital of the Caribbean, drawing in kitesurfers, wakeboarders and sailors from all parts of the world looking to catch gnarly waves during the day and knock back a beer at a beachside bar in the late afternoon.

The area is also a hotbed for ecotourism thanks to its natural preserves, lush botanical gardens and parks, and jungle-like rainforest environs. Fittingly, there's a strong focus on health, wellness, organic products and yoga establishments throughout the area that's embraced by the many condo-dwelling expats living in and around the town of Cabarete.

The northern region is also referred to as 'the Amber Coast' due to the abundance of the semi-precious stone being mined in nearby Santiago as well as neighboring Puerto Plata.

TOP TIP

If the nightlife in Cabarete is Disney Springs, neighboring Sosua is Vegas thanks to the casinos, nightclubs and a booming sex-work scene. While prostitution isn't illegal in the DR, the area of Sosua is known to exploit local Afro-Caribbean women with low economic mobility.

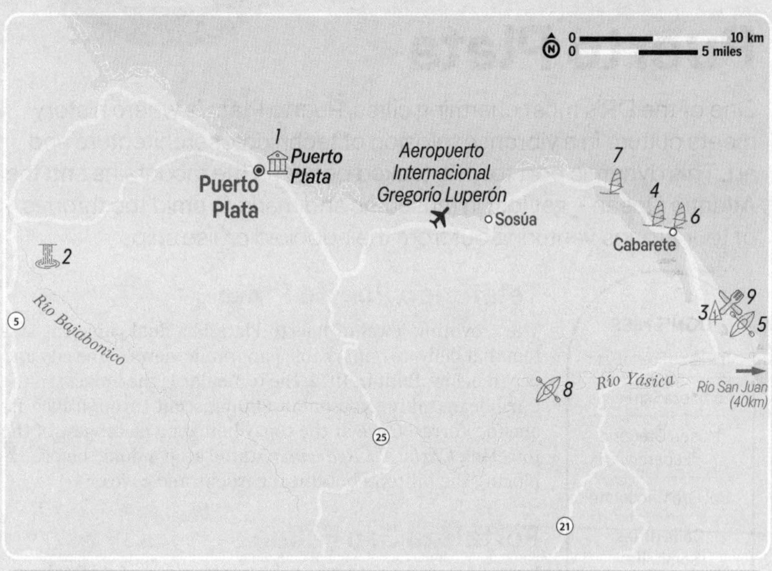

TOP SIGHTS
1 Puerto Plata

SIGHTS
2 Damajagua
3 Rugama Tours

ACTIVITIES
4 Kite Beach
5 La Boca Cabarete
6 Playa Cabarete
7 Playa Encuentro
8 Río Yasica

EATING
9 Wilson's at La Boca

MLIN/SHUTTERSTOCK ©

Scan this QR code for more information on the cable car (in Spanish).

TOP SIGHT

Puerto Plata

One of the DR's most charming cities, Puerto Plata is where history meets culture in a vibrant explosion of technicolor architecture and art. This dynamic port town is tucked between the mountains and the Atlantic Ocean – get lost in museums and markets amid the throngs of tour groups venturing out from their docked cruise ships.

DON'T MISS

- Teleférico Puerto Plata
- Fortaleza San Felipe
- Museo Gregorio Luperón
- Del Oro Chocolate
- Calle de las Sombrillas
- Paseo de Doña Blanca
- Museo del Ámbar Dominicano
- Ron Macorix

Teleférico Puerto Plata

The crowning jewel of Puerto Plata is a dual cable car system that delivers remarkable panoramic views of the city and ocean below. Built in 1972, the funicular is the longest in the Caribbean, taking you on an 800m ascent through Pico Isabel de Torres. Once at the top, you'll get a clear view of the towering *Christ the Redeemer* statue atop a dome before exploring the hilltop's botanical gardens and caves.

Fortaleza San Felipe

Located right on the bay, at the western end of the Malecón, San Felipe (pictured) is Puerto Plata's only early-colonial remnant. The fort, built in the mid-16th century to prevent pirates from seizing one of the only protected bays on the north coast, never saw any action. For much of its life, the structure's massive walls and interior moat served as a prison. Today, you can explore the monument (an audio tour is included with admission) and snap impressive photos of Puerto Plata's coastline.

Museo Gregorio Luperón

The life and times of native son and independence leader Gregorio Luperón are fleshed out inside this beautifully restored, pale-green, Victorian-era building. Photographs and period artifacts trace Luperón's life, from humble beginnings to his role as provisional president during the Restoration, as well as the story of Puerto Plata in the late 19th century.

Ron Macorix

After a quick informational tour of the barrel house and a short film on the history of Macorix, you'll get a chance to taste what you've come for – rum. After sipping your way through the brand's eight to 10 varieties, the gift shop awaits with a built-in bar serving rum cocktails and boozy popsicles.

Calle de las Sombrillas

More than 170 rainbow-hued umbrellas covering the alley aren't the only things fighting for your attention here – purple flowers bursting from their trellis, multicolored murals, and the occasional street performer with a monkey or parrot in tow are here too. Pop into **El Rincón del Café** for some of its chocolate-covered coffee beans or cool off with a cone from **Helados Ivon**.

Paseo de Doña Blanca

Right off Parque Central, Paseo de Doña Blanca was built as a memorial to Bianca Franceschini, an Italian who emigrated to Puerto Plata with her husband in 1898 and built Hotel Europa. The small alley is completely coated in bright pink, right down to the benches, flowers and floating bicycle display hanging on the wall.

Museo del Ámbar Dominicano

Within a 16th-century Victorian building, the Museo del Ámbar Dominicano houses a collection of amber exhibits including a small 50-million-year-old lizard and a 30cm-long feather. The museum also offers a tobacco experience with a lecture and a tasting for an additional cost. At the gift shop, you can purchase your own piece of amber and larimar jewelry, along with cigars and rum.

Del Oro Chocolate

When a tour starts with samples of hot chocolate and brownies, you're in for a treat. While you won't actually see the factory where Del Oro produces its organic chocolate, you'll learn how they grow their cacao, process their beans and make the chocolate through a short film and guided tour. An all-you-can sample tasting session at the end sweetens the deal – and the experience is free.

BRUGAL VS MACORIX

You'll find two rum juggernauts with facilities in Puerto Plata: Brugal and Macorix. As a local saying goes, Brugal gets the party started, but Macorix keeps it going. In other words, if you're looking for a strong party mixer, Brugal is your better bet. Macorix is more like wine – better for sipping slowly over good conversation.

TOP TIPS

- Get to the *teleférico* early – as soon as the cruise crowds roll in, you'll have to wait several hours to board the cable car.
- There are a couple of spots billing themselves as the official amber museum. The original is located in a Victorian building on Calle Duarte.
- Some tour operators still list a visit to the Brugal Rum Factory as part of their itinerary; however, the site stopped offering tours to the public in 2022.
- Make sure you have cash on hand for most of the museums and tours as several do not accept credit cards.

THE NORTH COAST'S BEST BEACHES

Allison Lockwood, owner of Nectar restaurant in Cabarete, shares her favorite beaches on the north coast (apart from the main beach Playa Cabarete):

Playa Sosúa
I love Playa Sosúa because it's very local. On Sundays, people bring boom boxes, play music and dance to reggae while kids play in the water. There are beach shacks selling excellent fried fish and lobster.

Río San Juan
Río San Juan is made up of three beaches: Playa Grande, Playa Preciosa and Playa Caletón. Caletón is my favorite because it's a family-friendly bay with very clear waters. Sculptures line the bay in honor of fishermen who have died off the coast.

Catch a Wave in Cabarete

A WATERY TRIPLE THREAT

One of the north coast's main hubs is Caberete, a one-time fishing and farming hamlet that's now the adventure-sports capital of the Caribbean and an ideal base for exploring the region. Beaches are its main attractions, and not just for sun and sand – each home to a different water sport, they are great places to watch beginner and advanced athletes alike.

The town's main beach, **Playa Cabarete** is ideal for watching windsurfing, though the best windsurfers are well offshore at the reef line. Look for them performing huge high-speed jumps and even end-over-end flips.

A sight to behold on windy days, **Kite Beach** is 2km west of town and welcomes scores of kitesurfers of all skill levels to negotiate huge sails and 30m lines amid the waves and traffic. On those days there's no swimming here, as you're liable to get run over.

The furthest beach from Caberete's center, **Playa Encuentro** is 4km west of town and home to the best waves – some up to 4m. It's the place to go for surfing, though top windsurfers and kitesurfers sometimes come to take advantage of the larger waves. The beach itself is a long, narrow stretch of sand backed by lush tropical vegetation; strong tides and rocky shallows make swimming here difficult. To find the beach, look for the Encuentro Surf Lodge and make a left at a security-staffed checkpoint. From there, follow the surfboards to parking on the beach. You'll find a variety of surf schools right on the shore for all skill levels – try your hand at balancing on a board and sign up.

Floating Down a River

EXPLORING THE YASICA

When you've exhausted the beach options around Cabarete, it's time to turn inland and take a look at **La Boca Cabarete**, about 7km south of Playa Cabarete right outside Sabaneta. It's only about a 10-minute drive to reach the entrance of La Boca. From there, it's another five minutes' jaunt on a sandy road that takes you to the shore and where the Atlantic Ocean meets the sand dunes and **Río Yasica**. The waters of Río Yasica are crystal-clear and flow from the mountains just outside town; on weekends, you'll find local families staking a spot along the river bed with portable stoves and barbecue in tow.

Compared to the Atlantic's tumultuous waves, the river's waters are considerably calmer and easy-flowing, making it an ideal spot for a variety of activities that don't involve a surfboard. Kayaks and paddleboards are an excellent way to explore the

WHERE TO EAT IN CABARETE

Fresh Fresh Cafe
Casual, cozy, no-frills eatery with a verdant back terrace selling smoothies, wraps, bowls and health supplements. **$**

Vagamundo Coffee & Waffles
Tropical Bohemian vibe at this outdoor cafe serving waffles with inventive toppings and coffee drinks. **$**

La Cocina de Mami
Small *comedor* run by the eponymous Mami and Angel serving traditional Spanish tapas and sangria. **$$**

Kitesurfing, Cabarete

SANTIAGO E. MOREL/SHUTTERSTOCK ©

waterway and its surrounding mangroves and coconut palms, but tubing also offers ample opportunity to observe the local flora and fauna (with a handy cup holder for your rum at the ready). You can find several tour operators in Cabarete that offer kayaking and tubing excursions on the Yasica.

Fishing and swimming are also popular activities on the river, along with a late afternoon meal at **Wilson's at La Boca**, a rustic waterfront shanty doling out fried seafood, plantains and tropical drinks. There's no electricity, and you'll need to board a questionable-looking dinghy to reach it, but the views and crispy fillets of parrotfish are worth the adventure.

A Playground of Waterfalls

NATURAL WATER SLIDES AND POOLS

A heady combo of adrenaline, nature and culture, the **27 waterfalls of Damajagua** are located about 71km from Cabarete or a 30-minute drive from Puerto Plata.

The history of the falls goes back centuries to the indigenous Taíno tribe, who believed that the waterfalls were a sacred place where they could communicate with their gods. Today, they're still considered a special place, and visitors are encouraged to treat them with respect.

BOTANICAL BEAUTY

To get a local taste of the north coast's ecotourism, book a day at **Rugama Tours**, a botanical garden and eco-park on the Río Yasica owned by Ruddy, a local ecology professor who's dedicated several years to collecting indigenous plants and letting them thrive on the property. You'll find an abundance of vegetation here – orchids, Hawaiian ginger plants, birds of paradise, hibiscus, and several varieties of fruits including mango, citrus, banana, dragon fruit and avocado – most of which Ruddy invites you to touch and interact with.

You can also grab a home-cooked meal in a treetop *palapa,* take a dip in the pool, check out the small zoo, rent a paddleboard or opt for a short boat tour.

WHERE TO STAY IN CABARETE

Surf Break Cabarete
Serene, *palapa*-topped budget accommodations in two lush complexes. Pool area and yoga studio. Great for solo travelers. **$**

El Encuentro Surf Lodge
Well-appointed bungalows and villas with a pool, restaurant, yoga platform, and direct access to Playa Encuentro. **$$**

Natura Cabañas
Thai-inspired bungalows with access to a secluded beach and two open-air restaurants serving health-conscious food. **$$$**

LEND A HAND

If you're looking to get involved with the sustainability efforts happening in the DR, several volunteering opportunities can put you directly in touch with the land and permaculture efforts in the area. **Cabarete Sostenible** is a nonprofit that started as a response to the food crisis brought about during the COVID-19 pandemic due to the fluctuations in global tourism. Currently, its goal is to create complete sustainability in Cabarete, from food sovereignty to entrepreneurship and wellness programs for the local population. Even if your stay is short, you can spend a day with Cabarete Sostenible helping with their efforts in civic agriculture, urban gardening, food packing and distribution, or local wellness programs.

ROB CRANDALL/ALAMY ©

Fishing, Río Yasica (p304)

This series of cascades and pools has been carved out of limestone by the rushing waters of the Río Damajagua. They range in height – some go up to 8m – and the water is cool and crystal-clear. Guides (mandatory at the falls) lead you up to the top via a path of stairs, over a suspension bridge, and through pools and cascading water before finally making a descent through a series of natural rock slides and heart-pounding jumps.

This experience isn't exactly a stroll in the park – you need to be in reasonably good physical shape and over the age of 12. But there's no minimum group size for the guided tour, so you can go solo if you wish. You can go up to the seventh, 12th or 27th waterfall; most jeep safari package tours only go to the seventh.

When planning your trip, set aside about four hours for the experience and wear water shoes with good traction. Note that backpacks aren't allowed within the falls, so most of your belongings will be left in the car or tour vehicle you arrived in – including towels and sunscreen.

GETTING AROUND

The roads around Cabarete are almost always narrow and busy; motorbikes are the main mode of transportation and they loudly weave their way in and out of traffic without much warning to other drivers on the road. In the city, the designated parking is scarce. Most people squeeze their vehicles somewhere along the shoulder of the road and hope that they don't get sideswiped or hit.

Aside from the shoreline, the towns aren't very pedestrian-friendly – sidewalks aren't common and vehicles like to test the road's boundaries, often brushing people walking to a restaurant or shop nearby. Keep a sharp eye on the road when walking around town or hop onto a *motoconcho* (a motorcycle taxi) if you're feeling brave, or use a taxi service.

PENÍNSULA DE SAMANÁ

Península de Samaná
SANTO DOMINGO

Samaná and Puerto Plata are a tale of two ports – the latter being more cosmopolitan and cultural while the former embraces a provincial and bucolic way of life, holding court among verdant, craggy cliffs. Samaná is a laid-back town defined by the humpback whales flocking to its warm waters in the winter and the industry that's flourished around observing them in their natural habitat and studying their behaviors and migratory patterns.

That's not to say that the Península de Samaná is myopically focused on these 30-ton mammals. In fact, within an hour's drive, you can find yourself in Las Terrenas, a sophisticated swirl of Dominican culture and European customs defined by the French, Italian and German communities cropping up on its shores and propping up chic cafes and restaurants. Nearby, Las Galeras beckons with several of the country's best and most secluded beaches. There are also waterfalls, underwater geography and natural parks ready for exploration.

TOP TIP

If you're driving into the Las Terrenas and Samaná area, be sure to take the toll road Blvd Turístico del Atlántico – it's a breathtakingly beautiful drive that's also easier to navigate than the alternative mountain passage.

Cayo Levantado (p310)

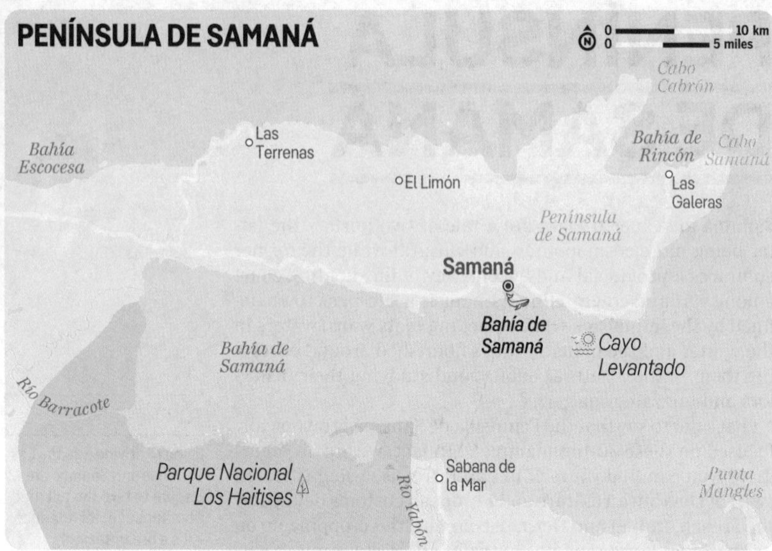

Whale-Watching in the Bay

SEARCHING FOR HUMPBACKS IN SAMANÁ

The town of Samaná – officially Santa Barbara de Samaná – is considered to be one of the world's top 10 whale-watching destinations. Around 60,000 people travel here every year between January 15 and March 25 to see the majestic acrobatics of these massive creatures.

It's a productive area for humpback whales, but researchers aren't exactly sure why. What they do know is that the whales spend six to seven months feeding in the North Atlantic waters before making their way to **Bahía de Samaná** for mating and, yes, birthing their baby calves (insert the obligatory 'awww' here). Interestingly, the whales do not feed while they're in the bay and females typically lose 25% of their body weight after birthing and feeding their calves.

Marine biologists camp out here in the winter months to observe the whales and record data on their activity during this busy time. How do they know they're studying humpback whales versus another species? Their 15m-long pectoral fins are white, and on their head, they have a set of knobs the size of a human first with two whiskers that help them feel what's around them.

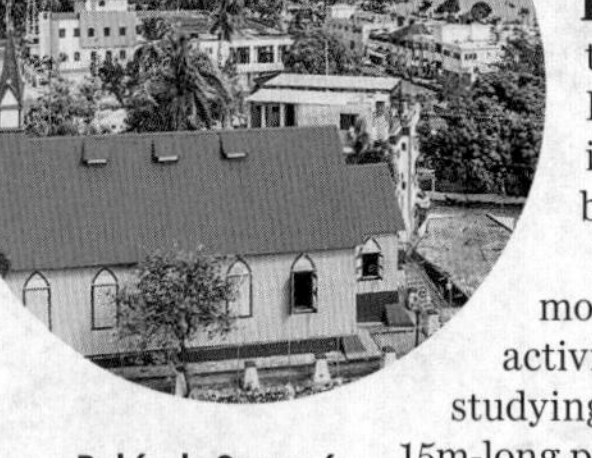

Bahía de Samaná

WHERE TO EAT ON PENÍNSULA DE SAMANÁ

Café Boulangerie Francaise
Flaky croissants, custard-filled brioche and hot espresso at this cozy French bakery and pastry shop. Cash only. $

Restaurante Luís en Cosón
Choose your own fillet at this seaside shack on Playa Cosón that will serve it with rice, beans and salad. $$

Paco Cabana
French cuisine meets Caribbean in this alfresco beachfront spot with cushy couches, candlelit tables and chilled cocktails. $$

KIT KORZUN/SHUTTERSTOCK ©

Whale-watching, Bahía de Samaná

Humpbacks, which get their name from the way they arch their backs when going down for a dive, are also famous for lifting their tail flute in the air after they go down for their dive. The tails have a distinctive black-white pattern that functions like a fingerprint and is unique to these whales.

They are the most active whales in the world – plenty of splashing and breaching – making an excursion to the warm waters of Bahía de Samaná an awe-inspiring thrill of a lifetime.

There are several tour operators offering excursions on the shore, although actually spotting a whale in the wild is never a guarantee. It takes about 15 to 20 minutes to reach prime whale-viewing territory, which – depending on the weather – can be quite a choppy and bumpy experience. Some tour operators will have motion sickness acupressure bands available for guests, but it might be helpful to bring your own pair, along with Dramamine, if seasickness is a concern.

Along the way, you'll be keeping your eyes peeled for tell-tale water spouts indicating that whales are nearby. Once you've reached an area with whales, only three ships are allowed to be within close proximity to the mammals for 30 minutes at a time. Any other vessels out on the water remain in a queue a good distance from the whales until it's their turn to approach the viewing area.

EATING IN SAMANÁ

Waves of expats, mainly hailing from France and Italy, have established little hubs of Euro-culinary joy in Samaná, where a house-baked *pain au chocolate* or a *bouillabaisse* are more common than local *comida criolla* (Creole food). A bounty of fresh fish ensures that a meal here always offers a cavalcade of flavors for seafood-lovers, whether taken in a sophisticated candlelit bistro or at a simple beach shack.

The majority of restaurants are located along Av Malecón, while cheaper eats can be found in converted wooden kiosks along the waterfront and along Av Francisco de Rosario Sánchez. **Playa El Valle**, a nice beach 10km to the north, has two informal beachfront restaurants.

El Cabito
Indulge in fresh seafood while perched over a cliffside with hawks soaring overhead and whales in the distance. **$$$**

Empanadas y Más
This hole-in-the-wall spot raises empanadas into an art form. Try the ceviche and *guanabana* (soursop) juice. **$**

Sol y Fresh
Sunny, colorful cafe for healthy-leaning fare including freshly pressed juices, smoothies, omelets and poke bowls. **$**

BELIPHOTOS/SHUTTERSTOCK ©

Los Haitises

A BOAT TRIP TO CAYO LEVANTADO

If the company hosting your whale-watching excursion offers an add-on experience to **Cayo Levantado** (aka 'Bacardi Island'), don't pass up the opportunity to dock for a few hours at this small island in the heart of the bay. Unspoiled sugar-white beaches fringed by swaying palms spill out into impossibly turquoise waters where visitors can kayak, paddleboard, swim or enjoy a lunch of freshly caught fish on the public side of the shore (half of the island is taken up by luxury resorts). Outside the whale-watching season, you can still take one of the boat taxis docked at Samaná port to the island or purchase a Cayo Levantado day pass through one of the area's tour operators.

Mother and calf coming up for air is a common sight, but if you're lucky you might spot a few males breaching in the distance, their powerful tails propelling them from the surf and exposing up to 90% of their body surface.

Bahía de Samaná is also home to several other species that are known to make guest appearances during a whale-watching excursion – on any given day, you might spot a curious pod of bottlenose dolphins engaging with the whales or a lone endangered leatherback turtle making its way through the waves.

Explore Parque Nacional Los Haitises

RAINFOREST WITH ANCIENT TAINO CAVES

Covering 1600 sq km, **Los Haitises** translates as 'land of the mountains' – its knolls were formed one to two million years ago when tectonic drift buckled the thick limestone shelf that had formed underwater. It's a worthy day trip by boat from Samaná town; most excursions cross the bay to reach the national park. It contains one of the DR's few remaining rainforests (used in the filming of *Jurassic Park*), but around it lies a terrain of rocky hills, multiple bays, ancient Taíno caves with pictographs, sinkholes, and tangled mangroves hosting a unique ecosystem for its resident manatees, frigate birds and over 700 plant species. Most excursions offer several options for exploring the park, including hiking, kayaking, zip-lining and boating.

GETTING AROUND

Reaching the Península de Samaná is best done by car – it's a winding path that will lead you through desolate country roads laden with speed bumps and potholes before reaching a picturesque cliffside road along the ocean.

Parking is a bit of a free-for-all in Las Terrenas, Las Galeras and Samaná – parking lots are scarce but street parking is typically free, although it can be crowded and difficult to maneuver. Parts of Las Terrenas and Samaná are walkable, but keep your head on a swivel – *motos* and cars are known to fly through intersections and drive dangerously close to curbs.

Beyond Península de Samaná

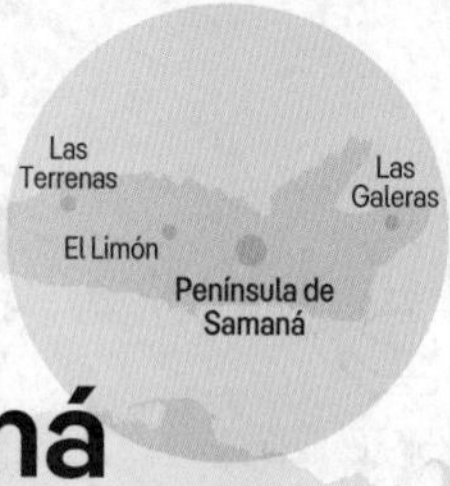

Outside Samaná town are tropical gullies with waterfalls and lagoons to explore. Along the way you'll find charming beachside towns with a European flair.

On the western coast of the Península de Samaná lies Las Terrenas, a busy, beachy town where French, Italian and Spanish languages fly fast and get lost within its chic cafes, alfresco bars and calm, palm-lined shores. On the peninsula's east side you'll find the quieter Las Galeras, a small fishing village that's the antithesis to Las Terrenas' constant hum, but no less infused with European expats.

Between the two towns is El Limón, a tall, cascading waterfall shrouded by thick forests that flows into a chilly pool. Just to the west outside the peninsula, you'll find the relatively secluded Dudu Lagoon, two crystal-clear pools that require an adventurous (or brave) spirit to be enjoyed.

TOP TIP

While parts of Las Terrenas and Las Galeras are walkable, you'll need a car – or the services of a tour operator – to get you to El Limón and the Dudu Lagoon.

Las Galeras (p312)

A Tale of Two Cities

EUROPE ON THE COAST

Once a rustic fishing village, **Las Terrenas** (an hour's drive from Samaná) is now a cosmopolitan town and seems as much French, Italian or German as it is Dominican. The balancing act between locals and expats has produced a lively mix of styles and a social scene more vibrant than anywhere else on the peninsula.

Motos and cars jockey for position on its crowded streets, where clothing, jewelry and home decor shops effortlessly mix bright beachy staples with well-known European brands. You can easily spend an afternoon drifting in and out of shops, stopping to enjoy a snack at one of the bakeries or gelaterias in town. Walking in either direction along the main beach road in Las Terrenas leads to a beachfront scattered with tall palm trees, calm aquamarine waters, and a smattering of restaurants and bars teeming with expats enjoying their evening cocktails and tapas while lapping up the salty ocean breezes.

Just 68km east of Las Terrenas is **Las Galeras**, the chill cousin of its western counterpart. One of the great pleasures of a stay in this small fishing village is losing all perspective on the world beyond – even the beautiful and isolated outlying beaches seem far away. By all means, succumb to the temptation to do nothing more than lie around your bungalow or while the day away at a restaurant. But if you summon the will to resist, Las Galeras offers a variety of land- and water-based activities including diving, hiking and ATV tours.

The town's laid-back charms have not gone unnoticed, drawing a cosmopolitan mix of European and North Americans who have also set up shop here.

BEACH BLISS AT LA PLAYITA

One of the most pristine beaches in the region, **La Playita** is perfect for an afternoon of unplugging from the more touristed areas without the disruptive noise of *motos* or blaring restaurant soundtracks. It's about 15 minutes from the main road in Las Galeras – take a quiet wooden path surrounded by trees and mangroves to a sugary sand cove that gives way to impossibly azure waters with small, gentle waves. There aren't typically many people here, save for a few patrons at the beachside shanties selling fried fish and cold drinks – but your best bet is to save your appetite for a restaurant in Las Galeras. Beach chairs, umbrellas and kayaks are available for rent.

Samaná's Stunning Waterfall

WATERY HEIGHTS ON HORSEBACK

The crown jewel of Samaná's waterfalls, **El Limón** is nestled within the lush greenery of the Parque Nacional El Limón, about half an hour's drive from Las Terrenas. Surrounded by rocky peaks, it's a tumbling 52m cascade into a beautiful swimming hole – the perfect spot to wash off the sweat and mud from the trip here, though it's often too deep and cold for a dip.

The trip to El Limón requires a 2.5km journey through thick tropical canopy either on horseback (expect a 15-minute ride; you can find several tour operators in Las Terrenas) or on foot (a 30- to 45-minute moderate hike). You'll travel through a

WHERE TO STAY IN LAS TERRENAS

Mahona Boutique Hotel
Whitewashed, Balinese-style bungalows featuring a small pool, plus an exceptional breakfast. **$$**

Mosquito Boutique Hotel
Family-run beachfront hotel with spacious and pleasant rooms, an on-site surf school and a hopping bar scene. **$$$**

Sublime Samana
Spacious villas with hot tubs, a spa and a 150m network of interconnected pools nestled within a modern luxury resort. **$$$**

Fruit shop, Miches (p316)

predominantly agricultural area, where farmers tend to their personal plots amid cacao, coffee, banana and coconut plantations. Along the way, you might spot the DR's national bird, the palmchat, as well as Hispaniolan woodpeckers and the broad-billed tody, along with once-endangered royal palm trees (they're now protected by the Dominican government). You'll also venture through several river crossings, so expect to get wet. If you've opted to hike, rubber sandals are your best friend here.

Once you arrive at the waterfall, there are a number of vendors selling snacks and water – you can take a break and admire the falls from here, or you can descend a set of steps to the base of the fall and dip your feet in the swimming hole or channel your inner Wim Hof and go for an icy dip.

PLUNGE INTO THE DUDU LAGOON

Drive about 73km northwest of Las Terrenas and you'll find the **Dudu Lagoon** – it's right off the DR-5. You'll see a welcome sign to your left and an area with plenty of parking. The lagoon is actually two connected bodies of water that branch out into the ocean through a more indirect route; it's surrounded by natural rocky cliffs and trees. Swimming here is a refreshing way to cool off from the punchy heat and humidity, but there's a catch: you'll have to jump 10m off a cliff or opt for a zip line that will shoot you over the lagoon before demanding that you drop into the water below. Or, just take the stairs for a less adrenaline-spiked entrance.

GETTING AROUND

Driving is one of the best ways to explore the areas in and around Samaná, whether it's renting a car or opting for a motorized tour. The roads are paved and in generally good condition, although areas in and around Las Terrenas can get quite congested in the morning hours and early evening. Designated parking spaces and lots aren't always a given – most drivers find street parking and wedge themselves into a nook that can safely accommodate their vehicles.

PUNTA CANA

Punta Cana
SANTO DOMINGO

For most people, visiting the Dominican Republic is code for spending a week at an all-inclusive resort in Punta Cana. To be fair, there's definitely some appeal in whiling your day away at a swim-up bar with access to limitless cocktails – and there's nothing wrong with doing just that. Sprawling resorts have taken up most of Punta Cana's prized coastline, so hassle-free access to its warm aquamarine waters is a bonus. Plus, there's a resort to suit just about anyone's needs – from kid-centric complexes with water slides and character breakfasts to adult-only escapes with private pools and beach bars galore.

But if you're willing to step outside the all-inclusive orbit, you'll find scenic mountaintops with tantalizing vistas, ancient caves and zip lines that soar over the green canopies of vibrant eco-parks, and a pretty darn convincing replica of a 16th-century Mediterranean village. The all-you-can-eat buffet will still be there tomorrow.

TOP TIP

Punta Cana, shorthand for the region as a whole, is somewhat of a misnomer. It actually refers to the area just east and south of the airport. The majority of resorts are scattered around the beaches of Bávaro and, increasingly, Playa Uvero Alto.

VALENTIN VALKOV/SHUTTERSTOCK ©

Barcelo Bávaro (p316)

SIGHTS
1 Montaña Redonda

SLEEPING
2 Barcelo Bavaro
3 Breathless
4 Club Med
5 Nickelodeon
6 Zoetry

ENTERTAINMENT
7 Scape Park

RUM WITH IT

It seems like no tour in the Dominican Republic is complete without a shot or two of rum. Like most Caribbean islands, Dominicans know their way around this popular spirit. Sugarcane grows exceptionally well on the island, so by the 1600s they had figured out that molasses (a by-product of refined sugar) could be fermented into alcohol. Dominican rum stands out because it's almost exclusively made in oak barrels – from fermentation and distillation, all the way through to the aging process (rum must be aged for a minimum of one year in the DR). With over 15 distilleries in the DR alone, the chances are you'll find a bottle that suits your palate and piña colada.

Living the All-Inclusive Life

CREATURE COMFORTS ON THE SHORE

You can't talk about Punta Cana without discussing the piles of resorts on its shores. The area carries the weight of the Dominican Republic's most dramatic beaches and turquoise seas on its tanned shoulders, hosting more all-inclusive stays than anywhere else in the country. Indeed, if you're looking to enjoy a small swath of sun, sand and water in the southeast DR, your best bet is to book a stay at one of these behemoths, with few exceptions.

Tourists flock to these sprawling city-states by the millions every year to be pampered and catered to with Disney-like precision and professionalism. And while it's difficult to get a true sense of Dominican history and culture within these gleaming towers and villas, you'll find bits and pieces of it woven throughout your stay, like the *mangú* (mashed plantains)

WHERE TO STAY IN PUNTA CANA

AC Hotel Punta Cana
Comfortable Marriott hotel (not all-inclusive) in the heart of Punta Cana with an infinity-edge pool, restaurant and bar. **$$**

Secrets Cap Cana Resort & Spa
Adults-only all-inclusive for poolside dining under a *palapa*, movies on the beach, spa treatments and golf course. **$$$**

Hard Rock Hotel Punta Cana
This den of decadence features a casino, several restaurants, poolside foam parties and in-room hot tubs. **$$$**

ECOPARK EXPEDITION

Nestled within the touristy bells and whistles of the Cap Cana area lies **Scape Park**, an eco-adventure experience for adventure seekers of all ages. The park's attractions have a rich history dating back to the indigenous Taíno people, including the Hoyo Azul, a stunning cenote with crystal-clear water that is perfect for swimming and snorkeling. You can also explore the park's verdant jungle on a zip-line tour or investigate its caverns and underground caves.

If you're looking for less of an adrenaline spike, you can take a peek at the parrots on Parrot Island or the rhinoceros iguana living in Iguanaland. In addition to its natural attractions, Scape Park has a small ranch with horses, goats and donkeys.

served for breakfast or the *bachata* and merengue rhythms that seep into the night's entertainment.

Just like their trademark buffets, you can find a resort that caters to your particular taste in travel or vacation. **Nickelodeon** – with its water slides, infamous slime buckets, and activities led by the network's beloved characters – has an outpost in Punta Cana for vacationing families. Meanwhile, resorts like the **Barcelo Bávaro** and **Breathless** promote an adults-only environment with nightclubs, in-room hot tubs and a plethora of bars to match. And if you're looking to tap into an experience that marries a bit of adventure with sun-soaked wellness, resorts like **Zoetry** and **Club Med** offer rock-climbing walls, trapeze classes, beachfront yoga, and excursions outside the resort walls.

Swinging in the Sky

MOUNTAINTOP VIEWS AND PHOTO OPS

The mountain views don't end at the Central Corridor – Punta Cana has its own rocky cliffs (albeit not as skyscraping in scope) with views that give the peaks in Jarabacoa a run for their money. To get a taste of that rocky mountain high in the southeast, drive about an hour from the heart of Punta Cana until you reach **Montaña Redonda** in Miches.

The family that owns this 300m-high hilltop has been inviting visitors to enjoy its peak since 1999, and they've made quite an operation out of the view. When you arrive at the base, you'll pay an entrance fee (RD$100) that includes a ride on the back of a truck all the way up the mountain.

Once you reach the top, you'll have a chance to take in the views of the Bahía de Samaná area, Playa Rincón, Playa Esmeralda, and the Limón and Redonda lagoons. But what Montaña Redonda is really known for is their perfectly placed photo-op props. Swings, hammocks and seesaws appear perched precariously on the edge of the hilltop, so if you angle your camera just right, it gives the illusion that you're flying through mid-air (don't worry – there's a small ledge beneath you). Guides who also double as photographers flit about the space snapping pics and offering photo packages for purchase. They can be quite pricey, so if you're on a budget, your smartphone's camera will do just fine.

There's also a small restaurant here offering *comida típica* (traditional Dominican fare) and a handful of shops selling Dominican crafts and souvenirs.

GETTING AROUND

Most of the resorts in Punta Cana offer round-trip transportation from the Punta Cana airport to their property – check with your accommodation provider to see how frequently shuttles arrive and depart. Road conditions and driving are considerably more developed in this area, so driving a rental car is less of a gamble than in other parts of the country. Taxis and rideshares are also widely available.

Beyond Punta Cana

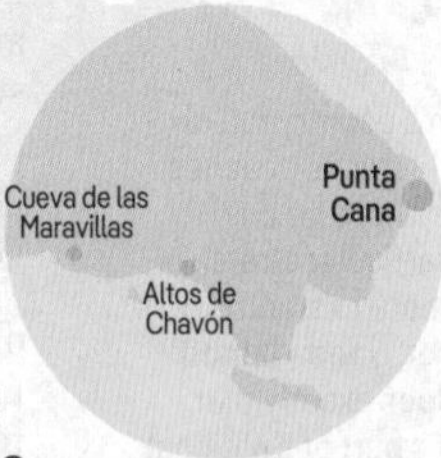

Cueva de las Maravillas
Punta Cana
Altos de Chavón

Punta Cana makes a great base for scouting out experiences beyond the beach, from Taíno caves to a Mediterranean village.

Outside the three-ring resort circus in Punta Cana lies a raft of unique destinations that offer a deeper look at the Dominican Republic, one that goes beyond its fabled beaches and sugary shores.

Before the Spanish docked their ships on Hispaniola's coast, the Taíno tribe were the principal inhabitants of the island and left their mark, quite literally, throughout the country – including the petroglyphs in an underground cave system situated between San Pedro de Macorís and La Romana. A bit further west from the caves in La Romana, a recreation of a 16th-century Mediterranean-style village watches over the Río Chavón, a stony vision conceived by an Italian set designer that's now home to artists and creatives.

TOP TIP

While the Cueva de las Maravillas and Altos de Chavón are near one another, dedicating a full day to each one is best for enjoying the site properly.

Altos de Chavón **(p318)**

SUNNING IN SAONA

In a country full of illustrious beaches, it's hard for any particular stretch of shore to stand out. Yet, **Saona Island** does exactly that. It's part of a national park – so while you can't stay overnight, you can spend a day snorkeling in its clear waters, observing the endangered starfish puckered to the bottom of the waist-deep Blue Lagoon, and lazing under the breezy palms. Saona is a popular excursion from Punta Cana, so there's no shortage of tour operators offering visits on a catamaran to its powder-white shores. You'll drive 79km to Bayahibe before sailing to the island (about two hours on a catamaran, or 45 minutes on a speedboat), but the music and drinks aboard make the time fly.

Cave Art from Long Ago

PRESERVED PETROGLYPHS UNDERGROUND

Located between San Pedro de Macorís and La Romana lies an underground network of caves that tells another side of the story of the Dominican Republic – prior to the brutal Spanish colonization efforts in the 1500s – and reveals the existence of a peaceful people whose way of life was all but eliminated from the island.

The **Cueva de las Maravillas** (Cave of Wonders) tells part of the story of the indigenous Taíno tribe. Part of the Arawak nation, the Taíno were generally peaceful, and were the first to meet Christopher Columbus in 1492 when he arrived to Hispaniola's shores. The caves – which were declared a national park in 1997 – are open to the public, but visits are carefully monitored and controlled to preserve the art and structures within.

After descending about 25m, you'll navigate through a 250m trail with 10 petroglyphs (rock carvings) and more than 500 pictographs (paintings on walls) that depict life among the Taíno tribe through images of people, animals and plants. One room, known as the **Water Mirror Gallery**, uses an artificial lake to mirror the ceiling of a cave with a pictograph of what appears to be a funeral ritual. Along the way, you may also spot a few snakes, diplopods, toads and bats living among the rocks.

This is also one of the few experiences in the Dominican Republic that accommodates visitors with disabilities via ramps, paved paths and an elevator.

An Artist Enclave Built from Stone

A MEDITERRANEAN VILLAGE COMES ALIVE

About 72km from the breezy beaches of Punta Cana lies a weathered village ripped from the pages of a Mediterranean fairy tale. It's a curious sight – a secret enclave founded by European pilgrims in the 16th century, perhaps?

Not quite. As convincing it appears, **Altos de Chavón** was built in 1976, not 1576. But the feeling of European influence isn't too far off. Conceived by the Italian master designer and cinematographer Roberto Coppa and designed by the Dominican architect José Antonio Caro, the town was made to look like the set of a 16th-century medieval village, complete with iron sculptures, cobblestone streets and timeworn stone buildings.

WHERE TO EAT IN PUNTA CANA

Wacamole
Good-time, open-air taqueria for Mexican street tacos, ceviche and fiery salsas made from organic ingredients. **$$**

Playa Blanca
Stylish and atmospheric beachfront restaurant within the Puntacana Resort complex serving seafood and pasta. **$$$**

SBG Punta Cana
The waitlist can be a bear, but this fine-dining den ups the fun factor with its roving tequila cart and cheese-wheel pasta. **$$$**

SANSARA/GETTY IMAGES ©

Cueva de las Maravillas

The village is located within the Casa de Campo resort complex, and you'll have to pay US$25 to enter. But the uniqueness of the experience is worth the pricey ticket. Altos de Chavón is considered an artists' haven – it even has its very own resident design school, partially founded by the US-based Parsons School of Design. That explains the avalanche of boutiques showcasing the talents of its resident artists, including pottery, weaving, silk-screening and jewelry making.

While perusing the shops, also take a moment to explore **St Stanislaus**, a stunning (and functioning) church that was named for Poland's patron saint after Pope John Paul II left some of his ashes there. Further along you'll find a 5000-seat Grecian **amphitheater** with magnificent views of the Río Chavón and the Caribbean Sea; it has hosted performances by Frank Sinatra, Elton John and Shakira.

PASTELES

The power of the plantain doesn't go unrealized in the Dominican Republic. One of the most sublime expressions of this starchy fruit is the *pastel*. While it's quite similar in appearance to tamale, there's no corn in the masa – it's simply mashed plantain and a meat filling all wrapped up in banana leaves, aka *en hoja*. (Versions using *yautía* or yuca are also quite popular.)

On your way to Punta Cana, make a stop in the city of **San Pedro** and pay homage to **Amables**, a no-frills restaurant specializing in *pasteles*. The large versions of these rich and savory plantain pockets can easily feed two people – but no one will blame you for keeping it all to yourself.

GETTING AROUND

If you're not using a tour operator to get you to destinations around Punta Cana, renting a car is your best bet. While not the most scenic routes, the roads – many of which are highways – are modernized and paved, offering a smooth ride between sites. Be sure to have Dominican pesos on hand to get past the occasional toll booth.

KRIKOF97/SHUTTERSTOCK ©

Arriving

Options for getting to the Dominican Republic include flights into any of the seven international airports, overland crossings and international cruise ships. The high season runs from mid-December to March, so expect busier airports. Depending on the airport, you'll find some cafes and shops in the arrivals hall, but they may be closed in the early morning and late in the evening.

By Air

Most of the major regions of the Dominican Republic have access to an international airport. Consider flying into one place, like Santo Domingo, and out of another, say, Puerto Plata, to see more of the country.

By Boat

The Dominican Republic is a popular destination for international cruise ships. The ports in Santo Domingo and Puerto Plata (Taino Bay) see the most action, but other regions of the island are equipped to host these large vessels.

Money

Currency: Dominican peso (RD$)

CASH

Cash is still king in the Dominican Republic. The more remote the area, the less likely you'll be able to use anything else. Have cash on hand to pay for excursions, souvenirs or meals in small roadside *comedores*. The Dominican currency is the peso, but US dollars are widely accepted.

DIGITAL PAYMENTS

Resorts and global businesses can process digital payments. Things may get tricky if you venture off the resort and head into town, but an increasing number of services and businesses are beginning to embrace money transfer apps like Remitly. In more remote areas, your digital wallet may be out of luck.

CREDIT CARDS

Credit and debit cards are becoming more common among Dominicans (and more widely accepted for use by foreigners). Visa and Mastercard are widely used, especially in areas frequented by tourists. However, Amex is pretty much a no-go at most places except for resorts and global businesses. Some businesses add a surcharge for credit card purchases.

Getting Around

The Dominican Republic is a fairly small, so it's easy to drive or take public transportation from one side of the country to another. Most destinations can be reached within three to four hours by car; however, the inadequate road infrastructure in some of the more remote regions – like the Southwest Coast and Samana Peninsula – will require the use of a 4WD.

PUBLIC TRANSPORT

Large cities like Santo Domingo and Santiago have public bus systems. In Santo Domingo, specifically, there's a rapid transit metro system (pictured). Other city buses are more or less like *guaguas*, where you board quickly and pay the *cobrador* when he comes round.

EQROY/SHUTTERSTOCK ©

BUS

Private buses are useful for travel between different regions. Three main companies (Caribe Tours, Expreso Bávaro and Metro) provide comfortable, frequent service along a network of major cities. Tickets can be purchased at bus terminals or online.

MOTOCONCHO

You can generally find a few *motoconchos* (motorcycle taxis) parked in front of the entrance to most resorts. They're fairly common around the DR and are an efficient way to get around. Fares run around RD$100 to RD$200, but can be higher in heavily touristed areas.

TAXI/RIDESHARE

Uber operates in the major cities (Santo Domingo, Santiago and Puerto Plata) at a fraction of the cost of a taxi. Cabify, which tends to be less expensive, can only be found in the capital. They're generally safe to use but can be hard to find outside major metro areas.

AIR

Flights are useful if you're short on time, though they're the most expensive option and are frequently unavailable. The main domestic carriers and air-taxi companies include Air Century, SAP Group and Sky Cana.

DRIVING ESSENTIALS

Drive on the right side.

Speed limits are 40km/h in the city, 80km/h outside the city and 120km/h on freeways.

Roads range from good to horrible.

Above: Levera Beach (p331); Right: St George's (p330)

GRENADA

HANDSOME TOWNS, RAINFOREST AND EMPTY BEACHES

With a multitude of fine beaches, adventurous jungle hikes and charming towns, the Spice Isle adds flavor to any Caribbean itinerary.

Despite being a nation that offers the full gamut of top-shelf Caribbean experiences, Grenada is not a heavyweight on the regional tourism scene. It remains a refreshingly authentic destination that absorbs international arrivals effortlessly without losing any of its beguiling charm.

While it may not be high on the must-visit list for the uninitiated, the vast majority of those travelers that are lucky enough to know the three islands that make up the country return again and again, called back by its wonderful white sandy beaches, lush rainforested interior, delicious rich cuisine and fascinating history.

Grenada is nicknamed the Spice Isle due to its extensive plantations of seasonings – nutmeg even appears on the national flag – and on the fertile main island you can often smell delicious sweet aromas in the air.

The hilly capital, St George's, with its colorful buildings overlooking an elegant old port, is one of the most charming towns in the region, while the slow-paced rural areas of the island are sprinkled with hiking trails, hidden waterfalls, tranquil lakes and even Cold War artifacts left behind by the infamous US invasion of the country.

And if you believe Grenada is relaxed, wait until you get to Carriacou. The second-biggest island in the country is home to many of its best beaches but not a single resort, and feels plucked directly from another, simpler era.

THE MAIN AREAS

GRENADA ISLAND
Rainforest, snorkeling, spices and chocolate. p328

CARRIACOU
Total relaxation on silky white sands. p334

Find Your Way

Grenada the country is made up of three islands, Grenada, Carriacou and tiny Petit Martinique, which are linked by passenger boat and small plane, although services are not daily so you'll need to plan your itinerary accordingly.

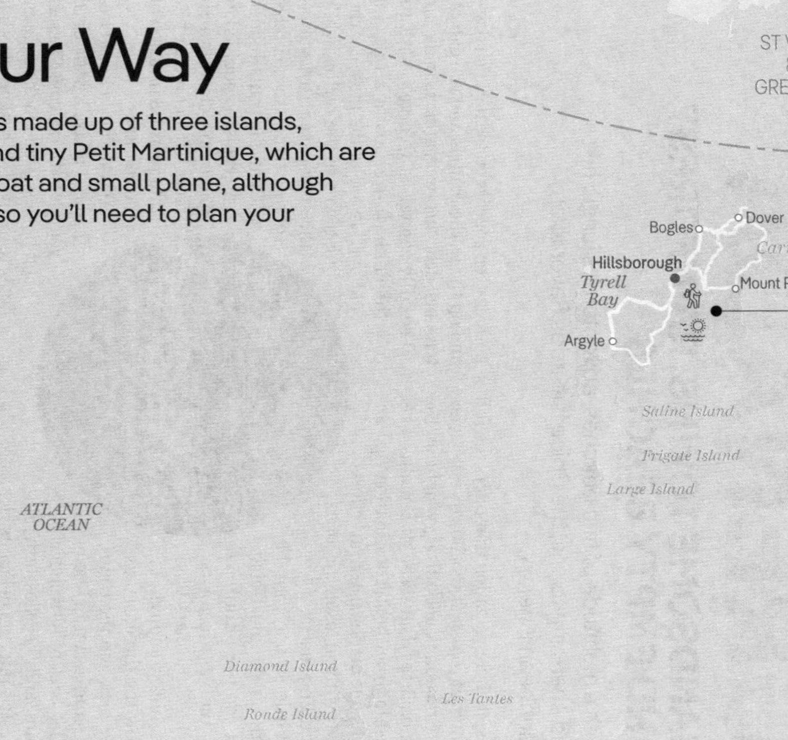

ST VINCENT & THE GRENADINES

Petite Martinique

Dover

Bogles

Carriacou

Hillsborough

Mount Pleasant

Tyrell Bay

Argyle

Saline Island

Frigate Island

Large Island

ATLANTIC OCEAN

Diamond Island

Les Tantes

Ronde Island

Carriacou, p334

A timeless Caribbean island with stunning white-sand beaches and deserted cays fronted by brilliant blue waters, with friendly locals and a vibrant carnival.

Grenada Island, p328

The country's main island is a lush wonderland rimmed by magnificent beaches, with colorful towns, epic rainforest hikes, and excellent diving and snorkeling.

LOCAL BUS

In Grenada, 'buses' aren't buses at all but rather crowded, privately run minivans running along a number of lines branching out from St George's in Grenada and Hillsborough in Carriacou to reach most parts of both islands.

WATER TAXI

Water taxis are small, usually colorful painted boats that take passengers from populated areas to remote beaches and smaller islands on both Grenada and Carriacou. You'll need to agree a fee beforehand and arrange a pickup time in advance.

TAXI

Taxis in Grenada have no meter and prices are technically fixed according to distance but you should check with the driver before getting in. There are no transportation apps but most businesses will call a trusted driver upon request.

FROM TOP: AISHA SYLVESTER/SHUTTESTOCK ©, WANDERING LEXICON/SHUTTESTOCK ©

Plan Your Time

It's a good idea to try to spend time on both Grenada and Carriacou to get a taste of these starkly different destinations, but wherever you're based fine beaches will be just around the corner.

OTORONGO/SHUTTERSTOCK ©

Anse la Roche (p336)

If You Only Visit One Place

- If you have limited time, pick a hotel somewhere around **Grand Anse** (p330) on Grenada, from where you can explore the gorgeous beaches of the southwest, including **Morne Rouge** (p331) and **Magazine Beach** (p331).

- After a couple of days of relaxation, take a trip to attractive capital St George's and climb up to **Fort George** (p330) for panoramic views over town and along the coast before taking a stroll around the bustling **Carenage** (p330).

- Next morning take a boat trip up to Molinere Bay to snorkel or dive in the **Underwater Sculpture Park** (p332) before returning to Grand Anse for a last-night sundowner right on the sand.

Seasonal Highlights

Grenada has warm weather year-round so the only real planning issues revolve around the rains. The heaviest rains usually fall from June until November but even then there's a fair amount of sun.

JANUARY

Calm weather and clear waters make for excellent **diving** at the Underwater Sculpture Park and elsewhere around Grenada.

FEBRUARY

Carriacou Carnival brings parades, concerts and non-stop partying to this otherwise sleepy island.

MARCH

Perennial sunshine paints the sands a brilliant white and makes the turquoise waters glow across the country.

R GOMBARIK/SHUTTERSTOCK ©, HEMIS/ALAMY ©, OTORONGO/SHUTTERSTOCK ©

One Week on Two Islands

- After spending four days getting to know the best of Grenada Island, take the fast boat to **Carriacou** (p334) and set up base close to the soft white sands of **Paradise Beach** (p335).

- Take a water taxi over to uninhabited **Sandy Island** (p336) for a swim or a spot of snorkeling before heading down to **Tyrrel Bay** (p336) for drinks and a meal overlooking the yacht-filled bay.

- On your second day, hike or take a water taxi to **Anse la Roche** beach (p336) to relax in spectacular solitude surrounded by dense forest, before taking a walk through the diminutive capital **Hillsborough** (p335).

If Time is No Constraint

- After returning from Carriacou, see more of the main island by exploring the interior and remote east coast. On your first morning, get up early to hike through the rainforest in **Grand Etang National Park** (p333) before continuing down to the pleasant seaside town of **Grenville** (p331) to enjoy a traditional meal.

- The following day go for an early swim in the protected waters at **Bathway Beach** (p331) before driving to remote **Levera Beach** (p331) to take in the fine Grenadine views.

- On your way back stop at the traditional **River Antoine Rum Distillery** (p331) then visit **Belmont Estate** (p332) to see the chocolate-making process up close.

APRIL
Music lovers descend on Carriacou for the lively **Maroon and String Band Festival**, featuring national and international artists.

MAY
There's still plenty of sun around but crowds are down and beaches are far less crowded.

AUGUST
The country's biggest party, the **Spicemas** carnival, gets going in and around enchanting St George's.

OCTOBER
Some risk of storms but rains begin to taper off and there are great low-season accommodation deals around.

Carriacou

GRENADA ISLAND

The island of Grenada is one of those rare destinations that really does have everything. Whether you're looking for shimmering sands, delicious cuisine, gourmet treats, unspoiled nature, fascinating history or fun nights out, the Spice Isle has you covered.

An almond-shaped, beach-rimmed tropical playground with around 75 miles of coastline surrounding a lush interior covered in swaths of verdant rainforest, it is absolutely stunning from top to bottom. But despite having so much to offer, it remains a down-to-earth and extremely relaxed place, with some of the friendliest residents anywhere in the Caribbean. Most of the population reside in colorful seaside villages and towns that are safe, welcoming and great to explore – that is if you're able to pull yourself away from the island's magnificent blue waters.

There are fine beaches everywhere but they're especially beautiful in the southwest where the esteemed Grand Anse takes pride of place.

TOP TIP

Both vehicle hire and taxis are fairly expensive in Grenada so mastering the local bus system is not only a great way to immerse yourself in Grenadian culture but can also lower costs significantly. It's usually possible to pay bus drivers extra to deviate a little from their path.

Above: St George's; Right: Coconuts for sale, St George's (p330)

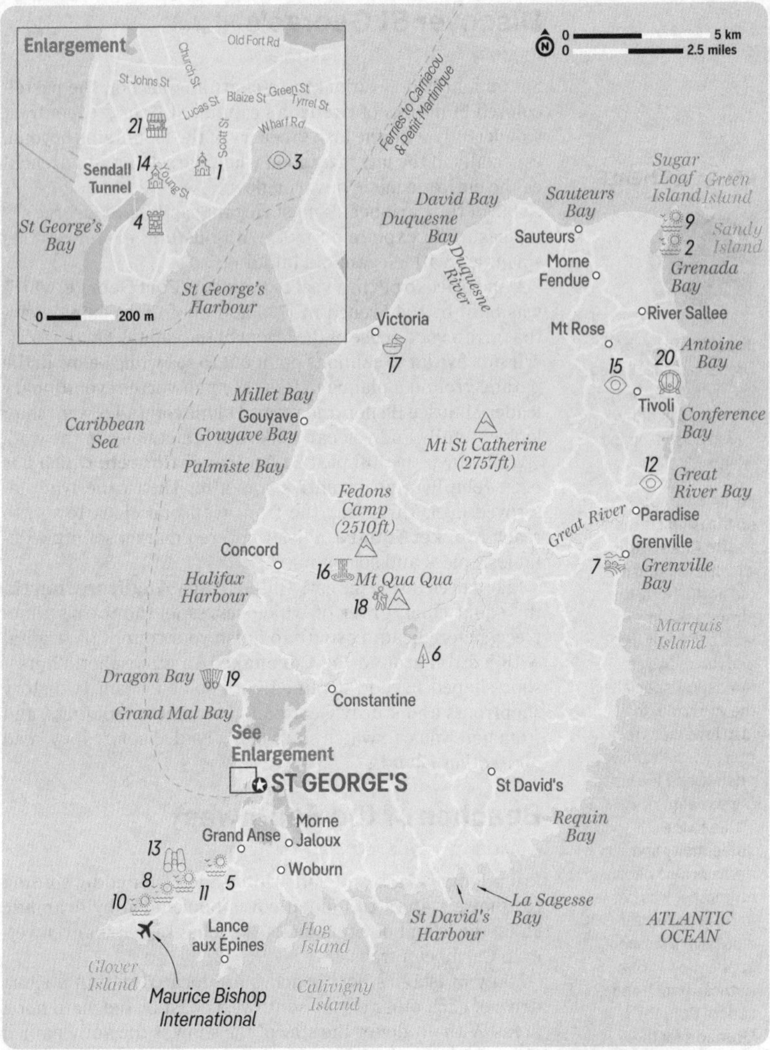
Enlargement
Old Fort Rd
Church St
St Johns St
Lucas St
Blaize St
Green St
Tyrrel St
Wharf Rd
Scott St
Young St
Sendall Tunnel
St George's Bay
St George's Harbour
0 200 m
21
14
1
3
4
0 5 km
0 2.5 miles
Ferries to Carriacou & Petit Martinique
David Bay
Duquesne Bay
Duquesne River
Sauteurs Bay
Sauteurs
Sugar Loaf Island
Green Island
Sandy Island
Grenada Bay
Morne Fendue
River Sallee
Victoria
Mt Rose
Antoine Bay
Tivoli
Conference Bay
Millet Bay
Gouyave
Gouyave Bay
Caribbean Sea
Palmiste Bay
Mt St Catherine (2757ft)
Great River Bay
Paradise
Great River
Grenville
Grenville Bay
Fedons Camp (2510ft)
Concord
Halifax Harbour
Mt Qua Qua
Marquis Island
Dragon Bay
Grand Mal Bay
Constantine
See Enlargement
ST GEORGE'S
St David's
Requin Bay
Morne Jaloux
Grand Anse
Woburn
La Sagesse Bay
St David's Harbour
ATLANTIC OCEAN
Lance aux Épines
Hog Island
Glover Island
Calivigny Island
Maurice Bishop International
2
5
6
7
8
9
10
11
12
13
15
16
17
18
19
20

SIGHTS
1 Anglican Church
2 Anglican Church
3 Bathway Beach
4 Belmont Estate
5 Carenage
6 Fort George
7 Grand Anse
8 Grand Etang National Park
9 Grenville
10 Grooms Beach
11 Levera Beach
12 Magazine Beach
13 Morne Rouge
14 Pearls Airport (abandoned)
15 Quarantine Point

ACTIVITIES, COURSES & TOURS
16 Underwater Sculpture Park

EATING
17 Diamond Chocolate Factory

DRINKING & NIGHTLIFE
18 River Antoine Rum Distillery

SHOPPING
19 Market Square

AGENTURFOTOGRAFIN/SHUTTERSTOCK ©

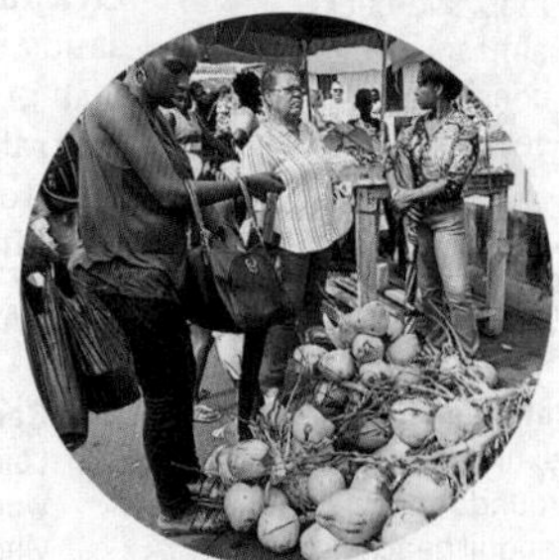

Discover St George's

GRENADA'S CHARMING CAPITAL

Set on a hillside overlooking a charming harbor, the pastel-colored buildings of Grenada's capital, St George's, contrast wonderfully with the lush greenery of the mountains beyond, especially in the late afternoon when the setting sun drenches the entire scene in a warm glow.

One of the Caribbean's most elegant capitals, St George's is a pleasure to explore on foot, with bustling narrow streets sprinkled with elegant old buildings.

A fine place to begin a visit to the city is **Fort George**, which was built by the French in 1705 and affords sweeping views that give a good sense of the layout of the capital. On the western side five large cannons point out to sea while below in the parade ground a plaque marks the spot where revolutionary leader Maurice Bishop and several of his comrades were shot; look carefully and you can make out bullet holes in the wall.

Walk down the hill past **St Andrew's Church**, which has been rebuilt in an inventive way after Hurricane Ivan destroyed everything bar the front wall and clock tower, to reach **Market Square**, a lively covered market selling vegetables, spices and souvenirs.

Take a peek inside the early-19th-century **Anglican Church**, the squat clock tower of which serves as the town's timepiece, before heading south to finish your tour of the capital with a stroll around the **Carenage**. An atmospheric horseshoe-shaped harbor, it's lined with some elegant two-story shopfronts and sturdy Georgian government buildings, and from here you can watch ships being loaded before they head off to other islands.

RELAXING MEALS

Joachim Joseph, a Grenadian chef based in Grand Anse, has pioneered healthy vegan cuisine on the island.

My favorite spot on the island is the **Petite Anse Hotel**, which is located in the north. Here, they always customize meals to fit my diet, and the drinks are fantastic, especially the virgin mojito. I also love their fresh fruit juices, the view is pristine and the vibes are so calm.

Due to the authenticity and perhaps also because my mother was born and raised there, I also have a strong connection to St Patricks parish and I adore **Punjabi Grenada** for their food, laid-back atmosphere and consistently fantastic service.

Beaches of the Southwest

EXPANSIVE SANDS AND HIDDEN COVES

From long expanses of soft white sands fronted by shining turquoise waters to hidden coves bookended by dramatic cliffs, the island of Grenada has beaches to delight even veteran Caribbean travelers.

Many of island's best beaches are located within a short drive of each other on the southwest coast by the main hotel areas Without doubt the star of the show is the aptly named **Grand Anse**, which boasts a full 1¼ miles of wide powdery sands running down to brilliant blue waters, all backed by lush green mountains. While the beach has the highest concentration of hotels on the island, it is big enough to never feel crowded and it attracts a mix of Grenadians and visitors, meaning there's always a vibrant atmosphere.

WHERE TO STAY ON GRENADA

Calabash Hotel
Luxurious rooms and spacious grounds on one of the most tranquil beaches on the island. **$$$**

Caribbean Cottage Club
Laid-back and great-value wooden cottages for those who prefer their digs with less concrete. **$$**

Lance aux Epines Cottages
Beautiful views, complete kitchens and large living areas make for a fine, family-friendly option. **$$$**

Just to the south, beyond the pretty picnic area with sweeping views at **Quarantine Point**, the beach at **Morne Rouge** has less development than its flashier neighbor but has equally soft sands that meet calm, crystal-clear waters and has a backdrop of shady trees.

Even quieter still is the hard-to-find **Grooms Beach**, a secluded strip of white sand strung between rocky headlands and backed by a wall of greenery. It's usually empty although a major hotel development on the northern headland may change that.

Towards the end of Maurice Bishop Hwy right in front of the airport, **Magazine Beach** is nicknamed the Caribbean's prettiest departure lounge and is indeed a fine place to get a last-minute shot of sun, sand and sea, with gentle waves of luminous blue water rolling onto swaths of fine sand.

Explore Eastern Grenada

HISTORY, BEACHES AND STRONG RUM

Grenada's remote east coast is the perfect place for slow-paced exploration along seldom-transited country roads that pass through gorgeous countryside.

Begin in the bustling fishing town of **Grenville**, which has several elegant old stone buildings, before heading north along the main coast road to the abandoned **Pearls Airport**, a remarkable reminder of Grenada's fleeting role as a Cold War battlefield. Once the main airfield on the island, it was seized by marines during the US invasion, stranding two Cuban planes beside the runway. These days it's a tranquil place with goats nibbling at the shrubs next to the tarmac. You can climb inside the Russian-made Antonov jet but you'll need good footwear – there's jagged metal everywhere.

Next stop is the historic **River Antoine Rum Distillery**, one of the most traditional rum manufacturers in the Caribbean. The facility has been run by residents of surrounding villages for generations and produces eye-watering overproof rum from locally grown sugarcane crushed by an antique waterwheel.

Continue northwards for refreshment of a different kind at **Bathway Beach**, the best of the east-coast beaches for swimming due to a long rock shelf running parallel to the shoreline that creates a deep, tranquil pool. There are shady picnic tables, making it a fine place to while away the afternoon. But make sure you leave time for isolated **Levera Beach**, a spectacular sea-turtle nesting area on the northeast corner of the island, where expansive soft sands afford magnificent views of the pyramid-like Sugar Loaf Island just offshore and the southern Grenadines further afield.

BEST BITES IN GRENADA

Melting Pot
Overlooking the sea in Grenville, this unpretentious diner has an excellent homestyle hot buffet. $

Andy's Soup House
Roadside place serving delicious traditional soups – come on Friday for the testosterone-boosting 'mannish waters.' $

Nutmeg
This Carenage institution does great rotis and mains. $$

Patrick's Local Homestyle Cooking
A no-frills restaurant serving a wide selection of local specialties. $

Coconut Beach
Unbelievably tasty Creole cooking and great rum punch right on Grand Anse. $$

Deyna's Tasty Foods
Salt fish and bakes for breakfast and a hot buffet lunch. Downtown. $

Jam Down
Follow the sweetly scented smoke to this roadside van selling the best jerk chicken on the island. $

My Place
Tasty rotis and tangy doubles fly out the door at this little Grenville winner. $

WHERE TO DINE OUT ON GRENADA

Aquarium
Fine dining beneath a wall of massive boulders on pretty Magazine Beach. **$$$**

BB's Crabback
Inventive modern Caribbean dishes bringing out the flavors of fresh island ingredients. **$$$**

Armadillo Restaurant
Reserve one of the eight spots on the communal dining table for multiple courses of gourmet delights. **$$**

Grenada's Boutique Chocolatiers

FROM BEAN TO BAR

While Grenada is known around the world for its spice plantations, another highly valued cash crop is also an important part of the island's economy: cocoa.

Although cocoa has been grown on the island for hundreds of years for export and local consumption as cocoa tea, the gourmet chocolate industry in Grenada has its origins in the late 1990s when Mott Green, an ecologically minded American, founded the Grenada Chocolate Company in Hermitage on the east coast.

Traditionally, cocoa farmers had been required to sell their crop to a national export body at a low fixed price, but the arrival of chocolate makers on the island meant they could bypass the monopoly and increase their profits.

These days several companies turn local cocoa into chocolate bars with rich, complex flavors. It's well worth visiting one of the factories to see how cocoa is processed to make the delicious bars that grace supermarket shelves.

Dating back to the 17th century, **Belmont Estate** was once dedicated to nutmeg but in the aftermath of Hurricane Ivan wiping out most of the crop in 2004, large areas have now been converted to cocoa plantations. The estate produces its own gourmet chocolates, including varieties imbued with island spices, and visitors can follow the chocolate-making process from the plantation to the finished product.

The **Diamond Chocolate Factory** is set in an 18th-century distillery by a river on the northwest of the island and produces the Jouvay brand, which can be found in shops across the island. The factory is focused on production rather than tourism so you're likely to see specific activities rather than the entire chocolate-making process.

PUTTING THE SPICE IN THE SPICE ISLE

Grenada's moniker 'Spice Isle' owes much to one humble tree. While a variety of seasonings are grown around the island, by far the biggest export is nutmeg, with the country producing 20% of the world's total. All of the trees on the island are descended from the first ones planted here by the British in 1843. Once ripe, the fruit is processed, with the nutmeg coming from the seed itself and mace being produced from the waxy surrounding fibers. A good place to see the process up close is the **Nutmeg Processing Cooperative** in Gouyave, where row after row of drying racks line the drafty old facility awaiting workers who sort the fragrant pods.

Molinere Bay's Underwater Sculpture Park

FINE ART BENEATH THE WAVES

You'd never know it at first glance but quiet Molinere Bay, just north of St George's, is home to one of Grenada's most extraordinary attractions, where art and nature come together in an otherworldly creative realm. Beneath the surface of this otherwise unremarkable stretch of water are more than 80 sculptures grouped into around a dozen main works that together form the **Underwater Sculpture Park**. Founded by British artist Jason deCaires Taylor with the intention to

WHERE TO DRINK ON GRENADA

Plywood Bar
Grenada's most intimate beach bar has good tunes, tasty snacks and awesome views.

61 West
An upmarket beach bar with drinks served on the sand under shady canvas.

West Indies Beer Company
A wide choice of real ales brewed on-site, with delicious bites and a fun atmosphere.

NANDANI BRIDGLAL/SHUTTERSTOCK ©

Belmont Estate

provide unique anchor points for new coral growth, the project has now expanded to include works by several other artists. The works in the park change in appearance over time as marine life takes hold, with aquatic plants, sponges and tropical fish adding splashes of color to the gray monuments backed by a translucent bluish canvas.

Rewarding Rainforest Treks

TOWERING PEAKS AND MOUNTAIN LAKES

Covered in tracts of dense rainforest, the mountains of Grenada's lush interior are several degrees cooler than the coastal plains, making the area the perfect place for long hikes among nature.

Just a short drive from St George's, **Grand Etang National Park** is home to some of Grenada's highest peaks as well as an expansive lake backed by lush greenery.

One of the best treks in the park is the three-to-four-hour round-trip climb to the boulder-topped **Mt Qua Qua**, where fine views to both the Atlantic and the Caribbean coasts as well as Lake Etang await. Serious hikers can continue on a challenging muddy path past several cascades to **Concord Falls** and down to the main west-coast road – an epic five-hour adventure.

BEST DIVING & SNORKELING IN GRENADA

Blessed with many coral reefs and an abundance of marine life, Grenada is a fine place for snorkeling and diving, with spectacular sites for novices and pros alike.

One of the best places for both snorkeling and diving is **Flamingo Bay**, just north of Molinere Bay's Underwater Sculpture Park, which has an ample array of healthy corals and colorful reef fish beginning just feet from the shore.

On the south of the island, secluded **Grooms Beach** is ideal for beginner divers, with a shallow reef covered with soft corals and sea fans, while the southern end of nearby **Magazine Beach** is perfect for snorkeling, with numerous shoals of fish closeby to the sand.

GETTING AROUND

Grenada has an extensive bus network, with privately operated minivans running along most main roads on the island, with the notable exception of the airport, where taxis cling tightly to their monopoly.

In the city you need to hail the vans at designated stops, but they're not clearly marked so you might have to ask a local to point you in the right direction. Outside built-up areas you can hail the vans anywhere. To get off you'll need to shout 'bus stop driver' above the music or tap the roof or window.

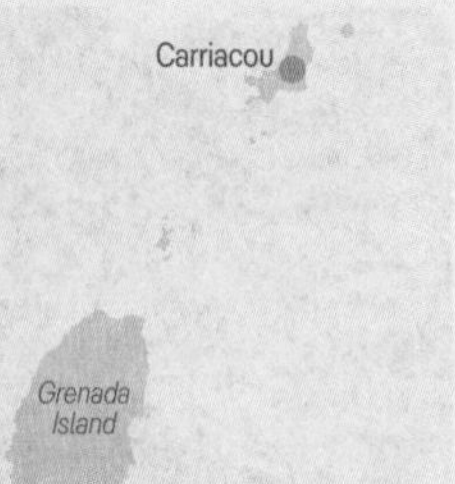

CARRIACOU

The southernmost of the inhabited Grenadine islands, tranquil Carriacou has somehow managed to avoid the tourism spotlight and remains almost unknown outside Grenada despite being blessed with powder-like sands and the most brilliant turquoise waters. And its fortunate residents wouldn't have it any other way. You won't find cruise ships, big resorts or tacky souvenir shops here – this is Caribbean life the way it was 50 years ago: quiet, friendly and so very relaxed.

Linked to the main island via an infrequent boat service and with very little traffic, it has a sleepy provincial feel that makes it the perfect destination for unwinding. There's enough space on its gorgeous beaches to ensure they never feel crowded, while just offshore, tiny uninhabited islets await those that want the full castaway experience. If all that relaxation gets old, there's also good hiking, great snorkeling and intrepid kayaking adventures on offer.

TOP TIP

The ride from Grenada to Carriacou on the fast ferry can be rough, especially the stretch between the main island's northern tip until just before Tyrrel Bay. If you're prone to sea sickness take a pill at least an hour before departure, or consider the short flight, which is not that much more expensive.

Above: Hillsborough; Right: Carriacou

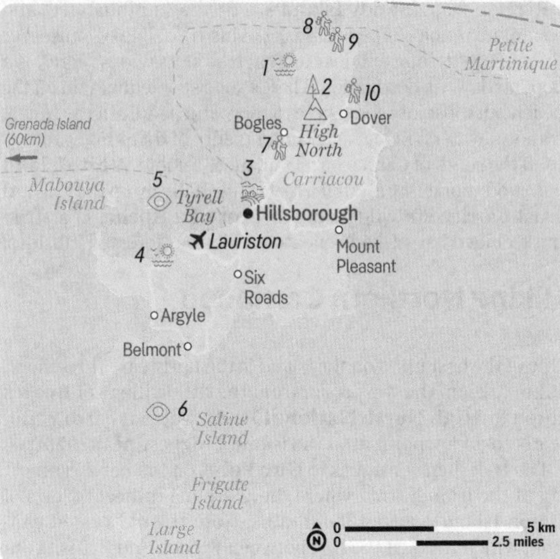

SIGHTS
1 Anse La Roche
2 High North National Park
3 Hillsborough
4 Paradise Beach
5 Sandy Island
6 White Island

ACTIVITIES
7 Bogles
8 Gun Point
9 Petit Carenage Beach
10 Windward

WHY I LOVE CARRIACOU

Alex Egerton, writer

One of the main reasons I love the Caribbean is the incredibly relaxed pace of life, and nowhere is that more apparent than on Carriacou. Once you step off the boat in Tyrrel Bay, modern stresses dissipate and you quickly connect with island time while waiting for the bus with a bunch of goats in a supermarket car park. It's impossible to rush here and the highlight of my visits usually involves just sitting under a shady tree with a cold drink, chatting with friendly islanders and marveling at the incredible colors of the sea.

White Sands of Carriacou

SHADY PALMS, TINY ISLANDS

While it may be far smaller than the main island, Carriacou punches well above its weight when it comes to beaches, with many of Grenada's best bathing spots found within walking distance of **Hillsborough** or just a short boat ride away.

Easily the island's most famous beach, the appropriately named **Paradise Beach** features a long stretch of soft sand backed by palms and sea-grape trees, with views across translucent turquoise waters to white-fringed islands just offshore. It's such an idyllic scene that even seasoned Caribbean beach bums will want to reach for their phone to try to capture its beauty, but photographs can't do it justice. Despite its charms, the beach is rarely crowded and while there are plenty of services, including two fun bars from which to take in the panorama, development is minimal and unobtrusive.

WHERE TO STAY IN HILLSBOROUGH

Mermaid Hotel
The most comfortable hotel in town with bright modern rooms and a good seaside restaurant. **$$**

Rosa Guesthouse
Gleaming well-equipped apartments across from the water right in the middle of Hillsborough. **$**

Green Roof Inn
A quiet and peaceful place to stay just north of Hillsborough, with simple, elegant rooms. **$**

BEST BITES

Slipway
Right on the water on Tyrrel Bay with a fun casual atmosphere and awesome burgers and fish. $$

Fig & Bluggoe
A welcoming garden restaurant with healthy homestyle Caribbean dishes that you won't find elsewhere. $$

Mom's Trini Roti
Cheap, filling and absolutely delicious, the Trinidadian treats here are perfect for a hike or beach picnic. Come early – they sell out fast. $

Green Roof Inn
Fresh seasonal ingredients and fine sea views from the veranda make this Hillsborough's best dining experience. $$$

Right in front, **Sandy Island** is a dreamy, uninhabited, and roughly banana-shaped reef islet. This tiny slice of sunseeker utopia, 1600ft long and just 165ft across at its widest point, is a popular day-trip destination. There's good snorkeling right off the beach but most just come here to relax and paddle in the warm, tranquil waters. Bring snacks and plenty of drinking water.

Off the south of Carriacou island, more remote **White Island** has good snorkeling around a reef, while halfway up the leeward coast Carriacou's wildest beach, **Anse La Roche**, is a striking secluded bay tucked beneath precipitous forested hillsides.

Hiking Northern Carriacou

A WALK ON THE WILD SIDE

One of the best hikes on the island is the fairly easy three-hour, 10km hike up the west coast from the little village of **Bogles** through **High North National Park**, where a narrow trail leads to a viewpoint atop the island's highest peak (920ft).

The trek then continues to **Gun Point** on the northernmost tip of the island, from where there are magnificent views of Union Island's jagged mountains. Note the old rusted cannon, which marked the line between French and British control in the area during the late 18th century.

To the east of Gun Point, the road continues to the seldom-visited **Petit Carenage Beach**, a turtle-nesting area with the most brilliant blue waters anywhere in Carriacou.

From the end of the beach, it's then just a short walk around the coast to **Windward**, a traditional village famous for its skilled boat builders and from where transport runs back to Hillsborough.

Carriacou's Curious Carnival

RUM, FEATHERS AND SHAKESPEARE

While Carriacou is normally the most chilled of islands, there's one week a year when it is anything but. Held just before the beginning of Lent, the **Carriacou Carnival** is five days of mayhem that sees what seems like half of Grenada descend on the island to party.

It builds to a crescendo on Jouvert morning at dawn when, after partying all night, revelers parade through the streets, with many covering themselves in black oil and donning horned helmets. But for many the highlight of the carnival takes place the next day with the quirky Shakespeare Mas, where brightly costumed men meet on crossroads across the island to recite lines from the Bard of Avon at each other in a battle of literary knowledge.

KEEP THE PARTY GOING

If Carriacou Carnival whets your appetite for rum-soaked bedlam, check out Barbados' raucous **Crop-Over Festival** (p163) in August – it's one of the largest and loudest carnivals in the region.

GETTING AROUND

Carriacou is a deceptively big island, which means walking between destinations often takes longer than anticipated. Fortunately there are a couple of bus lines running from Hillsborough south to Tyrrel Bay and northeast to Windward.

Taxis can usually be found waiting for fares around the capital and at the island's two docks.

LEONARD ZHUKOVSKY/SHUTTERSTOCK ©

Arriving

While most visitors to Grenada arrive by air or on a cruise, a small percentage reach the country under their own sails on either private or chartered yachts. It's possible to enter the country on both the islands of Grenada and Carriacou, but outside the main international airport the immigration and customs procedures can be extremely slow.

By Air

All long-haul and longer regional flights arrive at the Maurice Bishop International Airport on the south of Grenada island, a short drive from Grand Anse's main resort strip.

Irregular flights on small planes link Carriacou's Lauriston Airport with St Vincent and the Grenadines (SVG).

By Boat

Most sea arrivals are with cruises that dock at downtown St George's pier. A small passenger boat runs twice weekly between Carriacou and SVG's Union Island.

Yacht arrivals can get immigration clearance at one of several marinas on Grenada's west or south coasts or at Carriacou's Tyrrel Bay.

Money

Currency: Eastern Caribbean dollar (EC$)

CASH

For most smaller transactions in Grenada, cash remains the payment of choice. While US currency is widely accepted, the exchange rate for small transactions is often less than optimum.

CREDIT CARDS

Nearly all midrange and top-end hotels accept cards but at smaller places you should check in advance, especially on Carriacou.

Both debit and credit cards are widely accepted at supermarkets and larger restaurants but are rarely accepted at local bars and cafes.

TIPPING

In higher-end restaurants a service charge is sometimes added to the bill; in other situations a gratuity of around 10% is expected. Taxi fares are fixed and tips are not the norm.

GUADELOUPE

DREAMY AND DIVERSE FRENCH CARIBBEAN ARCHIPELAGO

Guadeloupe delights visitors with hundreds of beaches across several islands, towering waterfalls, verdant rainforest, an active volcano, scenic cliffs, hot springs and French Caribbean culture.

While mentioning Guadeloupe often elicits puzzled looks from English-speakers, French tourists have been flocking to this hidden paradise for decades. Yet this French overseas territory has a lot to offer to any intrepid traveler – especially if you can learn some basic French phrases. Guadeloupe is a jack-of-all-trades that ticks the boxes for an ideal Caribbean vacation. With more than a dozen islands (six inhabited), this geographically diverse archipelago boasts 270 beaches and more than 50 waterfalls.

The two main islands, Grande-Terre and Basse-Terre, have contrasting terrain and are separated by a narrow channel known as Rivière Salée (Salty River). Basse-Terre is a mountainous island with lush rainforest, dramatic waterfalls, an active volcano, black- and golden-sand beaches and natural hot springs. Grande-Terre is a flatter limestone island with majestic viewpoints and white-sand beaches ideal for swimming and surfing. Travel between the main islands is seamless via two bridges, while Guadeloupe's offshore islands are accessible by boat in 20 to 60 minutes. Island-hoppers can experience the sophisticated Les Saintes renowned for its cuisine, the rum-production powerhouse of Marie-Galante, and the wild and unspoiled La Désirade.

Smaller hotels and apartment rentals prevail in Guadeloupe, as tourism is a minor industry. Travelers can move easily amongst some 400,000 Guadeloupeans, experiencing the local culture of French, African, Indian and Caribbean influences.

THE MAIN AREAS

BASSE-TERRE
Mountainous adventure island. p344

GRANDE-TERRE
Beaches, surfing and viewpoints. p349

OFFSHORE ISLANDS
Gastronomy, rum and relaxed beach life. p354

MIRVA LEMPIAINEN ©

Above: Plage du Souffleur, La Désirade (p353); Left: Ste-Anne (p352)

Find Your Way

Basse-Terre and Grande-Terre form the mainland of Guadeloupe, dubbed the 'Butterfly Island' due to its shape. It's twice the size of Singapore. The significantly smaller offshore islands are all reachable by boat within an hour.

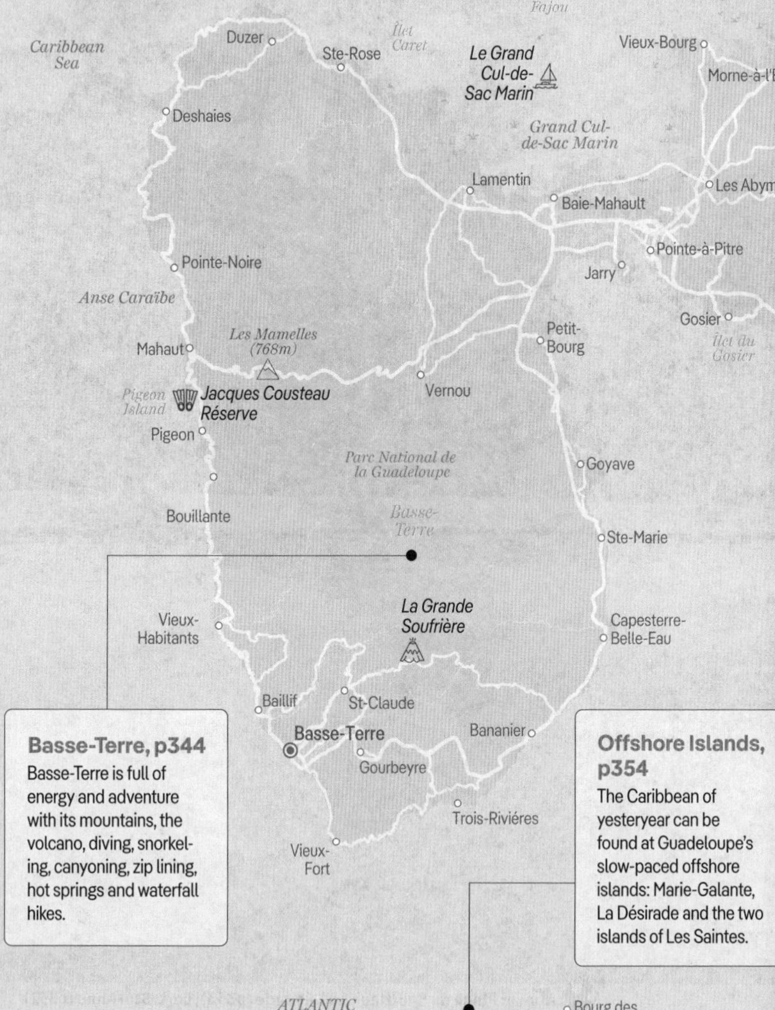

Basse-Terre, p344
Basse-Terre is full of energy and adventure with its mountains, the volcano, diving, snorkeling, canyoning, zip lining, hot springs and waterfall hikes.

Offshore Islands, p354
The Caribbean of yesteryear can be found at Guadeloupe's slow-paced offshore islands: Marie-Galante, La Désirade and the two islands of Les Saintes.

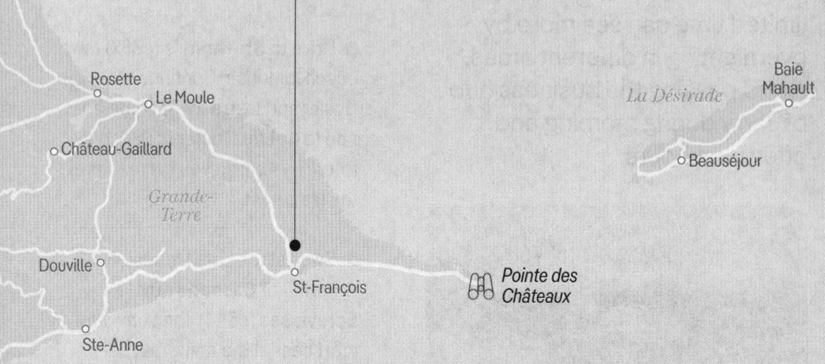

Grande-Terre, p349
It's all about relaxing here: lounging on white-sand beaches surrounded by turquoise waters, admiring majestic cliffside viewpoints and casually catching surf waves.

CAR

You need a car to properly explore mainland Guadeloupe and to visit its sights. It takes about three hours to drive around each wing of the Butterfly Island. A car is ideal in Marie-Galante, too: circumnavigation takes an hour. Taxis are sparse and pricey.

BUS

Buses run regularly in the daytime (Monday to Saturday) in parts of Grande-Terre, particularly between Pointe-à-Pitre and the coast up to St-François. The Karulis mobile application provides schedules that are not always faithfully followed. Bus transport in Basse-Terre is more limited.

BOAT

Several boat companies transport people to the offshore islands. The shortest trip is the 25-minute boat ride from Basse-Terre's Trois-Rivières to Terre-de-Haut on Les Saintes. La Désirade is 45 minutes by boat from St-François on Grande-Terre. Marie-Galante is the furthest, taking an hour from Pointe-à-Pitre.

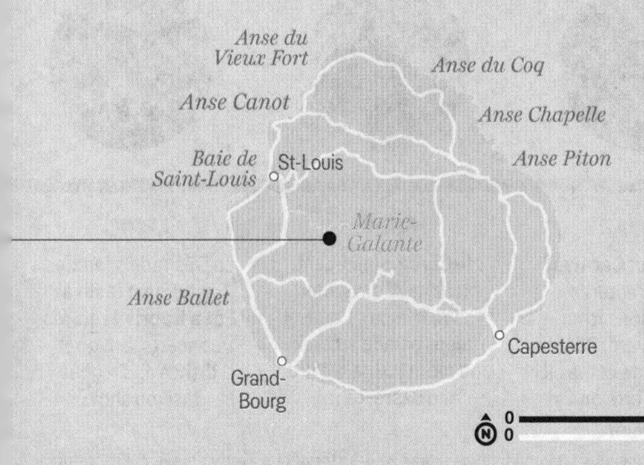

Plan Your Time

As Guadeloupe is vast and traffic jams are common, travelers with limited time can see more by overnighting in different areas. Avoid passing the business hub of Jarry during morning and afternoon hours.

MIRVA LEMPIAINEN ©

Pointe des Châteaux (p350)

If You Only Do One Thing

- Hike to the viewpoint of **Pointe des Châteaux** (p350) in St-François and get soaked at the natural splash pool of La Douche.
- Drive to **Ste-Anne's** (p352) town beach for lunch. Continue to Le Gosier and take a five-minute boat ride to **Îlet du Gosier** (p352), but return by 4pm so you can explore the rainforest.
- Swim at the small roadside waterfall of **Cascade aux Ecrevisses** (p344), then enjoy a craft beer at the rainforest beer garden, **Les Bières de la Lézarde** (p346).
- Have dinner at **L'Intemporelle** (p352) by the Memorial ACTe, not far from the nightlife hub of Marina Bas-du-Fort.

Seasonal Highlights

Guadeloupe's annual festivities and events reflect the archipelago's rich cultural heritage – a combination of French, African, Indian and Caribbean influences.

FEBRUARY

The colorful **Carnival** season features celebrations from January onward. See the largest parade in the city of Basse-Terre on Fat Tuesday.

MARCH

Mi-Câreme (mid-Lent break) is 22 days after Ash Wednesday. Carnival groups parade in black and red in Pointe-à-Pitre and Basse-Terre.

APRIL

La Désirade's famous Easter goat festival, **Fèt a Kabrit**, features concerts, art, goat dishes and a goat fashion show.

Three Days to Travel Around

- On the second day, drive to southern Basse-Terre to see **Les Chutes du Carbet** (p345) waterfalls.
- Continue further south to the heart-shaped 'Love Bath', **Le Bain des Amours** (p347).
- Visit **Fort Delgrès** (p347) in Basse-Terre, before admiring the sunset at the lighthouse of **Vieux Fort** (p347) and eating pizza at the adjacent Le Phare.
- Next day, drive up the west coast to Malendure to snorkel with turtles at the **Jacques Cousteau Réserve** (p346).
- Chill in the hot-spring bay of **Bouillante** (p347), then head north to see the sunset at **Grande Anse** (p348) beach and enjoy a waterfront dinner in **Deshaies** (p348).

More Than a Week

- Base yourself in **Le Gosier** (p352) if you have about a week. If longer, split time between Basse-Terre and Grande-Terre. Visit the aforementioned sights, the **Mémorial ACTe** (p349) and some additional waterfalls – alternate between active days and chilling on **Grande-Terre's** (p353) beaches.
- Do a road trip around **northern Grande-Terre** (p351)., and hop over to an offshore island: **Terre-de-Haut** is ideal for a day trip (p356).
- Take a boat trip to the nature reserve of **Petite-Terre** (p350) and the turquoise lagoon of **Le Grand Cul-de-Sac Marin** (p348).
- Finally, if there's a totally cloud-free day, hike up **La Grande Soufrière** (p348) volcano.

JUNE

Marie-Galante triples its population during the iconic **Terre de Blues Festival** showcasing acclaimed international and Caribbean artists.

AUGUST

Try local specialty foods and see colorful Creole dresses at **Fête des Cuisinières**, an event celebrating women chefs since 1916.

NOVEMBER

Visit Morne-à-l'Eau's historic cemetery on November 1 for **La Toussaint** (All Saints' Day). Its 1800 graves are illuminated with red candles.

DECEMBER

Experience **Chanté Nwel**, a Creole Christmas concert with cheerful, fast-paced songs. The events take place all over Guadeloupe through December.

La Désirade
Grand-Terre
Basse-Terre
Marie-Galante
Les Saintes

BASSE-TERRE

This volcanic island is Guadeloupe's biggest landmass. It's a nature hub and an active traveler's dream with its mountains, rivers, waterfalls and hot springs. A third of Basse-Terre is protected: it belongs to the 220-sq-km Parc National de la Guadeloupe.

Basse-Terre appeared from the sea only about three million years ago, making it a young Caribbean island (by comparison, La Désirade, the oldest island of the Lesser Antilles, dates back 145 million years). Thus natural erosion has not flattened it much. The island's highest point, the active volcano of La Grande Soufrière, rises to 1467m; it's the tallest peak in the Lesser Antilles. Basse-Terre's sand depicts a fascinating variety of colors. The beaches in the south, closest to the volcano, feature fine black sand; in the central part, the shade changes to gray; and in northern Basse-Terre, the beaches look golden brown or almost orange.

TOP TIP

Bring sneakers for waterfall hikes. Challenge-seekers should prioritize the tallest Carbet waterfall (three hours' round trip), the 40m Chute du Galion (three hours) and the turquoise Saut d'Acomat (30 minutes, steep climb). Bassin Bleu is family-friendly (1½ hours), as is the popular Cascade aux Ecrevisses with its flat paved path (10 minutes).

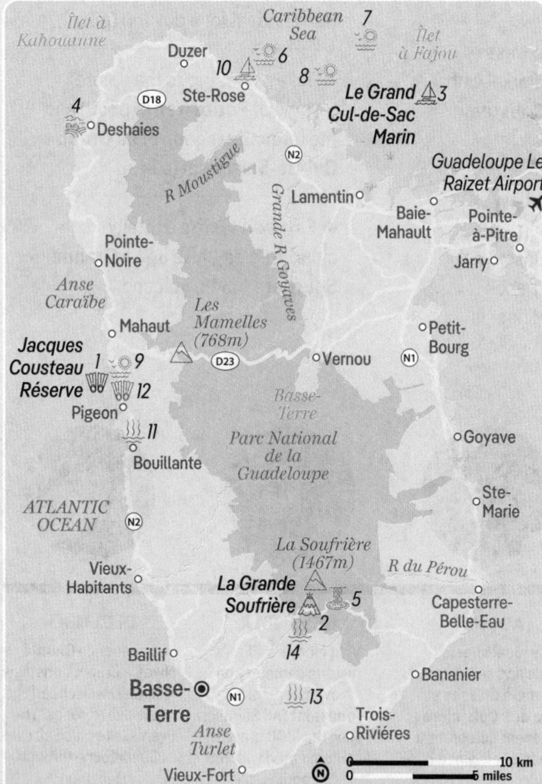

TOP SIGHTS
1 Jacques Cousteau Réserve
2 La Grande Soufrière
3 Le Grand Cul-de-Sac Marin

SIGHTS
4 Deshaies
5 Deuxième Chute du Carbet
6 Îlet Blanc
7 Îlet Caret
8 Îlet La Biche
9 Plage de Malendure
(see 9) Plage du Petit Malendure
(see 5) Première Chute du Carbet

ACTIVITIES & TOURS
10 Blue Lagoon
11 Bouillante
(see 9) Caraïbe Kayak
(see 9) CIP Guadeloupe
(see 10) Gwadaventure
12 La Rand'eau
13 Le Bain des Amours
14 Les Bains Jaunes
(see 12) Les Heures Saines
(see 1) Les Îlets Pigeon
(see 10) Nico Excursions

EATING
see 4 Le Madras

BENNY MARTY/SHUTTERSTOCK ©

Première Chute du Carbet

The Famous Carbet Falls

SEE THE TALLEST WATERFALLS

None of Guadeloupe's waterfalls are more highly acclaimed than **Les Chutes du Carbet**. While there are officially three Carbet waterfalls, only two of them are close to one another and measure over 100m each, putting them among the tallest waterfalls in the Lesser Antilles.

The drive to the park entrance in southern Basse-Terre is already an adventure: turn off the main road, N1, when you're between Capesterre-Belle-Eau and Le Bananier, and get onto D4 heading inland. Soon you'll find yourself deep inside Jurassic Park–like dense rainforest. The serpentine road takes many steep twists and turns before you reach the parking lot. This is the only nature destination in Guadeloupe that has an entry fee (€5.15 for adults).

On a clear day, an easily accessible viewpoint near the park entrance allows you to see the two waterfalls in the distance, snaking down the mountain. Apparently, Columbus also spotted this waterfall pair in 1493. Hike down to the riverbed for a closer view of the bottom waterfall, the 110m-tall **Deuxième Chute du Carbet**. It only takes 20 minutes one-way

RAINFOREST ADVENTURES

A unique way to experience Basse-Terre's waterfalls is to join a canyoning tour. You can use ropes and harnesses to rappel down cascades with companies such as **Vert-Intense**, **Canyon Guadeloupe** and **Canopée Forest Adventure**. Family-friendly canyoning routes are available from age eight onward.

Zip lining is another fun way to see the rainforest. **Le Tapeur** in central Basse-Terre has several long glides through the dense forest. The family-friendly **Akro Park** in Petit-Bourg has zip-lining tracks for ages three and up. It's located just next to the big botanical garden of **Valombreuse**.

For those enjoying slower activities, **Guadeloupe Zoo** has an impressive 400m-long rainforest canopy walk 20m above ground for ages eight and up.

WHERE TO STAY IN BASSE-TERRE

Hôtel St-Georges
Colorful hillside hotel with a cute S-shaped pool. Ideal for volcano hikers and those exploring southern Basse-Terre. €

Le Jardin Malanga
Upscale hillside cottages with a lush garden, a gourmet restaurant and a small infinity pool overlooking Les Saintes. €€

Tendacayou Ecolodge & Spa
A hilltop eco-luxury hotel oozing Bali vibes with a spa garden and hot tubs. Unique tree-house accommodations. €€€

THE MOST VERSATILE FRUITS

Nicaise Monrose, a Basse-Terre native, is an avid gardener and a passionate cook. She explains how to prepare Guadeloupe's most popular fruits:

Breadfruit
It's the tree of life. With breadfruit, we'll never starve. It works in casseroles, soups, sauces and as fries. When it ripens, it becomes sweet. It's full of vitamins and helps you live a long life.

Green banana
It's called *poyo*. You boil it and use it in salads, soups and casseroles. When it ripens, make banana pancakes and banana flambé.

Avocado
They're big and creamy here. Eat them salty or sweet, making *féroce* (codfish avocado balls) or chocolate avocado mousse. The season is June to September.

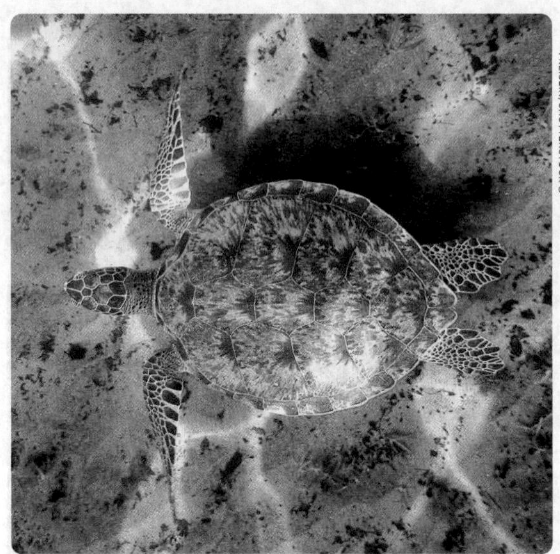

Turtle, Plage de Malendure

to walk to the viewing platform along the paved rainforest path made of 400 steps. Going under the waterfall is forbidden due to landslide risks.

From there, sporty types can continue hiking toward the highest Carbet waterfall, the 115m-tall and more narrow **Première Chute du Carbet**. The round trip takes around 2½ hours from this point – the rest of the way is unpaved. Be prepared to maneuver over some roots and muddy trails and to hold onto ropes. Swimming is possible at the highest waterfall, but the water is very chilly.

Cousteau Reserve's Underwater Wonders

SPOT COLORFUL FISH AND TURTLES

Plage de Malendure on the west coast of Basse-Terre (within the town of Bouillante) is Guadeloupe's unofficial underwater headquarters, as it is the jumping-off point for the **Jacques Cousteau Réserve**. The acclaimed French oceanographer once said this area was among the world's top diving sites. The corals may not be quite as colorful as before, but the reserve still offers excellent diving and great chances

UNIQUE BASSE-TERRE FLAVORS

La Maison du Cacao, Pointe-Noire
Indulge in locally produced dark chocolate with sumptuous flavors. (Open Tue-Sat.)

Les Bières de la Lézarde, Petit-Bourg
Try beer with chili, coriander and hibiscus flavors in a rainforest beer garden. (Open Tue-Sat.)

La Maison de Kassaverie, Capesterre-Belle-Eau
Buy manioc-flour pastries called *kassav*. Morning visitors may see the production process.

for seeing big schools of tropical fish by snorkeling, too (bring your own snorkeling gear to avoid needing to visit Malendure for rentals).

The fish are particularly plentiful around **Les Îlets Pigeon** (Pigeon Islands), though the reserve officially extends well beyond these two small islands. You can visit the islands independently by renting a kayak from **Caraïbe Kayak**, or go by boat with one of the companies operating at Malendure beach. Divers won't go wrong with any of the dive shops (**Les Heures Saines**, **Archipel Plongée** or **PPK Plongée Guadeloupe**). Snorkelers are best off with Caraibe Kayak, **CIP Guadeloupe** and **La Rand'eau**, as these companies do specialized snorkeling trips (two to 2½ hours). They usually include three stops: a deeper marine area dubbed the 'Japanese coral garden', the two Pigeon Islands and the bay of Malendure, where the guide helps you spot turtles. If you're a good swimmer, you can see turtles on your own, too. It's best to swim around 150m offshore from the gray-sand beach of Malendure and head to the right, toward the small cove of **Plage du Petit Malendure**. Tens of turtles live in this bay, feeding off the seaweed in the bottom. With any luck, you can spot at least a few.

THE BEST RESTAURANTS IN BASSE-TERRE

Le Rocher de Malendure
A cliffside restaurant with wooden terraces, resident iguanas and panoramic views over the Malendure bay. Portions are gourmet-sized. €€€

Hôtel Restaurant Le Rayon Vert
Decorative and tasty plates, plus an infinity pool with magnificent hillside views over the town of Ferry that guests can use on weekends. Reservations required. €€

Les Senteurs d'Asie
A rare find, an excellent Asian fusion lunch restaurant in Jarry, a business hub dubbed Guadeloupe's economic lungs. €

Guadeloupe's Hot-Spring Hubs

SOAK IN HOT VOLCANIC WATER

Guadeloupe's most unique hot spring is a whole bay full of hot water in the center of **Bouillante** (translating as 'Boiling'). People float in this giant hot tub all day. The water is hot due to the town's geothermic power plant generating electricity from volcanic steam and sending the excess boiling water into the sea via a rushing river. Bring your goggles: you can spot schools of sergeant major fish and see yellow corals.

For a more typical hot-spring experience, drive five minutes south to the shallow bath of **Ravine Thomas**, which has hot ground water mixing with sea water. Alternatively, head to Basse-Terre's other hot-spring hub, the town of Gourbeyre, where you'll find the heart-shaped 'Love Bath' – **Le Bain des Amours**. Surrounded by rainforest, this kid-friendly shallow concrete pool has warm volcanic water flowing in through pipes. Go on weekdays to avoid crowds. If you follow the path starting at the bottom of the concrete stairs, you can find natural hot springs in the river nearby.

SOUTHERN BASSE-TERRE HIGHLIGHTS

Fort Delgrès
Historic fortress in the city of Basse-Terre where a 2002 stone circle commemorates freedom fighter Louis Delgrès.

Phare de la Pointe du Vieux Fort
A 1955 lighthouse with amazing views of Les Saintes and a good restaurant called Le Phare.

La Plage de Grande Anse
A gorgeous, long black-sand beach in Trois-Rivières with Guadeloupe's darkest sand.

BEST BEACHES IN DESHAIES

Plage de la Perle
Long and winding golden-sand beach famous from the TV show *Death in Paradise.*

Plage de Grande Anse
Guadeloupe's longest beach with golden sand, popular restaurants and beach bars, and a mangrove swamp for kayaking.

Langley Resort Fort Royal's beaches
The lively Kawann Beach Bar is on the hotel's pretty main beach, near another gorgeous wild beach.

Hike to La Grande Soufrière Volcano

CLIMBING THE VOLCANO

Choosing the right day to climb up **La Grande Soufrière** is a form of art. The start of the hiking path is about a 10-minute drive from St-Claude. On a really clear day, you can enjoy spectacular views from the top, yet visibility is usually low due to the clouds. The edge of the crater is currently off-limits due to the volcano's increased activity, but you can see some varied vegetation on the hike. Upon your return from the three-hour round trip, you can soak in the rectangular concrete hot spring, **Les Bains Jaunes**, near the parking lot.

Boating in a Lagoon Reserve

TINY SAND ISLANDS AND TURQUOISE WATER

Guadeloupe's original Arawak name was Karukera, 'the island of beautiful waters'. The name definitely rings true at the 150-sq-km marine lagoon of **Le Grand Cul-de-Sac Marin**, located northwest of Basse-Terre island. This Unesco Biosphere Reserve features calm turquoise seas, mangrove forest and tiny white-sand islands. While storms have wiped out the islands' vegetation, a boat trip to the lagoon is still a fantastic experience.

Trips include snorkeling (gear included) and time spent on some or all of the sandbanks: **Îlet Blanc**, **Îlet Caret** and the already sunken **Îlet La Biche**. Note that shade on the small boats is limited. Other tourists tend to be French speakers, and the guides know very basic English at best. The boats leave from Blvd Maritime in Ste-Rose, where several companies have their booths. The full- and half-day trips offered by **Gwadaventure**, **Blue Lagoon**, **Guada Decouverte** and **Nico Excursions** offer good value; the first two can be booked online. Those who prefer to sail from Grande-Terre's Marina Bas-du-Fort can book online with **Le Flibustier**. This pirate-themed full-day catamaran trip is ideal for children (lunch is included but no snorkeling gear).

Wander Around Colorful Deshaies

SEE A CHARMING FISHING VILLAGE

Guadeloupe's most picturesque town is the cute **Deshaies** (pronounced 'day-hay'), a former fishing village with a rainforest backdrop. The town features just a few streets with colorful houses and a whole row of waterfront restaurants looking out to the bay full of sailboats. Deshaies' most recent claim to fame is the British-French TV series *Death in Paradise,* filmed in town and nearby. The thatched-roof beach restaurant **Le Madras** is a tourist favorite, as it portrays Katherine's Bar on the show.

GETTING AROUND

A car is essential in Basse-Terre. To bypass traffic, avoid heading toward Jarry in the mornings (6am to 9am), especially from the directions of Ste-Rose and the city of Basse-Terre. After-work traffic is heavy from 4pm to 7pm from Jarry toward the same areas. Parking is free everywhere except in parts of Bouillante and the city of Basse-Terre.

Grand-Terre
La Désirade
Marie-Galante
Les Saintes

GRANDE-TERRE

When you leave Basse-Terre via the Pont de la Gabarre or Pont de l'Alliance bridges and arrive in Grande-Terre seconds later, it doesn't exactly feel like a major change. Yet the difference in the landscape is fundamental: you have driven from a mountainous island onto a limestone plateau.

Most roads in Grande-Terre are straight and the terrain is flat, aside from hilly Le Gosier and the winding, hilly forest roads of Les Grands Fonds in the middle. With a coastline that alternates between cliffs and sandy stretches, Grande-Terre is a paradise for beach lovers, who can go from Ste-Anne's touristy white sands and shallow turquoise water to the beginner-surfers' pretty pebble beach of Helleux and onward to the remote, picture-perfect Anse Laborde. The dramatic cliffside viewpoints in the north and eastern tip of the island are also absolute highlights with their sharp rocks, steep cliff drops and wild waves.

TOP TIP

Guadeloupe's dilapidated main city, Pointe-à-Pitre, is hardly worth visiting if your time is limited but it has one ace up its graffitied sleeve: the Mémorial ACTe. This world-class cultural center focuses on the history of slavery in Guadeloupe and the world. Reserve two to three hours for visiting this massive waterfront building.

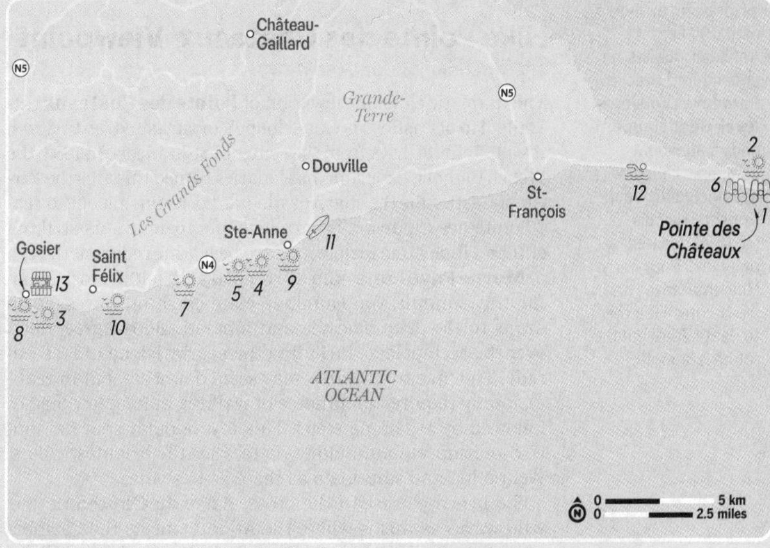

TOP SIGHTS
1 Pointe des Châteaux

SIGHTS
(see 1) Anse du Château
2 Grande Anse des Salines
3 Îlet du Gosier
4 La Caravelle
5 La Toubana
6 Morne Pavillon
7 Petit Havre
8 Plage de La Datcha
9 Plage du Bourg
10 St-Felix

ACTIVITIES, COURSES & TOURS
11 Anse du Belley
(see 10) Just In Kite – École de Kitesurf & Wing
12 La Douche
(see 11) Ste-Anne Kitesurfing School

EATING
(see 9) Fabienne Youyoutte
(see 9) Goune's Food
(see 9) La Rôtisserie de Ste-Anne
(see 9) Le Kontiki

SHOPPING
13 Le Gosier

THE NATURE RESERVE OF PETITE-TERRE

From the viewpoint of Pointe des Châteaux you can spot two flat islands in the distance. This is the palm-tree-fringed paradisiacal nature reserve of **Petite-Terre**. It's the only place in Guadeloupe where you are likely to spot a shark while snorkeling (a friendly lemon shark). Petite-Terre is also known for its turtles and schools of tropical fish, as well as for being the home of 10,000 Lesser Antillean iguanas, an endangered species. **Paradoxe Croisières**, **Awak Guadeloupe** and smaller boat companies run day trips including lunch from St-François (45 to 90 minutes one-way). Book early. Note that waves often get rough on the way to Petite-Terre but the return is smooth.

FRITZ DESIGNER/SHUTTERSTOCK ©

Pointe des Châteaux

Hike Pointe des Châteaux' Viewpoint

SPECTACULAR 360-DEGREE VIEWS

The dramatic cliffside viewpoint of **Pointe des Châteaux** (literally 'Tip of Castles') is Guadeloupe's most visited destination. It's a 15-minute drive from the center of St-François. In 1683, the French Catholic Capuchin missionaries named this area the Parish of Castles for the sharp castle-like rocks jutting out to sea.

Pointe des Châteaux is extremely photogenic – its striking cliff and limestone formations are best admired from the top of **Morne Pavillon**, a 43m hill topped with a 10m cross. From the tiny summit, you can appreciate crashing waves, steep drops to the deep blue sea and fantastic 360-degree views over the archipelago, including the nearby island of La Désirade. The hike to the cross may seem daunting, but in reality, it only requires 15 minutes of walking among low bushes followed by 150 stone steps. This is a popular spot for sunrise and sunset, but midday visitors see the brightest colors. Wear a hat and sunscreen as there is no shade.

The beach closest to the cross, **Anse du Châteaux**, has wild waves as this is where the Atlantic meets the Caribbean; swimming is forbidden. To cool off after the hike, walk instead to nearby **Grande Anse des Salines**. It's a long beach

WHERE TO STAY IN GRANDE-TERRE

La Toubana Hotel & Spa Guadeloupe's only five-star hotel with a beautiful infinity pool and stylish hillside bungalows. **€€€**

Creole Beach & Spa Hotel Classy hotel with bright rooms, three interconnected pools and a small beach on Le Gosier's hotel road. **€€**

Pierre & Vacances Village Club Ste-Anne A typical French family resort in a rural area with two big pools, two beaches and scheduled activities. No English spoken. **€**

NORTHERN GRANDE-TERRE ROAD TRIP

The sparsely populated northern Grande-Terre is wild, expansive and untamed. It features dramatic cliffside viewpoints, historical sights and remote white-sand beaches.

Start your exploration from Guadeloupe's oldest town, **1 Le Moule**, where the ruins of the historic port are still standing. Watch local talent riding the waves at the Damencourt surf spot before heading to the modern Damoiseau rum distillery for a visit. Then drive toward **2 Morne-à-l'Eau** for a stroll around the town's historic black-and-white hillside cemetery. Visit the artisanal bakery of Maison Cérès to buy a filled baguette as lunch options later are limited.

Drive to **3 Petit Canal** to descend the 54 Slave Steps leading to the esplanade where enslaved people were once sold. Posters of Unesco's Slave Route Project provide information in English. Then drive up the coast to the lagoon of **4 Port D'Enfer**. Walk for about 15 minutes around the (often seaweed-infested) lagoon to view the cave-like rock formation of Trou Madame Coco that's the starting point of a longer, scenic cliffside hike. Return to the car and drive up the hill to see Port D'Enfer from above before heading to **5 Pointe de la Grande Vigie**, Guadeloupe's second most famous viewpoint. Admire the 80m limestone cliff drops reminiscent of Portugal's Sagres.

Next, it's beach time. Visit the cute town of **6 Anse Bertrand** to swim at Anse Laborde, which has Guadeloupe's whitest sand. Clear turquoise waters, a row of palm trees and a tall cliff at the end complete the postcard look. Check out the pretty Plage de Chapelle before continuing to **7 Port Louis' Plage du Souffleur** for sunset. Have a cocktail in one of the beach bars while observing surfers riding some of the Caribbean's finest waves.

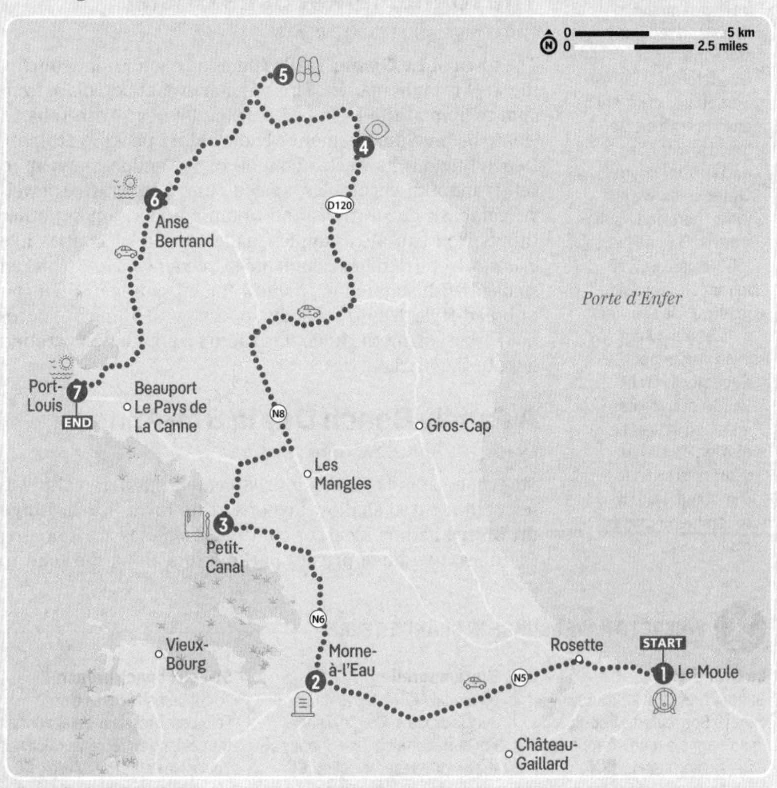

with a coral reef right offshore, featuring Grande-Terre's best snorkeling. Alternatively, you can drive about 5km back and search for the hidden natural sea pool of **La Douche** where waves sporadically splash over the rocks, providing an exhilarating salt-water shower. While most online maps recognize La Plage de la Douche, the actual splash pool is a stone's throw from there. Ask around for guidance.

Chill on a Paradise Island

ULTIMATE RELAXATION ON ÎLET DU GOSIER

Imagine a little island where palm trees sway over shallow turquoise waters and white-sand beaches contrast beautifully with green mountains on the horizon – that's **Îlet du Gosier** for you. This Robinson Crusoe island is the perfect place to spend a few hours, or all day (note that there's no toilet). It's quick to get to: the boat trip takes just five minutes from the pier next to Anse Tabarin in the center of Le Gosier. The boats run daily every 20 minutes from 9am to 5pm (with a longer midday break). Pack a picnic lunch or try the island's only restaurant, the rustic **Ti Robinson** (prepare to wait an hour for fish and rice). Check out the island's lighthouse for some beautiful sea views.

WHY I LOVE GRANDE-TERRE

Mirva Lempiäinen, writer

I am a beach bum and a water lover, so Grande-Terre is my ideal place to live. My favorite spot here is Îlet du Gosier. I have been swimming to the island regularly since moving to Guadeloupe in 2014. Sometimes my friends and I bring a picnic lunch in a dry bag and stay for hours. Other times, we just swim there and back from La Datcha beach (600m one-way, 20 minutes). Exercising in turquoise sea water sure beats doing laps in an indoor pool! Recently a row of yellow buoys was installed in the sea, making it safer for visitors to swim to the island. I highly recommend going for it!

The Night Market of Le Gosier

SOUVENIRS AND LOCAL TREATS

The town of **Le Gosier** really comes alive on Fridays during the weekly night market. This popular event takes place from 5pm to 9pm at the L-shaped parking lot near Anse Tabarin (come before 7pm, as many vendors start packing at 8pm). Depending on the week, about 50 to 80 vendors show up to sell fruits and vegetables, spiced rum, handcrafted jewelry, calabash decorations and organic honey, among other things. You can also sample Guadeloupean specialties like *accras* (deep-fried fish dough balls), *poulet boucane* (chicken smoked with sugarcane), *boudin* (blood sausage), *bokit* (pita-bread-style deep-fried dough pocket with fillings) or coconut sorbet. Bring the kids, too: there's a popular playground next to the market.

A Family Beach Day in Ste-Anne

ENJOY THE SHALLOW TURQUOISE SEA

Ste-Anne, Grande-Terre's tourist center, has very calm water within three shallow lagoons at its town beach. **Plage du Bourg** is thus ideal for children. Logistics are a breeze: there are two huge private parking lots along the road to

WHERE TO HAVE BRUNCH IN GRANDE-TERRE

Le Grand Bleu
Sunday brunch at La Toubana Hotel & Spa features free-flowing champagne, a room of appetizers and a grilling station. €€€

L'Intemporelle
Memorial ACTe's hip restaurant serves creative Creole dishes. For buffet brunch (first Sunday of the month), reserve online. €€

St-Felix beach brunch
To get brunch delivered on St-Felix beach (or elsewhere), contact the catering entrepreneurs Island You or Ma Petite Brunch Box. €€

DAVID SVESTKA/SHUTTERSTOCK ©

Îlet du Gosier

St-François. The walk to the sand is short, so transporting kids and the beach gear is easy. Lunch options are plentiful, too, between the casual **Le Kontiki** beach restaurant and a whole row of food trucks selling *bokits* (the vegetarian ones are yummy here). Alternatively, go to the main road to **Goune's Food** for gourmet burgers, or **La Rôtisserie de Ste-Anne** for lamb, pork and home fries. For dessert, try the Italian gelato place across from La Rôtisserie or the nearby local artisanal ice-cream chain **Fabienne Youyoutte**. Kids also love the beach vendors' *chi-chis* (mini-churros), *beignets* (jam-filled donuts) and coconut sorbet.

Beach-Hopping on Grande-Terre

FIND YOUR FAVORITE SOUTH-COAST BEACH

Grande-Terre's south coast consists of dozens of beaches. All are public, so just choose your favorite. The lively **Plage de La Datcha** has beach bars and kayak rentals, while the shallow **Petit Havre** is a family favorite with some scenic limestone cliffs. **La Caravelle**, the home of Club Med, is Guadeloupe's longest white-sand beach. The small turquoise cove of the five-star hotel **La Toubana** has a beach-club vibe with house music. Nature fans love the untouched **St-Felix** with its mangrove trees and hiking trails. Meanwhile, **Anse du Belley** with its regular trade winds is a kitesurfer's dream. For classes, contact **Ste-Anne Kitesurfing School** or **Just In Kite – École de Kitesurf & Wing**.

GRANDE-TERRE'S BEST SURF BEACHES

Aaron Djafri, a coach at Arawak Surf Club (@arawak_surf_club), shares his favorite surf spots on the island:

Plage de Petit Havre
I learned to surf here at 16. Along the south coast the waves are often small and soft. But there's a coral reef at Petit Havre so it's not for beginners, unlike Plage du Helleux in Ste-Anne.

Plage de Souffleur
You have all types of waves: small, big, hard. I surf at Mirador on the right side, beginners go to La Piscine on the left. I recently surfed with four dolphins and we see whales every year.

Plage de Chapelle
The waves are just perfect, good and strong, and there are waves with barrels.

GETTING AROUND

Buses frequently operate between Pointe-à-Pitre, Le Gosier, Ste-Anne and St-François. A car is necessary to visit other parts of Grande-Terre, including Pointe des Châteaux. Parking is free everywhere outside the narrow streets of Pointe-à-Pitre and the private parking lots of Ste-Anne. Roads tend to be straight and only slightly hilly, so driving in Grande-Terre is much easier than in Basse-Terre. Traffic is an issue between 7am and 9am from the directions of St-François and Morne-à-l'Eau toward Jarry, and vice versa afternoons from 4pm to 6pm.

OFFSHORE ISLANDS

Guadeloupe's dreamy offshore islands are the Caribbean of yesteryear, where beaches are nearly empty, traffic jams are caused by ox-pulled carts and restaurant visits take hours. Day trips are possible but staying overnight is better, as it takes a little while to get into the relaxed Creole West Indies mindset.

Each island is unique in its own way. The round Marie-Galante, called 'the Big Pancake', is the most populated with 11,000 residents. This agricultural island focuses on rum and sugar production, and has gorgeous beaches. La Désirade is the wildest island with a high mountain ridge ideal for off-roading. Its 1400 residents live near the coast and include Guadeloupe's best fisherfolk. The volcanic archipelago of Les Saintes charms with its beauty. The sophisticated Terre-de-Haut has 1500 residents, classy restaurants and a few fashion boutiques. Terre-de-Bas is more nature-focused, featuring hiking trails with amazing views; it has under 1000 residents.

LOCAL TOP TIP

Jah My, also known as Louis Cléonis, is a reggae artist whose biggest hit is 'Marie-Galante' (@jahmyofficiel). He says, "All the beaches are spectacular, but **Anse Canot** is away from the road noise and is protected by trees. There are nice waves and always people around."

PHIL O'NECTOR/SHUTTERSTOCK ©

Plage de la Feuillère, Capesterre

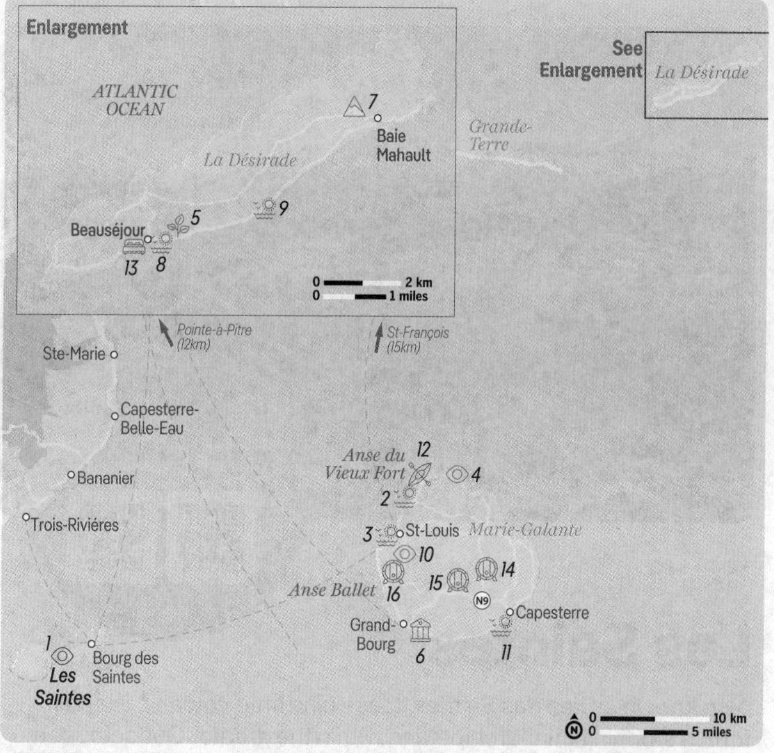

TOP SIGHTS
1 Les Saintes

SIGHTS
2 Anse Canot
3 Anse de Mays
4 Gueule Grand Gouffre
5 Jardin Botanique du Désert
6 L'Habitation Murat
7 La Grande Montagne
8 La Plage à Fifi
9 La Plage du Souffleur
10 Les Délices de Siblet
11 Plage de la Feuillère
12 Plage Vieux Fort

SLEEPING
13 Oüaliri Beach Hôtel

DRINKING & NIGHTLIFE
14 Bellevue
15 Bielle
16 Poisson

See Marie-Galante's Highlights

TAKE A MINI ROAD TRIP

Start the day with a swim at Capesterre's palm-tree-fringed **Plage de la Feuillère**. Then head to Grand-Bourg to visit **L'Habitation Murat**, Guadeloupe's largest sugarcane plantation turned eco-museum, where you can see the remnants of the old sugar factory and visit a historical exhibit. Continue toward St-Louis to the small syrup factory of **Les Delices de Siblet**, located behind the owner family's home that looks like a cute red-roofed gingerbread house. Provided the open-air factory is open, you can buy strong condensed syrup. Then it's time to relax on some amazing white-sand beaches, like **Anse de Mays** and **Anse Canot**. **Plage Vieux Fort** has a mangrove swamp across the road with kayak and paddleboat rentals available. End your mini road trip with a drive to the iconic rock arch of **Gueule Grand Gouffre**. This massive hole in the cliff is quite impressive when waves splash on it.

STAY, EAT & DRINK IN MARIE-GALANTE

Coco Beach Resort
Clean, basic rooms by a seaside pool and a small beach within Grand-Bourg. €€

Aux Plaisir des Marins
Popular restaurant with seating on the sand. Order the boiled fish, then go for a swim while you wait. €€

Sun 7 Beach
Relaxed beach bar with occasional live music. Ideal for sunset.

IRYNA SHPULAK/SHUTTERSTOCK ©

Use these QR codes to check for boat tickets from Trois-Rivières to Les Saintes.

TOP SIGHT

Les Saintes

Also known as Îles des Saintes, these nine little volcanic islands form a stunning mini-archipelago within the greater Guadeloupean archipelago. The bay of Les Saintes is often said to be one of the most beautiful in the world. Only two of the islands are inhabited: the slightly upscale but still relaxed tourist favorite, Terre-de-Haut; and the lesser-known nature destination, Terre-de-Bas.

DON'T MISS

- Fort Napoléon des Saintes
- Îlet à Cabrit
- Pain de Sucre
- Plage de Pompierre
- Grande Baie
- Top restaurants
- Hiking

Fort Napoléon des Saintes

This Terre-de-Haut hilltop fortress is an ideal first stop in Les Saintes as the views from 114m above sea level are jaw-dropping – bright blue waters and green hilly islands. The tough uphill walk from Le Bourg, the island's only town, takes 30 minutes, or you can rent a scooter or a golf cart. The fortress museum is open daily from 9am to 12:30pm.

Îlet à Cabrit

The uninhabited Îlet à Cabrit (Goat Island) has tons of friendly goats hiding among the ruins of Fort Joséphine at the island's peak, which offers incredible bay views. Kayaking here from Terre-de-Haut takes about 30 minutes and island circumnavigation takes 45 minutes (rent kayaks from **Clear Blue Caraïbes** or **Sunsea Balado**). Pack lunch and snorkeling gear.

Pain de Sucre

Called 'mini-Rio', Terre-de-Haut has its own Sugarloaf Mountain: a 53m volcanic hill. The lovely cove on the hill's Leeward (left) side is known as **Plage de Pain de Sucre** (Sugarloaf Beach). Featuring gorgeous turquoise waters and light sand, the beach is very thin and only about 30m long. If it gets crowded, go snorkeling and enjoy some of Guadeloupe's best underwater views. Most people arrive nearby with electric vehicles or scooters, then take a five-minute walk downhill to the beach. Others arrive by kayak (from Îlet à Cabrit, for example), and a few do the strenuous 45-minute hilly walk from Le Bourg.

Plage de Pompierre

The biggest beach in Terre-de-Haut is Plage de Pompierre, which consists of a crescent-shaped stretch of beige sand and a turquoise lagoon with an island called Les Roches Percées just in front – you can visit it by wading across the shallow water. Pompierre is a 20-minute walk from town, without many hills. When the lagoon has seaweed issues, head to the small gray-sand beach of **Anse Mire**.

Grande Baie

The best snorkeling spot in Terre-de-Bas is Grande Baie, a secluded bay with really clear waters. It can be reached from the port by a 15-minute walk. There are lots of corals and fish, and you may see the bay's resident turtles munching on the green seaweed in the bottom.

Top-Notch Food

Terre-de-Haut is known as the gastronomic capital of Guadeloupe, like St-Barthélemy 30 years ago. You have restaurant options bordering on fine dining – **Ti Kaz' La**, **Ti-Bo Doudou**, **La Fringale** – yet you can eat with your feet in or near the sand. **Les Balançoires** is perfect for sipping a cocktail in a beach swing. The restaurants in Terre-de-Bas are more casual, serving Creole comfort food. Call the modest home-style **Chez Eugenette** to reserve a fabulous lobster lunch. The hilltop restaurant **Ti Grille** has tasty meals and sprawling views over the great snorkeling beach of Anse à Dos.

The cultural specialties of **les Saintois** (the local people) include **tourment d'amour** (coconut-jam-filled flat sponge cakes) and the flat **salako** fishing hats.

Hiking Trails

Hiking the 7.6km loop trail to Terre-de-Haut's water tank, **Le Chameau**, is challenging but worth it for the stunning views from the top. The water tank of Terre-de-Bas is also at a high point, offering spectacular archipelago views, with an orientation table on site. Terre-de-Bas has over 10km of hilly hiking trails.

FANTASTIC FISH CREPES

Don't miss delicious *crêpes de poisson* (fish crepes; like long Dutch croquettes but with mild-tasting fish inside). They are sold as street food in Terre-de-Haut and occasionally in restaurants. Walk just past the Billabong store to find the vendors that sell the crepes for €1 to €2 euros each. Go early: by 9:30am everything is likely sold out.

TOP TIPS

- Book transportation in advance. In Terre-de-Haut, contact Savana Location TDH, Aqua Blue or Eco Car Location. Green Bike & Car also rents e-bikes fitted with child seats. In Terre-de-Bas, VV Location Terre-de-Bas and Iguana Location rent regular cars, micro electric cars, scooters and buggies.
- Terre-de-Haut's accommodations options range from Airbnb rentals to boutique hotels like Hôtel Bois Joli, Hôtel Kanaoa and Les Petits Saints. Terre-de-Bas has two guesthouses, Rêve de Robinson and Residence Soleil Demery, and private rentals.

FÈT A KABRIT

Nicole Polion performs at La Désirade's popular Fèt a Kabrit, an Easter weekend festival with goat-cart rides and a goat fashion show. Polion explains what you can experience at this family-friendly beach extravaganza.

Art
It's a beautiful celebration with ambience, harmony and creativity. We welcome visitors at the pier with traditional dances with the members of our retirees association, Soleil et Vie Désirade.

Goat dishes
You can eat lots of tasty goat dishes, like *colombo de cabrit* (goat curry) and *râgout de cabrit* (goat in caramelized sauce). Everyone owns goats here.

Sun and fun
Easter is the best time to visit. The sea is beautiful and the sun is hot.

Tour Rum Distilleries in Marie-Galante

LEARN ABOUT RUM MAKING

Marie-Galante is a rum-production powerhouse with three renowned distilleries producing *rhum agricole* from freshly pressed sugarcane juice: **Bellevue**, **Poisson** (also known as Père Labat) and **Bielle**. They all have historic estates and do free tastings before 1pm. If you only have time for one visit, make it Bellevue, the biggest rum exporter in Guadeloupe. Bellevue has new nonpolluting machinery as the first eco-positive estate in the Caribbean. After touring the facilities, you can taste rum in a green terrace setting. Don't miss coco punch – the local piña colada.

Experience La Désirade's Wilderness

OFF-ROADING ON THE MOUNTAINTOP

La Désirade is Guadeloupe's wildest island. It has a high mountain ridge ideal for off-roading with quads and buggies (from **Location 2000**) or e-bikes (from **Ti Paradi Location** or **JM Désirade Service**). Once you have wheels, you can visit the island's cactus garden, **Jardin Botanique du Désert**, and zoom over to La Désirade's furthest corner to see an old meteorological station and the ruins of a cotton plantation. Then climb up to the mountain ridge, the 276m-high **La Grande Montagne**. A 10km-long, dusty unpaved road eventually leads you to a historic white-and-blue mountainside chapel, **Notre Dame du Calvaire**, with fantastic island views. The way back to town is paved. Stay at the casual **Oüaliri Beach Hôtel** for a night to relax afterward.

Picture-Perfect Empty Beaches

APPRECIATE THE SANDS OF SOLITUDE

La Désirade's south coast has several long white-sand beaches and it's not unusual to have them to yourself. **La Plage du Souffleur**, in particular, looks picture-perfect: tall palm trees hover over the downward sloping shoreline and colorful boats bob around the bright turquoise sea. **Restaurant Keya** sports colorful cushioned waterfront seating and offers a slightly modernized Creole menu. **La Plage à Fifi** in the island's main town, Beauséjour, is also beautiful, but is more prone to collecting unsightly seaweed. The Fifi beach restaurant **La Payotte** and the nearby **Restaurant Lagranlag** are island favorites. A Karulis minibus offers daily island transport in the mornings and afternoons.

GETTING AROUND

The offshore islands can be reached by boat in 20 to 60 minutes. There are several companies serving Marie-Galante and Les Saintes, including CTM Deher, ValFerry and L'Express des îles. The only company going to La Désirade is Comadile. Advance bookings online are recommended, especially during high season.

Renting a car in advance is crucial in Marie-Galante: Magaloc, MagAuto and Cubix Location have booths in the parking lot to the left of the ferry port, and Bleu Location is in front of the port. In La Désirade, a quad or an e-bike rental will come in handy, and in Les Saintes many get scooters, e-bikes or golf carts (the latter also need to be booked in advance). Walking is also possible in Les Saintes, and regular bicycles and scooters are available without reservation.

Arriving

Guadeloupe's only international airport, Pôle Caraïbes, has the airport code PTP, which refers to Pointe-à-Pitre, though the airport is in the city of Les Abymes. High season runs November to April; the busiest times correspond with French school vacations. The arrivals hall has a pharmacy, a Carrefour Express minimarket and a baby-gear rental business Bblou (book online for car seats, strollers etc).

By Air

There are several daily flights from Paris. Miami is the only US airport offering direct flights to Guadeloupe year-round; flights from New York only operate during winter. Guadeloupe also has direct flights from its neighboring island of St-Martin, St-Barthélemy, Martinique and Dominica.

By Boat

European cruise lines MSC, Costa and Tui visit weekly from November to April, others sporadically. Ferries come from Dominica and Martinique (L'Express des Îles, ValFerry). Cruises and ferries arrive at Pointe-à-Pitre, though smaller ships visit Deshaies, the city of Basse-Terre and Les Saintes.

Money

Currency: euro (€)

CASH

You can use the ATM at the arrivals hall or visit the exchange office, Karukera Change Aéroport. Cash is mainly needed for small purchases, buses and taxis (there is no Uber). Tipping is not expected. You may see a tip jar at the restaurant counter when paying – some coins are appreciated.

DIGITAL PAYMENTS

Paying by phone is popular. Most businesses accept digital wallets, though some require a minimum purchase of €5 to €10 for non-cash payments. In some places paying by phone is also an efficient way to circumvent the €50 purchase limit otherwise imposed on contactless credit card payments.

CREDIT CARDS

Credit cards, especially Visa and MasterCard, are widely accepted; American Express less so. A chip card is necessary for purchases above €50. 'No CB' means no credit cards. In restaurants you should notify the server in advance if you wish to tip by credit card, as it's not typical.

ANDI DE BOER/SHUTTERSTOCK ©

Above: Citadelle Laferrière (p380); Right: Jacmel (p366)

HAITI

FOR THE INTENTIONAL TRAVELER

Haiti's plain-sighted beauty is not hard to find, but it's going beyond the headlines and misconceptions that will make you fall in love with this country.

Haiti sits on the western side of Hispaniola island, sharing it with the Dominican Republic. Home to a rich history, diverse scenery and people who know how to welcome visitors, it remains an excellent destination for travelers looking for an escape – or some thrills. A melting pot of unique sounds and dishes, Haiti is at the intersection of African, indigenous and European culture and offers a transformative Caribbean experience. Whether you travel during Carnival season to soak up the colors and rhythm of Jacmel or to explore the booming city of Cap-Haïtien, it's sure to leave you with the ache to visit again.

Haitian culture is wonderfully laid-back and welcoming – it's island life at its purest. You'll find that having been embraced by the local population, many fellow travelers have settled in the country.

Note that Haiti is currently experiencing a spike in violence and civil unrest, particularly in Port-au-Prince. There's an increase in kidnappings and an alarming presence of gangs in a large portion of the capital. For these reasons we've chosen to focus on two cities that remain safe to visit. With good planning, it's possible to travel to Jacmel and Cap-Haïtien directly or via a quick stop in Port-au-Prince, meaning that (barring a five-minute drive from the international airport to the small local terminal), you can travel safely without entering the capital.

THE MAIN AREAS

JACMEL
A colorful yet peaceful getaway. **p366**

CAP-HAÏTIEN
A fun door to Haiti's history. **p376**

Find Your Way

Haiti is a relatively small country, and the best way to travel around depends on where you are and where you want to go. Moto-taxis are a common and cheap way to move around, but driving and sometimes hiking is necessary. It's an adventure!

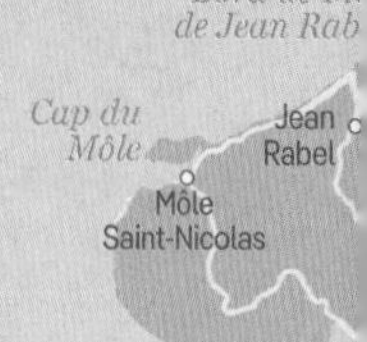

Golfe de la Gonâve

MOTO-TAXI

Moto-taxi (often just referred to as a 'moto') is the most common and cheapest way for locals to get around. Should you find a driver you like or are recommended a good one, stick with them!

WALKING

Wear comfortable shoes and carry around a water bottle. In the Caribbean, it tends to get hot and you want to be careful with the water you drink, so carrying your own is the safest option.

PLANE

Taking the plane to Jacmel is an option, but airlines offering services directly to Jacmel are limited. Your best bet may be to take a plane to Les Cayes and do the five-hour drive to Jacmel.

Cap-Haïtien, p376
Cap-Haïtien encompasses Haiti's history as it becomes the country's top spot for fun getaways, parties and adventurous excursions.

Jacmel, p366
With luscious green spaces, mesmerizing art, serenity and rhythm, Jacmel is Haiti's perfect escape.

Plan Your Time

Exploring Haiti is a group project – you will get the best outcome if you engage with local communities, which is what makes the experience so special. If you have the time, you can plan a day trip to a nearby waterfall or spend it exploring the town.

ROTORHEAD 30A PRODUCTIONS/SHUTTERSTOCK ©

Cathédrale Notre-Dame (p377)

A Quick Stop

- If you only have very limited time in Haiti, stay in **Cap-Haïtien** (p376) from where you can easily visit the **Citadelle Laferrière** (p380) and **Palais Sans Souci** (p380), located an hour or so outside the city.

- Head back into town and take a walk on the **Boulevard du Cap-Haïtien** (p377), stopping by any restaurant for a typical Creole meal with a side of ocean views.

- Alternatively, take a drive to **Cormier** (p379) beach, about 20 minutes from the city center, for a quick dip in the ocean and a delicious meal.

Seasonal Highlights

Haiti's weather tends to average above 26°C (80°F) year-round (in the mountains it tends to be a tad cooler) – a great advantage as it's always the right time to go to the beach or for a hike.

FEBRUARY

The **Carnival** season lasts from early January up to the three actual Carnival days in February. Cities like Jacmel and Cap-Haïtien come alive.

APRIL

As the weather usually brings lots of wind at this time of the year, **kites** can often be seen flying around.

JULY

Summertime in Haiti can mean whatever you want it to. It's possible to balance the quiet getaways with the immersive city experiences.

QUENTIN GUSTOT/SHUTTERSTOCK ©, LUMPPINI/SHUTTERSTOCK ©, SOLARISYS/SHUTTERSTOCK ©

A Week to Travel Around

- A week in Haiti is a good balance to explore without tiring yourself out too much. If you can, plan ahead and try to get a seat on a HAS flight to **Jacmel** (p366). Whether you're staying in or outside the city, carve out time for sightseeing and basking in its color and sun. You can opt for a hike to **Bassin Bleu** (p369) or a lot of beach time.

- It can be hard to choose between **Kabic** (p374), **Cyvadier** (p373) and **Raymond les Bains** (p372) – for the perfect beach day, or days if one just isn't enough.

More Than a Week

- A longer stay in Haiti can be both rejuvenating and exhilarating. For a thrilling start to your adventure, take a boat from Anse-à-Pitre to **Jacmel** (p366). Start slowly by exploring the city and enjoying its beaches.

- Drive to Les Cayes for a flight to Port-au-Prince with Sunrise Airways in the morning and catch a later flight to **Cap-Haïtien** (p376). From there you can pick and choose what you'd like to do – explore the city, visit **Dondon** (p379) caves or do more beach-hopping. Cap-Haïtien is currently the busiest city in Haiti, so finding things to do won't be a challenge.

AUGUST

Most Haitian cities honor their **patron saint** or ***fèt champèt***, with lots of music, dancing, eating and joyful festivities.

OCTOBER

Fall is rainy season in Haiti (specifically October and November), but it also gets quieter as the rush of summer tourists is usually gone by then.

NOVEMBER

On November 2, Haiti celebrates the **Day of the Dead**, an important event in both Vodou and Catholic religions. Expect public processions and ceremonies.

DECEMBER

This is a great month in Haiti as the **holidays** bring along many traditions, along with a special edition of Haitian partying.

RUI MESQUITA CORDEIRO/ISTOCK EDITORIAL/GETTY IMAGES ©, ROSTASEDLACEK/SHUTTERSTOCK ©, GUERINAULT LOUIS/GETTY IMAGES ©, GUERINAULT LOUIS/GETTY IMAGES ©

JACMEL

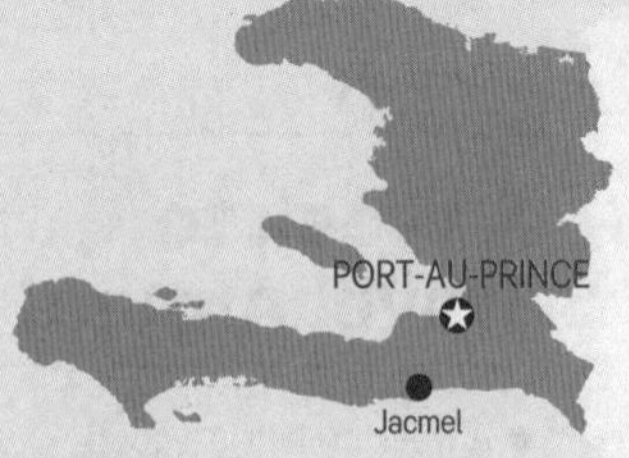

There is a Haitian saying – *dèyè mòn gen mòn* –which translates as 'behind mountains, there are more mountains,' and while this may be a philosophical way of saying there's always more to life, it's also an accurate representation of Haiti itself. If you were to drive from one end of the country to the other, you would find yourself in between large mountains more than anything else. Sheltered by a wide bay, Jacmel is a port city located right at the feet of a series of mountain chains. Painting a picture of this city is, quite frankly, very easy to do. Known for its colors during the Carnival period in February, Jacmel caters to most travelers. Art, culture, beaches, nature and exquisite food make the Jacmel experience one that can be rejuvenating or exhilarating, depending on your mood and needs.

TOP TIP

Jacmel is a good spot to recenter or find yourself. The pockets of silence, accentuated by breathtaking ocean and mountain views, are incredibly soothing. The sunsets at Kabic or Ti Mouillage (the smaller, quieter beaches), in particular, are must-sees. Take the time to enjoy it.

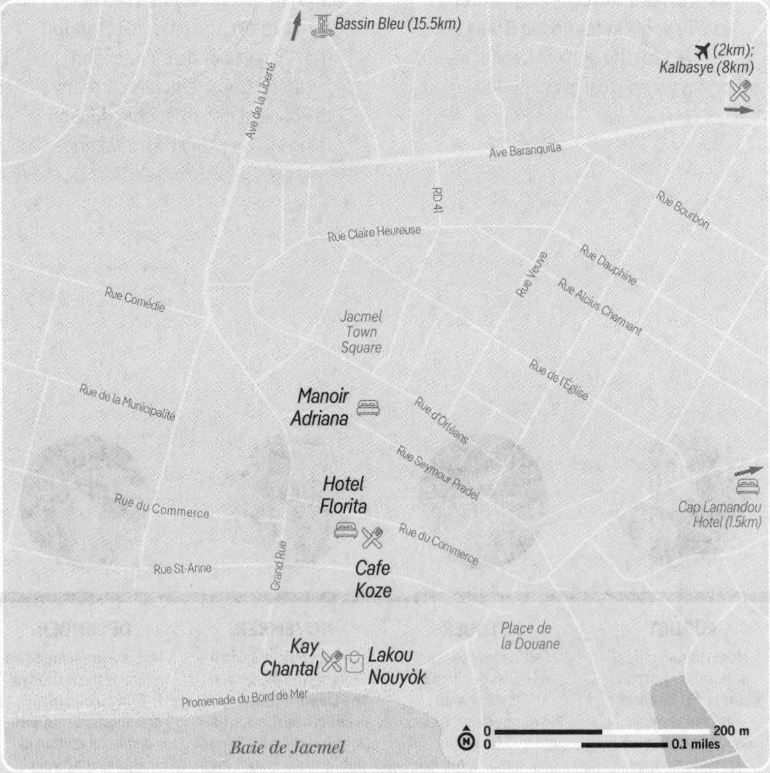

QUENTIN GUSTOT/SHUTTERSTOCK ©

Carnival, Jacmel

Experience the Carnival

THE SOUL AND THE RHYTHM

February is the most vibrant time of the year in Jacmel, when the city shines the brightest. The Carnival period in Haiti generally lasts from the first or second Sunday of January to the three actual Carnival days, beginning on the Sunday before Ash Wednesday. However, the entire country starts celebrating a month in advance. DJs and Haitian bands release their annual Carnival sounds early in the year and hold 'pre-Carnival' street parties (generally on Sundays).

This tradition, although celebrated widely throughout the country, is Jacmel's raison d'être. Every year, a city is picked by the government where the national Carnival will take place, but it doesn't mean that most other cities don't also celebrate. Jacmel has the reputation for the best Carnival. From papier-mâché artistic masks and colorful stands to beautiful parades and typical Haitian Carnival music, it's the happiest time of the year.

As with the festivities in other Caribbean countries, Haitian Carnival has a mystical, almost spiritual aspect to it. More than a festival, this is a celebration showcasing the country's culture and complex history. During the colonial

BEST STREET FOOD IN JACMEL

Griot
Fried pork shoulder marinated in *epis* (spices); get it with a side of *bannan peze* (fried plantains). For the best kind, check out **Kay Alix**.

Tassot
Goat meat prepared similarly to *griot* (citrus-marinated pork that's braised then fried), with the same spices. Locals recommend **Kay Jano** on Baranquilla Ave.

Akra
A great option for vegetarians – a fried mixture of *malanga* (a root vegetable and spices). It makes for a great crunchy snack.

Fish
At Raymond les Bains beach, **Madame Anette** is a local vendor selling incredible fish, prepared the Haitian way.

WHERE TO STAY IN JACMEL

Manoir Adriana
Referenced in René Depestre's book *Hadriana in all my dreams*, Adriana has great amenities and a nice pool to relax by. **$$**

Hotel Florita
Jacmel's oldest-standing hotel is an impressive structure and centrally located but does have a more dated feel to it. **$$**

Cap Lamandou Hotel
This hotel offers ocean views and great service, and the restaurant has a typically Haitian menu. **$$**

Bassin Bleu

SAMPLE THE BENYÈ

A delicacy of the season, *beignets* (pronounced *benyè* in Haitian Creole) are typically eaten around Carnival time. They are made from ripe sweet bananas, flour, sugar, eggs and appropriate spices. *Beignets* are generally made during large gatherings of family or friends and they embody the spirit of togetherness that emerges during Carnival.

period, enslaved people were not allowed to celebrate with their owners at the time, pushing them to create their own smaller celebrations where they expressed themselves in ways that aligned with their culture, faiths and traditions. This allowed for the preservation of African identity and with time was adapted to what would become modern Haitian culture with its ever-evolving identity.

Today, Carnival is celebrated with specific music, dances and artistic expression. The three-day street celebration features *rara* bands on foot, who play music mainly with drums and other folkloric instruments, lending the celebration a mystical, almost spiritual aspect. Schoolchildren also parade throughout the day in colorful costumes; come nightfall, the *djaz* (bands) generally perform the Carnival song of the year on a set path aboard a float.

Participating in such activity requires vigilance from even the most accustomed locals. It's better to get a spot on a stand, from which you can choose to join the crowd or enjoy from a bit of a distance – this also assures that you catch some performance from all the bands. Carnival is best enjoyed with a glass of Rhum Barbancourt or Prestige beer (both iconic local drinks) in hand.

WHERE TO EAT IN JACMEL

Kay Chantal
Located in Lakou Nouyòk, it's a more informal setting with excellent seafood. **$**

Cafe Koze
Great for those working remotely, Cafe Koze is also very LGBTIQ-friendly and hosts different events. **$$**

Kalbasye
Housed in the Tchaka Agrikòl Complex; everything from the utensils to the food is made from locally grown produce. **$**

Crafts & Drinks at Lakou Nouyòk

GET TO KNOW JACMEL

From Jacmel's city center, a few minutes' walk towards the beach will lead you to the area of **Lakou Nouyòk**. Previously known to Jacmeliens and frequent visitors as Congo Plage, this is a strip of beach harboring artists who sell their work; the colorful ceramics separate the sellers' area from the beach. This is where you can find everything Jacmel artisans have to offer when it comes to typical Haitian handmade crafts such as sandals or jewelry. Ensure you've honed in on your negotiation skills to get the best deals on art pieces. It's also a good spot to try local alcoholic drinks (if you're brave!). *Kleren* is made from pure sugarcane juice and has a very sharp but smooth taste; an alternative flavored version with added leaf or root is called *tranpe*. These drinks are generally made in artisan distilleries. The beautiful promenade is a great addition to any Jacmel trip.

JACMEL'S FIRE

Being in Jacmel is a great experience, but knowing this little piece of history gives its people and its beauty a different allure. In 1896, a fire broke in Jacmel (which was then known as the City of Lights, as it was the first one in the Caribbean to have electricity) that destroyed most of the city, particularly the gingerbread homes that are typical for Haiti. After the fire, homes were rebuilt, preserving the architectural heritage where it was possible and innovating elsewhere. The Jacmel you can now see is a place that had to reinvent itself and has managed to keep its people's creativity and passion intact.

Trek to the Waterfalls of Bassin Bleu

TAKE A HIKE TO JACMEL'S SOUL

Getting to **Bassin Bleu** is an experience in itself. A short drive from Jacmel's city center (about 12km to the northwest), Bassin Bleu is situated between luscious, imposing mountains. The waterfalls comprise four basins: Cheval, Yes, Palmiste and Clair. Bassin Clair is the most beautiful, but all four are worth the challenging hike – an effort rewarded by pristine views and incredible cascades. The great thing about having four basins on the way is that they may constitute pit stops, if you need them.

First on the way up is **Bassin Cheval**; being shallow, it's the safest to visit with children and also offers a view of the southeastern coastline. Following Cheval, you will find **Bassin Yes** (4.5m deep) and soon after, Bassin Palmiste (17m deep), where you can once again take a dip or take advantage of the seating area – in Jacmel fashion, it's made of concrete and fades into the surrounding nature – to eat or rest.

Reaching **Bassin Clair** is the most challenging part of the hike, where you'll need the assistance of a local guide who will help you descend the narrow staircase from the top of a rock using a rope. This is perfect for those seeking adventure. Bassin Clair is roughly 22m deep, and with piercing blue waters, it has a tranquil air. Coming down from the adrenaline of the hike is much easier than you think. If you've opted not to dive from the jumping-off point where locals often perform impressive backflips, you can simply enter, float and relax.

GETTING AROUND

Jacmel is walkable. Wear comfortable shoes but be careful and aware in the streets as motos tend to pass people by quite closely. If you don't feel comfortable walking and don't want to drive, a moto is usually how everyone gets around. If you like a driver, keep in touch with them during your stay.

Beyond Jacmel

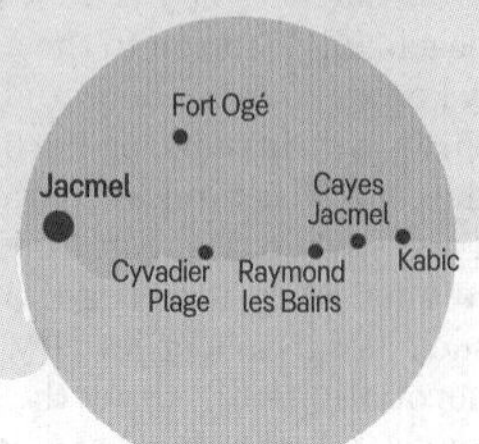

Ecotourism shines in Jacmel's surroundings. The green scenery and the endless choices of beaches provide the space to disconnect.

As described by locals, the Jacmel area has multifaceted beauty. Its proximity to the beach and location in a mountainous area highlights the diverse ecosystem in which it exists. The city is quite small, meaning that the experience is not truly complete without an exploration of its surroundings – the Cayes Jacmel and Kabic area in particular, which are home to white-sand beaches, great people and, as usual in Haiti, incredible food. A 45-minute drive along the eastern coast from the center of Jacmel will take you to the doorstep of small fishing settlements, where you can connect with nature and try out some of the best seafood on the island.

TOP TIP

If you're looking for a more quiet getaway, stay at a hotel outside Jacmel and go to the city by moto.

JAMESJONGPHOTOGRAPHY/SHUTTERSTOCK ©

Beach, Jacmel

JOHN SEATON CALLAHAN/GETTY IMAGES ©

Fried red snapper, Jacmel

A Beachside Feast at Raymond les Bains

BEACH DAY, THE LOCAL WAY

For a more local experience, driving down 15 minutes east from Cyvadier will lead to a beach, that's sometimes undetectable to the untrained eye. Awaiting you is **Raymond les Bains**, a popular spot where people come for the food, music and dancing.

As it is maintained by locals, entering Raymond les Bains and parking will cost you a small fee. This allows for the space to be kept clean, and shows support for the community. Once you've arrived, picking out where to eat will be your most difficult task of the day. The particularity of Raymond les Bains is that the informal restaurants are right on the beach, so you can simply pick a vendor and choose your table. And being so close to the water, the food cooked here is as fresh as it gets in Haiti – some vendors may even have you pick out your own fish.

WHY I LOVE JACMEL

Asley Carrénard is a tourism professional and a graduating student in tourism management.

Jacmel is, to me, a great place to step into my own peace. It's a place where creativity flows, you can see it on the walls or hear it in the music that plays at different bars at night. It's a place for expression of self and is extremely welcoming to others. The proximity to little isolated spots makes it one of my favorite places to go as Port-au-Prince tends to get crowded and loud. Jacmel is the reason I've never had to go on a meditation retreat. Why bother, when I can get there by a 45-minute flight?

WHERE TO STAY IN & AROUND JACMEL

Colin's Hotel
A Jacmel staple, this hotel is centrally located and often hosts salsa nights and other events (it can be on the louder side). **$$**

L'Auberge du Vieux Port
Located in a post-colonial-style building, offering spacious rooms along with typical local dishes. **$$**

Auberge du Mont Saint-Jean
For some cabin/lodge vibes, head 45 minutes west of Jacmel's center for this cozy place in La Vallée de Jacmel. **$$**

THE COMPOSITION OF A HAITIAN DISH

If you walk into a Haitian household, the chances of being offered a meal are quite high – this is what it will most likely be.

Haitians eat rice almost on a daily basis; if not it's substituted by cornmeal or wheat. On a typical plate, white rice is served with a bean sauce and accompanied by stewed meat. Rice can also be cooked with beans *(riz colé)* or with *djondjon* mushrooms to make *duri djondjon* (aka black rice). These main components may be accompanied by boiled root vegetables (plantains, sweet potatoes, yuca) or stewed legumes. And more likely than not, you'll end the meal with a fresh glass of juice made of whatever fruit is in season.

JANOS CSERNOCH/ALAMY ©

Fishing boat, Cyvadier Plage

A local recommendation: **Fafane** has the best *lambi* (conch) and fried fish in the area. You can expect a plate of food (whatever meat or fish you pick, along with some fried plantains and *pikliz,* or pickled vegetable relish) to cost around HTG800.

If you decide to make a day out of it, make sure you bring along your sunscreen (although there are plenty of palm trees to rest under), a swimsuit and a towel. The atmosphere on the beach is very lively, with *raboday* (traditional Haitian music) playing from the speakers, folks drinking Prestige (Haiti's most popular beer) and probably playing dominoes. If you're looking to be immersed in Haitian ambience and hospitality, Raymond les Bains serves that right up.

Relax on Cyvadier Beach

A HAITIAN SPIN ON '80S PARADISE

Many tourists have come to Haiti and never left, having fallen in love with its charm – it's common for small-town hotels to be owned by once-tourists, now-locals. Such is the case with **Cyvadier Plage Hôtel**, which sits on a stretch of road

WHERE TO DRINK IN JACMEL

La Reference Resto-Bar, Cayes Jacmel
Good drinks with even better music. DJs often play there at night.

La Taverne
Great spot for cocktails and a more social setting, occasional jazz or salsa nights; rum sours are highly recommended.

Belle Epoque
Nightclub in Jacmel with a more international crowd and range of music.

between Jacmel and Cayes Jacmel, about 25 minutes' drive from Jacmel. It was never renovated, conserving its '80s feel in a tropical setting, with palm trees surrounding the property and large swimming pool.

The private beach of **Cyvadier Plage** (nonresidents welcome with a day pass) is down a small track leading from the Cayes Jacmel road. This small half-moon-shaped cove flanked by rocky cliffs has no undertow. Should you go for a day pass, the terrace restaurant helmed by the Swiss-trained chef-owner Jean Christophe serves lunch and dinner; try *lambi* (conch) in Thai sauce. The hotel offers a variety of activities ranging from paddleboarding to boat excursions.

Go Back in Time at Fort Ogé

HISTORY AND COMMUNITY

When it comes to forts in Haiti, Citadelle Laferriere (p380) is everybody's first and main pick, and rightfully so – yet the smaller but mighty **Fort Ogé** is well worth the visit. As with many sites in Haiti, the thrill usually comes from getting to the destination, but the history around the fort is what keeps people coming back.

During the period of Haiti's fight for independence from its French colonial rulers, forts were constructed across the island to provide refuge for the previously enslaved people. Most major cities in Haiti have forts, each representing a source of pride for the local population.

Unlike the Citadelle Laferriere, Haiti's largest fortress, Fort Ogé sees far fewer tourists. Exploring the site is best done with a guide, who will share insights about the fort's background and construction. The entrance fee and the cost of a guide contributes to the community projects in the area.

Fort Ogé is at about an hour's drive east of Jacmel. Head toward Cayes Jacmel and turn left at the airport; from there, follow the signs to the fort. You can also make the trip by moto. At the airport, it won't be difficult to find moto drivers, so be ready to negotiate. Due to a scarcity of fuel, the fee to get to the fort will likely be close to HTG1000 and this should include the wait time at the fort.

LET'S PLAY DOMINOES

Walking around in any Haitian city on a lazy day or in the evening, it's very possible that you stumble upon a group of people playing dominoes, gathered around a table and slamming it strongly. If you look at the corner, you might find someone standing with clothespins all over their face – in Haiti, the loser of a domino game has to wear them for the remainder of the game. In fact, if you want to interact with local communities, try having a domino set – just be prepared for the *fawouch* (friendly teasing in Haitian culture) if you don't know how to play!

WHERE TO FIND ART IN JACMEL

Jacmel Mozaik Boutique
This small shop specializes in mosaic art, but also has a wide variety of other typical Haitian craft pieces.

Jacmel Arts Center
Self-described as an inclusive space for creatives to collaborate; paintings are sold in store and online.

Rue du Commerce & Rue Ste Anne
These two streets are key to finding small local artisan shops.

A Luxurious Escape at Cayes Jacmel

ECO-LUXURY AT ITS FINEST

From Raymond les Bains, a seven-minute drive further down the coast will lead you to **Cayes Jacmel**. A quaint fishing settlement, it isn't very busy except on market days (Wednesday and Saturday), where you can go and pick out the freshest produce before it makes it to Jacmel itself and other neighboring towns.

As a destination, Cayes Jacmel is perfect for visitors who wish to respect the environment, support local ecological endeavors and consume as locally as possible. In line with this, **Chic Chateau** (a further 10 minutes from Cayes Jacmel), is an eco-luxe hotel – or more of a B&B for the conscious adventurer.

Located on a large property, the solar-powered hotel stands on a high cliff with an ocean view. The property is adorned by mango and *kenèp* (a local favorite Caribbean fruit, in season during the summer) trees. Chic Chateau provides farm-to-table breakfast every morning; it's a great place to get acquainted with a typical Haitian breakfast (and coffee). Staying at Chic Chateau also means being within walking distance of a more quiet beachfront. With three bungalows (suites), it's also the perfect romantic getaway or spot to enjoy the quiet, as there aren't that many guests. Southern sunsets in Haiti are must-sees by any standard, and Chic Chateau's sunset boat rides (for a small fee) with a local fisherman render them much more memorable.

As with most hotels on the coast, it is perfectly possible to move around if you don't have a car, using a moto driver. Ask the hostess at Chic Chateau (Janet) for recommendations on trusted drivers.

BEST BOOKS TO READ BEFORE VISITING HAITI

Hadriana in All My Dreams (René Depestre; 1988)
This book follows Hadriana, who has just died, and her transformation as she is zombified. It's an attempt at reclaiming the narrative around Haiti's mystique.

Masters of the Dew (Jacques Roumain, 1944)
Haiti's perhaps most famous novel recounts the story of a man returning to his homeland after 15 years. The best way to understand its impact is to read it.

Les Cinqs Lettres (Georges Castera; 1992)
This collection of poetry reflects the Haitian charm like no other.

Surf the Waves at Kabic

HAITI'S FIRST SURFING SCHOOL

As you might expect, activities in the south of Haiti generally revolve around the beach. Located in a sleepy fishing village about 30 minutes east of Jacmel, **Kabic** beach is perfect for a quick dip but it's also home to Haiti's only surfing school. **Surf Haiti** is a nonprofit that encourages surfing as an activity for young Haitians in the area. They've become a part of the community, teaching kids to swim and surf while reinforcing positive community engagement. Surf Haiti has carved Kabic as a destination for surfers, particularly due to its emptiness – waves are common but not very crowded.

TOUR OPERATORS IN JACMEL

Annou Fè Touris
This Jacmel-based operator has a focus on supporting all things local; it can service the north as well.

Experience Jacmel
Think of an excursion or adventure, and Experience Jacmel will make it happen.

Bellevue Tours
Run by a Haitian-American couple who strive to provide country-wide tours that are both educational and exceptional experiences.

Surfing, Jacmel

Visitors can rent gear and receive lessons from Surf Haiti staff. Available to those who would rather stay close to the beach is the **Surf Haiti Guesthouse**. Perfect for eco-tourists, this guesthouse is located within the 'jungle' and provides closeness to nature in an unparalleled way. Depending on the size of the group, the entire guesthouse is available for rent.

Surf Haiti was founded in 2011 by Dr Ken Pierce, an emergency physician who came to Haiti after the 2010 earthquake. In a not-so-uncommon fashion, Dr Pierce decided to build a space that would support the local community and engage with younger folks.

With the current situation in Port-au-Prince, travel to Haiti and its provinces, in particular, has significantly decreased, forcing many young Haitian instructors to leave for better economic opportunities. Visits to Kabic, or any other place for that matter, are a big boost for local economies.

If you're looking for peace and quiet, **Ti Mouillage** (meaning 'small dip') beach offers one of the most spectacular sunsets on the coast and makes for a beautiful stop should you have the time.

JACMEL'S KITE FESTIVAL

Every January 2, a kite festival is organized in **La Vallée de Jacmel** (45 minutes outside Jacmel). It makes for a great spontaneous adventure and is perfect for anyone spending the New Year in Jacmel. The atmosphere is comparable to that of Carnival with displays of colors overtaking the sky, as though it were an art exhibition.

This event usually means heavy involvement from the community, particularly the youth who work to preserve its traditions. The fact that January 2 is a holiday in Haiti makes it even more popular for neighboring communities.

Visitors can also participate (for a small fee) and be a part of a unique and colorful celebration.

GETTING AROUND

To get around the area beyond Jacmel, you can always rely on a moto if traveling alone, especially if you've found a good driver. However, it may be more comfortable to rent a car, as travel times usually go over 45 minutes.

CAP-HAÏTIEN

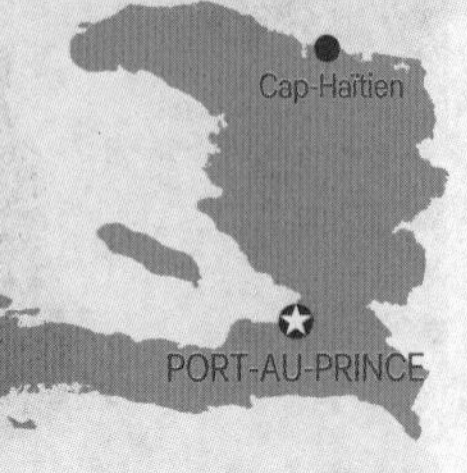

Cap-Haïtien (known to Haitians as Okap) has been Haiti's fastest-growing city for years. In recent times it has picked up a number of activities and tourists from Port-au-Prince. For many, it remains Haiti's historical treasure chest. Understanding Haitian or Caribbean culture is easier if you take a look at Cap-Haïtien's turbulent history and the role it played in the Haitian revolution.

This city is a perfect base for exploring Haiti's attractions while connecting to the island's soul. Okap is famous for the Citadelle Laferrière (a Unesco World Heritage site), but it has also become a spot for leisurely activities, from festivals to beach parties. The recent spike in interest in Okap as a tourist destination has caused festivals such as PAP Jazz to move here, and led to an increase in Cap-Haïtien restaurants participating in Burger Week. In short, something is always going on. Okap is growing into a tourist jewel in the Caribbean and is a must-visit on the island.

TOP TIP

The *fete patronale,* which can be seen as the city's birthday, is celebrated in mid-August, so things tend to ramp up around that time – but really, any time of the year is a good bet for visiting.

SIGHTS
1 Boulevard du Cap-Haïtien
2 Cathédrale Notre-Dame
3 Marché au Fer
4 Musée des Beaux Arts

EATING
5 Cap Deli
6 Coin Capois

DRINKING & NIGHTLIFE
7 Boukanye

Cap-Haïtien

BEST PLACES TO EAT IN CAP-HAÏTIEN

Cap Deli
Located on the Boulevard, it offers old-fashioned Haitian ambience paired with typical Capois food. $$

Coin Capois
This cafe provides a calmer atmosphere for a quick bite or coffee. $$

Boukanye
The Creole cuisine here is impeccable; they also host happy hours and have Haitian parties on weekends. $$

Lakay Bar-Restaurant
This restaurant has a homey feel and serves sugarcane juice, which isn't found on many menus in Haiti. $

Welcome to Okap

THE CITY THAT HAS IT ALL

Okap is an iconic city. During the French colonial era it was the richest city in the Caribbean, and the role it played in Haiti's independence struggle is not one locals joke about.

The most straightforward way to explore the city is on foot. Most landmarks have on-site guides who can tell you about the history or significance of the sight.

The **Bataille de Vertières Monument** symbolizes the deciding battle that took place on November 18, 1803 between the revolutionaries and Napoleon's army. This victory led Haiti to officially declare its independence from France on January 1, 1804.

The **Marché au Fer**, the city's main market, is named after Port-au-Prince's own, as both are mainly made of iron. Sprawling over four city blocks, you'll find a variety of local vendors selling both fresh produce and art pieces.

Another historic landmark is the **Cathédrale Notre-Dame**, built in 1670, along with the square right in front the church, where the liberation of enslaved people was proclaimed in 1793. Lovers of art can visit the new **Musée des Beaux Arts**, which often hosts conversations with artists.

Finally, to know this city is to know the **Boulevard du Cap-Haïtien** (or Boulva, as it's pronounced in Haitian Creole) – a stretch of road along the waterfront with ocean views. It has a tourist market and some of the city's best restaurants. You're sure to find *machann fritay* (street food vendors) too, if you're up for an authentic taste of Haiti.

GETTING AROUND

It's fairly easy to get around in Cap-Haïtien by walking or taking a moto. It's also faster and cheaper than driving. Transport from one end of the town to another shouldn't cost you more than HTG100.

Beyond Cap-Haïtien

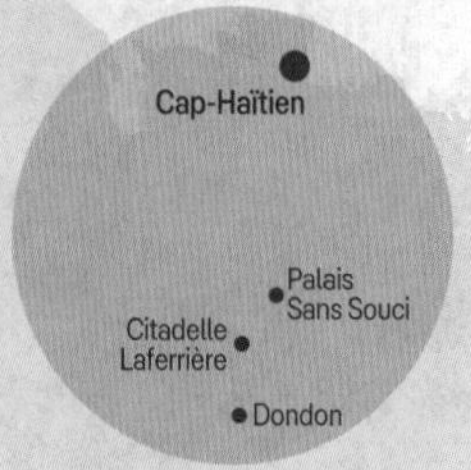

Cap-Haïtien
Palais Sans Souci
Citadelle Laferrière
Dondon

Explore the north to understand why Haiti, despites the many challenges, should be considered a top destination in the Caribbean.

Exploring the nothern part of Haiti is is an adventure you could dedicate months to – seeing the sights, getting to know local people and learning about the history, all while eating delicious food. Well beyond Cap-Haïtien and into neighboring communities, you'll find gems that make the island so alluring. A road leading west from Cap-Haïtien winds along the cape toward some of the loveliest coastal scenery in the country. Whether it's the hidden beaches or Dondon's caves, the natural beauty of this area gets travelers to come back. Meanwhile, if you can only do one day trip while you're in Cap-Haïtien, the must-sees remain Citadelle Laferrière and Palais Sans Souci (both Unesco World Heritage sites).

TOP TIP

Unlike the Jacmel area, attractions outside Cap-Haïtien are usually further away – if you are stepping out of the city, make it a day trip.

Citadelle Laferrière (p380)

VICHINTERLANG/GETTY IMAGES ©

Vodou shrine

Descend into Dondon's Caverns

EXPLORE THE CITY OF CAVES

Situated two hours south of Cap-Haïtien (by heading toward the town of Milot), Dondon makes an interesting addition to a Cap-Haïtien itinerary. Dubbed 'the city of caves,' it's an attraction due to its unique system of natural grottoes. There are a total of 10 caves in Dondon.

The small town itself, surrounded by coffee and cocoa plantations, is one of the few places in Haiti that conserves a piece of history from the island's indigenous Taíno culture. It's believed that the caves were places of devotion for the Taínos, a practice that continues to this day with Vodou ceremonies. The caves are now home to large numbers of bats, but the Taínos left their mark on many of the stalagmites, the tops of which have been carved to resemble skulls.

You can get a local guide in the communities surrounding the caves, or stop by the town hall and ask for a guide. The community involvement in tourism plays a key role in conserving the history of these caves through oral storytelling.

Dondon also hosts the **Festival des Grottes** (Caves Festival) every year in July. The event is as much about the caves as it is about the town – an incentive for Haitians along with foreigners to discover their island while supporting local economy.

Additionally, Dondon celebrates its patron saint for three days from November 9, when pilgrims from afar come here to celebrate **St Martin of Tours**. These celebrations are usually deeply rooted in Vodou practices, in which the *lwas* (spirits) are honored.

THE SIGNIFICANCE OF VODOU

Vodou is everywhere in Haiti. History shows that enslaved people often had to use Western religion to conceal the practice of their own. This created an interesting mix (often confusing to outsiders) of Western, African and even indigenous religions – for instance, the patron saint festivities in big cities are celebrated in both Catholic and Vodou circles. But Vodou represents much more than a religion. It played an important role in Haiti gaining its independence (the Bois Caïman ceremony was the very first gathering of enslaved people, which triggered the struggle for independence), and while most Haitians now practice Western religions such as Catholicism, the cultural impact of Vodou remains and is often honored.

WHERE TO GO TO THE BEACH

Ile a Rat
Small island with white sands, sparkling blue water, palm trees and fresh seafood – perfect for a beach getaway.

Kay Lolo
A secluded beachside B&B that's only accessible by boat, and surrounded by forest – great if you want to disconnect.

Cormier
All-inclusive beach resort a 20-minute drive away from Cap-Haïtien, offering day passes. Incredible sunsets.

THE ERA OF FORTIFICATION

After Haiti gained its independence from France, the focus was on safeguarding this newly acquired freedom. About 20 forts were built throughout the country for defense purposes, with the Citadelle Laferrière being the most famous. All of them were placed strategically to protect the country in case of a counterattack, and most major cities in Haiti have at least one fort. Nowadays, most forts are cared for by the communities surrounding them. With tourist numbers decreasing in recent years due to the increase of violence in Port-au-Prince, visits to these forts hold much more weight.

Palais Sans Souci

Admire the Vision of Henry Christophe

HAITI'S MUST-SEE HERITAGE

The **Citadelle Laferrière** is the largest fort in the Caribbean region. Sitting at the top of a mountain called Bonnet à l'Eveque, at an elevation of about 915m, it offers commanding views in every direction.

Built after Haiti's independence in 1820, the battleship-like fort was intended to protect the country's newfound freedom and repel the French. Building it took more than 15 years and employed about 20,000 people. Its construction was ordered and overseen by Henry Christophe, a key leader in the Haitian Revolution and Haiti's only monarch. Today, the Citadelle is a Haitian landmark – its image is included on the HTG100 bill.

A 20-minute drive away, in the town of Milot, the **Palais Sans Souci** is a collection of ruins of the palace built in 1813 by Christophe, who was known to throw lavish parties in order to build up the power and presence of people of African descent. The palace was designed to be the administrative capital of Christophe's kingdom; it has been abandoned since it was ruined in the 1842 earthquake.

GETTING AROUND

As with Jacmel area, it is possible to travel beyond Cap-Haïtien by moto, but it's more comfortable to rent a car to as travel times are usually longer than 45 minutes.

To get to the Palais Sans Souci and the Citadelle Laferrière, drive to the town of Milot.

To get to the fort, you can either hike or go up on horseback for roughly US$15; get a guide near the ticket office at the far end of Milot. The hike usually takes a little over two hours, with a distance of 6km and a steep climb at over 600m.

Arriving

You can fly directly to Haiti from Florida or from New York City (via Florida). There are also regular flights from the Dominican Republic to Haiti; small airlines are on the cheaper side. If going to the north, it's perfectly safe to take the bus from Santo Domingo to Cap-Haïtien with Caribe Tours. If arriving at the Port-au-Prince airport, you can get a SIM card for free from Natcom or Digicel.

By Air

Alirlines have daily scheduled flights to Port-au-Prince from Florida. For the north, you can fly directly to Cap-Haïtien. For Jacmel, take a Sunrise Airways flight to Les Cayes, and arrange for a driver to take you to Jacmel. Alternatively, Haiti Aero Solution SA provides flights from Port-au-Prince to Jacmel.

By Boat

It's possible to get to Jacmel by boat from the Dominican Republic via Pederales. Reach Pederales from Santo Domingo by flying to Cabo Rojo with Rep-Air. The airline can help organize a taxi to the border. From Anse-à-Pitres, you can take a boat to Jacmel.

Money

Currency: Haitian gourde (HTG)

CASH

Carry cash everywhere, particularly if you are spending the day outside and will be buying street food or anything from local vendors. Cash is also useful to pay for your moto-taxi along with any guide whose services you may use. Most major cities have ATMs and most places will gladly exchange any US dollars for HTG.

DIGITAL PAYMENTS

It's possible to make digital payments, as long as you have a Haitian SIM card with one of Haiti's service providers. Digicel users can make digitial payments via MonCash, and Natcom users can make payments via NatCash. However, prioritize using cash, in case the person you'd like to pay does not have a digital wallet.

CREDIT CARDS

It's possible to use credit cards at most restaurants and hotels (given that they are not street vendors), but to be on the safe side, having cash is always recommended.

JAMAICA

MUSIC, BEACHES, FOOD, CULTURE AND NATURE

A host of attractions awaits in exciting Jamaica, from reggae beats, spicy jerk and buzzy towns to rugged wilderness and roaring waterfalls.

Jamaica is a musical powerhouse that gave the world Bob Marley, the first global superstar from the developing world – a source of immense national pride. Music is life here, with its roots reaching back to the folk songs of West Africa and reflected in the electronic beats of dancehall, the bass of the omnipresent sound systems, the lyricism of the patois and the sounds of gospel. And just like its music, Jamaican food is a mélange of the country's many cultures, with a flavor all its own. African spice-rubs and Taíno cooking methods have evolved into the country's signature jerk; the Indians contributed curry; the Sephardic Jews brought punchy, vinegary escoveitch fish; and the country's rum and Blue Mountain coffee round off its rich culinary offerings.

Even in a region as full of natural beauty as the Caribbean, Jamaica holds its own. There's the allure of the white-sand beaches, lapped at by the crystal-clear Caribbean Sea, which entices you to dive in and explore its underwater world. In the lush, green hinterland, you can float along crystalline rivers on bamboo rafts, or frolic in the natural hot tubs of the island's many spectacular waterfalls. The caves riddling Jamaica's limestone-and-jungle wilderness entice the adventurous, who can also don hiking boots to explore the cloud forest covering the Blue Mountains, and summit Blue Mountain Peak – the range's highest.

JOHN B HEWITT/SHUTTERSTOCK ©

THE MAIN AREAS

KINGSTON
The capital that never sleeps. **p388**

TREASURE BEACH
Tranquil village life. **p397**

NEGRIL
Sea, sand and beach parties. **p404**

PHOTO SPIRIT/SHUTTERSTOCK ©

Above: Negril (p404); Left: Cooking jerk chicken on an oil-drum grill

MONTEGO BAY
Buzzy nightlife in Jamaica's second city. **p411**

OCHO RIOS
Adventure parks, waterfalls and swimming. **p417**

PORT ANTONIO
History and river rafting. **p422**

Find Your Way

Jamaica's attractions are spread out, and visiting them often takes longer than planned, due to road conditions. Some attractions are reachable by public transportation; others, by tour from the island's visitor hubs of MoBay, Ocho Rios and Negril.

Negril, p404
Jamaica's most popular beach town entices with its superb stretch of white sand, diverse dining options, nightly music events and multiple outlying attractions.

Montego Bay, p411
Luxury resorts, beaches and partying on the Hip Strip are the draws of MoBay, as is the 'greatest reggae show on earth,' held here in July.

Treasure Beach, p397
Numerous beaches, tranquil lanes, excellent restaurants and an addictively bohemian way of life await at this relaxed, timeless fishing village.

Ocho Rios, p417

This bustling beach town is the springboard for some of Jamaica's most famous watery attractions, and it boasts beach parties and resorts galore.

Kingston, p388

Jamaica's gritty, chaotic capital is a world-class destination for music lovers, with an excellent dining scene and street art to boot.

Port Antonio, p422

Waterfalls, low-key beaches, river rafting and Maroon culture await in the blessed environs of this unassuming, tranquil and historic town on the north coast.

BUS

Jamaica's major destinations are well connected to Kingston, the capital, via the air-conditioned Knutsford Express buses, while the rest of the country is covered by a network of minibuses that run to virtually every town and village.

CAR

Self-driving offers flexibility and access to out-of-the-way attractions and remote villages. Bear in mind that with the exception of the country's two highways, potholes are numerous and range from moderate to will-swallow-your-car. A 4WD is required to explore the Blue Mountains.

WALKING

The country's cities, towns and villages are very walkable and best explored on foot, with the exception of some outlying attractions. There are also a couple of exceptional treks in Cockpit Country and the Blue Mountains.

Plan Your Time

Jamaica is a remarkably diverse country comprising stunning coastlines, mountains, wilderness and cities, and its attractions are many. We've handpicked the places that best capture the country's unique cultural heritage and diverse landscapes.

ESTUARY_OF_DREAMS/SHUTTERSTOCK ©

Ruins, Port Royal (p395)

If You Only Visit One Place

- Spend a long weekend in loud yet beguiling **Kingston** (p388), soaking up its unique vibe and becoming slightly nocturnal because of its epic music scene, from street parties and overnight events to nightclubs.

- Give yourself at least half a day to explore **Downtown** (p391); swing by the **National Gallery of Jamaica** (p390) for a comprehensive intro to the country's art, admire **Kingston Creative** (p390) murals along **Water Lane** (p390), pop into **Life Yard** (p390) – an art project that works with urban youth.

- Treat yourself to a meal at **Swiss Stores** (p390) – a photography gallery and jewelry shop serving excellent Jamaican standards.

Seasonal Highlights

Jamaica hosts a diverse array of festivals year-round, from music and cultural extravaganzas to fairs and celebrations that highlight the best of Jamaica's fresh produce.

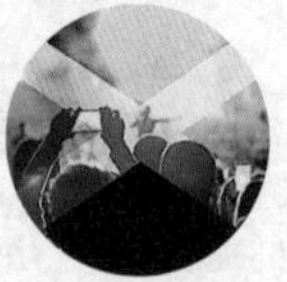

JANUARY

Accompong celebrates its Afro-Caribbean heritage and independence at its Maroon Festival, while St Ann's Bay rocks out to the rhythms of **Rebel Salute**.

FEBRUARY

It's **Reggae Month**, where Jamaica celebrates Bob Marley's birthday, with concerts and sound-system parties held across the island.

MARCH

Spring breakers descend on Ocho Rios and Negril to party, while sports fans hit Kingston for the **Boys & Girls Championships**.

TRYBEX/SHUTTERSTOCK ©, LOST MOUNTAIN STUDIO/SHUTTERSTOCK ©, ALEXANDER HASSENSTEIN/GETTY IMAGES FOR SPIEGEL ©

A Week's Adventuring

- Day-trip from **Kingston** (p388) to **Port Royal** (p395) to check out the remains of the former pirate capital of the Caribbean, and take a boat out to **Lime Cay** (p396) for some sunbathing.

- If you're a hiker, head into the Blue Mountains to conquer **Blue Mountain Peak** (p394) and sample some **Blue Mountain coffee** (p394).

- Drive east to the laid-back fishing village of **Treasure Beach** (p397), hang out with locals for two days, and take a boat trip to the **Pelican Bar** (p400), then press on to **Negril** (p404) for beach parties and great dining before finishing up in **Montego Bay** (p411).

If You Have More Time

- If you can set aside time for more in-depth exploration, then do it. Interested in Maroon culture? Visit **Accompong** (p403) come January 6. Love waterfalls? Throw in **YS Falls** (p402), **Reach Falls** (p424) and **Dunn's River Falls** (p418).

- Fancy tackling Jamaica's toughest hike? Head north for **Cockpit Country** (p403).

- If beautiful, undeveloped beaches are your passion, hit **Winnifred Beach** (p423).

- For beach parties, check out **Montego Bay** (p411) and **Ocho Rios** (p417).

- Finish with an epic road trip along Jamaica's east coast, stopping for the island's best jerk pork at one of **Boston Bay's** (p424) cookshops.

APRIL
Spring means **Carnival** in Jamaica. Parties in Kingston lead up to the main event of costumed revelry and live music.

JULY
The rainy season doesn't stop Montego Bay from hosting **Reggae Sumfest** – Jamaica's biggest music event, with a week-long party.

OCTOBER
Jamaica is pelted by heavy rains; coffee lovers converge on Devon House in Kingston to imbibe at the **Jamaica Coffee Festival**.

DECEMBER
Nights are cool, days are sunny, and **Sting** – Jamaica's biggest dancehall event – rocks Plantation Cove in St Ann's Bay.

GEOGPHOTOS/ALAMY ©, PHOTO BY SHELBY SOBLICK/GETTY IMAGES ©, PHOTO SPIRIT/SHUTTERSTOCK ©, ANDY MARTIN JR./ZUMA/ALAMY

KINGSTON

Nestling between a vast harbor and the ridges of the Blue Mountains, Jamaica's capital is an assault on the senses: scenic, noisy and full of hustle. The island's cultural and economic powerhouse, this tough, gritty city is the musical heart of Jamaica, with street parties, music events and nightclubs pulsating to a tireless beat.

Kingston is split into two, separated by the market hub of Half Way Tree. The tight grid of Downtown is home to historic buildings, street markets and the National Gallery of Jamaica – the Caribbean's greatest art museum. Off-limits after dark, Downtown is fringed by tough, impoverished neighborhoods resulting from decades of government neglect and inequality of opportunity and populated by the 'sufferers' whom Marley immortalized in song. However, they're renowned for their music, and their names (Trench Town, Tivoli Gardens) are legend to reggae and dancehall fans. Spread-out Uptown is home to high-rises, and the city's best hotels and restaurants.

TOP TIP

Downtown is compact and best seen on foot, so enjoy strolling through the sights. Uptown is considerably more spread out, but two of the city's most essential spots – the Bob Marley Museum and Devon House – are within walking distance of each other, just off Hope Rd.

MIHAI-BOGDAN LAZAR/SHUTTERSTOCK ©

Devon House (p392)

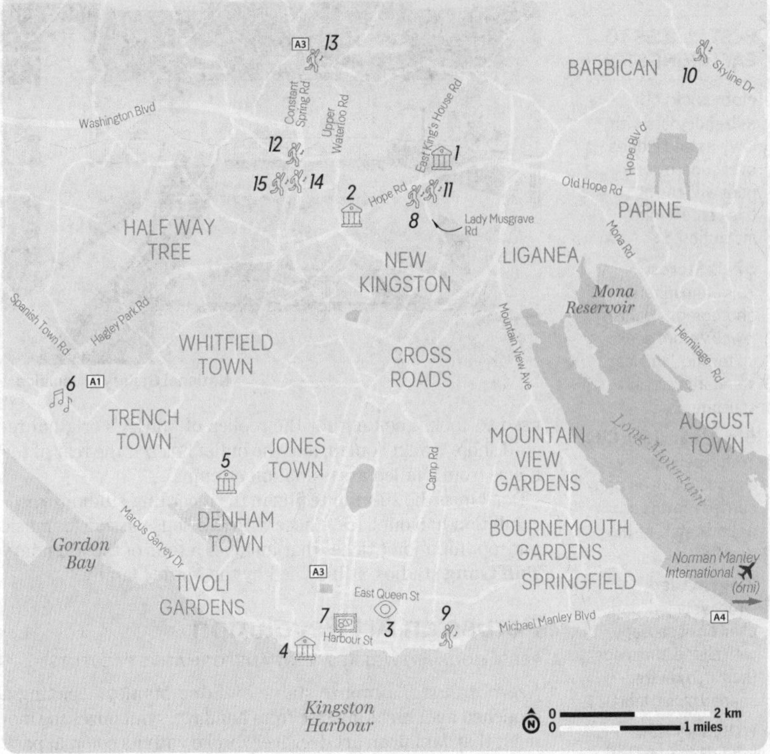

SIGHTS
1 Bob Marley Museum
2 Devon House
3 Life Yard
4 National Gallery of Jamaica
5 Trench Town Culture Yard
6 Tuff Gong
7 Water Lane

ENTERTAINMENT
8 Beer Mug Fridays
9 Capricorn Inn
10 Dub Club
11 Dubwise Café
12 MECA
13 Taboo Kingston
14 Uptown Mondays
15 Weddy Weddy Wednesdays

Chasing Marley's Ghost

THE FORMER HOMES OF A LEGEND

Few Jamaicans have made as great an impact on the world as Bob Marley. Upon arrival at the **Trench Town Culture Yard**, Marley's early home, a rusted-out carcass of a Volkswagen bus that belonged to the Wailers in the 1960s will greet you. Trench Town, a 1930s' housing project in Downtown Kingston, immortalized in Marley's 'No Woman, No Cry,' is widely credited as the birthplace of ska, rocksteady and reggae. Peek into the small bedroom that he shared with his wife Rita before heading to the **Bob Marley Museum** in Uptown, where Marley lived and recorded from 1975 until his death in 1981. The hour-long tour of this creaky wooden house provides an intimate insight into his life, with much of the house left as it was, from his simple bedroom and favorite denim shirt to the kitchen where he

BEST PLACES FOR A COFFEE

Danya's Coffee Barrel
Laptop-friendly cafe that employs hearing-impaired baristas to serve excellent Blue Mountain coffee, bagels and cakes.

Deaf Can! Coffee
An Uptown social enterprise specializing in Blue Mountain coffee, simultaneously employing hearing-impaired staff.

Café Blue/Deli Works
Smoked marlin sandwiches are washed down with large cups of Blue Mountain coffee by laptop-toting Uptowners.

BEST PLACES TO EAT IN KINGSTON

Moby Dick
Rub shoulders with lawyers and judges over superb curry goat with roti at this century-old institution. $$

Swiss Stores
This atmospheric photography gallery/jewelry store cooks up terrific Jamaican standards and jerk sausage. $$

Gloria's Seafood City
Watch pelicans fly by as you munch on zingy curried prawns or grilled catch-of-the-day. $$

Kingston Jerk
Order your jerk pork, chicken or sausage with all the trimmings, then enjoy at tree-shaded picnic tables. $

Mi Hungry Now
Incredible I-tal food bar, with delicious plantain burgers, 'pleaza' (raw pizza) and fruit juices. $

Usain Bolt's Tracks and Records
Bolt's takes on his favorite Jamaican dishes – janga soup, jerk chicken, pepper shrimp – wins gold. $$

Steak House on the Verandah
Kingston's best grilled meats in an unparalleled setting. $$$

National Gallery of Jamaica

used to cook. Look out for the replica of Marley's original record shop, Wail'n Soul'm, and the bullet holes at the rear of the house from a failed assassination attempt.

Don't miss the 20-minute film in the recording-studio-turned-exhibition-hall out back. Those with a serious passion for music may opt for a joint ticket that includes a tour of the legendary **Tuff Gong** studios, still owned by the Marley family.

Peruse an Art Revolution

REBELLIOUS ARTWORKS AND TRANSFORMATIVE PROJECTS

Negro Aroused, a bronze statue by Edna Manley depicting a crouched man breaking free from bondage, symbolizes the moment that Jamaican art decisively broke with its colonial past. The chronological art collection of the world-class **National Gallery of Jamaica** begins with Taíno carvings and continues with the dramatic shift away from British-style landscape paintings to authentically Jamaican forms of expression. Other highlights include more bold sculptures by Manley, 'intuitive' paintings by artists John Dunkley and David Pottinger, and Everald Brown's art, which examines Rasta beliefs. Also look out for the abstract religious works by Carl Abrahams, and realist Barrington Watson's take on the lives of ordinary Jamaicans.

Near the gallery, the vibrant murals along **Water Lane** depict different aspects of Jamaican life, from music and iconic movie scenes to Kingston street life, and are part of the Paint the City project by **Kingston Creative**, which aims to empower local creativity and transform Downtown. On the edge of Downtown, **Life Yard** is an innovative, Rastafari-run art and urban farming project that supports local youth with regenerating a neighborhood once beset with gang problems; call ahead for tours.

WHERE TO STAY IN KINGSTON

AC Hotel
The pick of New Kingston's business-style hotels, with Blue Mountain views from its Jamaican-art-filled rooms. **$$$**

Neita's Nest
Generous Jamaican breakfasts, friendly hosts and great views of Kingston define this B&B in Stony Hill. **$$**

Dancehall Hostel
Dancehall dance classes, DJ nights, a recording studio and hot tub are perks at this popular hillside hostel. **$**

DOWNTOWN KINGSTON WALKING TOUR

This walking tour pulls together Downtown Kingston's best sights. Begin at **1 Parade**, the central park of the city. Proceed north along Upper King St, past **2 Liberty Hall**, an excellent interactive museum dedicated to Marcus Garvey and the Back to Africa movement, then turn right along Charles St and follow it down to **3 Sha'are Shalom Synagogue** (p392), Jamaica's only remaining Jewish house of worship. Head east, where East St leads to the **4 National Museum**, worth a peek for its Taíno carvings. The **5 Music Museum** next door traces the history and development of Jamaica's music, while the adjacent **6 National Library** is a wonderfully rich literary resource. Two blocks south, detour east along Port Royal St and its moderately scenic **7 seafront promenade**, which runs past Kingston harbor and the 19th-century Tower St Penitentiary, then follow East St all the way south to the **8 Money Museum**, inside the Bank of Jamaica, where its display runs the gamut from Taíno beads to the first bills issued by an independent Jamaica. Follow Ocean Boulevard west to the **9 National Gallery of Jamaica**. A block north is the **10 African Caribbean Institute**, an extensive resource for the history of the Middle Passage and the African diaspora, while the Memory Bank audiovisual history archive preserves Jamaica's rich folkloric traditions. A block north, take Water Lane (p390) east for three blocks, then turn left up Temple Lane to reach the **11 Crying Child Memorial**, commemorating the youth of Kingston who have perished due to gun violence. Make your way up King St, past the courts, and detour west to the chaotic and buzzy **12 Coronation Market** for fresh produce and a slice of local life.

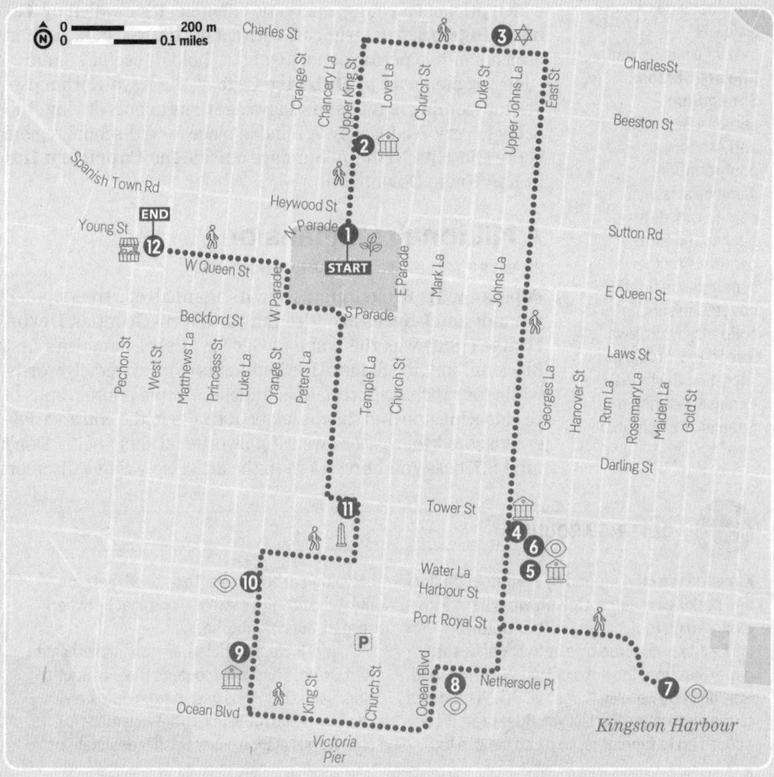

KINGSTON'S HOUSES OF WORSHIP

Both of Downtown Kingston's houses of worship are open to the public. In the devout Rastafarian community on Oxford St, at the 11am Sunday service in the Ethiopian Orthodox Church of **Ba Beta Kristyan Haile Selassie I**, women must wear dresses and keep their hair covered, while men must wear long trousers (shorts are forbidden). The two sexes must sit apart, on either side of the aisle.

At 92 Duke St, the **Sha'are Shalom Synagogue** serves a Sephardi and Ashkenazi congregation. Jamaica's Jewish community dates back to the 15th century, and the synagogue's floor is covered in sand in solidarity with Jews forced to worship in secret on the Iberian Peninsula during the Spanish Inquisition.

Bring on the Night

KINGSTON'S VIBRANT PARTY SCENE

Kingston never seems to slumber, a fact that is unsurprising given that it's Jamaica's number-one music destination, regardless of whether you're into old-school roots reggae or the latest dancehall moves. Kingston nightlife is divided into weekly events that take place in (mostly) Uptown venues: overnight reggae and dancehall events are advertised by flyers and typically involve a dozen performers, while impromptu sound-system parties in Downtown's neighborhoods consist of giant speakers set up in the middle of the street, with a 'selector' (DJ), a 'toaster' (MC) and dancers trying to outdo each other with the slickest moves and hippest outfits. While some visitors may be daunted by the idea of venturing into Kingston's infamous neighborhoods in the middle of the night (things often don't get going till 2am or 3am), street parties are generally safe, as residents are responsible for security and don't take kindly to violence. Still, it's best to leave your valuables behind and come with a local.

Your weekly party planner should include **Uptown Mondays**' reggae and dancehall party; **Weddy Weddy Wednesdays**, a dancehall event at 41 Burlington Ave, Uptown; **Beer Mug Fridays**' DJ sets at East Japanese Kazumi restaurant; and Sunday roots reggae at **Dub Club**, north of Papine. Popular Uptown dancehall clubs include **MECA**, located in the Marketplace, which attracts a young, energetic clientele. It's rivalled by **Taboo Kingston**, part strip-club with a more diverse audience and occasional live performances by household dancehall names.

For reggae, head to **Dubwise Cafe** at the Kaya Herbhouse: up-and-coming reggae stars showcase their talents during Dub School every Wednesday. A reliable place for old-school reggae is the Old Hits Night on Sundays outside the **Capricorn Inn** in Rae Town, Downtown.

A Millionaire's Mansion

EXPLORE THE HISTORY OF DEVON HOUSE

Popular with Kingstonians for its manicured, tree-shaded grounds and **I-Scream** outlet, the Caribbean-Georgian **Devon House** (1881) was the home of George Stiebel, Jamaica's first Black millionaire. Some of the highlights of its extremely worthwhile tour include porcelain chandeliers, sepia photographs of ye olde Kingston and the roundabout chairs in the entrance foyer, designed for visitors wearing swords on their belts. Don't miss Stiebel's gambling room in the attic. Now *that's* discreet.

GETTING AROUND

Kingston is a city gripped by perpetual gridlock, and parking is scarce. Downtown is best explored on foot, as are parts of Uptown.

The city is covered by a network of buses, departing from the hubs of Half Way Tree, and Parade in Downtown Kingston. Bus 98 connects to the airport and Port Royal. Buses rarely run according to timetable, so it can mean a lot of waiting at bus stops. Taxis and Ubers are the quickest and easiest way to get between spread-out neighborhoods.

Comfortable, scheduled, air-conditioned Knutsford Express buses to Montego Bay, Falmouth, Negril and Ocho Rios depart from Uptown. Minibuses and route taxis from Downtown's chaotic bus station cover smaller destinations.

Beyond Kingston

Beyond Kingston, cloud-forested mountains, Jamaica's highest peak, the former pirate capital of the Caribbean, and waterfalls and beaches await you.

Taking their name from the purplish haze that surrounds them and softens their contours when gazed at from a distance, the forest-covered Blue Mountains loom above the capital. The road toward them runs through small agricultural settlements and the well-to-do neighborhood of Stony Hill. The road then deteriorates into rough, rutted tracks, leading deeper into the cloud forest and to the Blue Mountain coffee plantations and mountain villages that act as gateways for the ascent of Jamaica's highest peak. On the coast, Port Royal – a former pirates' den of iniquity – and the seaside getaways of Lime Cay and Hellshire Beach make for some excellent day trips from Kingston.

TOP TIP

A 4WD is needed to explore the Blue Mountains. If you want to summit Blue Mountain Peak, arrange transportation and guides in advance.

Blue Mountains

PRACTICALITIES OF SUMMITING 'THE PEAK'

Of the 30 recognized trails in the Blue Mountains, the trail to 'The Peak' is the most popular. Go with a local guide if hiking overnight, since numerous spur trails lead off the main trail, meaning it's easy to get lost.

Most hikers overnight at Jah B's or Whitfield Hall in Penlyne Castle (call in advance to arrange dinner, guides and breakfast). Layers and rain gear are a must, and while sneakers will suffice, tough walking shoes are better.

Pay the park entry fee at the Portland Gap ranger station, where there are two basic cabins with bunks (BYO sleeping bag) and a camping area (BYO tent), run by the Jamaica Conservation and Development Trust. Reserve in advance.

Conquering Blue Mountain Peak

SUNRISE FROM JAMAICA'S HIGHEST MOUNTAIN

Your guide wakes you up at 2am. Disoriented and sleepy, you follow them through the forest, with sparks of fireflies dancing in the darkness. The first part of the 12km round-trip hike up the 2256m **Blue Mountain Peak** from **Penlyne Castle,** 37km northeast of Kingston, is a tough slog up scree-covered switchbacks referred to as Jacob's Ladder. You pause for a breather halfway up, at Portland Gap, then climb higher through the woodlands as the temperature drops.

You emerge in a clearing around 5:30am, and gradually the peak comes into view: a flat-topped hump, marked by a scaffolding pyramid. As the rays of the rising sun illuminate the sea of greenery beneath you and the Caribbean Sea beyond, you swear that you can see the faint outline of Cuba, 144km away.

After a brief celebratory drink, you set off back down the mountain, able to appreciate several distinct ecosystems now that you can see them – stunted elfin forest with hirsute soapwood and rodwood no more than 2.5m high (an adaptation to the cold), followed by cloud forest festooned with moss, dotted with wild strawberries, and dripping with filaments of 'Old Man's Beard' lichen. Further down, you encounter bamboo and primordial giant tree ferns. Your guide will point out the Blue Mountain coffee plants growing on the steep lopes, and you'll be greeted at your lodgings with the breakfast of champions, accompanied by the tastiest cup of joe.

For the Love of the Brew

BLUE MOUNTAIN COFFEE ESTATES

Coffee was first introduced to Jamaica from Haiti in 1728, and has grown from strength to strength since then, with Jamaica's **Blue Mountain coffee** a world-renowned variety growing high on the slopes of its namesake mountains, just north of Kingston. Several coffee estates offer tours, allowing you to follow the journey from coffee bean to cup.

North of Newcastle, and 21km from Kingston, is **Craighton Estate Great House** and coffee plantation, founded in 1805 by Scottish–Italian emigrant George Craighton. Learn the basics of coffee cultivation, and walk amid the coffee plants with views of the surrounding mountains and villages.

The B1 road ribbons further up into the mountains, and after 13km you'll reach **Old Tavern Coffee Estate**, known for producing the rare peaberry coffee variety. Owner David Twyman is happy to explain the growing and production process, and can treat visitors to a tasting session of their three arabica roasts (book ahead).

WHERE TO STAY IN THE BLUE MOUNTAINS

Lime Tree Farm
Luxe cottages on a working coffee farm near Mavis Bank with mountain views, bird-watching and hiking. **$$$**

RafJam B&B
Chill out in the terrace bar over a burbling river at this friendly guesthouse in Newcastle. **$$**

Mount Edge B&B
Quirky mountainside maze of bright rooms with great views and an organic garden in Newcastle. **$$**

TONI-ANN MCKENZIE/SHUTTERSTOCK ©

Blue Mountain coffee beans

STRAWBERRY HILL FOREVER

Record mogul Chris Blackwell's pet, **Strawberry Hill** is an iconic luxury retreat nested on a hilltop just north of Irish Town. A romantic bolt-hole for well-to-do weekending Kingstonians, it gives guests the opportunity to gaze at the views from deck chairs by the infinity pool, roam the bougainvillea-draped grounds or choose from a range of treatments at the Ayurvedic spa. The Caribbean-style cottages range from well-appointed mahogany-accented studio suites to four-bedroom, two-story houses built into the hillside.

Even if you're not staying, Strawberry Hill is worth the winding drive for the excellent fusion cuisine (think oxtail shepherd's pie and coconut curry prawn linguine). Coming here for the Sunday brunch buffet is a rite of passage.

The **Mavis Bank Coffee Factory**, established in 1923 and located 1km southwest of Mavis Bank, is the largest coffee factory in Jamaica, producing Jablum Blue Mountain. Call ahead for cupping (tasting) sessions, and to see the coffee beans drying (March to August) and undergoing processing; the roasted beans are sold here at bargain prices.

The Wickedest City on Earth

THE PIRATE CAPITAL OF THE CARIBBEAN

Arriving in the sleepy fishing village of **Port Royal**, a 45-minute drive from Kingston, it's hard to recognize Jamaica's former capital , which was once a thriving, wealthy town of merchants, rum traders, ladies of negotiable affection and buccaneers.

Settled by the English in 1655, Port Royal was initially circled by five forts. The Confederacy of the Brethren of the Coast (government-sponsored privateers) used Port Royal as a base to attack Spanish merchant ships; their ranks included Jewish pirates, including the notorious Moses Cohen Henriques, whose descendants live in Kingston. Wealth flowed into Port Royal's coffers as drunken sailors brawled in the streets or sought pleasure in its dens of iniquity, until June 7, 1692 when the town was devastated by a great earthquake,

WHERE TO EAT IN THE BLUE MOUNTAINS

EITS Café
Farm-to-table meals (including veggies from the garden) served with a side of valley views in Newcastle. **$$**

Café Blue
Irish-Town offshoot of the popular Kingston institution, known for gourmet sandwiches and Blue Mountain coffee. **$$**

Blue Brews Bistro
Hungry hikers walking Holywell Park's mountain trails are cared for with burgers and all-day breakfasts. **$**

BEACH ESCAPE, KINGSTONIAN-STYLE

Reachable by minibus from Parade and by bus from Halway Tree, **Hellshire Beach** is a favorite place for Kingstonians to hang out on weekends. It gets particularly lively in the afternoons, when sound systems compete for beachgoers' attention alongside hawkers selling herbal tonics, oysters with special sauce and bags of spicy crayfish. There are donkey handlers offering donkey rides, jet skis cutting foam trails across the water, and bright thatched-roof restaurants serving fish and seafood dishes.

Note that this is more of a people-watching experience than a tranquil day by the sea. If you're looking for a quieter experience, arrive in the morning, when fishing pirogues come in with their catch, and before the turquoise waters get too crowded.

ROSTASEDLACEK/SHUTTERSTOCK ©

Fort Charles

followed by a tsunami. The area never recovered, though the underwater remnants are being considered as a World Heritage Site by Unesco.

Today, you can wander around the remains of the sole surviving **Fort Charles**, peruse memorabilia rescued from the sunken city at the **Maritime Museum** and peek inside the **former quarters** of Horatio Nelson – Britain's greatest naval hero. Nearby **Giddy House** was used to store weapons and gunpowder, until half of it sank during the 1907 earthquake. Port Royal's only intact building is the **Old Gaol House** – a women's jail, pre-1692 earthquake. To date, it has also survived 14 hurricanes and two major fires.

Limin' on Lime Cay

PORT ROYAL'S ISLAND ESCAPE

One of several uninhabited, white sand-covered specks of coral, 3km by boat from from Port Royal, Lime Cay is facility-free apart from a couple of food shacks, and is perfect for a lazy day of sunbathing and swimming. Fans of the movie *The Harder They Come* may recognize it as the place where Ivan took his last stand against members of law enforcement. Organized trips run from Port Royal's **Morgan's Harbor Yacht Marina** (Wednesday to Sunday only; minimum four people), but you can talk one of the local fishers into taking you for a reduced rate; pay half on arrival, and the rest at the agreed pickup time.

WHERE TO EAT IN PORT ROYAL

Gloria's
Order the fish with all the trimmings or the honey jerk shrimp at this age-old institution. **$$**

Martin's Conch
Conch cooked up every which way by friendly chef Martin and his wife. **$**

Carlus Jerk
Mobile oil-drum grills that cook up amazing jerk chicken on Wednesday and Saturday nights. **$**

TREASURE BEACH

Set amid semi-arid countryside, Treasure Beach is the quintessential Caribbean experience: a fishing village spread across four coves that maintains a low-key, friendly vibe of yesteryear, having avoided major development. A lack of resorts, a handful of deserted beaches and a complete lack of hustlers contribute to the destination's appeal, with its emphasis on sustainable tourism. The welcoming, mellow community of artists, poets and fisherfolk will have you feeling right at home.

It's said that Scottish sailors were shipwrecked near Treasure Beach in the 19th century, accounting for the presence of fair skin, green eyes and reddish hair among the local population. Civic pride is strong here: the Treasure Beach Women's Group and the Treasure Beach Foundation bring locals and expats together to work on community projects, while visitors take part in impromptu drumming sessions or nod along to old-school reggae tunes wafting from chill beachside bars, along with the aromatic clouds of ganja smoke.

TOP TIP

Walking or cycling is the best way to get around Treasure Beach. Bikes can be rented from the juice shack in front of Jake's. Route taxis run to/from Black River, Santa Cruz and Junction. If you choose to drive, note that the roads are badly cratered, especially the direct Parrottee route.

Treasure Beach

TREASURE BEACH

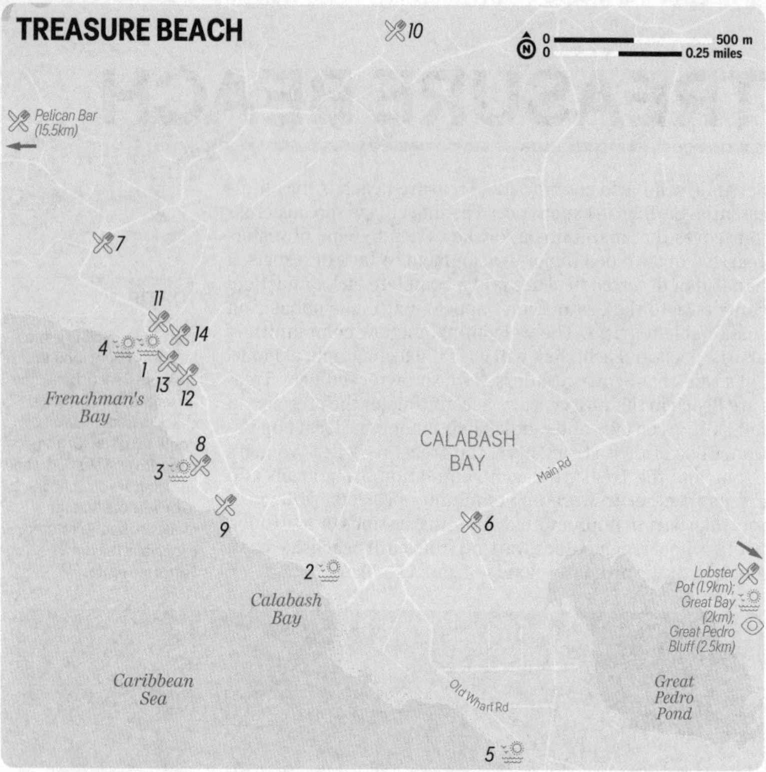

SIGHTS
1 Back Seaside
2 Calabash House
3 Fisherman's Beach
4 Frenchman's Beach
5 Old Wharf Beach

EATING
6 Gee Whiz
7 Hold a Vibz
8 Jack Sprat
9 Jake's
10 Joseph's Hideaway
11 Kim's Restaurant
12 Mellow Yellow
13 One Loave
14 Smurf's Café

TAKE A TOUR

Call ahead to book a morning walking tour with local historian Lilieth Lynch (876-572-8835). The daughter of a Treasure Beach fisherman, she points out notable landmarks while regaling you with stories about residents past and present, and can pinpoint the time when a humble fishing village began to transform into a hip retreat for bohos, artists and celebrities alike.

Beach-Hopping in Treasure Beach

TREASURE BEACH'S SEASIDE GEMS

Treasure Beach is spread along five bays. Going west to east, **Frenchman's Beach**, backed by several bars, is good for body surfing. Directly in front of Jack Sprat Restaurant, **Fisherman's Beach** is watched over by a landmark buttonwood tree, and its calm waters make for great sunning and swimming. Next up, the best spot to swim along the narrow arc of Calabash Bay Beach is in front of **Calabash House**, west of the fishing boats. Ask locals before venturing in, since there can be undertows. This applies to **Old Wharf Beach** as well – a pristine brown-sand beach that's just east of Taino Cove. In **Great Bay**, the long beach is safest for swimming and sometimes hosts impromptu soccer games. To the east, the bay is bookended by **Great Pedro Bluff**, a rocky headland

RALF LIEBHOLD/SHUTTERSTOCK ©

Treasure Beach

covered in thatch palms and enormous cacti, with several well-defined trails. The main trail leads to **Back Seaside** – a fine sunbathing beach that's a 20-minute walk away.

Eat Your Way Around Treasure Beach

EAT LIKE THE JAMAICANS DO

For breakfast, head to **Smurf's Café** for ackee and saltfish – a classic Jamaican staple – or else, mackerel rundown, with 'ground food' (three types of tubers; also typically eaten for breakfast) plus Blue Mountain coffee. **Hold a Vibz** is a great brunch spot, with a mix of homemade bagels and Jamaican standards.

Non-guests and guests alike dine on jerk sausage, yam and beans for breakfast and superlative versions of Jamaican standards the rest of the day at **Jake's**. No one does curry goat – another classic Jamaican staple – quite as well as **Joseph's Hideaway**, a short drive inland. **Kim's Restaurant**, a little cookshop shaded by a large cassia tree, serves excellent homemade burgers, jerk chicken with *festival* (deep-fried, slightly sweet cylindrical dumplings) and freshly caught fried fish in the evenings, while **Mellow Yellow** combines Italian and Jamaican flavors to great effect.

Jack Sprat is the go-to place for pizza with jerk sausage, along with Jamaican staples of brown stew fish and curry

FISH FEASTS AT ALLIGATOR POND

Locals and visitors converge on the fishing village of Alligator Pond, an hour's drive east of Treasure Beach, where hordes of hungry patrons wait in eager anticipation in the breezy dining areas of **Little Ochie** or **Oswald Seafood Restaurant**.

Overlooking the black-sand beach, both have chalk-scribbled blackboard menus and charcoal-blackened kitchens that cook curry lobster, jerk snapper and other ocean bounty on wood-fire grills over pimento wood, served with *festival*, *bammy* and other tasty sides.

Make your choice from whatever happens to be in stock, decide how you want it cooked, then hang with other diners and leave happily sated and covered in fish scales, like something from *Lord of the Flies*.

WHERE TO SHOP LOCAL IN TREASURE BEACH

Africa Village
Each pendant, calabash shaker, naturally dyed scarf and tambourine is handmade by local artist Sharon.

Calalloo Butik
Peruse hand-sewn and bold-patterned silk dresses, Jamaican prints and beauty products made from local ingredients.

Treasure Beach Women's Group
Handmade hats, woven bags, calabash dishes and 'jungle jewelry' made from seeds can be perused.

BEST PLACES TO STAY IN TREASURE BEACH

Shi Shed Africa Village
Three curved-walled adobe rooms decorated with original artwork by owner/artist/musician/writer/diva Sharon Martini. Two-night minimum; drumming sessions optional. $$

Waikiki Guesthouse
Eight simple rooms scattered across two cottages and a house in super-central Frenchman's Beach. $

Kudehya Guesthouse
Three comfortable Rasta-themed rooms with private terraces amid a lush garden, within splashing distance of the waves. $$

Katamah Beachfront Resort
Beachside space with three Moroccan-style rooms, sumptuous suites, breezy cabins with hammocks and glamping tents with thatched beachside gazebos. $$

Jack Sprat (p399)

lobster, and **Lobster Pot** is a charming shack restaurant right on the water, serving superlative lobster dishes. Hungry for I-tal food? (Rastafarian vegan dishes, cooked without salt.) **Gee Wiz** rustles up epic platters of Ethiopian-style green vegetables and tubers, simmered in coconut milk. Oh, and there's a terrific bakery in Frenchman's Bay, too: **One Loave**. Geddit?

All Aboard for Pelican Bar

A SANDBAR-BASED WATERING HOLE

As the boat gets closer to the apparition, you see what owner Floyd originally saw in a dream before he built it: a thatched hut on stilts, sitting on a submerged sandbar 1km out to sea. At first, it was an occasional beer stop for local fisherfolk. However, over the years, the original hut acquired a cook-shop that serves brown stew fish, curry lobster and barbecue wings made to order; a bar; and a powerful sound system that sees a mix of travelers and locals grooving to old-school beats while waist-deep in the shallows. Here at **Pelican Bar**, carve your name into the walls, play a game of dominoes or just shoot the breeze with Floyd himself. Local boat captains run trips from Frenchman's Beach (p398) and can combine these with outings to the Black River Great Morass (p403).

WHERE TO PARTY IN TREASURE BEACH

Eggy's Bar
Drink some beers, watch the sunset and eye the torpedo-sized spliffs at this local institution.

Fisherman's Bar
Slam down dominoes with locals or rock out to the powerful sound system out back.

Seasplash Pub
Colorful shack on Great Bay Beach, serving Red Stripes and strong rum cocktails by the water.

Beyond Treasure Beach

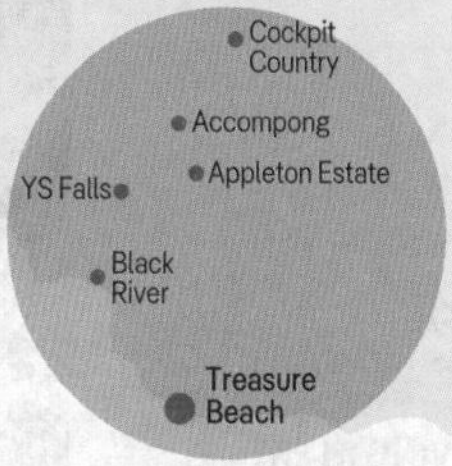

The historic sights of Black River, as well as some rum tasting and rugged hiking, lay beyond Treasure Beach.

A short drive northwest of Treasure Beach, the historic town of Black River beckons with faded mansions and Jamaica's largest wetlands, while to the northeast lies the mountain town of Mandeville, distinguished by its great house. Head beyond the mountains to reach the multi tiered cascades of YS Falls and the Appleton Rum Estate. Then you have Cockpit Country, 1295 sq km of limestone plateau, covered with dense jungle and riddled with caves that gave enslaved runaways shelter from their pursuers. In south Cockpit, Accompong is the place to delve into Maroon culture, while the faint trail between the hamlets of Troy and Windsor, through the very heart of Cockpit, presents you with Jamaica's toughest trekking challenge.

TOP TIP

Mandeville and Black River are reachable via frequent public transportation; for everywhere else, including Accompong, you'll need your own wheels.

Mangroves, Black River (p403)

CAVING IN THE COCKPITS

Of the hundreds of caves that riddle Cockpit's limestone, the **Printed Circuit Cave** is one of the most accessible, with hour-long tours organized by the Southern Trelawny Environmental Agency. The underground river that runs through the cave, near the tiny village of Rock Spring, is filled with crayfish that live in almost perpetual darkness. To venture into the cave, you have to scramble up rocky ledges and wade through cool water.

Near Windsor, **Windsor Great Cave** is one of Jamaica's chief bat habitats. Join a tour from Windsor Great House to watch the sunset bat vortex, or employ Franklin 'Dango' Taylor at the Rasta Shack near the trailhead to lead you into the chamber.

TONI-ANN MCKENZIE/SHUTTERSTOCK ©

Appleton Estate

Sampling Jamaica's Favorite Tipple

TOUR AN ENGAGING RUM ESTATE

Jamaica is one of the world's leading producers of rum, with tipples ranging from white rum (used in cocktails) to aged rums prized by discerning palates. **Appleton Estate** – the largest and oldest distillery in Jamaica – has been blending rums since 1749, and you can smell the fermented sweetness of molasses wafting from the property long before you reach it. You're welcomed with complimentary cocktails and a short video, before the slick 1½-hour tour walks you through the production process, from the squeezing of cane juice using a ye olde cane press (and willing members of the audience) to molasses production and the aging of the rum in oak barrels, with a heady tasting session of three rums to finish.

Watery Adventures at YS Falls

EXPLORE JAMAICA'S STAGGERING WATERFALLS

Enormous guango trees cast their shade over seven-tiered **YS Falls**, one of Jamaica's most splendid waterfalls, framed by lush jungle and fed by the YS River. Wannabe Tarzans swing out over one of the many limpid pools, and an occasional

WHERE TO STAY AND EAT IN BLACK RIVER

Cloggy's On The Beach
All-round pleaser with a beachfront terrace and reggae grooves; also serves conch soup and curried fish. $

Waterloo Guesthouse
Air-conditioned, motel-style rooms behind Waterloo Great House, with an bar resembling a Graham Greene haunt. $

Sister Lou's Crab Shack
Superlative jerk crab, at this shack reachable either by boat tour from Black River or by driving toward Cashew. $

screech pierces the air as the more adventurous fly over the falls along canopy zip lines. This is a great place for kids, who can play in the swimming pools at the foot of the falls, and you can easily spend a few hours here picnicking and swimming. From the parking lot, 39km north of Treasure Beach, it's a 5.5km drive from the A2 turnoff, and a tractor-drawn jitney can take you across the former sugarcane-growing YS Estate to the cascades.

Creatures of the Great Morass

BOAT TOURS OF THE WETLANDS

The **Great Morass**, 201 sq km of wetland accessed from the bridge in the town of **Black River**, shelters more than one hundred bird species, including jacanas, egrets, whistling ducks, water hens and herons, as well as roughly two hundred American crocodiles. Three main boat companies run scheduled 75-minute tours from both sides of the bridge on a daily basis. **J. Charles Swaby's Black River Safari** includes visits to its crocodile nursery (essential for maintaining croc numbers in the wild), while **Irie Safaris** and tucked-away **St Elizabeth Safaris** provide a more intimate experience. The tour boats glide serenely through a living corridor of mangroves that comes alive with bird calls in the mornings and at sundown. As the day heats up, you're likely to see the famous toothy denizens of the Great Morass sunning themselves on the riverbank.

Crossing Cockpit Country

JAMAICA'S TOUGHEST DAY TREK

The **Troy–Windsor Trail** snakes its way up and down steep hills and was built by British soldiers in the 1700s as a shortcut between two British military garrisons, across inhospitable Cockpit Country. The 19km hike is relentless, and if you're hiking from Windsor, it's mostly uphill. As you follow the faint trail through the jungle, your guide and 'cutlass man' will hack their way through undergrowth as you trip over creeping vines, skid on loose rocks and scramble over fallen logs. The views of the limestone formations and dangling curtains of vines are wondrous, especially when you know that you're seeing a part of Jamaica that few get to experience. Trekking requires excellent physical fitness, good footwear, ample food and water, a knowledgeable guide (US$200 per person) and at least one 'cutlass man' (US$100). The **Jamaican Caves Organisation** can provide knowledgeable guides.

ACCOMPONG'S MAROON FESTIVAL

Save the date for January 6 and come on up to **Accompong**, where the Maroons celebrate their ancestors' victory over British forces and Accompong's nominal independence in a riot of traditional dancing, drumming, mento bands, street food and clouds of ganja smoke. A pig is roasted overnight, and the Maroon dish of unsalted pork is consumed by the Maroon leader and community elders in the Old Town, before they proceed to the towering Kindah Tree amid the sounds of Coromantee chanting, goombay drumming and the echoing tones of the abeng horn. The procession culminates at Parade Ground with speeches, followed by a blistering sound-system party that rocks until daybreak.

WHERE TO STAY IN NORTH COCKPIT COUNTRY

The Last Resort
Basic rooms at the rustic home of archaeologist Ivor Connelly; riverside in Windsor. **$**

Windsor Great House
Remote, 18th-century mansion and biological research station with resident naturalists and bat-watching outings. **$**

Good Hope Jamaica
Choose between the breezy hilltop mansion or an 18th-century coach house that's now a seven-room villa. **$$$**

NEGRIL

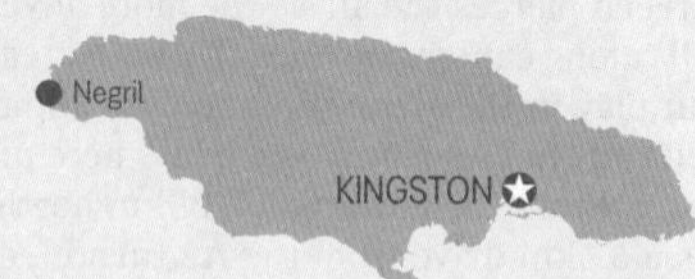

'Jamaica No Problem' is what the T-shirts proudly proclaim here, and you can buy a couple at the Rasta-colored shacks that line the road along the cliff top in Negril's West End. Its 'discovery' by hippies in the early 1970s transformed this once-tranquil fishing village and deserted beach into Jamaica's most popular resort town and a temple to unbridled hedonism.

In terms of geography and vibe, Negril can be split neatly in two. To the north of the town is the erroneously named yet still spectacular Seven Mile Beach, lined with resorts and restaurants, and with reggae and dancehall beats from competing beach parties ringing through the night. South of the village, the cliffs plunging into turquoise waters and low-key accommodations peeking out of the greenery of West End evoke the Negril of yesteryear, with some concessions to the present day, including cliffside boutique hotels, international restaurants and cafes selling ganja edibles.

TOP TIP

Negril stretches along more than 16km of shoreline, so either be prepared for a lot of walking, use frequent route taxis or hotel shuttles offered by the resorts, or hire a scooter or bicycle. Self-driving can be a headache, particularly in the West End, where there are few places to park.

RALF LIEBHOLD/SHUTTERSTOCK ©

Seven Mile Beach (p406)

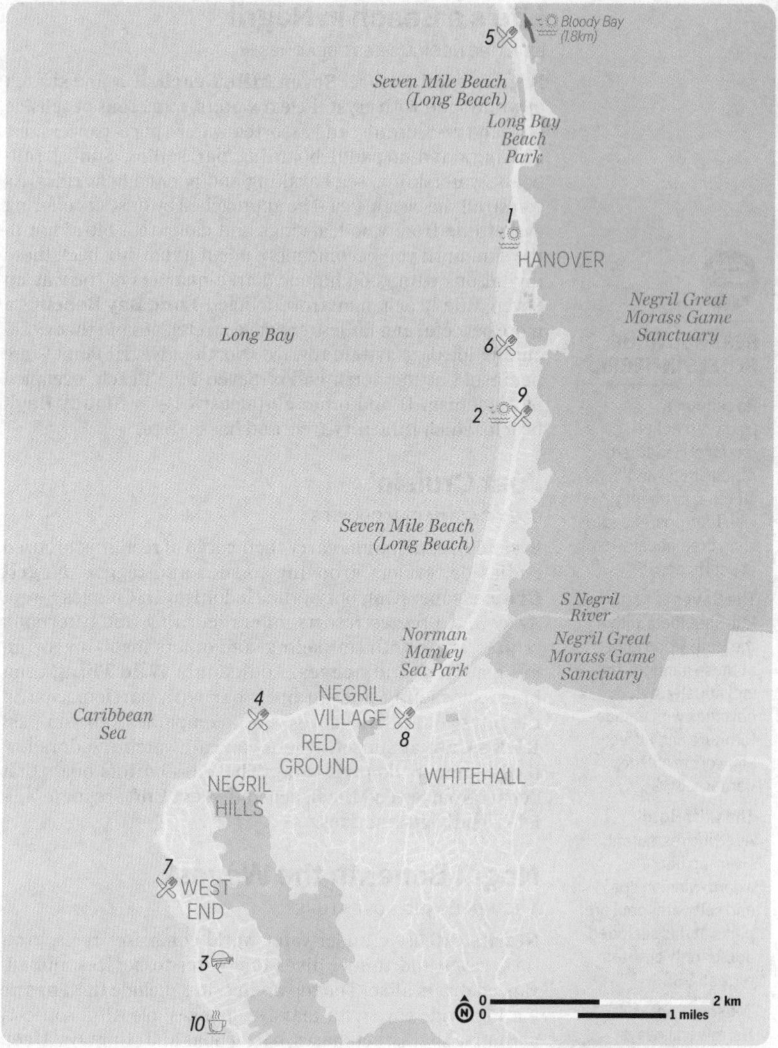
Bloody Bay (1.8km)
5
Seven Mile Beach (Long Beach)
Long Bay Beach Park
1
HANOVER
Negril Great Morass Game Sanctuary
Long Bay
6
9
2
Seven Mile Beach (Long Beach)
S Negril River
Norman Manley Sea Park
Negril Great Morass Game Sanctuary
4
NEGRIL VILLAGE
8
Caribbean Sea
RED GROUND
WHITEHALL
NEGRIL HILLS
7
WEST END
3
10
0 2 km
0 1 miles

SIGHTS
1 Long Bay Beach
2 Seven Mile Beach

ACTIVITIES & TOURS
3 West End Caves

EATING
4 Chicken Lavish
5 Fireman's Lobster Pit
6 Miss Lily's
7 Pushcart
8 Rockies Local Cuisines
(see 7) Rockhouse
9 Vinnes Grill N Bar

DRINKING & NIGHTLIFE
10 Rick's Cafe

Long Bay Beach (p406)
SHAMAR WHYTE/SHUTTERSTOCK ©

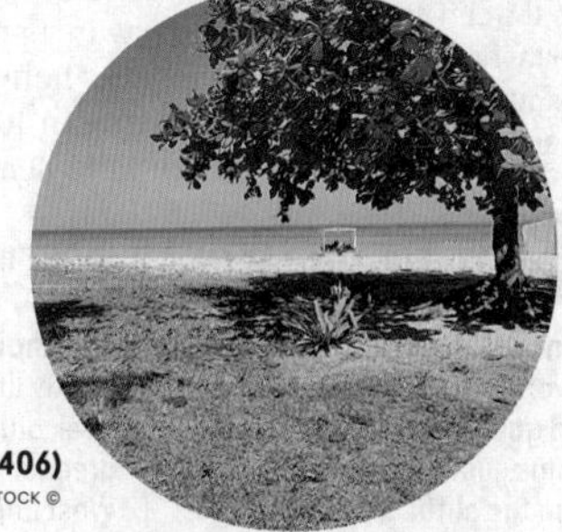

Life's a Beach in Negril

EXPLORE NEGRIL'S BEST BEACHES

Negril's main feature, **Seven Mile Beach**, is a fine stretch of white sand with crystal-clear waters, numerous beachside bars and restaurants, and assorted water-sports concessions offering stand-up paddleboarding, parasailing, Sunfish sailboats, waterskiing, sea kayaking and banana boat rides. As you stroll the beach, you'll be approached by hustlers offering everything from woodcarvings and ganja to a bit of fun in the sun, until you become more adept at batting back these invitations with good humor. Three-quarters of the way up Seven Mile Beach, mangrove-fringed **Long Bay Beach** is a more peaceful and far less crowded stretch of sand that weekending locals gravitate toward. North of Negril Point – the peninsula at the north end of Seven Mile Beach, occupied by Hedonism II and other all-inclusives – is **Bloody Bay**'s beach, which is facility-free, and hassle-free.

BEST BOUTIQUE HOTELS IN NEGRIL

Rockhouse
Luxury thatched *rondavels* (southern African huts) and studio apartments with four-poster beds cling dramatically to the cliffside. $$

The Caves
Rub shoulders with the Hollywood elite at these handcrafted, individually styled cottages with unique furniture and alfresco showers in cliff-top gardens. $$$

The Cliff Hotel
A terrific restaurant, swim-up bar, award-winning spa and saltwater pool are perks at this secluded, adults-only cliff-top retreat. $$$

Tensing Pen
Narrow walkways connect the pool to the cliff-top pillar houses, with exquisite bamboo and hardwood detail. $$$

Just Cruisin'

COZY CATAMARAN CRUISES

Every day, catamarans carry their cargo of reclining bronzed bodies or revelers grooving to soca and reggae. **Negril Cruises**, operating out of the Hedonism II, Couples Swept Away and Breezes resorts, offers morning and afternoon cruises, some with snorkeling, and others involving swimming at West End's **caves**. Adults-only **Wild Thing** combines snorkeling and an open bar with participation in the latest dancehall moves. Both companies sail you past **Rick's Cafe** at sunset, where you can watch the daredevil cliff jumpers do their thing. The glass-bottom boats that depart from Seven Mile Beach and **West End** are more wallet-friendly alternatives.

Negril Beneath the Waves

A SCUBA-DIVING ADVENTURE

Negril's extensive underwater world comprises reefs, grottoes, caves and tunnel dives that cater to novices and advanced divers alike. The top diving sites include the **Throne** – a 15m-wide cave with massive sponges, plentiful soft corals, nurse sharks, octopuses, barracudas and stingrays. **Deep Plane** is the remains of a Cessna airplane that lays 21m underwater and attracts an abundance of fish, with the nurse sharks hanging out at a nearby overhang. **Sands Club Reef**, sitting in 10m of water, lies offshore from the middle of Seven Mile Beach. From here, a drift dive to **Shark's Reef** leads

WHERE TO STAY ON A BUDGET IN NEGRIL

Conrod's Negril Guesthouse
A wonderfully hospitable West End guesthouse with spotless rooms, just a two-minute walk from the cliffs. $

Lighthouse Inn 2
Subtly lit and snug bungalows peek out of the hammock-hung greenery near the lighthouse in West End. $

Bak a Yaad
Choose between a dorm, double or cottage at this fairylight-adorned hostel with pool and garden. $

PHOTO SPIRIT/SHUTTERSTOCK ©

Rick's Cafe

you through tunnels and overhangs featuring huge sponges and gorgonian corals.

Dream Team Divers and **Marine Life Divers** are reputable outfits that offer a range of courses and dives to suit all levels.

A Gourmet's Tour of Negril

A TASTER OF NEGRIL'S BEST DINING

Negril's dining scene is almost as legendary as its show-stopping beach. At the north end of Seven Mile Beach, **Fireman's Lobster Pit** is a wallet-friendly stop for grilled lobster – a Jamaican staple. Further south, **Miss Lily's** jerk platters, comprising three types of meat, will get you through a siege, while **Vinnes Grill N Bar** serves up the best jerk chicken, grilled lobster and curry goat – all Jamaican classics – for miles.

Head to **Rockies Local Cuisines** in Negril village for escoveitch fish, steamed snapper and conch fritters, and to **Chicken Lavish** for fried and jerk chicken and curry goat at lunchtime and dinnertime, and ackee and saltfish for breakfast. West End's **Pushcart** serves highbrow versions of jerk fish, chicken, pork and sausage fresh off the grill, plus melt-in-your-mouth oxtail and beans, and curry goat, while **Rockhouse** offers cliffside vistas along with fusion bites, such as coconut shrimp, steamed snapper and jerk chicken fajitas.

PARTY ON THE BEACH

Negril's nightlife is legendary, with live performances every night in peak season, while its Margaritaville branch boasts year-round spring-break vibes. To make the most of your time in Negril, check out these venues at the south end of Seven Mile Beach, where you can party every night of the week.

Monday: live reggae at Roots Bamboo

Tuesday: reggae beach party at Alfred's

Wednesday: live reggae at Roots Bamboo

Thursday: live reggae at Bourbon Beach

Friday: reggae beach party at Alfred's; reggae and/or soul jam at Drifter's Bar

Saturday: live reggae at Bourbon Beach; Retro Saturdays at Woodstock Bar

Sunday: reggae beach party at Alfred's; Sun-Daze beach party at Woodstock Bar

WHERE TO EAT OLD-SCHOOL JAMAICAN FOOD IN NEGRIL

Rasta Ade Refreshments
Colorful beachside spot, serving vast helpings of curried chickpeas, callaloo, breadfruit, plantain and brown rice. $

Erica's Hideaway
Homey restaurant serving terrific curry goat and brown stew fish with veggies from Erica's garden. $

Just Natural
In a lush, hummingbird-filled garden, tables groan under the weight of epic Jamaican breakfasts. $

Beyond Negril

Tranquil fishing villages, inland waterfalls, hillside organic farms and arty retreats are found in Negril's gorgeous environs.

Head east of Negril, and you pass through the notorious ganja-growing village of Orange Hill, and the fishing village of Little Bay, which is as soporific as it was when Marley lived there with one of his girlfriends. Its main attraction, Blue Hole, entices many day-trippers. Further east, the coastal settlements of Bluefields and Belmont have an understated charm that invites you to come stay awhile. Inland and on the coast, attractions such as the Mayfield Falls and Roaring River offer plenty of fun, while up in the hills are organic farms, with some offering farm-to-table dining; a unique artistic property with historic roots; and a sculpture garden. North of Negril, fabulous beaches vie for your attention.

TOP TIP

Frequent public transportation connects to other parts of Jamaica, but you'll need your own wheels to reach Little Bay and inland attractions.

Belmont Beach (p410)

An Organic Farm-to-Table Extravaganza

ATTEND A MEMORABLE MOUNTAINSIDE MEAL

You and your fellow diners sit at the strikingly stylish yet rustic bar of **Zimbali Retreat** and watch with rapt attention as the chef explains how each of the five vegetable-forward dishes of your multicourse meal is made. You will have seen some of ingredients grown during the organic farm tour that preceded your meal. Many visitors come by tour from Negril, either for the lunch or the dinner slot, but it's extremely worthwhile to stay overnight in one of the bright and breezy rooms, and delve deeper into Rastafarian culture while you're here: enjoy a rustic I-tal cookout with Rasta Fiyah at his Camp Survival, learn about herbal remedies from Rasta elder Bongo Roache, partake in a drumming session, or watch Ishanti the sculptor work his magic with wood. Zimbali Retreat is 23km northeast of Negril; pickups can be arranged.

There be Giants

RASTA-THEMED OUTDOOR SCULPTURE

A half-hour's drive into the hills from Negril, a replanted tropical forest provides the backdrop for the works of sculptor-in-residence Fotzroy 'Fitzy' Russell at **Jamaica Giants Park**. Two of the giants – enormous cottonwood trees – frame the boardwalk that leads you to enormous Rasta heads carved from wood and stone, erotic tableaux and a breezy house displaying thought-provoking portraits of Rastafarian men and women in repose, done by resident painter Bruce Allen. Entry fee (US$20) includes tours – but they add little to the experience, so some visitors prefer to commune with the art in solitude. You'll need a high clearance vehicle to get here due to a rutted section of the road.

Into the Blue

SWIMMING HOLE

Reggae beats reverberate from the sound system at the open-air restaurant while a lively crowd launches into an impromptu dance party by the pool. A daredevil climbs a tree branch overhanging Little Bay's main attraction – **Blue Hole**, a sinkhole filled with turquoise water. Leaping in, she makes an almighty splash as onlookers strain to catch sight of her form somewhere in the blue depths of the sinkhole. Daytrippers come for the natural attraction, 14km southeast of Negril, plus the laid-back vibe of this spread-out fishing village that

MOUNTAMBRIN THEATRE: A WRITER'S RETREAT

At **Mountambrin Theatre**, the former estate of Alex Haley, author of the iconic *Roots*, phalluses are everywhere: in the carved bedposts and headboards of the individually styled rooms, and in the tableau on the door of the concert hall that once hosted a Jamaican piano prodigy. They are a labor of love by resident artist Lesbert Lee, while the thought-provoking paintings were created by Wilbert Gruhlke, father of the present-day owner.

Over the years, Mountambrin Theatre has hosted classical music evenings (and may do so again), as well as artists, writers and other dreamers seduced by the expansive views. Stay overnight, or tour the property. Mountambrin can be reached via Darliston-bound route taxis from Sav-la-Mar.

WHERE TO STAY IN BELMONT

Natural Mystic
German-speaking Lydia oversees two thatch-roofed cottages and a tree house in Rasta colors. Meals on request. $

Rainbow Villas
Friendly and spotless studios overlook the garden, where a bar is built into a turpentine tree. $

Nature Roots
'Bush Doctor' Brian rents out rooms in a shared cottage and runs hiking tours. $

BEST PLACES TO EAT IN BELMONT

Carlene Studniczka, owner of Rainbow Guest House, shares her recommendations for the best places to dine in Belmont.

Omar's Jerk
For my money, Omar makes the best jerk chicken on the island. Get to his cookshop around noon, when the grill's all fired up.

Cracked Conch
It's Belmont's fanciest restaurant. They do a mix of pastas, salads and burgers, plus expensive takes on oxtail and beans, and curry goat.

Blue Ocean Sands
A new restaurant at Belmont's east end, it's bright and breezy inside, with a nice seafront terrace. It's the best place for Jamaican breakfasts and fresh fruit juices. They do Mexican food, too, plus live music sometimes.

JOHN GREIM/LIGHTROCKET VIA GETTY IMAGES ©

Mayfield Falls (p408)

reminds old-timers of Negril in the 1970s. Ask locals to point out Bob Marley's former house, and while away an hour or two on the narrow main beach.

A Perfect Day in Belmont

BELMONT'S OFFBEAT ATTRACTIONS

Start the day early with a ganja plantation tour, or else a half-day birding and hiking tour in the hills above Belmont with naturalist Wolde Kristos of **Reliable Adventures Jamaica**, who's happy to point out endemic species in an engaging manner. In the afternoon, opt for snorkeling off the local reef with shoals of tiny reef fish; Reliable Adventures can help organize an outing with local fishers. Alternatively, a 10-minute uphill drive from the coastal road, just past Bluefields Beach, gets to you to Keith Wedderburn's wonderful (and family-operated) **Bluefields Organic Farm**. Call ahead for a tour (US$15) of his 22-acre property, where he will be happy to walk you around, pointing out produce such as soursop, star fruit, June plum, scotch bonnet peppers and breadfruit, all grown without pesticides. In the evening, watch the sun set over **Belmont Beach**, Red Stripe in hand, and lime with locals at **Natural Vibz** well into the night.

WHERE TO STAY IN BLUEFIELDS AND LITTLE BAY

Good Hope Retreat
Three snug cabins look out to sea from their private terraces in the hills above Bluefields. $

Coral Cottage
This secluded six-room house in Little Bay comes with a roof terrace, pool and generous breakfasts. $$

Judy House Backpacker Hostel
Camp under the stars or sleep inside a shipping container at this Little Bay backpacker haunt. $

MONTEGO BAY

Montego Bay

KINGSTON

Jamaica's second city ('MoBay' to the locals) has two distinct faces: there's the world of all-inclusive beach resorts, white-sand beaches, sunset cruises and visitors dressed in elegant outfits dining contentedly by the sea, which beckons from the pages of glossy Caribbean brochures; and there's MoBay proper, a sprawling, gritty city, second only to Kingston in terms of status. Most of the big, all-inclusive resorts are located outside the urban core, in the fancy suburb of Ironshore. In the city itself, where there's a clutch of historic sights and a couple of souvenir markets selling mostly mass-produced Chinese tattoos, you're greeted with a chorus of cacophonous car horns and bustling humanity that offers an unscripted and uncensored slice of Jamaican life.

The Hip Strip (aka Gloucester Ave), with its attendant hustlers, midrange hotels, excellent beach and crowds of *Homo margaritavillus* frequenting its nightspots, bridges the gap between the two.

TOP TIP

MoBay has a reputation for gang violence, which tends to be confined to MoBay's poorest neighborhoods. Standard precautions against petty crime apply.

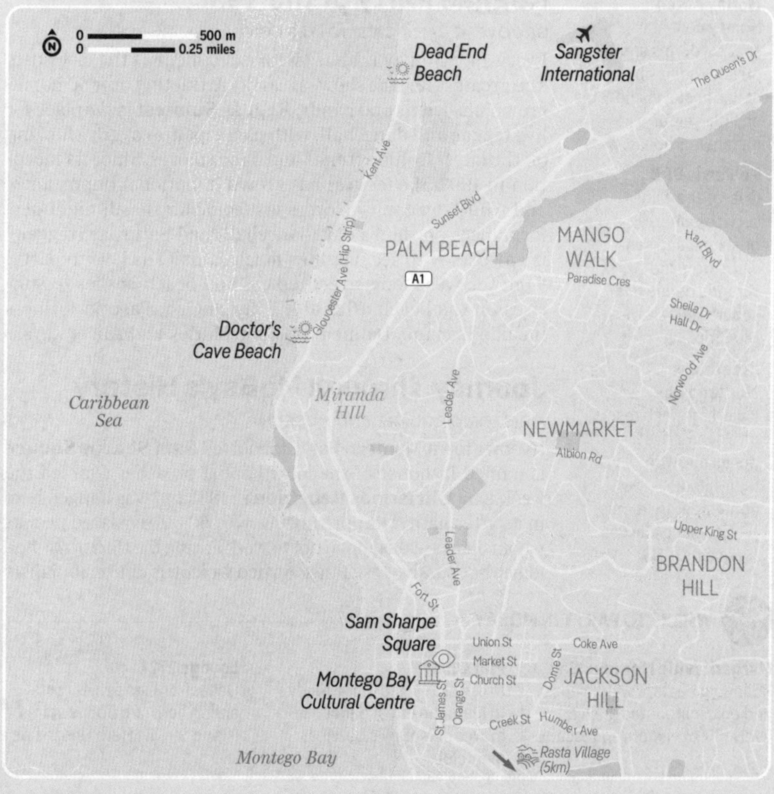

BEST PLACES TO STAY IN MOBAY

S Hotel
Splurge on an ocean-view room at this contemporary seafront hotel with suspended plunge pool and private beach. $$$

MoBay Kotch
Homey common spaces, dorms and private rooms abound at this hostel inside an 18th-century merchant's house. $

Polkerris B&B
One-of-the-family service, superb breakfast and sea views from the veranda define this superb B&B above the Hip Strip. $$

Breathless Montego Bay
Luxe, high-tech resort on a semi-private peninsula, with light-filled, contemporary rooms, plus cooking classes for guests. $$$

LEFT: SHELBY SOBLICK/GETTY IMAGES ©; RIGHT: CO LEONG/SHUTTERSTOCK ©

Reggae Sumfest

Reggae Party of the Year

GROOVE AT JAMAICA'S HOTTEST GIG

Every July, MoBay is abuzz with excitement as the city hosts 'the greatest Reggae show on earth.' Attracting over 50 home-grown musicians and bands, **Reggae Sumfest** is *the* place for live reggae and dancehall, with participants eagerly showing off the latest fashion trends and dance moves. Since its inception in 1993, the festival has grown in national importance, and while some music lovers just come for the all-night performances on the Friday (dancehall) and Saturday (reggae), it's also a joy to see just how much Jamaicans love to party: from the week-long street dances and beach bashes to sunrises on the beach after all-night dancing. Past performers include Luciano, Damien 'Jr Gong' Marley and Alicia Keys.

Journey Through MoBay's History

A HISTORIC SQUARE AND MUSEUM

In downtown Montego Bay, the cobbled **Sam Sharpe Square** is named in honor of the local Baptist preacher who led the week-long **Christmas Rebellion** in 1831 and was hanged here in its aftermath. The uprising involved 60,000 enslaved people, whom Sharpe called upon not to work during the Christmas holidays, but passive resistance turned violent, and 15 colonialists

WHERE TO PARTY IN MOBAY

Margaritaville Montego Bay
Pounding beats, a water slide and epic margaritas draw a lively mix of visitors and locals.

Pier One
Dress nicely and come ready to learn the latest dancehall moves at MoBay's buzziest nightclub.

Lounge 2727
Oceanfront terrace, DJ sets and 'di herb' are boons at this Island Strains Herb House bar.

were killed, along with over two hundred rebels. Retribution was swift and brutal, with over three hundred enslaved men and women hanged. The public outcry led to the passing of the Abolition Act in 1834. The square features the bronze National Heroes' Memorial, which depicts Sam Sharpe, bible in hand, as well as a cage from 1806 that was used as a lockup for drunk sailors, vagrants and enslaved people who broke curfew.

The **Montego Bay Cultural Centre**, built on the ruins of the courthouse where Sharpe was sentenced, houses a well-curated exhibition on western Jamaica's history, from the indigenous Taíno ceremonies and the arrival of the Spanish to the transatlantic slave trade, Maroon rebellions, emancipation, the rise of Rastafarianism and the Back to Africa movement. Also on-site is **National Gallery West**, which holds four annual exhibitions, ranging from contemporary painting and sculpture by Jamaican artists to cutting-edge photography.

BEST PLACES TO EAT IN MOBAY

The Pelican Grill
Sink into a leather banquette and dine on superlative curry goat and oxtail at this Hip Strip institution. $$

Usain Bolt's Tracks & Records
Excellent janga soup, jerk platters, seafood curries and milkshakes dominate the menu. $$

The Pork Pit
Pork is the star at this traditional jerk pit; eat it with all the trimmings under the 300-year-old cotton tree. $

Houseboat Grill
Enioy an eclectic meal at this converted houseboat in Bogue Lagoon. Reservations essential. $$$

Pon di Beach

MOBAY'S BEST BEACHES

MoBay's best stretch of sand is **Doctor's Cave Beach** (pictured right), in the middle of the Hip Strip. Founded as a bathing club in 1906, with dubious claims made about the waters' healing properties, it's an arc of sugary sand with floating dive platforms, a restaurant, ample water sports, and an admission charge. Just north of Gloucester Ave, **Dead End Beach** is a free, narrow strip of white sand that disappears at high tide, but makes for good sunset-watching and swimming the rest of the time.

Communing with the Rastafari

DELVING INTO RASTA CULTURE

Reachable via a 7km taxi ride from central MoBay, **Rasta Village** is best described as a living interpretive exhibit – a decent introduction to Jamaica's home-grown religion, Rastafarianism. Book your visit in advance, then prepare to be led around the appealing jungly settlement, complete with medicinal herb garden. You'll be given a coherent breakdown of what the Rasta followers traditionally believed in, including the divinity of former Ethiopian emperor Haile Selassie I, the significance of the vegan I-tal diet and the use of ganja in sacraments. The all-day tour includes trekking in the surrounding countryside and some glorious swimming in the nearby natural pools.

GETTING AROUND

The Hip Strip and downtown are very walkable, but you'll need transportation for anywhere further. Only drive in MoBay if you absolutely have to, since it's congested and has very few options for parking. Route taxis with red number plates ply specific routes (as indicated by the neighborhood names on the door). Flag them down or find them near Sam Sharpe Sq.

Licensed, pricey JUTA taxis ply Gloucester Ave and go to Montego Freeport (the cruise ship terminal), Greenwood and Ironshore. Knutsford Express buses connect MoBay to Negril, Falmouth, Ocho Rios, Port Antonio and Kingston. Smaller destinations are served by minibuses and route taxis from the transportation center on St James St; they depart when full.

Beyond Montego Bay

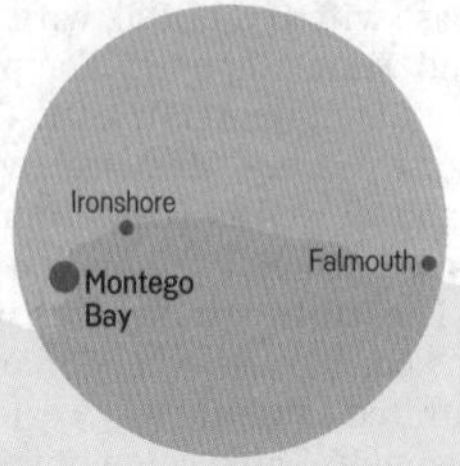

Plantation houses, an atmospheric rum estate, the historic city of Falmouth and assorted water-based adventures are found in MoBay's environs.

East of MoBay, along the north coast, which faces controversial mass development, are the top-end hotels of Ironshore, as well as plantation-houses-turned-museums. Further east, the 18th-century town of Falmouth, which grew its wealth thanks to the blood trade of plantation slavery, features well-preserved historic buildings, including a church that played a key part in slavery's abolition. Inland from Falmouth, raft along the tranquil Martha Brae River and visit the Hampton Estate – Jamaica's most atmospheric rum producer – while east of Falmouth, swim amid seasonal sparks of phosphorescence in the bioluminescent lagoon.

TOP TIP

Frequent public transportation connects MoBay to coastal towns and attractions, while inland sights are best reachable by tour or on wheels.

Falmouth

SOLARISYS/GETTY IMAGES ©

A Tale of Two Great Houses

A GLIMPSE INTO HISTORY

As you make your way out of the crimson silk-brocaded bedroom of the Haitian-born Annie Palmer – the 'White Witch of Rose Hall,' accused of murdering three husbands and several enslaved people, a figure in period costume leaps out at you from behind an antique mahogany wardrobe, and your heart nearly stops. The 1770s Caribbean–Georgian **Rose Hall**, 13km east of MoBay, is Jamaica's most famous great house. Burnt during the Christmas Rebellion (p412) of 1831 and rebuilt in 1966, it's hugely popular with Jamaicans and overseas visitors. However, the tours seem to focus more on the sumptuous furnishings and the ghostly aspect of the house rather than a sobering look at the house's history as a slave plantation.

The more intimate **Greenwood Great House** is a hilltop property just 23km east of MoBay, up a pitted road up from the coast. It survived the Christmas Rebellion with its authentic furnishings intact, and it's one of the few Jamaican historical homes whose displays directly address the cruelty of plantation slavery. Beyond the original library, look out for such rare musical instruments as the inlaid piano made for Edward VII, one of three working barrel organs in the world, and the two polyphones, one of which the guide is happy to bring to life. The resident ghost is decidedly low-key, and you can drink in the view of the entire coast from the upstairs veranda.

GLISTENING WATERS

On starry nights, the boats chug their way sedately out into the **Luminous Lagoon**, aka Glistening Waters, 35km east of Montego Bay. In the water surrounding the boats are the eerie green 'torpedoes' of fish that shoot through the dark water. Best experienced a couple of days after the full moon, and outside of hurricane season, the bioluminescence of Luminous Lagoon is a phenomenon caused by tiny aquatic organisms called dinoflagellates, found in the areas where salt- and freshwater meet. When disturbed, the organisms produce photochemical reactions, resulting in an eerie green glow.

Forty-five minute jaunts from the Glistening Waters marina also allow you to swim in the magic of the bioluminescence.

Wander Through Historic Falmouth

FALMOUTH'S HISTORICAL BUILDINGS

A port town founded in 1769, Falmouth grew wealthy on the proceeds of plantation slavery, sugar and rum. When the local sugar industry died as a result of emancipation, Falmouth languished in relative obscurity for almost two centuries, but these days, Falmouth is well worth a stroll for a glimpse of its well-preserved historic buildings that shine a light on its dark past. At its heart lies **Water Square**; to the east, the imposing wrought-iron **Albert George Market** (1894) was built on the site of slave auctions, while on the corner of the Tharpe and Lower Harbour St, the conical-roofed **Phoenix Foundry** (1810) marks the entrance to the wharf where enslaved people were brought ashore. The restored **Baptist Manse** on the corner of Market and Trelawny Sts was the house of nonconformist Baptist preacher William Knibb, who was instrumental in lobbying for the passage of the Abolition Bill. On

WHERE TO STAY AND EAT IN IRONSHORE

Sandals Royal Caribbean
Georgian-accented, adults-only hotel, with plantation-chic rooms, suites you can swim to, and several restaurants. **$$$**

Scotchie's
Some of the best 'sit-down' jerk in the northwest, served with breadfruit, *festival* and *bammy*. **$**

Far Out Fish Hut
Casual, thatch-roofed spot serving alfresco sea-view meals of grilled or escoveich fish and *bammy*. **$**

RUM TOURS AT HAMPDEN ESTATE

A palm-tree-lined lane leads to the landscaped grounds of **Hampden Great House Estate**, complete with its 18th-century great house (which isn't open to the public, unfortunately). Visitors assemble beneath an impressive century-old ficus tree, where guides will provide the history of the estate before showing you around the rum factory and fermentation house, replete with sweet molasses fumes.

A visit to Hampden includes lunch (typically curry goat), and if you're a rum connoisseur with an interest in the ins and outs of production, the factory manager can organize a private tour on demand, but it's recommended to book this ahead of time.

To get here, take the B15 south of Falmouth toward Wakefield, and follow the signs.

Martha Brae River

July 31, 1838, enslaved people gathered for an all-night vigil outside the **William Knibb Memorial Church** on Queen St to await emancipation at midnight.

Rafting the Martha Brae

FLOAT ALONG A TURQUOISE RIVER

The two-person raft is poled through a green tunnel of jungle vegetation, along the alternately jade-colored and occasionally murky waters of the **Martha Brae River**, sometimes slowing down so that you can swim alongside it and cool down in the refreshing waters. The raft makes a stop at **Tarzan's Corner**, and you can indulge your inner child as you propel yourself into the deep pool using the rope swing (splashing guaranteed). While the hour-long Martha Brae rafting trips along the 4.8km stretch of the river are touted as romantic experiences, be warned that the river can get quite crowded, meaning the 'romance' is lessened slightly by the presence of other boats. Nonetheless, it's great fun.

WHERE TO EAT IN FALMOUTH

Pura Vida
Cheerful yellow house with three studio rooms near Famouth, run by knowledgeable Richard; tours arranged. $

Pepper's Jerk Center
Thatched-roof jerk pit in central Falmouth with outdoor seating, reggae, and excellent pork and chicken. $

Flavaville Restaurant
Barbecue pigtail, oxtail and curry goat are all present and correct at this friendly, family-run restaurant. $

OCHO RIOS

It's hard to believe that Ocho Rios was a sleepy fishing village up until a few decades ago. The town has since become one of Jamaica's top tourist hubs and cruise-ship ports, with a wide variety of accommodations, a good dining and nightlife scene, and decent beaches. While the compact town is short on sights, it's within easy driving distance of some of Jamaica's most spectacular waterfalls and the island's best amusement park, Mystic Mountain. Untamed wilderness this ain't, and Ochi has a slightly 'packaged' feel to it, but outside cruise-ship days, it's a relaxed place lacking the hardcore hustle of MoBay and Negril, where you'll find yourself rubbing shoulders with weekending Kingstonians and other out-of-town Jamaicans.

TOP TIP

On cruise ship days (every day bar Saturday in peak season) and public holidays, top attractions get absolutely packed, so it's best to avoid these times. Ochi is connected to Kingston, Falmouth, Montego Bay, Port Antonio and Negril via the Knutsford Express bus, and numerous minibuses and route taxis serve smaller destinations.

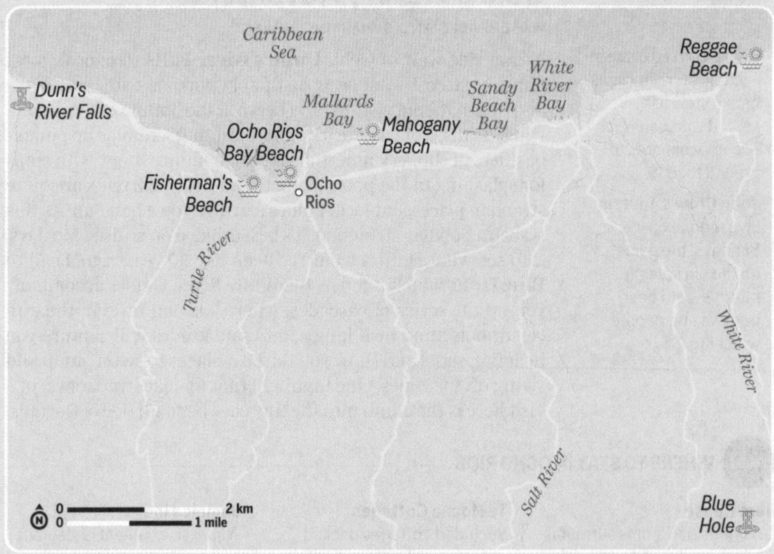

BEST PLACES TO EAT & DRINK IN OCHO RIOS

Ocho Rios Jerk Centre
A centrally located crowd pleaser, with ample jerk platters, plus curry goat, mannish water and other Jamaican standards. $

Miss T's Kitchen
Stop by this tin-roofed, brightly painted local favorite for large portions of Jamaican classics, including I-tal dishes. $

Mom's
Home-cooked dishes – oxtail, stew chicken, brown stew fish – served with generous accompaniments of ground food. $

John Crow's Tavern
Live reggae on Sundays, the game on the big screen, plus ice-cold beer, burgers and people-watching. $$

BYVALET/SHUTTERSTOCK ©

Ocho Rios Bay Beach

Beach-Hopping in Ochi

OCHI'S BEST BEACHES

Start off at Ochi's most central beach – the palm-shaded crescent of **Ocho Rios Bay Beach** (aka Turtle Beach). Then head to **Mahogany Beach**, 1km east of town, for a seaside lunch, where the smell of jerk will tickle your taste buds, and the impromptu soccer games might entice you to join. Further east, the beautiful white-sand **Reggae Beach** is good for swimming and also hosts occasional music events, while **Fisherman's Beach**, west of Ochi's cruise ship pier, has several fish restaurants.

Ochi's Watery Adventures

WATERFALLS AND SWIMMING HOLES

A 3km ride west of Ochi, **Dunn's River Falls**, Jamaica's most famous natural wonder, is justifiably popular with Jamaicans and international visitors. You begin at the bottom of the jungle-fringed falls, from where it's an exhilarating scramble up numerous tiers of slippery limestone amid pounding spray, with stops for splashing in the pools along the way. The currents are quite strong in places, but local guides can give you a hand up. As this is such a popular attraction, it's best avoided on cruise-ship days.

To see what Dunn's would've been like 20 years ago, head to **Blue Hole**, which is fed by the White River. Guides accompany you up the series of cascades, where you can revel in the gin-clear pools amid lush jungle, and said guides will capture you in action shots and show you the best places to swim, jump and swing off the ropes. One highlight (not for claustrophobes) of a visit here is the climb into the tiny cave beneath one of the falls.

WHERE TO STAY IN OCHO RIOS

Blue House
Luxurious bedrooms surround a bougainvillea-draped pool; creative breakfasts and dinners are Jamaica's best. **$$$**

Te Moana Cottages
Secluded cottages decked out with Caribbean art, with a cliff-top garden overhanging a coral cove. **$$**

Jamaica Inn
A spa, an excellent restaurant and ample water-sports facilities define this private cove hotel. **$$$**

Beyond Ocho Rios

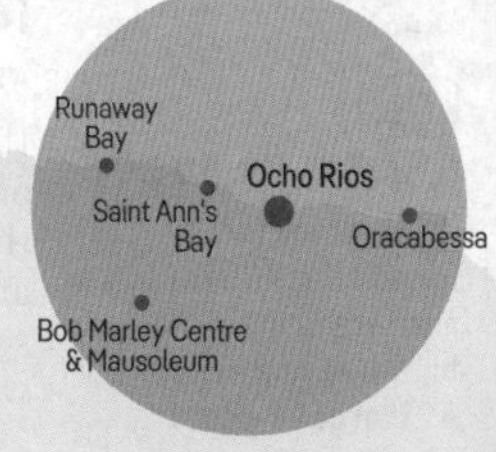

Historic homes, subterranean caves, Jamaica's biggest music festivals, Bob Marley's resting place and superb farm-to-table dining await you beyond Ochi.

West of Ochi, Plantation Cove in St Ann's Bay rocks Jamaica during the winter months, with two of the island's biggest music festivals: Rebel Salute in January, and Sting in December. Further west, explore the spectacular yet accessible Green Grotto Caves in Runaway Bay, and visit Seville Great House, which marks the site of the first Spanish capital in Jamaica. Venture inland for some exquisite farm-to-table dining at Stush-in-the-Bush, or head to Nine Mile to pay your respects at Bob Marley's final resting place. East of Ochi, Oracabessa allows you to visit or stay in the former homes of some of its famous residents, including Noël Coward and James Bond creator Ian Fleming.

TOP TIP

Coastal attractions in this area can be reached by minibus or route taxi. You'll need your own wheels to visit the inland sights.

Entrance to Green Grotto Caves (p421)

STUSH IN THE BUSH

Run by locavore Rastafarians Chris and Lisa Binns in the hills of St Ann's Bay, a 22km drive west from Ocho Rios, **Stush in the Bush** is a joyful merging of Jamaica's farming culture with gourmet elements to create an unforgettable I-tal farm-to-table dining experience. You start with a 30-minute 'earth walk' tour of the farm with Chris, who points out the ackee, coconuts and bananas, as well as various vegetables and herbs, before sitting to an eight-course meal (US$165) prepared by Lisa that merges local ingredients with international influences to create the likes of almond hummus, plantain ceviche and grilled pumpkin lemon ricotta.

Advance bookings are essential, and the views of the surrounding countryside sublime.

Rebels & Lyrical Clashes

ATTEND JAMAICA'S BIGGEST MUSIC FESTIVALS

If you're looking for pure, old-school roots reggae by the likes of Burning Spear, and Toots and the Maytals, then don't miss the **Rebel Salute** festival, which takes place in mid-January at Plantation Cove, near St Ann's Bay. The two-day festival serves I-tal food only, and the action takes place at night, wreathed in the fragrant smoke of 'di herb.'

Plantation Cove also sees the old year off with a bang, with **Sting** taking place on December 26. Known as a make-or-break event for up-and-coming artists, it sees lyrical 'clashes' between dancehalls stars such as Animosity and Mercenary, and A'mari and Queen Ladi Gangster, with additional sets by veterans such as Etana Gyptian and Jahmiel.

Farewell, 'Natural Mystic'

PAY RESPECTS TO BOB MARLEY

The setting is spectacular: the **Bob Marley Centre and Mausoleum**, a spectacular 45km drive southwest of Ocho Rios, is surrounded by green hills and deep gullies, and many Marley devotees come here, where the reggae great is seeing out eternity, in the hope of quiet reflection. Unfortunately, that hope is dashed by the presence of overly assertive 'community guides' vying for your attention. However, their desire to make a living in a struggling rural community is understandable. Once you've paid the steep entrance fee, you get to see the simple wooden house where Marley lived from age six to 13, the meditation stone from the song 'Talkin' Blues' and the simple marble tomb, surrounded by numerous (and heartfelt) handwritten tributes.

Enter the Spanish

VISIT JAMAICA'S ORIGINAL SPANISH CAPITAL

In 1494, Columbus first sighted Jamaica. In 1510, his son Diego, appointed Governor of the Indies, granted land to army officer Juan de Esquivel to establish Sevilla la Nueva, the first Spanish capital on the island, and **Seville Great House** (1745), 14km west of Ocho Rios, marks the spot. You can wander through the ruins of the castle house and the sugar mills, but the highlight is the museum inside the restored plantation house that shines a light on the *encomienda* system, under which the indigenous Taíno population was forced by the Spanish to work as serfs, with the majority perishing from disease, overwork and suicide. They were replaced by the first enslaved Africans in Jamaica, whose everyday lives are

WHERE TO STAY AND EAT EAST OF OCHI

Tamarind Great House
Antique-filled rooms with four-poster beds greet you at this 'plantation guesthouse' with superb valley views. **$$**

Kareema's Kitchen
Jerk snapper, curry mopped up with roti and innovative spins on Jamaican dishes served with aplomb. **$**

PG's Restaurant
Authentic risotto, osso buco and pasta delight the taste buds, as does the (mostly) Italian wine list. **$$**

Green Grotto Caves

reconstructed here with considerable sensitivity. On the front lawn is a touching memorial to the enslaved people whose remains were discovered here and reburied in 1997.

A Subterranean Wander

MARVEL AT GREEN GROTTO CAVES

The guide will lead you down the steep steps into the vast entrance chamber of the **Green Grotto Caves** – an impressive system of caves and tunnels 31km west of Ocho Rios – where the delicate rock formations and the Green Grotto, a glistening subterranean lake 36m down – will garner admiration. The guide regales you with stories of the Taíno, who used these caves for religious purposes. In the centuries that followed, the caves were used as hideouts – by the Spanish during the English takeover of Jamaica in 1655, by enslaved people escaping from the plantations in the 18th century and by smugglers running arms to Cuba between the two world wars. The banter during the family-friendly tour is peppered with humor, and if you're lucky, you'll spot some bats and the Jamaican yellow boa.

GOLDENEYE & FIREFLY

East of Ocho Rios, exclusive villas dot the manicured grounds above a cove, and butlers and private chefs serve gourmet meals to celebrities looking for a discreet getaway at **Goldeneye**, Ian Fleming's former home. Fleming wintered here until his death in 1964, and all of his James Bond books were written here, with five set in Jamaica.

Further along the coast, on a cliff-top above Oracabessa, is **Firefly**, the intimate home-turned-museum of English playwright and actor Noël Coward. Check out his art studio and the drawing room where he entertained the likes of Sophia Loren. Particularly moving is his poem, 'When I Have Fears,' which is carved into the stone near his final resting place.

WHERE TO STAY AND EAT WEST OF OCHI

High Hope Estate
Venetian-style villa with five individually styled rooms, a veranda with ocean views, and superb meals on request. **$$**

Jus' Coool Puddin' Man
Priory's 'Puddin' Man' cooks up to-die-for sweet potato pudding, plus other Jamaican standards. **$**

Scotchies Drax Hall
Well-established jerk pit with dependably good pork, chicken and sausage, served with *festival* and *bammy*. **$**

PORT ANTONIO

Port Antonio
KINGSTON

Nestling near the lush Rio Grande Valley and tucked into the green hills of the rainy Portland parish, Port Antonio seems a world away from the cruise-ship strips, resorts, and hustle and bustle that define much of Jamaica's northern coast. The main draw of this compact historic town – comprising small businesses, bustling markets, Georgian and Victorian architecture, and laid-back bars – is its relaxed vibe.

In the first half of the 20th century, Port Antonio was a major shipping port for bananas, with the backbreaking night labor of the dock workers immortalized in Jamaican–American singer Harry Belafonte's 'Banana Boat (Day-O).' Port Antonio ('Porty' to its friends) is also where Jamaican tourism first took off in the 1940s, when American actor Errol Flynn declared that the town was more beautiful than any woman he had known, and other celebrities followed, with the likes of Ian Fleming and Noël Coward building their secluded bolt-holes here.

TOP TIP

Pack an umbrella: Portland is Jamaica's rainiest parish. For transport, Port Antonio is linked by Ocho Rios, Montego Bay, Falmouth and Kingston by the Knutsford Express. Minibuses run to Moore Town (for Maroon culture), Kingston via Annoto Bay (change for Ocho Rios), plus the east-coast destinations of Boston Bay and Machioneal.

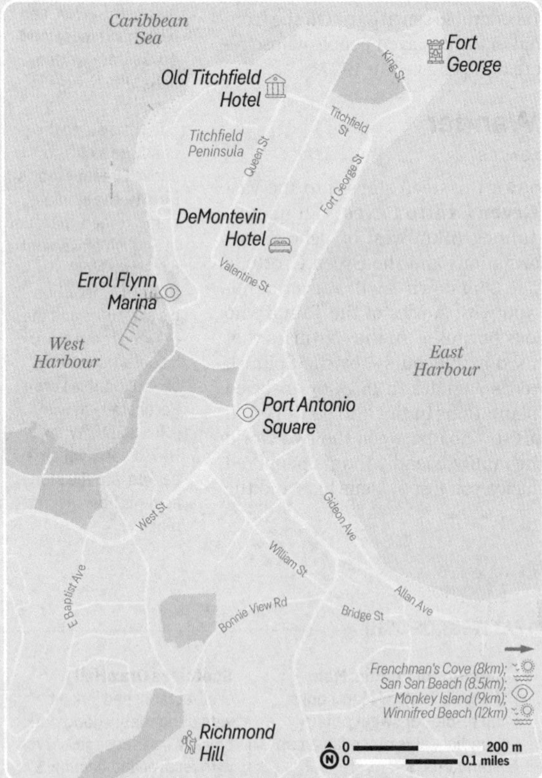

Frenchman's Cove

MARLON TROTTMANN/SHUTTERSTOCK ©

TRAVELLING JACK/SHUTTERSTOCK ©

Winnifred Beach

Pottering Around Porty

A STROLL AROUND PORT ANTONIO

Compact Port Antonio is a joy to wander through. From the center, it's a stiff 10-minute climb up **Richmond Hill** for a great view. In **Port Antonio Square**, admire the Georgian courthouse, clock tower and the Royal Mall – a mishmash of Tudor, Renaissance and medieval styles – then stroll the landscaped gardens next to the **Errol Flynn Marina**. Head to the tip of the Titchfield Peninsula, passing the late-Victorian gingerbread architecture of **DeMontevin Hotel**, the ruins of the **Old Titchfield Hotel** (once owned by Errol Flynn) and the rambling wooden houses, to check out the cannons and crumbling walls of **Fort George**.

Beach-Hopping Around Port Antonio

PORT ANTONIO'S BEST BEACHES

The coast east of Port Antonio has gorgeous beaches. Take a route taxi to **Frenchman's Cove**, just 8km away. A pristine, sugary-white half-moon, it has been immortalized in Hollywood hits like *No Time to Die*. Its calm waters are great for swimming. Nearby, **San San Beach** is fringed by a reasonably healthy reef that's ideal for snorkeling (snorkeling gear and kayak hire are available). Kayakers and strong swimmers can explore the small, uninhabited **Monkey Island**, 250m from the shore.

Just 3km further east is the hamlet of Fairy Hill. A narrow paved road leads steeply down to **Winnifred Beach**, a beautiful stretch of powdered white sand. The only truly public beach on this stretch of the coast, it has a terrific vibe, with competing sound systems on weekends, stalls selling grilled fish and coconut water, and an overwhelmingly local crowd.

BEST PLACES TO STAY IN PORT ANTONIO

Mesmerize Guesthouse
A super-central, friendly place behind a bamboo stockade, whose owners are a treasure trove of local knowledge. $

Geejam Hotel
Hillside villas and cabins owned by a music-industry veteran, with studio, celeb guests and superb cuisine. $$$

All Nations Guesthouse
Dine on ganja lobster on the private terrace of your Africa-themed suite at this handsome B&B. $$

Hotel Mockingbird Hill
Locally sourced slow food and art-bedecked, ocean-view rooms await your enjoyment at this renowned eco-hotel. $$$

WHERE TO EAT IN PORT ANTONIO

Yosch Café
Driftwood-and-bamboo spot for hearty breakfasts and sandwiches, plus seafood dishes in the evenings. $$

Portland Jerk Center
The best place in town for jerk chicken and pork, plus sausages and other meats. $

Wilkes Seafood
Coconut curried fish and other sea-based offerings are stars at this unassuming beachfront restaurant. $$

ROAD TRIP

The Best of the East

This driving tour takes you from Boston Bay to Kingston the long way, along Jamaica's least-developed, least-visited section of the east coast, pulling together such diverse attractions as the home of Jamaica's most authentic jerk pork, beautiful surf spots in low-key communities, Jamaica's most beautiful waterfalls, a remote lighthouse and hot springs. While the route can be driven as a one-day road trip, it's more rewarding to spread the journey over two days.

1 Boston Bay

Begin at Boston Bay, 20km east of Port Antonio. The cookshops at its north end are renowned island-wide for their jerk pork, where the practice of marinating meat with jerk seasoning first developed centuries ago. Beginner and intermediate surfers come here to ride the left-hander and right-hander breaks, while pro surfers are drawn by the challenging hurricane swells.

The Drive: From here, it's 7km to Long Bay, where the straight stretch of the A4 is beautifully paved.

2 Long Bay

Aptly named, Long Bay's beautiful, narrow beach stretches for 1.5km. The exposed break attracts surfers, with the most consistent swells during the fall. Whether you're hitting the waves or not, Pimento Lodge Resort and the Sea Cliff Resort are good spots to overnight.

The Drive: The 11km drive to the turnoff for Reach Falls near the village of Machioneal is well-signposted, winding and bumpy. From the turnoff, it's 3km uphill along a narrow road.

Downstream from Reach Falls

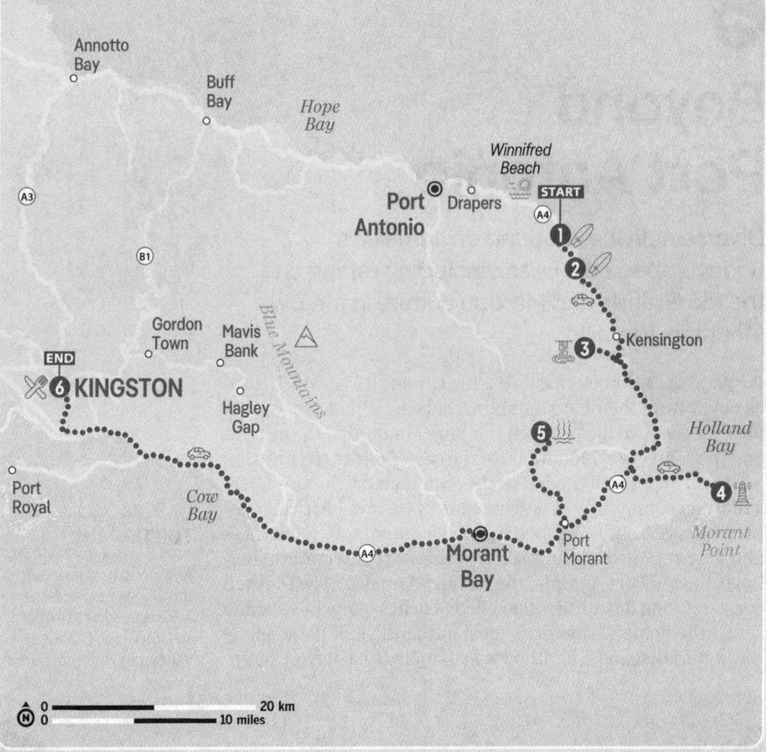

3 Reach Falls

Crystal-clear waters tumble down limestone tiers into jade-colored pools surrounded by jungle. The entry fee will buy you access to the main falls and pool; to climb to the upper pools, work your way up the river through a spray-battered cave and swim through an underwater tunnel; you'll need a guide for this.

The Drive: From Reach Falls, it's 19km to Golden Grove. Detour from the A4 to Duckenfield, pass the sugar factory on your left and take the dirt road through the cane fields for another 8km. A high clearance vehicle is a boon.

4 Morant Point Lighthouse

A surreal, wind-battered place, Morant Point is Jamaica's easternmost tip, crowned with a 30m red-and-white-striped lighthouse from 1842. The lighthouse keeper is happy to show you around, and the views over the sugarcane fields and the Caribbean Sea are tremendous.

The Drive: Return to the A4 and take the rutted 13km stretch west to Port Morant, and then the beautifully winding and hilly road north for 12km to Bath.

5 Bath

Hot mineral springs with medicinal properties made Bath a colonial socialite destination in the late 17th century, until the Morant Bay Rebellion. The springs are still popular with locals, and you can soak in the open air for free (though overly assertive 'guides' can be wearying), or stay in the pink Georgian Bath Fountain Hotel and use their spa.

The Drive: Retrace your steps to the A4, then follow the partially paved road west for 72km.

6 Kingston

Renowned for its tremendous music scene and excellent dining, Jamaica's capital (p388) makes a fitting end to your journey.

Beyond Port Antonio

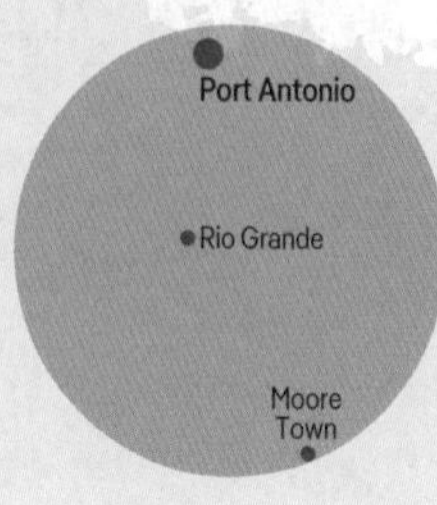

Diverse activities abound on Jamaica's undeveloped east coast, including rafting on the Rio Grande and Maroon culture in the Blue Mountain foothills.

Portland parish is bisected by the Rio Grande River, which rushes down from the Blue Mountains, carving a huge gorge that forms a deep wedge between the Blue Mountains to the west and the John Crow Mountains to the east. Besides river rafting à la Errol Flynn, you can follow the road inland to Moore Town, a Maroon community of descendants of enslaved African people who successfully escaped into the mountainous wilderness and have retained a strong sense of their African cultural heritage. East of Port Antonio, the A4 hugs Jamaica's least-visited coast, passing beautiful, unpeopled beaches; gorgeous surfing spots; the home of Jamaica's most authentic jerk pork; splendid waterfalls; and a lighthouse at Jamaica's easternmost tip.

TOP TIP

Allow plenty of time for driving the east coast. A 4WD is needed to explore the Upper Rio Grande valley, beyond Moore Town.

DOUGLAS PEARSON/GETTY IMAGES ©

Bamboo raft, Rio Grande

Sojourns on the Rio Grande

TRANQUIL RIVER RAFTING

In the 1940s, when Porty became the epicenter of Hollywood tourism, moonlight soujourns along the Rio Grande on bamboo rafts were allegedly popularized by actor Errol Flynn. Floating on the dark waters while crooning 'Moon River' into your loved one's ear is still possible when full moon trips are occasionally offered, but most rafting trips take place during the day, running for 13km from **Rafter's Village** to **Rafter's Rest** at St Margaret's Bay. During your two-to-three-hour float, the 'captain' poling your raft will stop to let you swim in the jade-colored waters. Ask to stop at **Belinda's**, a rustic riverside restaurant that serves fantastic crayfish stew and grilled snapper. Since the rafting trip is one-way, hire a driver to bring your car from Berrydale to St Margaret's Bay, hop in a taxi or get a local tour company to arrange transportation.

Communing with Windward Maroons

VISIT A HISTORIC MAROON COMMUNITY

Colorful murals greet you at the **Maroon Cultural Centre** in Moore Town, a one-street village along the Wildcane River. Founded in 1739 following the signing of a peace treaty that granted the Maroons their independence, Moore Town works hard to keep its lore alive. Arrange for a guide to show you **Nanny's Grave**, where Queen Nanny – warrior woman, freedom fighter, Maroon chieftain and national hero – is allegedly seeing out eternity. A scenic 30-minute walk uphill beneath huge ferns and tunnels of giant bamboo gets you to the beautiful Nanny Falls. Clamber over the rocks with your guide's assistance, then enjoy some splashes in the turquoise pools.

EXPLORING THE UPPER RIO GRANDE

Taking the right fork at the Seaman's Valley Y-junction and pressing on along the narrow, rough, 4WD-only road to **Bowden Pen**, 16km up the river valley, is as remote as it gets in Jamaica. Base yourself at Ambassabeth Ecolodge – a local tourism project with rustic cabin sans electricity for a genuine Maroon experience, complete with indigenous folklore and authentic Maroon meals.

Hiking is the only way to explore the rugged mountain terrain of the Upper Rio Grande Valley; your hosts can organize a local guide to take you along the **Cunha Cunha Pass Heritage Trail** or to the pristine cascades of **White River Falls** and the ruins of abandoned Maroon villages beyond.

WHERE TO EAT EAST OF PORT ANTONIO

Woody's
Dine on plantain burgers, or their meaty equivalents, plus superlative hot dogs and homemade ginger beer. **$**

Mille Fleurs
Book ahead for seasonal, locally sourced organic fare, served on a gorgeous terrace at Hotel Mockingbird Hill. **$$$**

Cynthia's on Winnifred
The pick of Winnifred Beach eateries, serving grilled fish with callaloo, roast breadfruit, and rice and peas. **$$**

MARCIN SYLWIA CIESIELSKI/SHUTTERSTOCK ©

Arriving

There are three ways to get to Jamaica: international flights into the two airports at Kingston and Montego Bay; by cruise ship to Kingston, Montego Bay or Falmouth; and by yacht. There are car rental facilities in the arrivals halls at the two airports. The high season runs from mid-December to March, with prices dropping during hurricane season (June to November).

By Air

Jamaica receives international flights from major cities in Europe and North America, as well as Caribbean destinations. If you're short on time and want to cover a major chunk of the island, consider flying into Montego Bay and flying out of Kingston.

By Boat

Jamaica is a popular destination for international cruise ships, which dock at Montego Bay, Falmouth and Kingston. One major criticism is that few locally owned businesses benefit from cruise ship tourism, with the majority of visitors whisked off to a set list of sights.

Money

Currency: Jamaican dollar (J$)

CASH
Cash is still king when traveling around Jamaica. You need it for public transportation, paying at budget restaurants and for excursions, souvenirs and many entry fees. The US dollar is widely accepted in tourist hubs but the exchange rate may be unfavorable. Some cash machines in touristy places dispense US dollars.

DIGITAL PAYMENTS
Resorts, hotels, guesthouses, many restaurants (particularly in touristy areas) and big-name businesses accept digital payments, but if you're visiting remote parts of Jamaica, you can forget about using that digital wallet.

CREDIT CARDS
Credit and debit cards are becoming more common among Jamaicans and foreigners, and are widely accepted. Visa and Mastercard are more common than Amex and are generally useful in areas frequented by tourists. Some businesses add a surcharge for credit card purchases.

Getting Around

Jamaica is a fairly compact island, and easy to get around. It's covered by an extensive public transportation network that reaches all but the remotest of destinations, though the condition of most roads means that getting there will invariably take longer than you think. Expensive charter flights connect major towns and cities.

PUBLIC TRANSPORT

Kingston is covered by a network of inexpensive city buses, though they rarely run according to schedule. Comfortable, air-conditioned Knutsford Express buses run between large towns and cities, while numerous minibuses and route taxis connect smaller destinations.

COLIN WHEELER/SHUTTERSTOCK ©

CAR

Renting a car gives you the greatest flexibility, allows you to reach isolated attractions, and is typically cheaper than taking taxis. Outside the toll motorways, watch out for potholes and aggressive driving. To explore the Blue Mountains, you'll need a 4WD.

BOAT & TRAIN

Boats are used for day trips and cruises, but the planned ferry service between Ocho Rios, MoBay and Negril is yet to materialise. There is talk of reviving the old railway connection between Kingston and Montego Bay.

TAXI/RIDESHARE

Expensive licensed taxis with set fares connect popular destinations, while moderately priced local taxis (call ahead or find taxi stand) cover major cities and towns. Uber operates in Kingston only. City taxis rarely use meters – agree on a price beforehand.

AIR

Jamaica's compact size makes domestic flights largely redundant, but expensive TimAir charter flights connect Montego Bay with Kingston, Ocho Rios, Negril and Port Antonio.

DRIVING ESSENTIALS

Drive on the left side

Speed limit is 50km/h in cities, 80km/h outside of cities and 120km/h on motorways.

Road conditions range from good to atrocious.

Above: Les Anses d'Arlet (p448); Right: Fort-de-France (p436)

MARTINIQUE

A WEST INDIAN SLICE OF FRANCE

Quaint fishing villages and charming architecture punctuate rugged volcanic landscapes, while the island's lively cultural scene reflects its French and African ancestry.

Martinique is a deceptively tiny island in the Lesser Antilles – and an overseas territory of France – teeming with a mélange of natural and cultural pursuits. The island's luscious greenery, which includes a riot of thick rainforests, soaring mountains and immaculate beaches, will initially draw your attention. Mont Pelée volcano, which famously wiped out the former capital of St-Pierre in 1902 and last erupted in 1932, towers proudly as a reminder of Martinique's fiery past. The island's volcanic origins are also evident in its rugged terrain.

But Martinique's appeal extends beyond its breathtaking scenery. The lively culture of the island is a fusion of its African, French and West Indian heritages. You'll savor French cuisine infused with the flavors of regional spices and ingredients, listen to the distinctive sounds of zouk, and hear rapidly spoken French blended with a Creole accent. Fort-de-France, the capital of Martinique, is a pulsating metropolis with a vibrant market, art galleries and museums that highlight the island's history and culture.

Forts, sugar plantations and slave quarters found across Martinique provide a glimpse into the colonial past for anyone interested in understanding the island's turbulent history. However, its present is equally fascinating, boasting a thriving arts scene, top-notch rum distilleries and various outdoor activities like hiking, snorkeling and kayaking.

THE MAIN AREAS

FORT-DE-FRANCE
Vibrant capital with exquisite architecture. p436

NORTHERN MARTINIQUE
Mountains and heavily wooded landscape. p443

SOUTHERN MARTINIQUE
Sun-kissed haven for beachgoers. p447

Find Your Way

Martinique is quite mountainous, with a tangle of narrow roads that can make navigating the island very challenging. But the scenic routes are well worth the effort to venture far out.

Northern Martinique, p443
A rainforested respite ripe for adventure, the north is an untamed wilderness flush with mountain peaks, cascading waterfalls and other hidden wonders.

CAR

If you want to truly explore Martinique, a car is a requirement. You can get a rental at the airport from companies like Sixt and Europcar. The roads are excellent, but Fort-de-France's rush hour traffic can be very heavy.

TAXI

Taxis are the natural alternative to a rental car, but they are a costly option. You can pay anywhere from 30€ to 70€ minimum from the airport to your accommodations. A 40% surcharge applies to night fares between 8pm and 6am.

BUS

There are two types of buses operating in Martinique: grand buses within Fort-de-France with a capacity for 40 passengers, and nine-passenger minivans called *taxis collectifs*. A TC sign identifies these privately owned minivans. Routes are very flexible depending on a passenger's destination.

Fort-de-France, p436
With the Pitons du Carbet mountains as a stunning backdrop and a gorgeous natural harbor, the city is both cosmopolitan and quintessentially West Indian.

Southern Martinique, p447
Detach and unwind at this coastal oasis replete with pristine white-sand beaches, shimmering turquoise waters and picturesque fishing villages.

ON-PHOTOGRAPHY GERMANY/SHUTTERSTOCK ©

Plan Your Time

The island is relatively small but culturally and naturally rich. Idyllic black- and white-sand beaches, imposing mountain peaks and lush tropical rainforests are all found within its rugged volcanic landscape.

SIMON DANNHAUER/SHUTTERSTOCK ©

Jardin de Balata (p439)

If You Only Do One Thing

In Martinique, finding a beach is not a difficult feat. From soaking up some sun to gliding through the azure waters, the perfect beach awaits. Visitors can conveniently access all of these sun-drenched stretches by car. Among all of Martinique's beaches, **Grande Anse des Salines** (p448) is one of the most spectacular seashores on the island. With its fine, powdery sand, exquisite coral reefs and swaying palm trees, it's postcard-perfect. It's located in **Ste-Anne** (p448), which is close to other picturesque spots like **Les Anses d'Arlet** (p448) and **Le Rocher du Diamant** (p448) on the southwestern coast.

Seasonal Highlights

November through March is the sweet spot for travel to Martinique during the dry season. However, November and December bring an influx of travelers escaping winter for the holiday season.

JANUARY

Pick up ***une galette des rois*** (king cake) at a bakery for **Fête des Rois**, a festival celebrating the Epiphany.

FEBRUARY

An explosion of parades, music, costumes and dancing takes over the island during **Vaval** (p437), the biggest festival in Martinique.

JUNE

Free performances and concerts are held all over the island to honor music as part of **Fête de la Musique**.

AYGUL BULTE/SHUTTERSTOCK ©, T PHOTOGRAPHY/SHUTTERSTOCK ©, MONITOR6/GETTY IMAGES ©

Three Perfect Days

- Start your journey in the vibrant **Fort-de-France** (p436) market. Immerse your senses in aromatic spices, and discover rare delicacies and unique crafts.

- Take a 20-minute drive to the **Jardin de Balata** (p439), the botanical heart of the island.

- Continue your cultural exploration at **Distillerie Depaz** (p445) in St-Pierre or **Distillerie JM** (p445) in Macouba.

- If you're a hiker, **Mont Pelée** (p444) is a highlight in the northern region.

- No visit to Martinique is complete without a day in the charming village of **Les Anses d'Arlet** (p448) and the beautiful beaches perfect for a lazy afternoon of sunbathing and swimming.

A Week to Travel Around

- Start with **Fort-de-France** (p436). Check out the fish and spice markets, visit **Fort St-Louis** (p438) and take a stroll through the city's streets.

- On day two, take a boat from the capital to Trois-Îlets and explore **La Savane des Esclaves** (p449) eco-museum.

- The following day, head out on a drive along the Route de la Trace and see **Sacré Cœur de Balata** (p439) and the **Jardin de Balata** (p439), among other attractions. The next stop is southwest to **Les Anses d'Arlet** (p448) for the beaches and snorkeling; end your day watching the sunset over **Le Rocher du Diamant** (p448).

- Close out the week by visiting **Ste-Anne** (p448) in the southernmost tip and the gorgeous snow-white sands of **Grande Anse des Salines** (p448).

JULY

Le Tour de Martinique is a multiday, nine-stage road cycling race held annually on the island.

AUGUST

It's a summer highlight as thousands of enthusiastic spectators cheer on sailors and boaters at **Le Tour des Yoles Rondes**.

SEPTEMBER

The colorful **Big In Jazz Festival** is billed as the world's premier Afro-Caribbean musical celebration.

DECEMBER

Chanté Nwel features traditional West Indian Christmas carols – music groups singing outdoors – and celebrates the spirit of Christmas.

FORT-DE-FRANCE

Since 1680, the city formerly known as Fort-Royal has served as the island's capital. It is the largest city in Martinique and the French West Indies, with roughly 150,000 inhabitants. A popular destination for cruise ships and international yachties, it also operates as a major transportation hub and the island's administrative and economic center. You can explore Fort-de-France's history and culture through its various museums and landmarks, including Bibliothèque Schoelcher, Fort St-Louis and La Savane park. The French influences are evident in the narrow cobblestone streets, intricate wrought-iron balconies and the cluster of Euro-style shops. The city is brimming with a variety of superb dining options. The market scene is bustling at local institutions like the Grand Marché, a sensory paradise where visitors can meander around searching for Creole spices, souvenirs, locally produced rum and handicrafts.

FORT-DE-FRANCE

TOP TIP

Don't be surprised if a bartender invites you to fix your Ti' Punch at a restaurant. The French term for this style is *Chacun Prépare Sa Propre Mort,* which translates as 'Everyone Makes Their Own Death'. The amount of rum in your glass is entirely up to you.

Bibliothèque Schoelcher (p438)

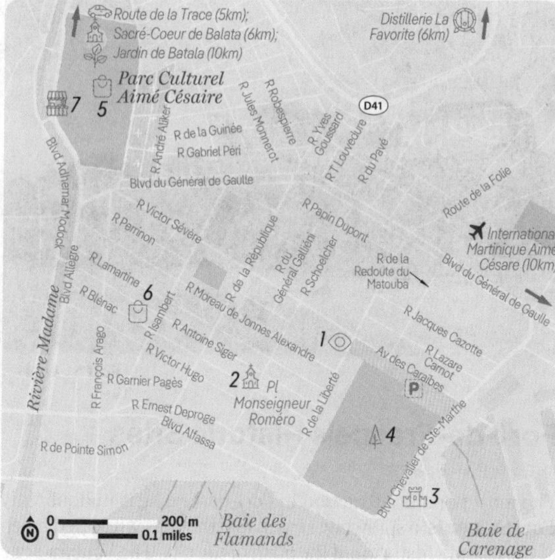

SIGHTS
1 Bibliothèque Schoelcher
2 Cathédrale St-Louis
3 Fort St-Louis
4 La Savane

SHOPPING
5 Centre des Métiers d'Art
6 Grand Marché
7 Marche aux Fruits et Légumes

The Tradition of Vaval

A WEEK OF REVELRY

The much anticipated Carnival celebrations take place in February. During these five days of revelry, locals and tourists can dance to nonstop music, let loose and appreciate the creativity of the costumes. Months of planning go into the parade, but the official festivities begin on the first Sunday after Epiphany. Early risers and partygoers returning home late at night can join together for a *vidé,* a parade through the streets to the sound of drums. Men traditionally dress as brides and women as grooms for 'Burlesque Weddings', which occur on Mondays. On Mardi Gras, also known as Fat Tuesday, revelers flood the streets dressed in the color of the Red Devils while being led by street orchestras, marching bands and floats equipped with sound systems. Ash Wednesday symbolizes the death of the devil.

Carnival
JVPHOT/SHUTTERSTOCK ©

WHERE TO STAY IN FORT-DE-FRANCE

Fort Savane
A home away from home conveniently located close to Fort-de-France's most popular landmarks. €€

Redoute Paradise
A mix of apartments and B&Bs located in Redoute, serving a daily gourmet continental breakfast. €€

Karibea Valmenière Hotel & Spa
La Valmenière's location places a multitude of dining options and entertainment venues at your fingertips. €€

THE NATIONAL COCKTAIL

In French Creole, the *ti'* in Ti' Punch is a derivative of the French *petit* or *petite,* meaning 'small'. The significance of this national treasure, however, is enormous. T-shirts bearing the name are widely available as mementos all over town, and for some Martinicans, getting their daily dose is a ritual. The flavor is equally robust, with a fiery intensity that sweeps across the palate. Ti' Punch is traditionally made with *rhum agricole,* sugarcane syrup and local lime, and served neat. But this is no shot – like any good French beverage, this scorching libation should be savored and appreciated.

NANCY C. ROSS/GETTY IMAGES ©

Fort St-Louis

Fort-de-France's Historic Sites

THE FOUNDATION OF THE CITY

The most popular attraction in Fort-de-France is undoubtedly **Fort St-Louis**, a sprawling stronghold that has witnessed much of the island's history and the birth of the city. The Vauban-style seaside fortress dates back to 1640; however, the current structure differs from the original incarnation. It's in the city center, a stroll away from **La Savane** and the ferry terminal. The fort is still in use as a French naval base, so only certain areas are open to the public, and visitors aren't allowed to take pictures of military personnel. Still, tours of the fort are entertaining and educational. Go up to the roof for fantastic city views.

Just across La Savane you'll find the **Bibliothèque Schoelcher**, a 19th-century wood-and-glass art deco library. The building was designed by French architect Henri Picq in Paris for the 1889 World's Fair before being dismantled and shipped to Martinique. This impressive structure is a memorial to Victor Schoelcher, a French abolitionist author who donated more than 9000 books and 250 musical scores to Martinique on the condition that they be made accessible to the people. The library is still in use, so visitors should refrain from making any unnecessary noise or taking any pictures.

The city's **Cathédrale St-Louis** was originally constructed in 1657. However, the current building dates from 1895 and is the seventh version due to the natural disasters that have ravaged Fort-de-France over the years. Its all-metal frame is designed to withstand fire, earthquakes and cyclones. A lofty tower, vibrant stained-glass windows and an iron balustrade further enhance the historical landmark's combination of Romano-Byzantine and neo-Gothic architectural elements.

WHERE TO EAT IN FORT-DE-FRANCE

Chez Carole
Chez Carole's Creole cuisine, cozily tucked inside the Grand Marché, is a Fort-de-France institution. €

Coco Mango
Dine on delectable tapas and full courses in a picturesque waterfront setting. €€

The Yellow
The French and Creole fusion menu is constantly evolving and features only homemade items. €€€

MAURITIUS IMAGES GMBH/ALAMY ©

Steam engine, Distillerie La Favorite

Tour a Family Rum Distillery

TASTING THE SWEET ISLAND RUM

Distillerie La Favorite, which dates back to 1842, is one of only two family-run distilleries on the island. In 1905, Henri Dormoy purchased the farm and modernized it by installing a steam engine, which is still functional today. The self-guided tour of the compact factory is free and traces the history of the operation. Visitors can also observe the various stages of the artisanal rum-making process right in the middle of the active machinery, and the tour concludes with a tasting. La Favorite produces some of the best white rum on the island, with a natural sweetness derived from sugarcane and notes of citrus. You can purchase one of their signature wax-sealed bottles at the gift shop.

A Slice of Serenity

FIND THE ETHEREAL AND ENCHANTED

Fort-de-France is peppered with Parisian influences, starting with **Sacré Cœur de Balata** (a 15-minute drive north of the city). This basilica is a miniature version of the original in Paris' Montmartre neighborhood. The church rises amid verdant surroundings, providing a breathtaking panorama of the countryside and the bay of Fort-de-France.

Less than 10 minutes away, a visual feast awaits at **Jardin de Balata**. There are more than 3000 different species of flora in this expanse of gorgeous greenery. The grounds are immaculately kept, the ponds are adorned with lotuses and water lilies, and the view from the rope bridges is nothing short of heavenly. The hour-long walk around the garden is clearly marked.

A DEEPLY ROOTED TRADITION

Martinique has earned worldwide renown as the source of exceptional rum. Only about 2% of the world's rum comes from Martinique, but the brands made there are known for their unique *agricole* method of distillation using only pure sugarcane juice rather than the more common industrial rum made from molasses. According to French law, the *appellation d'origine contrôlée* (AOC) may be awarded to rums made entirely in Martinique that meet certain production standards. *Rhum agricole* (agricultural rum) is often sipped neat and savored, much like a fine vintage brandy, due to its heady aroma and crisp flavor. Martinique has 14 distilleries that make *rhum agricole,* including brands like Clément, La Favorite, Saint James, Depaz and Maison La Mauny.

WHERE TO DRINK IN FORT-DE-FRANCE

Garage Popular
A small car-themed bar with inexpensive drinks and good food in downtown Fort-de-France.

Le Cloud
Enjoy fruity and colorful homemade cocktails while gazing at the sunset from the rooftop.

Ubuntu
A chic African bar with a welcoming atmosphere and expertly crafted drinks.

MARTINIQUE'S SCENIC ROUTE

If you only have time for one tour in Martinique, make it the **Route de la Trace**, a scenic ribbon of N3 highway that stretches from Fort-de-France to Mont Pelée.

The 30-to-40-kilometer route was carved out of the Carbet mountains by the Jesuits in the 17th century as a shortcut and now takes about two hours. It snakes its way through spectacular expanses of lush rainforest, offering glimpses of Martinique's untamed natural splendor. For a truly immersive experience, venture onto the stunning hiking trails that branch off from the main route.

If you have the time, detouring to **Alma** for a refreshing swim in the crystalline river waters is highly recommended.

MARC BRUXELLE/SHUTTERSTOCK ©

Grand Marché

Retail Therapy in Fort-de-France

GRAB SOME GOODIES IN THE CITY

Visit the **Marche aux Fruits et Légumes** (fruit and vegetable markets) for a glimpse into everyday life and to purchase some of the island's freshest and most succulent produce. All of them sell spices, liqueurs, medicinal plants, handicrafts and local foods like *accras* (fritters) and *boudins* (sausages). Small, locally owned eateries also serve delicious, authentic fare. **Grand Marché** on Rue Antoine Isambert has been serving locals since 1885 as the primary market for spices, fresh produce, rum, crafts and more. It's well worth getting up early to peruse the colorful stalls of the Marché aux Épices (spice market) here. Stroll over to Rue Blénac to pick up a few handicrafts like pottery, shells, painted fabrics and baskets at the **Centre des Métiers d'Art**. The well-crafted trinkets you'll find in this shop will be a reminder of your island getaway for years to come.

GETTING AROUND

If you prefer more flexibility and independence, you can rent a car in Fort-de-France. However, remember that rush-hour traffic in the city center can be quite heavy.

There are a few sights within walking distance of each other. Taxis are usually quite pricey. There is also the option of taking the bus, though its schedule is inconsistent.

Beyond Fort-de-France

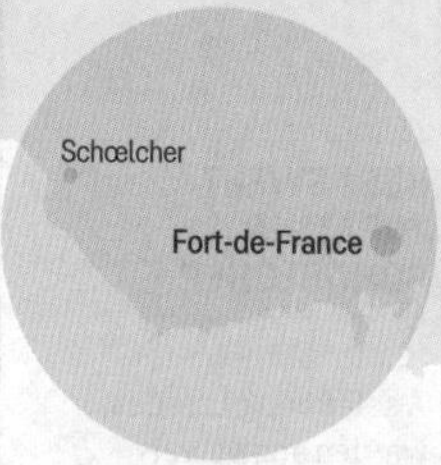

Schœlcher

Fort-de-France

There's a certain 'it' factor to Schoelcher that makes visitors want to linger a while and poke around.

The town of Schoelcher is the fourth-largest commune on the island of Martinique. Until 1889, the town was known as Case-Navire, but then it was renamed to honor the French abolitionist Victor Schoelcher. It is said that Schoelcher convinced the French government to end slavery in the French colonies in 1848. Schoelcher was one of the first communes in Martinique to be free of slavery after the abolition decree was issued. The small coastal town is often thought of as an extension of the capital, Fort-de-France, and has many hidden but pleasantly surprising qualities.

TOP TIP

Schoelcher has several accommodations options a short walk from the beach, including La Tita, Hotel La Batelière and Hotel Pelican.

Statue of Victor Schoelcher, Fort-de-France

PACK-SHOT/SHUTTERSTOCK ©

Schoelcher

BEST SWEET TREATS IN SCHOELCHER

Boule de Neige
A selection of crêpes, waffles and velvety ice cream at a low-key beach location. €

La Bonne Glace
All natural, homemade ice creams and sorbets made with fresh, in-season fruit. €

Passion Givrée
A variety of artisanal ice creams showcasing the incredible fruits grown on the island. €

Fun Times in Schoelcher

BEACHCOMBING AND INDOOR ROCK CLIMBING

Those looking for a place to swim without venturing too far north or south often head to **Plage de Madiana**. It's also a popular spot for early-bird joggers. The beach isn't typically crowded, and small groups of palm trees provide natural shade. Take a dip in the clear, turquoise waters, relax on the warm sand or play some volleyball. Since it's so close to the road, this beach is very convenient to get to. There's parking right on the beach, and restaurants nearby.

If you're feeling adventurous, take the whole family indoor rock s at **Clip'n Climb Martinique**. All ages and skill levels are welcome and safety is always prioritized, with dedicated instructors present for all activities. There are three progressively difficult traditional climbing challenges that participants can try their hand at. Valo Climb, the first interactive game platform for climbing walls, is another fun alternative. Spaces are limited, so book a spot in advance. Be sure to pack appropriate clothing and sneakers.

A Gastronomic Extravaganza

GET INTRODUCED TO CREOLE CUISINE

Martinican cuisine primarily comprises seafood, fruit and vegetable dishes, which are then seasoned with fresh herbs and spices. But the French influence is also apparent. Sign up for one of **Les Ateliers Médélices** gourmet workshops to learn more about Creole cuisine or even French classics. The workshops are designed for both complete culinary novices and seasoned pros. Local chefs offer classes in both French and English, and they cover dishes like *accras* (fritters), *colombo* (curried meat dish) and *terrine de foie gras,* among other specialties. Classes last for up to three hours throughout the year.

GETTING AROUND

Schoelcher's hilly terrain makes it unsuitable for pedestrians and cyclists to travel the area. A taxi, rental car or bus are more practical modes of transport.

NORTHERN MARTINIQUE

Northern Martinique
FORT-DE-FRANCE

The northern part of Martinique is a windswept area of sublime scenery, with towering mountains dominating the horizon. This is not a coastal hot spot like the southern region, but some great beaches are hidden away. Hiking enthusiasts will find some of the best trails and most breathtaking views in northern Martinique, thanks largely to the island's active volcano, Mont Pelée. Before the eruption of Mont Pelée, former capital St-Pierre was the site of the island's first French settlement, and many of the structures from that era have been preserved as archaeological sites today. Grand-Rivière, a tiny and colorful fishing village wedged between Potiche River, the cove of L'Anse Dufour and Dominica Canal, also has a certain allure and authenticity that visitors will enjoy. Black-sand beaches line either side and the neighboring island of Dominica is visible on a clear day.

TOP TIP

Visit Coeur du Carbet, a unique photo spot sure to tug at the heartstrings of romantics. The heart-shaped structure is perched in the heights of Morne aux Bœufs in the picturesque town of Carbet. The photo op is even more heart-melting as the sun disappears into the horizon.

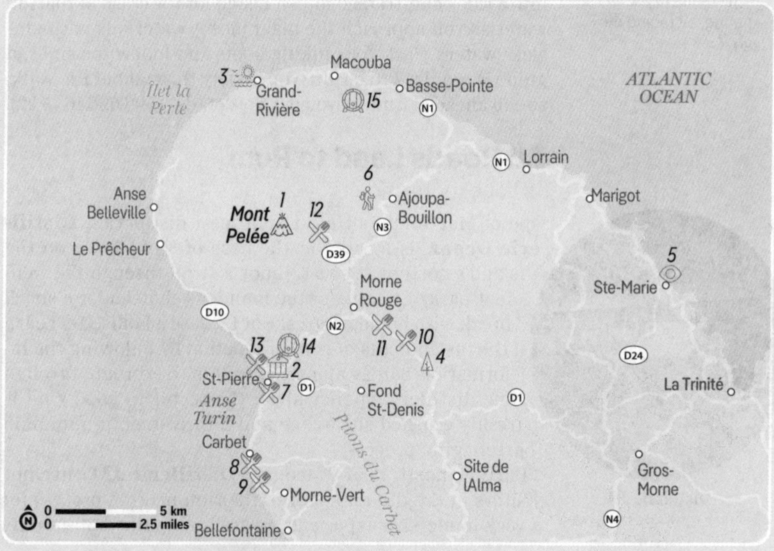

TOP SIGHTS
1 Mont Pelée

SIGHTS
2 Frank Perret Museum
3 La Plage de Sinaï
4 Le Domaine d'Émeraude
5 Tombolo de l'Îlet Ste-Marie

ACTIVITIES, COURSES & TOURS
6 Les Gorges de la Falaise

EATING
7 Arhum Glacé
8 Beach Grill
(see 7) Créole Arts Café
9 Effet Mer
(see 9) Flamingo Beach Bar
10 La Chaudière
11 Le Bambou
12 Le Refuge de l'Aileron
13 Snack La Roxelane

DRINKING & NIGHTLIFE
14 Distillerie Depaz
15 Distillerie JM

A Sleepy Volcano & Hidden Falls

HIKING MONT PELÉE AND LES GORGES DE LA FALAISE

Mont Pelée is an active volcano that erupted on May 8, 1902, destroying then-capital St-Pierre and irreparably changing the island's topography and history. Today, nature lovers flock to Mont Pelée because it's the island's premier hiking destination for scenic trails and incomparable panoramas. The difficulty of the routes varies, starting with the most popular one, **L'Aileron**, which hikers can complete in a four-hour round-trip trek. It takes two hours to finish the moderate **Grande Savane** hike, which includes sections along ridgelines and culminates in a fantastic view of St-Pierre. Another moderate hike that will reward you with excellent vistas of the Macouba valley and the island's east coast is the **Morne Macouba** trail, which cuts through a tropical rainforest. The approximately 4½-hour hike begins in **Désiles**. If you want to get the best views, no matter which route you take up the slope, start your ascent first thing in the morning. Unfortunately, Mont Pelée is frequently shrouded in clouds, reducing visibility – but when the haze lifts, the views are outstanding. Remember to pack plenty of water, a hat, rain gear and an extra sweater for good measure.

Another worthwhile hike is to the falls of **Les Gorges de la Falaise**. The gorge is embedded in Ajoupa Bouillon, a mile into a thick cliff-framed forest. Listen for the crash of roaring water as you approach the magnificent waterfalls with gin-clear waters. Pack your hiking boots and follow the signs; a guide is required to ensure your safety throughout the walk, so call ahead of time to iron out the details (+596 696 16 75 22).

BEST BEACH BARS IN CARBET

Flamingo Beach Bar
Enjoy refreshing cocktails or sushi à la carte on La Plage du Coin. €

Effet Mer
Indulge in upscale, locally sourced Caribbean fare or sip a cocktail in the chic lounge. €€

Beach Grill
A large airy terrace on Grande Anse beach with comfortable seating, all facing the sea. €€

All Roads Lead to Rum

AN EDUCATIONAL RUM TOUR

One of Martinique's tiniest and finest distilleries, **Distillerie Depaz**, is located at the base of Mont Pelée on the island's northwest coast. Enjoy a stroll through the well-kept park, a tasting at the founder's château, or a snack break with homemade cake at La Case à Louisette. Learn the ins and outs of rum production by following the information panels along the well-marked route through the distillery. Spoiler alert: the secret to good rum is freshly crushed sugarcane and a three-month-minimum barrel-aging process.

Further north near Macouba, **Distillerie JM** envelops visitors in the din and odor of the rum-making process for a very immersive experience. A free self-guided 30-minute

Distillerie JM

WHERE TO EAT IN GRAND-RIVIÈRE

Le Grill Riverain
Enjoy a meal prepared with fresh ingredients in a well-ventilated setting with a sea view. €

Tante Arlette
Tante Arlette welcomes guests to her casual bistro serving seafood and other regional specialties. €

Le Glacier du Boulevard
Classic flavors and original creations come together to delight adventurous taste buds. €

DAMIEN VERRIER/SHUTTERSTOCK ©

Mont Pelée (p444)

tour takes you past a small sample sugarcane plantation, the impressive machinery for processing the cane, and several other steps before the anticipated tasting.

Exploring Coastal Attractions

VOLCANIC SANDS AND A DISAPPEARING BRIDGE

Resting at the foot of the magnificent cliffs of Grand-Rivière, **La Plage de Sinaï** is the northernmost beach of the island, with panoramic views of Dominica. The volcanic black sands, warm water and a mixture of coconut trees and shrubs enhance its natural beauty. You won't have to fight your way through crowds of people here – spread out your towel and soak in the scenery. Strong currents make the beach unsuitable for children and inexperienced swimmers; don't wander too far from the safety of the beach's edge.

In the island's northeast, **Tombolo de l'Îlet Ste-Marie** is a narrow strip of sand that connects the islet of Ste-Marie to the main island. As part of the phenomenon, the land bridge strengthens for walking, horseback riding and biking to the islet during the Lenten months, then disappears as summer approaches. The *tombolo* currents are strong in the early and later parts of the season, so be careful on the journey.

BEST PLACES FOR A SNACK IN ST-PIERRE

Créole Arts Café
The decor of this restaurant, tea room, delicatessen and art gallery is a Parisian throwback. €

Snack La Roxelane
The proprietor of this colorful snack bar serves small plates of tasty Creole dishes. €

Arhum Glacé
Beat the heat and sample ice cream from a variety of delicious and unique flavors. €

WHERE TO STAY IN ST-PIERRE

Hôtel Villa Saint-Pierre
The waterfront hotel serves free breakfast and is close to several popular restaurants. €€

La Maison Rousse
Located in the Fonds St-Denis hills, this exquisite hideaway is one of Martinique's sweetest escapes. €€

Hôtel de l'Anse
A reasonably priced cluster of airy rooms wedged between Carbet and St-Pierre. €

JVPHOT/SHUTTERSTOCK ©

Le Domaine d'Émeraude

Reconstructing St-Pierre

GONE BUT NOT FORGOTTEN

St-Pierre was once a cosmopolitan city known as *petit Paris* or the 'Little Paris of the West Indies'. The town was rebuilt following Mont Pelée's cataclysmic eruption and is now referred to as 'Little Pompeii', but its tragic past will never be forgotten. You can learn more at the town's **Frank Perret Museum**, which is named after the American volcanologist who founded it and depicts the horrifying destruction. Photos and artifacts from before, during and after the eruption document the lives of St-Pierre's residents. A sobering addition to the collection includes a room dedicated to the victims. Thanks to the preserved records, the room's walls are covered with the names of 7045 people who perished in the 1902 disaster.

BEST PLACES TO EAT IN MORNE ROUGE

Le Bambou
This place is an homage to authentic, hearty and flavorful Creole fare. €

La Chaudière
Delicious gourmet Creole cuisine served in a peaceful and tropical plant-filled garden setting. €

Le Refuge de l'Aileron
This is the highest restaurant in Martinique, perched on the slopes of Mont Pelée. €

Get Lost in Nature

SEE MARTINIQUE'S EXCEPTIONAL BIODIVERSITY

Discover why Martinique is known as 'The Island of Flowers' (L'Ile aux Fleurs) by visiting **Le Domaine d'Émeraude**. The reserve explores the diversity and beauty of the island's flora through an immersive and interactive experience. A well-curated museum provides information about the local fauna and flora (entirely in French). The highlight is the three clearly marked trails, each lasting 15 to 60 minutes. However, if you frequently pause to take in the sights and sounds of the forest as you go, it might take a little longer. Although the terrain is quite hilly and there are lots of steps, all the paths are concrete so it is not difficult to navigate.

GETTING AROUND

The easiest way to get around the island's northern half is to rent a car. While you can certainly find rental options once you arrive on the island, you may find better rates if you book in advance.

SOUTHERN MARTINIQUE

FORT-DE-FRANCE

Southern Martinique

Southern Martinique's coastline is simply stunning, with white-sand beaches extending for miles along the Caribbean Sea's turquoise waters. The gentle lapping of the waves on the shore and fluffy white clouds dotting the azure sky overhead create a calming atmosphere for beachgoers to unwind. With Trois-Îlets and activity hub Pointe du Bout at the forefront, this is unquestionably the island's epicenter of sun-and-sand tourism. Apart from the natural wonders of the greater Trois-Îlets area, visitors can explore a wealth of historical and cultural landmarks. Musée de la Pagerie is the childhood home of Empress Josephine, wife of Napoleon Bonaparte, and La Savane des Esclaves sheds light on the island's identity. Les Anses d'Arlet, with its beautiful coves and sleepy villages, is a more charming and less crowded alternative to the ultra-touristy resort town. The beaches here, Grande Anse and Petite Anse, are well-known favorites among island visitors.

TOP TIP

Try some of the island's signature dishes: *accras de morue* (fritters made with codfish and various seasonings), *colombo* (a curried meat dish seasoned with *colombo* powder), *boudin* (a local sausage), *fricassée de chatrou* (an octopus stew), *dorade grilée* (grilled sea bream) and *féroce d'avocat* (spicy avocado salad).

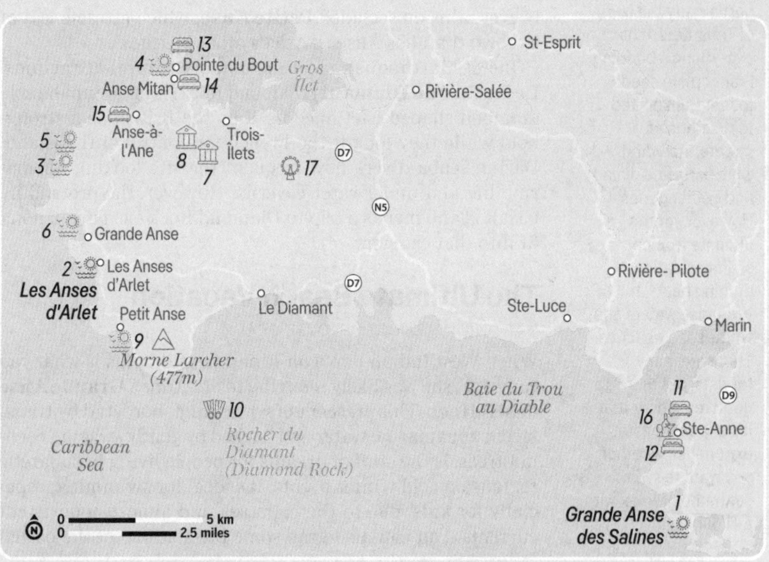

TOP SIGHTS
1 Grande Anse des Salines
2 Les Anses d'Arlet

SIGHTS
3 Anse Dufour
4 Anse Mitan
5 Anse Noire
6 Grande Anse
7 La Savane des Esclaves
8 Musée de la Pagerie
9 Petite Anse

ACTIVITIES
10 Le Rocher du Diamant

SLEEPING
11 Airstream Paradise
12 Anoli Lodges Village
13 Carayou Hotel & Spa
14 Hotel Bambou
15 Le Panoramic Hotel

DRINKING & NIGHTLIFE
16 La Dunette

ENTERTAINMENT
17 Mangofil Martinique

A Bounty of Beaches

CHOOSE YOUR ADVENTURE

One of the most frequently photographed areas in Martinique is **Les Anses d'Arlet**. A long pier connects the charming Église St-Henri to the water, where you can enjoy a 180-degree view of the bay. The coastal town also gets high marks for its chill vibe and serene beaches, making it a popular spot for swimming, snorkeling and sunbathing. The distinctive black sand of **Anse Noire** is the byproduct of volcanic activity in the region. The contrast between the dark sand and the turquoise waters of the Caribbean Sea is arresting. The rich seabed, replete with sponges, tropical fish, turtles and a variety of sea creatures, is reason enough to descend the 130-plus steps from the parking lot to the beach. A few hundred meters away, **Anse Dufour** is also popular with snorkelers and divers. This area is fantastic for watching sea turtles, especially green sea turtles. They are plentiful and the bay's primary draw, but remember to respect the ecosystem by not disturbing or touching the turtles. Despite its close proximity to Anse Noire, Anse Dufour's sand is a brilliant blond due to the erosion of shells and corals. **Grande Anse** is a stretch of white sand and calm water that has maintained its purity despite being a popular tourist destination. It's the largest beach in Les Anses d'Arlet and allows unobstructed views of Le Rocher du Diamant. It hardly ever rains on secluded **Petite Anse**, which attracts less of a crowd than Les Anses d'Arlet's other beaches.

One of Martinique's most memorable natural attractions, **Le Rocher du Diamant** (Diamond Rock) is an uninhabitable diamond-shaped islet once used by the British as a stronghold while they fought the French for control of the island. Daring scuba divers now frequent the site looking for marine life and underwater caverns. However, the protruding basalt island merits a trip to Diamond Rock even if you don't fit into that category.

WHY I LOVE SOUTHERN MARTINIQUE

Nasha Smith, writer

It takes less than two hours to sail from St Lucia to Martinique, and I've done it many times over the years. Even though I adore the buzz of Fort-de-France, my favorite part of the island is the southern region, particularly the town of Trois-Îlets. It has everything a budding Francophile needs to feel transported to the Parisian streets, including wine bars, fine dining and boulangeries. However, for the ultimate tropical sailing vacation, nothing beats its turquoise waters and white-sand beaches. There are many tourists, but there's a good reason for that. It's a great coastal experience whether you want to swim, sunbathe or relax with a Ti'punch.

The Ultimate Beach Vacation

MARTINIQUE'S MOST BELOVED BEACH

When West Indian pop icon Rihanna said, 'This is what you came for', she was likely referring to Ste-Anne's **Grande Anse des Salines**. This crescent of white sand, bordered by translucent aquamarine water and backed by gently swaying coconut trees, is the stuff of dreams for people living in subarctic regions on cold winter nights. It's ideal for swimming, especially for kids, due to the calm sea and almost nonexistent currents. You can also grab some bites at one of the casual

WHERE TO EAT IN LES ANSES D'ARLET

L'Escale
Excellent musical performances and a rotating menu of innovative dishes. €€

Snack Frédo
Unassuming but welcoming, it's perfect for a laid-back meal and some Ti' punch. €

L'Oasis
Exceptional hospitality and delicious, beautifully plated food; situated close to the beach. €€

EL GRECO 1973/SHUTTERSTOCK ©

Grande Anse des Salines

restaurants nearby. A popular beach like this one is bound to get busy, but if you walk out to the corners, you should be able to carve out some peace.

Tracing the Past in Trois-Îlets

THE ISLAND'S ANCESTORS AND ROYAL BEGINNINGS

It's easy to forget the region's history of slavery amid the Caribbean's idyllic beaches and exotic drinks, but in Martinique, public spaces and museums commemorate the stories. Visit **La Savane des Esclaves**, a living museum dedicated to preserving the history of the Caribbean's ignoble era with replicas of Maroon villages, sculptures and murals. Aside from the harrowing tales, the site also features an exhibition about the indigenous peoples who originally inhabited the Caribbean islands and displays of herbs, fruits, vegetables and medicinal plants native to the region. The guided tours are typically in French, but written versions are available in multiple languages.

An unassuming cottage in Trois-Îlets, **Musée de la Pagerie** has a rich royal history that belies its modest exterior. The museum was Marie-Josèphe-Rose Tascher de la Pagerie's childhood home. She is better known to the world as Napoleon's wife, Empress Joséphine de Beauharnais. Paintings,

BEST PLACES TO STAY IN STE-ANNE

La Dunette
A hotel that caters to families and places all of Ste-Anne's attractions within easy reach. €€

Airstream Paradise
The park's collection of restored Airstream travel trailers makes for an out-of-the-ordinary stay. €€

Anoli Lodges Village
Twenty-one Balinese-style lodges with a stunning view of the Caribbean Sea and the Diamond Rock. €€

WHERE TO EAT IN TROIS-ÎLETS

La Petite Crêperie
Delicious Breton crêpes with inventive flavor combinations and refreshing cocktails right on the bay. €

Ti Case
Treat yourself to an upscale dining experience featuring Creole and metropolitan fusion cuisine. €€

La Mandoline
Superb traditional French meals prepared with a lot of imagination and high-quality local ingredients. €€

BEST PLACES TO STAY IN TROIS-ÎLETS

Le Panoramic Hotel
An impressive location with 36 fully equipped rooms, bay views and a tropical garden setting. €€

Carayou Hotel & Spa
Situated in a tropical garden at Pointe du Bout, this complex has 207 rooms with sea or garden views. €€

Hotel Bambou
Charming bungalow rooms, a trendy cocktail bar, buffet dining and direct access to the beach. €€€

CLAUDIO306/SHUTTERSTOCK ©

Anse Mitan

sculptures and even Napoleon's handwritten love letters to Joséphine are just some of the Napoleonic-era artifacts that can be seen here, along with the young empress' maiden bed. There is a beautiful garden on the property where hummingbirds flit from flower to flower.

Leisure Time in Trois-Îlets

FOR BEACH LOVERS AND THRILL-SEEKERS

A slender strand of delicate white sand and clear, placid waters are the hallmarks of **Anse Mitan**, at the northern tip of Trois-Îlets. Crossing the bay from Fort-de-France to Anse Mitan via ferry is very easy, so this is not the most tranquil area. However, there are a lot of useful amenities, restaurants and bars close by. Moreover, Fort-de-France looks stunning from the beach.

To the southeast of town, **Mangofil Martinique** is an exhilarating adventure park that caters to both thrill-seekers and nature lovers with its wide variety of outdoor activities and attractions. Visitors can explore the park's lush foliage while traversing treetop trails on suspended bridges, zip lines and rope courses. Activities include mini-golf, bungy catapult, parkour and motorsports. Mangofil's flourishing plant life fully immerses guests in the island's thriving biodiversity.

GETTING AROUND

Instead of paying for expensive taxi rides, fighting through traffic and looking for a parking spot, take the *vedette* (ferry) between Fort-de-France and the various towns in the southern region.

CHRIS ALLAN/SHUTTERSTOCK ©

Arriving

Aimé Césaire International Airport is the only airport in Martinique, but cruises and ferries also frequent the French Caribbean island. The busiest time is from December to April, which also happens to be the island's dry season. Expect slightly busier restaurants and beaches during these months, as well as higher flight and hotel costs.

By Air

Aimé Césaire International Airport is a 15-minute drive east of Fort-de-France in the village of Lamentin. Flights to Martinique typically require a stopover on a neighboring island; there are few nonstop flights from the US. However, there are direct flights from Paris and Montréal to Fort-de-France.

By Boat

L'Express des Îles operates a ferry service from Dominica, Guadeloupe and St Lucia to Martinique multiple times a week. It can take anywhere from one to 4½ hours, depending on the port of departure. The fast catamaran vessels can accommodate 360 to 420 passengers.

Money

Currency: euro (€)

CASH

Martinique is one of France's overseas territories, so the euro is the local currency. Some businesses accept US dollars, but visitors should still have some euros on hand. Bank-operated 24-hour ATMs (DABs or *distributeurs automatiques de billets*) dispensing euros are found throughout Martinique. If you need to change some foreign currency, visit the nearest *bureau de change* (currency exchange office).

DIGITAL PAYMENTS

Paylib is a digital payment service offered by the main French banks. It allows users to make online purchases and in-store payments using their mobile phones or computers and is available wherever contactless payment is accepted.

CREDIT CARDS

Visa and Mastercard are widely accepted, but only a few merchants accept American Express or Discover cards. A few local businesses, especially the smaller ones, may not have a credit card machine, so be sure to get some cash for convenience.

PUERTO RICO

NATURAL WONDERS, SLOW-ROASTED IN SUNSHINE

Sugary beaches, sizzling pork and salsa beats, certainly – but it's the Boricua spirit that's really responsible for this archipelago's enduring allure.

Palm-fringed coastlines and cloud-shrouded mountain peaks; the scent of gold-fried fritters and the infectious beat of *bomba*. There's a reason it's called *La Isla del Encanto* (The Island of Enchantment). Puerto Rico might be the smallest island of the Greater Antilles, but it packs tons of Caribbean charm into every inch. Between diamond-dusted beaches and gushing jungle waterfalls lay centuries-old cities and rum-soaked *malécons* (main streets) – the postcard-perfect destination for tropical vacations.

While it's possible to spend an entire trip sipping piña coladas at seaside resorts, the heart of Puerto Rico beats beyond the hotel walls. Here, you'll experience a culture influenced by indigenous Taíno roots, Spanish colonization, African enslavement and American control. Pain and suffering color the island's history, and resilience is a cornerstone of life. Despite natural disasters like Hurricane Maria and an ongoing recession, the people here remain strong, turning challenges into opportunities for change.

Street artists in San Juan have transformed blocks of rundown buildings into open-air galleries. Farmers across the island are planting seeds for an agricultural revolution. Ancient Taíno traditions live on in the Central Mountains, and settlements in the northeast burst with Afro–Puerto Rican pride.

Join locals eating pork slabs at street-side *chinchorros* (food kiosks) or dancing salsa at fiery clubs. You'll soon find that it's the Boricuas (the Taíno-inspired name for Puerto Ricans) who make this island most enchanting.

THE MAIN AREAS

SAN JUAN
Puerto Rico's historic, cultured capital. p458

RÍO GRANDE
Home of a prized tropical rainforest. p465

VIEQUES
Laid-back islands off the mainland. p470

PONCE
Rich history and creative cuisine. p476

SUDARSHAN MONDAL/SHUTTERSTOCK ©

Above: Vieques (p470); Left: Isla Verde (p463)

JAYUYA
Hiking, coffee and Taíno culture.
p484

UTUADO
River excursions and ancient petroglyphs. p488

RINCÓN
The Caribbean's top surf spot.
p493

Find Your Way

Puerto Rico is an archipelago, with over 100 islands, islets and cays dotting the mainland's perimeter – a jewel of pearl-white beaches and emerald mountains. Seeing it all requires a mix of driving, boating and walking.

Jayuya, p484

Spot Taíno petroglyphs along the Río Saliente and crest high peaks on trails similar to El Yunque's; sample homegrown brews at the abounding coffee haciendas.

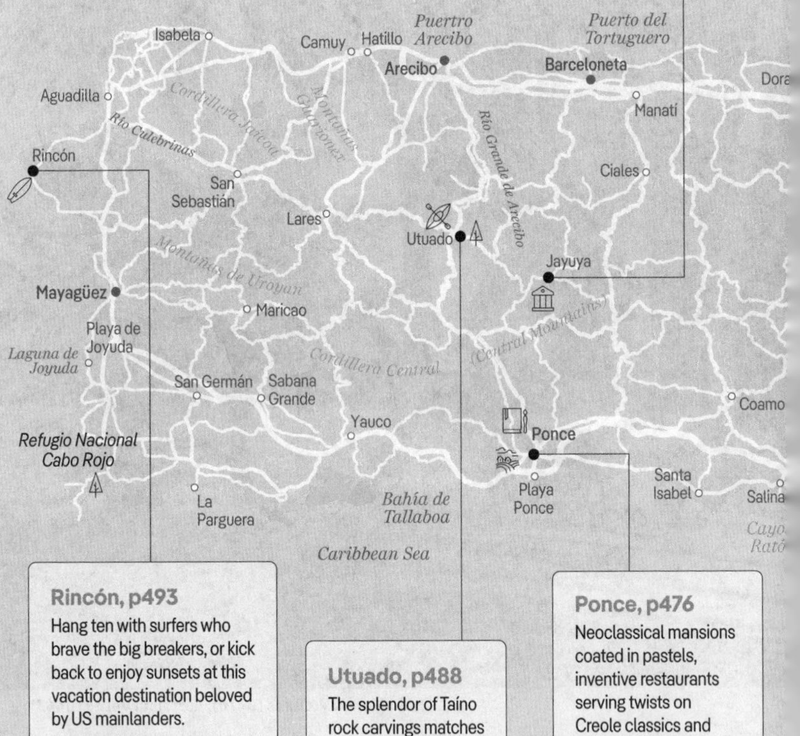

Puertro Arecibo
Puerto del Tortuguero
Isabela
Camuy
Hatillo
Arecibo
Barceloneta
Dora
Aguadilla
Manatí
Cordillera Jaicoa
Montañas Guarionex
Río Culebrinas
Río Grande de Arecibo
Rincón
Ciales
San Sebastián
Lares
Utuado
Jayuya
Montañas de Uroyan
Mayagüez
Maricao
(Central Mountains)
Playa de Joyuda
Laguna de Joyuda
Cordillera Central
San Germán
Sabana Grande
Coamo
Yauco
Ponce
Refugio Nacional Cabo Rojo
Santa Isabel
Playa Ponce
Salina
La Parguera
Bahía de Tallaboa
Cayo Rató
Caribbean Sea

Rincón, p493

Hang ten with surfers who brave the big breakers, or kick back to enjoy sunsets at this vacation destination beloved by US mainlanders.

Utuado, p488

The splendor of Taíno rock carvings matches the superior collection of limestone caves and swimming holes sprinkled around this karst landscape.

Ponce, p476

Neoclassical mansions coated in pastels, inventive restaurants serving twists on Creole classics and historic sites honoring indigenous heritage: it's called the 'Pearl of the South' for a reason.

San Juan, p458

From Old San Juan's cobblestone streets to industrial Santurce's graffiti-strewn blocks, Puerto Rico's biggest city is glamorous, gritty and on the cutting edge.

Río Grande, p465

Lace up your hiking boots before scaling the mountains of El Yunque National Rainforest, then soak your feet in the ocean that laps the north coast's beaches.

Vieques, p470

Leave the stress of urban life behind on these easy-breezy islands, where tropical fish, aquatic birds and semi-wild horses outnumber people.

CAR

Exploring the island is best with your own set of wheels. In most places, driving is the only way to get around. Urban congestion can be hairy and rural roads harrowing, so plan for some time to decompress after long stretches in the car.

TAXI/RIDESHARE

There's no need for a car rental if you're staying in San Juan, the capital. Taxis are ubiquitous and Uber is accessible. Just don't expect car services to act as chauffeurs outside the city – they're either super expensive or hard to find.

BOAT/FERRY

Reaching the islands of Vieques and Culebra requires a ferry ride from Ceiba (unless you decide to fly). To reach the other isles and cays, charter a boat, rent a skiff or consider kayaking.

Plan Your Time

After seeing the major sights of San Juan, venture to the tiny sand-swept towns and remote mountain enclaves where Puerto Rico's heart beats loudest.

BOOGICH/GETTY IMAGES ©

El Yunque National Rainforest (p466)

A Long Weekend

- Experience quintessential Puerto Rico by sticking to **San Juan** (p458) and its verdant surroundings. Stroll around Old San Juan's cobblestone streets to admire Crayola-colored architecture and imposing Spanish forts.
- Join the city's cool crowd in **Santurce** (p460) by dining at food-truck parks and imbibing at bars blaring reggaeton.
- Budget at least one day to summit the peaks and swim in the waterfalls around **El Yunque National Rainforest** (p466).
- After working up an appetite on the trails, drive to **Kioskos de Luquillo** (p469) and wolf down fritters for a taste of the simple life, sand beneath your feet.

Seasonal Highlights

Caribbean breezes might be most popular in winter, but Puerto Rico delights year-round with a perpetually packed calendar of events. There's always a reason to celebrate life on *La Isla*.

JANUARY

Christmas continues into January, bookended by parties celebrating **Día de Los Reyes** and San Juan's **Fiestas de la Calle San Sebastián**.

FEBRUARY

Carnaval Ponceño turns Ponce into a Mardi Gras madhouse, with ***vejigantes*** (demons) taunting crowds behind papier-mâché masks.

MARCH

Rivers shine like turquoise due to a lack of rain – the ideal time to jump into swimming holes around **El Yunque** (p466).

J ERICK BRAZZAN/SHUTTERSTOCK ©, BOB KRIST/GETTY IMAGES ©, VILINTA GRICIUTE/SHUTTERSTOCK ©

Five Days to Travel Around

- After visiting the capital, drive west with the surfers to see why longboarders love **Rincón** (p493). Ride the waves or walk the nose on big-time breaks at beaches like **Tres Palmas** (p495).

- Next stop is **Refugio Nacional Cabo Rojo** (p496), perched on Puerto Rico's southernmost expanse.

- Spend an afternoon wowing over the pink salt flats and golden cliffs leading to **La Playuela**'s (p497) sun-bleached sands, then zip east to **La Parguera**'s (p480) buzzy *malecón* to see the bioluminescent bay's nightly light show.

- Before returning to San Juan, pause in **Ponce** (p476) to ogle the *criollo Ponceño* architecture around **Plaza Las Delicias** (p478).

A Week or More

- With more time you could journey through the island's adventure-crammed core to experience the majestic Central Mountains: start by climbing into **Cañón de San Cristóbal** (p483), the island's deepest canyon.

- After a day of hiking, kick back in **Ponce** (p476) to try **Don Q** (p479) at the founder's former mansion, followed by a night of upscale dining.

- Brave the vertiginous roads of **Adjuntas** (p491) to find swimming holes like **Charco el Ataúd** (p492), then bop around the karst boulders and petroglyphs of **Cañón Blanco** (p490).

- You can't leave Puerto Rico without a dip, so spend your last day on the beaches of **Luquillo** (p469).

JUNE
Slip on a bathing suit for **Noche de San Juan**, when crowds jump backwards into the ocean for good luck.

JULY
As school lets out, local families cram into southwest hotels around **Cabo Rojo** (p496) and **La Parguera** (p480) for vacation.

NOVEMBER
Jayuya's roots are on full display during the **Festival Nacional Indígena**, featuring traditional food, ceremonies and a 'Miss Taíno' pageant.

DECEMBER
Families gather for **Nochebuena** (Christmas Eve) to snack on ***lechón*** (pork), sing ***trullas*** (Christmas songs) and sneak ***pitorro*** (rum).

SAN JUAN

Puerto Rico's capital is a patchwork of indigenous culture, imperial history and modern grit, stitched together by 16th-century cobblestone streets and high-rise hotels overlooking silky strips of sand.

Established by the Spanish in 1521 on a largely deserted peninsula, the city started as a military outpost – evident in the stately fortresses framing Old San Juan's pastel-painted buildings. After the US took control in 1898, San Juan became the island's primary port, and by the mid-20th century, rapid industrialization caused the population to boom. Highways sprouted like tentacles to accommodate the growth, eventually strangling the city as industries died in the coming decades.

But in San Juan, quick reinvention has been critical to its survival. Derelict buildings are now canvases for colorful murals. Old factories serve as sanctuaries for trendsetting food and music scenes. Despite a relentless recession, the city remains fearless – making it one of the Caribbean's most lively destinations.

TOP TIP

San Juan might *look* like a walkable city, but at 77 sq miles, getting around requires a combination of walking and driving (or taking taxis). Apps like Skootel and other scooter rental services are available between Old San Juan, Condado, Miramar and Ocean Park and are a low-cost alternative for zipping between neighborhoods.

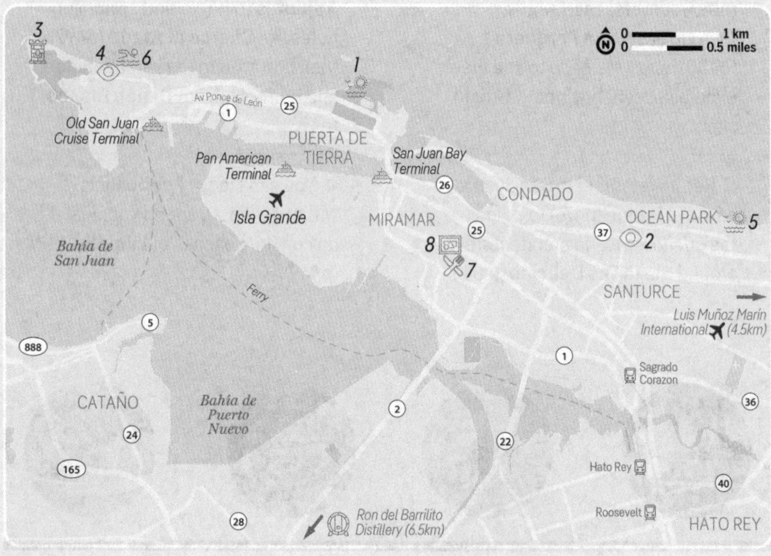

SIGHTS
1 Balneario El Escambrón
2 Calle Loíza
3 Castillo San Felipe del Morro
4 La Perla
5 Playa Ocean Park

ACTIVITIES, COURSES & TOURS
6 El Bowl

EATING
7 Esquina Watusi

DRINKING & NIGHTLIFE
8 Calle Cerra

Castillo San Felipe del Morro

TIME FOR A DRINK?

Jump-start your morning with an espresso or *cortadito* (espresso with steamed milk). The Spanish introduced coffee here in the 18th century, and it quickly became an island staple – it was even endorsed by the Vatican.

Cool off in the afternoon with **Malta**, a non-alcoholic beverage brewed with barley. Prefer a higher ABV? **Medalla Light** goes down like water, but for complex brews, try artisanal ales from local companies like **Ocean Lab Brewing Co.** When the sun goes down, **Don Q** comes out. Puerto Rico is the world's largest rum producer, and this smooth sipper is top-shelf. Enjoy it solo or in sweet-tooth cocktails like the piña colada, invented in San Juan in the 1950s.

A Sentry's Perspective

HISTORIC RAMPARTS WITH SWEEPING VIEWS

The six-level **Castillo San Felipe del Morro** is an impressive feat of military engineering, constructed over 250 years (between 1539 and 1790) along the turbulent Atlantic Ocean. It guarded the city from pirates and other conquerors for centuries of Spanish rule, then served as a US military base during WWI and WWII.

Wear comfortable shoes to wander around the steep ramps, spiral staircases, artillery tunnels, dungeons and portholes, just as soldiers once patrolled and observed the churning waters below. Don't miss the rooftop ramparts, where it's possible to see the city spilling out before you. On weekends, join families and their kite-flying kids to picnic on the green fields outside the fort.

The Taste of Puerto Rican Excellence

REFINING THE CRAFT SINCE 1880

Ask a Puerto Rican to pull out a special bottle of rum from their cabinet, and most will show you a bottle of Ron del Barrilito. The rum's particular color and flavor come from

BAR HOPPING ON CALLE SAN SEBASTIÁN

La Factoría
A labyrinth of six bars buzzing with salsa music where world-class mixologists craft fruity cocktails. **$$**

La Taberna Lúpulo
Local and international brews served alongside greasy bar food underneath soaring beamed ceilings. **$$**

La Sombrilla Rosa
An LGBTIQ+ centric hang for cheap beer and reggaeton tunes that spill out onto cobblestone streets. **$**

PHOTO SPIRIT/SHUTTERSTOCK ©

La Perla

BEACH BUMMING

Drive east of San Juan to **Isla Verde** (p463), where the only problem you'll encounter is deciding which beautiful beach is right for you.

FUEL UP AT FOOD TRUCKS

Meals in Puerto Rico aren't always centered around rice, beans and delectable pork. New and established chefs at **Lote 23**, a food truck park in the middle of Santurce, serve everything from Mexican food at La Neta Urban Tacos to creative vegan dishes at Malanga and fried chicken at The Hen House. Special events and live music occasionally add a festive flare.

For more food-truck fare, head to the **Miramar Food Truck Park**, where you can gorge yourself on dumplings, bubble tea and poke bowls while hanging out at picnic tables under the sun.

its aging process in cognac barrels, brought directly from France to Hacienda Santa Ana, where the rum is produced.

Located in Bayamón – a 20 to 25-minute drive from Old San Juan – Hacienda Santa Ana, home of the **Ron del Barrilito Distillery**, offers one of the best tours for learning about small-batch rum production. Whether you choose the tasting, mixology or history tour, end at the Bar del Barrilito, where bartenders prepare excellent rum cocktails, including a dreamy piña colada and the Bayamón Mule.

Dip in the Atlantic

TREAT YOURSELF TO THE BEACH

San Juan's most splendid public beach is **Balneario El Escambrón**, a swath of golden sand between Old San Juan and Condado. Walk east of the palm-shaded shore to see the remnants of a 17th-century Spanish fort.

Playa Ocean Park is at its finest in the morning, with few crowds and plenty of places to set down a blanket and bask in the bright sun. It's a 10-minute walk from **Calle Loíza**, a hip strip for shopping and dining. Heads up: this beach is known to have rip currents. Make sure you check weather and government advisories regarding tide conditions before attempting to swim.

WHERE TO EAT CRIOLLO IN SAN JUAN

Ruben's Café
This neighborhood pillar has delectible *mangú* (mashed plantain) and *carne frita* (fried pork). **$$**

La Alcapurria Quemá
Its namesake yucca-root-and-plantain fritter is the star, but its other Boricua staples are must-haves. **$$**

Asere Cubano Kitchen and Bar
With a terrace overlooking the plaza, this place will make you feel like you're in Havana. **$$$**

A Different Side of San Juan

THE CITY BEYOND THE WALLS

The world first met **La Perla** when its paradisiac boardwalk, precariously close to the treacherous Atlantic tide, was immortalized by pop star Luis Fonsi and reggaeton king Daddy Yankee in 2017's 'Despacito.' The colorful houses, snaking alleyways and welcoming community make for a perfect afternoon hang. But it wasn't always this way.

La Perla's oceanside location was established in the 19th century by enslaved people and servants forbidden to live inside San Juan's citadel walls. Government neglect and discriminatory socio-economic policies, including the US government's Operation Bootstrap in the 20th century, have kept the community stuck in poverty for generations.

Through it all, the resilience of the community is undeniable. Taking advantage of the tourism boom brought by 'Despacito,' La Perla boasts one of the coolest public art projects on the island. Murals decorate bars, houses, plazas and derelict buildings, painted by local and international artists celebrating the history of salsa and some of La Perla's beloved public figures. On weekends, the *malecón* – where you can take a picture with the 'I Love La Perla' sign – comes alive with *bomba* music and dancing. If you're lucky, you might even catch **El Bowl** (a seaside pool) filled with water and open for swimming.

Santurce's Outdoor Art Gallery

SELF-GUIDED MURAL TOURS

El Gandul and neighboring Tras Talleres are two of **Santurce**'s historic sub-*barrios,* both industrial epicenters of San Juan in the mid-20th century known for agriculture and railroad mechanics. But when their industries tanked, the areas started to crumble and the region became known as a no-man's-land.

Then, around 2010, artists began taking it upon themselves to spruce up forgotten buildings, transforming them into a public art-and-history project. Today, walls along streets like **Calle Cerra** serve as giant canvases for expert muralists who tell stories of the neighborhood's past in paint. Walk around the area to see works by world-renowned street artists like Alexis Bousquet, Pun 18 and Vero Rivera. Extra points if you can find Bikismo's hyperrealistic chrome rabbit.

After walking around the outdoor art gallery, head to **Esquina Watusi** to enjoy an authentic *chinchorro* (food kiosk) experience – Medalla Light, music and all. If you're interested in guided tours, book an experience with the Art Walk PR.

SUPERIOR SPRAY PAINT

The most famous murals along La Perla's promenade are those honoring musical heroes. The distinctive grayscale artworks are made by Peruvian muralist **Alexis Abel Villanueva Puente** (@elsalsadklle). You can follow the story for each mural on Instagram (@lascarasdelaperlapr).

If you're serious about street art, consider a trip to **Yauco**, a south coast town terraced in the hills above Guánica, and a two-hour drive from San Juan. Thanks to **Yaucromatic**, an urban paint project that started in 2017, over 50 murals have transformed once-drab walls into picture-perfect eye-poppers. Beyond their selfie-snapping allure, each mural holds a key to Puerto Rico's culture, with references to local food, fauna, heroes and history.

GETTING AROUND

If you're staying in San Juan proper and don't intend to leave the city, taxis and Ubers can usher you around. Walking is best if you're staying in Condado and Old San Juan – both neighborhoods are compact and easy to explore on foot, but avoid driving around Old San Juan, as parking is a hassle. If you're planning on day trips to other areas of the island, consider renting a car.

San Juan
Isla Verde
Piñones
Cayey

Beyond San Juan

Skip along the coastline's splendid white sands or drive into the mountains to dine on slow-roasted delicacies.

Head east of San Juan for Isla Verde, a strip of boutique hotels facing wide beaches that lure travelers as soon as they land at SJU. Further afield is Piñones, a seaside community with kiosks hocking snacks and crafts central to Afro–Puerto Rican and indigenous culture.

For gastronomes, consider trading the beach for Cayey, unofficial kitchen of the Central Mountains. Barbecue smoke from Guavate's roadside *chinchorros* beckon drivers to pull over for Creole classics, while a mix of upstarts straight from San Juan add new-age spice to the regional restaurant scene. This might be the gateway to *jíbaro* (country people) country, but it's still bursting with modern flavor. Plan on spending at least half a day here.

TOP TIP

Isla Verde and Piñones are accessible via taxi or rideshare from San Juan, but you'll need a car for Cayey.

PHOTO SPIRIT/SHUTTERSTOCK ©

Piñones

ISRAEL PABON/SHUTTERSTOCK ©

Isla Verde

Beach Day Bliss

PICK THE PERFECT PLAYA

The number of inviting beaches between **Isla Verde** and **Piñones** can be overwhelming – walk along the coast and one sandy expanse seems to blow into the next. But each shoreline has a distinct personality, and to find your ideal spot, it's essential to know the basics.

Playa Isla Verde, just 15 minutes outside San Juan and a quick drive from SJU, is a tourist magnet split into three separate beaches. **Balneario de Carolina** (Carolina Public Beach) is an excellent option if you're traveling with children, with facilities like bathrooms, showers and gazebos. **El Alambique** is the beach closest to San Juan, perfect for sunbathing. Residential buildings and hotels block some of the entrances, but there are public passages – like the one on Calle José Tartak – that will get you straight to the sand. **Pine Grove Beach** is a quiet area with a sheltered sandbar and consistent breaks beloved by local surfers; you can find street parking on Calle Violeta.

In Piñones, **La Pocita** is a cool wading pool created by a seawall. Park across the street, set up some chairs along the shoreline and spend a day dipping in the shallow water and dining on finger food from nearby *chinchorros*. Head east, and you'll eventually reach **Playa Vacía Talega** – a crescent beach backed by a seagrape forest. This spot tends to get crowded on weekends, but if you follow trails heading east, you'll find solitude among distant coral rocks and caves.

ALIEN BEAUTY

It's easy to spot the **African tulip tree**, native to the continent's tropical dry forests and brought here for ornamentation: lipstick-red petals reach above the forest canopy to capture all the sunlight and rain they can swallow. Economic upheaval after WWII caused a decline in agricultural activity on the island, spurring a mass migration of Puerto Ricans to the US mainland. Abandoned farmland was quickly colonized by the African tulip trees, effectively reforesting the land. The trees are both a blessing and a curse – a truth captured in its nickname, *meaíto*, which means 'little pisser.' Squeeze the bud and water shoots out – delight for the pisser, aggravation for the pissed.

WHERE TO HAVE CHEAP EATS IN PIÑONES

Donde Olga
Amazing octopus salad, *alcapurria* fritters (fried, meat-stuffed plantains) and drinks overlooking the bay. **$**

Kiosko El Boricua
Arrive early – lines can get long for these hand-made empanadillas and fritters, made fresh. **$**

Kiosko La Comay
Patrons describe this restaurant's *arroz con jueyes* (rice and crab) as heavenly. **$**

Lechón (suckling pig), Guavate

WHY I LOVE CAYEY

Crystal Diaz, Cayey-based owner of the culinary farm and lodge, El Pretexto, on her municipality's many charms:

I decided to live in Cayey for the weather. It's breezy and, temperature-wise, there's a difference from the coast. It's only one hour from San Juan, so there's a rural-modern mix of families who have been here forever and younger people who decided to leave the city and start a new life. This is also the highest elevation along the highway linking San Juan and Ponce – you get amazing views of the southern coastline. Take advantage of the lush green spaces and traditional food. At night, look up to see some of Puerto Rico's starriest skies.

Spit-Roasted Road Trip

IT'S A LECHONERA PORK PARTY

Chinchorro-hopping goes whole hog in Guavate, a tiny *barrio* (neighborhood) in the municipality of **Cayey**, where cars create a pork-fiend processional along Rte 184. The road is better known as **La Ruta del Lechón**, or 'Pork Highway' – a serpentine strip lined with *lechoneras*. These open-air, cantina-style restaurants, famous for slow-roasting whole pigs over hot coals, serve more than food – they also deliver religious experiences. The line of hungry visitors? A congregation. The occasional live band? A boisterous church choir. The machete maverick behind the counter, carving tender meat like Carrara marble? A priest of pork. Communion comes in a styrofoam box crammed with hearty helpings of traditional island cuisine. La Ruta del Lechón is open daily, but it's best on weekend afternoons, when crowds stuff the highway snout-to-tail, stopping whenever the sounds of salsa or the scent of barbecue pique their palate's interest.

If driving from San Juan, start at **Lechonera Los Amigos**. It's tempting to overdo it on *pernil* (pork shoulder) and *morcilla* (blood sausage) – but pace yourself. This is a marathon, not a sprint. **Lechonera El Mojito** delivers on its name with fruity versions of its namesake cocktail. Place an order at the front window, then grab a drink while your designated driver waits in line to pick up a heaping pork plate. **Lechonera Los Pinos** is where the party begins. On weekends, a band lures seasoned dancers to strut their stuff on a tiled dance floor. The route's head hog is **Lechonera El Rancho Original**, and not just because of its stream-side gazebo and massive two-floor pavilion – it also claims to be the highway's first-ever *lechonera*.

DISHES WORTH DRIVING FOR

Bacoa Finca + Fogón
Local farms and fisherfolk provide the seasonal ingredients for this hacienda, one hour from San Juan. **$$**

Casa Vieja
The antique-core interior matches the *abuelita*-style 'mountain food' at this rustic Ciales restaurant. **$**

Pa'l Pueblo
Sit plaza-side in Cayey to whistle with whiskey while dining on burgers, tacos and fried delicacies. **$$**

SAN JUAN
Río Grande

RÍO GRANDE

Río Grande is best known as the home of El Yunque National Rainforest – the only tropical rainforest in the US National Forest System. The park covers nearly 29,000 verdant acres, over 10,000 of which sprawl across Río Grande's southern edge. Within the rainforest, you'll find rambling rivers, gushing waterfalls and hiking trails that scale some of the area's highest peaks. On top of the natural beauty, there's plenty of historical pedigree: pre-Columbian petroglyphs and structures built by the US Civilian Conservation Corps in the 1930s dot the landscape.

Head north of El Yunque to explore the Espíritu Santo River Nature Reserve, home to Puerto Rico's only navigable river. Further east, you'll find Las Picuas Beach, with soft golden sand and shallow blue waters.

As for accommodations, visitors can choose between lux hotels, spartan campgrounds and cozy haciendas – or drive in for a day trip from San Juan.

TOP TIP

Instead of paying for expensive tours to visit El Yunque, book your ticket through recreation.gov and explore the area by yourself. Ridesharing apps hardly reach the region – even if you get here, you'll have difficulty finding a ride back – so you're better off renting a car to explore the area.

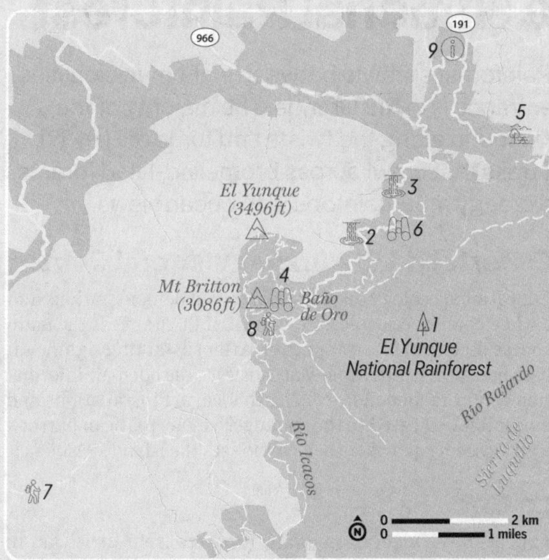

TOP SIGHTS
1 El Yunque National Rainforest

SIGHTS
2 Juan Diego Falls
3 La Coca Falls
4 Mount Britton Tower
5 Puento Roto
6 Yokahú Observation Tower

ACTIVITIES
7 El Toro Wilderness Trail
8 Mount Britton Trailhead

INFORMATION
9 El Portal de El Yunque Visitors' Center

El Yunque National Rainforest
INFINITE_EYE/SHUTTERSTOCK ©

PRACTICALITIES
Scan this QR code for El Yunque's ticket prices and opening hours.

TOP SIGHT

El Yunque National Rainforest

El Yunque National Rainforest sprawls between eight municipalities, but the park's main entrance is in Río Grande. The majority of the park's top sites can be found along the twists and turns of Hwy 191, including 23 miles of trails that crawl across bromeliad-filled forests, babbling brooks and craggy mountaintops with ocean views.

DON'T MISS

- Juan Diego Falls
- La Coca Falls
- El Portal de El Yunque Visitor Center
- Mount Britton Tower
- Yokahú Tower
- Puente Roto
- El Toro Wilderness Trail
- Angelito Trail
- Baño Grande

El Portal de El Yunque Visitors' Center

Educational ecology displays, ranger-led demonstrations and a wheelchair-accessible garden trail: if El Yunque is the main course, El Portal is the appetizer. After sustaining significant damage during Hurricane Maria in 2017, the open-air information center reopened in 2022 with local art installations and an exhibit dedicated to the endangered Puerto Rican parrot – a viridescent squawker that symbolizes the island's resiliency.

La Coca Falls

Expect to see visitors snapping pictures from their cars in front of this 85ft waterfall, which welcomes visitors to El Yunque along Hwy 191 as it begins its steep southern ascent. For those who want a closer look, hike along the trail to the left of the road's barrier until you reach the boulders at the bottom of the cascade. A challenging 3.6-mile path near the falls crosses a slippery section of El Yunque's tabonuco tree forest as it heads to the Río Mameyes.

Juan Diego Falls

Park on the shoulder of Hwy 191 near the 6-mile mark for access to Juan Diego Creek and its sparkling cascades. The very short hike to the falls is steep and covered in tangled roots, but the trail is well-marked and easy to follow. Multiple pools along the path may coax you into taking a cold-water plunge. Getting to the highest cataracts is a muddy mission best attempted by physically fit adventurers.

Mount Britton Trail & Tower

The 0.8-mile ascent to Mount Britton Tower snakes through a forest of sierra palms before disappearing into the mist that hovers above El Yunque. Although visibility here is usually low, an observation deck delights with views of the Atlantic, the Caribbean and the eastern coast when the clouds disappear. The tower, built between 1937 and 1938, is the island's tallest Civilian Conservation Corps structure to be made with stone masonry.

Yokahú Observation Tower

Rising 1575ft above sea level, Torre Yokahú is a prime spot for viewing El Yunque's palo colorado, tabonuco, palm and cloud forests. The tower is 69ft tall, with a spiral staircase leading to an observation deck. On clear days, it's possible to glimpse Puerto Rico's coastline and the Virgin Islands from the top. Although lower than the Mount Britton Tower, there's usually less cloud cover, making this a more consistent location for expansive views.

Puento Roto

Puente Roto, meaning 'Broken Bridge,' refers to a recreation area along the Mameyes River where locals throw weekend barbecues, wade in the water and hop around big riverbank boulders. Unlike some El Yunque swimming holes, this spot requires little hiking, making it an excellent option for families with children.

El Toro Wilderness Trail

Prepare to get dirty on this hike to El Yunque's highest peak (3524ft). Slipping and sliding around the muddy 4.9-mile trail is nearly unavoidable. Lace up your hiking boots, consider walking sticks for extra support and wear long pants to contend with razor grass. The three-hour slog, which starts in the town of Canóvanas, is best suited for experienced hikers, but the 360-degree views from the top can be appreciated by just about anyone – if you can make it that far.

QUICK TOUR

If you're short on time, stick to the northern section of La Mina Recreation Area for a one- or two-hour adventure. With your reservation.gov ticket ready to go, zoom past La Coca Falls and stop at the Yokahú Tower for a panoramic park view. Juan Diego Falls is a two-minute drive south of here, where you can take a short but rewarding trek before leaving.

TOP TIPS

- Book tickets to La Mina Recreational Area (which starts near La Coca Falls) in advance – passes run out during winter's busy season. Tickets are available at recreation.gov.
- If you can't secure a ticket, visit Angelito Trail, Las Paylas and Charco El Hippie, which are free to access.
- Avoid hiking alone and always stay on designated paths – the rainforest has poor cell reception.
- Wear water shoes if you plan on exploring the cascades and rivers.
- Consider bringing a poncho or extra clothes to contend with the rain.
- Rivers are prone to flash flooding. Even on sunny days, stay vigilant.

Río Grande
Luquillo

Beyond Río Grande

After an arduous hike through El Yunque, drive east to Luquillo, where food kiosks, beautiful beaches and bustling bars abound.

Luquillo's most-lauded destination is its same-named beach, a curving shore backed by the Kioskos de Luquillo – a strip of roughly 60 food stands. A perfect weekend afternoon could be spent sampling fried snacks and sipping cocktails from beachfront stalls, then floating for hours in the beach's azure waters. But limiting yourself to Playa Luquillo would be a shame. A diversity of waterfronts throughout the area lend themselves to all kinds of aquatic activities. You could paddle along the Sabana River, watch for wildlife at Playa San Miguel or hang ten at La Pared, the east coast's best surf spot. Sick of the sand? Head inland and you'll eventually enter El Yunque's eastern forests.

TOP TIP

Visiting Playa Luquillo and the Kioskos de Luquillo is free. Avoid expensive tours that offer visits to the area.

Luquillo

FUTURISTMAN/SHUTTERSTOCK ©

La Pared

Beach-Hopping in Luquillo

CROWDED SANDS TO QUIET SHORES

A trip to **Luquillo**, just 10 miles from Río Grande, presents a serious problem for beach bums: with over 12 miles of pristine coastline, how do you choose which sandy strip to visit?

For lazy beach days, find a palm-shaded patch on **Playa Fortuna**, located along Luquillo's western border. If you're looking for something more sceney, stop by the calm-water shores of Playa Luquillo, also known as **La Monserrate**. On weekends, crowds bounce to salsa beats blasting between the beach and the **Kioskos de Luquillo**, where they snack on fritters and sip Medalla Lights. As La Monserrate gives way to **Punta Bandera**, the noise from beachside bars gets overpowered by waves crashing on distant reefs. The water here is shallow, making it easy to walk far into the waves without getting your head wet.

For surfers, the 3–5ft breaks at **La Pared** offer some of the best waves to ride on Puerto Rico's east coast. If you want to hang ten with the pros, take a lesson from a local surfing school (try **Surfing Puerto Rico**) or admire the board show from the shore.

Head east of La Pared for the area's most secluded beaches, located along the coastal forests and mangroves of the Northeast Ecological Corridor. **Playa San Miguel**, a nesting ground for turtles, is the all-natural, laid-back antidote to buzzy La Monserrate – though navigating the dirt road to get here can be challenging for compact cars.

Still unsure where to go? Try playing Goldilocks for the day, stopping at every beach until you find the one that's just right.

LUQUILLO'S BEST BEACH ADVENTURES

Surfing Puerto Rico
Book classes or rent a board from this Luquillo-based surfing school.

Luquillo Flyboards
Live out your superhero fantasy on a 30-minute flyboarding experience at Luquillo Beach.

Puerto Rico Bike Tours and Rentals
Call ahead to rent bikes or join guided tours that zip around Luquillo's beaches.

Sun Capital Paddlesports
Kayak along the Sabana River, located within the Northeast Ecological Corridor Nature Reserve.

Carabalí Rainforest Adventure Park
Gallop on horseback along Luquillo's shoreline to the Mameyes River.

WHERE TO EAT IN LUQUILLO

Vive La Vida Brunch & Waves
This food truck at Playa Costa Azul serves breakfast and brunch with a Puerto Rican twist. **$$**

La Fonda Gourmet
Surf, turf and *comida criolla* (Creole food) classics will fill you up at this La Pared restaurant. **$$**

Kioskos de Luquillo
This strip of food kiosks has everything from Puerto Rican-style finger food to international cuisine.**$$**

VIEQUES

The islands of Vieques and nearby Culebra are two of the most ecologically diverse and culturally unique municipalities in Puerto Rico. Their relative isolation has made them havens for indigenous populations, prizes to be won by international imperialists and, today, vacation destinations for tourists seeking solitude.

Vieques comes from the Taíno word *bieké,* meaning 'small island' – and what it lacks in size, it makes up for with a panoply of magnificent beaches, bountiful wildlife and a history of resilience. Isabel II (pronounced 'Isabel Segunda') is the first sight you get of Vieques when arriving via ferry. This quaint and colorful town serves as the island's capital, filled with enough groceries, bakeries, restaurants and bars to satisfy all cravings.

Most tourists spend their time in Esperanza, a seaside neighborhood along a lovely stretch of shore. Don't be alarmed by all the horses and roosters roaming around – they're semi-wild staples of local life.

TOP TIP

Getting to Vieques requires a combination of car rides and ferries, or plane trips. Once on the island, hailing a cab from the Isabel II ferry dock is easy – taxis and buses are almost always available – or you can rent a scooter or utility vehicle to hop around the beaches and towns.

Esperanza

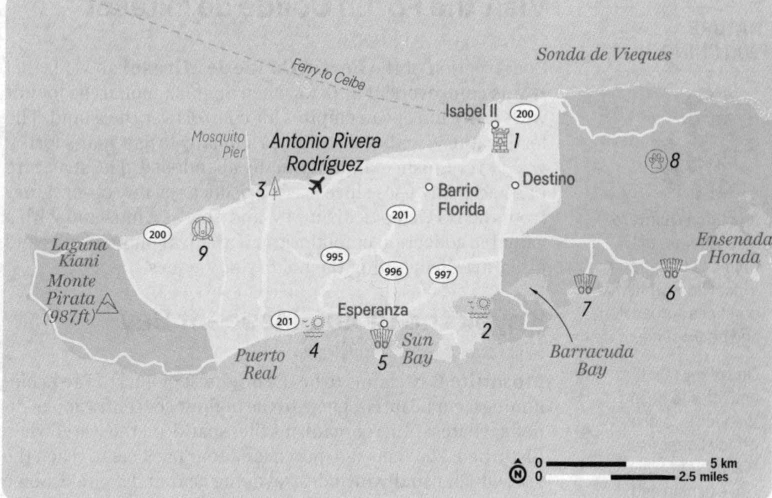

SIGHTS
1 Fortín Conde de Mirasol
2 Mosquito Bay
3 Parque de la Ceiba
4 Playa Negra

ACTIVITIES, COURSES & TOURS
5 Fun Brothers
6 La Chiva
7 Playa Caracas
(see 5) Taino Aqua Adventures

8 Vieques National Wildlife Refuge

DRINKING & NIGHTLIFE
9 Crab Island Rum

Sample Rum at Crab Island

ARTISANAL RUM AND SPECIALTY DRINKS

The first hand-crafted rum distillery on Vieques is helmed by lifelong local Iván Torres Ortíz, who witnessed first-hand the end of military target practice and the removal of US naval bases on the island. In a former Navy yard known as Camp García (you can still see the old barracks and decommissioned military vehicles), Torres Ortíz set up **Crab Island Rum**, a distillery and bar where you can taste liquor infused with orange and coffee.

The operation also grows most of its own produce. Visit the on-site garden to check out the fruit and herbs that might end up in your cocktail. If you're hungry, right in front of the terrace is **La Tabla del Chef**, which has excellent *mofongo* balls (mashed plantains with pork rind), empanadas and corn fritters, among other *criollo* delicacies. You can book a distillery tour and learn about the rum-making process at crabislandrum.com.

OPENING & CLOSING TIMES

One of the potentially frustrating things about Vieques is that most businesses function by demand. If the ferries come in empty, there's a chance that many businesses, including cafes and kiosks, will be closed – even if their operating hours say otherwise. The same goes for public transportation and taxis, so be patient, call ahead and always make alternative plans. Life here runs on island time.

WHERE TO STAY IN VIEQUES

Finca Victoria
A rustic, vegan-forward B&B with morning yoga and an edible garden. **$$$**

El Blok
This modern concrete building is an adults-only boutique hotel with a chic cocktail bar. **$$**

Amapola Beach Inn
This charming guesthouse, home to El Bilí restaurant, has rooms and apartments at reasonable rates. **$$**

NATURE WATCHING

Ana Elisa Quintero is co-director of La Colmena Cimarrona, a local non-profit that practices agroecology and beekeeping.

One of my favorite activities to do in Vieques is to dive off the Esperanza Pier and snorkel. I love fishing and beachcombing at Gallito Beach. Bird-watching there is great, but the waters are not always safe for swimming. La Chiva is a really good hiking trail, but swim with caution. The Mosquito Pier wave break is a cool spot to just sit and fish.

Visit the Fortín Conde de Mirasol

SPANISH FORT TURNED ART MUSEUM

Construction of the **Fortín Conde de Mirasol** above Isabel II was controversial in 1845, when Spanish monarchs fought with other European empires for control over the island. The fortification – with walls planned similarly to San Juan's forts – was never finished and eventually abandoned. The structure has had many uses since – as a prison, a seismic observatory from the US Geological Survey, and now as a museum with a valuable collection of folkloric art, archival photographs and other artifacts telling the history of Vieques.

Kayak the Bioluminescent Bay

GLITTERING WATER AT NIGHT

Mosquito Bay claims to be the brightest of Puerto Rico's bioluminescent beauties, home to the highest concentration of dinoflagellates – microorganisms that sparkle in the water when disturbed. You'll need to purchase a tour package to reach the site, which usually includes kayaking gear and a guide. Some rental companies, like **Taino Aqua Adventures**, have clear kayaks for exploring, making the experience extra magical.

Before you go, freshen up your knowledge on waxing and waning moons. Bright lights dim the shimmering spectacle, and it's best to wait for a new moon to join the paddling party.

Honor a Centuries-Old Tree

THE ISLAND'S RESILIENT ROOTS

The ceiba tree – also known as the kapok or silk-cotton tree – is a sacred symbol for Puerto Ricans, with roots so strong it can withstand relentless storms. At the **Parque de la Ceiba**, you can spot one of these trees, which dates back more than three centuries. In 2019, its flora made a dramatic comeback after getting battered by Hurricane Maria two years prior. The surrounding nature park is best for bird-watching and meditating.

Join a Snorkeling Expedition

FANTASTIC OCEAN FAUNA

With its abundance of isles, cays and beaches, Vieques boasts adventures for underwater enthusiasts of all levels. It's common to find kids and adults alike snorkeling near shore to spot the sea urchins and reefs. Colorful fish abound at **La Chiva** and **Playa Caracas** – both popular places to dip masks in the water.

For deeper diving, book a guided expedition with a rental company, who will lead you to the island's most exceptional snorkel spots. **Fun Brothers** offers DIY and guided options

BEST BEACHES FOR SUNSETS

El Gallito Beach
Pause at this solitary lookout point for the best views of Culebra and Puerto Rico's mainland.

Mosquito Pier
This former US Navy pier is a tranquil spot to watch fiery sunsets on the western coast.

El Malecón La Esperanza
The sunset bathes this sandy strip in mesmerizing golden light around 6pm.

MIKEHOP.FL/SHUTTERSTOCK ©

Fortín Conde de Mirasol

for $20 to $50 per person. Other companies offer tours to idyllic, uninhabited islands offshore.

Climb Down to Playa Negra

SPARKLING VOLCANIC SAND

Looking to trade white-sand beaches for a shimmering black shoreline? Drive down hilly Rte 201 and stop at a marked clearing to park your vehicle. A 20-minute hike from the road leads to **Playa Negra** (Black Beach) – an isolated coastal area with volcanic sand and stunning Caribbean views. Many Viequenses (people from Vieques) refer to this beach as their natural spa: the sands contain magnetic properties that supposedly benefit cardiovascular diseases and joint pain.

You might be tempted to swim after a sandy exfoliation, but use caution. The waters are choppy and the tide swells without warning.

Beach-Hopping in the East

WILD SHORES AND WARM WATERS

Several services, like the Vieques Beach Bus, offer shore-hopping tours within the **Vieques National Wildlife Refuge** – an 18,000-acre collection of coastal lagoons, mangrove wetlands, forest uplands and beaches. If you want to move at your own pace, rent a car for a self-guided excursion – but ensure your vehicle has 4WD before traveling down rough dirt roads. You can also get around by taxi or public van.

Beaches inside the reserve include La Plata, Pata Prieta, Playuela and **Playa Caracas** – a favorite thanks to facilities such as gazebos, showers and umbrella rentals.

PROTECT THE LOCAL LANDSCAPE

Two of the most pressing concerns for longtime Vieques residents are overtourism and gentrification. Government-sponsored tax incentives have created a boom in real-estate sales, most of which are scooped up by outside investors and turned into temporary rentals, leaving residents unable to find affordable housing. When visiting, be mindful of these issues and considerate of Viequense culture: support local businesses and respect the fragile ecosystems around you.

GETTING AROUND

Walking isn't always an option – roads and sidewalks aren't always up to par. Renting a vehicle is the best way to tour at your leisure.

Remember to follow road rules – the island hasn't had a fully functioning hospital since Hurricane Maria, so safety should be extra high priority.

Beyond Vieques

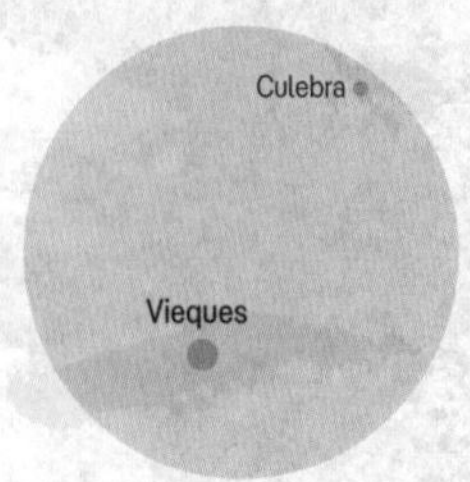

Pearl-white beaches, world-class reefs and ocean as far as the eye can see: Culebra is the postcard picture of Caribbean relaxation.

Culebra has lured a hodgepodge of human inhabitants over the centuries. First, there were the Arawak and Taíno, followed by pirates who hid along the curving coastline during Spain's Caribbean reign. Then, after the US took over in the late 19th century, Culebra became a bombing range for the Navy until locals reclaimed the land in the 1970s. Today, you'll find a mix of full-time beach bums and San Juan weekenders looking to live stress-free.

This isn't the kind of place where you'll find historical landmarks or late-night entertainment – the underwater reefs are more lively than the main town, so enjoy the salty air and dive into the blue. This is your cue to exhale.

TOP TIP

Culebra is off the coast of Fajardo. Take the ferry from Ceiba or catch a plane from SJU or Isla Grande.

Playa Flamenco

Superlative Shores

SHORT HIKES TO STUNNING BAYS

There are many reasons why people call **Playa Flamenco** one of the world's most beautiful beaches – turquoise waters, sugary sands and graffiti-splashed tanks from the island's US Navy days are just a few. There are plenty of amenities, too – bathrooms, food stands, lifeguards and umbrella rentals. (Don't skimp on umbrellas – the sun means serious business and you'll find no shade here.) On weekends, crowds jockey for the best bay-front real estate. Plan a weekday visit so you're not elbowing strangers.

If you're searching for superb snorkeling, take a 20-minute trek to **Playa Carlos Rosario**, or see reefs filled with colorful fish at nearby **Playa Tamarindo**, located on the Luis Peña Channel Natural Reserve.

Swim Through Clear Waters

WILDLIFE AT CAYO LUIS PEÑA

Culebra's **National Wildlife Refuge** covers roughly one-quarter of the island. It serves as a haven for three species of sea turtles and 13 types of nesting seabirds, including the long-winged sooty tern. If you want to swim with marine creatures and gawk at tropical birds, plan a snorkeling trip to **Cayo Luis Peña** – an uninhabited islet within the refuge. The only way to reach the deserted shores is via kayak or water taxi, which must be booked in advance.

Immerse Yourself in Culebra's History

STORIES OF RESILIENCE

Housed in a remodeled military munitions warehouse, the **Museo Histórico de Culebra** showcases the island's culture and ecology. The tiny museum packs quite a punch, highlighting everything from indigenous history to the island's US military occupation and the local struggle to take back the land. Once you're finished, stroll to Culebra's town center, a 20-minute walk away.

THE ART OF WAR

The two tanks at **Playa Flamenco** are reminders of a time when these pristine lands were off-limits to locals. From the early 1900s until 1975, this beach – along with much of the island – was used as a shooting range by the US Navy. Although the military personnel eventually left, their waste remains. Clean-up efforts have moved at a snail's pace, and some beaches and public lands remain closed; the occasional chain-link fence warns trespassers of explosive dangers buried in the sand. As for those rusting war machines, they always seem to have a fresh coat of paint, as graffiti artists regularly tag the hulking battle tanks, turning Culebra's dark past into an idyllic spot for a photo-op.

WHERE TO EAT IN CULEBRA

Dinghy Dock
Fresh seafood and a festive atmosphere; don't miss the frozen chocolate-and-rum Bushwhackers. **$$**

La Lobina Sports Bar
Karaoke bar with pool tables, pub fare and a wraparound deck for lakefront views. **$**

Mamacitas
Excellent seafood and the best skirt steak in town, served in a bohemian tin-roof restaurant. **$$$**

PONCE

With strings of stately plazas covered in neoclassical ornaments, it's no wonder Ponce is known as the *Perla de Sur* (Pearl of the South). At the dawn of the 20th century, Ponce was Puerto Rico's most populous city – a bourgeois metropolis that grew rich from coffee, rum and tobacco production. A mash of European, Caribbean and West African cultures gave birth to music, art and architectural styles that set Ponce apart from the rest of the island.

But after the US invaded Puerto Rico in 1898 and an 1899 hurricane destroyed Ponce's sugarcane fields, Ponce never fully recovered. Today, the city is a curious mix of old-world glamour and working-class grit – its historic district an elegant time capsule; its outskirts a mess of modern strip malls. Stick to the center, and you'll understand why Ponceños remain proud: fantastic museums, inventive restaurants and its hallmark *ponceño criollo* architecture shine like gems.

TOP TIP

Consider flying directly to Ponce if you plan on basing yourself in the south. Non-stop flights from New York City and Orlando, Florida, land at Ponce's Mercedita International Airport. The drive from San Juan is a scenic route along Hwy 52, while Hwy 2 makes the west coast sights easily accessible.

Museo Castillo Serrallés (p479)

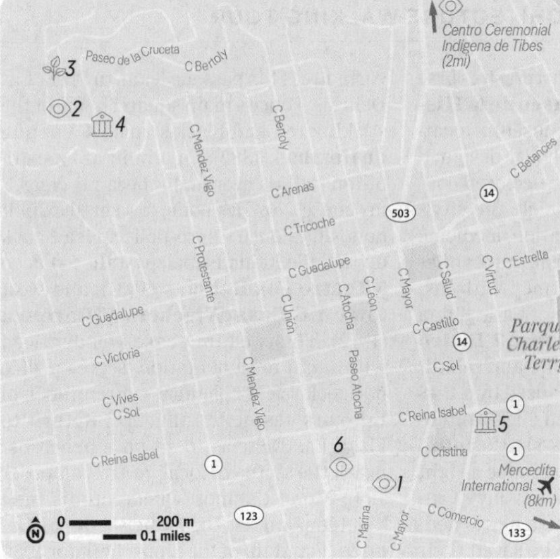

SIGHTS
1 Calle de Amor
2 Cruceta del Vigía
3 Japanese Garden
4 Museo Castillo Serrallés
5 Museo de la Música Puertorriqueña
6 Plaza Las Delicias

Indigenous Beginnings

TAÍNO RUINS AND HISTORY

One of Puerto Rico's most enthralling archaeological sites wasn't uncovered until 1975, when receding flood waters from a tropical storm unearthed the ruins of an ancient ceremonial ground north of Ponce. Now known as the **Centro Ceremonial Indígena de Tibes**, this site prospered from roughly 400 CE to 1000 CE, starting with the Igneri (the area's oldest-recorded inhabitants) and followed by the Taíno.

Begin your tour at the attached museum, filled with artifacts like *cemíes* (deities) and a skeleton found buried in the fetal position – a pre-Taíno tradition. The highlight is an outdoor exhibit exploring indigenous heritage in the Caribbean that serves a searing critique of European colonization.

Outside the museum, a bridge over the Portugués River leads to remnants of seven stone-rimmed *bateyes* (ball courts), two ceremonial plazas and a botanical garden filled with calabash trees, their green gourds hanging like oversized Christmas ornaments. Entrance is free.

BEST PLACES TO DRINK IN PONCE

Velada
Craft cocktails and jazz lend this upscale bar and restaurant old-school sophistication. $$$

Papa Rupe
Suds heads will salivate over the selection of local and imported beers at this small-batch brewery. $

Vistas
Grab a table along the edge of this rooftop restaurant to sip sangria as the sun sets. $$

Gallo Espresso
Sit down street-side with your morning joe at this coffee shop along Plaza Las Delicias. $

Mirrors
Shake your hips to pop anthems at the only LGBTIQ+ bar for miles. $

WHERE TO STAY IN PONCE

Hotel Bélgica
It's chic or shabby, depending on your style – but the neoclassical facade and 20ft ceilings are first-rate. **$$**

Ponce Plaza Hotel and Casino
Ponce's first all-girls school is now a sun-yellow dream where the gals can gamble. **$$**

Meliá Century Hotel
Vintage furniture dipped in bright paint delivers a bit of colonial kitsch near Parque de Bombas. **$$**

ARCHITECTURE WALKING TOUR

Start this walking tour with a crash course in local history at the **1 Museo de la Historia de Ponce**. This free museum, located inside a *ponceño criollo* house designed by Blas Silva in 1911, is a rose-colored confection. Ten galleries chronicle the city's evolution through art, education, medicine and politics. Text is in Spanish; guides offer English-speaking tours. Armed with historical context, head south of Calle Reina Isabel on Calle Mayor Cantera to **2 Teatro la Perla**, constructed in 1864 and rebuilt in 1941 following damage caused by a 1918 earthquake. Although closed due to another earthquake in 2020, its six Corinthian columns stand tall. Next, make a right on **3 Calle Amor** to see artist Javy Cintrón's *Sangre y resistencia* – a mural dedicated to seven Ponceños who saved their city from disaster during the 1899 El Polvorin fire. This passage leads to Plaza Las Delicias, Ponce's main square, home of the striking red-and-black-striped **4 Parque de Bombas** (1882). First built as an exhibition hall, it eventually became Ponce's firehouse. Now, it's home to a small exhibit honoring Ponce's pyro-police. Head back up to Calle Reina Isabel, past the art deco **5 Teatro Fox Delicias** (1931), and west toward **6 Casa Wiechers-Villaronga** (1912). This wedding-cake wonder, iced with floral ornamentation, serves a slice of neoclassical splendor – a reminder of Europe's aesthetic influence. Return to Plaza Las Delicias to sit on a bench beneath the statue of local *danza* composer Juan-Morel Campos. Queue up his tune 'Contémplame' as the **7 Fuente de los Leones** (Fountain of the Lions; built for 1939 New York World's Fair) gushes before you.

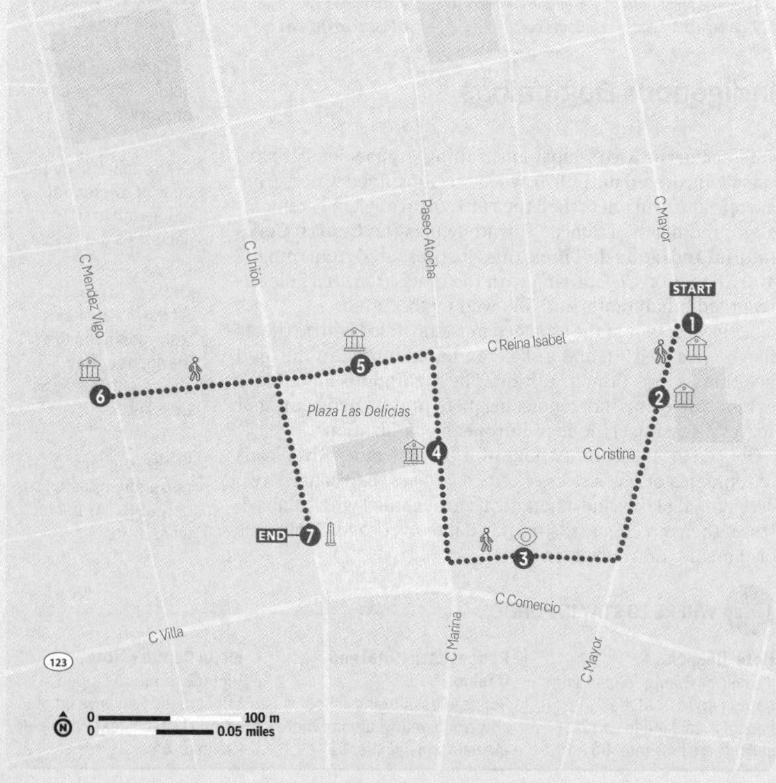

The Don Q Rum Castle

EXPLORE THE SERRALLÉS' MANSION

The four-story Spanish-revival mansion towering atop Cerro del Vigía starkly contrasts with the crumbling buildings and packs of stray dogs below. This is the **Museo Castillo Serrallés**, once home to Ponce's **Don Q** dynasty and now a museum showcasing the Serrallés family legacy.

The home, built between 1930 and 1934, is a decorator's rum-drenched daydream. Almost all of the furniture is original, including Tiffany lamps, hand-carved dining chairs and European glassware. Manicured gardens and breezy balconies along the mansion's south side deliver princely views over Ponce and the Caribbean.

It's easy to get swept up in the fairy-tale fantasy of the fortress, but it's important to remember that the Serrallés family initially built their wealth on the backs of forced labor. In 1872, one year before Spain abolished slavery in Puerto Rico, Juan Eugenio Serrallés (the original Don Q rum baron and head of Castillo Serrallés) had over 100 enslaved people working for him.

After a peek at Puerto Rican royalty, scan the city from the **Cruceta del Vigía**, built above the mansion grounds in 1984 to take the place of a 19th-century lookout used to spot pillaging pirates. Views from this Brutalist cement cross give the Serrallés 'castle' a run for its money. Behind the cross, you'll find a small **Japanese garden** – pagoda, bonsai trees, koi fish and all.

Walking tours of Castillo Serrallés, now owned by the municipality of Ponce, last 45 minutes and cost $15. Entrance to the cross and garden is included. On-site Don Q rum-tasting tours, including a mixology class, cost $60; book tickets at rondonq.com.

From Bomba to Salsa

EXPLORE THE ISLAND'S SONIC SOUL

The history of Puerto Rican music is the history of the island: a clash of African beats, Spanish strings, American jazz and indigenous dance. The **Museo de la Música Puertorriqueña** does a fine job of distilling the complexity of sounds into a single-floor museum, with Spanish-language galleries dedicated to salsa, *bomba y plena* (two folk-music styles with African roots) and *danza* (an elegant Ponce-born musical style similar to a waltz). The museum is due for an update – there's no section showcasing reggaeton, Puerto Rico's most recent musical invention – but it's worth a short visit. The neoclassical building, constructed in 1911, was another home owned by the rum-rich Serrallés clan. Touring the museum is free.

SUNDAYS IN THE SQUARE

Melina Aguilar Colón (@islacaribepr), founder of Ponce-based tour company Isla Caribe, shares a historical tidbit about the Pearl of the South:

In 19th-century Ponce, 'fan language' was the equivalent of Tinder. Instead of swiping right, women walked in circles around Plaza Las Delicias and fanned themselves in particular ways to show if they were single, looking or interested in someone specific. After flirting, couples met along Calle de Amor. This all happened with *danza* music playing in the background. Starting in 1883, *danza* composer Juan-Morel Campos organized a band that gave free concerts every Sunday in the square. The tradition lives on: every Sunday at 6pm, the band plays their romantic soundtrack for adoring crowds.

WHERE TO EAT IN PONCE

Diverso
Cosmopolitan restaurant, cocktail bar or chocolate shop? This expert spot is difficult to label. **$$**

Enlaspapas
Expect leftovers with the stuffed baked potato or burrito from this Plaza Las Delicias food truck. **$**

The Kitchen by Chef Teissonniere
Gilded staircases and low lighting set a classy tone for upscale Caribbean fare. **$$**

Beyond Ponce

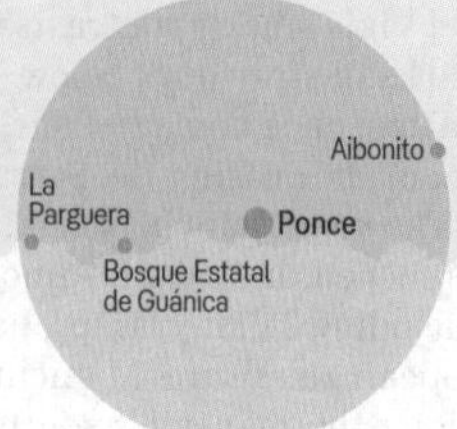

Explore the cacti-packed trails, glittering bays and waterfall-fed swimming holes that wait in the wilderness surrounding Ponce.

Ponce's diverse outskirts give good reason to leave urban life behind. Drive west to reach Bosque Estatal de Guánica, a 10,000-acre United Nations Biosphere Reserve with over 700 types of plants, including 48 endangered species. More than 30 miles of trails weave through dry cactus scrublands, deciduous forests and patches of evergreen.

Further afield is La Parguera, a town that splits itself between gentle surf and rowdy turf. Offshore, tranquil mangrove isles and a vibrant coral reef protect underwater wonders. On land, the town exerts big spring-break energy along its mojito-soaked *malécon*.

Northeast of Ponce lies the island's deepest canyon, ironically located near Puerto Rico's highest-elevated town, Aibonito, which soars around 2000ft above sea level.

TOP TIP

Guánica and La Parguera are reachable via Hwy 2 west of Ponce. The roads to Aibonito are treacherous, so drive in daylight.

Fuerte Caprón

PHOTO SPIRIT/SHUTTERSTOCK ©

CHRISTIAN OUELLET/SHUTTERSTOCK ©

Bosque Estatal de Guánica

Native Roots

AN ANCIENT SYMBOL OF SURVIVAL

The Guánica dry forest is full of fantastic flora, but none hold a candle to the **Guayacán Centenario** – a tree that's somewhere between 700 and 1400 years old, depending on who you ask. It's hard to miss the ancient wonder, located 700ft off the **Ballena Trail** that links Hwys 333 and 334. There are other impressive trees in its midst – including a gnarly gumbo limbo tree – but the Guayacán Centenario, with its swirling bark and sturdy foundation, exudes the gravitas of a giant that's weathered countless storms.

The trail, including the Guayacán detour, covers 2.5 miles round-trip and can be reached via Hwy 333 or near the Bosque Estatal de Guánica ranger station, 30 miles from Ponce.

Historic Overlook

GUÁNICA'S BAYSIDE OBSERVATION TOWER

Climb the staircase to **Fuerte Caprón**'s turreted tower and you'll understand why this is Guánica's most popular hike. Unobstructed views stretch from the tiny town and bay toward distant mountains. The vantage point is so good that Spanish colonizers originally built a tower here in the 16th century as a lookout to spot pirates. The tower was rebuilt in 1898, during

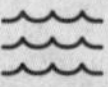

BIO BAY 101

Puerto Rico's bio bays may seem like midnight magic, but the visual stunt is rooted firmly in science. The glowing water is caused by dinoflagellates, a type of microscopic, single-celled plankton called the 'whirling fire of The Bahamas' (or *Pyrodinium bahamense*, if you're feeling nerdy). When luciferin, a chemical within these organisms, reacts to oxygen, it creates a blue twinkle as a byproduct. A reactive dinoflagellate swimming solo might not cause a stir, but when millions gather together, the results are electric.

This is precisely what happens in bays like the one at **La Parguera**: dinoflagellates get trapped together in shallow, semi-enclosed spaces – and once disturbed by movement, the chemical light show begins.

GREAT ADVENTURES NEARBY

Vereda Meseta Trail
The scent of ocean brine and the sight of desert succulents make this 6.5-mile Guánica hike unique.

Yauco
Skip around this tiny hillside town to see over 50 murals, part of the Yaucoromatic project.

The Wall
Blow bubbles with guides at Paradise Scuba along the continental shelf paralleling La Parguera.

Cañón de San Cristóbal

FOR HARDCORE HIKING

If Guánica's trails seem like child's play, join a guided tour of **Cañón de San Cristóbal** (p483), a nature-made amusement park for cliff jumping, river swimming and strenuously steep climbs.

BEST BEACHES IN GUÁNICA

La Jungla
Guánica's safest bet for seaside solitude. Arrive early to score a sand patch concealed by mangroves or join the families along two quiet beaches looking toward Cayo Don Luis.

Playa Santa
On weekends, families set up picnic spreads and nurse Medalla Lights until the sun sets along this free public beach.

Gilligan's Island
Rent a kayak or charter a private boat to play castaway for a day on this popular mangrove cay near the Copamarina Beach Resort.

the Spanish–American War, then replaced by the Civilian Conservation Corps in 1936 with the observation tower seen today.

You can reach this lookout along two different hikes. For a lengthy trek along a forest-flanked fire road, take the 6-mile out-and-back trail that starts near the Bosque Estatal de Guánica ranger station on Hwy 334. For a shorter ascent, park along Hwy 333 near **Playa Jaboncillo** and follow a steep, unmarked trail for a 1-mile round-trip. After working up a sweat, drive down to Playa Jaboncillo and finish with a well-deserved splash.

Underwater Disco

LA PARGUERA'S BIOLUMINESCENT BAY

Vieques might boast the island's brightest bio bay, but La Parguera's **Bahía Fosforescente** (Phosphorescent Bay, 32 miles from Ponce) is the only one where it's legal to swim. Paddling through the glittering water is a psychedelic experience – and a bright-blue highlight of a south-coast trip.

At sunset, boat tours trade La Parguera's busy docks for the bay's fringing mangrove forests. As darkness takes over, the magic begins: disturbances in the water cause dinoflagellates to light up like shimmering stardust, and each stroke of a swimmer's hand ignites a sparkling symphony. Pictures don't do the dinoflagellates justice, so let the magic of the underwater disco live in your memory rent-free.

WHERE TO STAY NEAR LA PARGUERA

Hacienda Verde Tahití
Curious puppies welcome guests to this *pitahaya* farm with two-story glamping, 9 miles from La Parguera. **$$**

Copamarina Beach Resort & Spa
This property has it all: restaurants, swimming pools and a beach; steps from Guánica's forest. **$$**

La Jamaca
Swing in poolside *jamacas* (hammocks) on a quiet hill above La Parguera's rowdy main street. **$$**

Paradise Scuba and Snorkeling Center leads some of the best tours in town; trips start with empanadillas and beer ($60). **Fondo de Cristal** leads bigger, non-swimming groups on glass-bottom boats ($15). The visibility of the bioluminescence depends on darkness, so plan your trip during a new moon to maximize the spectacle.

Before booking a tour, consider its ecological impact. Harmful chemicals introduced by humans can decrease the density of dinoflagellates. Play the role of seawater steward by washing off sunscreen, perfume and bug spray before taking a dip, and consider kayaks as an alternative to boats with combustion engines.

Canyon Quest

TOUGH TREKS TO HIDDEN MARVELS

After a 40-mile drive involving the hour-long ascent from Ponce into the mountains around Aibonito, the ground plummets around 500ft into the **Cañón de San Cristóbal**. This 5.6-mile chasm, chiseled by the Río Usabón, is a dramatic highlight of the Central Mountains and a must-see for leisure hikers and adrenaline junkies alike.

Gawk above the gorge by following the 3-mile out-and-back trail to **Vereda El Ancón**, a well-maintained path that starts roadside on Rte 162. After walking 1.5 miles along fields of native flora, it's possible to glimpse the El Ancón waterfall showering Río Usabón in the distance.

But the real jaw-droppers here delight from the canyon floor, including **La Niebla**, a three-tiered cascade, and the peerless **Charco Azul**, a sky-blue dunk-pad punctuated with an avalanche of water. Careful where you step: rusted remnants from waste dumped in the 1960s and 70s have fused with rocks to form Richard Serra-style earthworks. (Today, the land is a Natural Protected Area.)

Hiking into the canyon shouldn't be done on a whim. Rain can cause dangerous rapids and unexpected landslides, turning the site into a death trap. Even on dry days, navigating trails requires technical skill and athleticism. To ensure a safe visit, join a guided expedition. Samuel Oliveras Ortiz, the Barranquitas-based geography and history teacher behind **Go Hiking PR** (gohiking4@gmail.com), practically grew up in the canyon and leads weekend tours ranging from straightforward hikes to all-day odysseys packed with rappelling, cliff jumping and climbing through waterfalls. Non-profit conservation group **Para La Naturaleza** also leads treks, often in Spanish. Call ahead to check for availability in English.

SATISFYING SOAKS

Unwind post-hike by dipping into the **Baños de Coamo**, located 13 miles south of Aibonito. Local legend says the water, heated by the remnants of a dormant volcano, was the Fountain of Youth that Ponce de León searched for. Joke's on him. Taíno people enjoyed the healing powers of the *aguas termales* long before Spanish colonizers arrived – a practice that remains popular today. Two pools pipe in thermal water at 89°F and 108°F (32°C to 42°C), and though a dip won't leave you looking younger, it's bound to relieve stress. The site is well maintained, with changing rooms and refreshments. Soft jazz emanating throughout the space might be cheesy, but it sets the tone. Boisterous kids can splash elsewhere.

CHEAP EATS IN AIBONITO

Placita Aibonito
Built in 1830, this warehouse now serves healthy fare, as well as smoothies and sweets. $

Bokita Vegana
Aibonito loves its chicken, but with plant-based sandwiches this tasty, you might forgo the *pollo*. $

La Curva Del Bacalao
Gobble up fritters from this unfussy food stand, open on weekends and near the Vereda trailhead. $

JAYUYA

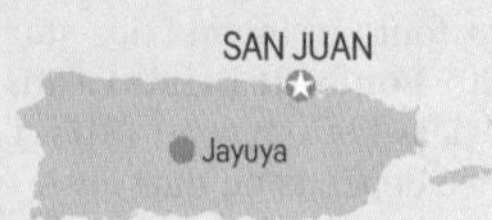

Puerto Rico's soul sings in this remote mountain town, named after the Taíno chief Hayuya and known as the island's indigenous capital. Jayuya's Taíno pride dazzles year-round with museums and archaeological sites honoring native culture, but the Boricua spirit shines brightest during late November's Festival Nacional Indígena, which celebrates the island's ancient traditions.

Crowned by mountains and cross-hatched with rivers, it's easy to see how Jayuya held fast to its Taíno heritage: the imposing geography largely protected this area from outside influence until 1911, when it became a municipality. Even today, getting here requires deft driving skills when weaving through mountain roads that spiral like a petroglyph.

Verdant hiking trails and coffee haciendas fringe areas outside downtown, and when night falls, a shot of locally made moonshine rum will send you to sleep to the sweet song of coquís.

TOP TIP

Cell service is unpredictable, so download maps and other necessary information before hitting the road. As a general rule, GPS hurts more than it helps – instead, stick to main roads like Hwys 141, 143 and 144. Avoid unnamed backroads – they aren't always well-maintained and can be dangerous, particularly in the rain.

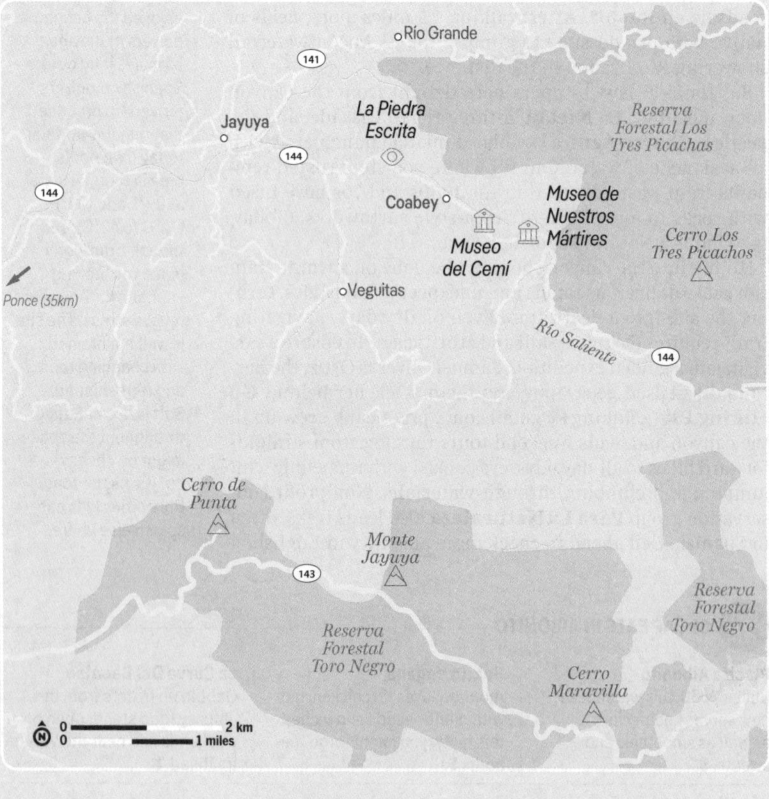

Río Grande
141
La Piedra Escrita
Reserva Forestal Los Tres Picachas
Jayuya
144
144
Coabey
Museo de Nuestros Mártires
Museo del Cemí
Cerro Los Tres Picachos
Ponce (35km)
Veguitas
Río Saliente
144
Cerro de Punta
Monte Jayuya
143
Reserva Forestal Toro Negro
Reserva Forestal Toro Negro
Cerro Maravilla
0 2 km
0 1 miles

PHOTO SPIRIT/SHUTTERSTOCK ©

La Piedra Escrita

A Magnifying Glass on Taíno Culture

ANCIENT ARTIFACT TURNED MODERN ARCHITECTURE

The **Museo del Cemí** is an eye-catching building shaped precisely like one of the indigenous artifacts it displays. Here, the *cemí* – typically a tiny spiritual figurine carved by Taíno people to embody ancestral spirits – is transformed into a two-story wonder designed by Río Piedras architect Efrén Badia Cabrera. Look west toward the peaks of Tres Picachos to clock some similarities. Scholars believe the three-pronged mountain range, considered sacred by the Taíno, inspired the *cemí*'s shape. The exterior outshines the museum's actual exhibits, though a cheery mural depicting Taíno petroglyphs is worth a gander.

The adjacent **coffee plantation house**, a reconstruction of the 19th-century original and filled with authentic furniture and antiques, belonged to Jayuya's first mayor, Rosario Canales.

Ancient Etchings

A SCENIC ARCHAEOLOGICAL SITE

When it comes to indigenous petroglyphs, the best examples are free to see along public waterways. One of the most impressive examples is **La Piedra Escrita** (The Written Stone) – a granite boulder that is 13ft tall and less than five minutes from Museo del Cemí by car. Park at La Escrita, a pork-heavy restaurant, and descend a wooden boardwalk to see the famous slab in the center of the Río Saliente. The stone, awash with Taíno carvings, sparkles like polished marble.

The scenery alone is worth the trek: egrets hunt for fish, tangled trees climb to distant peaks and rocks along the riverbank seem tailor-made for picnicking. Bring a swimsuit for the small pool beneath the boulder.

BASEMENT REBELLION

In 1950, nationalist Blanca Canales (daughter of Jayuya's first mayor, Rosario) led an armed rebellion in the city of Jayuya to win Puerto Rico's independence from the US. The US National Guard quickly quelled the uprising, arrested the conspirators and sentenced Canales and other revolutionary leaders to prison time.

Today, the tumultuous event lives on in the private basement of Ernesto Marín, whose uncle and four cousins were imprisoned for participation in the uprising. Marín's 'martyr's museum,' called the **Museo de Nuestros Mártires**, features artwork, photographs and newspaper clippings from the uprising, honoring activists who sacrificed their lives for the island's freedom. Marín is the museum's charming guide, often followed by his pack of friendly German Shepherds.

WHERE TO HAVE SIPS AND SNACKS IN JAYUYA

La Destileria Craft Spirits
Small-batch distillery making alcohol-forward rums and legal *pitorro* (moonshine rum). Tours end with a tasting flight. **$$**

La Herencia
Guava-flavored yogurt, grass-fed meat, fresh-picked veggies and locally made art at a teeny grocer-and-specialty store. **$**

Café Nativo
Come for the decadent brunch-and-bistro menu – French toast, waffles, sandwiches and locally made coffee. **$**

Beyond Jayuya

It's possible to spot Ponce from the mountains above Jayuya, but city life feels far away from the lush jungles that await here.

Before Hwy 149 zig-zags along Jayuya's eastern border, it cuts through Ciales, which connects the northern karst region to the Central Mountains. The actual town of Ciales, surrounded by rounded limestone cliffs, is a haven for coffee connoisseurs and Caribbean-cuisine fiends – a prime spot to fuel up before Bosque Estatal de Toro Negro.

Toro Negro's 10-plus miles of hiking trails might not be as popular as El Yunque's well-worn paths, but it's not for lack of beauty. Fern-filled jungles, rushing rivers and Puerto Rico's three highest peaks make this park a stunner, as do local flora and fauna – including the endangered Puerto Rican sharp-shinned hawk and orchids that'll make your house plants green with envy.

TOP TIP

Pack plenty of water and snacks before hitting Toro Negro's trails. Food options are scarce, as are amenities at the ranger station.

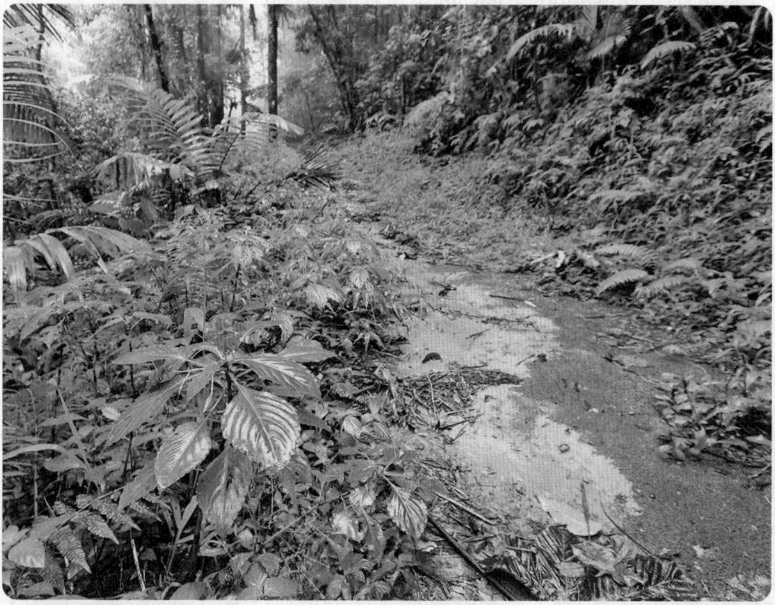

Toro Negro Reserve

Orocovis

Jungle Adventure

TREK TO CERRO DOÑA JUANA

The **Toro Negro Reserve** sprawls over 7000 cloud-shrouded acres within the municipalities of Ciales, Jayuya, Juana Díaz, Orocovis and Ponce, but the best hiking trails all begin at the Orocovis ranger station, off Hwy 143.

From here, visitors can choose from several excursions with varying levels of difficulty. For the most dynamic adventure, you can Frankenstein three trails into one 4-mile monster of a climb, with Cerra Doña Juana (the highest peak in Orocovis) – as the prize. Consult a park map before taking off – the trails aren't always well-marked or maintained, but they're easy to navigate if you know what to look for.

Start on **Camino El Bolo** – which ascends for 1.5 miles through a forest shaded by sierra palms and bamboo trees – then continue onto **Vereda la Torre** (Path to the Tower), a half-mile scramble to the summit. The name doesn't lie: choirs of coqui and flutters of butterflies line the trail to an observation tower that delivers panoramic views, 3500ft above the Caribbean. Switch up the descent by taking La Piscina, a rocky route through a vine-dripped jungle leading to a now-defunct pool and Charco de los Suspiros – a series of small cascades. A short jaunt along Hwy 143 returns to the ranger's station.

If one trail isn't enough, the 1.2-mile out-and-back path to **Charco La Confesora**, a turquoise swimming hole, makes a pleasant coda. Bring a bathing suit for a refreshing post-hike soak.

GRINDERS & GOATS

You smell it before you see it: caramel notes of roasted coffee beans create an olfactory path to the **Museo del Café de Puerto Rico**. Owner and curator Pedro 'Pichy' Maldonado Ramírez presides over this quirky Ciales coffee museum, which includes everything from a jumble of international coffee grinders to documents from the island's heyday as a coffee exporter in the late 19th century. For an inside scoop, call ahead to book a Ramírez-led tour – scant information accompanies the museum's two display rooms.

After a quick spin around the museum, pop over to the adjacent cafe, with farm animals nestled nearby. Cap the visit with a cup of Café Don Pello, produced by Ramírez.

UNIQUE LODGING IN THE CENTRAL MOUNTAINS

El Pretexto, Cayey
Relax on swinging hammocks with mountain vistas after meals prepared with farm-grown ingredients. **$$$**

Hacienda Pomarrosa, Jayuya
Curl up in a casita for views of this coffee plantation, run by a German expat. **$$**

Casa Grande Mountain Retreat, Utuado
The nearby waterfalls and hiking trails here provide plenty of reasons to unplug. **$$**

UTUADO

This is karst country – a limestone landscape of sinkholes, canyons and caves decorated with rounded hillocks called *mogotes*. Utuado, named after the Taíno chief Otoa, means 'between mountains' – and in the morning, misty veils blanket the valleys between the *mogotes*, lifting midday to reveal glistening rivers and reservoirs.

Before colonization, Utuado played a principal role in Taíno rituals, and the Parque Ceremonial Indígena de Caguana, unearthed in 1914, remains one of the most important indigenous ceremonial sites discovered in the Caribbean. By the late 19th century, the town grew rich on coffee production, but the renaissance was short-lived. US colonization in 1898, followed by a devastating hurricane, disrupted the industry and made sugarcane the island's new crop, stunting Utuado's economy.

Today, Utuado's biggest draws are its enduring assets – the great outdoors. Hiking, spelunking and swimming among rock formations is proof of the area's stay-power: the beauty is unbeatable.

TOP TIP

The town of Utuado is easily accessible by car via Hwy 10, which traverses the Central Mountains from Arecibo to Ponce. Although the town is great for grabbing food, it's a concrete-smacked departure from the region's natural beauty. To see the municipality's attractions, whip around the windy, wild backroads.

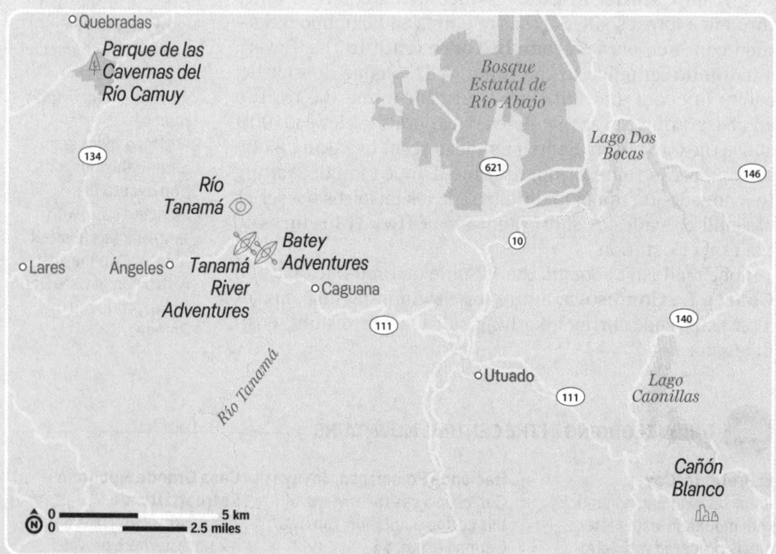

EFRAIN PADRO/ALAMY ©

Hiking, Río Tanamá

FOR MORE FRESHWATER FUN

Some of the most stunning swimming holes in the Central Mountains can be found along rivers flowing through **Adjuntas** (p492), a bucolic municipality neighboring Utuado.

Flit Along the Río Tanamá

ONE-STOP SHOP FOR ADVENTURE

Fill your water bottle from a fresh spring while touring the **Río Tanamá**: this natural hydration station is a necessary pitstop while engaging in activities that might include hiking, tubing, caving, cliff jumping, kayaking along a 1000ft tunnel, and rappelling down a 250ft cliff.

The Río Tanamá spent millions of years carving Utuado's limestone rock-bed with the precision of a Renaissance sculptor, its glittering caverns and deep canyons part of a miles-long masterpiece. Tanamá, Taíno for 'butterfly,' is a fitting description for the fragile ecosystem, but an incomplete list of what you'll find here. Tiny tarantulas bury holes in the forest floor, bat colonies cling to stalactites in caves, and if you're lucky, you might spot a 25-inch *guabá* – the tailless whip scorpion, which hides in caves and feasts on crickets. (Don't worry – they're harmless to humans.)

Most of the river is on private land, so hiring a tour company is best for seeing the sites. Both **Batey Adventures** and **Tanamá River Adventures** offer information-rich excursions with varying degrees of difficulty. Still, none of the options are walks in the park – they're treks through the tropics. Wear

MODERN MYTHS

Leathery skin. Crimson eyes. Chugs animal blood like cheap sangria. Its name? The *chupacabra*, or 'goat sucker' – a folkloric creature that feasts on livestock, first spotted in Puerto Rico.
Soon after reported sightings began in the mid-1990s, the worldwide hysteria was so real that the mayor of Canóvanas conducted hunts for the vampiric predator using a caged goat as bait. The Island of Enchantment's dark caves and deep canyons have ignited imaginations for centuries, starting with the Taínos, who believed in *hupia* – shape-shifting spirits that sometimes appear as bats and birds. Could *hupia* be the *chupacabra*'s mythical relatives?

WHERE TO EAT IN UTUADO

Finca Vista Bella
Pair a floral wine from this mountainside vineyard with cheese boards, pastas or steaks. **$$$**

La Aldea
Wash down delicious tapas in the yolk-yellow interior with fruit-forward cocktails, mocktails or coffee. **$$**

Bier Garden Utuado
Cool off with a craft beer on the AstroTurf backyard of this brew bar and restaurant. **$$**

strong-soled water shoes and quick-dry clothing for maximum comfort. Tours leave in the morning, and are generally best during winter's dry months, when the river is easily navigable and glistens jade-green.

SPELUNKING EXPEDITION

If you're coo-coo for karst country's limestone features, take the hour-long trek from Utuado to Camuy for a two-hour tour of Puerto Rico's most famous cave system, **Parque de las Cavernas del Río Camuy**. After purchasing a ticket from the main office (cash only) and watching a short educational film, you'll receive a hard hat, flashlight and audio guide before entering this ancient underworld.

Once inside, the audio and human guides provide information on the house-size stalagmites and stalactites, the fauna that inhabits them (bats and spiders) and the devastating flooding caused by Hurricane Maria. A limestone roof soars 170ft above your head and an underground river gurgles beneath your feet – a magical subterranean spectacle.

Jump into Cañón Blanco

NATURE'S PEARL-WHITE PLAYGROUND

As the Río Caonillas slithers through Utuado, it carves a half-mile-long canyon through creamy white limestone. Secret swimming holes, gurgling cataracts and rounded rock formations make this a veritable jungle gym, while the stone formations seem fit for a modern art gallery. In many ways, the site is already an alfresco museum, with Taíno petroglyphs decorating some of the most magnificent boulders.

The road to **Cañón Blanco** comes at a sharp turn near the 15km marking on Hwy 140 – part of a hair-raising drive that's par for the course while navigating the Central Mountains. After crossing a small bridge, park at one of the lots along the river's eastern banks. A sandy beach at the canyon's northern mouth might be the finish line for some travelers, while the craggy mountains and shimmering stones make this a scenic spot to picnic.

But for strong swimmers and sure-footed hikers, the beach is only the beginning. Paddle upstream through the canyon's colossal western walls, where a karst grotto awaits. This hidden, open-air chamber comes equipped with a mini limestone slide, smoothed to hip-width by centuries of water. Crawl into the canyon 400ft upstream of here to find 'El Sofa,' a boulder shaped like a *Flintstones*'-style loveseat. For Taíno carvings, walk downstream of the bridge to a nearly 6ft-high boulder blocking the river's heart. Sacred symbols adorn its crown – tiny remnants of the indigenous people who once populated the area.

Cañón Blanco might be beautiful, but it can also be dangerous. Avoid visiting during or after a rainstorm – flash floods make the river unnavigable, and the water turns the rocks into slip-and-slides. Wear proper footwear to explore the area safely.

GETTING AROUND

The Central Mountains are only accessible by car (or bike, if you're daring). Get your own set of wheels to come and go as you please, and don't expect cabs to haul you around. Most of the region's gems shine along remote roads with little reception.

Before hitting the highway, plan your route and download maps in case you lose cell service. GPS can give faulty directions. Once on the road, drive slowly and honk liberally around blind turns.

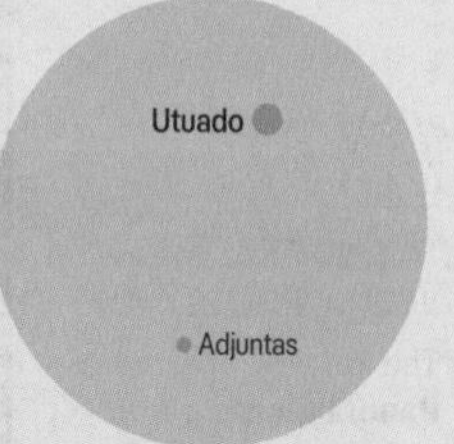

Beyond Utuado

Pack some snacks and pump the brakes to savor the scenery in Adjuntas, south of Utuado.

Gaze toward Cerro El Gigante to see how Adjuntas earned its nickname, 'City of the Sleeping Giant.' Three points of craggy peaks create the crude silhouette of a stone-faced man. As the nickname suggests, it's not the shop-lined streets of Adjuntas that spark excitement – it's the magical mountains outside of town, filled with forests and farmland.

Loving the wild landscape is an integral part of local life. After the Puerto Rican government granted permits to dig mines around Adjuntas in the 1980s and '90s, community activists fought back. The lush paradise you see today is proof that the activists won: no mining pits here – just coffee haciendas and swimming holes at the end of woodland roads.

TOP TIP

Adjuntas is an easy day trip from Utuado and Ponce, located half an hour from both destinations via Hwys 10 and 123.

Adjuntas

Charco el Ataúd

TAKING THE SCENIC ROUTE

The **Ruta Panorámica**, a 167-mile rollercoaster of interconnected roads that slices into the island's heartland, runs through Adjuntas – and while its name might suggest a breezy road trip, this highway isn't for the faint of heart. Roaming dogs and chattering chickens pop up around bends that S-curve into clouds, and razor-thin stretches along misty mountain saddles will shake a novice driver's confidence. But for seasoned adventurers, the trip from Mayagüez to Maunabo can be a soul-stirring quest – it's called the 'panoramic route' for a reason. Just don't expect to drive faster than 25 mph – oncoming drivers, including the occasional horse-riding *jíbaro* (country person), will be glad you're taking it slow.

Turquoise Trifecta

SPLASH AROUND THREE MOUNTAIN POOLS

Slap on a swimsuit to jump into Adjuntas. The municipality's most striking sites are secluded swimming holes in fairytale forests, and a day spent driving to these gems is an opportunity to bathe in mountain-studded splendor. Visit on dry, sunny days to see the water shimmer like thousands of emeralds.

Start at **Charco el Ataúd** (also called Cascada Las Garzas), located along Carretera Garzas Centro. A steep cliffside trail leads to three tiers of cascade-fed pools. The Olympic-sized tub at the base is most impressive, framed by slate-gray stone. Swim across the pool to sunbathe iguana-style on warm rocks and appreciate the area's best view – but only if you're ready for a near-vertical scramble back to the trail.

There's less need for fancy footwork at **Charco el Mangó** – a pristine swim spot in the Río Yahuecas. Park roadside near Hwy 525, part of the Ruta Panorámica, then hike for 10 minutes along a dirt road until the pool appears. (Attempting to navigate the road's potholes in a car will likely lead to disaster.) Framed by boulders, bolstered by a pebble beach and decorated with the white petals of Angel's trumpets, the landscape is heavenly.

Arriving at **Salto Santa Clara** requires a bit of sweat equity. On this 1.2-mile out-and-back trail, hikers ford a small river and use a rope to assist one short, slippery descent – two obstacles worth overcoming for a dip in the waterfall-swept pool that awaits. This well-marked path near the Adjuntas-Yauco border begins on a dead-end road off Rte 372.

BEST BITES IN ADJUNTAS

Re-creos Coffee Shop
Stop by this cheery cafe and kitchen for late brunch or lunch treats. **$**

Restaurante Hacienda Maribó
Admire artfully plated Puerto Rican fare before meeting the bleating goats and sheep outside. **$$$**

Sandra Farms Coffee
Tour this sustainable coffee-and-cacao plantation to taste the fresh brew and decadent chocolate. **$$**

RINCÓN

As distant from the bright lights of San Juan as you can get without falling into the Atlantic, the 'Corner' is an apt name for this triangle of Puerto Rico that juts into the ocean. You'll likely see plenty of people falling into the briny, too, for on top of being Puerto Rico's surfing epicenter, this is also one of the best places to catch a wave in the Caribbean.

Disciples of the board began colonizing this area in the late 1960s, lured by images of the 1968 World Surfing Championships. Today, they're joined by a rolling population of students and snowbirds who party their winters away in tandem at beach bars and food truck parks. You'll find the island's highest concentration of US mainlanders in Rincón – a mix of chilled surfers, digital nomads and sun-tanned hippies who sell beach glass and driftwood sculptures at the weekly Rincón Art Walk.

TOP TIP

Many accommodations, restaurants and bars don't use their street addresses, making them a nightmare to find, even with GPS. Calling ahead for a route description is often a good idea.

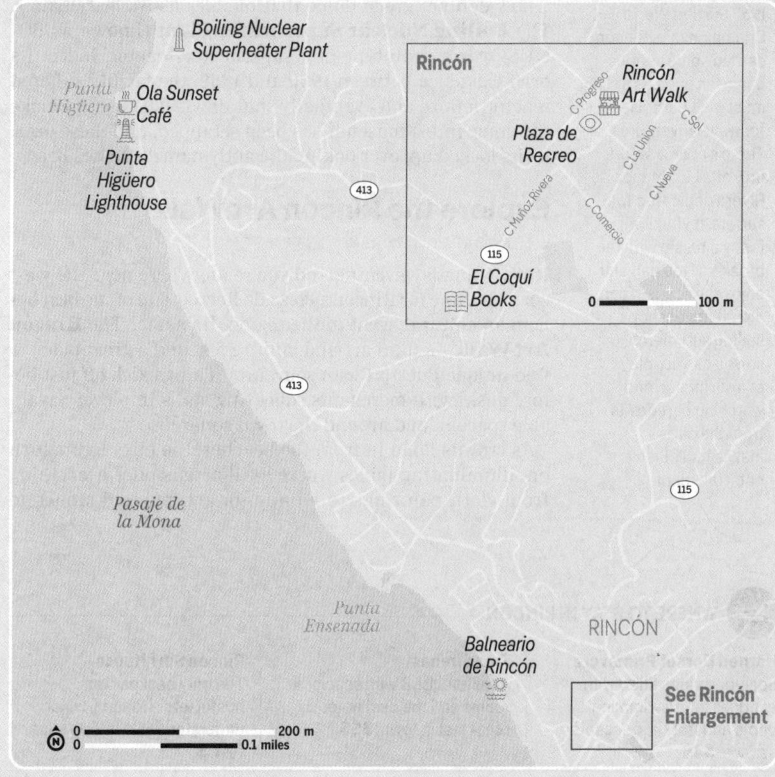

Around Rincón Town

TOURING THE MARITIME COMMUNITY

Rincón's epicenter is the **Plaza de Recreo**, a cozy space packed with plants and benches and surrounded by busy restaurants and bars. During the day, it's an excellent spot for ice cream, but it really comes into its own after dark, especially on Thursday evenings, when it hosts the impressive Rincón Art Walk.

Rincón has no seafront or promenade, but the main public beach is the **Balneario de Rincón**, equipped with restrooms, showers, restaurant and a lookout tower, which is currently closed.

Continuing north, the **Punta Higüero Lighthouse** dates from 1892 and rises almost 100ft. It was restored in 1922 after being trashed by a tsunami set off by the devastating 1918 earthquake. The 26,000-candlepower light has been automated since 1933 and still helps ships navigate the Pasaje de la Mona (Mona Passage). The best reason to come here is to watch the sunset over the Atlantic with a passion fruit mojito in hand (grab one at the **Ola Sunset Café**) – a quintessential Rincón experience. It's also a great place for whale watching between January and April.

A short walk north from the lighthouse is Rincón's most bizarre attraction – the Caribbean's first nuclear power station, a now-defunct green dome that bubbles above leafy palms. The **Boiling Nuclear Superheater Plant** (known as BONUS) was a prototype of a superheater reactor, but in its brief existence between 1960 and 1968, the facility suffered reactor failure and eventually shut down. The idea to make the dome into a museum has been scrapped, and these days, it sits locked up, overlooking the aptly named Domes Beach.

RIDING THE NOSE

'In Rincón they're riding the nose...' goes the Beach Boys lyric in 'Surfin' Safari.' The phrase 'riding the nose' is surfer slang for moving forward on the board toward the front.

Rincón is arguably the Caribbean's premier surfing destination. After hosting the legendary 1968 Surfing World Championship, Rincón earned some serious hang-ten hype as a must-visit paradise for wave adventures. There's even a statue on Calle Luis Muñoz Rivera dedicated to surfers. If you don't fancy a tussle with the breakers, you can still enjoy the scene. There are plenty of shops selling surf merch, so you can cosplay at a surfer bar, and watching daredevils from the cliffs makes for splashy entertainment.

Explore the Rincón Art Walk

WEST COAST CULTURE AT ITS FINEST

If it's Thursday evening and you're anywhere near the west coast, beeline for Rincón's Plaza de Recreo, site of the best bohemian cultural event in the region. Its name? The **Rincón Art Walk** – a mini art-and-culture fest and a great place to find unique Puerto Rican souvenirs. Things kick off just before dusk, with merchants squeezing stalls into every available space in and around the town square.

As crowds flood in from the beaches, the fairy lights turn on, illuminating tables where local artists offer everything from cloth paintings to aluminum art, painted stones to

WHERE TO STAY IN RINCÓN

Horned Dorset Primavera
Secluded villas filled with antiques, plus swimming pools and truly impeccable service. **$$$**

Tres Sirenas
A tasteful B&B with spacious rooms and the best hotel breakfast in town. **$$$**

Rincón Surf House
The only backpacker hostel left in Rincón, which understandably fills up super fast. **$**

EDTORORO/SHUTTERSTOCK ©

Punta Higüero Lighthouse

sea glass jewelry, bamboo lamps to homemade soaps, woolen dreamcatchers to coffee sack bags. There's no hard sell, and stall owners are usually glad to chat about their wares. Grab a snack or a cold beer from the bars and cafes ringing the plaza and peruse the stalls at your leisure. Plan on coming hungry – the artisanal food vendors sell some seriously tempting treats.

The evening's highlight happens around 8pm when a musical act entertains from the columned bandstand facing tiers of concrete seating. Arrive early to grab a good spot. Couples show off their hottest salsa moves in the cool evening breeze, and kids hop around the base of the stage. Some businesses, like **El Coquí Books**, stay open late on Thursday, and the bars are always rocking till the bewitching hour. The easy-breezy atmosphere is the epitome of west coast 'cool.'

RINCÓN'S BEST SURFING BEACHES

Little Malibu
Just north of the marina. Good for beginners.

Tres Palmas
The big kahuna, with breaks of up to 25ft.

Steps
The 'inside' break to Tres Palmas' 'outside' break. Good snorkeling spot when it's calm.

Dogman's
Expect waves that are high and hollow.

The Point
Just south of the Punta Higüero Lighthouse, this isn't for amateurs.

Domes
A classic surf spot, probably the most consistent overall in the Rincón area.

Maria
A good right, but needs a decent swell.

WHERE TO EAT IN RINCÓN

Estela
If you've had enough surfer chic and want something higher end, this gourmet place won't disappoint. **$$$**

English Rose
This morning-only spot in the hills is known for its big breakfasts and prime views. **$**

Harbor
Filling dishes of seafood and *mofongo*, topped by its location – just steps from the waves. **$$**

Beyond Rincón

Leave the surf behind for open-sea adventures, or find peace along the southwest's coral-pink salt flats and remote white sands.

Head west from Rincón and you're in the Mona Passage – a strait between Puerto Rico and the Dominican Republic prized for exceptional fishing, snorkeling and diving.

Drive south through Mayagüez, and you'll eventually enter Cabo Rojo (Red Cape) – the name of both a small administrative town and the infinitely more enticing municipality that extends out from the town on all sides. To add to the confusion, it's also the name for the rugged coastline that constitutes Puerto Rico's extreme southwestern tip. Got it?

The top reason to head here is the Refugio Nacional Cabo Rojo – a remote area with rolling hills tumbling into mangroves, replete with limestone cliffs diving into the sea.

TOP TIP

There's little shade in the Refugio Nacional Cabo Rojo, so bring a hat and sunscreen, as the sun's rays are grueling.

Isla Mona

Sea Trips

OUT INTO THE BLUE

Diving may not seem particularly promising while looking at the west coast surf, but the reef near the uninhabited **Isla Desecheo** is among Puerto Rico's best scuba sites. Lack of run-off from the main island makes for crystal-clear waters, which means better views of the coral and underwater caves. For divers who can manage the long haul to **Isla Mona** (dubbed the Puerto Rican Galápagos), this oval island 13 miles west of Rincón's coast is equally promising for underwater escapades.

Prefer plucking creatures out of the sea? Several companies in and around Rincón can arrange deep-sea fishing, live bait fishing and kite-fishing trips. There's also exceptional whale watching between December and March, when humpbacks migrate through the Mona Passage. If you want to try to see whales breaching from dry land, head to the Punta Higüero Lighthouse (p494).

Most sea-going excursions depart from **Black Eagle Marina** at the northern end of Black Eagle Beach (which blends seamlessly with the Rincón public beach). Perhaps the most popular trips out of the marina are sunset cruises, offered by most outfits and often including drinks or dinner.

THE BEST SEA TRIP COMPANIES

Rincón is the easiest place on the west coast to arrange a boating excursion. These are the best companies for hitting the high seas.

Taíno Divers
Arguably the best of the west coast bunch. Based at Black Eagle Marina, they specialize in diving at Isla Desecheo and also offer courses and sunset cruises.

Katarina Sail Charters
Join wildlife-watching cruises, snorkeling trips and sunset sailings offered by this outfit at Black Eagle Marina.

Makaira Sportfishing
Deep-sea-fishing charters for up to six people.

Half-Moon Heaven

RELAX ALONG A TRANQUIL COVE

The sugar-sand icing on top of remote **Refugio Nacional Cabo Rojo** is **La Playuela**, 35 miles from Rincón and arguably Puerto Rico's most magnificent wild shoreline. This crescent beach, strung between two headlands and shelving gently into a calm, reef-protected lagoon, is isolated from development (aside from a nearby lighthouse). Scrub and bushes provide shade, and the extra-salty water is ideal for a therapeutic float. You'll rarely be alone, but it's never too crowded.

WHERE TO DRINK IN RINCÓN

Rincón Beer Company
Superb brewpub opposite the Plaza de Recreo that specializes in local and US ales and lagers. **$$**

Tamboo Tavern
Join the bronzed bodies at this après-surf beach bar for cocktails and filling food. **$$**

Caddy's Calypso
Rub shoulders with salt-encrusted surfers at this restaurant and bar along Maria's Beach. **$$**

PATRICK HORTON/SHUTTERSTOCK ©

Arriving

Travelers usually arrive in Puerto Rico via plane at Luis Muñoz Marin International Airport (SJU), located 13km east of Old San Juan. Other entry points include Old San Juan's cruise port, Aguadilla's Rafael Hernández Airport and Ponce's Mercedita International Airport. Between mid-December and early April, expect greater airport congestion as snowbirds fly south to escape the winter.

By Air

SJU is the island's most convenient airport, with 48 direct flights from international destinations. You can also fly into Aguadilla or Ponce, but renting a car at SJU and zooming to your destination on wheels is just as handy.

By Boat

Most cruise ships dock at the San Juan Bay terminal, located near Old San Juan, or at the Pan American terminal, which requires hiring a taxi or rideshare. Some cruise ships also (rarely) port at Ponce in the south.

Money

Currency: US dollar (US$)

CREDIT & CASH
All major credit cards are accepted at establishments around San Juan and at hotels. Cash is handy in smaller towns, particularly in the Central Mountains, where remote tourist sites and street-side *chinchorros* are often cash-only. It's easy to find ATMs in most towns, but it's safest to pull out greenbacks in San Juan before heading inland.

TIPPING
The local restaurant industry relies on tips, just like the mainland US. If you're sitting down for a meal, tip 15–20% – unless the service is terrible. It's customary to tip around $1 for a drink at a bar. There's no need to tip at fast-food joints.

TRAVEL ON A BUDGET
Dining out in big cities gets pricey. Save money by stocking up at grocery stores or farmers' markets to self-cater your meals. If you're sticking to San Juan, you can save money by not renting a car and walking instead; if you're looking for free activities, head to the beach.

Getting Around

Puerto Rico is relatively small and easily navigable – as long as you have a car. Traffic around San Juan can get chaotic, and the serpentine Central Mountain roads aren't for the faint of heart, but if you want to explore, there's no better option. Ferries, chartered boats or group tours are the best way to visit islands off the coast.

PUBLIC TRANSPORTATION

It's possible to navigate San Juan via city buses called *guaguas*, but service can be unpredictable. There's also a city metro, the Tren Urbano, which serves San Juan's major universities. Don't rely on public transportation outside of the city.

BLACKREGIS/SHUTTERSTOCK ©

CAR

A rental car is the most convenient (and sometimes the only) way to get around outside San Juan. While most expressways are well maintained, roads in remote towns and the Central Mountains can get hairy.

BOAT

To access Vieques (pictured) and Culebra, take the daily ferry service from Ceiba. Other islands, like Isla Mona, require chartering a private boat. Smaller skiff rentals in towns like La Parguera make it possible to zip around the coastal cays.

TAXI/RIDESHARE

Taxis are easy to find in San Juan, Ponce and other tourist-trafficked cities. Most drivers don't use their meters – always agree on a price before taking off. Uber is the most convenient around San Juan and the north coast.

AIR

It's possible to take domestic flights from SJU and Isla Grande to Mayagüez, Vieques and Culebra, but driving or boating is the faster and cheaper alternative.

DRIVING ESSENTIALS

Drive on the right side

Speed limit is generally 25 mph in cities and 65 mph on freeways.

GPS can be faulty in the Central Mountains. Plan your route before hitting the road.

EQROY/SHUTTERSTOCK ©

Above: View toward Nevis Peak (p515); Right: Basseterre (p507)

ST KITTS & NEVIS

TWO ISLANDS, ONE COUNTRY

Go beyond the beach to hike volcanic mountains, snorkel in reef-filled waters, and discover the rich history of this two-island nation.

Shared history, cultural similarities and close proximity unite St Christopher (St Kitts) and Nevis in one federation. Separated by the Narrows (a channel only 1.9 miles wide), the two Leeward Islands are the summits of a submerged mountain range; majestic volcanoes – now extinct and covered with greenery – loom over both islands. They share a complex history of contested colonial rule and sugar-plantation prosperity, and you can still visit the fantastic Brimstone Fortress and many former plantations, both ruined and preserved. Blissfully under the tourist radar, these two scenic islands entice visitors with opportunities for rugged hiking, beach lounging, and plenty of *limin'* (the national pastime: hanging out and having a good time).

For all their similarities, however, the two sister islands have very different vibes. St Kitts is larger and more commercial, with a busy cruise-ship terminal at Port Zonte and several sprawling resorts (although this development has been curtailed significantly in the wake of the Covid-19 pandemic). The scene on 'the Strip' at Frigate Bay is pretty much nonstop. By contrast, Nevis is smaller and more serene – and quite content to stay that way. By avoiding mass tourism, the little island offers all the natural attractions and irresistible amenities, without the crowds. Fortunately, it's easy to cruise across the Narrows to get a taste of both of these beauties.

THE MAIN AREAS

BASSETERRE & FRIGATE BAY
St Kitts' capital and buzzing beach.
p507

CHARLESTOWN
Busy port city in Nevis.
p512

Find Your Way

Public ferries and water taxis shuttle between St Kitts and Nevis, the two islands of this two-island nation. You'll need wheels to explore either island, although taxis and tours are plentiful.

Basseterre & Frigate Bay, p507
Side-by-side centers in St Kitts, with the capital city on the west coast and the idyllic beach-facing Frigate Bay on the east side.

INTER-ISLAND TRAVEL

Public passenger ferries make the one-hour trip between Basseterre and Charlestown. The so-called Sea Bridge is a car ferry from Majors Bay to Cades Bay. There are also water taxis that run between Reggae Beach and Oualie Beach in about 15 minutes.

DRIVING

Rent a car for maximum flexibility on both islands. Depending on the rental company, you can transport the car between islands or trade in your car for a vehicle on the other island. Don't forget to drive on the left!

TAXIS & TOURS

Taxis (usually Toyota minivans) double as tour guides and are plentiful on both islands. Fares are usually US$15 to US$30 (or up to US$60 if you're traveling the length of the island). Resorts and tour operators also provide transportation for their guests.

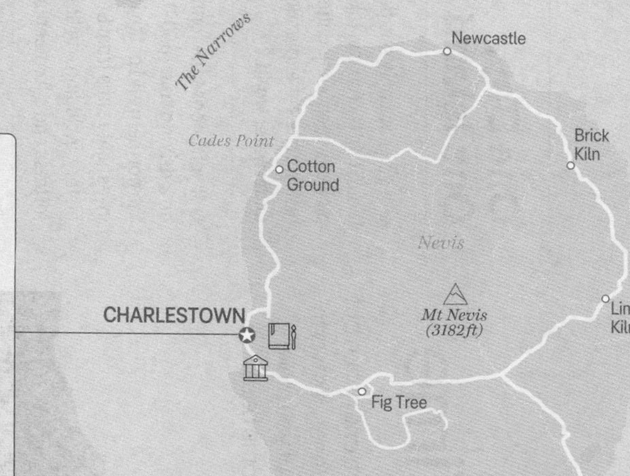

Charlestown, p512
The historic port city on Nevis was the birthplace of Alexander Hamilton and is still the home base for many island adventures.

FROM TOP: EQROY/SHUTTERSTOCK ©, BARBARA788/SHUTTERSTOCK ©

Plan Your Time

St Kitts and Nevis are one nation but two very different islands. It's worth exploring both, even if you make a day trip from your home base.

JASON PATRICK ROSS/SHUTTERSTOCK ©

Mt Liamuiga (p509)

One Day, One Island

- If you have only one day, spend it on St Kitts. You can take your pick between visiting the island's historic sites or exploring the underwater world.
- If you choose the former, go on a **driving tour** (p509) around the northern end of the island to investigate sites from St Kitts' history, including a military fortress and a former plantation.
- For the latter, book a snorkel tour to **Shitten Bay** (p510) – or hike there if you're feeling adventurous.
- End the day with an indulgent dinner at **Marshall's** or casual fare at **Cathy's Oceanside Bar & Grill** (p507).

Seasonal Highlights

The driest months in St Kitts and Nevis are from February to May, but you shouldn't let a little rain deter you from the lively cultural calendar from June through December.

JANUARY

St Kitts' six-week Carnival – aka Sugar Mas – ends with **Parade Day** on January 1 and the **Last Lap** on January 2.

MARCH

Swimmers speedy and sedate take part in the festive **Nevis to St Kitts Cross-Channel Swim**, a 2.5-mile race between the two islands.

JUNE

One of the region's biggest music events, the three-day **St Kitts Music Festival**, takes place over the third weekend in June.

MICHAEL RUNKEL/ROBERTHARDING/ALAMY ©, HEDELIN F/ANDIA/UNIVERSAL IMAGES GROUP VIA GETTY IMAGES ©, DIANA HALSTEAD/SHUTTERSTOCK ©

Four Days to Explore

- With four days to explore, you have time to visit the historic sites and the best beaches on St Kitts, as described previously.

- On your third day, venture up **Mt Liamuiga** (p510) for a wonderfully challenging and rewarding hike.

- Afterwards, celebrate your summit with sunset drinks on **The Strip** (p507).

- On your fourth day, depart early for a day trip to Nevis, where you can see **Alexander Hamilton's old stomping ground** (p513) or explore the hills by **mountain bike** (p515), stopping for lunch at **Bananas Restaurant** (p516) or **Golden Rock Inn** (p515).

A Week or More

- With a week or more, spend several days on each island.

- You can take in all the activities described in the previous itineraries, including the history and culture, as well as some adventurous activities like snorkeling, hiking and mountain biking. Best of all, you will have plenty of time for a few dedicated beach days on both islands.

- Go beach-hopping on the **southeast peninsula** (p511) on St Kitts and choose your favorite **secret beach** (p515) on Nevis.

- Before leaving the islands, be sure to stop off at **Sunshine's** (p516) to sample the famous killer bee cocktail.

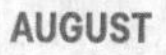

AUGUST
During the first week of August, **Nevis Culturama** includes parties, parades, and pageants to celebrate Nevisian heritage.

SEPTEMBER
On September 19, both islands celebrate **St Kitts & Nevis Independence Day** with parties, parades, and a speech by the prime minister.

NOVEMBER
Kittitian Carnival – known as **Sugar Mas** – kicks off during the third week of November, with a calypso show and many fêtes to follow.

DECEMBER
Sugar Mas culminates on December 26 with **J'ouvert Morning**, a massive street party that starts at dawn.

BASSETERRE & FRIGATE BAY

Occupying a prime location overlooking its namesake bay, Basseterre is St Kitts' historic heart, political capital and main population center, with cruise and cargo ships shuttling in and out of its busy ports all day (although it quiets down pretty quickly when the working day is over). Basseterre is a gritty little city, tinged with local color at every turn. The vibe is pure Caribbean, with just a touch of Victorian England (eg, the grand Berkeley Memorial clock tower that is the centerpiece of the central Circus roundabout). Just 3 miles south of the city center, the bustling mood mellows out at Frigate Bay, a narrow isthmus with beaches on both sides. A sprawling resort faces the wild Atlantic, while beach bars line 'the Strip' on the Caribbean side. This is a top spot for sunsets, beach parties, and after-dark bar-hopping. Side by side, these contrasting areas form a sort of microcosm of St Kitts.

TOP TIP

A Kittitian favorite drink is the grapefruit soda Ting. Add a shot of rum – especially Cane Spirit Rothschild – for Ting with a sting. This refreshingly sweet drink plays an important role in the national pastime, *limin'*, which refers to hanging out, drinking and talking with friends.

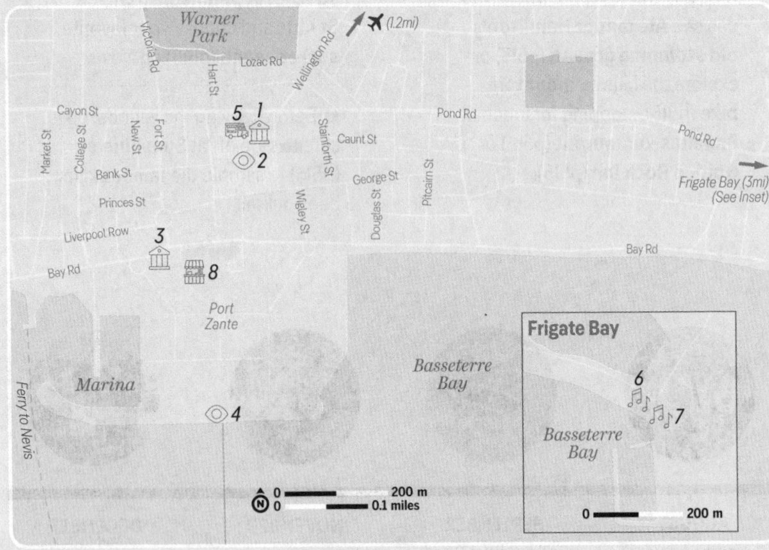

SIGHTS
1 Basseterre Gallery & Restaurant
2 Independence Square
3 Port Zante

EATING
4 North Square

ENTERTAINMENT
5 Mr X's Shiggidy Shack
6 The Dock

SHOPPING
7 Amina Craft Market

The Strip

BEACH PARTY!

Some beach bums might spend their entire vacation on 'The Strip' in Frigate Bay – and there's no shame in that! A long row of beach bars lines this attractive stretch of sand, each offering sun umbrellas, chaise longues, rum punch and good vibes. By day there are beach volleyball and soccer on the sand, in addition to swimming in that inviting Caribbean blue. By night the volume turns up a few notches, with music and dancing into the wee hours. **Mr X's Shiggidy Shack** is a local favorite, especially for its Thursday-night bash, which comes complete with live music and beach bonfire. Sunday nights are hopping at **The Dock**, with live music and drink specials.

Basseterre Then & Now

HISTORIC SITES AND CONTEMPORARY CULTURE

Basseterre is a colorful, crowded, buzzy city, with vendors selling coconut water and pumpkins on the sidewalks, and chickens scrambling away from passing cars. There is a lot of action around **Port Zante**, where stallholders sell souvenirs and handicrafts at the **Amina craft market**. The most prominent building in town is an austere stone Georgian edifice now housing the **National Museum**. A few blocks north, **Independence Square** was so renamed in 1983, after St Christopher and Nevis gained its independence from Britain. During the 18th century, this was the city's main venue for slave auctions. The surrounding streets contained various government administration buildings, some of which had holding cells for enslaved people in their basements. Nowadays, colorful Caribbean-style houses can be seen along N Independence St, including the inviting **Basseterre Gallery & Restaurant**, and food trucks congregate in nearby **North Square**, making this a pleasant pit stop.

Independence Square

EQROY/SHUTTERSTOCK ©

THE BEST RESTAURANTS IN BASSETERRE & FRIGATE BAY

Marshall's
The finest dining in St Kitts. You can't go wrong with the mixed grill (lobster tail, lamb chop, beef tenderloin, and shrimp). $$$

El Fredo's
A popular lunchtime spot for Kittitian specialties, such as oxtail, or lobster and conch stew. Open 11am to 3pm. $$

Sweet Cane
Casual luncheonette with crispy conch fritters and attentive service. $

Cathy's Ocean View Bar & Grill
Eat ribs and lobster with your toes in the sand at this welcoming spot on Frigate Bay. $$

GETTING AROUND

Basseterre is small enough to stroll around, with easy access to Port Zante, the historic downtown, the ferry terminal, and pretty much anywhere else you might want to go in the city. It's about 3 miles to Frigate Bay, so you'll probably want to hop into a taxi or drive to the beach.

Beyond Basseterre & Frigate Bay

Hike forest-covered mountains, lounge on glorious beaches, and discover the intriguing history of paradisiacal St Kitts.

One main road runs around the perimeter of St Kitts, connecting the colorful villages crowded along the shore. At the center of the island, a lush volcanic mountain range with Mt Liamuiga as its centerpiece towers over the 70-sq-mile land mass. Here, outside the city, the country's natural splendor is on full display, with rolling hills, verdant farmland, and ocean views at every turn. Also in evidence is the island's checkered history of colonial geopolitics and slavery-based economics. Present-day visitors to this now peaceful island can enjoy a wealth of enticing blue waters and stunning sandy beaches, especially on the southeast peninsula. But St Kitts is also a trove of culture and adventure awaiting discovery.

TOP TIP

Driving in St Kitts can be nerve-wracking, especially if you're not used to driving on the left. Take your time – and beware the roundabouts!

BARBARA788/SHUTTERSTOCK ©

Wingfield Estate

DRIVING THROUGH ST KITTS' HISTORY

Skirt the northern perimeter of St Kitts, taking in the island's most interesting historical and natural sights. Spend a few hours or spend all day, depending on how long you linger at each stop. From Basseterre, drive along the island's western coast to the village of Old Road Town. Your first stop is the ruins of the **1 Wingfield Estate**, a sugar plantation dating to 1625. Some of the structures are partially restored, with signs explaining how enslaved people toiled to produce sugar, molasses and rum. Nowadays, the small-batch Old Road Rum Co offers tours and tastings on this spot (reservations recommended). Nearby, the estate's residential building **2 Romney Manor** now houses Caribelle Batik, where craftswomen give demonstrations of their art practice and purvey their work. Continuing along the coast, you'll pass **3 St Thomas Anglican Church**, founded in 1625. Just before Sandy Point Town, the mighty **4 Brimstone Hill Fortress** perches high above the coastline. This British fortification – constructed by enslaved people in the 1690s – consists of citadels, bastions, and barracks all open for exploration, with informative exhibits about the history of the island and of the fort. The island and ocean views are spectacular all around. Your lunch stop is **5 Belle Mont Farm**, where you can feast on views of Saba and Sint Eustatius along with your meal. Continuing to circle around the northern end of the island, you'll come into Bellevue Village, home of the picturesque **6 Black Rocks**. These dramatic rock formations are the result of an ancient eruption by **7 Mt Liamuiga**, the now-dormant volcano that looms over this end of the island. Continue south along the east coast to return to Basseterre.

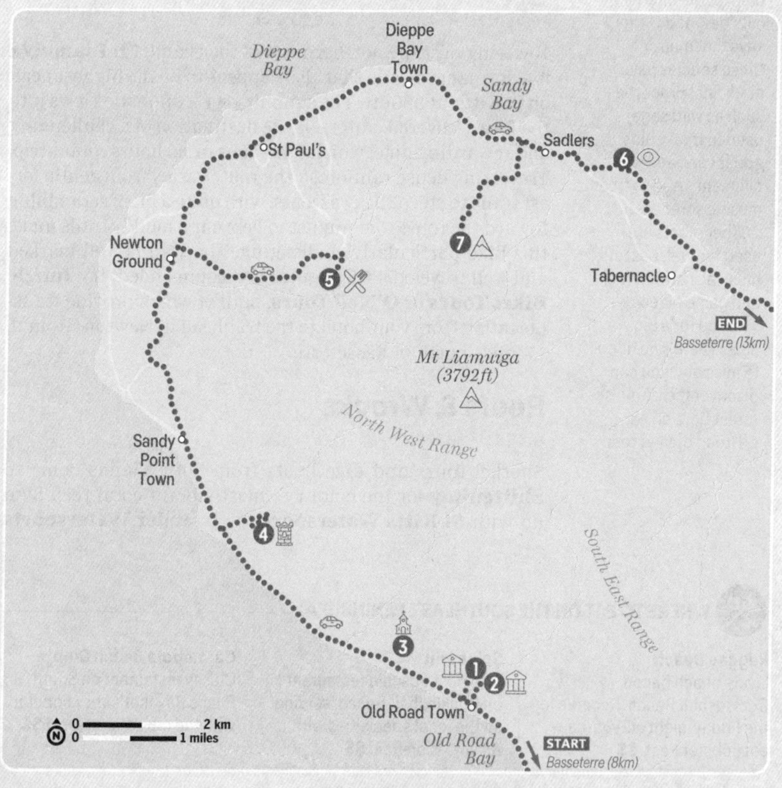

DISCOVER THE RAINFOREST

O'Neil Mulraine (*@oneiltours*) is a sportsman, tour guide and herbologist who has been leading hiking trips for 40 years.

O'Neil recommends that visitors should take a break from the beach and explore the rainforest while they're in St Kitts. Plants and trees blanket the interior hillsides, and O'Neil says that many of these species have medicinal properties, such as wild sage, used to treat colds and fevers, and wild cilliment, used to treat muscle soreness.

Other plants are used for fuel, baskets, musical instruments, and game pieces.

Not up for a big hike? There's no need to miss out: you can discover the island's forest flora on an off-road driving tour.

Cockleshell Beach

Volcano Hike

PEER INTO A FOREST-COVERED CRATER

Towering over the northern end of the island, **Mt Liamuiga** is a dormant volcano that also happens to be the highest peak on St Kitts, at 3800ft. The summit – with fantastic views into the forest-covered crater – is the destination of a challenging and rewarding hike, which takes four to six hours round-trip. Traversing dense rainforest, the route varies from gentle forest trails to steep rocky ascents, with quite a bit of scrambling toward the top. From August to February, muddy trails make this hike particularly challenging. The trail is well marked and well traveled. Still, a guide is recommended: try **Jungle Bikes Tours** or **O'Neil Tours**, both of which provide transportation from your hotel to the trailhead in Newton Ground, 15 miles north of Basseterre.

Reefs & Wrecks

HIKE TO SHITTEN BAY

Snorkel tours and dive boats from both islands come to **ShittenBay** for the country's most vibrant coral reef. Sign up with **St Kitts Watersports** or **Islander Watersports**

WHERE TO EAT ON THE SOUTHEAST PENINSULA

Reggae Beach
Lively beach bar on Cockleshell Beach. Reserve for the Friday-night all-you-can-eat Lobster Fest. **$$**

Spice Mill
The most upscale restaurant on Cockleshell Beach, serving all the local specialties with Asian-fusion flair. **$$**

Carambola Beach Club
Classy restaurant on South Friar's Bay that's very popular with the cruise-ship set. **$$$**

Nevis. Or, if you're up for a little adventure, you can also hike to this unfortunately named spot at the southwestern corner of St Kitts. The hike begins at Majors Bay (departure point for the SeaBridge car ferry). Follow the beach to its western end and look for the orange markers painted on the trees. Eventually, you'll follow a dry creek bed straight over the mountain and down the other side to Shitten Bay. The hike takes 30 to 40 minutes each way; sturdy, closed-toe shoes are a must. Besides the thriving reef, there's also an intriguing shipwreck to explore, so it's worth the effort to get here.

Beach-Hopping Around the Southeast Peninsula

SWIM, SNORKEL AND SUN-WORSHIP

Starting about 3 miles south of Basseterre, the southeast peninsula is St Kitts' long and unruly tail, reaching playfully toward its sister island of Nevis. Here you'll find St Kitts' most beguiling beaches. Rent a car or a taxi to go beach-hopping around the peninsula to find your favorite.

Your first stop is not a beach but a scenic lookout over the peninsula: **Timothy Hill Overlook**. With the Atlantic on the left, the Caribbean on the right and Nevis in the distance, the overlook allows you to take in the southern tip's spectacular landscape and seascape in one sweeping panorama.

A tiny strip of sand, **Whitehouse Bay Beach** is dominated by the dock and building of an abandoned restaurant. It creates a weird atmosphere, for sure, but this is one of the island's top spots for snorkeling. Swim off the southern end of the beach to find the reef and an intriguing shipwreck, recently revealed to be a British warship from the 1782 Battle of Frigate Bay.

At the southern tip of the island, **Cockleshell Beach** is a slender beauty with enticing views across the Narrows to Nevis. Waves lap gently at the sand, where lounge chairs and beach umbrellas are lined up in front of a row of beach bars.

At **South Friar's Bay**, take your pick from two beloved beach bars serving up rum punch and good vibes. There's decent snorkeling around the rocks at either end of the beach. This is a terrific place to be around sunset, when the bustle of the cruise passengers is long gone and the sky turns magnificent shades of pink and orange. The vervet monkeys like it here, too.

MONKEY SEE, MONKEY DO

Kittitians like to say there are more monkeys than humans on their small island, and it's easy to believe that when you see troops of primates congregating on the beaches and trails.

Expressive they might be, but these long-tailed creatures are an invasive species that was brought to the islands by European settlers in the 17th century.

The monkeys thrived (to say the least) and now their ravenous descendants are best known for devouring crops and destroying local farms. Various programs are in place to reduce and isolate the monkey populations, but so far these clever and extremely adaptable beasts have not been hampered in their colonisation of the island.

GETTING AROUND

A rental car will give you the most flexibility to visit the sights on the island and explore the beaches on the southeast peninsula. That said, taxis and tours are plentiful and will transport you where you need to go. You'll also see minivans, known as 'H buses,' which cruise the main road around the island. There are bus stops in town and in the villages, but the buses stop on demand. The inexpensive fares are payable in East Caribbean dollars. H buses do not run to Frigate Bay or to the southeast peninsula.

St Kitts

CHARLESTOWN

Charlestown

Nevis

In this two-island family, Nevis is the sweet and serene little sister to bigger, brasher St Kitts. And the Nevisian capital, Charlestown, is fittingly charming: quaint and colorful by day, and quiet after dark. Aside from the ferry terminal – which is front and center – there's not a lot of tourist infrastructure to draw a visitor into Charlestown. But this is the historical and cultural capital, so the island's rich heritage is on display here. It's worth a wander around the narrow streets to admire the old wooden houses with their gingerbread trim, as well as the impressive Georgian facade of the Old Courthouse and other government buildings. This is also where you can discover some unique aspects of Nevisian history, including the site of the island's first luxury hotel and the earliest stomping grounds of US founding father Alexander Hamilton.

TOP TIP

Islanders always offer a rather formal greeting – 'Good morning', 'Good afternoon' or 'Good evening' – before proceeding with business or conversation. This may feel like unnecessary formality if you're not used to it, but it's an important custom that visitors are advised to respect and return.

EQROY/SHUTTERSTOCK ©

Museum of Nevis History

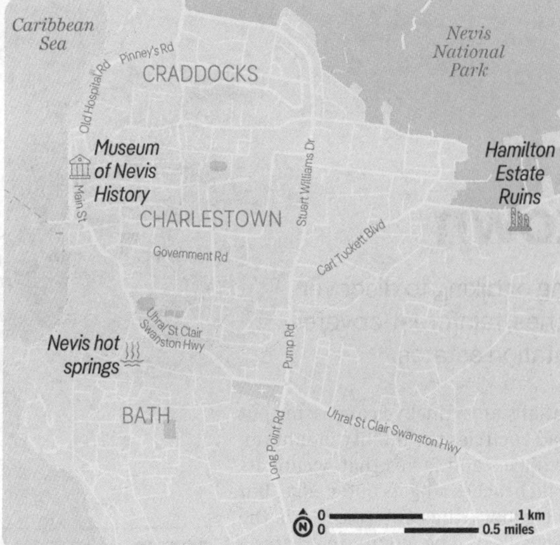

Alexander Hamilton's Nevis

WALK IN A FOUNDING FATHER'S FOOTSTEPS

Anyone who has seen the musical *Hamilton!* knows that the statesman Alexander Hamilton was 'dropped in the middle of a forgotten spot in the Caribbean...' That was Nevis (although it was a thriving port and not exactly a forgotten spot). Hamilton only spent a few years here before he was abandoned by his father and then moved with his mother to St Croix. But the island proudly claims him as a native son, with the small **Museum of Nevis History** on the site of his supposed birthplace. About 2.5 miles east, in the hills above Charlestown, the **ruins of the Hamilton Estate** include the old sugar mill, the chimney, and other crumbling structures. Alexander never lived at this property, but it remained in the family until it ceased operation in 1951.

Hot-Spring Therapy

SOAK IN VOLCANIC THERMAL POOLS

In central Charlestown, the historic **Nevis hot springs** have long served as a gathering and bathing place for islanders. In fact, the Bath Hotel – built in 1778 – was the island's original luxury hotel and spa. The ruins of the old bathhouse are still on the site, and the former hotel is now a government building. But the hot springs still feed a series of thermal pools ranging in temperature from 97°F (36°C) to 108°F (42°C) where islanders go to bathe, relax or soak in the therapeutic waters.

BEST BOOKS SET IN NEVIS

Noreen Meguid and **John Maher** are owners of the Mount Nevis Hotel (@MountNevisHotel). Here are their recommendations for the best books to read on your Caribbean vacation.

Don't Stop the Carnival
Herman Wouk's hilarious novel is set on a fictional island resembling Nevis.

The Moon Also Rising
Alice Early takes her readers from Scotland to New York to Nevis in this wonderful ghost-story-meets-love-story.

Rivers of Time
Historian June Goodfield researches the life of a Nevisian woman after discovering her mysterious 17th-century gravestone.

GETTING AROUND

Streets are narrow and parking is sparse in Charlestown, so you're best off strolling around (although it's a hike up to the Hamilton Estate, so you might want wheels for that).

Beyond Charlestown

Lovers' Beach
Nesbit Beach
New Castle
Rawlins
Pinneys Beach
Nevis Peak
Golden Rock Inn
Charlestown
The Hermitage
Montpelier Plantation

Explore Nevis by hiking or biking to discover secluded sandy beaches, rainforest-covered hills, and historic plantation estates.

The island of Nevis is essentially an extinct volcano rising out of the Caribbean Sea. A road encircles the mighty mountain, connecting the scattered villages and farms that occupy its slopes. And yes, splendid wild beaches ring its outer edge. But the indisputable star of the show – the centerpiece – is the majestic, forest-covered Nevis Peak. The mountain creates a topographic playground for hiking, biking and exploration of all sorts. It's hard to imagine that these same forested slopes were once agricultural land – namely, sugar plantations. But just as the rainforest has reclaimed the land, so too has the new economy claimed some of the farms, converting them into unique and exquisite boutique hotels.

TOP TIP

For independent explorers, there are several hiking trails on the slopes of Nevis Peak, starting from the grounds of the Golden Rock Inn.

Nevis Peak

Cycle the Island

ROLLING HILLS AND SEA VIEWS

From a cyclist's perspective, Nevis has two things going for it: it's small (20 miles around) and there aren't many cars. Add the gorgeous Caribbean views and the challenging hills, and you've got yourself an ideal place to explore by bike. Book a tour with **Nevis Adventure Tours**, or rent a bike from **Bike Nevis** (at Oualie Beach Resort, 5.6 miles north of Charlestown) to explore on your own. An easy place to start is the hills and trails around the villages of **New Castle** and **Rawlins**, where you can stop at the picturesque ruins of the 19th-century Cottle Church and climb to the summit of Maddens Mount. Alternatively, ride 'around the rock', circumnavigating the island on the (mostly paved) main road, with potential stops at hidden beaches and satisfying restaurants. Ambitious riders might detour to the haunted ruins of the Eden Brown Estate (said to be haunted) or stop for lunch at one of the other former sugarcane estates in the hills. The route offers a fair amount of climbing when the road turns inland, especially around Zion Hill.

Summit Steep

CLIMB A CLOUD-SHROUDED MOUNTAIN

Looming over the eponymous island, **Nevis Peak** is a steep, volcanic mountain, thick with greenery and often shrouded in mist. Indeed, the constant cloud cover earned the island its name, which comes from Nuestra Señora de las Nieves (Our Lady of the Snows) – a reference to a miraculous snowfall on Esquine Hill in 4th-century Rome. There's actually no snow but rather dense rainforest on the slopes of Nevis Peak, which dominates the center of the island. At 3200ft, it's not as high as Mt Liamuiga on St Kitts, but it is extremely steep. Reach the summit on a four-hour excursion with **Nevis Nature Tours** or **Nevis Adventure Tours**. While the first half is a mostly straightforward rainforest hike, the second half is an all-out four-limb climb over rocks and roots, with ropes to assist. Make sure you have proper footwear and plenty of water. Both companies provide transportation to the trailhead, which is 4.5 miles east of Charlestown.

Secret Beaches

BEYOND PINNEY'S BEACH

Many sun-worshippers make a beeline for **Pinneys Beach** for high-quality beach time, frequenting the bars and snorkeling the breakwater. It's not the worst way to spend your vacation, but Nevis is practically lined with beaches, so there's no need

NEVIS' BEST HIKE

Reggie Douglas is a cyclist, nature lover, and owner of Nevis Adventure Tours 9nevisadventure-tours.com). Here he describes one of his favorite hikes, which he calls Russell's Rest.

It starts around 500ft above sea level and it takes you into the interior of the mountain to a series of waterfalls.

When it rains, the upper falls are running very well. It's just so beautiful and peaceful. One of the bigger falls is called 'the shower' because you can actually go under. And the two bigger falls that are up above it have pools for a dip.

The hike gets difficult as you go up higher to the bigger falls, but it's worth it.

WHERE TO EAT IN NEVIS

Bananas Restaurant
Head deep into the hills to sample the best of local cuisine, enhanced with international flavors. **$$$**

Driftwood
Serves seafood and other delicacies in a stunning waterside setting near the airport. **$$**

Yachtsman Grill
Welcoming beachfront restaurant serving thin-crust pizza with myriad toppings. (Lobster pizza? Yes, please!) **$$**

HELLO, SUNSHINE

An island institution, **Sunshine's Beach Bar** is a rasta-colored, rum-fueled beacon of happiness and good vibes on Pinney's Beach. It's a pleasant place by day, when beach bums take a break from the sun to feast on lobster salad, conch fritters, and spicy chicken wings. But the party ramps up just before sunset, thanks to reggae beats and free-flowing drinks. The signature cocktail is the strong and tasty killer bee. The recipe is a secret, of course, but it involves some combination of rum, passionfruit juice, and club soda, plus honey, lemon and bitters. Be careful: it goes down easy, but the sting of the killer bee is strong!

to fight the crowds. If you want your own private beach, hitch or drive 6 miles to the northern end of the island. Romantic, wild and windswept **Lovers' Beach** is a turtle nesting ground from April to November; otherwise it's often empty. Look for the turnoff about half a mile past Oualie Beach. Just past the airport, **Nesbit Beach** is another gorgeous strip of blinding white sand, facing the Atlantic. The beach bar is now closed, which means this place is often deserted. About half a mile further along, you can't miss the sign for **Herbert's Beach**, another unruly Atlantic-facing strand. The only living beings you're likely to see are the resident goats. There are no facilities at any of these beaches, so bring your own food and water, and swim at your own risk.

Repurposed History

STAY AT A FORMER PLANTATION

Nevis' sugar plantations thrived on the backs of enslaved people's labor. It's a sordid history that permeates the island – and especially the picturesque ruins and restored buildings of the former plantations. In the hills of Nevis, 3 to 5 miles east of Charlestown, several estates have become boutique hotels with restaurants. The intention is not to romanticize plantation life but to give new purpose to grounds and buildings that carry the weight of history.

Dating to the turn of the 18th century, **The Hermitage** preserves its historic atmosphere. Its Great House is supposedly the oldest house on the island (and one of the oldest wooden houses in the Caribbean). Reminiscent of the era, the library and dining room are open to guests, with signs explaining the history of the farm. The restaurant on the veranda overlooks an orchard of mango trees, while the guest rooms are in colorful 'gingerbread' cottages built in traditional style. The Wednesday-night **West Indian feast** is a highlight.

Set in spectacular grounds and gardens, the **Montpelier Plantation** was founded in 1687, and several structures remain from that era. By contrast, the classy guest rooms are contemporary, and bedecked with art. The restaurant is highly recommended, especially the private dining in the remains of the sugar-mill tower.

Finally, the gorgeous **Golden Rock Inn** is lush with palms and native grasses. The innovative design incorporates several 19th-century plantation structures into the hotel: the huge stone oven is now the hotel bar, while the old sugar mill contains an atmospheric guest suite. The remaining rooms are eclectic, arty and inviting, as is the sublime poolside restaurant.

GETTING AROUND

Rent a car to explore Nevis with the greatest flexibility. Otherwise, it's possible to get around the island by taxi (sample fare: US$20 from Charlestown to New Castle in the north). Tour companies almost always provide transportation from your hotel. Minivans ('H buses') travel along the main perimeter road, picking up and dropping off passengers on demand. Fares are cheap (payable in East Caribbean dollars), but there is no schedule.

LEFT: RAKSYBH/SHUTTERSTOCK ©, RIGHT: HENNING MARQUARDT/SHUTTERSTOCK ©

Arriving

Most folks arrive at the airport in St Kitts, and take a ferry or water taxi to Nevis, if necessary. There's also a small airport in Nevis, and additional ferries to and from more distant islands.

By Air

On St Kitts, Robert L Bradshaw International Airport (SKB) has daily direct flights from Miami, USA, and seasonal flights from Atlanta, Charlotte, Newark and New York, USA, and Toronto, Canada. There are regional flights to Antigua, Dominica, Dominican Republic, Puerto Rico, Sint Maarten, St Croix, St Thomas, and Tortola.

On Nevis, tiny Vance W Amory Airport (NEV) receives direct flights from Anguilla on Air Sunshine and from St Thomas on Cape Air. Air Sunshine also runs the 10-minute flight between St Kitts and Nevis.

By Boat

Makana Ferry runs a commuter service several times a week, with boats running to St Kitts from Sint Maarten, as well as Saba and Statia.

Money

Currency: East Caribbean dollar (EC$)

CASH

The East Caribbean dollar (EC$) is pegged to the US dollar: EC$2.70 equals US$1. US dollars are widely accepted, and are dispensed at some ATMs. If you pay in US dollars, you will receive change in East Caribbean dollars. Use cash for tips, and taxi and bus fares.

DIGITAL PAYMENT

Some independent tour guides prefer payment by Venmo, Apple Pay or other digital payments instead of cash.

CREDIT CARDS

Mastercard and Visa are accepted by most hotels, restaurants, grocery stores, tour companies and rental-car companies. (American Express is not as widely accepted.) Some local stores and restaurants, and independent tour operators, may not accept credit cards at all.

ST LUCIA

ICONIC LANDMARKS AND BEAUTIFUL BEACHES

The majestic Pitons, volcanic-sand beaches and mountains blanketed with deep, verdant green foliage make St Lucia one of the most paradisiacal islands.

St Lucia is blessed with all the tropical trappings, including year-round sunshine, shimmering sands and cerulean waters. However, there's also plenty to do away from the beaches. Emerald-coated mountains, rushing waterfalls and exotic flora and fauna also helped establish the reputation of 'Helen of the West' as one of the world's most picturesque travel spots.

From zip-lining through the rainforest canopy to hiking up the iconic Pitons – two enormous volcanic peaks that rise dramatically from the water – there's no shortage of adrenaline-pumping activities to fill your days. St Lucia's pellucid waters are fantastic for scuba diving and snorkeling, where you can see coral reefs and abundant colorful marine life.

Indulge in the island's delectable cuisine, built on succulent seafood, fragrant spices, ground provisions and a cornucopia of tropical fruits. Whether you fancy gourmet dishes that meld contemporary techniques with locally sourced ingredients from the island, or yearn for the flavorful home-cooked food offered by community restaurants and food trucks, your palate is in for a treat.

Traditional dance and music, like soca and calypso, are woven into festivals and events throughout the year, including Carnival celebrations, Jounen Kwéyòl and the Saint Lucia Jazz and Arts Festival. The island also takes pride in promoting genuine local experiences that highlight the landmarks, gastronomy, cultural heritage and values of St Lucian people.

THE MAIN AREAS

SOUFRIÈRE
Iconic mountains and thermal healing.
p524

CASTRIES
The bustling capital.
p530

RODNEY BAY
The epicenter of activity.
p534

SOUTH COAST
Cliffsides and sandy beaches.
p539

FOKKE BAARSSEN/SHUTTERSTOCK ©

Above: Sugar Beach (p709); Left: Moule à Chique (p540)

Find Your Way

Measuring just 238 square miles, St. Lucia is small, which makes it fairly simple to get from one end to the other. The island is also mountainous with a maze of narrow roads, sharp turns, and blind corners, so always proceed with caution.

Rodney Bay, p534
A popular entertainment hub, with a dizzying array of dining and shopping options, stretches of sandy beaches, nightlife and show-stopping sunsets.

Castries, p530
The vibrant and lively capital is the heartbeat of the island, home to historic landmarks and a hub of commercial activity.

CAR

To travel at your own pace, a car is essential. A temporary permit costs US$20 and is valid for three months; it can be obtained from the immigration desk at the airport, a car rental agency or a police station.

TAXI

Taxis are easily accessible. Arrange a pickup through your hotel, or you can find drivers waiting at stands in front of transportation hubs like the airport, the grocery store and the shopping areas. Authorized taxis carry a light-blue license plate with a TX prefix.

BUS

The local minibus is an inexpensive way to navigate the island. Drivers ply several routes in the towns, cities and villages within the island's 10 districts. You will recognize authorized buses by the green license plates beginning with the prefix M.

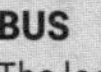

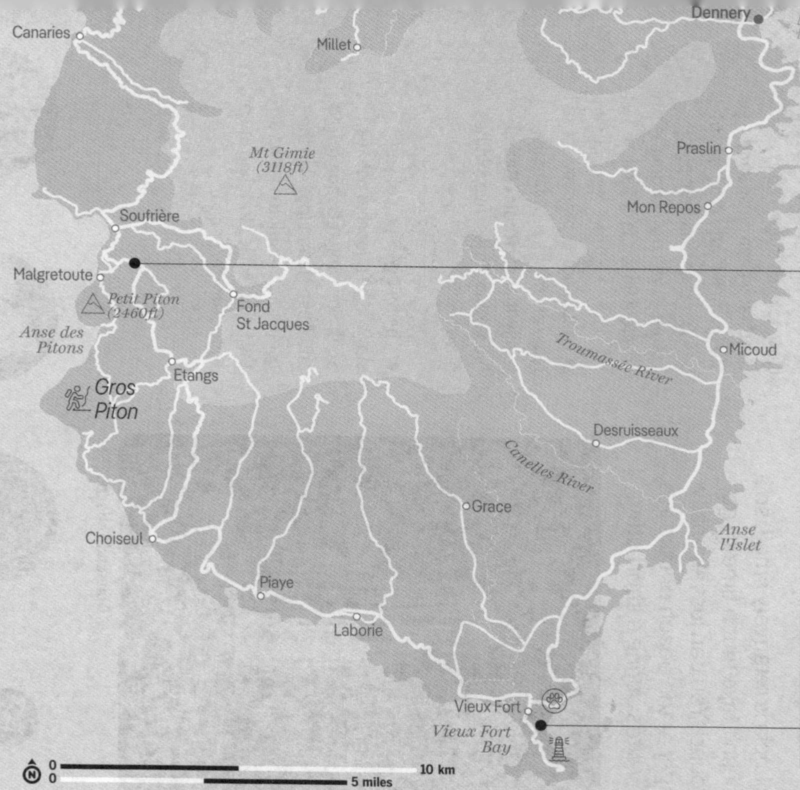

Soufrière, p524
A picturesque coastal town with stunning volcanic scenery, an overflow of natural wonders, gourmet cuisine and warm hospitality.

South Coast, p539
Come here for a respite from the constant flow of activity; grab a drink beachside or sail out to explore rare wildlife on a secluded island.

FROM TOP LEFT: MAGICBONES/SHUTTERSTOCK ©, BENUS C MATHURIN/SHUTTERSTOCK ©, NOAH DENSMORE/SHUTTERSTOCK ©

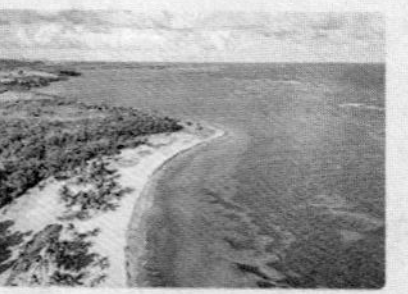

Plan Your Time

St Lucia is relatively small, so it doesn't take much time to get around. You can just as easily linger at the beach or take in a few sites during a short stay.

CHRIS HARWOOD/SHUTTERSTOCK ©

Diamond Falls (p525)

If You Only Do One Thing

- Visit St Lucia's ethereal beaches. While many are sprinkled throughout the island, most are close to each other. The crystal-clear waters and plush sand of **Pigeon Island**'s (p538) two beaches is an excellent place to start as you travel from the northern tip to the capital.
- A multitude of restaurants and other amenities surround the family-friendly **Reduit Beach** (p535) and it's just five minutes' drive away.
- The toughest part of your stay will be choosing between Soufrière's **Sugar Beach** (p709) and **Anse Mamin** (p527) in the south for unrestricted views of the Pitons while stretched out on warm, powdery sand.

Seasonal Highlights

St Lucia's pleasantly warm temperatures extend year-round. But it's mildly cooler from December to April, at the tail end of the rainy season, making it perfect for sightseeing.

JANUARY

St Lucia pays homage to its two Nobel laureates, Sir Arthur Lewis and Sir Derek Walcott, during **Nobel Laureate Week**.

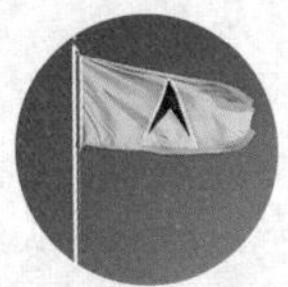

FEBRUARY

Parades and multiple island-wide celebrations mark St Lucia's **Independence Day** on February 22.

MAY

The **Saint Lucia Jazz and Arts Festival**, the Caribbean's premier music event, has welcomed icons ranging from Rihanna to Sting.

ANNA KRASNOPEEVA/SHUTTERSTOCK ©, RAILWAY FX/SHUTTERSTOCK ©, TRODLER/GETTY IMAGES ©

Three Days to Travel Around

- Set up camp on the island's western coast in **Soufrière** (p524). The charming area is popular with locals and visitors, thanks to its unspoiled quality and a seemingly infinite trove of natural wonders.
- Any visit to Soufrière warrants a stop at the famed volcanic twin peaks, the **Pitons** (p525).
- The volcanic mud at the **Sulphur Springs** (p527) makes for a great exfoliant, and the locally crafted ice cream at **Au Poyé Park** (p527) is arguably the best.
- Take a dip at **Toraille Falls** or **Diamond Falls** (p525). Enjoy authentic Creole cuisine at the local haunts peppered throughout Soufrière town.

More Than a Week

- Start at the northern end of the island and work your way down the coast or vice versa.
- Visit **Pigeon Island** (p538), one of St Lucia's most significant landmarks.
- Dine in one of several bars and restaurants dotted along the **Gros Islet** (p538) town streets.
- Head south to **Rodney Bay** (p534) to indulge in more varied culinary options and nightlife.
- Immerse yourself in local customs with a trip to the capital to meander through the **Castries Market** (p531) or learn the craft of cassava bread at **Plas Kassav** (p533) further west.
- Cool off at the beaches or waterfalls along the east and west coasts.

JULY
St Lucia's **Carnival** heats up with soca and calypso competitions, the queen show, various fêtes and the main costumed parade.

AUGUST
Chocoholics indulge in the island's cocoa-producing prowess during **Chocolate Heritage Month**. Locals also celebrate **La Rose Flower Festival**.

OCTOBER
Explore St Lucia's Creole roots through culinary and cultural events during **Creole Heritage Month** and **Jounen Kwéyòl** (Creole Day).

DECEMBER
The **Atlantic Rally for Cruisers**, a transatlantic competition for racer and cruiser yachts, makes its annual stop in St Lucia.

SOUFRIÈRE

This waterfront town was the island's original capital before that designation was passed on to Castries in the early 1800s. Soufrière has earned a reputation as a respite for romantics and nature lovers with its paradisiacal surroundings. The town's landmark, and arguably the island's most lauded feature, are the Pitons, the now-dormant skyscraping volcanic peaks that loom proudly over the west coast. But this Unesco World Heritage site is just one of several natural attractions dispersed around the charming fishing town. The second-biggest draw is the living 'drive-in volcano' known as the Sulphur Springs, a large caldera emitting steam plumes and boasting mineral-rich 'healing' mud. The sulfuric scent is so pervasive that it's fitting Soufrière takes its name from the French word for sulfur. Mineral-infused waterfalls, unique land formations, unmissable views, lush scenery and flavorful Creole cuisine have made Soufrière a mandatory stop on any St Lucian getaway.

TOP TIP

While hiking in Soufrière, it's highly recommended that you do so with a well-informed and experienced guide. Longer hikes, in particular, should be done before noon, when the sun is at its peak intensity and less likely to cause discomfort.

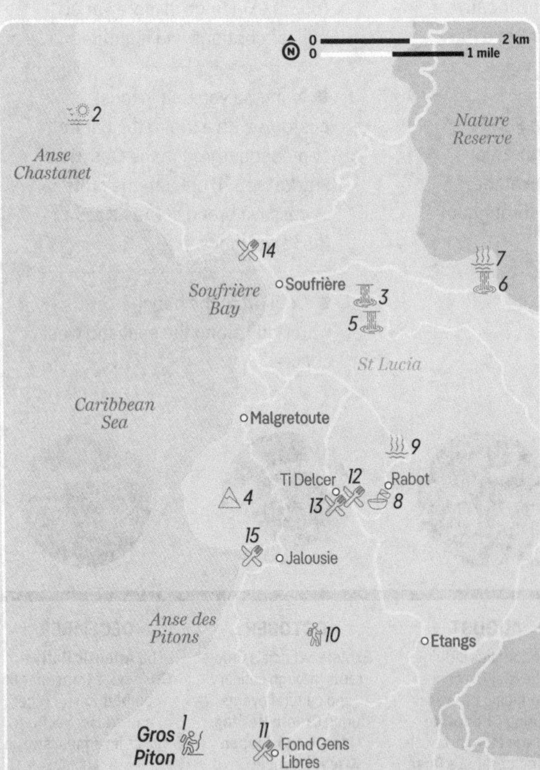

HIGHLIGHTS
1 Gros Piton

SIGHTS
2 Anse Mamin
3 Diamond Falls
4 Petit Piton
5 Superman Falls
6 Toraille Falls

ACTIVITIES, COURSES & TOURS
7 New Jerusalem Mineral Pools
8 Project Chocolat
9 Sulphur Springs
10 Têt Paul Nature Trail

EATING
11 Au Poyé Park
12 Boucan Restaurant & Bar by Hotel Chocolat
13 Dasheene at Ladera
14 Orlando's Restaurant & Bar
15 Saltwood at Sugar Beach

Soufrière

Walk an Ethereal Nature Trail

HEAVEN IN THE SOUFRIÈRE HILLS

The **Têt Paul Nature Trail** is a short loop hike, ideal for novice hikers and those who want a relaxed walk with some educational value. The nature reserve houses traditional medicinal herbs and local fruits like guava, soursop and avocado on 6 acres of land in Château Belaire. If they're in season, you might even get to sample some of the delicious bounties. The aptly named 'Stairway to Heaven' – a fabled all-natural staircase – rewards visitors with expansive views of the southern coast, including Mt Gimie, Maria Island, Vieux Fort, the majestic Pitons and the nearby islands of Martinique and St Vincent. The trek is approximately 1.5 miles long and takes a cool 30 to 45 minutes to complete. It's signposted, 3.1 miles south of Soufrière.

Climb the Towering Pitons

AN ODE TO VOLCANIC ORIGINS

St Lucia's volcanic origins forged the formidable **Pitons** twin peaks that are now the most recognizable feature of the island. The volcanic spires gained Unesco World Heritage site status

ST LUCIA'S BEST WATERFALLS

Diamond Falls
The Diamond Falls' colorful hue comes from a mix of minerals, rainwater and volcanism, resulting in a breathtaking, gushing kaleidoscope. This waterfall is for viewing only.

Toraille Falls
The waterfall cascades over a 50ft cliffside drop into a plunge pool ensconced among verdant foliage.

Superman Falls
Trek past a mélange of tropical plants and fruit trees to a 50ft waterfall famed for its appearance in *Superman II* and *Romancing the Stone*.

WHERE TO STAY IN SOUFRIÈRE

Sugar Beach
A secluded luxury resort experience set between the dramatic Piton peaks. **$$$**

Fond Doux Eco Resort
An assortment of cottages hidden in the Soufrière Hills and surrounded by tropical gardens. **$$$**

Stonefield Villa Resort
A smattering of bungalows with private plunge pools overlooking the Pitons. **$$$**

Mud bath, Sulphur Springs

in 2004, solidifying their significance as a natural attraction. The world-renowned peaks are an optical illusion: they appear to be next to each other along the coastline but, in reality, are apart. **Petit Piton** (2457ft), the smaller and steeper of the two, is located in Malgretoute, while **Gros Piton** (2617ft) extends into the neighboring fishing village of Choiseul. Petit Piton is a dangerous climb and generally off-limits. However, Gros Piton's more manageable but tough terrain offers unobstructed views of the entire southern landscape and an incomparable look at Petit Piton. Allow roughly four hours there and back. A guide is strongly recommended; contact the Pitons Management Area (PMA) for suggestions.

BEST FINE-DINING RESTAURANTS IN SOUFRIÈRE

Dasheene at Ladera
Spectacular close-up views of the Pitons and cuisine created from locally harvested ingredients. $$

Saltwood at Sugar Beach
Gourmet cuisine is sustained by rare cuts of beef in an elegant setting with an open-air bar. $$

Orlando's Restaurant & Bar
Sustainable food and innovative culinary creations from award-winning chef Orlando Satchell. $$

Boucan Restaurant & Bar by Hotel Chocolat
A unique sweet and savory cocoa spin on fresh seafood, vegetables and fruit. $$

Project Chocolat's Sweet Treats

GET IMMERSED IN THE COCOA CULTURE

Project Chocolat marries chocolate decadence with sustainable farming. Hotel Chocolat's Rabot Estate is the oldest working cacao estate on the island, and the site of an interactive Tree to Bar tour that takes guests through the entire process of cacao production, from grafting a tree to tasting the pulp, roasting cacao beans and making a chocolate bar. Each step is based on a deep respect for history and the environment. Break for lunch with unique culinary selections and drinks from The Cacao Bar. Saturday evenings are spent watching the sunset turn into a starry night, while listening to DJs and enjoying cacao-infused food and drinks. On the last Saturday of every month, a group of Caribbean musicians get together to perform live for an unforgettable evening.

WHERE TO EAT IN SOUFRIÈRE

Marie's Local Cuisine
A small family-owned restaurant a few steps from the Botanical Gardens, serving home-cooked local meals. **$$**

Michael's at Jen Mwen
Local cuisine, wood-fired pizzas and cocktails at a waterfront location with a fantastic view. **$$**

Saltfish at Green Fig Resort
Caribbean cuisine crafted with fresh local ingredients served against a stunning mountainous backdrop. **$$$**

A Feast in Au Poyé Park

A LOCAL FAMILY LEGACY

The **Au Poyé Park** sits at the base of Gros Piton, in the small community of Fond Gens Libre. The plot of land has been in the Charles family for nearly 80 years and takes its name from the surrounding *poyé* trees. Hurricane Allen destroyed the family home in 1980, but now wooden, canopied structures occupy the property among the thicket of trees and plants. Learn about the area's rich history on a guided tour, and enjoy a lunch of breadfruit fingers, ripe plantain and other local delicacies under one of several mini huts as the waterfall gently hums in the background. The highlight of the menu is the ice cream made from seasonal local fruits and even Piton beer. For those who want to spend the night, camping is possible.

BLACK-SAND BEAUTY

Hidden away behind the Anse Chastanet Resort, the beach of **Anse Mamin** is typically very peaceful and quiet, which adds to its appeal for those who want to disconnect. At certain hours, it can feel like your own private paradise.

You can always count on palm trees swaying in the wind and turquoise water, but the sand is a bit darker than you might expect.

Snorkeling here is a must, but if you're in the mood for something a little more strenuous, there are bike lanes and hiking trails in the vicinity.

Those who are willing to spend the day or late afternoon at Anse Mamin will be rewarded with breathtaking sunsets.

Detoxify at the Sulphur Springs

MAGICAL MUD THERAPIES

It's hard to imagine being able to casually wander into a volcano, but St Lucia famously lays claim to the world's only drive-in volcano. The **Sulphur Springs** have been dormant for more than two centuries, but sulfuric steam still belches out from cracks in the ground, and what remains of the collapsed crater are four warm pools of mineral-rich water. The geothermal mud baths are reputed to have detoxifying, therapeutic properties. The smoothing effect of the dark mud on the skin and other reported benefits – including soothing sunburn, joint soreness, arthritis and eczema – are enough to make up for the pungent rotten-egg stench of sulfur. The springs are a couple of miles south of Soufrière, off the Vieux Fort Rd.

Escape to New Jerusalem Mineral Pools

A HOT-SPRINGS HIDEAWAY

The term 'off the beaten path' gets bandied about a lot, but it's appropriate in this case. A five- to 10-minute walk along a trail through the rainforest reveals the hidden **New Jerusalem Mineral Pools**. The space features three different pools of varying temperatures, from very hot to invigoratingly cold. Jets of cascading water along the hillside provide a rejuvenating natural shower. The hot springs are cocooned by a thick brush of greenery, adding another layer of serenity, solitude and privacy. It's located a short distance from the more popular Sulphur Springs, which gives it a less touristy feel.

GETTING AROUND

Getting to Soufrière from either end of the island is a breeze. In Castries, catch a bus on Jeremie St. There are also buses from Vieux Fort, adjacent to the roundabout. Plan your trip carefully, as service on many St Lucian bus routes is reduced or nonexistent on Sundays. The roads on the west coast are unforgiving, so exercise caution if you plan to drive a rental vehicle. As part of the itinerary, some tours sail to Soufrière. Once in town, it's easy to walk around. You can prearrange a taxi ride with a local driver or get help from one of the tour guides.

Beyond Soufrière

The hassles of some more heavily traveled areas are absent from the traditional, unhurried villages of Choiseul and Laborie.

Choiseul and Laborie are two charming towns in southern St Lucia that offer a genuine and special glimpse into the island's cultural heritage. Both are traditional fishing villages – laid-back and unhurried. Choiseul has birthed many skilled artisans who create intricate handicrafts and pottery. Visitors are often welcome to try their hand at the various art forms. Before it was christened Laborie, the other fishing village was called Quartier de l'Isle Caret (Caret loosely translates as 'sea turtle' in French Creole), honoring the loggerhead sea turtles found in the vicinity. Listen closely, and you'll hear the conch shell sound as fishermen return with their catch from a day at sea.

TOP TIP

Two flower festivals, Kolasyon Nwèl (December) and monthly Festen Labowi are among Laborie's cultural events.

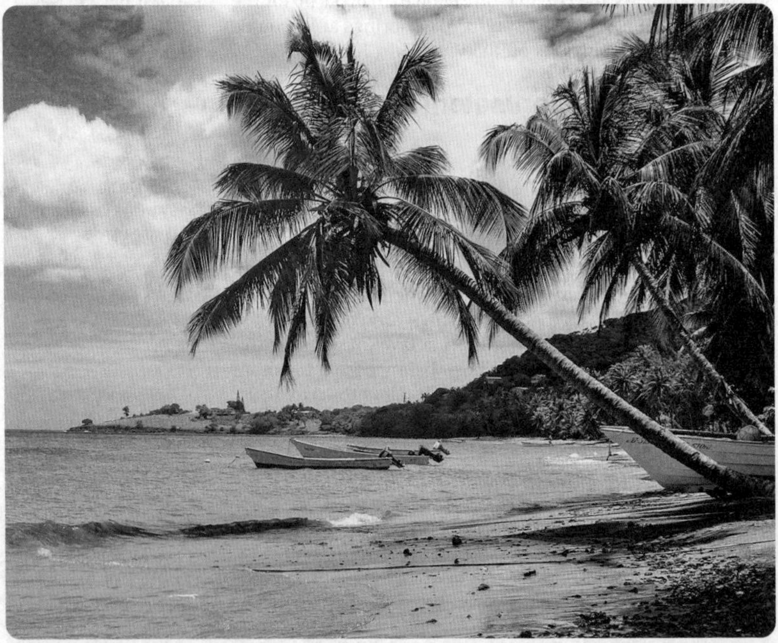

Laborie

A Community Reveals its Crafty Side

A DISPLAY OF LOCAL ART

Overlooking picturesque Rudy John Beach Park in Laborie (a half-hour drive from Soufrière), the **Papèl Craft Centre** is a showcase for the village's thriving handicraft industry. Members of the Anse Kawet Crafters Association use the center as a marketplace to sell and show off their wares, which include basketry, crochet, doll-making, handmade soap, knitting and needlework. The **Aquarius on the Bay Café** at Papèl is open daily, so you can enjoy the scenery with some local fare. The community also hosts Festen Labowi, a street party that takes place on the last Friday of the month, featuring local cuisine, artists and music.

Basket weaving, Choiseul Art Gallery

OLIVER BENN/ALAMY STOCK PHOTO ©

In Choiseul, just off the main road in River Dorée and about a 20-minute drive from Soufrière, Hattie Barnard's **Choiseul Art Gallery** has an extensive range of paintings, prints and other unique locally made crafts that incorporate the island's culture.

Hike Up Morne Le Blanc

A VIEW FROM THE TOP

Morne Le Blanc, less than 10 minutes' drive from Laborie Beach, is one of the island's many peaks. And like with any St Lucian mountain, the views are almost guaranteed to be spectacular. Because of its commanding vantage point, this area once housed a radar station during the Cold War, and its concrete structures are still there. The summit features a wide range of plants and trees, picnic tables and a viewing platform that overlooks the southwestern coast. You can drive to the top for easier access because the hill is a bit steep, but it's also manageable if you prefer to hike the trail. It's about 45 minutes uphill.

BEST LOCAL CUISINE IN LABORIE

Mama Tilly's
Come here for flavorful barbecued chicken and grilled fish. $

Mama Rose's by the Market
A Laborie institution, with local favorites and a well-stocked bar. $

La Bwizan
A seafood-centered haunt with everything from fish to vegetable rotis. $

A&A (Miss Ann Marie's)
Miss Ann Marie's chicken and beef rotis are legendary in the village. $

Zoe's Place & Bar/ by Clue
Hot bakes, tender chicken, homemade pizza and other local treats with a view of the bay. $

GETTING AROUND

From the city, you can take a bus to Vieux Fort, before switching to a bus bound for Laborie or Choiseul. Naturally, the trip is much less complicated if you're coming from the south. Both communities can be easily explored on foot.

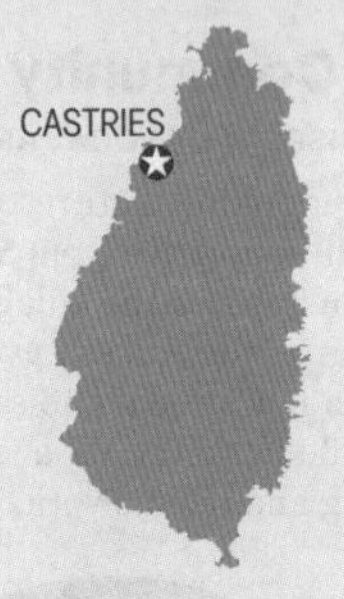

CASTRIES

The capital is home to almost a third of the population and is the island's heartbeat, with the soaring Morne Fortune (853ft) serving as a scenic backdrop. Known initially as Carenage, the city was renamed Castries in 1785 after the French Minister of the Navy and Colonies, Marquis de Castries. Although the 1948 fire destroyed close to 75% of the city, remnants of its French and British history are still detectable in the architecture, making for an interesting stroll.

The center of the port city is typically bustling with activity from locals and tourists alike, who come to shop at the city market and shopping complexes.

TOP TIP

Avoid driving if you plan to spend the day in Castries. The roads are narrow, and some areas are restricted on certain days and hours, making parking challenging. If you must drive, parking is available at the Conway Castries Car Park Facility on the waterfront.

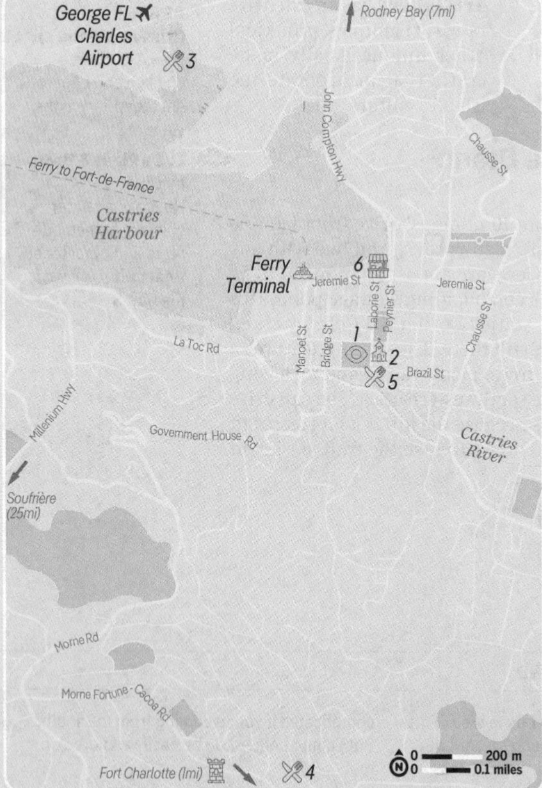

SIGHTS
1 Derek Walcott Square
2 Minor Basilica of the Immaculate Conception

EATING
3 Coal Pot
4 Pink Plantation House
5 The Balcony

SHOPPING
6 Castries Market

Derek Walcott Square

NENAD BASIC/SHUTTERSTOCK ©

NANDANI BRIDGLAL/SHUTTERSTOCK ©

Minor Basilica of the Immaculate Conception

A Tour of Castries' Highlights

A LESSON IN ST LUCIAN HISTORY

Start exploring the city at the large, open-air **Castries Market**, where you'll find fresh local produce, spices and the catch of the day. In the adjacent Vendor's Arcade, locally handcrafted straw items, pottery, wood carvings and other trinkets make for ideal souvenirs. It's closed on Sunday.

Among Castries' main sights is the **Minor Basilica of the Immaculate Conception**, a cavernous stone structure that's one of the largest cathedrals in the Caribbean. St Lucian artist Dunstan St Omer, who also designed the national flag, painted the brightly colored interiors with murals depicting biblical scenes and the image of the island's patron saint, St Lucia, prominently positioned above the altar. Join the locals for one of the masses to experience the communal atmosphere.

The iconic **Derek Walcott Square** is a tribute to the 1992 winner of the Nobel Prize in Literature. Both Sir Walcott and Sir William Arthur Lewis (winner of the Nobel Prize in Economics in 1979) are celebrated with bronze busts amid the flowers, a gazebo and pristinely manicured lawn. That the square is now named after Walcott is serendipitous – the wordsmith's legendary career started with 'A City's Death by Fire', a poem he wrote as an 18-year-old to memorialize the devastating Castries blaze.

For sublime views of the capital and harbor, head to **Morne Fortune** (about 3 miles south of the center). Steeped in history, the 'Hill of Good Luck' isn't made for pedestrians, but the commanding view is worth a ride. The formidable **Fort Charlotte**, once home to French barracks, now houses the St Lucian campus of the University of the West Indies.

BEST PLACES TO EAT IN CASTRIES

Coal Pot
Fresh ingredients and local spices provide an innovative take on Creole cuisine on the waterfront. $$

The Balcony
Fresh, hot and modern cuisine with a breathtaking panorama of Derek Walcott Sq. $$

Pink Plantation House
Creole dishes prepared with local ingredients are complemented by unbeatable veranda views. $$

GETTING AROUND

Most bus routes run through Castries and are stationed at various points around the capital.

Walking around the city is fairly easy since most of the attractions are in close proximity to each other. It's also a good idea to get around on foot because parking is typically difficult to come by on the narrow streets.

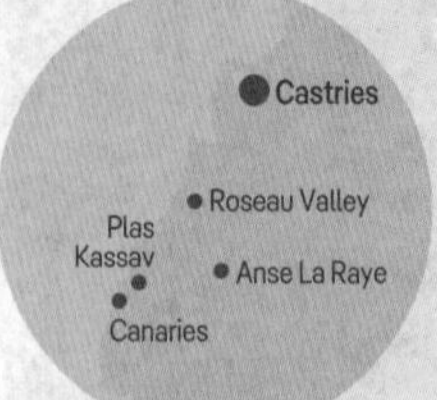

Beyond Castries

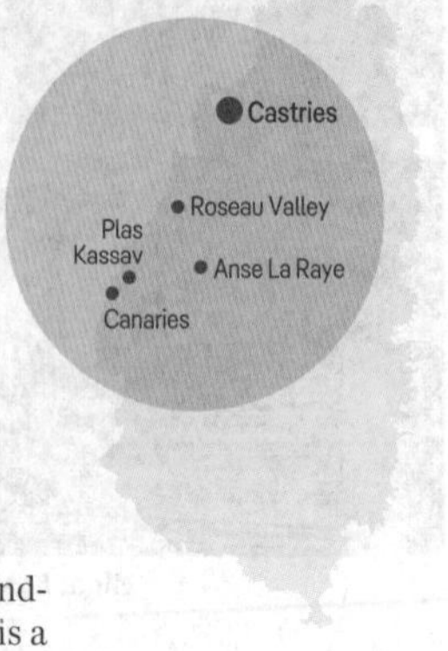

The waves of the Caribbean Sea gently lap the west coast as slow-paced villages beckon.

St Lucia's western front is known for its undulating and winding roads, but it's worth the effort. Sheltered Marigot Bay is a picturesque yachties' haven and a palm-studded oasis. South of Marigot Bay, in Roseau, is the island's only remaining rum distillery. About 20 minutes south of Castries, you will find the serene west-coast fishing village of Anse La Raye. Outwardly unassuming, a trek further inland reveals natural treasures like the River Rock Waterfall. Canaries is another small neighboring fishing village with a close-knit community aura. There are a few shops and bars, and it's where you can find some of the best cassava bread and micro-batch chocolate courtesy of Plas Kassav and Cacoa Sainte Lucie.

TOP TIP

The underrated River Rock Waterfall is a tranquil enclave with picnic tables and a changing room.

Anse La Raye

A Decadent Road Trip

HANDCRAFTED CHOCOLATE AND WORLD-CLASS RUM

The quaint **Anse La Raye** village is bustling on Fish Fry Fridays. The community streets come alive with the cacophonous sounds of soca, reggae, local classics and raucous laughter, while villagers serve up succulent, freshly caught seafood prepared on grills and coal pots.

Wedged comfortably between Anse La Raye and Canaries, **Plas Kassav** hugs the shoulder of the Anse La Verdure roadside. The family-owned bakery produces freshly baked, chewy cassava bread in various flavors, including banana, coconut and saltfish.

Chocolate nirvana lies in Belvedere, Canaries, the home of St Lucia's first female chocolatier. A former pastry chef, Maria Jackson poured her knowledge and skill into **Cacoa Sainte Lucie**, a micro-batch chocolate agro-processing company handcrafting decadently rich gourmet bars. The locally grown cocoa beans, nourished by volcanic soil, and a slow roasting and stone-grinding process are at the foundation of the handcrafted chocolate. Cacoa Sainte Lucie primarily produces premium dark chocolate; it also offers demonstrations, tutorials and chocolate-infused culinary masterpieces like cocoa-crusted grilled mahi doused in a sweet-chili sauce at a new on-site restaurant.

For years a famous St Lucian jingle has proclaimed the spirit of St Lucia to be Bounty Rum. The line is a double entendre on the people's joyous spirit and the actual booze. Its purveyors, **St Lucia Distillers**, provide more background on Bounty and its other world-class rums – including the award-winning Chairman's Reserve – and liqueurs on a Rhythm of Rum tour at the distillery's headquarters in Roseau Valley (it's off the road to Anse La Raye). Bounty's Coconut Rum paired with pineapple juice is an otherworldly experience.

St Lucia Distillers

CHRIS ALLAN/SHUTTERSTOCK ©

BEST PLACES TO STAY IN MARIGOT BAY

Ti Kaye Resort & Spa
An eco-friendly cliffside resort perched above Anse Cochon cove, featuring red-roofed cottages. $$

Marigot Palms Luxury Caribbean Guesthouse and Apartments
Five-star hospitality and incomparable Marigot Bay views are the hallmarks of this property. $$

Villa Pomme d'Amour
Villa apartments in the secluded Marigot Bay Hills, just steps away from a private swimming cove. $$

Oasis Marigot
All-inclusive villas equipped with personal concierges and panoramic Marigot Bay views. $$

GETTING AROUND

There is no public transportation that goes directly to Marigot Bay, but you can take a bus from Castries to Jacmel and get off at Marigot Village, then walk down the hill for about 10 minutes. Usually, you can get all the way to the port if you tip the driver. Should you need a taxi, drivers are stationed outside the marina. For EC$5, a ferry will take you from the bay to the beach and back.

RODNEY BAY

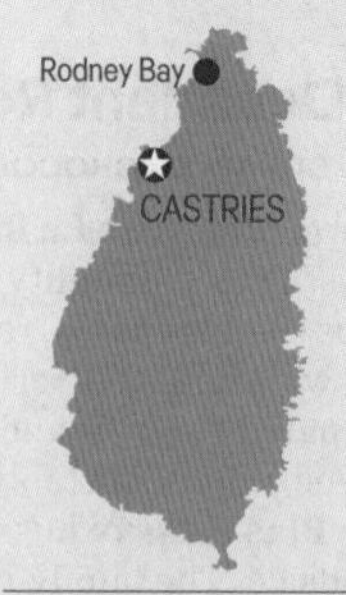

On the island's northwestern tip, Rodney Bay is the unofficial epicenter of nightlife and cuisine. The village streets are lined with an assortment of restaurants representing multinational cuisine, trendy bars, hotels and nightclubs. You'll also find two major shopping malls, banks and other amenities. On weekends, the horseshoe-shaped bay is crackling with energy as the strip comes alive with music and an influx of people looking for a good time or running errands. Further north is the state-of-the-art Rodney Bay Marina, which offers even more dining options and, during December, plays host to participants from the Atlantic Rally for Cruisers. Several companies organize sailing trips along the west coast from Rodney Bay. Of course, you're never too far away from a beach in St Lucia, and the long stretch of white sand at Reduit Beach is one of the best on the island.

TOP TIP

If you're headed to Reduit Beach, note that it can get crowded, particularly when cruise ships are in port. There are also multiple hotels along the fringe of the beach. Head south away from the central portion for a more relaxed, peaceful experience and shadier spots.

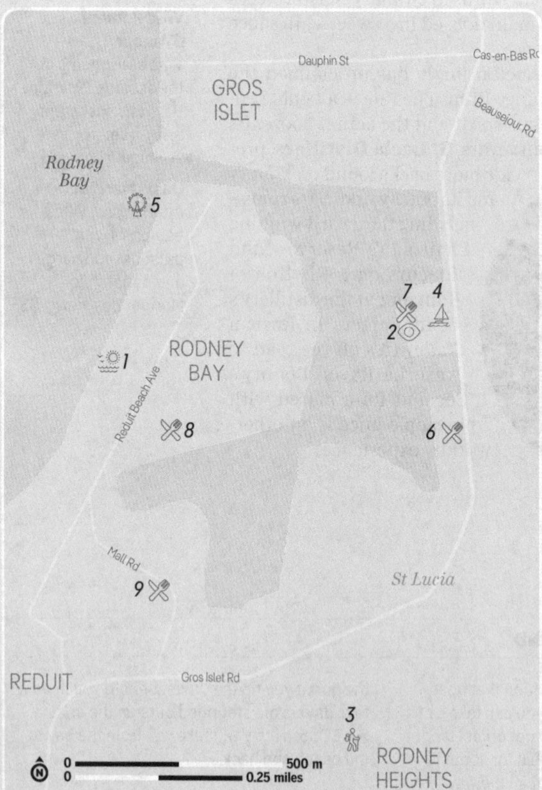

SIGHTS
1 Reduit Beach
2 Rodney Bay Marina

ACTIVITIES, COURSES & TOURS
3 Mount Pimard
4 Sea Spray Cruises
5 Splash Island

EATING
6 7th Heaven Bakery
7 Café Ole
8 Cockpit Pub
9 Rituals Coffee Shop

Reduit Beach
STBARI964/SHUTTERSTOCK ©

Choose Your Adventure at Reduit Beach

AQUATIC ADVENTURES AND UNDERRATED HIKING

Many people have a soft spot for **Reduit Beach**, also known as 'The Ramp', due to its seemingly endless expanse of golden sand and calm, impossibly blue waters. Come here to swim, sunbathe or enjoy water sports, with a clear view of Pigeon Island National Park across the bay. There are plenty of places to eat, drink and relax within walking distance of the beach.

The perfect addition to Reduit Beach in Rodney Bay village, **Splash Island** is the Caribbean's first floating, inflatable water park. The fun, family-friendly festivities includes around 20 different inflatables with everything from a trampoline, slides and a climbing wall to water volleyball. All activities are executed under the watchful eye of certified lifeguards, and the park's optimal location means that it's easy to grab a snack or meal from one of Rodney Bay's multiple dining establishments. Water-park users must be six or older and at least 3.5ft tall.

Literally steps away from Reduit Beach rises **Mount Pimard**, and it's a relatively moderate hike to the top of the more than 600ft peak. The out-and-back trail starts with a cool 10-minute walk before the intensity ramps up during an almost mile-long 45-minute journey. Hikers will find ropes available for the final 20-minute scramble to the top. But the trek is rewarded with stunning views of the west coast, Rodney Bay and the island of Martinique. The path can be slippery, so wear proper shoes for your adventure.

BEST BRUNCH SPOTS IN RODNEY BAY

7th Heaven Bakery
Select from savory breakfast favorites or an assortment of light, flaky French pastries. $$

Rituals Coffee Shop
Offers a variety of breakfast options, from the traditional Creole to a full English breakfast. $

Café Ole
A waterside breakfast featuring omelettes, pancakes, parfaits, sandwiches and vegan options. $

Cockpit Pub
Tuck into a traditional English breakfast or the quintessentially St Lucian hot bakes and cocoa tea. $$

Drop Anchor at Rodney Bay Marina

A WATERSIDE COMMUNITY

Rodney Bay Marina is the Caribbean's second-largest yachting hub and the official finish line for the annual **Atlantic Rally for Cruisers** in December. The modern complex is the nerve center of the well-heeled boating community with its state-of-the-art facilities, full-service boatyard furnished with a 75ft travelift and dry storage, and berths for up to 253 sailboats and yachts. It's a lovely place for an evening stroll among the floating yachts, and visitors can dine on everything from Italian cuisine to sushi or hang out for drinks while taking in the stunning waterfront views.

Rodney Bay Marina

WHERE TO STAY IN RODNEY BAY

Harbor Club St Lucia
A tranquil getaway close to some of the island's best beaches, attractions and entertainment. **$$**

Bay Gardens Beach Resort & Spa
A magnificent beachfront retreat offering water sports and other activities. **$$**

Sol Sanctum
A boutique wellness hotel and studio located steps away from Reduit Beach. **$$**

WHY I LOVE RODNEY BAY

Nasha Smith, writer

I moved to Gros Islet at 18 from Entrepot, a Castries suburb. But even before we moved up north, my childhood and adolescence were tied to the area.

Long before the erection of the two malls, the highlight of a weekend was a trip to the classic pizza parlor, Capone's, or treats at Sweet Dreams. Both are long gone, but I am still partial to 'liming' at the marina for waterside gab fests with my friends, where I always order either a Margherita pizza – the best on the island – or chicken and chips from Elena's, accompanied by whatever fresh local juice is available that day and topped off with their creamy gelato. And I will never turn down a late-afternoon sunset cruise.

Rodney Bay

Sail Away with Sea Spray

BASK IN THE SUNSET'S GLOW

Set sail with **Sea Spray Cruises**, a family-owned company operating since 1991. What started with a small catamaran has turned into a day-sailing powerhouse offering tours to the west coast's waterfalls, mud baths, volcanic wonders, and excursions like rum tasting, chocolate making, hiking, swimming and snorkeling. There are options to visit the neighboring French island of Martinique for a day of shopping, and plans for a similar sojourn to the Grenadines, a small chain of islands between St Vincent and Grenada. But the highlight is the unforgettable golden-hour sunset cruise. Passengers on the two-hour cruise nibble on savory hors d'oeuvres while sipping various beverages, including fruit punch, rum punch, champagne and rum mixes. If you're lucky, you might even catch the elusive green flash, an optical phenomenon you can see shortly after the sun dips into the horizon.

GETTING AROUND

Passengers hop on the 1A public bus from Castries to get to Rodney Bay. In Rodney Bay, taxi drivers frequently hang out in front of the malls, and there is a bus stand with service to Gros Islet and Castries. The Rodney Bay strip is very walkable, but a bus is practical if you plan to head to the marina. A water taxi from the Reduit Beach area to Gros Islet is the quickest and most enjoyable option.

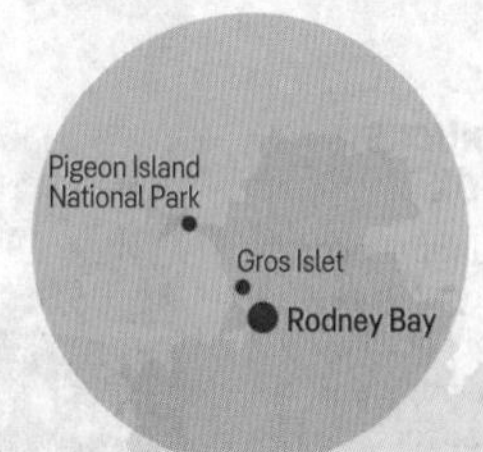

Beyond Rodney Bay

Once remote, Gros Islet is now a blossoming hot spot full of historic sights and a thriving street jam.

Gros Islet is one of St Lucia's 10 districts. Within this expansive district is Gros Islet town, a small fishing community straddling the edge of the northern coast. If Rodney Bay is the epicenter of nightlife, Gros Islet town is the unofficial afterparty. The renowned Friday night Street Party is ideal for experiencing the island's culinary and musical culture, and the popular jump-up never fails to attract a substantial crowd. During the day, visitors can explore the nearby Pigeon Island National Park or lounge on one of two beaches on the property. Pop into one of the bright wooden cottages found along the streets for a refreshing local drink or some authentic St Lucian fare.

TOP TIP

Cas en Bas Beach occupies the wild and windy Atlantic side of the island; it's a kitesurfing paradise.

Pigeon Island

FOOD-TRUCKS RUN AMOK

With the introduction of the Food Village, Beausejour quickly became a popular destination for foodies in Gros Islet. A collection of food trucks serving a variety of cuisines have set up shop in the courtyard.

J's Wrap City serves burgers, pitas, pulled-pork sandwiches, wraps and quesadillas.

Shawarma King has Mediterranean fare, local staples and vegetarian options.

Authentic Jamaican jerk, rice and peas, and oxtails are on the menu at **Deez Diner**.

Jus Good Food delivers tasty fast food and hot meals.

Vegans and vegetarians are well served at **Empress Sabrina**.

Get St Lucia's best burger and loaded fries from **Burnz Food Truck**.

Mr Sweet's vegan ice cream, made with breadfruit and mango, will satisfy your sweet tooth.

STYVE REINECK/SHUTTERSTOCK ©

Fort Rodney

The Historic Ruins at Pigeon Island

THE ISLAND'S ANCIENT HISTORY

The hiking trails and historic ruins of **Pigeon Island National Park** cover 44 acres. The sweeping views across the bay, as far as the neighboring island of Martinique, positioned it as an advantageous strategic outpost during France and Britain's battle for control of St Lucia. History buffs will appreciate the remnants of the colonial fracas, including an old military fort, ancient powder rooms and other relics sitting atop **Fort Rodney**. The gentle climb to the summit also unveils sprawling vistas of the northwest coastline. Nearby, the 359ft **Signal Peak** is a more arduous climb, but the view is equally phenomenal. Bring a picnic and make a day of it, or relax at the private beach tucked off to the side, just past the park entrance.

Good Times in Gros Islet

STREET PARTYING AND CRICKET GAMES

Next to Carnival, the Gros Islet **Street Party** is the biggest fête in St Lucia, and unlike the parade, the local 'lime' is a weekly event. It is the town's main attraction, drawing people together over cold drinks, flavorful grilled and barbecued meals, and the pulsating West Indian rhythms blaring from surrounding sound systems.

Even if you don't understand the sport, the party atmosphere also makes any West Indies cricket match a good time. The **Daren Sammy Cricket Ground** is named the first cricketer from St Lucia to play internationally and the first to be named West Indies captain. The Micoud native led the team to two T20 world titles and cemented his place in sports history. Catch a match at Beausejour during the season.

GETTING AROUND

The 1A route travels deep into the heart of Gros Islet. From Rodney Bay, you can take a quick taxi ride or a water taxi from Reduit Beach. Although there are no public buses that go to Pigeon Island, there are usually minivans waiting at the town entrance that will take you there. Walking to Pigeon Island along the Gros Islet beach is also possible.

SOUTH COAST

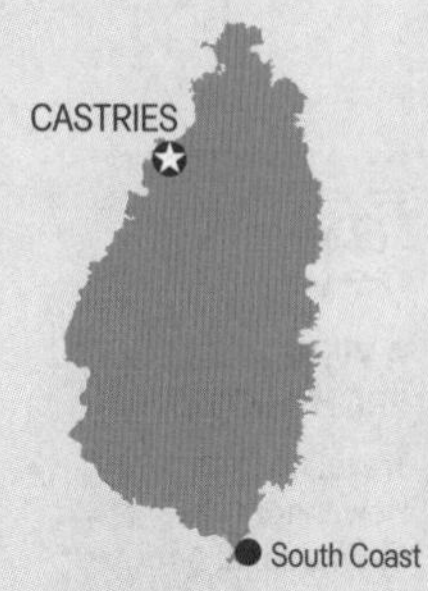

Hewanorra International Airport in Vieux Fort on the island's southern tip is the primary point of entry for tourists. Large swathes of agricultural land and emerald-colored mountains surround the town, which is 730ft above sea level. You can find several banks, supermarkets and shopping complexes in Vieux Fort, which is widely regarded as the de facto capital of the south. Fresh seafood and locally grown produce play essential roles in the cuisine, as they do in many of the island's other districts. One of the town's standout landmarks is the Moule à Chique lighthouse that provides unparalleled views of the southern coastline. Laze the day away on Sandy Beach or take a 20-minute trip across the water to the Maria Islands Nature Reserve, a sanctuary for rare and exotic wildlife like *kouwés* (St Lucia racer), the world's rarest snake, and *zandou* (St Lucia whiptail).

TOP TIP

Sandy Beach, or Anse des Sables, sits right outside Hewanorra International Airport. Expect choppy water and stiff winds because this is the Atlantic coast. However, before catching your plane, this is a great beach to grab a drink or meal with a view.

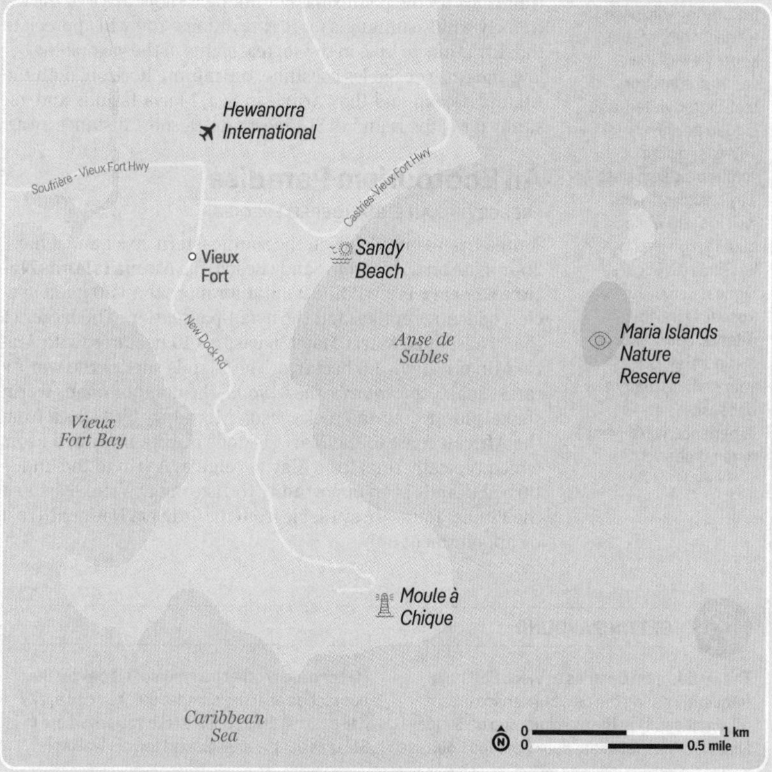

Hewanorra International
Soufrière - Vieux Fort Hwy
Castries-Vieux Fort Hwy
Vieux Fort
Sandy Beach
New Dock Rd
Anse de Sables
Maria Islands Nature Reserve
Vieux Fort Bay
Moule à Chique
Caribbean Sea
0 1 km
0 0.5 mile

A VIEW FROM ABOVE

Traveling from Hewannora International Airport is an opportunity to catch a first glimpse of St Lucia. But if your accommodations are in the north, the journey can take almost two hours depending on the traffic.

Consider a ride from **St Lucia Helicopters**, which whisks passengers above the photogenic island for an incomparable aerial view of the verdurous interior, teal-tinged waters and jagged peaks.

It's a sensible solution and the best way to kick off your visit in style while gliding high over Mt Gimie (St Lucia's highest peak), the Roseau Dam, the Atlantic coast and Marigot Bay. Get your camera ready because it's an experience you'll want to remember.

JASON PATRICK ROSS/SHUTTERSTOCK ©

Anse de Sables

Take in the Views from Moule à Chique

SURVEY THE SOUTH COAST

Standing 730ft above sea level on a sharp cliff face at the southern edge of Vieux Fort, **Moule à Chique** is believed to be the world's second-highest lighthouse. It was erected in 1912 as a guidance mechanism for sailors navigating choppy waters. The weathered lighthouse is a piece of industrial and maritime history. A tight trail leads up the peninsula, but taking a short drive to the extremely windy summit is more expeditious. You will appreciate the extra time to take in the surreal sights of the vast plains below, the Anse de Sables coastline, the infinite horizon, both the Atlantic Ocean and the Caribbean Sea, Maria Islands and, on sunny days, the island of St Vincent just a short distance away.

An Ecotourism Paradise

PRESERVING AN ENDANGERED SPECIES

A mile from Point Sable on the southeastern coast and a mere 20-minute boat ride from Sandy Beach, the **Maria Islands Nature Reserve** is a wildlife habitat for more than 80 plant species, endemic reptiles and the avian population. The larger of the two islands, Maria Major, measures 10 hectares, with Maria Minor a slight 1.6 hectares. The islands shelter the world's rarest snake, the *kouwés*, the *zandou,* the non-poisonous worm snake, plus pygmy and rock geckos. Migratory birds flock from the African coast to the Maria Islands during nesting season, which typically runs from May to August. A trip to the undisturbed islands is an opportunity to gaze out at Vieux-Fort and the Pitons. Tours are available from the St Lucia National Trust by appointment only.

GETTING AROUND

The 2H bus from Castries to Vieux Fort runs frequently during the day, but service drops off significantly in the evenings and on Sunday. Minibuses run between Vieux Fort and Soufrière (4F) and many other communities. Look for the bus station near the roundabout. You can easily hail a taxi at the airport to take you anywhere in St Lucia but the area around town is walkable.

Beyond the South Coast

The east coast of St Lucia is battered by ferocious Atlantic waves and features gorgeous bays.

St Lucia's west coast gets a lot of attention, but don't sleep on what the east coast has to offer. Micoud is ensconced between an impressive stretch of coastline, rolling hills, lush vegetation and a riot of forest reserves. Plunge into the refreshing natural pools at La Tille Waterfall, or take a leisurely stroll through the bounty of flora and fauna at Mamiku Gardens. Drive north of Micoud to Dennery, yet another fishing village on the island. The fresh catch supplies the weekly Saturday-night fish fiesta. Remember to stop along the way for fresh local Creole bread from Tomazo Bakery – the hot loaves are the best on the island.

TOP TIP

Public transportation gets you to La Tille falls drop-off point on Micoud Hwy, but it's a 30-minute walk to the entrance.

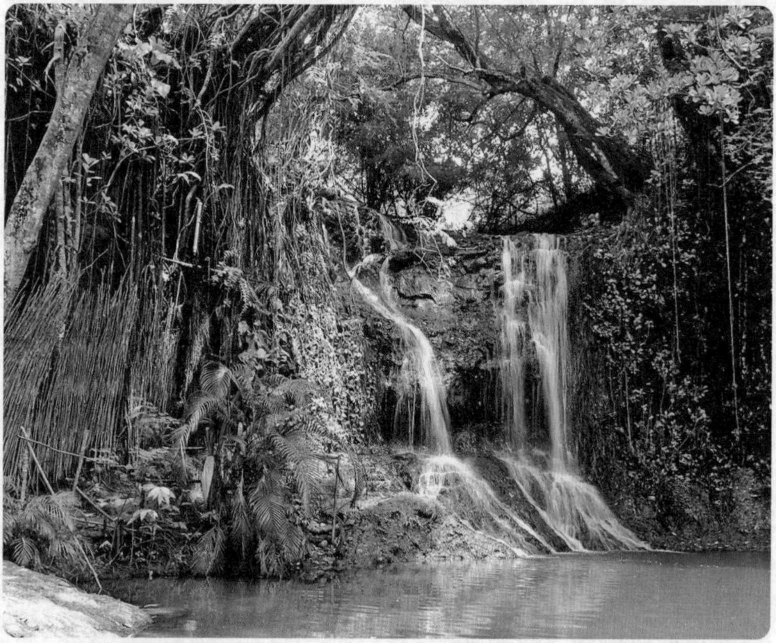

La Tille Waterfall (p542)

IN FULL BLOOM

One of St Lucia's most exquisite botanical gardens continues to blossom on the remnants of the former Micoud Estate. The estate once belonged to the Baron de Micoud, and the **Mamiku Gardens** moniker comes from his wife, Marie Anne Devaux. Locals abbreviated Madame de Micoud to Ma Micoud, which eventually morphed into the gardens' name.

Although the estate is now primarily a banana plantation, many private or 'secret' gardens on the property are brimming with exotic flowers, delicate orchids and scented herbs.

Bird-watchers will delight in trying to spot the golden oriole, endangered white-breasted thrasher and hummingbirds that flit through the gardens.

MEGAN M. WEBER/SHUTTERSTOCK ©

Creole bread

The Sweet Serenity of La Tille Falls

A NATURAL SPA EXPERIENCE

La Tille Waterfall is a 30-minute drive from Vieux Fort and yet another natural retreat. A flight of shrubbery-canopied stairs leads to the waterfall, flanked by fortified handrails for support. The cold water from the 20ft drop shocks the system at first contact, but it doesn't take long to acclimate and enjoy the pseudo-massage from the pressure. The spa vibe continues with an island pedicure in a tilapia pond, where the fish nibble at your feet. There are plenty of sheltered areas and some hammocks to lay out and chill, or maybe catch up on some reading. Restrooms are available on site for changing.

Tomazo Bakery's Magical Bread

LET YOUR TASTEBUDS GUIDE YOU

Stopping at **Tomazo Bakery** is practically mandatory, whether you are traveling up or down the east coast's road. Just off the Micoud Hwy, this family-run bakery operates in a galvanized offshoot of their home. The long, hot loaves are baked perfectly in a wood-fired oven and deposited in large handwoven baskets. With steam still gently swirling, the loaves are sliced open and filled with generous cuts of unbranded local cheddar cheese or luncheon meat. Wash it down with freshly squeezed juices (the tangy lime squash is excellent). The large, coconut-stuffed turnovers are equally delectable. If in doubt about the exact location, follow the unmistakable smell of fresh bread or look out for the throng of salivating bystanders waiting for the next batch of goodness.

GETTING AROUND

Getting to Dennery village and Mabouya Valley is easy from Castries via bus or taxi. If you're headed to Micoud, you'll need to take a bus south to Vieux Fort, but it will let you off along the highway. The east coast's roads provide a better driving experience than the west so a rental would be useful.

GALINA SAVINA/SHUTTERSTOCK ©

Arriving

Fly direct from the United States and Europe, enjoy a stopover on a cruise, or sail across from one of the neighboring islands – there are multiple options to visit St Lucia. The weather is typically welcoming year-round, but December to mid-April draws a high influx of visitors escaping cold temperatures and sailors from the Atlantic Rally for Cruisers.

By Air

Two airports service St Lucia. Hewanorra International Airport is located in Vieux Fort in the island's south. George FL Charles Airport is 40 miles north, in the capital city of Castries. Direct long-distance flights are available from the US, Canada and the UK.

By Boat

St Lucia is accessible to those who prefer water-based travel. L'Express des Îles operates ferries between St Lucia and Martinique, with continuing service to Dominica and Guadeloupe. Cruise ships and yachts also frequent the island.

Money

Currency: Eastern Caribbean dollar (EC$)

CASH

Cash is still the preferred payment method, particularly in more remote areas. Carry smaller notes for shopping from roadside vendors or paying for public transportation. Many establishments accept US dollars and euros, but you will receive any change in Eastern Caribbean dollars.

DIGITAL PAYMENTS

St Lucia-based digital wallet provider Penny Pinch is available for download on Google Play and the App Store. Customers can use the mobile application to pay for items and services at several local merchants.

CREDIT CARDS

American Express, MasterCard and Visa are widely accepted at hotels, resorts, supermarkets, car-rental agencies and large shops and restaurants. ATMs are available throughout the island and will issue Eastern Caribbean dollars.

Above: Musician playing steel pan, Philipsburg (p550); Right: Grand Case (p555)

ST-MARTIN & SINT MAARTEN

A MULTICULTURAL ISLAND WITH A CARIBBEAN SOUL

Relish this delicious mash-up of European and Afro-Carib cultures – all against a backdrop of Caribbean beachy bliss.

At 96 sq km, Sint Maarten/St-Martin is the world's smallest area of land that is shared by two countries. But don't let the small size fool you. This island is not *only* Dutch and French; it is a multicultural mélange, celebrating its deep-rooted Afro-Caribbean heritage and welcoming more than a hundred nationalities from around the globe. Fondly called SXM (for its airport code), the island is a breeding ground for fusion cuisine, musical mash-ups, cross-lingual communication, and rich cultural commingling.

SXM is proud of its melting pot of peoples and cultures, but the two 'sides' also maintain their own distinct identities. Even though they share close quarters, they feel like the two separate countries that they are. Sint Maarten has more cars, more casinos, more cruise ships and more construction of all types. Anything goes in this land of laissez-faire – a vestige of its ties to the Netherlands. St-Martin, by contrast, carefully restricts development, as evidenced by the low-rise buildings, pristine beaches, and forest-covered hillsides. French food, fashion and, *oui*, language are the norm on this side of the island, which makes it feel like the French Riviera *aux Caraïbes*.

Fortunately, there's no border control between the two countries – just a set of flags at the side of the road – so it's easy to experience all the facets of the aptly named 'Friendly Island.'

THE MAIN AREAS

PHILIPSBURG
The commercial and cosmopolitan capital.
p550

GRAND CASE
French food, fashion and fun.
p555

Find Your Way

This two-nation island is only about 96 sq km. One main road runs around its perimeter, with smaller roads leading off to beaches and villages. It's easiest to get around by car, but taxis and buses also do the trick.

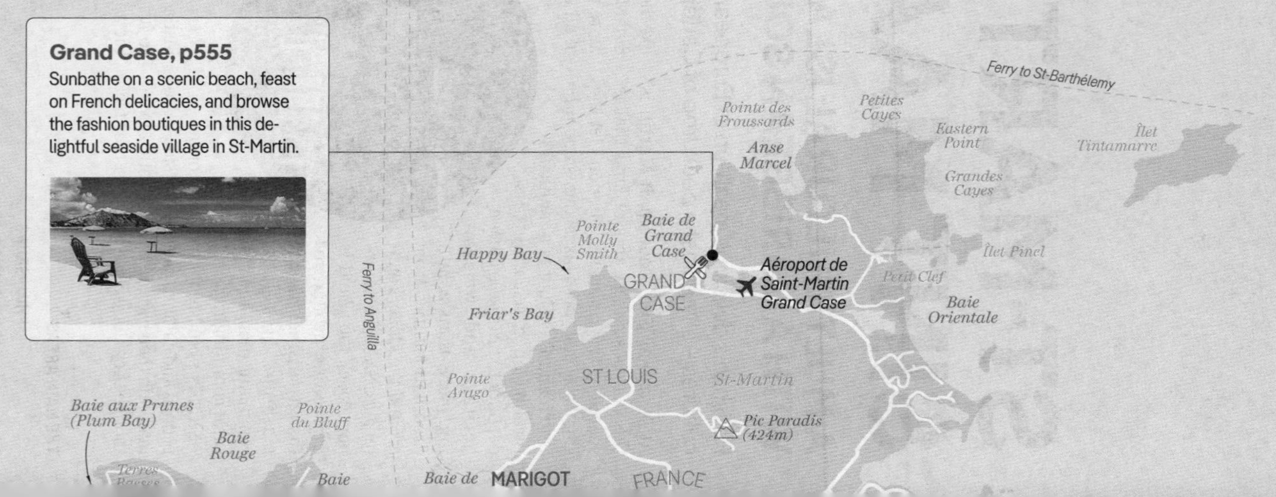

Grand Case, p555
Sunbathe on a scenic beach, feast on French delicacies, and browse the fashion boutiques in this delightful seaside village in St-Martin.

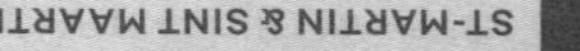

Philipsburg, p550

Cruise ships, casinos, shopping, and nightlife keep things hopping in and around the Sint Maarten capital.

BEEP BEEP

Honking is usually friendly! Drivers honk to say 'Hello', 'Thank you' or 'After you'. It's rarely an expression of impatience or aggression.

TRAFFIC

There are a lot of cars on this little island. Traffic jams are common, especially around Philipsburg, Simpson Bay and Marigot. Budget more time than you think you'll need to reach your destination.

BUSES

Look out for minivans with BUS in the license plate. These are passenger buses that connect the main towns of Sint Maarten and St-Martin for about US$2 per ride. They stop on demand and do not run on a schedule.

Plan Your Time

Considering the close quarters, Sint Maarten and St-Martin are remarkably different from each other. Fortunately, it's easy to experience both, as the island is small and border-crossing is a breeze.

TOMIKL/SHUTTERSTOCK ©

View from Pic Paradis (p560)

If You Only Have One Day

- Even with just one day, you can still experience both sides of this island's dual personality.
- Spend your day at one of the stunning shores on the French side, whether you choose to hike to **Petites Cayes** (p560), kayak to **Îlet Pinel** (p562) or bare it all at one of the **clothing-optional beaches** (p561).
- For dinner, feast on French fare in **Grand Case** (p556).
- Then retreat across the border to catch a live jam at one of the music clubs in **Simpson Bay** (p552).

Seasonal Highlights

The two-nation island has two countries' worth of festivities, which means the cultural calendar is pretty packed year-round. The rainy season is July through November, so be sure to bring an umbrella!

FEBRUARY

Parades and pageants take over the streets on the French side for three weeks before Ash Wednesday during **St-Martin Carnival**.

MARCH

Sint Maarten hosts three days of boat races and beach parties during the **Heineken Regatta**, followed by the five-day **SXM Music Festival**.

APRIL

The island's biggest event is **Sint Maarten Carnival**: two weeks of food, drinking, dancing, music, costumes, and unbridled fun in Philipsburg.

VAUGHNTHOMPSON/ISTOCK EDITORIAL/GETTY IMAGES ©, GLOWIMAGES/GETTY IMAGES ©, TIMSIMAGES.UK/SHUTTERSTOCK ©

Three Days of Sun & Fun

- On your second day, you have more time to explore Sint Maarten, with **scuba diving** (p551) or **horseback riding** (p554).

- Follow up your adventure with rum tasting at **Topper's Rhum** (p553) and dinner at **Jae's Contemporary Fusion Cuisine** (p553).

- On your third day, return to France to hike up **Pic Paradis** (p560) in the morning, then spend the rest of the day recovering at **Loterie Farm** (p560) or on the beach of your choice.

- Be sure to sample the island's most authentic Caribbean cuisine at one of the Grand Case **lolos** (p556).

One Week in Paradise

- With a week on this two-nation island, you'll have plenty of time to discover both the French side and the (former) Dutch side.

- In addition to the activities described above, you can spend a morning exploring charming **Marigot** (p559) and eating croissants in French cafes.

- Spend another morning hitting the duty-free shops in Philipsburg, followed by lunch (and beer) at **Dutch Blonde** (p551).

- Discover some of the island's lesser-known **beaches** (p560) and choose your favorite one.

- Did we mention dining in Grand Case? Well, you'll probably want to do it again.

MAY

May 27 is **Emancipation Day**, with programs and celebrations commemorating the abolition of slavery on the island.

JULY

In honor of the esteemed abolitionist, the **Fête de Victor Schœlcher** features sports, games, and music in the streets of Grand Case.

NOVEMBER

On **St Martin Day**, islanders celebrate the 1493 'discovery' by wearing traditional dress, listening to steel-pan music, and eating ribs and johnnycakes.

DECEMBER

Island **Christmas** celebrations include a Christmas village in Grand Case, and parades and puppets in Marigot.

PHILIPSBURG

The capital of Sint Maarten, colorful Philipsburg is wedged between Great Bay on the coast and the Great Salt Pond inland. The city's beach and streets wrap around the bay, anchored by the ruins of Fort Amsterdam at one end and the massive cruise-ship terminal at the other. In between, duty-free shops line narrow Front St, while boisterous bars and souvenir stalls fringe the boardwalk. The whole scene caters to the thousands of passengers that disembark from cruise ships most days.

When there's no ship in port, Philipsburg is a pleasant place to stroll, shop, and stop for lunch. A hike up to Fort Amsterdam will reward you with wonderful views of Great Bay and Little Bay. Snorkel tours and dive boats depart from picturesque Bobby's Marina, on the eastern side of the bay.

Philipsburg is small enough to walk almost everywhere, but taxis are also plentiful, especially near the cruise-ship terminal.

TOP TIP

The island's official elixir is guavaberry liqueur, made from oak-aged rum, cane sugar, and wild guavaberries. The berries – sometimes orange, sometimes black – have a woody, spicy, bittersweet flavor, as does the liqueur. Sample it (and buy some to take home) at the Sint Maarten Guavaberry Co on Front St.

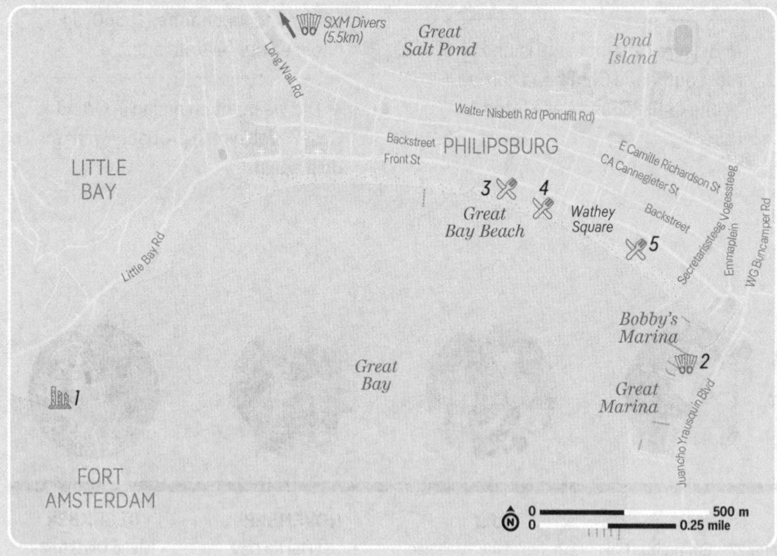

SIGHTS
1 Fort Amsterdam

ACTIVITIES
2 Dive Sint Maarten

EATING
3 Caribbean Blend
4 Dutch Blonde Beach Bar
5 Ocean Lounge Restaurant

MULTIVERSE/SHUTTERSTOCK ©

St Maarten

Descend into the Deep

DIVE WITH SHARKS GALORE

Sint Maarten is a fabulous scuba-diving destination with 50-plus dive sites, mostly located in the protected **Man of War Shoal Marine Park**. Most dive sites have an average depth of 18m, which makes this a great place for less experienced divers. In addition to the vibrant coral reefs, there are also interesting rock formations and a few wrecks to explore. The most accessible wreck is **HMS Proselyte**, a frigate of the British Royal Navy that sank in 1801. Nowadays, resting on its starboard side at 15m, it is covered with coral and is a haven for marine life. Another favorite destination is **Fish Bowl**, so named for its colorful reef and abundant fish. Barracuda are particularly numerous, especially around the beautiful archway swim-through. But what makes diving in Sint Maarten unique is the abundance of reef sharks, nurse sharks, and the occasional hammerhead. See them at sites such as **Big Momma**, **Mike's Maze** and **Coralita**, all in the Man of War Shoal Marine Park.

Dive Sint Maarten and **SXM Divers** are two recommended dive shops. Note that several dive shops offer special 'shark dives' to which they bring tuna or other snacks to attract sharks. However, feeding sharks can be detrimental to the animals' hunting instinct and dangerous for divers. There's no need to feed the sharks! Shark sightings are very common at dive sites around Sint Maarten, so it's not recommended or necessary to engage in this harmful practice.

FLYING DUTCHMAN

There is no rainforest on Sint Maarten, but never mind that. Just north of Philipsburg, **Rainforest Adventures** is an 'eco-adventure park' with chairlifts to the top of Sentry Hill, where there are fabulous views in all directions. The main attraction is the zip line back down, known as the **Flying Dutchman**, which claims to be the steepest zip line in the world, dropping more than 320m in altitude across an 850m span. Other attractions include a mountain slide and the leisurely gondola ride to the summit. Note that Rainforest Adventures caters mostly to cruise-ship passengers, so it's often crowded when there's a cruise ship in port, and often closed when there isn't.

WHERE TO EAT AND DRINK IN PHILIPSBURG

Dutch Blonde Beach Bar
Friendly place located in a windmill (for real), serving the namesake beer alongside pub favorites. **$**

Caribbean Blend
Small, colorful beach shack tantalizing the senses with jerk chicken wings and fresh grilled fish. **$$**

Ocean Lounge Restaurant
The breezy terrace at this classy Holland House restaurant is perfect for seafood and sundowners. **$$$**

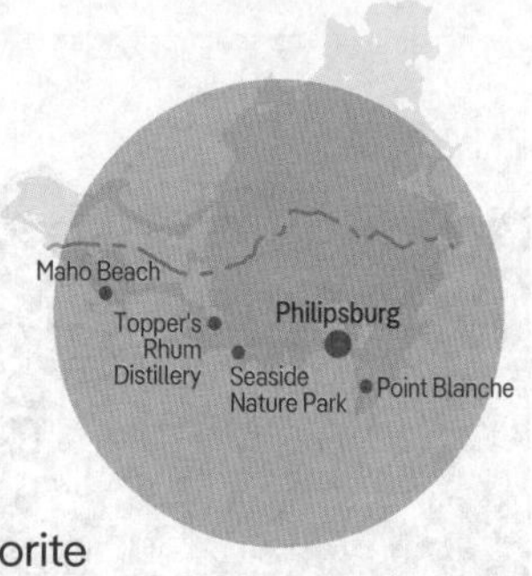

Beyond Philipsburg

Choose your favorite beach – and your favorite beach activity – amid the hustle and bustle.

Sint Maarten's merrymaking continues outside the city, with casinos and nightclubs keeping people buzzed. Heading west from Fort Amsterdam, the coastline is a series of picture-perfect coves facing the Caribbean blue, most marked by hotels and condo developments. Simpson Bay is the center of the action, site of the international airport (an attraction in its own right) and a large marina, as well as resorts, restaurants, and rum-tasting. Nearby, Mullett Bay is Sint Maarten's most popular beach, backed by seagrass and a lovely golf course beyond. The smaller coves offer their own brand of beachy fun, from snorkeling to horseback riding to plane-spotting. It's not that peaceful or pristine, but the atmosphere is hard to beat.

TOP TIP

SXM is the code for Princess Juliana Airport in Sint Maarten, but it's also a nickname and term of endearment for the island as a whole.

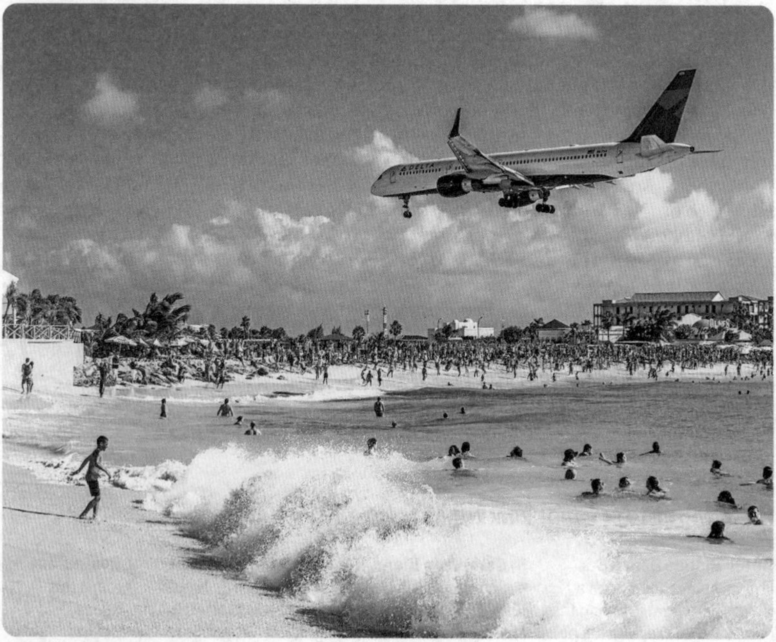

Maho Beach

GREG BALFOUR EVANS/ALAMY ©

Philipsburg

Island Elixirs

GET YOUR (LOCAL) DRINK ON

If you want to learn more about the most seductive spirit of the Caribbean, sign up for a tour at **Topper's Rhum Distillery**, 7km west of Philipsburg. Topper and his wife, Melanie, started distilling rum in their kitchen and serving it to friends. One thing led to another and now they work out of a state-of-the-art facility in Simpson Bay, complete with restaurant and gelateria. The tour includes a quick refresher on the history of rum, as well as a demonstration of how to distill it, how to cook with it and how to bottle it. You'll have the chance to sample a dozen flavors of rum, and you can even bottle one to take home.

If you're more of a beer drinker, take a tour of the **Caribbean Brewing Co**, maker of the award-winning Dutch Blonde Ale. At the facility in Point Blanche, 3km south of Philipsburg, you can see the whole process from milling the ingredients to brewing and bottling. Afterwards, the tasting room is open, so you can sample all the brews, including a pilsner, an IPA and a stout. Alternatively, skip the tour and just drink beer at the Dutch Blonde Beach Bar (p551) on the boardwalk in Philipsburg.

Plane Spotting

WATCH THE SKY FROM THE BEACH

Where the runway ends, the beach begins. That's **Maho Beach**, 12km west of Philipsburg and immediately west of the runway at Princess Juliana Airport. The planes fly in low over

BEST BEACHES IN SINT MAARTEN

Mullet Bay Beach
A sweet, serene spot with a few snack bars and **Mullet Watersports** providing active entertainment.

Cupecoy Beach
A small, secluded beach surrounded by limestone cliffs. This beauty is (unofficially) the only clothing-optional beach on the Dutch side.

Indigo Bay
A little-known beach with minimal development and good snorkeling. **Indigo Beach Restaurant** provides sustenance.

WHERE TO EAT AND DRINK IN SIMPSON BAY

Dinghy Dock
A fun waterside bar with a sassy attitude, a generous pour and satisfying pub food. **$$**

Jae's Contemporary Fusion Cuisine
Delicious combinations of Caribbean and Indian flavors, in a contemporary setting. **$$**

The Palms SXM
Warm hospitality and unique preparations of Caribbean delights. The drunken ribs are an island favorite. **$$$**

'THE DUTCH SIDE'

Vera Verbruggen, stable manager at Seaside Nature Park *(@seasidenature parksxm)*, explains why calling Sint Maarten 'the Dutch side' is not exactly correct.

Everyone calls it 'the Dutch side,' but this is sort of a misnomer. Around 2010, the Netherlands offered its overseas territories a choice between staying part of the Netherlands or going it alone. Sint Maarten chose independence and is now a self-governing sovereign nation.

Another reason why it's not really the Dutch side: Sint Maarten is extremely multicultural, with more than 100 nationalities represented in the population, and no clear ethnic majority.

English is the dominant language of communication, and the US dollar is the predominant currency.

FRANS LEMMENS/ALAMY ©

Horseback-riding near Philipsburg

the beach when they are coming in for a landing, making for some great photo ops. Often, they clear the beach by only 3m to 6m! Also exhilarating, when the jet airplanes take off, they create a storm of wind and sand and sound and spray that blows across the beach. Located at the southern end of the beach, the famous **Sunset Beach Bar** posts the incoming flight schedule, so you know exactly what you're looking for. At the other end of the beach, **Driftwood Boat Bar** is also a great option, with a more local vibe. Both bars have beach chairs and umbrellas for rent.

You can ride the bus to Maho. Or, if you're driving, get a validation from Sunset to park in the lot for free.

Seaside Horse Ride

RIDE THROUGH SURF AND TURF

At the southernmost tip of the island, 6km west of Philipsburg, **Seaside Nature Park** has a herd of free-range Antilliano horses. Mount one for a ride along the coast, through the scrub and cactus of the dry coastal forest and down to the beach, with fabulous views all around. The outing culminates with a cooling dip in the Caribbean blue – a treat for the horses as well as the riders. The pace of the ride is leisurely: there is no trotting or running over this steep, rocky terrain. But the scenery is gorgeous and the horses are gentle. And, of course, swimming with the horse is a thrill. The basic 'trail and beach ride' is one hour – and the time flies by – while the 'sunset ride' tags on a champagne toast and marshmallow roast for a two-hour affair.

GETTING AROUND

A rental car makes things easy, but there are also taxis and buses. The most useful bus route runs between Philipsburg and Mullet Bay, traversing Cole Bay, Simpson Bay, Airport Rd and Maho Bay. Buses also run between Philipsburg and Marigot, via Cole Bay. Buses leave from Clem Labega Sq in Philipsburg.

You'll want to make advance arrangements for any evening or nighttime transportation you need, as taxis and buses are sparse after dark.

GRAND CASE

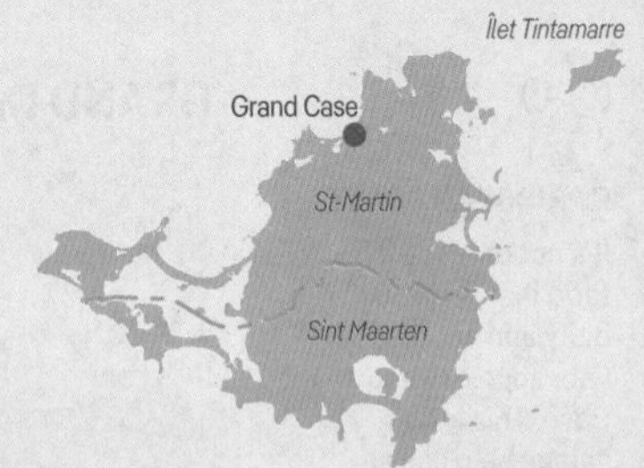

Grand Case seduces with its snazzy beach bars, chic boutiques and classy restaurants – not to mention that certain *je ne sais quoi* that confirms you're in France. In 2017, Hurricane Irma washed the beach away in some places, and there are still ruined buildings along the main drag, but the town's food, culture and French flair are as vibrant as ever. And in the midst of all the French restaurants, you'll find a collection of lively *lolos* (roadside food stalls) serving up the tastiest barbecue on the island.

Boulevard de Grand Case is less than 2km from end to end (with limited parking), so the best way to get around town is to walk.

Grand Case is a perfect base for exploring the island: it provides easy access to the fabulous beaches at the northern end, and it's only 20 minutes to the airport and other amenities on the Dutch side.

TOP TIP

The St-Martinois love Carnival so much they replicate it every Tuesday from February through April in Grand Case. They call this weekly street festival Le Mardi de Grand Case (Grand Case Tuesday), with food, music, crafts, parades, and plenty of joie-de-vivre.

Boulevard de Grand Case

CARIBBEAN FEAST

It's not only French food that fills your belly and soothes your soul in Grand Case. This little village also has an excellent collection of **lolos**, the casual open-air grills at the main crossroads in town. Here, you can feast on huge portions of traditional island favorites, especially barbecue ribs, chicken and lobster, along with side dishes such as johnnycakes, slaw and fried plantains. Sassy staff members stand at the entrance doing their best to entice customers to their stalls. The atmosphere is informal, the food is satisfying, and the price is right. It's hard to single out particular places, but **Sky's the Limit** and **Talk of the Town** are among the best.

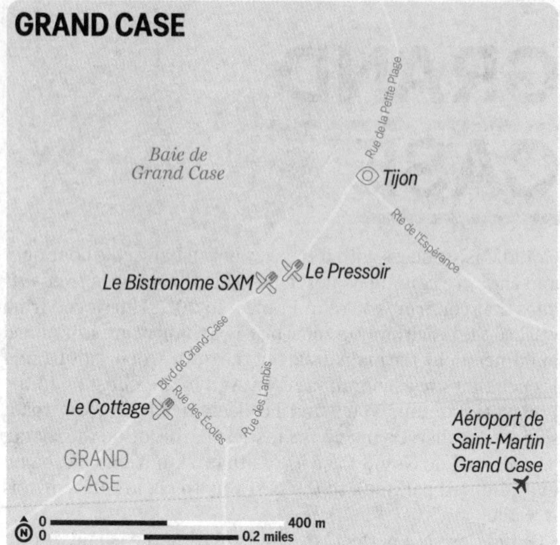

The People's Parfumerie

SCENTS TO DELIGHT THE SENSES

Tijon is a perfumerie, where master perfumer John Berglund (aka 'Le Nez' – the Nose) sells the fragrances he has created from fine natural ingredients. Even better, Tijon is a laboratory, where you become a master perfumer and create your own fragrances, mixing and matching from the menu of 300 scented essential oils. Various classes guide you through the perfume-making process, ending with a vial of perfume to take home.

French Foodie Delight

THE CARIBBEAN'S CULINARY CAPITAL

They say Grand Case has the best French cuisine outside of *la belle France*. Agree or disagree, but don't miss the chance to form your own opinion. Forty-some restaurants line the 2km stretch of Boulevard de Grand Case, so you are spoiled for choice. Here are a few recommendations to get you started.

In an 1871 Creole house, **Le Pressoir** is a long-celebrated establishment that is lauded for its sophisticated dishes

WHERE TO EAT AND DRINK IN GRAND CASE

Le Sucrier
Divine fresh bread and pastries; order sandwiches here for your beach picnic. **$**

Captain Frenchy Beach Bar
Cool, casual beach bar with picnic tables in the sand. **$$**

Rainbow Café
Elegant international restaurant with a sweet rooftop terrace overlooking Grand Case Bay. **$$$**

MATT BILLS/GETTY IMAGES ©

Lobster meal, St Maarten

A SALTY HISTORY

Tucked in between the sea and a salt pond, Grand Case was home to a thriving salt industry in the 19th and 20th centuries.

Using channels and sluices, the pond was filled with sea water, which would later evaporate under the hot sun. The remaining salt crystals were harvested for trade to Europe. A giant salt press would crush the crystals before packing. Le pressoir, as it was called, is still on display across from its namesake restaurant on Blvd de Grand Case.

The vestiges of the *salinas* are still visible around the Aeroport de Grand Case-L'Espérance.

and innovative presentations, including classic French fare and unique fusion inventions. The truffle egg parfait is the stuff of legend.

A newer arrival, **Le Bistronome SXM** is a standout for its personal service and relatively affordable prices. The menu does not disappoint, with decadent dishes such as slow-cooked beef with foie gras, and seven-hour lamb stew. With mango puff pastry for dessert, this place is a delight from start to finish.

Le Cottage is a superb option that offers a four-course lobster menu (bisque, ravioli and lobster tail, plus dessert) that is hard to resist. But the other menu items are also on par, from the escargots to the caramel soufflé.

MORE BARBECUE, PLEASE

Another great place to feast on authentic Caribbean delights is at the *lolos* near the **marché de Marigot** (p559).

GETTING AROUND

Grand Case is a one-street town, and the street is the Blvd de Grand Case, running for about 2km along the edge of the eponymous bay. It's easy to explore on foot. Leave your car at the parking lot just north of the main intersection (next to the basketball court).

Beyond Grand Case

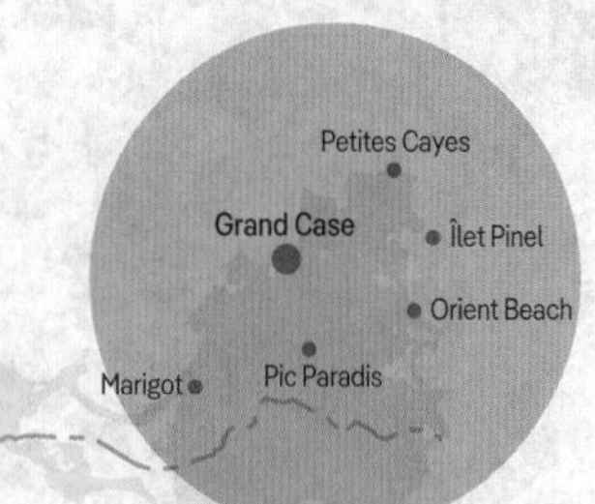

Hike to a hidden cove, kayak to an offshore island, or just bliss out on a spectacular sandy shore.

So many beaches, so little time. St-Martin is endowed with some absolutely jaw-dropping coastlines: long, sandy stretches lined with trendy bars; wild beaches tucked into hidden coves; tiny offshore islands that are just begging to be explored. In St-Martin, the beaches are not just for swimming and topless sunbathing – although both of those happen, of course – but also for snorkeling, kayaking, kiteboarding, and hiking. And when you are ready to take a break and catch some rays, you might just choose to bare it all. In addition to luscious sands and Caribbean breezes, the French side has wonderful hiking trails and a colorful capital, Marigot, that's made for shopping and strolling.

TOP TIP

Looking for the perfect beach read? *Hide and Seek Paris-SXM* by Valérie Lieko is a fun, romantic thriller set in St-Martin.

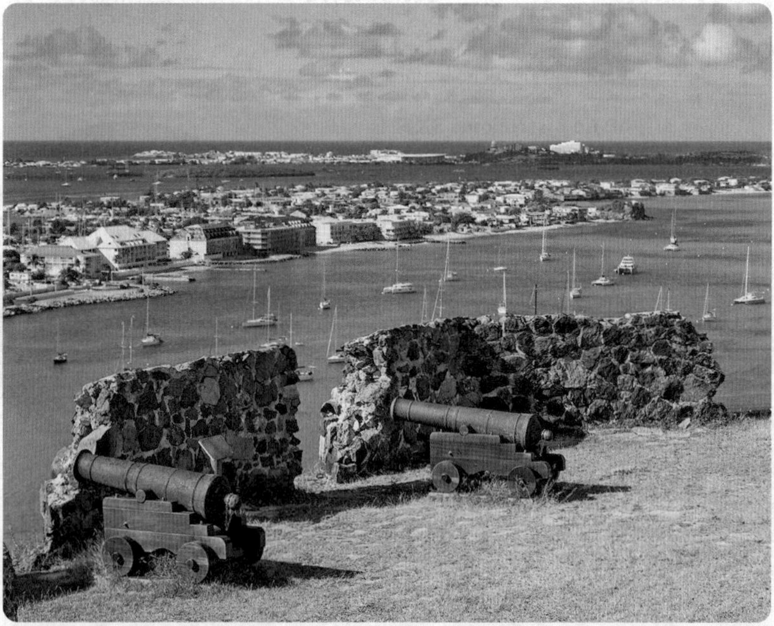

Fort Louis

DARYL BROOKS/SHUTTERSTOCK ©

Juice bar, Marigot

City Sights

A MORNING IN MARIGOT

Tourist attractions are limited in Marigot, 6km south of Grand Case, but this is the heart of the island, where the St-Martinois are busy working, shopping, and socializing. When there's a cruise ship in port, lively, colorful **marché de Marigot** has handmade jewelry and handicrafts for sale (in addition to more generic souvenirs). Bring cash and be prepared to haggle. Nearby, the **food market** features fresh fish and produce, as well as a strip of **lolos** offering traditional Caribbean fare. A **sculpture** by Martin Lynn depicts the hard-working women of the market.

From here, you can walk three blocks north and climb the hill to **Fort Louis** for 180 degrees of spectacular seascapes all the way to Anguilla. If you need to refuel afterwards, several fantastic French bakeries, such as **Serafina** and **Chez Fernand**, are just south of the market. Traffic is usually clogged and parking is a challenge, so grab a spot when you can and explore the city on foot.

BEST LIVE-MUSIC VENUES

Thomas Krider, a long-time St-Martin radio host, talks about the island's music scene and shares his favorite places to hear live music: Super-talented musicians play a mix of genres, from Caribbean to French to good old-fashioned rock-n-roll. The best is when these varied musicians get together for a fusion jam session, or *faire le boeuf*.

Lagoonies Bistro & Bar
Friendly vibe and excellent wide-ranging music, from acoustic rock to Latin jazz to African beats.

Red Piano
Supremely talented pianists take requests and play on demand. Mondays are reserved for a legendary blues/reggae jam fest.

Friars Bay Beach Cafe
Gorgeous setting, gourmet food and live music are there to be enjoyed at Friars Bay.

WHERE TO EAT IN MARIGOT

Le Sous Marin
Delightful lunch spot serving sandwiches, salads, quiches and stews – all delicious and made with love. **$**

Rosemary's Creole Cuisine
Rosemary still oversees the oldest *lolo* in Marigot. Melt-in-your-mouth ribs and other grilled goods. **$**

O Plongeoir
Decadent French food in a seductive setting near the marina. **$$$**

BEACHES OF TERRES BASSES

Here in the 'Lowlands' at the island's western tip, there are no restaurants and almost no resorts – just private villas, swanky estates and three long, glorious beaches that are often deserted. Don't be deterred by the gated entrance to the residential area: the beaches are public. Bring food, water and a beach umbrella, as there are no facilities.

Baie Rouge is a 3km pinkish strand against a backdrop of red cliffs. Swimming can be dangerous, but sunbathing is glorious (and clothing optional). Smaller, west-facing **Baie aux Prunes** has views out to Saba. On the southern shore, **Baie Longue** is another stretch of loveliness with a glamorous resort occupying one end.

Orient Beach

Island Topper

REACH THE ISLAND'S HIGHEST POINT

The island's highest point is 424m **Pic Paradis** (Paradise Peak), where you can marvel at the views over Orient Bay, Oyster Bay, and all the way to St-Barth. The most rewarding way to get here is a somewhat strenuous but invigorating forest hike, which takes about two hours round-trip. The trailhead is 4km south of Grand Case at **Loterie Farm**, a private nature reserve that charges €10 to access the well-marked trail system. (Afterwards, you can have lunch in the Jungle Room restaurant, cool off in the 'jungle pool' or zip on the zip line for an extra fee.) If you don't care to hike up, you can also drive almost all the way up, on the same road past Loterie Farm. Park at the last house, just before the Paradise Peak Hotel, and walk the final 800m to the lookout point.

Rugged Beauty

HIKE TO A HIDDEN BEACH

Who doesn't love a (nearly) deserted beach? **Petites Cayes** is a splendid, pristine cove with turquoise waters, soft sand and a green mountain backdrop. It's a stunner, and if you're

WHERE TO SHOP IN ST-MARTIN

Ma Doudou
Unique shop in Cul-de-Sac selling the perfect St-Martin souvenir: homemade rum in hand-painted bottles.

Busco
Grand Case's go-to shop for specialty local food products, including rum, sauces and spices galore.

Voila SXM
Eclectic boutique in Grand Case selling fashion and artwork, with many items by local makers.

lucky you might have it all to yourself. That's because the only way to get here is on foot, via the **Sentier des Froussards** (Trail of the Fearful). (Don't be alarmed! There's nothing to fear.) This rugged 4.5km trail connects Anse Marcel to Grande Caye, traversing the island's last stand of coastal dry forest. Iguanas and cacti populate the terrain, as well as the classic prickly-pear cactus *(raquette volante)* and the curious Pope's head cactus. Petites Cayes is about halfway along the trail – 40 to 60 minutes' hiking from either end. Bring plenty of water and anything else you'll need, as there are no facilities at the beach.

The trailhead is on the outskirts of Anse Marcel, which is a 20-minute drive north of Grand Case. Coming into town, take the first right (about 600m after the boom barrier) to find a small parking area with a 'Reserve Naturelle' sign. Walk along the service road to the water-treatment plant, where the narrow, rocky trail begins. You'll want your closed-toe hiking shoes. Spend a few hours at Petites Cayes, then hike back to Anse Marcel for a luxurious late lunch at the **Anse Marcel Beach Restaurant**. There, you have a pretty perfect beach day.

RIDE THE WIND

You'll see kiteboarders riding the wind at many different places around the island, but Orient Bay is the most popular and most user-friendly place to surf, especially if you're a beginner.

You can sign up for private lessons or kitesurf school with **Wind Adventures**, which is located right on the beach. It also offers kite rental and storage, if you already know what you are doing.

If you prefer to ride the wind the old-fashioned way, Wind Adventures also has Hobie Cats for rent. You can sail to Îlet Pinel (p562) or nearby Green Caye (with or without a guide).

Beaches in the Buff

ENJOY THE ISLAND AU NATUREL

If you like to feel the sun on *all* your parts, you've come to the right island. Topless sunbathing is acceptable on any beach in St-Martin, and there are a few beaches where nude is the norm. The only official clothing-optional beach in St-Martin is the famous **Orient Beach**, 6km east of Grand Case. The namesake nudist resort closed after Hurricane Irma, but the southern end of the beach is still the domain of the clothing-free. It is also the only naturist beach with any facilities to speak of (lounge chairs, umbrellas and a snack shop). Note that Orient Bay does get crowded – especially on weekends – so it may not be for you if you're self-conscious about your nudity.

Elsewhere on the island, nudity is not technically permitted, but it's generally tolerated on remote beaches with few people. One unofficial option for skinny dipping and nude sunbathing is the aptly named **Happy Bay**, located about 2km west of Grand Case. Tucked into a hidden cove, this lovely little coastline has no development at its western end, making it a prime spot to bare it all. On **Îlet Pinel** (p562) most people plop down on the southern side of the island, near the ferry dock and the beach bars.

NUDE ATTITUDE

Opportunities for nude swimming and sunbathing are plentiful on the French side, but more limited in Sint Maarten. The only (unofficial) naturist beach on the Dutch side is **Cupecoy Beach** (p553).

WHERE TO EAT AND DRINK IN ORIENT BAY

Good Morning Cafe
Dark coffee, irresistible pastries, fluffy quiche and fresh baguette sandwiches hit the spot for breakfast or lunch. $

Le String Beach
Sophisticated food in a very stylish setting – not your typical beach-bar fare. $$

Astrolabe
Artistically presented, splurge-worthy French food, served in a romantic poolside garden. $$$

WHY I LOVE ST-MARTIN

Mara Vorhees, writer

One of my favorite aspects of travel is discovering the places where cultures mingle – border regions, ethnic enclaves, multicultural melting pots – and seeing how they enrich each other. This is where St-Martin excels. I love the French food, spiced up with Scotch bonnet peppers, nutmeg and cloves. The French music, set to calypso beats. The Creole, French and English overheard on the streets – and their speakers still communicating with each other. I acknowledge that the colonial history is deeply problematic. But the current manifestation of this mix is undeniably enchanting.

But if you follow the trail for 10 minutes to the northern side, you'll find a deliciously secluded beach that's perfect for sunning and swimming freestyle.

It's a 40-minute hike to reach **Petites Cayes** (p560), so there's rarely more than a few people on this sublime stretch of sand. As such, it's an ideal place to work on your all-body tan. **Baie Rouge** (p560) is another oft-deserted beach where you can shed your layers.

Wherever you disrobe, remember your naturist etiquette: don't stare, or take photos (obviously). And most importantly, don't forget the sunblock!

The Littlest Island

KAYAK TO AN OFFSHORE PARADISE

About 5km east of Grand Case, just off the coast from Cul-de-Sac, **Îlet Pinel** is a delightful destination for a sun-soaked day. Rent a kayak from **Caribbean Paddling** for the trip out to the petite Pinel. Stop on the way at **Petite Clef**, a tiny isle with a few good snorkeling spots, especially for sea turtles and stingrays. Once you reach Îlet Pinel, you'll come ashore at the main beach, which is a west-facing beauty, with soft sand and placid turquoise waters. It's a perfect swimming spot and you can snorkel around the rocks at the southern end. Two beach bars provide rest, shade and sustenance (and even wi-fi).

The rest of the island is completely undeveloped – and absolutely gorgeous – so it's worth exploring. Follow the narrow path up the hill and across the scrubby landscape to two other beaches with rough waters. The long, secluded stretch of sand on the northern side is one of St-Martin's most spectacular spots, with lots of vegetation providing privacy nooks for sunbathers.

Depending on the wind, it takes about 30 minutes to kayak out to Îlet Pinel. If that seems daunting, a small ferry runs every 30 minutes (€10 each way, cash only).

GETTING AROUND

The easiest way to get around St-Martin is to rent a car and drive yourself. Taxis are also available, but they are not cheap. A network of buses connects the main towns and villages on the island, including Marigot, Grand Case and Orient Bay, as well as Philipsburg and Simpson Bay in Sint-Maarten. Buses stop running around 7pm (and taxis are scarce after dark), so it's best to make advance arrangements for your evening transportation.

Arriving

Most visitors to the island arrive at Princess Juliana Airport (SXM; pictured) in Sint Maarten – the airport that gives the island its nickname. There's also a much smaller regional airport in Grand Case and a few boats and ferries to neighboring islands.

By Air

Princess Juliana Airport (SXM), in Simpson Bay, Sint Maarten, is a major international airport with flights to/from North American cities, Paris and Amsterdam, and regional flights to many other islands. Much smaller Aeroport Saint-Martin Grand-Case mainly has flights to/from Guadeloupe, plus Anguilla and St-Barth charters.

By Boat

Great Bay Express runs to Philipsburg, Sint Maarten, from St-Barth three times a day. Several times weekly Makana Ferry runs to Sint Maarten from St Kitts, Saba and Statia, and The Edge runs between Sint Maarten and Saba. Ferries and charters connect St-Martin and Sint Maarten with Anguilla (p71).

Money

Currency: St-Martin: Euro (€); Sint Maarten: US dollar (US$); East Caribbean dollar (EC$)

CASH

Since St-Martin is part of France, its currency is the euro. The main currency on the (formerly) Dutch side is US dollars, and it also uses the East Caribbean dollar. ATMs dispense euros in St-Martin, and US dollars and/or East Caribbean dollars in Sint Maarten. You can use euros or US dollars anywhere on the island, although you'll get change in the local currency. Use cash for buses, taxis, and tips.

DIGITAL PAYMENT

Digital payments are not usually used for official business, but some independent tour guides or charter-boat captains may accept Venmo, Apple Pay or some other form of payment in lieu of credit-card payment.

CREDIT CARDS

Credit cards (especially Visa and Mastercard) are widely accepted on both sides of the island. Hotels, restaurants, shops, car-rental agencies and most tour companies will accept credit-card payments. You cannot pay for taxis using a credit card.

ST VINCENT & THE GRENADINES

SAIL AN ENCHANTED ARCHIPELAGO

Whether you hike the slopes of an active volcano or swim with turtles off desert islands, in St Vincent and the Grenadines adventure is guaranteed.

St Vincent and the Grenadines is a country with a split personality. This fascinating yet seldom-visited nation is made up of a lush, green main island, where fertile farmland runs from the slopes of a brooding volcano down to striking black beaches, and a chain of bone-dry smaller islands with snow-white sands and luminous blue waters.

Just the exotic name evokes visions of tropical splendor. It's hard to look at a map of the tear-shaped island trailed by a long chain of islets, some barely a speck in an expanse of blue, and not dream of sailing to uncharted lands or being shipwrecked beneath swaying palms.

The main island, St Vincent, gets very few visitors due to its paucity of white sands, but those who do make the effort will discover one of the most fascinating destinations in the region. One of the last islands to be bought under European control, rebellious St Vincent retains a marked indigenous influence; in its earthy rural heartland, subsistence farming and weed smoking are a way of life.

A short boat ride south, the Grenadines feel like another world altogether. Inhabited by unassuming fisherfolk and a few salty yachties, these utopian islands are the place to indulge Caribbean fantasies that you assumed were no longer possible in a world of mass tourism.

THE MAIN AREAS

ST VINCENT
Lush main island and cultural heartland.
p570

BEQUIA
Beaches, sailing and seaside dining.
p576

MAYREAU & TOBAGO CAYS
Fantasy-like tiny desert islands.
p579

UNION ISLAND
Hiking, wind sports and luminous waters.
p581

LARWIN/SHUTTERSTOCK ©

Mayreau (p579)

Find Your Way

With 32 islands in the country, getting around St Vincent and the Grenadines (SVG) can be a challenge. Set up base in destinations with good transportation links, from where it's possible to explore surrounding attractions.

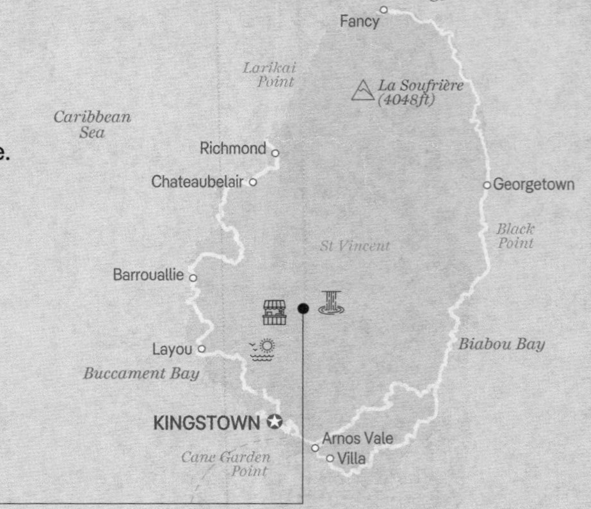

St Vincent, p570

The country's main island isn't your classic Caribbean postcard; it instead offers striking black-sand beaches backed by walls of jungle watched over by a brooding volcano.

BUS

Vincy's buses are the stuff of travel legend: packed, brightly painted old Toyota HiAces with booming speakers that fly around tight mountain bends at full speed. You'll need nerves of steel to ride them, but they're the cheapest and most entertaining way to get around.

BOAT

It's no surprise that boats are the backbone of the SVG transportation system. Regular ferries link the main island with the Grenadines. Cargo boats also accept passengers and are cheaper but significantly slower.

PLANE

Small prop planes link St Vincent with several of the Grenadine islands; there are also flights between these islands, although schedules are fluid and online bookings can be complicated.

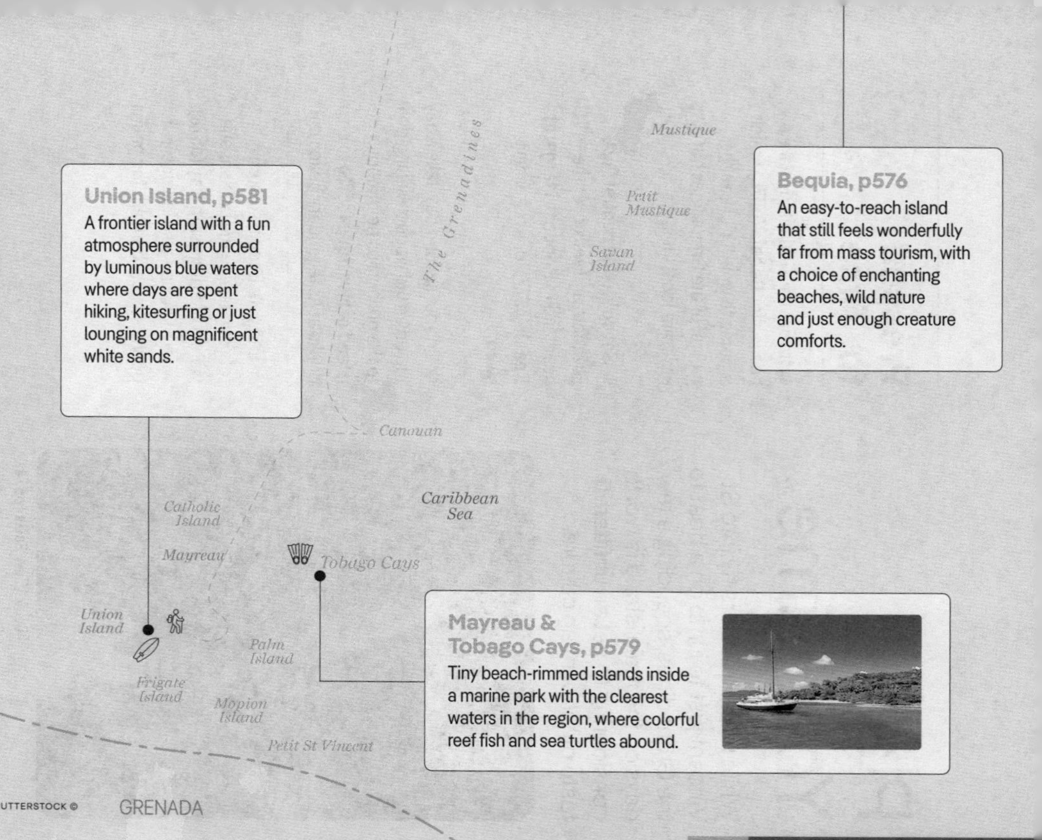

Union Island, p581

A frontier island with a fun atmosphere surrounded by luminous blue waters where days are spent hiking, kitesurfing or just lounging on magnificent white sands.

Bequia, p576

An easy-to-reach island that still feels wonderfully far from mass tourism, with a choice of enchanting beaches, wild nature and just enough creature comforts.

Mayreau & Tobago Cays, p579

Tiny beach-rimmed islands inside a marine park with the clearest waters in the region, where colorful reef fish and sea turtles abound.

Plan Your Time

While many travelers fly into St Vincent just to jump on a boat to the Grenadines, spending a few days on the main island is worth considering to get an unfiltered taste of Vincentian culture.

FLAVIO VALLENARI/GETTY IMAGES ©

Dark View Falls (p574)

Pressed for Time

- If your time is limited, make a beeline for **Bequia** (p576), which is home to wonderful beaches typical of the Grenadines but also a vibrant local lifestyle.

- Set up around central Port Elizabeth and walk over the headland to **Princess Margaret Beach** (p577) for a refreshing swim.

- On your second day, take a day trip on an old wooden sailing boat to the glamorous neighboring island of **Mustique** (p578) to enjoy drinks at its legendary beach bar.

- End your Bequia sojourn relaxing beside the brilliant still waters of **Friendship Bay** (p578), where you can also indulge in a gourmet meal beneath the palms.

Seasonal Highlights

While temperatures don't vary much between seasons in SVG, rainfall certainly does, with the heaviest downpours from July to November. The southern Grenadines are much drier than the main island.

JANUARY

The **Bequia Music Fest** sees top international acts across many genres descend on the island for four days of concerts.

FEBRUARY

Seafood lovers get their fill at the **Union Island Conch Festival**, with the island staple served in a variety of mouthwatering ways.

MARCH

Dry weather and warm waters are great for **diving and snorkeling** in St Vincent and throughout the Grenadines.

INTS VIKMANIS/SHUTTERSTOCK ©, DENNIS WILDBERGER/SHUTTERSTOCK ©, BCAMPBELL65/SHUTTERSTOCK ©

A 10-Day Adventure

- Spend a couple of days on **St Vincent** (p570) in order to visit the bustling streets of the capital Kingstown with its busy **market** (p572) and to drive up the west coast to **Dark View Falls** (p574) and the black sands of **Richmond Beach** (p575).

- Leave a morning to snorkel in the shallow waters off Indian Bay and to climb the rock monolith to stunning **Fort Duvernette** (p573) for 360-degree views of the south coast.

- Take an afternoon boat to **Bequia** (p576) and spend a couple of days here before heading south to end your trip on the powdery white sands of **Union Island** (p581).

If You Have More Time

- After a week exploring **St Vincent** (p570) and **Bequia** (p576), board a boat to the southern Grenadines to reach the enchanting little island of **Mayreau** (p579), where tranquility abounds.

- While away your time sitting beneath the coconut palms at breathtakingly beautiful **Saltwhistle Bay** and snorkeling among the corals of **Saline Bay** (p580).

- Take a day trip out to the uninhabited **Tobago Cays** (p580), to swim with turtles and indulge in shipwreck fantasies.

- Finally, cross the channel to **Union Island** (p581) to spend your last days in the country hiking to panoramic hilltops or swimming in the secluded waters of **Chatham Bay** (p584).

JUNE

Vincentians switch to full party mode, with the **Vincy Mas** carnival taking over the streets of Kingstown.

AUGUST

Tobago Cays are blissfully quiet, with hurricane season seeing most yachts moored in calmer waters.

OCTOBER

Low season means **better accommodation deals** and **quieter beaches**, with sunny stretches between intense downpours.

DECEMBER

Strong trade winds blowing over Union Island make for great **kitesurfing** for beginners and pros alike.

St Vincent

Bequia

Mayreau & Tobago Cays

Union Island

ST VINCENT

Despite being the largest island in SVG, St Vincent is viewed by most visitors as little more than a necessary stop on the way to the much better-known Grenadines. But while Vincy, as it's affectionately known, might not have the white sands and luminous waters of the nation's other islands, it is nevertheless blessed with incredible natural beauty.

The verdant rainforest-covered interior is like one big enchanted tropical garden, while in the north of the island, the majestic cone of the highly active La Soufrière volcano is capped in wisps of white cloud. Awesome hikes abound and there are also thundering waterfalls, enigmatic indigenous carvings and invigorating natural pools to explore.

St Vincent is also the cultural heart of the nation. The diminutive capital Kingstown bustles with the energy of small-scale commerce, while in the countryside, laid-back farming folk eke out a living in total harmony with nature.

TOP TIP

When large cruise vessels are docked in Kingstown, the narrow beaches at Indian Bay and Villa can get overcrowded, so it's a good idea to plan activities further afield on these days. The crowds usually dissipate by 3pm so there's plenty of time after your excursion for an afternoon swim.

CHRIS ALLAN/SHUTTERSTOCK ©

St Mary's (p572)

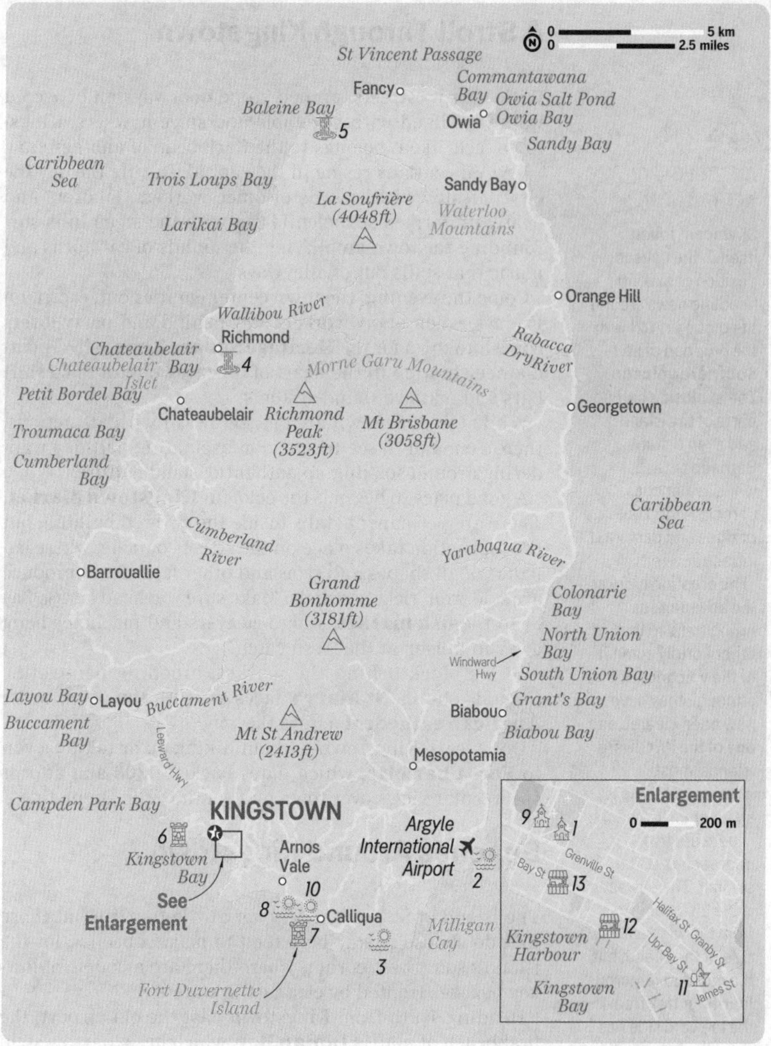

N 0 5 km
0 2.5 miles

St Vincent Passage
Fancy
Commantawana Bay
Owia Salt Pond
Owia
Owia Bay
Sandy Bay
Baleine Bay
5
Caribbean Sea
Trois Loups Bay
Sandy Bay
La Soufrière (4048ft)
Waterloo Mountains
Larikai Bay
Orange Hill
Wallibou River
Richmond
Rabacca Dry River
Chateaubelair Bay
4
Chateaubelair Islet
Morne Garu Mountains
Petit Bordel Bay
Chateaubelair
Richmond Peak (3523ft)
Mt Brisbane (3058ft)
Georgetown
Troumaca Bay
Cumberland Bay
Caribbean Sea
Cumberland River
Yarabaqua River
Barrouallie
Colonarie Bay
Grand Bonhomme (3181ft)
North Union Bay
Windward Hwy
South Union Bay
Layou Bay
Layou
Buccament River
Grant's Bay
Biabou
Buccament Bay
Mt St Andrew (2413ft)
Biabou Bay
Leeward Hwy
Mesopotamia
Campden Park Bay
KINGSTOWN
6
Kingstown Bay
See Enlargement
Argyle International Airport
2
Arnos Vale
10
8
Calliqua
7
Milligan Cay
3
Fort Duvernette Island

Enlargement
0 200 m
9
1
Grenville St
Bay St
13
Halifax St
Granby St
12
Upr Bay St
Kingstown Harbour
Kingstown Bay
11
James St

SIGHTS
1 Anglican cathedral
2 Argyle Beach
3 Brighton Salt Pond Beach
4 Dark View Falls
5 Falls of Baleine
6 Fort Charlotte
7 Fort Duvernette
8 Indian Bay
9 St Mary's
10 Villa Beach

DRINKING & NIGHTLIFE
11 Heritage Square Lime

SHOPPING
12 Fish market
13 Kingstown Market

Kingstown

A Stroll Through Kingstown

EMBRACE THE OLD CARIBBEAN

With narrow streets, arched stone doorways and covered walkways lined with vegetable and spice hawkers, Kingstown feels like it belongs to the Caribbean of another era.

Few Vincentians reside in the capital. During the day the city pulsates with crowds of office workers, laborers and neatly uniformed schoolchildren, with the steep hills surrounding the town amplifying the sounds of car horns and music that spills out of alleyways.

Come the evening, the town center empties out, except on Fridays, when many workers stay behind and party lovers come into town for the **Heritage Square Lime**, a lively outdoor celebration in the heart of downtown with makeshift bars and massive sound systems.

While the downtown area is not awash with attractions, there's enough to see to spend a fascinating half-day wandering around soaking up authentic island culture.

A good place to begin is the colorful **Kingstown Market**. There are permanent stalls inside the covered building but the real action takes place on the streets outside, where bananas of all shapes and sizes and other farm-fresh produce are sold from rickety stands. Make sure you head across Bay St to the **fish market**, where cleavers and machetes bang away in unison at the fresh catch.

Just a block behind the market, brooding neo-Gothic Catholic church **St Mary's** faces off with the prim, white **Anglican cathedral** across the way.

Don't leave Kingstown without hiking up or taking a van to **Fort Charlotte**, which dates back to 1803 and affords spectacular views over town and south to the Grenadines.

AN EXPLOSIVE ATTRACTION

St Vincent found itself in the unusual position of making headline news around the globe in 2021 with the eruption of **La Soufrière volcano**. The explosion bathed parts of the island and even distant Barbados in ash, while avalanches of rocks wiped out bridges and damaged infrastructure.

The eruption blocked the adventurous hiking trails to the otherworldly summit of the volcano, although they have now been cleared and one of the Windward Islands' most spectacular hikes is again open to visitors.

There are two approaches to the summit. The easiest is the 2½-hour hike from the windward side of the island, but the more adventurous four-hour trek from the leeward side has more bush and fine sea views all the way up.

Beaches Around Kingstown

SWIM, SNORKEL AND CLIMB

The island of St Vincent sees very little tourism but those that do choose to stay here tend to make a beeline for the island's southwest corner, where there are a couple of low-key beaches fronted by clear, calm waters.

Heading south from Kingstown past the old airport, the first beach of note is **Indian Bay**, which has a narrow strip of brown sand overlooking some muscular rock formations. There is good snorkeling in the shallow waters right off the beach, with large shoals of small fish and some colorful reef dwellers.

WHERE TO STAY ON ST VINCENT

Grenadine House
Whitewashed luxury in the hills overlooking Kingstown, with views over the city to the Grenadines. **$$**

Beachcombers Hotel
Great-value rooms right on Villa Beach with a good restaurant and sea-view pool. **$$**

Young Island Resort
A private island just off the south coast, with 29 elegant villas set among lush gardens. **$$$**

NICOLA PULHAM/SHUTTERSTOCK ©

Fort Charlotte

Just around the corner, **Villa Beach** is wider, with some shady trees at the northern end, and overlooks the pretty, forested private resort of Young Island.

You can hire a boat at the dock here to reach the marvelous **Fort Duvernette**, which is perched atop a rock monolith protruding from the sea. Built to defend the nearby town of Calliaqua, it affords fantastic 360-degree views of the southern shoreline. There are 225 steps in the spiral staircase that has been carved into the rock; your boatman will sprint up in minutes, but take care as it can be slippery, with small stones often covering the walkway. At the top, 200ft above sea level, there are two batteries of cannons and the island's most scenic picnic area.

Due to their limited dimensions, both Indian Bay and Villa Beach can get crowded when cruises are in port; further south there are a number of inviting but rarely visited beaches, including palm-lined **Brighton Salt Pond Beach** and windswept **Argyle Beach**.

BEST RESTAURANTS ON ST VINCENT

Basil's Bar & Restaurant
Great Caribbean and international food draws crowds to this dungeon-like stone-walled Kingstown classic. $$

Sapodilla Room
Elegant dining in the hills above town, with a small menu of rich Caribbean Creole flavors. $$

French Veranda
Open-air restaurant that's the only place on the island to sate escargot cravings. $$$

Veejays
A popular spot with a buffet of traditional Vincentian dishes and tasty, filling rotis. $

Young Island Restaurant
Fresh seafood at romantic beachside tables surrounded by nature at this first-class resort restaurant. $$$

Skyblue Apartments
Cheap, cheerful and well located, these tidy little apartments feature fully functional kitchens. $

Cobblestone Inn
An old stone warehouse converted into a comfy urban hotel in the heart of Kingstown. $$

Blue Lagoon Marina
Comfortable modern rooms with bright paint jobs and views of bobbing yachts. $

BIRD-WATCHING IN THE JUNGLE

While the verdant interior of St Vincent is a veritable paradise for nature lovers, it is for the most part impenetrable, with few roads or good trails into the heart of the jungle. However, there is one excellent hike just a short drive north of Kingstown.

The **Vermont Nature Trail** climbs up to around 1640ft above sea level in a stunning two-hour loop through thick rainforest inhabited by the rare endemic St Vincent parrot.

Other species in the forest to look out for include the whistling warbler and the crested hummingbird. While the trail is not long, the heat and humidity can make it tough going so it's best to arrive early.

St Vincent's Jungle Waterfalls

SWIM IN REFRESHING MOUNTAIN STREAMS

In Richmond Peak's jungle-clad foothills, the thundering **Dark View Falls** are the most spectacular waterfalls on the island you don't need a boat to reach.

Surrounded by sturdy trees and heliconias, the falls are divided into two sections. The lower cascade is higher, falling for 65ft over a vine-covered cliff face into a deep pool. The path to the upper falls is a bit shoddy; staff will try to dissuade you from climbing, but it's worth the effort. The diagonal cascade is enclosed in a natural rock amphitheater, full of ferns and fluttering butterflies, resembling an enchanted tropical garden.

It's an adventure to get here, but the remote **Falls of Baleine** are one of St Vincent's most energizing natural attractions and a must-visit for nature lovers. The falls are accessed from a rocky beach on the far north of the island, only reachable by boat and where disembarking in rough seas can be challenging.

The walk up the river to the falls requires good balance, but the reward is a towering cascade of water thundering over a plateau into a tight rock canyon with a refreshing natural swimming hole.

Party at Vincy Mas

JOIN SVG'S BIG BASH

St Vincent's biggest party is the wonderfully entertaining **Vincy Mas** carnival, a raucous two weeks of parades, boat trips, concerts and general mayhem that gets underway across the island at the end of June. Accompanied by a loud and fast soca soundtrack, Vincy Mas might not be as big as some carnivals in the region, but it's every bit as fun and visitors are welcomed with open arms. Among the not-to-be-missed events are the **Soca Monarch** song competition and the closing **Mardi Gras** parade, where islanders cut loose decked out in lustrous sequins and feathers.

RAINFOREST TREKS

More impressive waterfalls surrounded by lush tropical rainforest can be found at the **Grand Etang National Park** (p333), which spreads over some of the highest mountains on the island of Grenada.

GETTING AROUND

From Kingstown, regular vans run along both the Windward and Leeward Highways, but note that during peak hours they can be packed to the rafters. Outside these main thoroughfares, on secondary roads public transportation can be quite limited and a rental car is recommended for exploring the interior of the island.

LEEWARD HIGHWAY ROAD TRIP

St Vincent's Leeward Highway runs along the island's west coast for 25 very slow miles and is the most scenic drive on the island. The road winds around forested hillsides and into deeply cut coastal valleys covered in coconut plantations and banana plants to reach beautiful desolate bays with striking black sands.

Beginning in **1 Kingstown**, the highway climbs into the mountains before descending back to the sea at **2 Buccament Bay**, a lovely beach with imported white sands backed by beautiful craggy mountains.

Heading north, the next stop is the fishing village of **3 Layou**, which has some pre-Columbian petroglyphs, before reaching **4 Walliabou Bay**, which doubled as the town of Port Royal in the Pirates of the Caribbean film franchise. Some of the building facades remain, but even those who aren't film buffs will enjoy the tranquil narrow beach.

Less than five minutes further on, **5 Walliabou Falls** is a pretty waterfall that fills an inviting swimming pool surrounded by lush greenery above an old dam that has been reclaimed by the forest.

The next stretch of the highway winds through a labyrinth of forested hilltops covered with yellow-leafed trees before emerging at the coast again at secluded **6 Cumberland Bay**, home to jungle-covered headlands and sheltered waters that are great for a dip. After the turnoff to gorgeous beach **7 Troumaca Bottom**, the road crests a hill, affording sweeping views of La Soufrière volcano.

Turn off on the dirt road just south of Chateaubelair to reach the **8 Thirteen Stones of Chateaubelair**, an ancient indigenous site with wonderful views up and down the coast. The highway ends at the extraordinary **9 Richmond Beach**, where wide swaths of midnight-black sands contrast dramatically with walls of green foliage clinging to the lower slopes of the volcano.

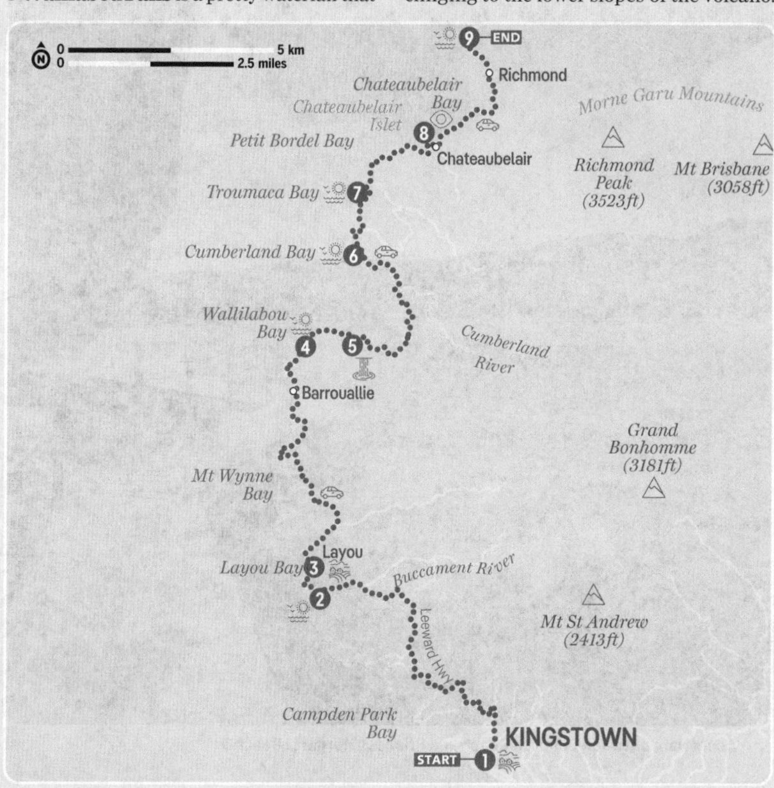

BEQUIA

St Vincent

Bequia

Union Island

Mayreau & Tobago Cays

Magical Bequia is the busiest of the Grenadines, but on an island chain that redefines the word 'tranquility', that doesn't mean a lot. Indeed, stepping off the boat in Port Elizabeth you'll soon discover that despite its popularity and fame, on Bequia a wonderfully relaxed village atmosphere reigns.

Approaching the island on the short boat ride from St Vincent, Bequia's near-vertical forested mountains emerge from the tranquil water like some kind of magic illusion and it's not until the very end of the journey that any buildings come into view.

The size of the island means there's no shortage of hidden coves and panoramic hilltops to explore, but the main reason to visit is Bequia's stunning beaches. Throw in elegant accommodations to fit most budgets, a fine selection of restaurants and fun bars, and it's easy to see why many travelers keep on coming back.

TOP TIP

While Bequia does have a fair range of accommodations across different price brackets, the total number of beds on the island is quite limited, especially alongside the best beaches. In high season, book in advance to lock down a place in your chosen area.

NAPA/SHUTTERSTOCK ©

Boardwalk between Belmont Beach and Princess Margaret Beach

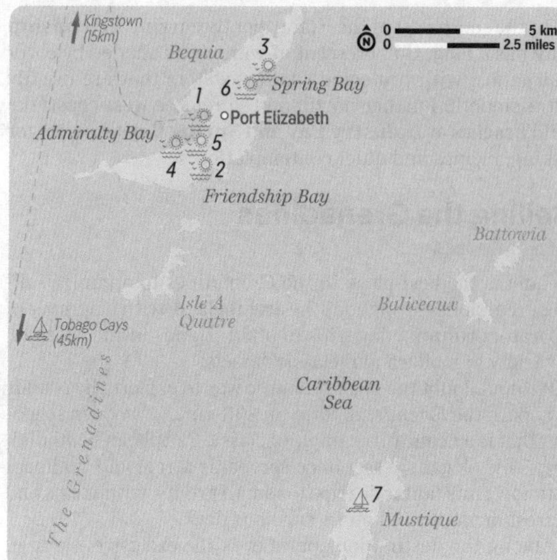

HIGHLIGHTS
1 Belmont Beach
2 Friendship Bay
3 Industry Bay
4 Lower Bay
5 Princess Margaret Beach
6 Spring Bay

ACTIVITIES, COURSES & TOURS
7 Mustique

Brilliant Beaches of Bequia

MAXIMUM WATERSIDE RELAXATION

While Bequia is rightly lauded for its great restaurants, fun social scene and striking forested mountains, the main reason most visitors travel to the island remains its magnificent beaches. From the soft sands and bright waters of the west coast to the wild, seldom-visited bays of the northeast, Bequia has more beaches than most visitors have time to get to.

The closest beach to Port Elizabeth, **Belmont Beach** is at the end of the walkway of the same name. It's fairly small so can feel a bit crowded, although the still, clear waters are great for spotting marine critters.

Follow the path up and over the headland and around the rock face to the much more spacious **Princess Margaret Beach**, a delightful wide expanse of golden sand backed by a wall of lush greenery, with deep waters perfect for swimming. It's thoroughly relaxing to sit back on the sands and look over through the masts of anchored yachts to the colorful houses nestled below the steep mountainsides opposite.

If you're looking for even more tranquility, follow the narrow path over the next headland to **Lower Bay**, a long stretch of powder-like sands with small, fun waves and a couple of good beach bars for whiling away the day.

BEST GRENADINES FESTIVALS

Bequia Easter Regatta
Competitive yacht races in the waters of Bequia, with plenty of partying once the crews are back on terra firma.

Bequia Music Fest
Beginning as a spinoff from the legendary Mustique Blues Festival, this festival in January now extends far beyond blues, with artists from SVG and beyond playing all over the island.

Union Island Conch Festival
Union Island locals have a taste for conch and this passion is celebrated each February with mass cook-ups and concerts.

WHERE TO STAY ON BEQUIA

Gingerbread Hotel
Plucked straight from a fairy tale, this charming hotel has just six rooms and great bay views. **$$**

Bequia Beach Hotel
A sprawling low-rise resort that manages to exude elegance while remaining relaxed and unpretentious. **$$$**

Sugar Apple
Bright and spacious apartments with sea views just a short walk from Friendship Bay. **$$**

On the southwest of the island, gently curving **Friendship Bay** has a long, thin crescent of white sand shaded by coconut palms, with protected shallow waters that are usually ultra-smooth. Further north, on the remote west coast, the wild beaches at **Industry Bay** and **Spring Bay** are great for hiking, picnics and quiet contemplation.

BEST BEQUIA DINING

Bagatelle
The menu is small but the top-notch seafood justifies the trip over to Friendship Bay. $$$

Fernando's Hideaway
Relax on the brightly painted porch surrounded by nature and enjoy fresh seasonal Caribbean food. $$

De Reef Cafe
Enjoy some of the best fresh seafood on the island washed down with potent rum punch. $$

Fig Tree
Delicious homestyle Caribbean cooking and a vibrant atmosphere with live bands. $$

Laura's
A sociable place with top service and great pasta and soups. $$

Sailing the Grenadines

EXCLUSIVE ISLANDS, TINY CAYS

Bequia is the best place in the Grenadines to organize sailing excursions throughout the archipelago, with a number of operators running day trips to other islands in the chain on a variety of modern and classic vessels.

Without doubt the most romantic way to explore the islands is aboard the *Friendship Rose*, an 80ft vintage wooden schooner that is a beautiful example of classic Caribbean boatbuilding. This elegant vessel once served as a regional mailboat but now runs fantastic trips for small groups with meals and refreshments served on its spacious deck.

Among the destinations on offer is the exclusive island of **Mustique**, an international haven for royalty and the uber-affluent, where TV stars and prominent musicians keep private villas. If you're not in a position to fork out thousands for luxury accommodations, an authorized day trip is your only chance to get an up-close look at the manicured lawns and mansions of this opulent isle. You'll need to register in advance for the tour to get clearance – paparazzi are not welcome – but once given the green light, visitors are free to join the local residents for drinks at the legendary Basil's Bar, one of the Caribbean's best beachfront watering holes. The magnificent sunsets here go a long way to explaining the island's price tags. Visitors are also free to relax on one of Mustique's many brilliant white-sand beaches, although some areas may be off-limits depending on which heir to a throne is on the island at the time.

Another popular destination for day cruises are the Tobago Cays (p580), one of the Windward Islands' premier snorkeling spots.

GETTING AROUND

Bequia has just one bus line that runs from Port Elizabeth past the turnoff to Lower Bay and through Friendship Bay to the airport on the southwest of the island.

If you're going elsewhere, you'll either have to walk or take a taxi, which are usually open pick-ups or vans. While fairly expensive, they can carry a large group.

MAYREAU & TOBAGO CAYS

St Vincent

Bequia

Union Island

Mayreau & Tobago Cays

Breathtakingly beautiful yet for the most part completely undeveloped, the compact palm-covered island of Mayreau is everything you dreamed the Grenadines would be. Despite boasting some of the finest beaches and best snorkeling in the Windward Islands, it remains pretty much unknown outside the country.

With only a handful of vehicles, no airport, no resorts and just a smattering of residents, it's an ideal Caribbean destination for independent travelers looking to get away from the crowds. During sailing season it's a popular anchorage, but at other times you'll pretty much have the island to yourself.

Across a narrow channel from Mayreau, the five coral-ringed islands of the Tobago Cays are the southern Grenadines' star attraction. Sitting within the boundaries of the national park of the same name, these uninhabited islets are fronted by strips of brilliant white sand, while sea turtles, parrotfish and manta rays swim just offshore.

TOP TIP

Accommodations options on Mayreau are limited, with just one top-end villa complex and a couple of budget guesthouses, so advanced bookings are essential. Groceries are also sparse on the island, so if you're self-catering, bring supplies from St Vincent. Fortunately there are rarely shortages of Hairoun beer.

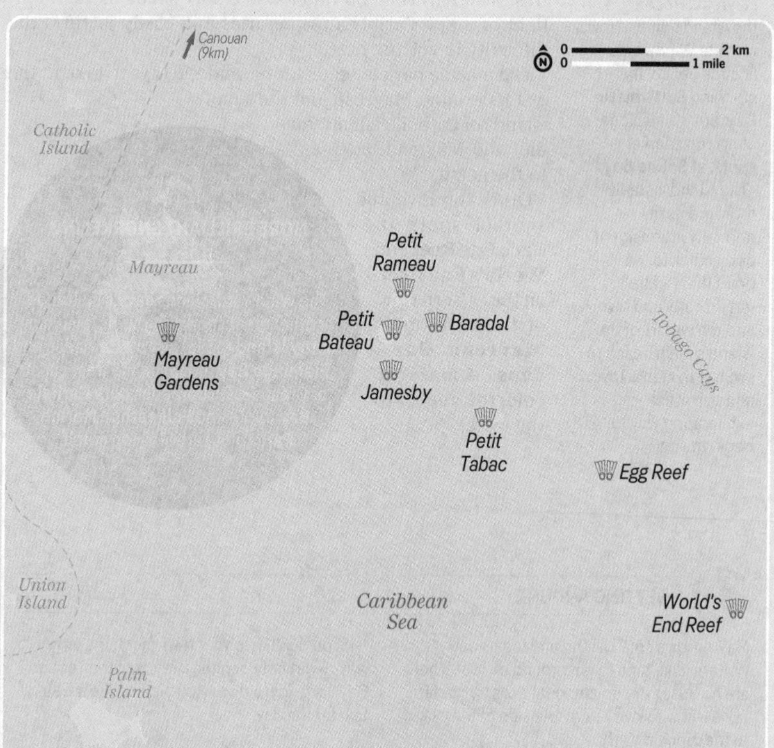

Snorkeling the Tobago Cays

SWIM WITH TRANQUIL TURTLES

While incredible blue waters and snow-white sands are something of the norm throughout the Grenadines, the small islands of the **Tobago Cays Marine Park** take the idyllic landscape to the next level.

As you bounce over the surface of brilliant turquoise waters in a small water taxi, the tiny islands begin to take form until you're suddenly ringed by empty palm-lined beaches in every direction in the middle of a screensaver-worthy panorama that seems too good to be true.

Home to some of the most transparent waters in the Windward Islands, the five cays – **Petit Bateau**, **Petit Rameau**, **Jamesby**, **Baradal** and **Petit Tabac** – offer superb snorkeling right off the beach.

Four of the cays sit above a large sand-bottomed lagoon protected by the 2½-mile-long Horseshoe Reef, an important habitat for sea turtles. There is a marked sea-turtle observation area for snorkelers around the long sandy beach of Baradal Cay, where boating activity is prohibited and sightings are pretty much guaranteed.

Wading in from a deserted beach to swim through the warm, clear water with marine creatures, followed by a delicious fresh-fish barbecue on otherwise empty sands, is the highlight of many Caribbean itineraries and easily justifies the difficulty in getting here.

The marine park extends far beyond the cays to take in the waters around Mayreau and the small islands of Catholic Island, Jondall and Mayreau Baleine to the north.

Other top dive and snorkel spots include **Egg Reef** and **World's End Reef** on the eastern side of the cays, and **Mayreau Gardens**, a maze of colorful reefs, to the west.

WHY I LOVE MAYREAU

Alex Egerton, writer

Whenever I'm traveling through the Grenadines, I always make sure you set aside time to relax on Mayreau. Not only is the island home to my favorite Windward Islands beach, the stunning **Saltwhistle Bay**, but it's also one of my top snorkel spots, at **Saline Bay**.

The island instantly reprograms my normally intransigent body clock to the point that I willfully get up early and dive into the waters of the island's main beach to swim with manta rays and parrotfish – an exhilarating way to begin the day.

MORE BRILLIANT SNORKELING

The Windward Islands have a multitude of other great snorkeling spots, including **Sandy Island** (p336) just off Carriacou and **Flamingo Bay** (p333) on the west coast of Grenada. On Barbados both **Carlisle Bay** (p160) and **Folkestone Marine Park** (p160) are also top notch.

GETTING AROUND

Mayreau is a small island and locals and visitors alike tend to get around on foot. There are no buses or conventional taxis but water taxis will whisk you from one side of the island to the other in a jiffy.

If you don't own your own yacht, the only way to get between the islands of the Tobago Cays is to join a dive excursion or hire a water taxi for the day.

St Vincent

Bequia

Mayreau & Tobago Cays

Union Island

UNION ISLAND

The southernmost island in SVG, Union Island feels every bit the outpost at the end of a country tentatively joined to a distant administration. Before the advent of fast boats, the island's remote location enabled it to become a center for contraband from across the Caribbean. These days the island depends more on fishing and tourism, with travelers descending to soak up the sun on its powdery white beaches, kitesurf over its luminous waters and hike its jagged mountain peaks.

Unlike some other nearby islands, which are mostly populated by visitors and resort workers, Union has a sizable local population, making it a good place to add some culture to your beach vacation.

A key transportation hub for travelers heading onto Grenada by sea, Union is also an important yacht anchorage, as evidenced by the wine and gourmet groceries on sale around town.

TOP TIP

If restaurants, nightlife and socializing are important, look for accommodations in Clifton. Nature lovers might prefer to find a base near quieter Ashton, which is closer to a number of trailheads. Both locations are just a short walk from excellent beaches that are never crowded.

UMOMOS/SHUTTERSTOCK ©

Union Island

ACTIVITIES, COURSES & TOURS
1 Ashton Lagoon
2 Chatham Bay
3 Fort Hill
4 Frigate Island
5 Kite Beach
6 Mt Taboi

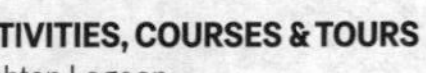

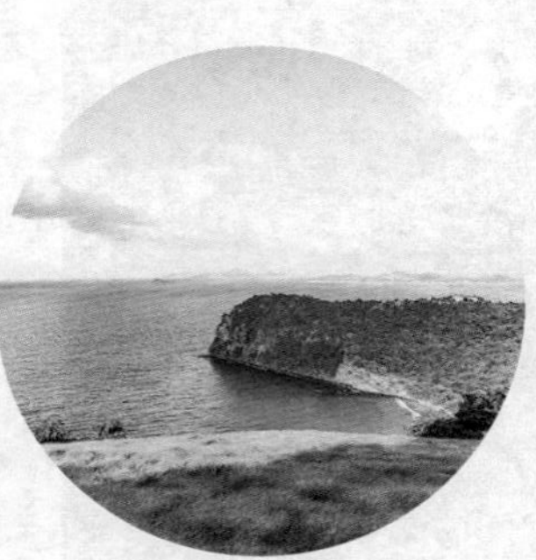

Chatham Bay (p584)
GREENS AND BLUES/SHUTTERSTOCK ©

UNION ISLAND

Kingstown (St Vincent) (65km)
Caribbean Sea
2
Mt Taboi
6
Ashton
Union Island
3
5
Clifton
1
4
Frigate Island
Palm Island
0 1 km
0 0.5 miles

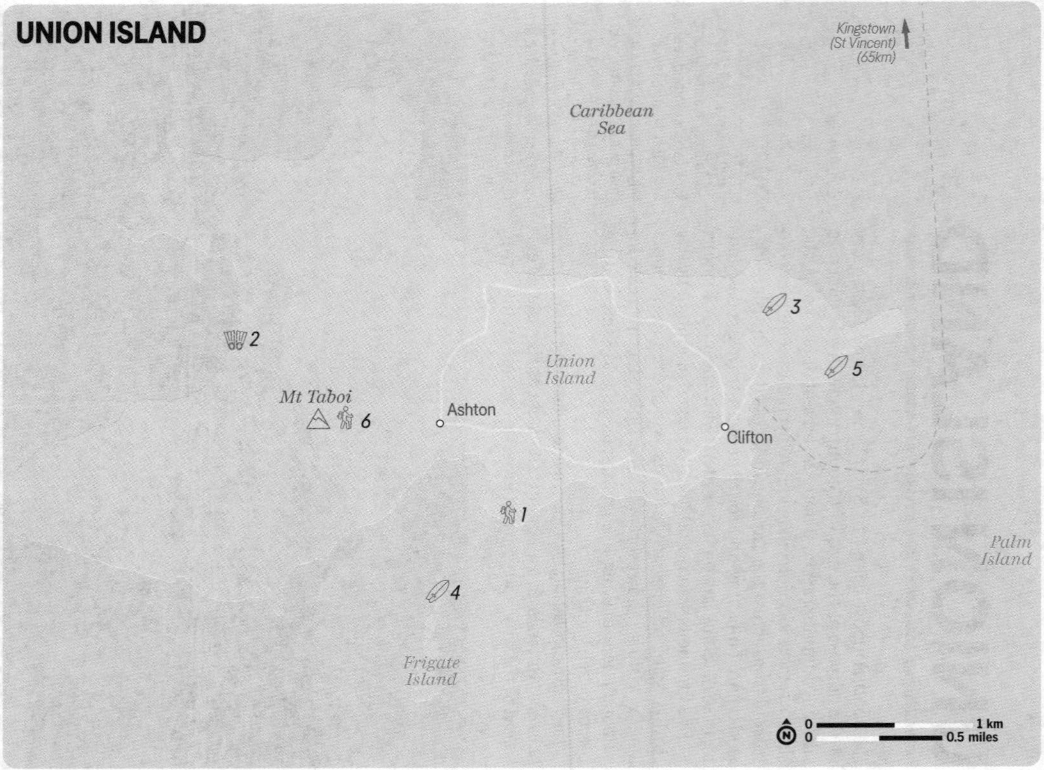

Frigate Island (p584)

CROSSING TO CARRIACOU

The Grenadian island of Carriacou lies across a narrow channel from Union Island, and it's possible to travel between the two countries by sea.

The fastest way between the islands is to hire a water taxi to take you across but, in addition to being quite expensive, the small boats slam down hard on the choppy waters and both you and your luggage might get soaked.

A more relaxed way to cross is to take the mailboat *MV Pride*, which leaves from Union on Monday and Friday mornings and returns from Carriacou in the afternoons. You'll need to get in touch with the captain at least a day before to complete immigration formalities.

Hikes on Union Island

CLIMB TO PANORAMIC VIEWPOINTS

With a spine of sharp mountain peaks, breathtaking hidden bays and causeways leading out into brilliant blue waters, Union Island has some of the best hiking in the Grenadines. From a distance, the serrated peaks of the island look a daunting prospect for hikers, but once up close the sharp features mellow and simple trails emerge from the undergrowth.

The premier hike on the island leads to the top of **Mt Taboi** for fantastic 360-degree views across the southern Grenadines. From the top it's possible to see as far as Bequia and St Vincent to the north and Grenada to the south. To reach the peak from Clifton, follow Back St to the Salt Pond, where you can often spot migratory waterbirds, before continuing along the soft white sands of Water Break Beach to then climb the mountain road after the Ashton turnoff. Keep an eye out for turtles and iguanas beside the track.

An easier hike but with equally magical views is the short walk up to **Fort Hill** on the eastern edge of the island. A vehicle track winds up the hill before turning into a foot trail a few hundred yards from the summit. At the top you'll find a

WHERE TO STAY ON UNION ISLAND

Bougainvilla
A French-accented hotel with inviting, warmly painted rooms and touches of art throughout. **$$**

Tenuta Chatham Bay
The only hotel on Union's most enchanting bay is a spacious, luxurious affair. **$$$**

Kings Landing
It's not fancy but the rooms here are breezy and the price and location are spot-on. **$**

IRRESISTIBLE ISLES

Just off the south coast of Union Island are a number of stunning, small, coral-ringed islands.

Both **Palm Island** and **Petit St Vincent** are private islands that house exclusive resorts, and visits are usually prohibited or involve a hefty landing fee.

But the highlight of these waters is totally free. Right in the middle of the channel, the tiny islet of **Mopian** is a snow-white sandbank surrounded by a shallow reef with a solitary thatched umbrella in the middle. Standing in the knee-high water surrounded by deep-blue seas in all directions is truly magical.

On your way back to Union stop in at **Happy Island**, a fun bar built atop an artificial island formed by discarded conch shells.

pair of gazebos with picnic tables and two rusting cannons as well as uninterrupted views of the Tobago Cays.

If heights make you dizzy, try the short sea-level hike through the **Ashton Lagoon** nature reserve along the causeway to wild Frigate Island. On the way you'll traverse two suspension bridges over possibly the most luminous waters in the Grenadines.

Snorkeling at Chatham Bay

WHERE THE FOREST MEETS THE SEA

It takes quite a long walk to get to remote **Chatham Bay**, but once you step out of the bush and catch a glimpse of the curving bright white sands bookended by forest-covered hills and fronted by kaleidoscopic waters you'll be in no doubt it was worth it.

On an island famed for its magnificent beaches, Chatham Bay stands out from the pack due to its unspoiled backdrop and calm, inviting waters. It is a favorite picnic and relaxation spot for locals, but many visitors come to Union Island and never make it this far – big mistake!

The bay is nestled among dense nature, where harmless gray snakes slither up rock faces and hummingbirds flutter above the flowers.

It's a stunning scene that's hard to take your eyes off, but perhaps the best reason to visit Chatham Bay is not visible from the sand. Beneath the waters you'll encounter some of the best snorkeling in the Grenadines, with an incredible variety of colorful reef fish darting among the maze of rocks.

Kitesurf the Trade Winds

SKIM ACROSS FLUORESCENT BLUE WATERS

With steady winds and warm waters that range from completely flat to fun, small waves, Union Island is one of the best places in the Windward Islands for kitesurfing. And you don't need experience to get involved – conditions around the island are great for beginners and a couple of schools offer classes.

There are two main kite spots: just south of the airport, scenic **Kite Beach** has reliable easterlies and is favored by more experienced riders, while **Frigate Island**, near Ashton, features tranquil waters and offshore winds perfect for beginners.

GETTING AROUND

Most of the main attractions on Union Island are located within walking distance of the towns of Ashton and Clifton, which are situated just 1¼ miles apart.

Minivans run between the towns fairly regularly, usually along the south-coast road but occasionally looping up around Richmond Bay. If you pay the driver a little extra you can be dropped down spur roads. Alternatively, if you're in a hurry, a couple of taxis can usually be found near the Clifton dock.

Water taxis service remote bays and smaller surrounding islands.

LEFT: BYVALET/SHUTTERSTOCK ©, RIGHT: HENNING MARQUARDT/SHUTTERSTOCK ©

Arriving

Many visitors to St Vincent and the Grenadines only see the country briefly as part of a cruise, with most boats docking in Kingstown.

For independent travelers, the principal gateway to the country is the main airport on the southeast of St Vincent island, from where many visitors head to Kingstown to board boats to the Grenadines.

By Air

While there are a handful of direct long-distance flights each week to St Vincent's Argyle International Airport, getting here often requires transiting through Barbados or Grenada.

Small airports on Bequia and Union Island also receive irregular flights from neighboring islands.

By Boat

Cruise vessels dock at the port on the south of Kingstown Bay, walking distance to town. Some smaller cruises call directly at Bequia's Port Elizabeth.

When arriving at SVG by yacht, it's possible to clear documents at St Vincent, Bequia, Canouan and Union Island.

Money

Currency: Eastern Caribbean dollar (EC$)

CASH

For everyday purchases, cash is the most common form of payment throughout SVG, and it's a good idea to have small banknotes, as many places don't keep much change. US currency is widely accepted, though not always at the official rate.

ATMS

ATMs are found around Kingstown and the built-up southwest of St Vincent island, but elsewhere they're few and far between. On the Grenadine islands there are often only one or two temperamental ATMs, and Mayreau doesn't have any at all.

CREDIT CARDS

At hotels and restaurants around Kingstown, credit and debit cards are usually accepted, but in smaller towns on the main island and in most places throughout the Grenadines, usage is very limited.

STYVE REINECK/SHUTTERSTOCK ©

Above: Pigeon Point (p607); Right: Archbishop's House (p598)

TRINIDAD & TOBAGO

FORGED FROM THE LOVE OF LIBERTY

Find the perfect travel symphony in Trinidad and Tobago, where preserved culture, pristine natural resources and perfect weather reign supreme.

The southernmost country in the Caribbean, Trinidad and Tobago offers a variety of unbridled adventures between both islands. With a population of 1.3 million people, T&T offers more than the 'sun, sea and sand' attraction that has been inextricably aligned with the tropical circuit.

Contrary to popular belief, tourism exists in multiplicity in this twin-island nation which gained its independence from Britain in 1962 and subsequently obtained republic status in 1976. In modern Trinidad, the national economy is propelled by oil and petroleum, and this reality makes it an inviting destination for various industrial investments and business tourism offshoots.

Moving further away from the southern government-run oil refineries and heading to 'The Sister Isle', Tobago is well versed in the quintessential tourism draw of beach-filled bliss. Here, you will find 310 sq km of Creole traditions, captivating beaches and wildlife wonders. The forested areas in Tobago slope into the world-renowned coral reef, attracting both hikers and marine lovers.

T&T is the birthplace of Carnival and its euphoric revelry; sacred nesting grounds for leatherback turtles; the steelpan, a musical instrument created in the 20th century – and much more. Visitors are imbued with the allure of sights, sounds, tastes and experiences that represent this country's multiethnic, multireligious unity that Nobel Peace Prize–winning Archbishop Desmond Tutu aptly described as the 'rainbow nation'.

THE MAIN AREAS

CENTRAL & SOUTH TRINIDAD
The heart of mainland Trinidad.
p592

PORT OF SPAIN
Urban life of the party.
p597

NORTHEAST COAST
Sustainability and serenity unencumbered.
p601

CROWN POINT
A blend of beach and bustle.
p605

CASTARA
A showcase of Tobago's rural beauty.
p610

Find Your Way

Trinidad and Tobago roughly covers 5128 sq km in total. With lots to discover on the cultural, historical and ecological landscapes, there's a favorite find in these picks for your next twin-island adventure.

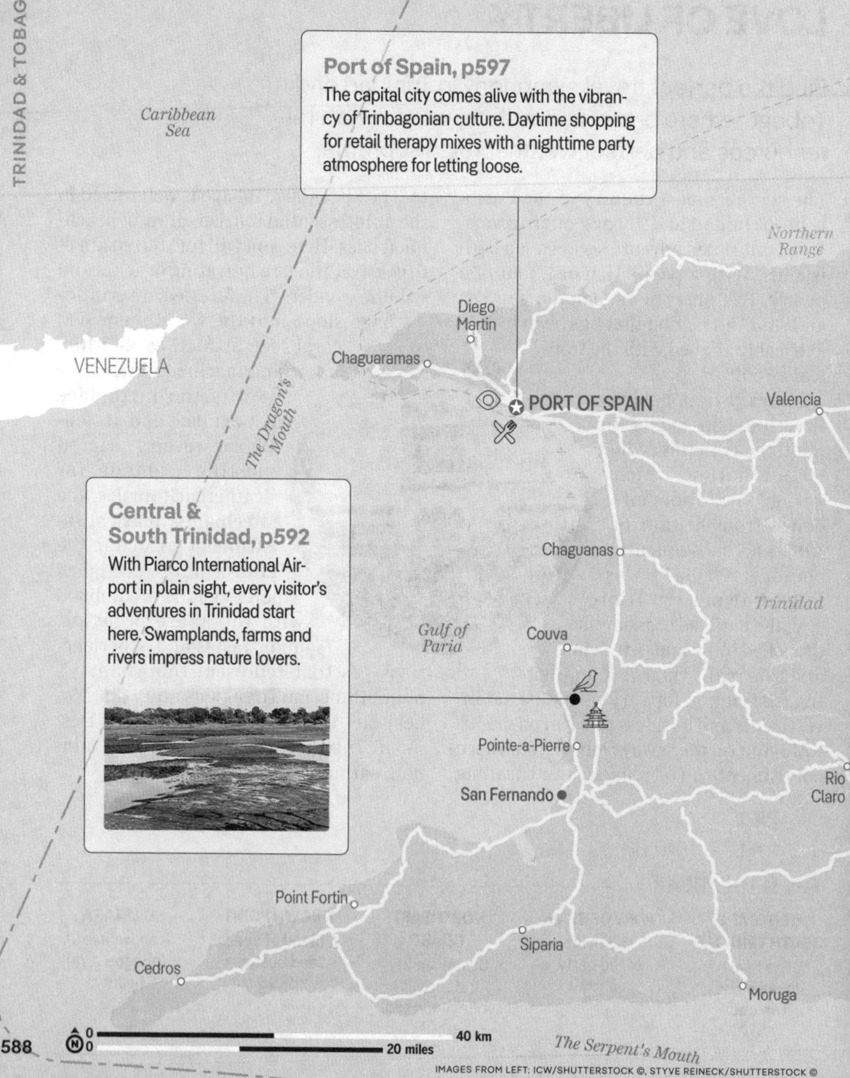

Port of Spain, p597
The capital city comes alive with the vibrancy of Trinbagonian culture. Daytime shopping for retail therapy mixes with a nighttime party atmosphere for letting loose.

Central & South Trinidad, p592
With Piarco International Airport in plain sight, every visitor's adventures in Trinidad start here. Swamplands, farms and rivers impress nature lovers.

IMAGES FROM LEFT: ICW/SHUTTERSTOCK ©, STYVE REINECK/SHUTTERSTOCK ©

Crown Point, p605

Southwest Tobago's vibrant activity hub, this town is known for water sports and sunbathing. It's also home to the ANR Robinson International Airport.

Castara, p610

A countryside Tobago community with a proud fishing heritage, Castara basks in the sustainable sights and sounds with forests and birds in abundance.

Northeast Coast, p601

Rekindle your love for nature, bird-watching, sandy beaches and rich heritage in this mountainous area, historically settled by First People communities.

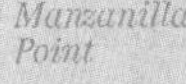

ATLANTIC OCEAN

CAR

Road trips give you the freedom to roam both islands. For many key spots in remote areas, renting a car is ideal for accessibility. Gas at the pumps is considerably cheaper in T&T than on other islands, due to the oil- and gas-based national economy.

BUS & MAXI-TAXI

The Public Transport Service Corporation (PTSC) is the state-owned public transport provider for T&T. Buy tickets at ticket booths and show them to the driver. Maxi-taxis are private minibuses that are color-coded based on service areas. Fares for both transportation options vary with distance.

TAXI & RIDESHARE

Taxis for hire are available across both islands at various rates based on start and end point. Alternatively, mobile rideshare applications have risen in popularity since the COVID-19 pandemic as a safer, slightly cheaper means of commute – with cost calculated based on distance traveled.

Plan Your Time

Start your day with breakfast the Trinbagonian way, by devouring doubles – the ultimate street food – while rush-hour morning traffic dissipates. Then, begin exploring with your crew or solo, as fun-filled escapades await.

CHRIS HARWOOD/SHUTTERSTOCK ©

Coconut stand, Port of Spain (p597)

If You Only Have One Day

- Take a brisk morning walk around Port of Spain's **Queen's Park Savannah** (p598) for fresh coconut water.
- Heritage awaits at the nearby **Magnificent Seven** (p598) buildings, which offer guided tours to explore the nation's.
- Grab lunch at the chic **Chaud Cafe** (p598) in Woodbrook, where the upscale vibe is matched by the delicious menu offerings.
- As the sun sets, the city's west end transforms to a foodie's dream on **Ariapita Ave** (p598), where culinary worlds collide in a crescendo of flavors to satisfy any craving.
- End the night with a seaside stroll along the **Chaguaramas** (p600) boardwalk.

Seasonal Highlights

Multireligious and multiethnic T&T celebrates the most holidays in the Caribbean. The national anthem rings true: 'Here every creed and race find an equal place'.

FEBRUARY

Trinidad Carnival, aka 'The Greatest Show On Earth', is a two-day street parade featuring music, dancing and thousands of costumed revelers.

MARCH

The jazz season enjoys local and international talent at events such as **Jazz Artists on the Greens** and **Tobago Jazz Experience**.

APRIL

Easter in Tobago highlights the **Goat Races**, an 80-year tradition where jockeys and their goats compete for top honors.

JOHN DE LA BASTIDE/SHUTTERSTOCK ©, SEAN DRAKES/LATINCONTENT VIA GETTY IMAGES ©, STICKNEY DESIGN/GETTY IMAGES ©

Three Days to Travel Around

- Spend a night at the HADCO Experiences at **Asa Wright Nature Centre** (p601) in Blanchisseuse for hiking, bird-watching or a dip in the freshwater pool.

- Then, a day-long adventure awaits, starting with the **Caurita Carvings** (p604) – the petroglyphs at the foot of El Tucuche mountain etched by Trinidad's First People.

- Finally, make it a northeast coast family affair with a day trip to **Maracas Bay** (p604), where the sun gently kisses your skin, sand caresses your toes and families flock to the food stalls to consume bake and shark.

If You Have More Time

- A week in Tobago is well spent at **Naturalist Beach Resorts** (p611), conveniently located on Castara Bay, with fresh breakfast served daily. The infectious community spirit extends to the Thursday night feature – the Bonfire Party preceded by dinner at **Cascreole Restaurant and Bar** (p612). The party lasts until the wee hours of the morning.

- Visit the **Tobago Main Ridge Forest Reserve** (p614), some 140 sq km of land that's home to hundreds of birds, animals, plant varieties and a waterfall; cool down at the beach of your choice.

- Return southside to **Crown Point** (p605) for a day of water sports at **Pigeon Point Heritage Park** (p607).

JULY

The **Tobago Heritage Festival** is a delightful showcase of traditional culture, such as 'Ole Time Wedding', dancing and folklore storytelling.

AUGUST

During **Hosay**, the Muslim community parades mosque-shaped model tombs through the streets, then ritually takes them out to sea.

OCTOBER/ NOVEMBER

The Hindu community celebrates **Divali** – 'The Festival Of Lights' a triumphant celebration of good over evil.

DECEMBER

Trini Christmas unites the Spanish musical influence of parang, indigenous foods like pastelle and rum cake, and **Paramin Harvest**.

CENTRAL & SOUTH TRINIDAD

Trinidad
Central & South Trinidad

Before you land at Piarco International Airport, look down while your plane descends and spy the murky marshlands and lush farmlands of Central Trinidad and its arterial throughways of sodden agricultural landscape. You'll see where the mouth of the Caroni River meets the sea, and eventually where rivers meet the Uriah Butler Hwy – a four-lane portal into new patterns of Trinidad's topography. Rural scenes set the tone for the quintessential landscape, embodying simplicities of good living in the heart of mainland Trinidad.

Its popular sibling, south Trinidad, is characterized by scenic plains, inclines, dips, flat stretches and winding, orbital roads as you near the southernmost tip. And that is just the drive along the highway.

TOP TIP

Central Trinidad's experiences tend to be easier to group for same-day adventures than the south's. Hired transportation or use of a rental vehicle is strongly recommended, though public transportation is an alternative. Consider all options with a resident tour guide when choosing your next adventure.

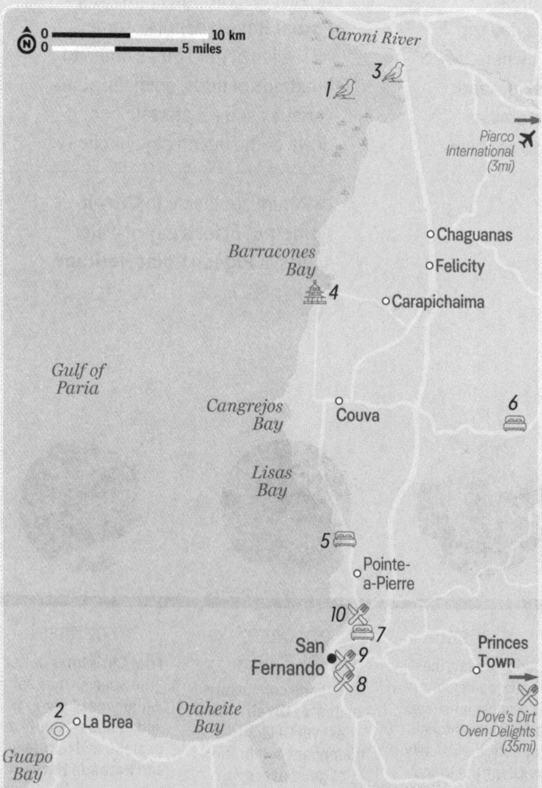

SIGHTS
1 Caroni Swamp and Bird Sanctuary
2 La Brea Pitch Lake
3 Nanan's Caroni Bird Sanctuary Tours
4 Temple in the Sea

SLEEPING
5 Cara Hotels
6 Gran Couva Eco Lodge
7 Tradewinds Hotel

EATING
8 Cross Crossing Food Strip
9 Homestyle Delights
10 Mona's Roti Shop

CHARLIEHARDY192/SHUTTERSTOCK ©

Flamingos, Caroni Swamp and Bird Sanctuary

Bird-watching Bliss By Boat

BLINK AND YOU'LL MISS IT

Though hidden behind clusters of trees along the Uriah Butler Hwy (14km south of Port of Spain), the **Caroni Swamp and Bird Sanctuary** is easy to access. This 48-sq-km swamp is Trinidad's largest mangrove wetland, known for several birds native to the island – including the scarlet ibis, T&T's national bird – along with caimans, swamp boas and crabs. Once common in the swamp, red flamingos from South America stopped settling in T&T for many years, but recently they've resumed nesting and reproducing in large numbers. On tours, you can spot congregations of scarlet ibises in flight overhead, while pink flamingos mill below in full marine glory. **Nanan's Caroni Bird Sanctuary Tours** is conveniently based at the sanctuary and operates for both research and leisure.

Honoring Sacred Ground

PILLAR OF REVERENCE AND RESILIENCE

On approach to the village of Carapichaima (a 40-minute drive from Port of Spain), a succession of towering palm trees signifies your proximity to the **Temple in the Sea**.

BEST PLACES TO STAY IN CENTRAL & SOUTH TRINIDAD

Gran Couva Eco Lodge
This all-inclusive eco-resort offers gorgeous rainforest views and convenient access to historical tours and nature trails. $$

Cara Hotels
Overlooking the Gulf of Paria, this Claxton Bay hotel is a short driving distance from San Fernando in south Trinidad. $$

Tradewinds Hotel
Located in San Fernando, this hotel is perfect for sunset gazing and dining at a well-rated restaurant. $$

WHERE TO DINE IN SOUTH TRINIDAD

Freebird Restaurant
This farm-to-table restaurant in Pointe-a-Pierre is a crowd favorite. **$$**

Bottles and Bites
Sushi and tapas; conveniently located at the Tradewinds Hotel in San Fernando. **$$**

Palki Authentic Indian Restaurant
This San Fernando food haven is for lovers of authentic Indian and Hakka cuisine. **$$**

SOUTH TRINIDAD'S BEST EATS

Trevor Benjamin, manager at a taxi service, shares some of his favorite food spots in south Trinidad.

Cross Crossing Food Strip, San Fernando
Also known as D'Cross, this is where you get a variety of street food: corn soup, hot dogs, hamburgers, barbecue, even gyros.

Homestyle Delights, San Fernando
Better known as Aunty Anne's. Good for breakfast like coconut bake or sada roti with vegetables or meats. Get there by 9:30am!

Mona's Roti Shop, San Fernando
For a mouth-watering roti, get here before 11:00am.

Dove's Dirt Oven Delights
If you want to taste traditional, airy bakes, head to Guayaguayare. Really authentic dirt-oven baking.

After the original temple was destroyed in 1952 because it had been built on the property of a sugar company, indentured laborer Sewdass Sadhu singlehandedly rebuilt this site for Hindus to worship. According to local media personality Karen Dass, Sadhu defiantly said, 'I'll go out on the ocean – nobody owns the sea.' After Sadhu's death in 1970, the temple's condition deteriorated due to high tides and a lack of maintenance. Reconstructed in 1995, it honors religious traditions and commemorates T&T's first indentured laborers from India.

Visit a Pineapple Farm

PRICKLY PATH, BUT SWEET CENTER

Tour the **Mahabir Maharaj Pineapple Estate Tableland** – featured on *Sesame Street* in 2017 – to learn more about pineapple farming in Trinidad. Along with boundless views and fascinating facts, the passion of the people behind it is worth the rocky road to visit. It's a sprawling 8-hectare estate that grows over one million pineapples for the local market; the farmers converted swathes of cocoa land to create the booming pineapple industry of today. The cultivation of pineapples is arduous, spanning over 13 months of labor. But the sugar loaf pineapple – a variety of the fruit indigenous to T&T – is a slice of foodie heaven with every bite.

Bathing in the Asphalt Lake

EIGHTH WONDER OF THE WORLD

It might be a point of irony that the road to the **La Brea Pitch Lake** (about 25km southwest of San Fernando) is quite a wonky one, but you can't have the world's largest asphalt deposit without it doing some damage to the surrounding infrastructure. The Pitch Lake welcomes visitors with open plains and an information center. Spread across 40 hectares and approximately 75m deep, it's the world's biggest commercial deposit of natural asphalt and a top supplier to the international market – boasting 10 million tones of asphalt at any given time. The lake has fascinated explorers, scientists and curious visitors for centuries.

Come with a change of clothes and immerse yourself in the purportedly healing properties of the sulfur pools. Careful where you walk, though – even spots that seem solid may swallow your shoes.

GETTING AROUND

While renting a vehicle is recommended, taxis, maxi-taxis and buses are also available for commuting. Many roads in San Fernando are steep and hilly, so bear this in mind while venturing throughout the city.

Beyond Central & South Trinidad

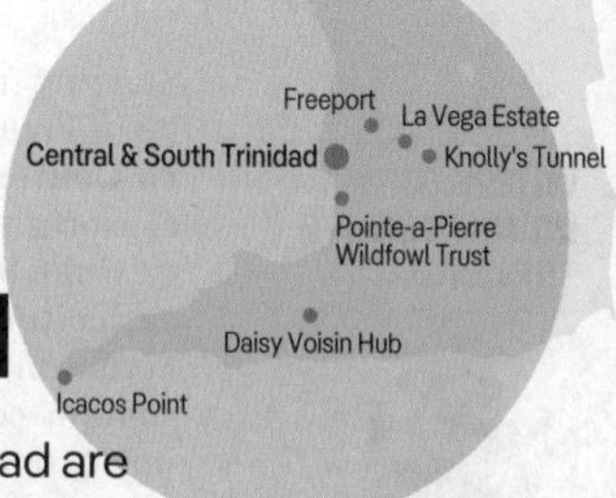
Freeport
La Vega Estate
Central & South Trinidad
Knolly's Tunnel
Pointe-a-Pierre Wildfowl Trust
Daisy Voisin Hub
Icacos Point

On the fringes of central and south Trinidad are natural and historical attractions in abundance – make time for both during your travels.

Wildlife conservation, tropical permaculture, a musical icon and panoramic views from Trinidad's southwestern tip – there's so much to explore beyond central and south Trinidad. If you know where to look, you'll find an unexpected, brilliant blend of commercial and cultural offerings. Above all else, the area is still full of somnolent rural villages, where generations of families proudly live off the land.

Locations such as the Great Icacos Lagoon or the Galfa mud volcano are a treasure in plain sight. You can also tap into your historical knowledge with a tour of the WWII-era US bunkers at Green Hill. Drive safely and enjoy where each detour takes you.

TOP TIP

This region involves more driving than meets the eye. Cater for a full day to experience most locations.

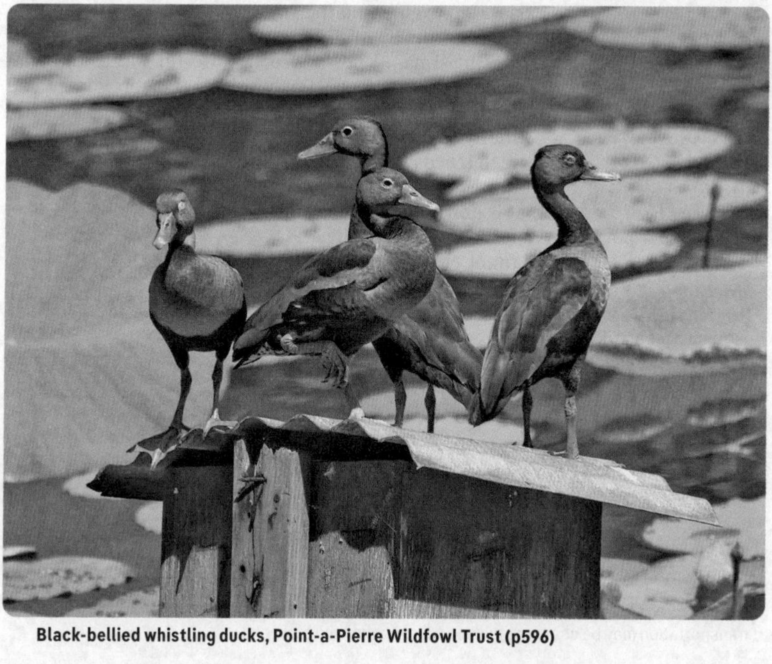

NANDANI BRIDGLAL/SHUTTERSTOCK ©

Black-bellied whistling ducks, Point-a-Pierre Wildfowl Trust (p596)

Nature's Finest & Other Finds

WILDLIFE, PERMACULTURE AND EXPLORING UNDERGROUND

Starting from the Caroni Swamp and Bird Sanctuary, you'll be in Freeport in a little over 20 minutes. Here, **El Socorro Center for Wildlife Conservation** hosts educational workshops and events on preserving T&T's biodiversity, while **Wa Samaki Ecosystems** focuses on regenerative agriculture and permaculture, offering farm tours and its Permaculture Design Course. The Wildlife Conservation has committed to the rescue and rehabilitation of over 700 animals, some of which permanently reside at the center and, in some instances, are appointed ambassadors in the facility's educational program.

In Gran Couva, visit **La Vega Estate**, a garden, nature park and recreation center with a swimming pool, for a nice day out. Should you still want adventure, head to Tabaquite to see **Knolly's Tunnel** – a 200m-long subterranean passage that reminds visitors of the national railway system.

WHERE TO DRINK IN SOUTH TRINIDAD

Linzi Jeremiah, director of Sixth Speed Media, shares his recommendations for drinks in south Trinidad.

Atherly's Restaurant and Lounge
Usually for people over 45; they play music from the '70s, '80s and '90s.

Seon's Bar
Has a down-to-earth vibe. You buy your drink and lime outside.

San Fernando Yacht Club
Place to go for a more chill vibe by the water.

Happy Hill
It's one of the few bars owned by women; also known as Pink Bar.

Rising Star
They tend to have live performances and if you're into hookah, this is the place to go.

Straight to the Edge

A ROAD TRIP FROM SAN FERNANDO

With San Fernando as your base, begin just under 20 minutes away at the **Pointe-a-Pierre Wildfowl Trust**, a bird sanctuary that also includes its guesthouse, Petrea Place, and Freebird Restaurant (p593) – a farm-to-table haven with an ambience that befits nature lovers.

Heading deeper south, visit the **Daisy Voisin Hub** in Siparia. Here, you'll find the statue of this undisputed Queen of Parang – the Spanish folk music genre synonymous with 'Trini Christmas'. Known for her powerful vocals and tempestuous stage presence, Daisy Voisin was a prominent cultural ambassador for Trinidad and Tobago.

Finally, enjoy the breathtaking drive to **Icacos Point**, Trinidad's southwesternmost peninsula that is only separated from Venezuela's coastline by a channel called the Serpent's Mouth.

Icacos Point
DAVID.KERNAHAN/SHUTTERSTOCK ©

GETTING AROUND

Renting a vehicle is strongly recommended. Many key locations are remote, so public transportation may be challenging depending on the time of day.

PORT OF SPAIN

Capital cities can be unreliable when it comes to learning about countries. Sometimes, the gaudy buildings give a dishonest history, and the industrious nature or the tawdry structures misrepresent where you are. But that's not the case with Port of Spain. This city tells you everything, and you don't even have to look that hard. Fall in love with the noise, the lights, the business, the happiness – the heart of Port of Spain.

The St Vincent Jetty Lighthouse will welcome you first. From there, you'll learn about the way citizens hustle by day and party by night. Come hungry to enjoy cuisine from any part of the world, remembering that the indigenous spin on a few classics is the real stunner. You can do a lot in one day, but not everything, so pace yourself. Trinidadians love this city and they're never tired of sharing it with somebody new.

TOP TIP

You won't get the best out of Port of Spain with a tour guide in a printed shirt. Your best bet is to make a Trinidadian friend, one who is open and able to take you through their beloved city and will give you a varied experience.

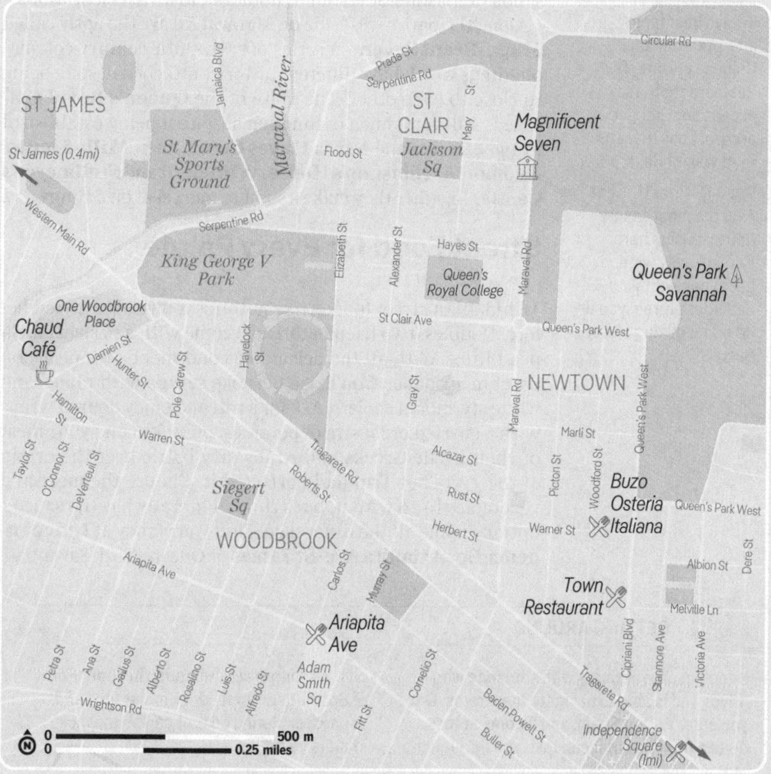

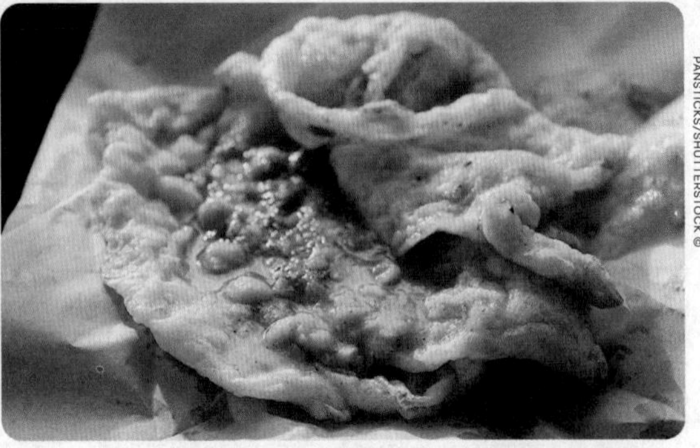

Doubles (two fried flatbreads with chickpea filling)

Open Greenery to Open History

BOTANIC HAVEN AND COLONIAL REMINDERS

The **Queen's Park Savannah** is a cultural amalgamation of the very best that Trinidad and Tobago has to offer. With a sprawling green landscape of over 1000 sq metres, this historical landmark sits in Port of Spain as a sustainable beacon. The park features the notorious Savannah Stage that hosts thousands of masqueraders for Trinidad's Carnival celebrations.

Along the park's west side on Maraval Rd are the aptly called **Magnificent Seven** – a series of early-20th-century colonial buildings which have different histories attached despite being so close to each other. The noise of the **Queen's Royal College** is still very much in function despite it being established in 1859. Across the way is **Hayes Court**, then **Mille Fleurs**, **Roomor**, **Archbishop's House**, **Whitehall** and **Stollmeyer's Castle**. Together they make a sight to marvel at on a sunny day.

Street Food for Every Palate

PORT OF SPAIN FOR FOODIES

Trinidadian street food is like nothing you've ever tasted before. Doubles (two fried flatbreads) come with a perfect chickpea filling. With all the delectable condiments, it's peace on parchment paper. You'll see bespoke setups with tables and white styrofoam coolers. Ask for a roti and enjoy floured wraps with a curried orchestra of potatoes, pumpkin and your meat of choice. The Greeks and Arabs may battle over the origin of the gyro, but Trinidad perfected it. Choose the meat and vegetables to go with it, but Trinidad literally has the sauce – options make all the difference. Find your fancy at **Independence Sq**, **Ariapita Ave**, **St James** or Queen's Park Savannah.

DINING IN STYLE IN PORT OF SPAIN

Chaud Café, One Woodbrook Place
Enjoy a lifted touch to a familiar cuisine. Chaud has a lovely view of downtown Port of Spain and flavors you can't resist. $$

Town Restaurant
Known best for its interpretation of Chinese cuisine, Town Restaurant offers exceptional service and portions that can feed you for days. $$

Buzo Osteria Italiana
Find the most savory Italian cuisine here. With a lovely wine list to pair with your delicious entrée, you'll go home talking about Buzo. $$

GETTING AROUND

Head out on weekends with someone who drives and is able to navigate the streets. Once you enter Port of Spain, you'll come across quite a few taxis that can take you through the city. Walking is also an option in upper Port of Spain. To properly drink in the sites and sounds, exploring on foot can be the most immersive option.

Beyond Port of Spain

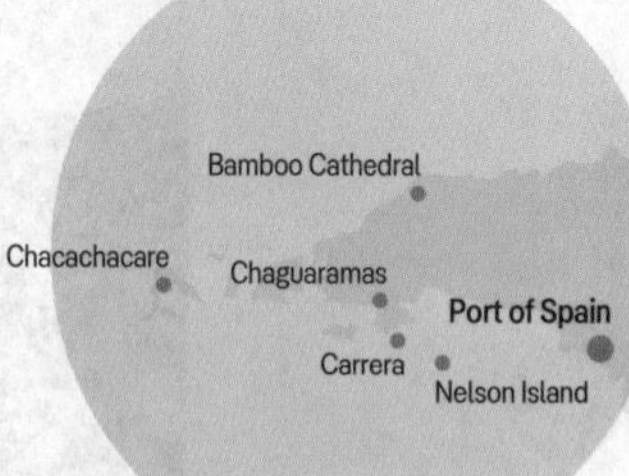

Port of Spain is highly metropolitan, but to Trinidadians, the city is also quite enshrined in its surroundings.

If you leave the city and head west, it won't be ridiculously long before you come upon Chaguaramas – that is, if you don't stop at Carenage for a quick bite. You'll know it by the unfettered sea views before you, or by the meandering curvature of the paved stretch. It's almost poetic how the busy highway quickly calms to become a lone main road. Venture into kayaking near the shore as you look out to the Five Islands (the real ones or the amusement park nearby), but we recommend you keep going. Venturing toward Trinidad's northwestern tip, the Chaguaramas Peninsula is the jumping-off point for exciting tours to a chain of offshore islands, the Bocas.

TOP TIP

Make your western adventures a group affair, since transportation is easily affordable by renting a maxi-taxi or minibus.

Tufted capuchin monkey, Bamboo Cathedral (p600)

View from Chacachacare

Chaguaramas & Westward

HEAD OUT INTO THE COUNTRYSIDE

A 25-minute drive west from Port of Spain takes you to Chaguaramas. Swing right just after Pier 1 and soon you'll doubt you're so close to the city. Lounge at the **Chaguaramas Boardwalk**, enjoying the seaside views and people-watching. Then, look for the signs leading to **Bamboo Cathedral**. As you walk down the path, you might hear monkeys calling in the distance; you might see a few, too. Bamboo stalks on each side merge at the centre, mimicking a couple's first wedding kiss. It's called a cathedral because the branches meet to make an archway, but it might also be because few experiences make you feel closer to God. An hour's hike further will take you to a 1975 **plane crash site**. It remains interesting to many, though the story is simple – bad weather caused the pilot to collide with the mountainside.

BEST PLACES TO EAT BEYOND PORT OF SPAIN

Don's Roti Shop
It's dubbed one of the best in the country. Find traditional roti and curries next door to a popular bar in Diego Martin. $

Carenage Fish Fry
On weekends, fisherfolk return from the sea with their catch. While it's fresh, seafood is seasoned and cooked for a waiting crowd. $

Caffe del Mare
This sweet spot among the sailboats at Crews Inn in Chaguaramas offers breakfast and lunch, with breathtaking views of the coast. $$

Down the Islands

HISTORY BY THE SEA

Further west, you can tour the smaller offshore islands by boat. There are five islands in all, each with a deep – and sometimes sordid – history. Learn about the diverse past of **Nelson Island**: a bartering point for First People tribes, a detention centre for Holocaust refugees, a quarantine station for East Indian immigrants, and a holding facility for political prisoners. Then, there's the prisoners living on **Carrera**, and the former leper colony of **Chacachacare**. Whether it's a day trip or a couple of days, heading 'down the islands' is an excellent way to enjoy some time away from the city bustle. Activities including hiking, bird-watching and historical excursions can be arranged with **Island Experiences**.

GETTING AROUND

Public transportation is unpredictable in this area, particularly after Carenage. It's best to rent a vehicle or to enlist someone you know who can drive you. Download a rideshare app to link up with a driver for the day; be mindful of peak periods or a lack of drivers on the app.

NORTHEAST COAST

Northeastern Trinidad envelopes the synergy of both islands. Residents aren't strangers to modern technology, but they cling dearly to simplicity. The origins of the people and their stories are still carried heavily in last names and lineage. There's also advanced ecological awareness and pride in the act of environmental preservation.

Despite the ruggedly beautiful coastline, waterfalls, hiking trails and swimmable rivers, tourism remains very low-key here. Water sports may feature on this coast, but they don't represent its main character. The 600-hectare Asa Wright Nature Centre, located amid the rainforest of the Northern Range, blows the minds of bird-watchers, while leatherback turtles come annually to lay eggs on the Grande Rivière and Matura beaches; the former, in particular, is among the world's major turtle-nesting sites.

Inaccessible from Blanchisseuse, where the North Coast Rd ends, this quiet region is bounded by Matelot in the north and Matura in the southeast.

TOP TIP

The experiences covered here can be booked and done as a tour. To have your own freedom, however, it's best to rent a car and get a data roaming plan or a SIM card at the airport so that you can navigate the area.

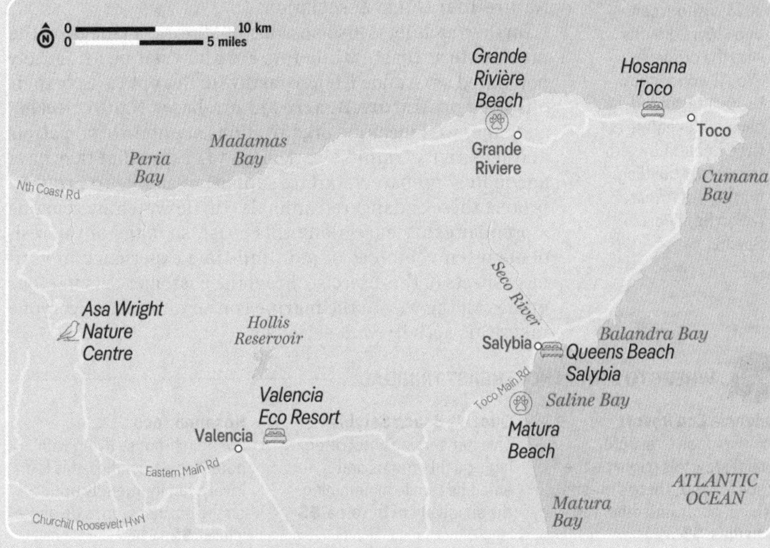

ECO-EXPERIENCE OF A LIFETIME

If nature and wildlife entices you, HADCO Experiences at **Asa Wright Nature Centre** in Blanchisseuse is for you. A former cocoa and coffee plantation transformed into a huge nature reserve, it's synonymous with the northeast countryside. Some 160 species of birds have been recorded here, including 14 species of hummingbirds.

Spend a night at the lodge and arise to lush greenery and the sounds of birdsong, or book a tour if you're short on time. Refurbished facilities were launched in 2023; visitors can book tours directly with the property.

You'll wonder how the uninterrupted calm of the nature can fit so beautifully with the nearby bustling borough of Arima (26km from Port of Spain).

MARK MEREDITH/GETTY IMAGES ©

Leatherback turtle, Grand Rivière Beach

The Nomadic Life of Turtles

A HOME FOR WILDLIFE

Book your ticket to Trinidad between March and May. As the skies darken, dozens of huge leatherback turtles slowly make their way to **Grande Rivière Beach**. They take their time looking for the best nesting spots and then they begin to dig. As a proper hole forms, a daze comes over them as they face the ocean and they begin to lay their eggs into the hole. It can be up to 110 eggs at once, but be patient. The turtles will carefully cover the hole with the precious offspring nestled safely inside and then make their way back to the beckoning sea bed. Later in the year, near September, you can visit again with the hope of seeing some of the hatchlings make their way to the sea. It can all be witnessed with the assistance of qualified guides from the Grande Rivière Nature Tour Guide Association.

Turtle-watching is also possible in Matura, a village on the northeastern coast. While this area may not be as densely populated as Grande Rivière, many turtles opt to leave their offspring on **Matura Beach**. Matura-based Nature Seekers and other well-meaning organizations maintain legal patrols and sensitivity training workshops to ensure that they have adequately prepared staffing support available to properly protect these endangered animals. Turtle-watching remains a premier experience along this coast, so many of the residents often volunteer or gain full-time experience in various aspects of this exercise. From the customer-serving tour guides all the way to the marine conservationists, everyone takes this activity very seriously.

WHERE TO STAY IN NORTHEAST TRINIDAD

Valencia Eco Resort
If you're open to a more quaint stay, this might be the place for you. There's on-site fishing, pools and other fun activities. **$$**

Queen's Beach Salybia
This full-service hotel offers high-quality rooms and amenities while maintaining the simplicity of the area. **$$**

Hosanna Toco
For beach-house living with hotel-type amenities, this is a lovely, family-friendly option on the northeastern side of the island. **$$**

Beyond Northeast Coast

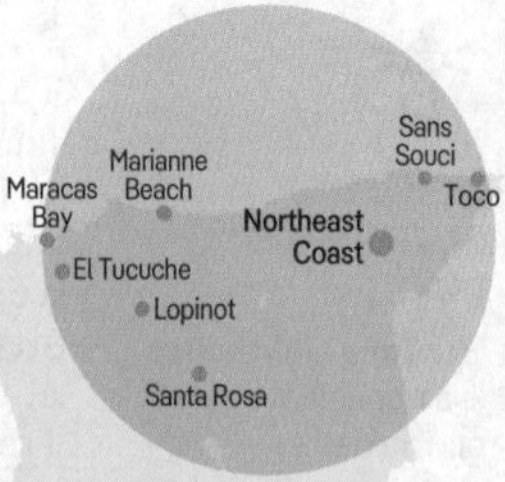

Exploring beyond Trinidad's northeast coast is an adventure. Some gems are obvious, but the best ones require more effort.

Cultural richness awaits beyond the northeast coast. There are food options aplenty, but your tastebuds will dance regardless. There's nothing like the seasonal Creole flavors offered in Rampanalgas on a Saturday morning or Maracas Bay on a Sunday. Or maybe your tongue would be put to better use with a new language. Patois has different flavors on every Caribbean island, but T&T's is perched in the north. It spittles off the tongues of the elderly, passed down through generations. In Trinidad, patois' main influences are French and West African, but many nations came here and brought their languages, so patois is often taught by those of Venezuelan and Eastern Caribbean descent. It's a language that succinctly embodies a multicultural story.

TOP TIP

Wear long, dark clothing that can protect you from any critters or insects you may stumble across on your adventures.

JOHN DE LA BASTIDE/SHUTTERSTOCK ©

Lopinot Historical Complex (p604)

TRINIDAD'S EASTERNMOST POINT

The **Toco Lighthouse** is a popular attraction on Trinidad's northeastern coast. Formerly known as the Galera Point Lighthouse and renamed after decorated Trinbagonian Olympic champion (and Toco resident) Keshorn Walcott, the 2m-tall structure was recently restored and now features a welcome center and seating areas for those looking to picnic at the historic site.

It was built by the British in 1867 and originally came equipped with 4 million candles and a kerosene light. A quick trod down some precarious rocks will lead you to breathtaking views of the ocean from this easternmost tip in Trinidad. As the waves swell and break onto the rocks, you might even spot some sea life.

Where Vast Waters Meet

BEACH LIFE IS THE BEST LIFE

The Northeast Coast has some of the best beaches on the island. See where the river meets the sea at **Marianne Beach** in Blanchisseuse. Located in what was once a secluded fishing village, it's the final stop along the North Coast Rd. Have a dip in the sea or try freshwater swimming in a lagoon mere steps away. The bluest water you'll find is at the very tip, in **Sans Souci**. Its French name means 'without worry', and carefree you will be: Sans Souci's aggressive waves are perfect for surfing. Further west lies the world-famous **Maracas Bay**. The beach is just the beginning at Maracas: discover the bake and shark, a local foodie favorite. Regardless of where you choose to splash, find your way there on a sunny Sunday and refresh yourself for the week ahead.

Maracas Bay

MARK MEREDITH/SHUTTERSTOCK ©

Indigenous History & National Foundation

THE HERITAGE OF THE FIRST PEOPLE

Trinidad's name is believed to come from the Spanish, who saw the three peaks of the Northern Range and labelled the island with the Spanish word for 'trinity'. With trained guides from **Island Hikers**, tackle the two-hour hike from Caura Valley to the second-highest peak, **El Tucuche**, which is moderately challenging. Many revere El Tucuche as a sacred mountain because of its petroglyphs, etched in the rocks by Trinidad's First People. The so-called **Caurita Carvings** are protected by the National Trust; they can be observed near the foot of the mountain.

There are also historic sites in **Lopinot** and **Santa Rosa**, including a historical museum on a rumoured haunted estate which displays pre-colonization indigenous artifacts. Today, the First People preserve the island's heritage within their language, way of life and teachings.

GETTING AROUND

More than anywhere else in the northeast, it's important to travel in a private vehicle and to have GPS here. Turns can become very confusing, especially after dark. With winding roads and unreliable street lighting, it's advisable to go with someone who's been to these places before.

Tobago
Crown Point
Trinidad

CROWN POINT

Tobago is Trinidad's more reserved sister, but it doesn't mean she lacks her own identity.

Crown Point is a hub of electrifying tastes, sounds and experiences. To enjoy limitless adventures, fantastic food and inviting accommodations all within easy distance of the ANR Robinson International Airport, Crown Point is where you want to be. Nothing is more calming than a Crown Point sunset, but you can awaken your senses at the brilliant crack of dawn, too.

This tourist hub is relatively small but mighty. The area packs in a full slate of experiences for any type of traveler, but it is especially true for the solo excursionist. With busy streets, well-lit areas and good access to prime spots, this town makes it easy for even the most unfamiliar tourist. On the best-planned day, you can interact with everything Crown Point has to offer and still have time to unwind in nature.

TOP TIP

It's important to know that when going to Tobago, you'll have a better time in the dry season (December to May). Many of the activities in Crown Point are best enjoyed under the Caribbean sun. Easter, especially, will give you the perfect weather to enjoy your trip.

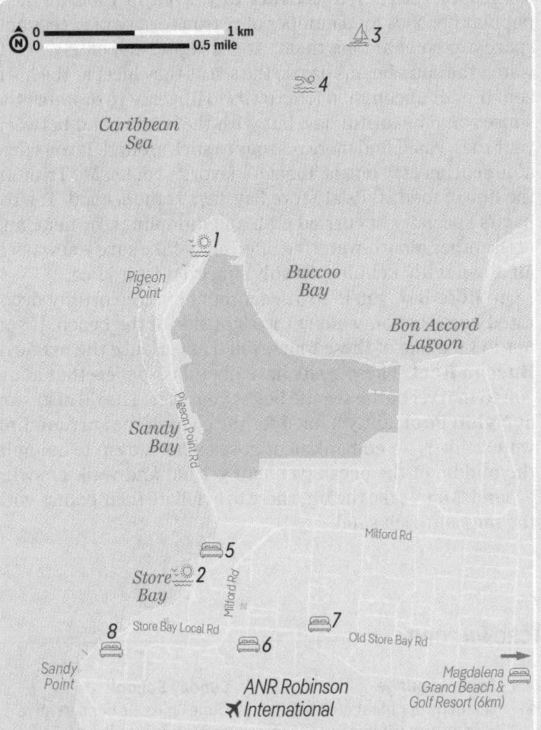

SIGHTS
1 Pigeon Point Heritage Park
2 Store Bay

ACTIVITIES, COURSES & TOURS
3 Buccoo Reef
4 Nylon Pool

SLEEPING
5 Coco Reef Hotel
6 Kariwak Hotel
7 Shepherd's Inn
8 Tropikist Hotel

Crown Point
NANDANI BRIDGLAL/SHUTTERSTOCK ©

BEST PLACES TO STAY IN CROWN POINT

Kariwak Hotel
Welcoming place known for its green surroundings and lovely Tobagonian breakfast. $$$

Tropikist Hotel
A great option for those wanting all-inclusive accommodations. $$

Coco Reef Hotel
All about the location, this hotel is adjacent to Store Bay and other attractions. $$$

Shepherd's Inn
Intimate place perfect for relaxation featuring Caribbean-style teakwood decor. $$

Magdalena Grand Beach and Golf Resort
Sprawling resort on Tobago Plantations Estate offering oceanfront suites with private balconies. $$$

AMY.LEZAMA/SHUTTERSTOCK ©

Curry crab and dumplings, Store Bay

Sail Away to Store Bay

BLUE SKIES AND BRIGHT EYES

It's unassuming at first, but take a deep breath before you come upon the shoreline. **Store Bay** is one of Tobago's most popular beaches for a number of reasons – ease of access and space are chief among them. At the right time of day, you'll watch the sun's beams dazzle the sea as they meet at the horizon. It's not uncommon for crowds to linger here to watch the sunset on a beautiful day, but with the warm sand between your toes, you'll find more reasons to stick around. If you come at lunchtime, try one of Tobago's favorite cooks: Ms Trim. In the line of food stalls at Store Bay, hers is the second. Try Tobago's specialty of curried crab and dumplings, or taste any of the other mouth-watering offerings. Make sure you wash it all down with a chilled, freshly squeezed fruit juice.

On Store Bay, you'll also see a number of colorfully decorated boats bobbing along the right side of the beach. If you opt to take one of these tours, you'll experience the magic of **Buccoo Reef**. These boats have fiberglass panels that allow you to marvel at the sea life below your feet. They'll also stop at **Nylon Pool**; aptly named for the color of the surrounding water, this is an embankment at sea where, despite being in the middle of the ocean, you can get out and walk or swim around. Many take the time here to exfoliate their bodies with the nutrient-rich sand.

WHERE TO DRINK IN CROWN POINT

Jade Monkey
A lively spot that often features live performances from soca entertainers.

Sahara Lounge
Quench your thirst at this spot with an array of drinks options and live music.

Sunday School
Quite unlike its conservative name, this is a vibrant representation of Tobago social life.

Windsurfing, Pigeon Point

Tobago's Heritage-Filled Escapade

A VACATION IN A DAY

From the moment you enter the arches, **Pigeon Point Heritage Park** has a special talent for making you feel like the outside world doesn't exist. Passing the coconut-tree-lined driveway relaxes you with every second that goes by. As you drink in the scenery – clear seas on your left, lush greenery on your right – you'll see why Pigeon Point is such a hit. Make your way to the shoreline and bask in the warmth. Go for a stroll along the water and take in the length of this popular spot, stopping by the iconic jetty to snap a few photos. A beachside bar provides drinks, and there are several vendors with a wide range of foods ready to awaken your palate.

There's no shortage of water-sports outfitters on the northernmost side of Pigeon Point, such as **Tobago Waterholics**. The premier rental offerings include glass kayaking, jet skis, stand-up paddleboards and the 'Super Mable' ride if you have a need for speed.

If you'd like to take a few trinkets home, the vendors at Pigeon Point are a great place to start. Indigenous stores offer a homely range of jewelry, swimsuits and clothing, along with classic souvenirs. The real treasures are bracelets made from materials found on the island. Sweet snacks are available as well; try tamarind balls, preserved mangoes or benne sticks (a brown-sugar-and-sesame-seed combination) for a unique taste of Tobago. Even Trinidadians stock up on them to share with people at home.

BEST PLACES TO EAT IN CROWN POINT

Skewers
Casual Middle Eastern dining and takeaway options; expect hefty portions. $

House of Pancakes
Quaint dining atmosphere with a healthy local and international mixed menu. $$

Pasta Gallery
Handmade pasta dishes define a small but intimate Italian dining experience. $$

Brown Cow Restaurant
Imaginative fusion cuisine featuring lots of local ingredients. $$

Frontline Flavours
Look no further for satisfying traditional Tobagonian dishes. $$

GETTING AROUND

If you stay in Crown Point, you can comfortably get around on foot, but there are several rental car operators in the area if you intend to venture out. Public transport is a bit too unpredictable to have that dictate how you spend your precious time.

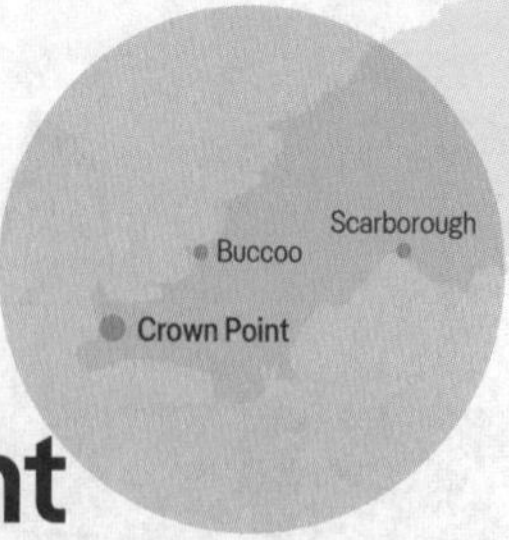

Scarborough
Buccoo
Crown Point

Beyond Crown Point

Tobago has a lot to offer, so even the smallest jaunt outside Crown Point will entice any traveler.

Buccoo and Scarborough are among the bigger activity hubs beyond Crown Point. In fact, if you opt to take a ferry to Tobago from Trinidad, they would be in plain sight first. While Scarborough, in particular, has pristine views of the deep blue sea, there's a buzz of activity which proves that this paradise still operates a busy economy. Even the trip from Crown Point on the Claude Noel Hwy takes you past many of the island's shopping malls and other business centers. Nevertheless, the culture and uniqueness of Tobago still thrive along with the surrounding noise, and the hospitality and vitality are as ripe as ever.

TOP TIP

Keep your GPS on. Whether you're driving or you have a guide, the roads can be confusing, so stay alert.

M. TIMOTHY O'KEEFE/ALAMY ©

Wedding re-enactment, Tobago Heritage Festival

History, Harmony & Heritage

HONORING TOBAGONIAN TRADITIONS

Tobagonians believe the best of their diverse history has been preserved, and it all culminates in the **Tobago Heritage Festival**. This island-wide affair has several events happening between mid-July and August 1. It borrows elements of Carnival, with stick fighting and Blue Devils, as well as Easter's goat and crab races, but it radiates richer traditions. Re-enactments of 'ole time' weddings native to the village of Moriah bring out the people's creativity; grooms in pseudo-tuxedos sporting wooden pipes dance with their well-endowed brides through the streets. There's something special about Tobago's oral traditions; learn about the folklore characters and urban legends (if it won't scare you away). Competition is on, too, as performing arts groups do traditional dances and skits which tell the history that Tobago holds dearly. The timing is no mistake: August 1 marks Emancipation Day – a yearly reminder of the liberation of African enslaved people.

Buccoo's Goat Races

TOBAGO'S EASTER FUN

Buccoo (about 15 minutes' drive from Crown Point) is a quiet community most of the year, but over Easter weekend, the area is awash with energy. The **Buccoo** and **Mt Pleasant** goat and crab races are a sight to behold. For weeks leading up to the event, Tobagonians train goats – and, somehow, crabs – to race against each other. Communities from all over the island gather to watch these unlikely creatures perform. Despite the eccentricity, there's no shortage of the competitive spirit. Residents make a day of the festivities with other games and light sports, and of course, there's food and drinks for the public. The event is usually held on the Tuesday after Easter, but you can catch participants practicing their strategies ahead of the event; they're always ready to entertain a visitor.

PARTY AT THE GREAT RACE

The **Great Race** is a fabulous way to enjoy this side of the island. In August, speedboaters stage a race from Port of Spain in Trinidad all the way to Scarborough in Tobago. Spectators often watch the start of the race on television and then head down to Scarborough to see the contestants come in.

Nothing happens without a party, though; after the race ends, crowds linger on the beach, whether they're celebrating their favorite boat's win or licking their wounds from an unfortunate loss.

If you gather up a few friends – perhaps those you made on the island – there's no doubt you'll have a memorable time at the Great Race.

Racing facility, Buccoo

NANDANI BRIDGLAL/SHUTTERSTOCK ©

GETTING AROUND

Having a rental car on a trip to Tobago is recommended to fully enjoy your trip. Bumper-to-bumper traffic isn't a normal occurrence on the island, so for absolute freedom of movement, renting a vehicle is the best way to go.

CASTARA

More than just a fishing village, Castara offers a rustic, charming warmth to visitors seeking a mixture of play and peace on Tobago's Leeward coastline. With a verdant, mountainous landscape that's punctuated by a lush tropical rainforest and the breathtakingly blue Caribbean Sea, Castara embodies the traits of 'olden but golden'. It's also where everybody knows your name: with a population of approximately 600 people, there is an elevated sense of close-knit community that adds to the serene vibe for visitors. Awake to the sounds of crashing waves at your doorstep with animated birds and other wildlife, and explore at your own pace. Whether you choose to go snorkelling in Englishman's Bay, or end your day by having a surreal dinner experience in the picturesque Jemma's Treehouse, there's plenty of choice.

One thing is for certain: Castara is an ecological paradise filled with adventures. Get ready to dive in.

TOP TIP

Castara Bay isn't your only choice for a sun-kissed beach day in the area – there are a number of stunning beaches within a small radius. Englishman's Bay, Bloody Bay, Parlatuvier Bay and Cotton Bay are some great options to explore. Bonus: they're family- and pet-friendly, too.

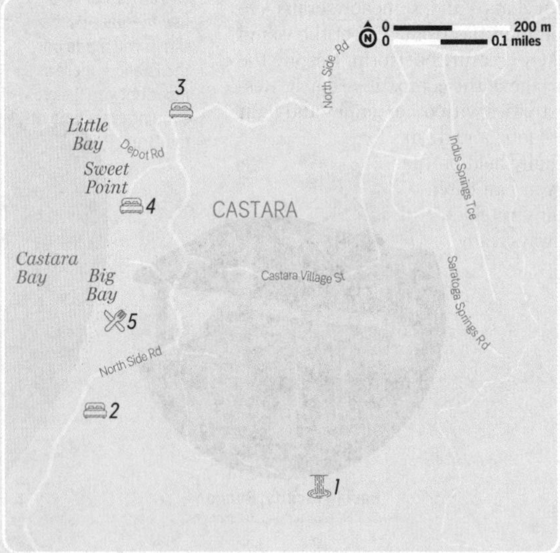

SIGHTS
1 Castara Waterfall

SLEEPING
2 Castara Retreats
3 Castara Villas
4 Naturalist Beach Resorts

EATING
5 Cascreole Restaurant and Bar

Path to Castara Waterfall (p612)

STYVE REINECK/SHUTTERSTOCK ©

Fishing, Castara

The Ultimate Caribbean Fishing Experience

THE THRILL OF MARINE LIVING

Connect with any Castara fisher on the local beaches or speak to your hotel host to book a boat trip out to sea for a glorious day of fishing. The half-day excursion will take you on a journey along the electric-blue coastline to fish for some of the most popular species including bonito, flying fish, salmon, tuna and kingfish. Fishing boats normally sail daily, unless the seas are too rough to navigate. Don't be late: fishers prefer to depart between 8am and 10am. Beat the scorching midday sun and make some stops along the way – some of the most gorgeous beaches in Castara are only accessible by boat.

Fishing is an integral custom in Castara village, a lived experience that the community shares with its nearest Caribbean island neighbors. But traveling a fair distance out from the northeastern shoreline may land you in some 'hot water' with authorities, as the Leeward tipping point of Tobago shares its marine borders with nearby Grenada (only 97 nautical miles away). Even with the allure of adventures on the sea, it's a good idea to make the trip with a seasoned Tobagonian fishers.

FISHER'S PARADISE

Shammon Walker is a lifelong fisher who was born and raised in Castara.

I am from here; I grew up here. My brother and I used to run around and explore as children, and go fishing with my father. Castara is more relaxed: there are so many places here that you can't find if you go searching online. It won't do it justice.

Beaches like Paradise or Cotton Bay and Back River are only reachable by boat and by trail – and sometimes it's a long walk, because you have to come from the hills. Now that I have my son, I want to teach him how to discover everything in the community, the same as my father let me find my way.

WHERE TO STAY IN CASTARA

Naturalist Beach Resorts
Wake up to the sounds of the seashore: Castara Bay is right at your doorstep. **$$**

Castara Retreats
A tree-house–style ecolodge with a difference, featuring panoramic sunset views and relaxing yoga classes. **$$**

Castara Villas
Perfect for families and groups, this rustic, wooden home is steps away from various amenities. **$$$**

WHY I LOVE CASTARA

Tenille Clarke, writer

Many of my fondest memories of Tobago's rural life were shaped as a child, when my grandfather and father religiously sent me to spend my July/August vacation with my paternal family.

In my impressionable years, I eagerly took those trips with great joy and wanton abandon – sights and sounds of lapping beach waves, home-cooked Creole meals and drives along meandering, precipitous roads were standard.

Today, the beauty of Castara remains in those unspoiled qualities. Here, there is a distinct sense of community, where smiles are as brilliant and warm as seaside sunrises. It is, indubitably, where everybody knows your name.

Glowing Inferno: A Beach-Bound Treat

BRING THE HEAT AT NIGHT

The fun doesn't stop when the sun sets in Castara village. Have an early dinner at **Cascreole Restaurant and Bar** – make sure to finish by 7:30pm on a Thursday evening. Villagers begin their ritual of hollowing wild bamboo to create a large pyre for the weekly **Bonfire Party**. Once the fire is lit, the party begins! Indulge in the sweet sounds of Caribbean music from the resident DJ, have a few drinks from the bar and watch the bamboo crackle and form embers that burn brilliantly into the night sky. Taking an after-hours swim under the stars is encouraged, and don't miss out on the performances from the traditional drummers or the steelpan players. Dance the night away until 3am.

Cascades Worth the Chase

MAJESTIC WATERFALL AND WILDLIFE SPOTTING

Castara's magic can be found in almost every tourist adventure, but there's a special allure to the **Castara Waterfall**. Visitors usually park on River Rd next to the open, grassy field by the Castara Government Primary School and walk across the river, where the trailhead is located. After about a 10-minute trek, this splendid 4.5m chute appears. Cascading into a natural freshwater pool that will draw you in for a quick swim, the falls provide a great view of the riverbank and rocky terrain. As you float in the water, look up to the sky: you are greeted with the sights and sounds of the surrounding rainforest canopy.

Access to the Castara Waterfall is free, which is a plus for visitors wanting to appreciate Mother Nature's wonders. Early morning visits, though not mandatory, are highly recommended since there is a variety of wildlife constantly spotted while crossing the creek. Agoutis, armadillos (known in T&T as tattoos), lizards and many birds are just some of the animals that inhabit the area, making it the ideal Caribbean spot for nature lovers.

AIM TO GO THE DISTANCE

The village of **Charlotteville** (p614) is neatly tucked away on Man of War Bay, and it's not only accessible from Tobago's mountainous roadways – you can take a 30-minute boat ride with a fisher from Castara Bay.

GETTING AROUND

Castara is a bit more remote. To enjoy this area to the fullest, it's recommended to have the luxury of your own vehicle.

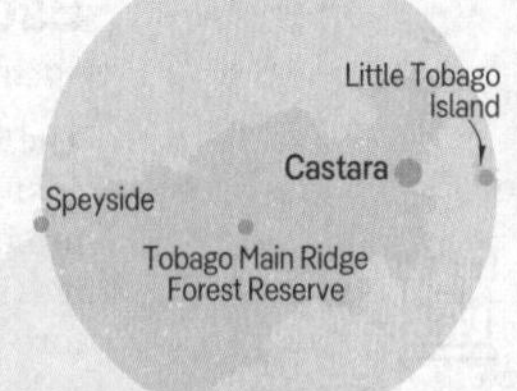

Beyond Castara

While Castara is the rural nucleus for good living in Tobago, nearby villages offer equal doses of balance and beauty.

The hospitable communities on the outskirts of Castara make for a welcome change of pace for visitors who seek moments of peace in the bucolic settings of Tobago. These rural hubs are the antithesis of the hustle and bustle that defines global metropolises. Parlatuvier, Bloody Bay, L'Anse Fourmi, Hermitage and Charlotteville – the far northeastern point in Tobago – are laden with culture. Here, street names and seaside stretches hint at a complicated colonial history of French, English, Spanish and Dutch influences from the 16th century. With lapping waves, quaint restaurants, and proud residents who focus on preserving traditions, commercialization isn't the priority. Instead, learn about the spirit of collaboration, where the beach is only the beginning.

TOP TIP

Split your time between two beaches per day and hire a taxi driver on standby for your convenient, sun-kissed commute.

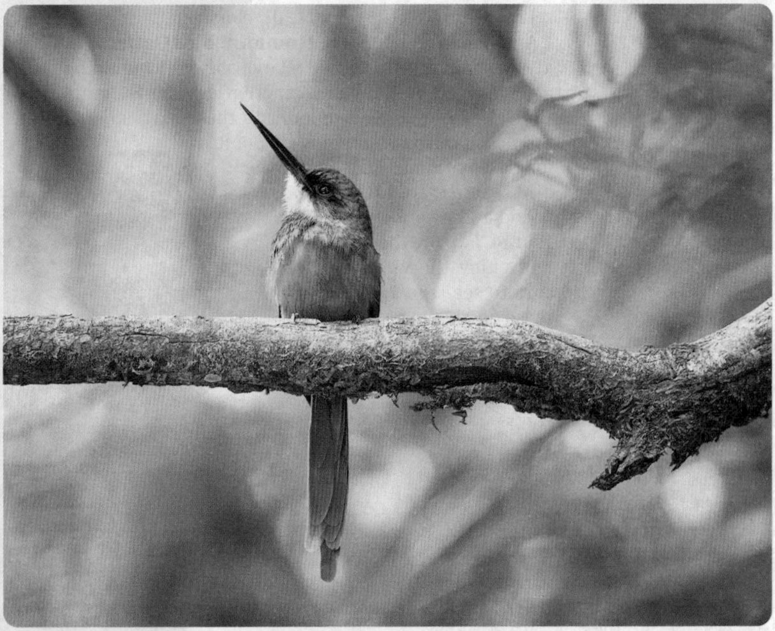

Rufous-tailed jacamar, Tobago Main Ridge Forest Reserve (p614)

Escape into the Ridge

PROTECTED WILDLIFE THRIVES

The **Tobago Main Ridge Forest Reserve**, a 20-minute drive east of Castara, is a point of pride for any environmentally minded Tobagonian. The reserve was established in 1776 and it's the oldest protected rainforest in the Caribbean. Long before that, back when Tobago was still linked in soil to South America, the Main Ridge shared most of its fauna. Through careful and deliberate preservation by stakeholders, the reserve is a quiet reminder of how nature can thrive under the right circumstances. Visitors are welcome to tour the reserve, but only with the assistance of qualified and authorized personnel. A number of trailheads lead off the main road into the rainforest, where there's excellent bird-watching, and tour guides – such as internationally acclaimed expert Errol Roach – provide commentary on the forest ecosystem.

FORTRESSES OF TIMES PAST

If you'd like to learn about Tobago's storied history in times of war, it may be useful to tour some of the forts. **Fort King George** in Scarborough, built by the British in the 18th century, is the best known one; it also houses the Tobago Museum. Meanwhile, **Betsey's Hope** in Roxborough and **Campbelton Battery** in Charlotteville decorate the eastern side of the island. While they have picturesque backgrounds and offer magnificent views, the forts also stand as tall reminders that Tobago had much to defend in the 1770s; remain preserved for visitors to learn a bit about the island's past.

The Mecca of Coral Reefs

WAYSIDE IN SPEYSIDE

Speyside is a small village on the northeastern edge of Tobago (about an hour's drive from Castara), but there's a lot to experience here. Enjoy the quiet, or kick things up a notch with blood-pumping water sports. The **Speyside Waterwheel**, originally from Scotland, once created enough energy to provide electricity for the entire community. It's perched on a former sugar estate where many of the ruins still exist. This National Trust–protected site is a good example of Tobago's relationship with sustainable development.

Another attraction is the **Hummingbird Gallery**. T&T has always maintained a special relationship with hummingbirds, as evidenced by the many sanctuaries. The Hummingbird Gallery is Speyside's love letter to these magical creatures. Speyside is also the jumping-off point for glass-bottomed boat trips to the bird sanctuary of **Little Tobago** island and neighbouring **Goat Island**. Explore the coral reefs and enjoy the views; you're sure to see several species of these quick-winged beauties.

Copper-rumped hummingbird

GETTING AROUND

Renting a vehicle that has a bit of height to it, like an SUV or a pickup truck, is most suitable for the roads in this area. While the infrastructure is quite stable, the added height assists in navigating the winding roads.

Arriving

Getting to Trinidad and Tobago is possible via international flights and cruises. High season runs from January to March, coinciding with annual Carnival celebrations; anticipate a busier pace this time of year. Trinidad's airport has a wider range of food and shopping than Tobago's, but across both islands, you'll find more to choose from in nearby communities.

By Air

Trinidad's Piarco International Airport (pictured) is typically 35 to 50 minutes' drive from Port of Spain. Tobago's ANR Robinson International Airport is much closer to Crown Point. Taxis for hire and vehicle rentals are available immediately outside both airports.

By Boat

International cruise lines are slightly more popular in Tobago but common across both islands. Cruise ships dock at Port of Spain in Trinidad, making it easy to explore the capital city after disembarking. In Tobago, ships arrive in Scarborough and Charlotteville.

Money

Currency: Trinidad & Tobago dollar (TT$)

CASH

Cash on hand is a must in Trinidad and Tobago, especially for public transportation, tours and similar activities, as well as for most street vendors and independent sellers. The further you go into rural areas, the more of a necessity it becomes. This is particularly the case in Tobago.

You can exchange currency at authorized banks, exchange offices and certain hotels or withdraw at the nearest ATM. The Trinidad and Tobago dollar is generally preferred for cash transactions, but some establishments accept the US dollar as well.

DIGITAL PAYMENTS

Currently, Endcash is the only digital wallet app available – restricted to T&T bank account holders.

CREDIT CARDS

Many establishments in T&T accept debit and credit cards. Visa and Mastercard are the most commonly accepted options. Select places also take American Express, Discover and Diner's Club. Have a popular alternative on hand just in case.

TURKS & CAICOS ISLANDS

WHERE LUXURY MEETS THE TROPICAL OUTDOORS

With the exception of Providenciales, the most developed island in the country, most islands ar e a throwback to a world untamed by modernity.

The Turks and Caicos archipelago sits on an underwater plateau, split by a deep ocean channel into two island clusters: the Caicos Islands, low-lying coral outcrops of which six are inhabited, and the Turks Islands (Grand Turk and Salt Cay). Providenciales (aka Provo) is the booming tourism epicenter. West Caicos is a wetlands ecosystem and flamingo habitat with a 200-hectare saline lake. The Twin Islands of North and Middle Caicos represent the quiet countryside. South Caicos is a growing luxury tourism center, bordered by the uninhabited East Caicos. Parrot Cay is the original private enclave for the rich and famous.

Peel away the luxurious trappings of tourism development in Provo, and you'll find Grand Turk – the capital and historic heart – standing proud at the core of the country's identity. The seat of government remains there, even as the island's population and economy have dwindled. The Turks Islands were the birthplace of tourism centuries ago when they served as salt-producing engines for the colonial government.

There's an inescapable tension between the capital's tight-knit community culture and the cosmopolitan vigor of Provo. Nevertheless, the islands blend together with a spirit of simplicity and sophistication.

The country is a British Overseas Territory and British royals sometimes visit to stay at Waterloo, the governor's residence in Grand Turk, but it's an underwhelming property that fits the diminished stature of monarchies the world over.

THE MAIN AREAS

PROVIDENCIALES
Upscale hospitality on a cosmopolitan eco-island.
p622

TWIN ISLANDS
A tropical wilderness with sacred soil.
p629

GRAND TURK
The historic capital and diving paradise.
p635

DANITA DELIMONT/SHUTTERSTOCK ©

Above: Lobster meal, Grace Bay Beach (p625); Left: School of snapper

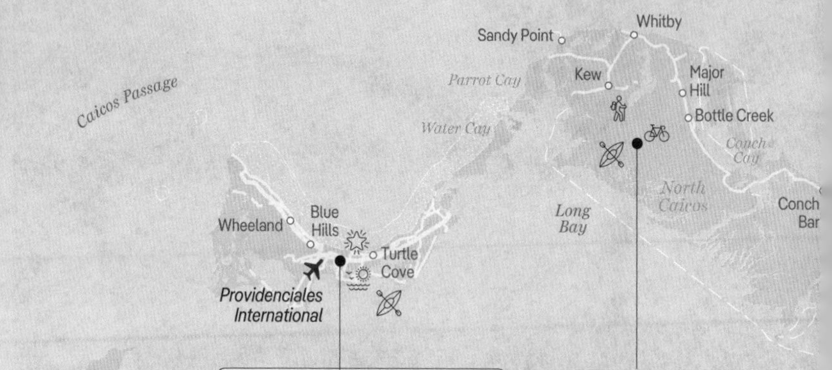

Caicos Passage
Sandy Point
Whitby
Parrot Cay
Kew
Major Hill
Bottle Creek
Water Cay
Conch Cay
North Caicos
Long Bay
Conch Bar
Wheeland
Blue Hills
Turtle Cove
Providenciales International
West Caicos
ATLANTIC OCEAN
West Sand Spit

Providenciales, p622

A balance of relaxation and entertainment in a stunning natural setting, without sacrificing luxury. Find tranquil beachfront landscapes and a lively island atmosphere.

Twin Islands, p629

Outdoor adventurers will delight in the peace and tranquility of beach landscapes and the subtle thrill of exploring nearshore shallow banks and the outdoors.

WALKING

On each island, walking is a great way to explore individual settlements, although a car is usually necessary for inter-town travel. Grace Bay's hip strip on Providenciales is designed for walking. It's the ideal way to explore top-rated restaurants, shops, hotels and beaches.

CAR & TAXI

An all-terrain vehicle is best to fully enjoy a stopover visit on the Twin Islands. Otherwise, rent a vehicle for a day's road trip across North and Middle Caicos or Providenciales. To only visit a few attractions, a taxi or tour service will suffice.

BOAT & JET SKI

Island-hopping by jet ski is a thrilling and unique way to zip across the shallow waters of Turks and Caicos, particularly around the Caicos Islands. Small passenger ferries are readily available with daily service to the other major and minor ports and moorings.

Find Your Way

The Turks & Caicos Islands (TCI) are remarkably interconnected. In most cases, island-hopping is easy by passenger ferry, jet ski or boat. Domestic air travel is commercially available. Although a British territory, the archipelago has no nonstop direct flights to the United Kingdom.

Grand Turk, p635

A quaint and quiet town with rustic island charm, floating on the edge of the great abyss of Grand Turk Wall, a snorkeling and diving marvel.

Plan Your Time

Keep in mind that your proximity to the resort district determines how much seclusion you can expect, ranging from a complete wilderness escape to a mix of outdoor thrill and city fun.

FLAVIO VALLENARI/GETTY IMAGES ©

Grace Bay Beach (p624)

If You Only Do One Thing

- Head to **Sunset Beach** (p624) on Providenciales and join a kayaking or stand-up paddleboard tour of **Mangrove Cay** (p625), a marine nursery in the Princess Alexandra Nature Reserve. It's a mild paddle to reach the thriving sea-turtle lair. The turtles are highly visible; they share the shallow mangrove creeks with juvenile sharks, conches and other wildlife.

- You'll have time afterward to relax on **Grace Bay Beach** (p624) and have lunch at **The Grill at Grace Bay Club** (p625).

- For something less active, the calm, shallow beach cove at **Sapodilla Bay** (p624) is the spot for a relaxing picnic.

Seasonal Highlights

Most activities are year-round except for whale-watching. The end of hurricane season between September and November, also known as mosquito time, brings unpredictable weather and budget deals.

JANUARY

This is the high season with prices peaking all around. In Long Bay, weather conditions are great for **kiteboarding** and **windsurfing**.

FEBRUARY

Put on your swimsuit for **whale-watching** in Grand Turk. You just might get to swim with a mother and calf pair.

APRIL

This is the tail end of the busiest time for **scuba diving**, when visibility is excellent down to 100ft (30m).

ALEXANDER KOLOMIETZ/SHUTTERSTOCK ©, ETHAN DANIELS/SHUTTERSTOCK ©, BLUE-SEA.CZ/SHUTTERSTOCK ©

Three Days to Travel Around

- Make **Grace Bay** (p624) on Providenciales your base to enjoy a diverse selection of restaurants and boutiques.
- Find handcrafted souvenirs at **Island Organics** (p626), and stop at **Lemons 2 Go** (p626) coffee shop for breakfast or a light lunch.
- Allot a day for a **Twin Islands road trip** (p631) – take the ferry over and rent a car to explore.
- Spend your evenings enjoying **Provo's nightlife** (p626). On Wednesdays, residents and visitors gather at **Da Conch Shack** (p626) for a fun beach party; on Thursdays, don't miss the **Fish Fry** (p626), a local cultural experience with music, food and crafts.

If You Have More Time

- Fly to **Grand Turk** (p635) for the day and join a morning **whale-watching tour** (p636) if you're visiting between January and March.
- You'll be finished by the early afternoon with enough time to stroll old **Cockburn Town** (p635), have lunch at **Jucky Jerk Food Truck** (p636) and tour the **Turks and Caicos National Museum** (p638).
- Alternatively, take a taxi to the **Grand Turk Lighthouse** (p638). Snack on conch fritters at the old lighthouse keeper's house before retiring to the airport.
- Return flights are notoriously delayed.

MAY

South Caicos is enlivened by the annual **South Caicos Regatta**, a long-standing festival with boat races and cultural competitions.

JUNE

Travel three to five days after the full moon to catch the bioluminescent mating ritual of glow worms on a **sunset cruise**.

JULY

Fishing is a year-round pastime, but July is the peak season for **marlin fishing**. Start trolling just 2 miles (3km) off the beach.

DECEMBER

The annual **Maskanoo** street festival is a Boxing Day tradition in Grace Bay honoring the island's African heritage with music, drumming and vibrant costumes.

Turks & Caicos Islands

Providenciales

Grand Turk

Salt Cay

PROVIDENCIALES

Before the 1980s, Providenciales (Provo) was a far cry from the modern tourism hub it is today. It was a minor agricultural town subsisting on fishing, sponge farming and ship salvaging. Schoolchildren traveling from Provo to the capital on Grand Turk risked being labeled 'country folk' and scorned, for their big island was little in stature. Today, Provo is a cosmopolitan island, an economic powerhouse and a celebrity magnet. The 1984 opening of Club Med Turkoise on Grace Bay Beach marked a turning point for mass tourism.

Development continues to move through like an unstoppable force. With many upscale amenities and nature at your fingertips, Provo is the place to indulge in the country's enviable beaches and laid-back atmosphere, along with a vibrant restaurant scene and lively entertainment. Provo is a compact island where traveling off the beaten path is as close as right down the road.

TOP TIP

The adventure can extend beyond Provo to the other Caicos Islands, accessible by air and boat: West Caicos, a biodiverse land and sea wilderness; East Caicos, a sanctuary for endemic plants and endangered birds; South Caicos, a growing tourism center still untouched by development; and Parrot Cay, a private resort island.

JADE PREVOST MANUEL/SHUTTERSTOCK ©

Sapodilla Bay (p624)

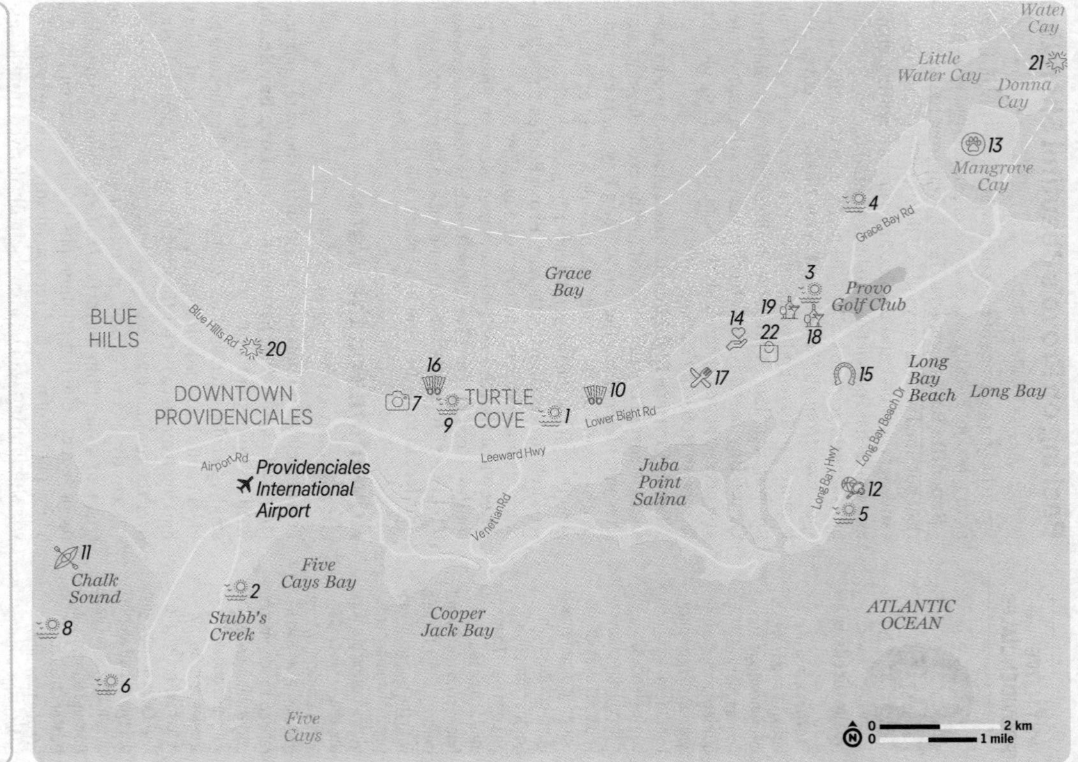

SIGHTS
1 Bight Beach
2 Five Cays Beach
3 Grace Bay
4 Leeward Beach
5 Long Bay
6 Sapodilla Bay
7 Sunset Beach
8 Taylor Bay
9 Turtle Cove

ACTIVITIES, COURSES & TOURS
10 Bight Reef (Coral Gardens)
11 Chalk Sound
12 Long Bay Beach
13 Mangrove Cay
14 Potcake Place K9 Rescue
15 Provo Ponies
16 Smith's Reef

EATING
17 Fish Fry
(see 14) Lemons 2 Go

DRINKING & NIGHTLIFE
18 Aziza Restaurant & Lounge
(see 14) Blue Bar & Lounge
19 Infinity Bar
(see 14) Shisha Lounge

ENTERTAINMENT
20 Da Conch Shack
(see 14) Danny Buoy's Sports Bar
21 Noah's Ark

SHOPPING
22 Island Organics
(see 14) Wellington Collection

WHY I LOVE PROVIDENCIALES

Noelle Nicolls, writer

Provo is a hub of activity, and I love it for the range and accessibility of outdoor experiences with close proximity to modern conveniences.

In one direction you can kayak Chalk Sound in meditative bliss, or kitesurf in another direction on Long Bay. Then, dine at a casual or fine-dining restaurant before a sunset cruise with the possibility to see bioluminescent glows worms blanket the sea.

In a single day, I flew to Grant Turk, had a rare and phenomenal underwater encounter with humpback whales, and on my return, although the flight was annoyingly delayed, I had ample time for pizza in Grace Bay and dancing at Da Conch Shack's Wednesday night beach jam.

Basking on Provo's Beautiful Shoreline

A GUIDE TO THE BEST BEACHES

Provo has no shortage of crystalline waters and idyllic beaches to relax on. Locally, beaches are often referred to as bays.

Sapodilla Bay is a gorgeous beach away from the hotel district but lined with luxury villas. There are makeshift restaurants serving food and drinks, and vendors renting chairs and umbrellas, plus jet skis to buzz around the bay. Because of its length, you can walk to the more secluded end to find a spot away from all the action. **Taylor Bay**, a few coves over, is more exclusive and compact, with a section of very shallow water, making it great for families with young children. **Grace Bay** is the island's busiest beach, with many hotels and access points. There's always something going on, from frisbee to Hobie Cat sailing.

Turtle Cove and **Bight Beach** share a phantom border along a single cove. They're renowned for the excellent snorkeling sites just meters from the shore. **Long Bay**, on the secluded southern side of the island, can provide a sense of isolation even though it's the revered kiteboarding beach where you'll see kiteboarders enjoying the surf. **Provo Ponies**, a small stable, runs horseback riding tours on Long Bay.

Leeward Beach has the best sunset views in Provo. The southwestern end of **Five Cays Beach** is part of a residential area with popular beachfront bars to enjoy a meal with your feet in the water and local island vibes.

Adventures on the Water

KITEBOARDING, KAYAKING AND SNORKELING IN PROVO

Providenciales is known for adventure on the water, particularly water sports that harness the wind. **Long Bay Beach**, with its consistent trade winds, shallow waters and wide sand, is a celebrated spot for kiteboarding. The location has ideal conditions for both beginners and experienced riders, making it a must-visit for those who crave the power to glide over the turquoise waters.

Recently, Provo gained increased prominence due to frequent visits of hip-hop artist Drake and the viral popularity of seductive aerial photographs in clear-bottom kayaks. These photos of modeling tourists, floating blissfully on Provo's shimmering waters, aren't actually derived from kayaking. You can participate in a clear-bottom kayak photoshoot at **Sunset Beach** to capture your own visual keepsake. Actual

PROVO BEACH BARS

Omar's Beach Hut
Jerked lobster tail and conch fritters are on the menu – authentic Caribbean food at the water's edge. $

Bugaloo's Conch Crawl
Enjoy good food, cocktails and music under the shady coconut trees on the water's edge of Five Cays Beach. $

Flamingo Cafe
The most popular spot for New Year's Eve fireworks. Enjoy the spectacle of sunset cocktails, any day. $

Smith's Reef

kayaking tours launch from the same beach to explore the **Mangrove Cay** turtle sanctuary across the Leeward Channel, with an active paddle in a traditional or clear-bottom kayak. **Chalk Sound** is where you'll go for a peaceful and meditative kayak. As you glide through the flats, the mesmerizing expanse of blue is interspersed with tiny islands resembling peaks of a mini mountain range.

Travelers in search of diving and snorkeling adventure will also find plenty of options in Provo. Two snorkeling sites that are renowned for their accessibility from the beach are **Smith's Reef**, which has multiple coral heads and reef systems near the Turtle Cove Marina; and **Bight Reef (Coral Gardens)**, which sits a bit further out at 107m from the beach and has a single impressive coral ridge.

Shop & Stroll Along Grace Bay

THE RESORT, RESTAURANT AND SHOPPING DISTRICT

Embark on a culinary journey with countless restaurants to choose from on the vibrant, cosmopolitan strip of Grace Bay Rd. This walkable district is turned on day and night.

CASUAL DINING IN PROVO

Mr Grouper's
Dine on authentic, down-home native food away from the tourist strip. $

Patty Place
Freshly baked Jamaican patties with flaky crust and flavorful seasoning – perfect snack food. $

Sweet T's
Inexpensive, finger-licking chicken wings and fries from a walk-up counter. $

Kin Khao Thai Restaurant
Quick service, casual setting, affordable prices and delicious, authentic Thai food. $

The Grill at Grace Bay Club
Soak in remarkable beach views and dine on international bistro fare under a shaded patio. $$

WHERE TO STAY IN GRACE BAY

Grace Bay Club
Resort campus with beachfront suites (adults-only), a section for families with villa suites and exclusive estate residences. **$$$**

Ritz Carlton
The first and only high-rise hotel in Provo with luxury rooms and 12-story residences, a steakhouse and a small casino. **$$$**

The Oasis at Grace Bay
Tucked-away, lush garden property within walking distance of the beach. A luxe atmosphere for a midrange price. **$$$**

BEST PLACES TO STAY IN SOUTH CAICOS

South Caicos Ocean & Beach Resort
Hilltop hotel overlooking Cockburn Harbour with spectacular sunset views toward Ambergris Cay on calm days. $

Sailrock Resort
The resort's luxurious villas with glasshouse design style are perched atop a sand dune in a secluded area overlooking Long Beach. $$

East Bay Resort
There are no crowds to worry about on East Bay Beach, where this large, full-service resort has all ocean-view suites. There's an on-site PADI dive shop. $$

On the road's northern side, adorned driving entrances lead to mega-resorts, and both sides have chic strip malls filled with restaurants and shops. **Lemons 2 Go** is a cozy coffee shop and meet-up point for breakfast and lunch. Two boutique souvenir shops, **Island Organics** and **Wellington Collection**, have unique, handcrafted finds. Refresh yourself with one of four varieties of beer and lager from Turk's Head Brewery, available at all bars in the area. The island's only two casinos, both modest in size, sit on the strip along with a few bars and nightclubs. Grace Bay Rd is completely pedestrianized each Christmas season for the **Maskanoo** street parade.

Get Your Daily Dose of Puppy Love

JOIN POTCAKE PLACE'S RESCUE MISSION

Adorable, tail-wagging potcake dogs prancing around town on a leash are a common sight in Grace Bay. Named after the local mongrel breed, these puppies are likely to be from **Potcake Place K9 Rescue**, a dog rescue charity that's one of Provo's most heartwarming experiences. Early in the mornings, a long line of visitors eagerly wait in the courtyard of Saltmills Plaza for the shelter's doors to open. On a first-come/first-serve basis, the rescue provides leashes and treats for a fun walk on the beach and around Grace Bay, aimed at helping these lovable dogs become more socialized. The ultimate goal is adoption, and many visitors who fall in love with their new furry friends do just that.

The Best of Provo Nightlife

DINNER, DANCING AND PARTY VIBES

Wake up when night falls to see the Grace Bay strip alight with dozens of bars and restaurants catering to different levels of hype and maturity, including **Danny Buoy's Sports Bar** and **Blue Bar & Lounge**. However, there's an unofficial local schedule for where to go each night to find the liveliest atmosphere.

On Tuesday evenings, just before sunset, enjoy traditional ripsaw music and an educational presentation of music and dance by cultural icon David Bowen and his son at **Infinity Bar**. A DJ performs at **Da Conch Shack** on Wednesday nights; every picnic table at this beach bar and restaurant fills out for this fun party under the stars. It's an absolute must to visit **Fish Fry** on Thursday nights, when the Stubbs Diamond

ALL-INCLUSIVE RESORTS IN PROVO

Club Med Turkoise
Adults-only resort isolated on the eastern end of Grace Bay, a broad and spectacular section of beach with calm seas. **$$**

Beaches Resorts by Sandals
This expansive property on Grace Bay Beach, with 21 restaurants and a water park, is tailor-made for families. **$$**

Blue Haven Resort
Boutique hotel with a small private beach in the upscale residential community of Leeward; adjoining marina. **$$**

PROVO'S EASTERN CAYS BY JET SKI

This exhilarating sea safari explores the uninhabited coastlines of the Caicos islands to Provo's east. Start at the **1 Heaving Down Rock Marina**. Head out over the Caicos Banks, off from Long Bay Beach, and stop at **2 La Famille Express** shipwreck. If you're fearless, climb the rusty ladder to jump from the ship's bow.

Continue in the direction of the Pine Cay private island, turning into the **3 Pine Cay Channel**. This is a thrilling part of the journey. The curved channel is completely protected from wind and waves, so the ocean carpet is flat and fast. Swirl through for a stop at the **4 Fort George Sandbar**, across from Sand Dollar Cove. Continue a bit further to glimpse the luxury cottages of Meridian Club Hotel along Pine Cay's north-coast beach.

Circle back into the channel and head to **5 Little Water Cay**, for a stop to see the protected rock iguanas in the Princess Alexandra Nature Reserve. Along the way, you will zip past Water Cay and Half Moon Bay, currently adjoined into a single landmass. The channels between these islands are filled with shifting sands, influenced by dynamic weather events. Next, head to **6 Noah's Ark** floating bar for a quick bite and a cold drink. Generally, jet skis are not allowed in national parks. However, in this area, there are designated channels separate from the protected islands and flats.

For the final leg, swing around to **7 Emerald Point**. Enter the **8 Leeward Going Through Channel** and pass the protected **9 Mangrove Cay** turtle sanctuary on the way to the **10 Blue Haven Marina**. Touring this phenomenal area on a jet ski is a wild and wonderful adrenalin rush.

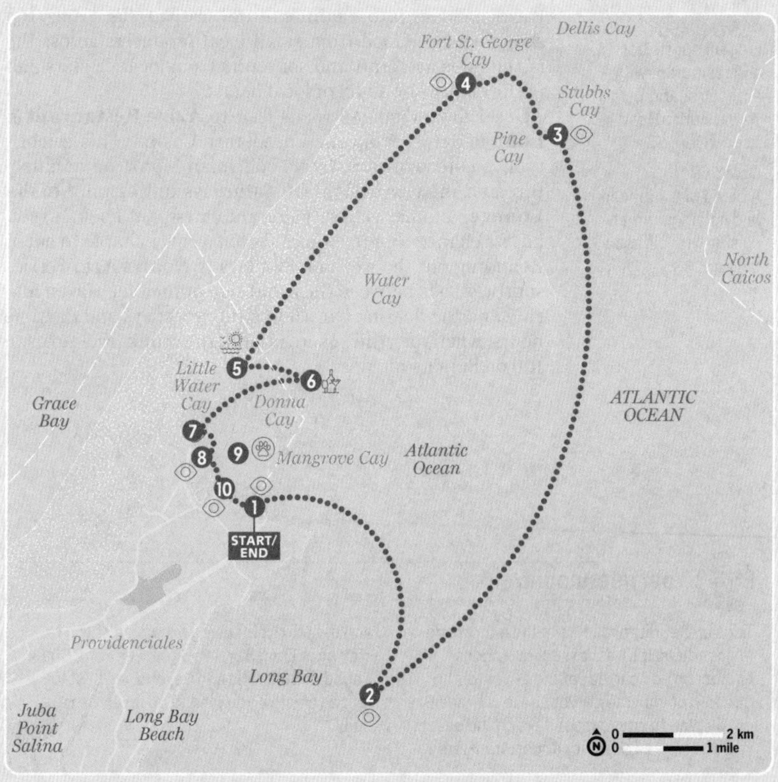

FINE DINING IN PROVO

Bella Luna Ristorante
Full range of classic Italian pasta and a pizzeria. Reservations recommended. $$

Coco Bistro
Fine dining in a coconut grove with an upscale menu that changes regularly. $$

The Deck at Seven Stars
Romantic setting with sultry live music and dinner on the beach. $$

The Terrace on Grace Bay
Elegant sports bar and restaurant with alfresco seating; serves Turk's Head beer on tap. $$

Caicos Cafe
A blend of Caribbean and Italian gourmet cuisine with alfresco dining. $$$

RENEE MCMAHON/ALAMY ©

Da Conch Shack (p626)

Plaza explodes into a mini cultural festival. It's a one-stop shop for native food from small local producers across the island, plus art, craft and souvenirs from local vendors and performances by a mix of local bands.

On Friday nights, all roads lead to **Aziza Restaurant & Lounge** across from the Casablanca Casino. This celebrity hive is recognizable by its bohemian Moroccan architecture and interior design. On Saturdays until 2am, **Shisha Lounge**, another celebrity lair and late-night hookah spot, has its chance to shine; there's often a cover charge to enter. Rounding out the week on Sundays is **Noah's Ark**. Ferries shuttle guests between the canal side of the Blue Haven Marina and the floating bar. Unlike the weekdays and daytime hours, when the atmosphere is chill, the crunk level turns to 100 on Sunday nights.

GETTING AROUND

Taxis are readily available at the airport and major hotels. It's best to secure a phone number so you can adopt the driver for the duration of your stay. If your base is Grace Bay or you plan to spend most days on the beach, you'll only need a taxi for airport transfers and the odd sightseeing excursion. If you're staying in Long Bay, the Bight, Leeward, Chalk Sound or Blue Hills and beyond, it's best to rent a vehicle if you plan to be up and about daily.

Turks & Caicos Islands
Twin Islands

TWIN ISLANDS

The sparsely populated Twin Islands of North and Middle Caicos, in the center of the Caicos archipelago, have storied histories featuring indigenous Taínos, British loyalists and enslaved Africans. These are the largest islands in the country and are best explored together given their proximity, shared history, cultural ties and ecology.

The main draw is the tranquility of beach landscapes and the subtle thrill of a banks ecosystem; however, outdoor adventurers can dive into history through the islands' heritage sites. The soil of this tropical wilderness is nourished by the sweat and bones of Africans, once enslaved on an infamous cotton and sisal plantation in North Caicos, and their Taíno predecessors, who largely settled in Middle Caicos.

Before 2007, when a causeway joined the islands, the families inhabiting both had to traverse the shallow channel at low tide by wading across on foot or traveling by boat. It's an easy drive today that has strengthened the community bonds.

TOP TIP

A day trip isn't enough for aquatic adventures to cram in kayaking the mangroves, bonefishing the flats or snorkeling the offshore dive sites. Many resorts have a three-night minimum, so plan an extended stay for a full eco-travel experience, and a day trip for an unhurried, rustic adventure.

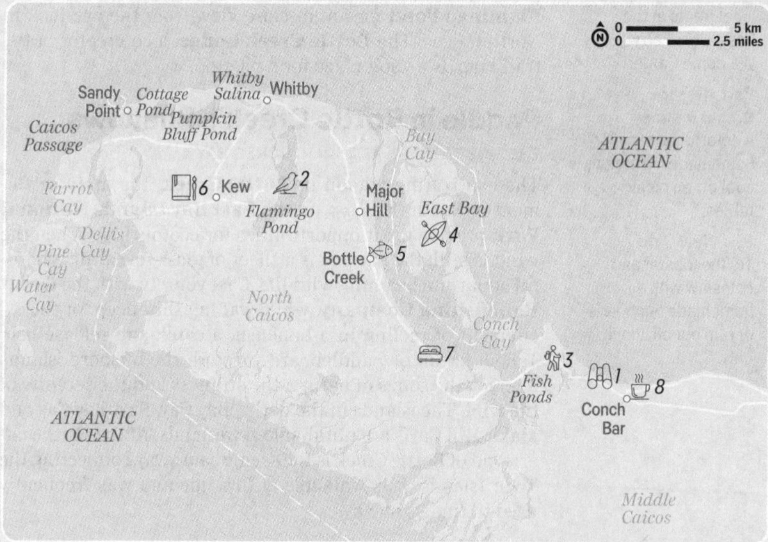

SIGHTS
1 Dragon Cay Overlook
2 Flamingo Pond
(see 1) Mudjin Harbor

ACTIVITIES & TOURS
3 Crossing Place Trail
4 East Bay Islands National Park
5 Great Bonefishing Company
6 Wade's Green Plantation

SLEEPING
7 Bottle Creek Lodge

DRINKING & NIGHTLIFE
8 Sea View Cafe

The Twin Islands' Great Outdoors

SCENIC BEACHES, BLUFF WALKS AND CYCLING TRAILS

Hike a portion of the historic **Crossing Place Trail** that once traversed settlements and plantations from Middle to North Caicos. Now, largely overgrown, sections of the coastal walk are still intact. Note that the surface is uneven and markers are poorly maintained – do not wear flip-flops. Hike between the trailheads at **Sea View Cafe** in Conch Bar settlement and **Dragon Cay Overlook** in Mudjin Harbor. Some of the best beaches and the most spectacular views of the Twin Islands are along the trail, especially at the most iconic site, **Mudjin Harbor**. Two sun-toasted beach coves collide to form a sandbar; at their meeting point is **Dragon Cay**, a cluster of nearshore barrier rocks washed by breaking waves loosely resembling a sleeping dragon. A naturally formed swimming pool, cradled between the beach and the rocks, beckons travelers to take a dip. In both directions along the coast are sandy ridges and rolling hills that encase many hidden beach coves.

Road bikes, cruisers and mountain bikes are also a great way to explore (don't forget to ride on the left). Rent a bike from **Caicos Cyclery** in Providenciales to carry on the ferry over for a self-guided tour along the **Caicos Cycle Trail** from Sandy Point to Lorimers Landing. While there are off-roads, the main 107km-long trail runs entirely along the paved public road. Bring binoculars or a zoom lens for the stop at the **Flamingo Pond** for an up-close view from the overlook in North Caicos. The **Bottle Creek Lodge**, a co-creator of the trail map, is a good place for a pit stop.

TWIN ISLANDS CASUAL DINING

Mudjin Bar & Grill
Known for its famous Jerk Burger, spicy fries, fresh seafood and specialty cocktails. $

Ms B's Restaurant
Casual North Caicos restaurant with tasty local breakfast, lunch and dinner. $

Hog Road Restaurant & Bar
Rest stop serving local treats at the Passenger Ferry Welcome Center. $

Parrotice Ice Cream & Snow
A colorful pit stop for homemade ice cream; cool off on picnic tables. $

Sea View Cafe
Try the lobster and coleslaw with a homemade lemonade or rum punch; lunch only. $

Paddle in Bottle Creek's Shallows

THE MOST SERENE AND UNTOUCHED BAY

The captivating lagoon in **Bottle Creek**, the main settlement in North Caicos, a nd the **East Bay Islands National Park** provide great opportunities for ecotourism. When the wind is still, the surface is a sheet of glass revealing a natural aquarium beaming with life. Cast your fly with the **Great Bonefishing Company**, while wading shin-deep for the excitement of reeling in a bonefish, a catch-and-release fish. Take a kayak or paddleboard through the offshore islands to enjoy the songs of nature, the stillness and the serenity of the wild. The islands in the park – Bay Cay, East Bay Cay and Major Hill Cay – are uninhabited wetlands. At the southeastern end of Bottle Creek is the scenic causeway connecting the Twin Islands; it is walkable at low tide and was frequently used in times gone by.

WHERE TO STAY ON TWIN ISLANDS

Bottle Creek Lodge
Rustic hillside ecotourism retreat on Bottle Creek Lagoon with tuckaway cabanas and concierge service. **$**

Dragon Cay Resort
A secluded property with spacious cottages and villas in Mudjin Harbor. Walking trails and easy beach access. **$**

Pelican Beach Hotel
Laid-back beachfront hotel in North Caicos with modest accommodations and an onsite bar and restaurant. **$**

ROAD TRIP

Island-Hopping from North to Middle Caicos

Although worthy of an extended stay, a driving tour of the Twin Islands will uncover an endearing tropical wilderness: swaths of undeveloped land, secluded beaches and undulating ocean cliffs. Tiny residential communities survive off subsistence farming, public service and tourism. The aging populations are monuments of cultural heritage. The extensive wetland and aquatic ecosystems nurse indigenous wildlife including flamingos and turtles, some in offshore enclaves accessible only by paddle craft.

Bambarra Beach (p633)

1 Wade's Green Plantation

Lizards and birds are the primary residents at Wade's Green Plantation (p630) in North Caicos today. They make themselves known on the long walkway from the parking lot to the start of the tour. A visit here is necessary to understand the island's sobering history. Book a guide and allow your imagination to step into the shoes of the plantation's inhabitants as you wind through the small portion of the property where buildings stand in ruin.

The Drive: Back at the main road, take the Kew Settlement bypass on the left. Turn at the next left towards Whitby. Continue until the next T-junction and turn right. Drive for 12km.

2 Bottle Creek Settlement

Enjoy dessert for breakfast with a first stop at Parrotice Ice Cream & Snow. Then, detour from the main road to the Bottle Creek promenade road for a perfect panoramic view of Bottle Creek Lagoon. The shallow lagoon glistens for miles into the blue horizon until it seamlessly kisses the sky.

The Drive: The Bottle Creek Main Rd leads to the North and Middle Caicos Causeway, along the most scenic part of the drive, and into Mudjin Harbor, 17km away.

3 Mudjin Harbor

Head straight for the secret beach. The concealed cove has strikingly beautiful 360-degree vistas at sea level and from high, including views of the entire Mudjin Harbor. Find the trail under the balcony of the Mudjin Bar & Grill. Pass the bronze cast sculpture of praying hands at the Circle of Hope lookout point, and hike until the walkway hollows into a narrow, hidden stairwell. It winds down into an open-faced beach cave, revealing the secret beach.

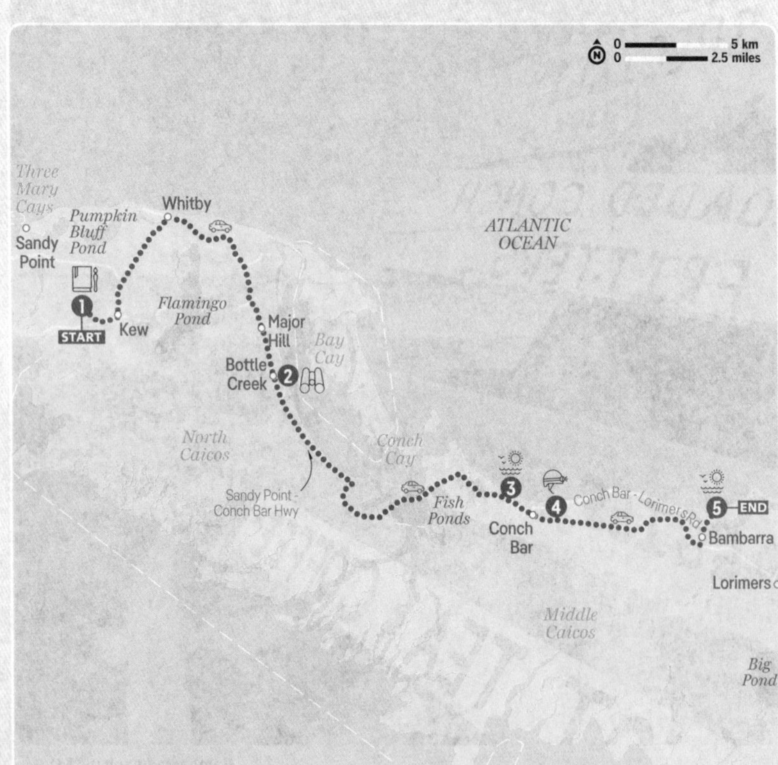

ROBERT A. METCALFE/SHUTTERSTOCK ©

Mudjin Harbor

The Drive: Once you pass the derelict Middle Caicos Airport, the paved road ends. Continue for 1.2km and turn left on the unnamed road marked with a sign for the caves.

4 Conch Bar Caves

Turn off your flashlight, and no amount of dark adaptation will help your eyes see figures in the Christmas Tree room of Conch Bar Caves. It's pitch black in every direction, except on rare occasions when a sliver of blue light bounces off stalactites to squeeze its way into this section of the live cave system. Wear sneakers for a guided tour of this chambered cave that was once mined for guano and used as shelter from hurricanes by the Taínos.

The Drive: Drive through Conch Bar community, past the Sea View Cafe turnoff. For 9km you'll pass wild greenery. The Bambarra Beach off-road is on the left and easy to miss.

5 Bambarra Beach

You could spend hours on Bambarra Beach, a tranquil bay with warm shallow waters that glow turquoise. Casuarina trees create a shaded borderline along the beach entrance. Fishing boats anchor offshore to the east. Pelican Cay, an uninhabited rock just off the beach, is reachable at low tide in waist-deep water. Dine on picnic tables and order fresh seafood and coconut water from the food shacks catering to beachgoers. Windsor Creek Cafe & Bar and the Official Bambarra Beach Bar serve local beer and rum punch.

Conch Bar Caves

KAREN WUNDERMAN/SHUTTERSTOCK ©

RESOURCES FOR NAVIGATING THE ISLANDS

Turks & Caicos National Trust
The National Trust operates three heritage sights on the Twin Islands with a mandate for natural, historical and cultural preservation.

Caribbean Cruisin
Comfortable passenger ferry to North and Middle Caicos and South Caicos, with convenient online booking.

Al's Rent-A-Car
Book in advance for the best vehicle selection. Look for the banner at the ferry landing; they operate from the back of a car.

MICHAEL DEFREITAS CARIBBEAN/ALAMY ©

Wade's Green Plantation

Unearthing a Plantation's Past

A HISTORIC WALKING TOUR

On North Caicos, the past is marked by the remains of a sprawling 400-hectare cotton and sisal plantation that enslaved 384 Africans at its peak in the 1700s. 'I still feel a connection to the ancestors who worked on that plantation,' said Vernia Duncombe, an elderly craftswoman, describing the land and history of **Wade's Green Plantation**. The ruins are notably preserved by the Turks and Caicos National Trust and warrant paying US$15 for the 30-minute guided tour of remembrance. The tranquil ruins of hand-cut limestone buildings – the main house, a chapel, an overseer's house and others – mask the atrocities of the times. Although not required, it's best to make a reservation.

GETTING AROUND

Ferry service to North Caicos runs multiple times daily from the Heaving Down Rock Marina on Providenciales. The 30-minute crossing stops at Bellefield Landing. It's best to rent a car to access all the attractions; book in advance to secure an all-terrain vehicle. Don't rely on taxi service, and don't expect built-in Bluetooth. Navigating the public paved roads is easy, as most sites are marked on Google Maps and useful tourist maps are readily available. Cycling is an option if you bring a bike or reserve one through a hotel or tour company; it doesn't require off-roading.

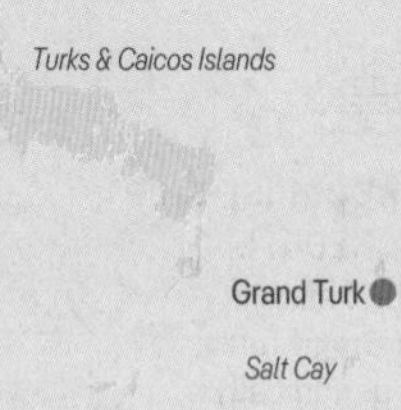

GRAND TURK

At sunrise, boats emerge along the northern coastline of Grand Turk to load passengers set for their morning dives, just as early risers step onto their balconies for coffee at dawn. At night, Front St becomes the beachfront viewing gallery for the sunset, with people meandering about the guesthouses and restaurants along the quiet main street. These rhythmic cycles are unfussy and easygoing, just like the communities on Grand Turk and its sister island Salt Cay. Both islands make up the grouping known as the Turks Islands.

The tranquility of Grand Turk, home to the capital city of Cockburn Town, is disrupted periodically by the frenetic energy of cruise-ship passengers that arrive in droves and take over parts of the island. Thankfully, these floating vacationers descend at set times, leave on a schedule and stay close to the cruise port on the south end of Grand Turk.

TOP TIP

It's discourteous to pass strangers on the street without greeting them. Visitors are easily recognizable and should feel comfortable engaging residents as though friends of a friend. There is a community spirit that's palpable on the island; it's part of the old family values that run the town.

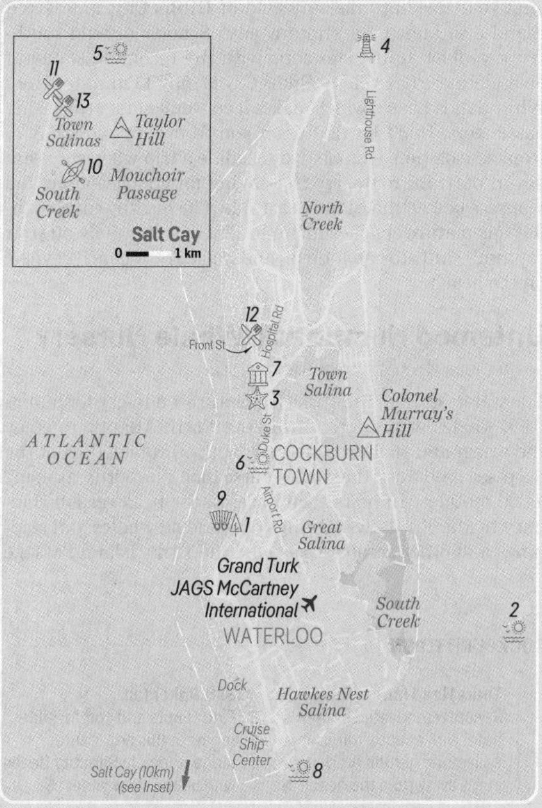

SIGHTS
1 Columbus Landfall National Park
2 Gibbs Cay
3 Government Dock
4 Grand Turk Lighthouse
5 North Bay Beach
6 Sandbar Beach
7 Turks and Caicos National Museum
8 White Sands Beach

ACTIVITIES, COURSES & TOURS
9 Grand Turk Wall
10 South Creek

EATING
11 Coral Reef Bar and Grill
12 Hakuna Matata Restaurant
(see 4) Lazy Donkey Bar
13 Oceanaire Bistro and Bar
(see 6) Secret Garden
(see 6) The Sandbar

SHOPPING
(see 11) Salt Cay Dive Shop

THE CRUISE-SHIP SCHEDULE

The tranquility of Grand Turk is periodically interrupted by the frenzied arrival and departure of cruise-ship passengers that take over **White Sands Beach**, **Governor's Beach** and **Jack's Shack Beach Bar & Grill**.

You can dodge these flurries by avoiding the **Grand Turk Cruise Center**, on the south end of the island. Consult the port schedule on the cruise center website for arrival days and times; it's updated regularly and used by residents. When ships are not in port, the cruise center and its 15 retail and duty-free stores and multiple restaurants are closed and the island finds its equilibrium. The northern end of the island is undisturbed by the port's ebb and flow.

Taste the Island Life

LOCAL FOOD NOT TO MISS

Eat your way across Grand Turk, enjoying classic local fare from diverse restaurants. Delicious cracked conch is served on a gorgeous sunset beach at **The Sandbar**, a popular lunch spot with a covered beach deck. It often hosts live music on Fridays. Jamaican delicacies at **Jucky Jerk Food Truck** include the red-peas soup with pig's tail or chicken; it's open in the late afternoons when many others are closed. Eat fried fish, meet locals and knock dominoes at the **Fisherman's Paradise Fish Fry** on Thursdays in the residential community Over Back. Sample traditional peas and grits with steamed conch or fish on weekends at **Secret Garden Restaurant & Bar**. **Poop Deck** is a local chicken shack known for its pork and chicken souse every Saturday morning. At **Hakuna Matata Restaurant**, feast on grilled lobster prepared by a trained gourmet chef; a saxophonist plays on some Friday nights.

Gibbs Cay Deserted Island Getaway

SANDY TOES AND STINGRAYS

Sink your toes into the soft sand of **Gibbs Cay**, a deserted island also known as 'stingray city'. Schools of wild southern rays flock to the shoreline with the incoming sound of boat engines. The ride to Gibbs Cay is only 15 minutes from White Sands Beach, which makes it convenient for cruise-ship passengers. Don't let that deter you from a relaxing day of tropical isolation – it's easy to schedule a trip when ships are not in port. En route, try free-diving for conches along the seagrass bed on the island's east side. The healthy conch habitat has mature conches in 4m to 12m of water. Rely on your captain's skills to catch them, and make fresh conch ceviche on the beach.

Untamed Humpback-Whale Nursery

INCREDIBLE WHALE SIGHTINGS AND SONGS

The waters around the Turks Islands are a nursery for humpback whales who migrate from the North Atlantic to enjoy the warm and sheltered shallow banks. Protected from the deep-sea predators, the whales nurse their newborns, as many as 20 mother-calf pairs each cycle. In the peak season (January to March), daily sightings of whale blowholes, tail slappings and other acrobatics around the Turks Island Passage

WHERE TO STAY IN COCKBURN TOWN

Osprey
Fall asleep to the lull of waves at this small, full-service beachfront hotel. Dine poolside with a beach view. $

Turks Head Inn
Recently renovated boutique hotel with antique furnishings on historic garden property steps away from the beach. $

Salt Raker Inn
Find simple and comfortable rooms at this 19th-century lodge opposite Sandbar Beach with ocean-view suites. $

MAURICIO HANDLER/GETTY IMAGES ©

Stingray, Gibbs Cay

are common. The fast-moving whales sometimes stop right by the boats. Tours leave from multiple locations, including the **Government Dock**, **Sandbar Beach** and **White Sands Beach**. Residents have grown accustomed to the presence of these gentle giants, even though they're a major attraction drawing visitors to the island.

Barrier Reef & Wall Dives

HANDPICK FROM 40 DIVE SITES

Cherry-pick from 40 named dive sites along the **Grand Turk Wall**, a dramatic drop-off with lush coral gardens and abundant marine life. An equally impressive barrier reef defines the borderline between the ledge and the 2000m abyss. This protected area in the **Columbus Landfall National Park** spans the entire west coast of Grand Turk, with novice and experienced sites including the Amphitheater, Aquarium and the Tunnels. No dive is more than 15 minutes from the beach before you descend into an aquarium where dolphins play, humpback whales sometimes sing, and on special occasions, manta rays and whale sharks visit. Dive sites are so close to

DIVE SITES ON THE WALL

Algrove 'Smitty' Smith, owner of Grand Turk Diving Company *(@grandturkdivingco)*, a dive master and local legend known as 'the real merman'.

The Pits, near Government Dock, is a typical safety stop. A creature hunt will reveal obscure fish, including frogfish, scorpion fish and batfish. **The Library** is great for night diving to see parrotfish sleeping in their lair, or crabs, eels and other nocturnals waking up to feed. Night dives three days after a full moon are alight with bioluminescence, creating a starry galaxy underwater.

At **McDonald's Reef**, swim through an impressive living coral arch. The black coral at **Black Forest** resembles branches of a cedar tree billowing in the underwater currents.

GRAND TURK BOATING EXCURSIONS

Emerald Escapes
Dive master, historian and Salt Cay native Captain Tim leads whale-watching tours, island getaways and private charters.

Screaming Reels Fishing Charters & Guesthouse
Multi-line trolling offshore. Catch different giant pelagic fish depending on the time of year.

Grand Turk Diving Company
Guided tours of the Grand Turk Wall and reefs around Salt Cay for novice and experienced divers, plus other cruises and excursions.

RETIRED DONKEYS REIGN FREE IN PARADISE

Wild donkeys roam freely throughout Grand Turk, having retired from their former duties as essential workers in the island's salterns dating back to the 1600s.

Their job in the now-defunct industry was to pull fully loaded salt carts from the commercial salt pans. Today, they simply take up space: an oddity of the island.

Though they can be a nuisance to some residents, they mostly mind their own business, lounging about unconfined in parking lots, by the roadside and along the beach. Their unbothered and sluggish nature is well suited to Grand Turk, where economic growth is desired but the island's rustic small-town charm and historical ruins are proudly maintained.

shore, you can easily hop on and off dry land between dives without the need for lengthy boat rides. Tours leave from Cockburn Town.

An Imagination Tour Fueled by History

MAKING THE INTANGIBLE PAST REAL

The construction of the **Grand Turk Lighthouse** in 1894 ended a boycott by ships which refused to collect salt in Grand Turk because of the frequent shipwrecks along the north-shore barrier reef. The government acquiesced to the demand to build the lighthouse that stands today; visit this historic sight to learn more on a guided or self-guided tour. Eat conch fritters at the **Lazy Donkey Bar** and take photos from the elevated North Point, where whales blend seamlessly into the horizon. The **Turks and Caicos National Museum** is located steps from the beach in Cockburn Town. Its collection of historic artifacts includes those from the islands' original inhabitants, Taínos, that bring history to life.

360 Degrees of Salt Cay

THE OLDEST HARBOR IN TCI

Explore the unpaved trails of Salt Cay along the island's sand dunes with a rented golf cart from the **Salt Cay Dive Shop** at Deane's Dock. Salt Cay was the first in TCI to enter the commercial salt industry dating back to the 1600s; the roads still run around the old salinas. Rent kayaks or paddleboards to venture into the shallow mangrove channels of **South Creek**, a natural bird sanctuary that conceals an underwater cave system. Visit the pristine **North Bay Beach**, a secluded swimming beach sheltered from the east trade winds.

You'll surely meet some of the island's 100 residents at one of the three restaurants: try home-style cooked meals at **Pat's Restaurant**, grilled seafood at **Coral Reef Bar and Grill**, or seasonal dishes at **Oceanaire Bistro and Bar** (book ahead for dinner). For overnighting, there are a few guesthouses on the island.

GETTING AROUND

Domestic flights to Grand Turk on Caicos Express Airways and InterCaribbean leave multiple times daily from the Providenciales International Airport. The former has a reputation for being the more prompt local airline. The 30-minute flight is convenient for day trips. There's also a tiny airport on Salt Cay with domestic flights from Grand Turk, Provo and South Caicos, and a passenger ferry service between Grand Turk and Salt Cay.

Most visitors arrive by cruise ship; they largely confine themselves to the Grand Turk Cruise Center, although you'll see caravans of ATVs and 4WD carts touring the island. These are available to rent along with cars, golf carts and bicycles. There's no bus service or public transport in Grand Turk. It's best to secure a taxi at the airport or the Cruise Center; save your driver's number.

NAN728/SHUTTERSTOCK ©

Arriving

Regional flights to the Turks and Caicos Islands (TCI) are available from The Bahamas, Jamaica, Haiti, Dominican Republic, Cuba and Antigua. There are also direct flights from major cities in the United States and Canada. From elsewhere in the world, you can connect through one of these cities or countries and get to TCI with one or two stops.

By Air

TCI's two international airports are Providenciales International Airport and Grand Turk JAGS McCartney International Airport. The South Caicos Airport is awaiting a planned upgrade as an international hub. Domestic flights operate regularly between the main hub in Provo, Grand Turk, Salt Cay and South Caicos.

By Boat

Yachts and sailboats have many marinas, ports and deep-water moorings to choose from on all of the islands when entering TCI and stopping over. However, not all of these ports of entry have permanently stationed customs officials. Grand Turk has the nation's only cruise port.

Money

Currency: US dollar (US$)

CASH

The further you move from Providenciales, the more you'll need to carry cash. When using ferry services, in particular, many captains expect cash payments. Despite the nation's status as a British Overseas Territory, the British pound is not exchanged – the US dollar is the only official currency. Head to a local bank for foreign exchange services.

CREDIT CARDS

Credit cards are widely accepted across TCI, mostly reliably in Provo. However, the type and size of a business can determine if it typically accepts credit cards. Small local food joints outside Grace Bay are less likely to take credit cards, for example.

TAXES & TIPPING

Tourism-related businesses charge a 12% hotel and tourism tax that's collected by the government. This is sometimes labeled as a sales tax in a company's system – however, there's no sales tax in TCI. The standard tip for service workers is 15%. Some businesses add this automatically to your bill.

Above: Cinnamon Bay (p652); Right: St Croix (p646)

US VIRGIN ISLANDS

A WORLD AWAY FROM THE MAINLAND

A far-flung national park, bountiful coral reefs and captivating cities welcome travelers to the US Virgin Islands.

Thriving, green jungles cover St Croix, St Thomas and St John. In the US Virgin Islands (USVI), visitors can hike beneath palm, sea-grape and fiddlewood trees on slithering trails that lead past 16th-century Danish ruins to secluded beaches and lagoons teeming with sea turtles, angel fish and barracudas. And though hurricanes Irma and Maria pummeled the chain in the recent past, leaving them stripped of vegetation and isolated from the world, the islands are methodically returning to their pre-storm form.

The snorkeling here is among the best in the world, and often just steps away from the beach bars and cafes that dot roadside stretches of these islands.

In towns like Charlotte Amalie, Cruz Bay, Frederiksted and Christiansted, kitchens waft with aromas from Africa, Europe, Latin America and the US mainland. Meanwhile, the sounds of music ranging from drum machines to saxophones and steel drums can be heard as faint echoes while wandering through the city streets at night, blending with the omnipresent rooster crows.

With three distinct main islands and another 50 small islands and cays to investigate, travelers should be prepared to spend several weeks in the Virgin Islands. They are living proof that Americans don't always need a passport to see another side of the world. And the combination of charisma and culture prove that these islands are worthy of more time than a cruise stop.

THE MAIN AREAS

ST CROIX
The USVI's most populous island.
p646

ST JOHN
Beaches, camping and hiking, National Park.
p651

ST THOMAS
Houses 17th-century trading port Charlotte Amalie.
p655

Find Your Way

Vibrant St Thomas, relaxed St John and spacious St Croix, each island carries its own vibe worthy of experience. Here's how to get around.

ATLANTIC OCEAN

BRITISH VIRGIN ISLANDS (UK)

Little Hans-Lollik Island

Hans-Lollik Island

Outer Brass Island

Inner Brass Island

Hull Bay

Magens Bay

Thatch Cay

Mingo Cay

St Thomas

Brewers Bay

Cyril E King

CHARLOTTE AMALIE

Red Hook

St Thomas Carnival

Saba Island

Bolongo Bay

Great St James Island

Capella Islands

Coral Bay

St John

Saltpond Bay

0 10 km

0 5 miles

St Thomas, p655
The most-visited USVI also feels the most urban. The island revolves around Charlotte Amalie's kaleidoscope of communities, cafes, shops and government buildings.

St John, p651
Roughly 60 percent of St John is encompassed by Virgin Islands National Park. This rugged, jungle paradise is most easily accessed by ferries from St Thomas.

VIRGIN ISLANDS NATIONAL PARK

Caribbean Sea

St Croix, p646

With two cities to explore alongside mountains, reefs and agricultural areas, the largest of the USVI is well worth the 40-mile crossing from its neighbors.

Buck Island

Christiansted

St Croix

Point Udall

Frederiksted

Henry E Rohlsen

Sandy Point

SAFARI BUS

Modified pickup trucks with bench seating stand in as public transportation in the USVI. While rides can be found for US$5, many 'safari' buses carry boatloads of cruise passengers and charge a premium of US$20 or more to hop onboard.

CAR

Rental cars are the most efficient way to get around each island. Jeep and Bronco rentals are the most popular, due to generally rough road conditions. Expect to pay between US$90–130 per day for the convenience.

TAXIS

Taxis are available in the USVI and can certainly get travelers out of a pinch. Expect to pay for the privilege, though, as rates are charged per passenger and can range from US$15–30 per person.

Plan Your Time

Captivating cultural history and an abundance of outdoor activities speed up famously laissez-faire days in the USVI. Blend the best of both worlds like this.

CHRIS ALLAN/SHUTTERSTOCK ©

Buck Island Reef National Monument (p649)

If You Only Do One Thing

- Base yourself in Christiansted and focus on **St Croix** (p646). Convenient access to Henry E Rohlsen Airport means you save time otherwise spent on interisland ferries.

- From Christiansted, you'll have access to snorkel tours full of marine life at **Buck Island Reef National Monument** (p649), dazzling pelagic dive sites like **Cane Bay Wall** (p647) and a topside world of mountains to hike, restaurants to savor and rainforest trails to ride.

- The largest of the USVI feels like a healthy blend of both St John and St Thomas, though Crucian culture is completely distinct from the nearby islands you will miss.

Seasonal Highlights

Each season brings its own unique twist to the USVI. While temperatures are almost always comfortably warm, shifting seas and weather patterns dictate harvests, local festivals and outdoor adventure opportunities.

JANUARY

Carnival, which kicked off in mid-December, comes to a conclusion with the **Three Kings Day Parade** on St Croix.

FEBRUARY

Toast-to-the-Captain brings an 8.4-mile road running race to St Croix, and Cane Bay gears up for **Mardi Croix**.

MARCH

St Thomas hosts the **Rolex Cup Regatta** for yacht-racing enthusiasts, while St Croix celebrates **Mardi Croix**.

EA GIVEN/SHUTTERSTOCK ©, SORAPOP UDOMSRI/SHUTTERSTOCK ©, LEIGHTONOC/SHUTTERSTOCK ©

Five Days to Explore

- Settle in at **Charlotte Amalie** (p657) and make the most of **St Thomas** (p655) and **St John** (p651). Ferries carrying both vehicles and people make the 45-minute run between islands, making it possible to get a sense of place for these two dynamic islands in one trip. Cyril E King Airport puts travelers just minutes from downtown Charlotte Amalie, where a hive of modern storefronts meld with 17th-century architecture and a global gallery of flavors.

- A day trip to St John opens the doors to the jungle canopies, mystifying ruins and spectacular reefs of **Virgin Islands National Park** (p652).

Two Weeks to Travel Around

- Two weeks in the USVI gives travelers enough time to adequately absorb all three major islands.

- Start on **St Croix** (p646), where wide open spaces and leisurely city centers make the introduction to island life a breeze.

- After a crash course in Crucian customs (and a probable tour of the Cruzan Rum Distillery), hop a seaplane or ferry to **St Thomas** (p655) and indulge in the comparatively frantic scene of downtown **Charlotte Amalie** (p657) before venturing over to outdoor-centric **St John** (p651) for a few well-earned, lazy nights lying under the stars at **Cinnamon Bay Campground** (p652).

APRIL
Stilt walkers and street bands are in full force, as the islands celebrate **Virgin Islands Carnival.**

JULY
St Croix celebrates its **Mango Melee** and **Tropical Fruit Festival**, while St John cranks up its own version of **Carnival**.

AUGUST
Emancipation celebrations are held throughout the Virgin Islands, with reggae and fungi bands along with parades.

OCTOBER
Virgin Islands Fashion Weeks brings mainland, Caribbean and West African fashions and designers to St Thomas.

ST CROIX

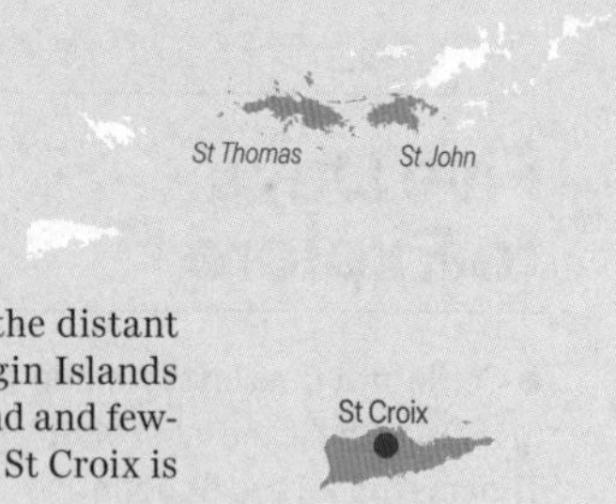

Located 40 miles south of Charlotte Amalie and the distant din of St Thomas, the largest island in the US Virgin Islands can feel positively quiet in contrast. With more land and fewer floating villages of tourists transiting through, St Croix is an island to slow down and savor.

Its two major population centers – Christiansted and Frederiksted – each hide a rich history of colonization, turmoil and liberation that is best absorbed in poignant sips. Ample harbor walks and cozy downtown streets make waltzing through the historic archways and ramparts of these cities an eye-opening, educational experience. Meanwhile, St Croix's outdoor attractions bristle with opportunities for hikers, divers and beachgoers to experience secluded spaces that highlight the ecological abundance of the Caribbean.

Cruzans rightfully take pride in the thriving culture of their island, which offers some of the most captivating stories as well as the clearest seas in the Caribbean.

TOP TIP

There are two primary ways to reach St Croix from St Thomas: a seaplane or a ferry. Short seaplane flights are preferable, owing to the often rocky conditions on the ocean crossing. Check out Seaborne Airlines and the QEIV ferry to choose your own in-transit adventure.

SUSAN M JACKSON/SHUTTERSTOCK ©

Christiansted Harbor

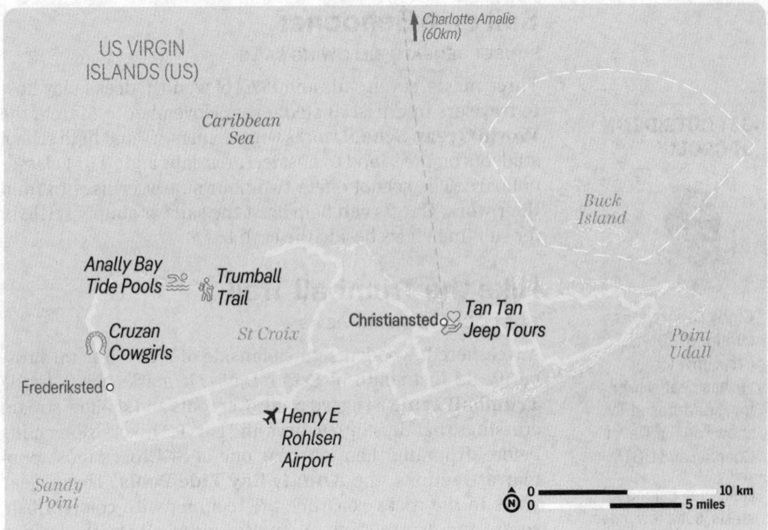

Saddle Up with the Cruzan Cowgirls

RIDING FOR A CAUSE

The **Cruzan Cowgirls** rehabilitate malnourished and abused horses across St Croix. A guided trail ride through the rainforest and along the coast at – where else – Cowboy Beach—helps fund that work. Horse hooves clip-clop along dirt paths while birds chirp and insects buzz as the natural sounds of St Croix come to life. Riders can feel the salty breeze blowing in across the Caribbean and inhale the scent as it mixes with the sweet fragrance of tropical flowers from wild ginger and flamboyant trees.

Ride the Path Less Traveled

RUTTED ROADS AND ROCKY BEACHES

Tan Tan Jeep Tours runs tours to places like the **Anally Bay Tide Pools** and **Anally Sugar Mill Ruins**. These are especially powerful experiences, as owner Wave Phillips and many of the team at Tan Tan are descendants of people brought to the islands by the transatlantic slave trade, whose voices are not always heard by tourists. Tan Tan's 4WD expeditions traverse lush rainforests, seaside hideaways and former plantations, often ascending to lofty peaks far above the coastline. The team's local insight into the area makes this trip a perfect introduction to St Croix and is an ideal way to start your trip.

THE STORY OF THE FIREBURN

The figures are intriguing, impossible to ignore. Across the USVI, depictions of three women bearing a torch, a lantern and a sugarcane knife can be seen. These are Mary Thomas, 'Agnes' Salomon and Mathilda McBean. They are known as the Queens of the Fireburn.

Together, the three women are credited with starting a 1878 labor revolt that saw the burning of homes, mills and plantations across St Croix in response to low wages and harsh living conditions.

WHERE TO DIVE ON ST CROIX

Cane Bay Wall
A legendary wall with frequent visitors.

Butler Bay
Deep and shallow wrecks like freighters and barges.

Frederiksted Pier
Arrow crabs, brittle stars and fireworms.

Sail on a Schooner

SUNSET BENEATH BILLOWING SAILS

Three masts, seven sails and 137ft of wooden decks play host to travelers in Christiansted. From November to March, the **World Ocean School** works with elementary and high school students on the island to host lectures, labs and STEM classes onboard. The school offers two-hour sunset cruises to fund their work. Guests can help hoist the sails or simply settle in for sublime views beside the cash bar.

GET OUTSIDE ON ST CROIX

Cindy Clearwater, curator of *My St Croix* (mystcroix.vi), has been a fixer for island-based TV shows on the Travel Channel and HGTV.

Deep-sea fishing starts just a few miles offshore. Captain Ryan at **Lioness Sportfishing** was born on St Croix and honed his skills as a fisher in Alaska, à la *Deadliest Catch* (US reality TV series).

Caribbean Sea Adventures gives visitors a chance to float above the sea while paired together on a tandem parasail. The sail flies from their luxury boat, *Smooth Recovery*, which can also be chartered for a private trip to Buck Island.

Hike the Trumball Trail

TIDE POOLS AND EPIC VIEWS

A weathered, wooden sign sits inside of a tree line on Prosperity Rd just south of Estate Davis. It marks the 2.3-mile **Trumball Trail**, a rugged route over roots and shallow stream crossings that dips into valleys and carries hikers along cliffs before dropping them off near one of St Croix's most popular attractions, the **Annaly Bay Tide Pools**. These clear pools in the rocky coastline are teeming with colorful fish, corals and crustaceans. A smattering of 4WD vehicles can be found parked along the shell-strewn beach leading to the pools; however, hiking in gives travelers the opportunity to immerse themselves in the rainforest and investigate its smaller creatures – such as reptiles, insects and birds. Newcomers should take a guide, as rough seas can create dangerous conditions on the rocks.

Sample Original Crucian Flavors

DELVE BEYOND THE BOARDWALK

Locally owned restaurants, specialty food shops and St Croix's signature rum take center stage with chef and self-described foodie Anquanette Gaspard's **Taste of the Twin City Food Tour** (VIFoodTours.com). These two- to three-hour tours bring visitors to six savory locations in downtown Christiansted. Dip into fascinating history and little-known facts about St Croix, as Antoinette guides you through plates of traditional fare, such as jerk chicken and callaloo, as well as the avant-garde flavors of Caribbean fusion that incorporate Latin and Trinidadian dishes. The entire tour takes place along the infinitely walkable streets and alleyways of Christiansted. This walking tour is one of the best ways to introduce yourself to the city while exploring areas and flavors often overlooked by other travelers.

GETTING AROUND

Unless you plan to spend all of your time in Christiansted, do yourself a favor and grab a rental car on St Croix. The highways here are the best in the USVI – you can even speed up to an astonishing 55mph on some stretches of the island. Doing so opens up a world of far-flung beaches, snorkel spots and vistas, so it's worth having time and freedom to appreciate them.

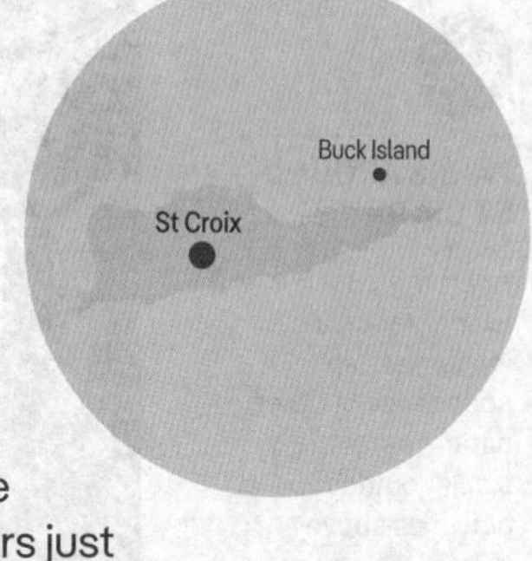

Beyond St Croix

One of the world's most marvelous marine ecosystems beckons adventurous travelers just off the coast from St Croix.

Buck Island Reef National Monument is one of just two submerged national monuments in the US, the other being the USS Arizona Memorial in Hawaii. Only a mile and a half off the coast of St Croix, the island is home to an underwater snorkel trail tracing its way between a staggering reef system filled with dolphins, sea turtles and eagle rays. This uninhabited area also serves as a nursery for lemon sharks, a safe haven for sea birds and the home of important biological research on Caribbean ecosystems. Big Beard's Adventure Tours and Caribbean Sea Adventures operate guided tours and sunset cruises to Buck Island from Christiansted.

TOP TIP

Take the short, 45-minute hiking trail across Buck Island to Diedrichs Point and a breezy walk back down West Beach.

Snorkeling, Buck Island Reef (p650)

PARKS AROUND ST CROIX

Apart from Buck Island National Monument, an abundance of other natural parks offer similar outdoor activities above ground, as well as underwater worlds to explore.

Jack & Isaac Bay Preserve
Staghorn coral reefs and turtle-nesting beaches located near Point Udall.

Christiansted National Historic Site
18th-century Danish fort complex with parapets, walls and support buildings.

Salt River Bay National Historical Park & Biological Preserve
Mangrove forests, beaches, estuaries and an indigenous village site.

Sandy Point National Wildlife Refuge
Protected habitat for rare and endangered birds, as well as leatherback sea turtles.

EA GIVEN/SHUTTERSTOCK ©

Tour boats headed for Buck Island

Dive into a Marine-Based National Park

REEF TRAILS, UNDERWATER ADVENTURES

While mooring your own boat is allowed via permit through the National Park Service, the best way for most travelers to access **Buck Island Reef National Monument** is to take a guided tour out of Christiansted. Both half-day and full-day tours are available from numerous outfitters. The journey takes about 40 minutes from Christiansted.

Two thirds of the island is surrounded by an elkhorn coral barrier reef, which means most of the recreational opportunities here are below the water. Swimming, snorkeling and diving are all popular activities, and the **Buck Island Reef Underwater Trail** is the star of the show. The reef's enormous, branching elkhorn form fortress walls that line a lagoon with plaques that depict and describe the marine life encircling snorkelers at every turn. Some 250 species of fish can be found here, including colorful tangs, rays and the occasional reef shark.

All tour operators on Buck Island must be licensed by the National Park Service, and most offer snorkel lessons for those less comfortable in the water. Entry-level divers can take advantage of the reef's pair of shallow 30ft and 40ft dives that are a perfect introduction to diving via a Discover Scuba experience.

Topside, **Turtle Beach** on the island's west end offers expansive views of St Croix along with a powdery, white sand surface that often lands this swatch of remote land on lists of the world's most beautiful beaches. This beach is aptly named, as a quick dip into the aquamarine waters here often yields encounters with green sea turtles grazing on perennial beds of sea grass.

GETTING AROUND

Taking a private boat to Buck Island is possible. Sailors at heart will need an anchoring permit from the National Park Service to moor up, but more advisable is a guided tour from Christiansted. The entire topside of the island is walkable. Marked hiking trails connect West Beach and Diedrichs Point.

ST JOHN

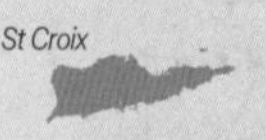

The adventurous little brother of St Thomas and St Croix, St John is a place for hiking boots, beach towels, kayak paddles and snorkeling fins. Roughly 60 percent of St John is covered by Virgin Islands National Park, where white-sand beaches mingle with jungle-encrusted ruins and the tragic past of the sugarcane industry. Though the island is only 19.6 sq miles, St John is packed with outdoor activities for the adventurous at heart. Here, visitors can paddle Caribbean waters to secluded beaches largely inaccessible by automobile; hike to sacred, ancient waterfalls; or explore bountiful coral reefs brimming with colorful marine life.

Cruz Bay, the island's primary hub, is home to a menagerie of restaurants, from casual taco stands to romantic fine-dining and leading-edge fusion kitchens. Remote Coral Bay offers mind-bending mountain vistas alongside the casual, braying interjections of free-roaming donkeys.

TOP TIP

Grab a rental car to gain unfettered access to trailheads, campsites and beaches. Jeeps are by far the most popular way to navigate the windy, often rocky roads of St John.

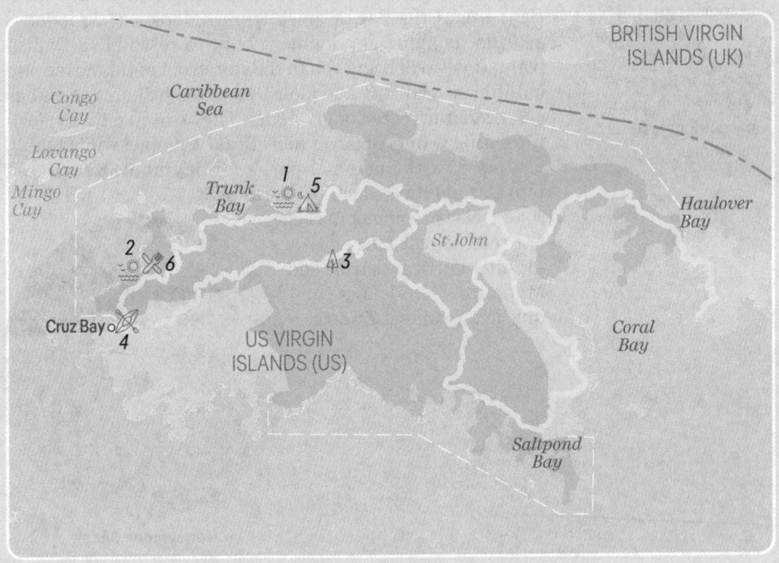

SIGHTS
1 Cinnamon Bay
2 Honeymoon Beach
3 Virgin Islands National Park

ACTIVITIES & TOURS
4 Arawak Expeditions

SLEEPING
5 Cinnamon Bay Campground

EATING
(see 5) Rain Tree Cafe
6 ZoZo's

WHY I LOVE ST JOHN

Joe Sills, writer

Larger parks like Yosemite and Yellowstone may dwarf Virgin Islands National Park in scale, but this pint-sized jungle getaway on St John rivals the best of them. I can't recall any other park in the US that features a combination of prehistoric settlements and European ruins with an endless array of vines, crabs and coral.

Plus, the digs at Cinnamon Bay are versatile enough for any outdoor lover to call home.

Camp at Virgin Islands National Park

STARLIT NIGHTS BY THE BEACH

One thousand years ago, Taíno people established a village beside the sea-grape trees and azure waters at St. John's . Today, you can stroll over sands where archaeologists have unearthed tools Taínos used in their lives, while meandering beside the ruins of a plantation whose tragic history left the graves of enslaved people beneath the waters of the bay.

At **Cinnamon Bay Campground** inside Virgin Islands National Park, flights of butterflies dabble nectar from carambola and breadfruit trees while deer waltz between tents. Aficionados of primitive campsites may find the restaurant running water at Cinnamon Bay luxe; however, there's no disputing the convenience of this campground. Tent rentals are available on-site, and the campground even offers upgrades with actual beds. Campsites come equipped with a grill; however, a food truck and outdoor dining at **Rain Tree Cafe** mean visitors won't have to work hard for a meal. Kayak, SUP and snorkel gear rentals also make enjoying the bay itself a breeze.

Kayak the North Shore

REEFS AND ROCKEFELLER RUINS

Arawak Expeditions offers North Shore kayaking tours right from Cruz Bay. A quick trip to Mongoose Junction – a 1970s shopping development built to resemble a Danish plantation – will bring you to the storefront of this adventure outfitter specializing in paddle tours. North Shore excursions can last either three or six hours. They traverse the typically exciting waters of Sir Francis Drake Channel while taking visitors past the national park's **Honeymoon Beach** and into **Caneel Bay**, where the ruins of St John's most prominent Rockefeller-era retreat rest much as they did after hurricanes Irma and Maria in 2017. Visitors can dine in the ruins at **ZoZo's**.

Honeymoon Beach

THE BEST HIKES ON ST JOHN

Reef Bay Trail
Six miles out-and-back through forest canopies, ancient sites and ruins.

Ram Head Trail
A 0.9-mile beach trek from Salt Pond and up a 200ft hill to cliffside views.

Johnny Horn Trail
This 1.8-mile North Shore trail includes Windy Hill ruins and views of Coral Bay.

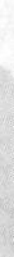

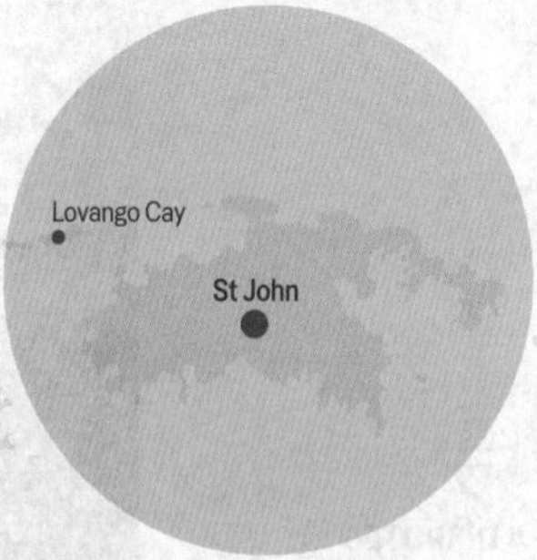

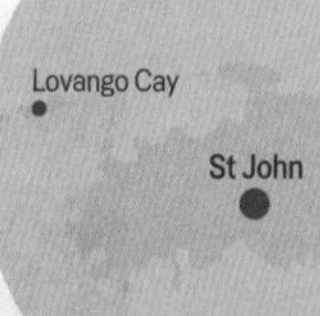

Beyond St John

Home to an eco-lodge and beach club, Lovango Cay opens its doors to day-trippers from St John.

Situated just off the coast of St John, Lovango derives its name from its colorful history as a haven for brothels. As the story goes, sailors leaving the West Indies would make a pit stop on the island for their last 'love and go' before setting off to sea.

Today, most of Lovango Cay is privately owned; however, Lovango Resort + Beach Club welcomes guests who want to experience their own slice of private paradise for a day. Visitors can lounge comfortably by the swells, with food and beverages from the beach club, or choose to hike to the top of the island for views of Tortola and Jost Van Dyke.

TOP TIP

Sublime snorkeling around the docks next to the beach club is one of the best kept secrets on the islands.

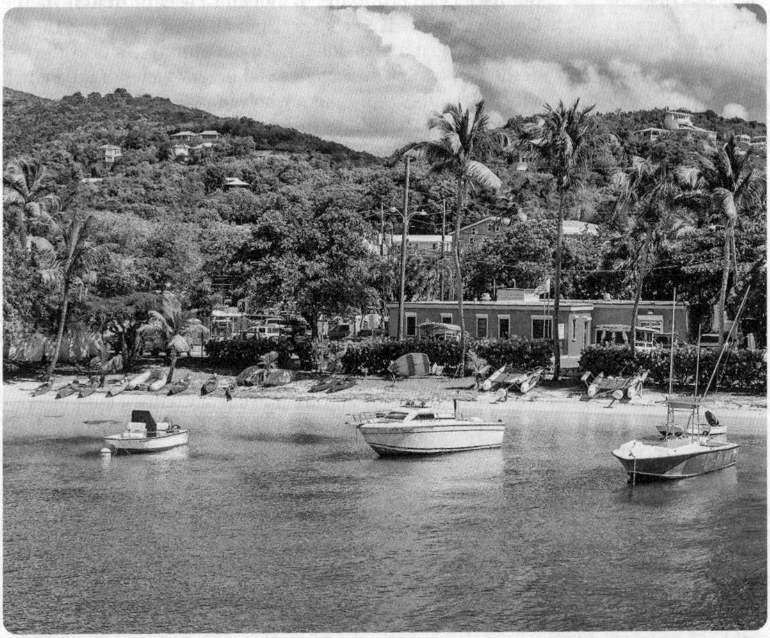

JONATHAN A. MAUER/SHUTTERSTOCK ©

Cruz Bay

A DISPUTED DESIGNATION

Local legends tell of an 18th-century brothel located on the island. Those stories attribute its modern name to pirates, who coined the term 'Love and Go Island'. As always in the Caribbean, pirate tales are to be taken with a grain of salt.

According to the St John Historical Society, the name most likely comes from the title of an African trading post in the Congo. The nearby cays of Congo and Mingo also feature African names, adding credibility to the claim.

PICS721/SHUTTERSTOCK ©

Mingo and Lovango Cays

A Voyage to Lovango Cay

HIKING TINY TRAILS

A 10-minute ferry ride from St John's Cruz Bay, **Lovango Cay** – at just 118 acres – is small even by island standards. The trails here are pint-sized, too, at under a mile each. Hiking from the **Lovango Resort + Beach Club** to the summit via the **BVI Trail** or linking to hidden **Crescent Beach** via the **Congo Cay Trail** takes less than an hour. However, the reward may last a little longer. An old gum tree sits at the top of the BVI trail, where chairs and breezy views of the British Virgin Islands greet hikers who've made their way to to the summit in the burning sun. Surrounded by dense jungle fauna, the **Congo Cay Trail** connects near the base of this tree, offering a cool, tranquil path crisscrossed by soldier crabs and yellow-feathered bananaquits. This trail saunters down to the steel hues of Crescent Beach, where hikers can catch views of crashing waves beneath the cliffs of the resort's tree houses and a view of uninhabited Congo Cay next door. This is an excellent place to investigate conchs and fan corals that have washed ashore on the stones; and during calm seas, it doubles as a fantastic place to go for a swim or snorkel on a seldom accessed reef.

Lovango also serves up an unusual day trip – a landing craft from the beach club's docks back to St John, where visitors can literally step off the boat and onto Honeymoon Beach.

GETTING AROUND

The easiest way to access Lovango Cay is to either take a private boat or use one of the beach resort's ferries from St Thomas or St John. Doing so deposits visitors on the doorstep of Lovango Resort + Beach Club, where the friendly staff is happy to propel you around the island on golf carts, provided you pay the daily club fee.

ST THOMAS

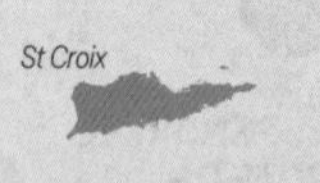

The scintillating aroma of johnnycakes and conch fritters permeates downtown Charlotte Amalie, the hub of St Thomas that brims with stout, 17th-century structures seeming more at home on a movie set than in real life. And yet, they are real. Since the 1600s, this mountainous island has been home to a global network of traders who brought African, Caribbean and European cultures into a melting pot here.

St Thomas is the most-visited Virgin Island for cruise ships, which take advantage of the same protected harbor that brought the Dutch West India Company here centuries ago. And yet, there's a hive of activity to explore here that goes largely untouched by those only able to spend a few hours away from their ships. St Thomas is a culturally rich, vibrant place in the midst of a renaissance fueled by its incredibly talented people – a place ripe for investigation.

TOP TIP

Keep track of cruise traffic. The more ships in port at once, the more difficult it can be to find a safari bus that has not been temporarily commandeered as a tour bus. Instead, consider budgeting for a cab or simply walking between places.

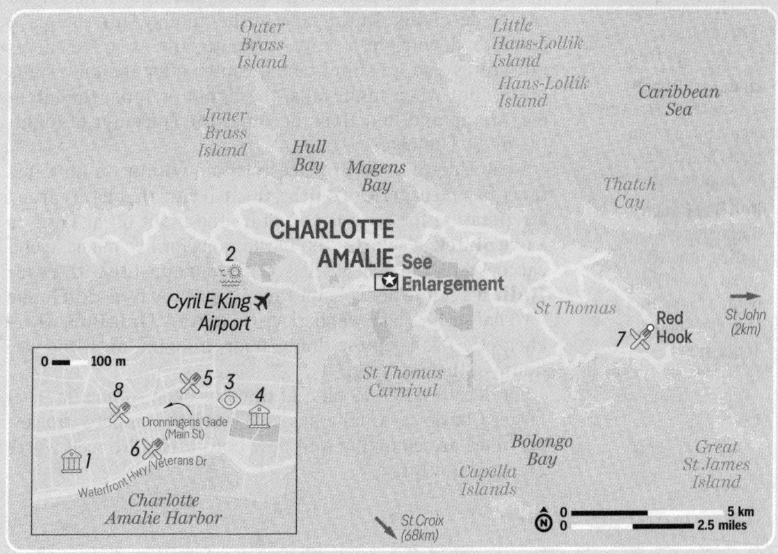

SIGHTS
1 81C
2 Brewers Bay Beach
3 Charlotte Amalie
4 Creative Native

ACTIVITIES, COURSES & TOURS
(see 7) Island Time Pub

EATING
5 My Brothers Workshop Cafe
6 Parley Cafe
7 Pesce Italian
(see 7) Saki House
8 Virgilio's

DRINKING & NIGHTLIFE
(see 7) Duffy's Love Shack

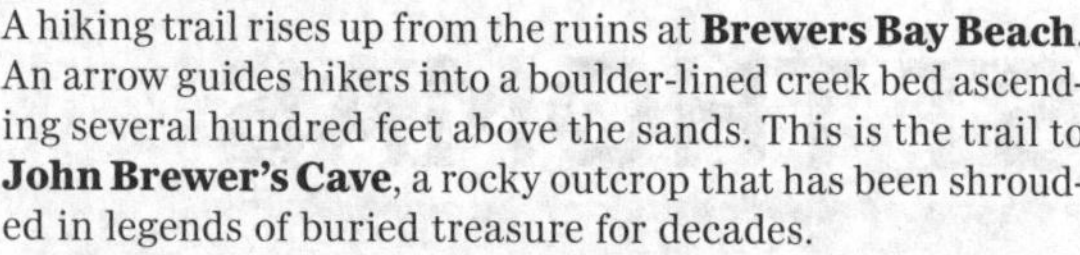

Hike John Brewer's Cave Trail

A LEGENDARY VIEW

A hiking trail rises up from the ruins at **Brewers Bay Beach**. An arrow guides hikers into a boulder-lined creek bed ascending several hundred feet above the sands. This is the trail to **John Brewer's Cave**, a rocky outcrop that has been shrouded in legends of buried treasure for decades.

Today, the trail to John Brewer's Cave is as rugged as it was nearly a century ago, though arrows are now interspersed with graffiti of Nintendo characters also making their way uphill. Hikers here must navigate a rumbling path of smooth boulders, hulking gum trees, bewitching air plants and yellow jacket nests before making a final push to the top aided by ropes. As for the cave itself? It's inaccessible to most.

The trail takes approximately one hour to ascend and slightly less to descend. It's a trek best capped by a golden hour visit to Brewers Bay Beach, where a row of food trucks will be waiting to serve up johnnycakes (corn-flour griddle cakes), conch fritters and cold beer.

BEST SNORKEL SPOTS ON ST THOMAS

Coki Point Beach
Easy access to gear rentals and crystal-clear water with fish, crabs and rays. Also popular with shore divers.

Secret Harbor Beach
Palm trees and hammocks line a beach with a floating raft, seagrass meadows and reefs.

Lindqvist Beach
A protected area with picnic tables, tide pools and reefs off the beaten path.

Hull Bay Beach
Barracuda, sea turtles, lobster and squid, as well as guided tours from Homer's Snorkel Tours.

Dance All Night in Red Hook

CLASSIC CARIBBEAN NIGHTLIFE

By daylight, the dockside bars and restaurants of Red Hook can be deceiving. In the heat of the midday sun, the place can look downright sleepy – a smattering of coffee shops, gift stores and a fishing tackle center offer the only signs of life. But when night falls, the lights turn on, the kitchens fire up and Red Hook becomes the epicenter of nightlife on St Thomas.

A cab ride to Main St places visitors within walking distance of a menagerie of quirky, themed bars that have earned a reputation for good times. Start the night off at **Duffy's Love Shack**, a colorful tiki bar famous for live music, tropical cocktails and upbeat vibes. Curb your appetite with **Pesce Italian's** renowned lobster ravioli or a stop by **Saki House** for Thai sushi. Then, wander over to **Island Time Pub**, where energetic DJs keep the dance floor grooving until the wee hours of the morning.

For decades, Red Hook nightlife has been so popular that larger Charlotte Amalie has struggled to compete. However, times are changing and now both areas are well worth an evening visit.

WHERE TO STAY ON ST THOMAS

Pink Palm Hotel
Edgy, chic boutique hotel in the heart of downtown. **$$**

Villa Santana
Built by an exiled Mexican president and steeped in lore. **$$$**

At Home in the Tropics
Former Danish barracks turned hotel. **$$$**

Charlotte Amalie

Uncover Charlotte Amalie

AN ONGOING RENAISSANCE

It seems out of place, at first. A Sicilian restaurant sits at the foot of a hill, a block from the waterfront in Charlotte Amalie. **Virgilio's** and the linguini here are as at home as the conch or jerk wings down the street. Such is the scene in **Charlotte Amalie**, where generations of cultures have coexisted and clashed to form a diverse community of creatives, cooks and craftspeople. It's the only 'city' on St Thomas and one worth several days of exploration. A burgeoning art community is beginning to supplant the jewelry stores that once dominated downtown. Led by galleries **81C** and the **Creative Native**, a new generation of expression is taking center stage in Charlotte Amalie. Elsewhere, islander-led projects like **My Brothers Workshop Cafe** give visitors a chance to support at-risk youth while sampling rum cake and banana bites, while the baristas at **Parley Cafe** dish out waffles behind 17th-century stonework.

EXPERIENCE ST THOMAS CULTURE

Anna Monica Villa, owner of Touring the Islands, was raised on St Thomas and has been giving walking tours of its storied streets for more than a decade.

E's Garden Teahouse
E's is at the top of my list in the historical district. Owner Judith Watlington Edwin is a treasure and a cultural icon.

Bordeaux Farmers Market
This market blends vegan food with a reggae vibe on the island's west side.

Zora's
Leather sandals and bags made by Miss Zora. St Thomians have been walking in her shoes since 1962.

GETTING AROUND

The best way to get around St Thomas is to either establish a relationship with a taxi driver or rent a vehicle. The roads here are a maze, and local knowledge comes in handy when making your way from Charlotte Amalie to Red Hook or one of the many beaches. Mapping apps are notoriously unreliable here, too. Safari buses will theoretically take you around the island for a few dollars. In practice, though, they are often converted into island tours when cruise ships arrive. This effectively renders the default public transportation on the island out of service until ships depart again.

Beyond St Thomas

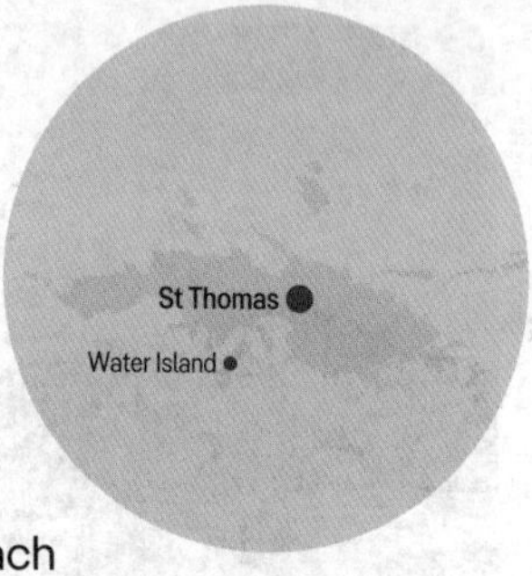

St Thomas
Water Island

Water Island could be your cup of tea if a beach getaway is on the calendar.

Cheekily dubbed the 'fourth' US Virgin Island by some and scoffed at by others, Water Island carries a vibe that feels more Florida panhandle than Caribbean, but it's nonetheless a worthy day trip for visitors in search of a lazy day at the beach. It's also home to a smattering of activities that offer many beachgoers an idyllic view of the Caribbean: white sand beaches and an island where the primary modes of transportation are flip-flops and golf carts. Honeymoon Beach (not to be confused with the identically named beach on St John) is a legitimately gorgeous place to lounge. Beachgoers can also swim with ever-present green and hawksbill sea turtles just offshore.

TOP TIP

Skip the dockside golf-cart rental if you're headed for Honeymoon Beach. The walk is short and free.

Snorkeling, US Virgin Islands

MATT MAY/STOCKIMO/ALAMY ©

Dingy's Beach Bar & Grill

Lounge Away at Water Island

ECCENTRIC ENCLAVE NEAR ST THOMAS

Just a 15-minute ferry ride from Crown Bay Marina in St Thomas, **Water Island** offers a reprieve from the high-paced energy of Charlotte Amalie that can give travelers in a time crunch a postcard-like vantage point of the Caribbean. Whether that view reflects reality is up to the traveler's discretion.

As soon as you step off of the dock, you'll see the golf carts for hire. **Rachael's Rentals** has carved out a niche by loaning visitors this miniature means of transportation for more than a decade. The staff are friendly enough and the rates really aren't that bad. However, unless you're determined to reach the remnants of a 20th-century battery and bunkers at **Fort Segarra**, it's wise to forgo the golf cart and walk 15 minutes to Honeym oon Beach.

Plop down beneath a palm tree – as long as you're wary of falling coconuts – or slide into a chair at **Dingy's Beach Bar & Grill** for a better-than-average tuna poke and an excellent rum cocktail. Just offshore, a small armada of catamarans are likely to be moored outside of a swim area, which features a convenient floating raft that draws the eye of curious sea turtles. **Honeymoon Beach** is a pleasant place to sunbathe and swim that is (fair warning) very popular among other mainland US tourists.

On the way back to the dock, be sure to swing by **Heidi's Honeymoon Grill** for its famous fish tacos before setting a timer to catch the last ferry back to St Thomas by 9pm.

A SUBTERRANEAN TOUR

Water Island's Fort Segarra is unusual among Caribbean forts. Though colonial-era fortifications bristle at key ports on most islands, Fort Segarra is a product of WWII.

Designed to protect a US Navy submarine base on St Thomas, the majority of this fort lies underground. Though the war ended before the fort was completed, Fort Segarra's lingering underground chambers and tunnels are open for exploration for visitors willing to make the drive from Philips Landing.

GETTING AROUND

Regular daily ferries depart for Water Island from Crown Bay Marina on St Thomas hourly throughout the day. After a 15-minute ride to Water Island, visitors are deposited at Phillips Landing, where Rachael's Rentals awaits. Booking a golf cart in advance is recommended, though not necessary.

EGROY/SHUTTERSTOCK ©

Arriving

The majority of visitors arrive by cruise ship, though direct flights from the US mainland have made air travel more popular. High season runs from December to March while hurricanes threaten July through October. Domestic air passengers from the mainland will not need to clear customs on arrival; however, boat passengers from the British Virgin Islands may encounter a passport check.

By Air

International airports on both St Croix and St Thomas operate direct flights from the US. Flying into St Thomas will put visitors within arm's reach of St John. Travelers entering via St Croix should catch another flight/ferry to the other two islands.

By Boat

Charlotte Amalie is by far the most prolific cruise port in the USVI. The city's St Thomas harbor has been welcoming ships since the 1600s. On St Croix, Frederiksted has a more sparingly used cruise terminal.

Money

Currency: US dollar (US$)

CASH

Cash rules everything around the US Virgin Islands, so get the money and bring dollar bills before arriving. The more paper you have, the more products and services will be at your disposal. Taxis and safari buses almost exclusively run on cash, and some restaurants do, too.

DIGITAL PAYMENTS

Tour guides may take digital payments through Cash App or Venmo but, in general, digital payments are not a major player here. Don't rely on a digital wallet to take you far in a place that learned the hard way how vulnerable electronic payments are to severe weather and power outages.

CREDIT CARDS

Hotels, most restaurants and most retail stores accept credit-card payments. Visa and Mastercard are widely accepted; however, a number of merchants do not take American Experss. Some but not all businesses may add a nominal surcharge for credit-card usage. ATMs are available in a pinch.

Getting Around

Despite their small stature, the USVI can be tricky to get around in. Driving distances are short, but trips can be frustrated by fidgety smartphone apps and unusual traffic patterns. The roads here are usually rough, too, which explains the omnipresence of off-road vehicles.

EQROY/SHUTTERSTOCK ©

PUBLIC TRANSPORT

Safari buses are the so-called public transport of these islands. Mostly comprising customized pickup trucks with bench seating, they do service 'bus stops' when cruise passengers aren't in. Consider taking these on slow days, but don't rely on them.

CAR

Renting a car takes more time on arrival but pays off for the duration of your trip. Rates are typically reasonable and most outfitters have a fleet of vehicles capable of handling the road conditions on the islands.

BOAT

USVI water taxis will bail you out of a bind – if you get stuck on Water Island after the last ferry departs – but they also charge a premium. Ferry companies operate mass transit across the islands and are generally reliable, if a tad pricey.

TAXI/RIDESHARE

It's unlikely that rideshare services are destined for operation in the USVI anytime soon. The local taxi drivers have too much political sway and their high rates offer little value other than technically getting you from point to point, sometimes wildly.

AIR

The most convenient way to travel from St Croix to St Thomas is by seaplane. Rates are surprisingly competitive in comparison to their ocean-bound competition. It's smoother and about the same price as the boats.

DRIVING ESSENTIALS

Drive on the left side.

Know where you're going beforehand; GPS does not always work.

Get ready for a bumpy ride.

BERMUDA

AN ATLANTIC PARADISE FOUND

Surrounded by nothing but stunning shades of blue, Bermuda is an unspoiled oasis of nature and culture.

Bermuda defies categorization: Caribbean in culture but not geography, historically English but politically independent, tropical but also temperate. This archipelago is something fully its own, as evidenced by its fascinating history and revered and (often feared) position in nautical lore.

The Devil's Isle – as it was named by sailors fearful of its treacherous reefs and storms – has assumed many roles throughout the centuries. It's been a military base, a penal colony, a haven for blockade runners, an island getaway for continental travelers and a home for people hailing from Portugal, the West Indies and the Americas. It was also believed to be the inspiration for Shakespeare's *Tempest*.

Today Bermuda maintains a breezy spirit – literally and figuratively – that invigorates everyone who visits its shores. Humble Hamilton curls around the harbor like a friendly cat, inviting travelers into a crash course of Bermudian culture and history. South Shore and West End balance flashy beaches and big-name historical sites with a laid-back pace that invites you to slow down and stay a while. The nature reserves and rustic beaches of East End compliment the small-but-sophisticated St George's, Bermuda's original capital and a Unesco World Heritage Site.

Offshore, Bermuda's underwater world astounds. Reefs studded with centuries-old shipwrecks make for some of the most amazing diving on the planet.

THE MAIN AREAS

HAMILTON & CENTRAL BERMUDA
History and gardens.
p668

ST GEORGE'S & EAST END
Nature reserves and Unesco Heritage.
p673

SOUTH SHORE & WEST END
Beaches and ruins.
p676

YINGNA CAI/SHUTTERSTOCK ©

Above: Tobacco Bay (p674); Left: Royal Naval Dockyard (p678)

Find Your Way

Bermuda is an archipelago of small islands, the largest of which are nestled together in the shape of an 'S'. The six main islands form the contiguous area that makes up Bermuda in the colloquial sense.

South Shore & West End, p676

Bermuda's signature beaches mingle with cozy waterside parks, while the imposing Royal Naval Dockyard welcomes tourists with a big dose of history and culture.

Hamilton & Central Bermuda, p668

The financial and cultural hub of the island, Hamilton and its surrounds boast several fascinating museums and historical sites, along with numerous lovely outdoor parks.

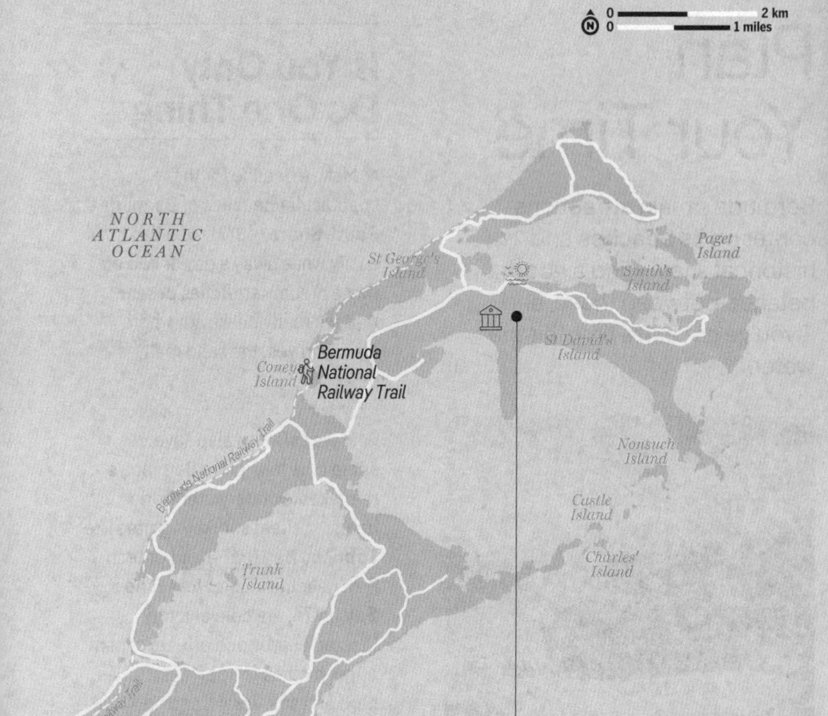

NORTH ATLANTIC OCEAN

St George's Island

Paget Island

Smith's Island

St David's Island

Coney Island

Bermuda National Railway Trail

Bermuda National Railway Trail

Nonsuch Island

Castle Island

Charles' Island

Trunk Island

Bermuda National Railway Trail

Bermuda

St George's & East End, p673

Bermuda's original capital city, St George's perches at the top of windswept East End; visit for well-preserved 17th-century architecture and reserves teeming with flora and fauna.

CAR & SCOOTER

If you're a tourist, cars aren't an option here – even Bermuda residents are only allowed one per household. Instead, you have two options: a motorized scooter or electric mini-car Twizy. Oleander Cycles and Elbow Beach Cycles are good options for rentals.

BUS

If you aren't pressed for time, Bermuda's reliable bus system makes for an excellent transportation choice. The pink and blue buses run across the entire island, so you'll be able to get to all the major sites easily.

TAXI

Bermuda's taxis are plentiful, but they're very expensive and really only a budget-worthy option if you're in a group. Call ahead of time to book or use the island's rideshare app, Hitch, which contacts local taxis on demand.

Plan Your Time

Bermuda's main attractions center on its beaches and historical sites – find a good balance between these, and if you've got extra time, hit the water.

YINGNA CAI/SHUTTERSTOCK ©

South Shore Park (p677)

If You Only Do One Thing

- Make a beeline for the spectacular beaches of Bermuda's **South Shore** (p677)– you can easily while away a day or two on these dreamy stretches of sand that are really unlike anywhere else. And yes, the sand really is pink!

- Make sure you also save some time to explore Bermuda's remarkable underwater world here; excellent snorkeling sites like **Tobacco Bay** (p674) and Church Bay, near the iconic **Horseshoe Bay** (p677) are conveniently located nearby and offer excellent opportunities to spot rays, turtles, hard and soft corals, and an innumerable variety of reef fish.

Seasonal Highlights

Bermuda's weather experiences a fluctuation between summer and winter, but its subtropical location means things don't get too extreme. Expect cool temperatures and rain November through March, and warmer climes from April to October.

MARCH

Keep your eyes turned to the horizon – this is peak season for spotting **humpback whales** migrating past Bermuda's shores.

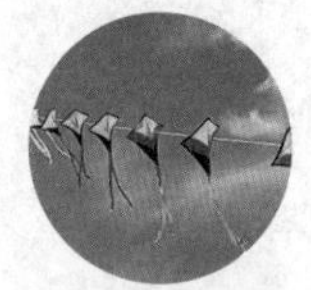

APRIL

On Good Friday, the Bermudian sky turns colorful (and noisy) at the **Bermuda Kite Festival** on Horseshoe Bay Beach.

MAY

Bermuda Day kicks off the summer season by celebrating the island's unique culture with parades, boat races and dance parties.

TRUDIE OTTOLINI/GETTY IMAGES ©, NOOM HH/SHUTTERSTOCK ©, ANDRE PLACE/SHUTTERSTOCK ©

Three Days to Travel Around

- Spend a day lounging on **South Shore** (p677) before heading to quaint **St George's** (p673) – grab a bite to eat by the water, tour the historic town and wander the museums that will give you an insight into Bermudian history.

- On your last day, make your way to **West End** (p676) and head to the **Royal Naval Dockyard** (p678), where you should dedicate a few hours to exploring the **National Museum of Bermuda** (p678) – the building dedicated to underwater archaeology is a highlight.

- Peruse the artisan shops at the dockyard before heading down the road to **Woody's** (p677) for the island's best fish sandwich.

More Than a Week

- Bermuda invites you to slow down, and a longer itinerary allows you to see what the Devil's Isle is all about. Make the most of the island's mid-Atlantic location by adding a boat trip or **offshore diving excursion** (p680) to see some of Bermuda's most striking reefs and interesting shipwrecks.

- The island is also known for its sailing culture; take a lesson at one of the many clubs and learn all the skills.

- If you're a hiker or biker, explore sections of the **Railway Trail** (p670), taking the time to savor the cliffside paths and domed tree tunnels.

JUNE
Bermuda's biggest celebration, the **Bermuda Carnival** turns things up with a long weekend of parades and 'raft-ups' (on-the-water boat parties).

AUGUST
Bermuda's rival cricket teams face off at the **Cup Match**, a two-day event that's one of the island's most significant sporting events.

OCTOBER
A celebration of Bermuda's famous traditional dancers, the **International Gombey Festival** showcases the island's various gombey troupes.

NOVEMBER
International rugby stars descend upon Bermuda for the **World Rugby Classic**; eight teams from around the world compete for the title.

Hamilton & Central Bermuda

HAMILTON & CENTRAL BERMUDA

Established in 1793, Hamilton was built to provide Bermuda with a centralized trading center – the deep waters of the harbor made for easier shipping lanes, and before long Hamilton was the island's commercial hub. In 1815 it replaced St George's as the island's capital.

Today Hamilton has become an international destination thanks to Bermuda's position in finance and tourism, and the city has a business-oriented air. That's not to say there's nothing to do – Hamilton has a number of lovely parks, plus several top-notch museums. You'll also find some of Bermuda's swankiest hotels and trendy bars. While a lot of Hamilton's dining and drinking feels old-school, some coffee shops, brunch stops and breweries bring a hip energy.

TOP TIP

Pay attention to place names when you are booking hotels and transport options in Hamilton. Despite sharing its name, the capital city is not located in Hamilton Parish – somewhat confusingly, it's actually located in Pembroke Parish!

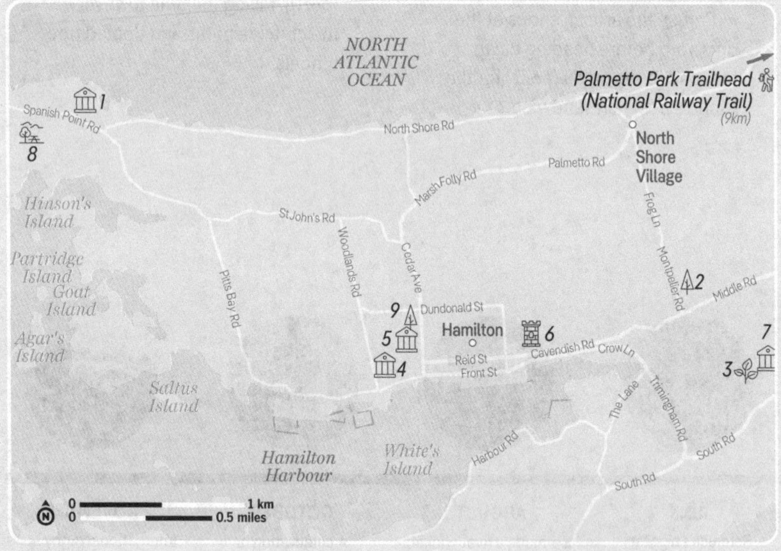

SIGHTS
1 Admiralty House
2 Arboretum
3 Bermuda Botanical Gardens
4 Bermuda Historical Society Museum
5 Bermuda National Gallery
6 Fort Hamilton
7 Masterworks Museum of Bermuda Art
8 Spanish Point
9 Victoria Park

The Marvelous Museums of Historic Hamilton

EXPLORING BERMUDA'S GALLERIES AND MUSEUMS

As the country's capital, Hamilton contains a treasure trove of national heritage in the form of art, architecture, and historic documents and artifacts. These aspects of history can be found in a solid collection of excellent museums and galleries, all well worth a visit.

Start your tour at the **Bermuda Historical Society Museum** – while smaller than the national museum, it gives a good taster of Bermuda's early years and contains a sea chest owned by the founder of the colony of Bermuda, George Somers himself. The enthusiastic volunteers who work here will be happy to answer any questions you have.

Swing north to dive into Bermuda's art scene, both historic and contemporary, at the **Bermuda National Gallery**. This airy space houses rotating exhibitions that feature both Bermudian and international artists, showcasing everything from photography and abstract art to Renaissance paintings.

Head due east to find **Fort Hamilton** – this open-air museum is DIY, but you'll enjoy wandering the battlements of this 19th-century fortification. Don't miss the moat, which has been converted into a green space with prehistoric feels; if you're feeling brave, you can even walk through the passages inside the fort walls.

If you haven't had enough Bermudian art, head to the **Masterworks Museum of Bermuda Art**, located on the grounds of the Bermuda Botanical Gardens; this museum focuses on works inspired by the island, and the collection features pieces from art icons like Georgia O' Keeffe and Winslow Homer.

Hamilton Alfresco

APPRECIATING HAMILTON'S NATURAL BEAUTY

Hamilton may indeed be a capital city, but it's also located on a stunning island in the Atlantic; the city and the surrounding parish boast plenty of places to take in the green (and blue) vistas, so lace up those walking shoes and take a jaunt through Hamilton's parks.

We recommend starting up top and working your way down, beginning with the small park known as **Spanish Point**. Gaze across the water to the Royal Naval Dockyard, and if you've got the time, light up one of the grills and stay for a while. Practically next door sits the **Admiralty House** and its adjacent park, a fascinating combination of history and nature.

BERMUDA'S ARTS SCENE

Jennifer Phillips, member of the Advisory Committee for the Bermuda Festival of the Performing Arts.

Music

Tino Martinez Quintet. Saxophonist Tino Martinez hosts weekly, must-see jazz pop-ups across the island. The locations – anywhere from social clubs to hotel lounges – are updated on his Instagram *@tmq.bda*

Culture

Harbour Nights. On Wednesday evenings during the summer months (May–August), Front Street is transformed into a pedestrian festival along Hamilton Harbor, with local artisans, food and entertainment, headlined by Bermuda's cultural icon, the Gombey dancers, whose rhythmic drumbeats, vibrant costumes and lively dancing will energize you.

WHERE TO STAY IN HAMILTON

Oxford House
A 12-room bed and breakfast located in a historic townhouse built in 1938. **$$$**

Rosemont Guest Suites
A midrange option in downtown Hamilton with rooms and suites, and epic views of the harbor. **$$**

Bermuda Princess by the Fairmont
This hotel doubles as a modern art museum; spot the Warhol and Banksy art. **$$$**

ANDRE PLACE/SHUTTERSTOCK ©

PRACTICALITIES
Scan the following QR code to find out more about the Bermuda National Railway Trail.

TOP SIGHT

Bermuda National Railway Trail

Bermuda's Railway Trail follows an out-of-commission mid-century railway that spans the entire length of the island. Divided into nine different sections, the trail allows visitors to string together Bermuda's sights while experiencing the best of the country's outdoors. Whether you're walking, hiking or biking, this 29km trail is a fantastic way to see the island's hidden corners.

DID YOU KNOW?
Bermuda banned cars from 1908 to 1946 in an effort to keep the island serene. The railroad filled a much-needed transportation gap and carried 1.5 million passengers during its tenure, but eventually closed due to maintenance-related costs.

Follow our itinerary from West End to St George's for the full railway experience.

Somerset Station to Somerset Bridge

This section of the trail winds through friendly Somerset, Bermuda's westernmost town, before cutting over to the harbor-side coast. All paved, this area winds through tree-lined tunnels before passing over the tiny bridge connecting the two halves of Sandys Parish. Take a quick detour to visit the photogenic Fort Scaur, which overlooks the island's pretty bays.

Somerset Bridge to Evans Bay

Continue through Sandys Parish, a scenic route that takes you along dirt paths beneath overhanging palms. As you move toward Evans Bay, the trail runs alongside – and occasionally joins – Middle Road. Don't miss small-but-charming Whale Bay Park, where you can spot migrating humpbacks and explore an old battery.

Evans Bay to Church Road to Khyber Pass

The trail runs alongside Middle Road on the sound side of the island. Take Tribe Road #2 to check out Gibb's Lighthouse before proceeding through Warwick Parish; this is also the stretch of the trail that passes closest to the South Shore beaches.

Khyber Pass to Rural Hill

The route moves through the middle of Paget Parish, winding beneath tree tunnels that feel like they belong in fantasy tales, and on to Rural Hill, where the trail will continue to Hamilton.

Hamilton

The trail breaks in Hamilton, making it an ideal spot to take a rest and enjoy the creature comforts of Bermuda's capital. With a little research, diehards can trace the approximate path the railway used to take through the area, but we say to skip it and head to the trailhead at Palmetto Park.

Palmetto Park to the Railway Museum

Hop back on the trail and make your way along the north coast, through more of Bermuda's signature greenery. Cross the bridge at Flatt's Inlet to arrive at the Railway Museum trailhead. Unfortunately, the museum is permanently closed.

The Railway Museum to Coney Island

Perhaps the most dramatic part of the Railway Trail, this section hugs the cliffs on its way to Bailey's Bay – and ultimately Coney Island Park – delivering views of Bermuda's signature blue water via a series of small waterside parks. Note that the trail gets a bit confusing here, winding up to North Shore Road and back again at several points.

Section 8: Ferry Point to the Oil Docks

The trail dead-ends at Coney Island, so you'll have to backtrack and head toward St George's Island via North Shore Road and St David's Island to tackle the last sections. Once on St George's, hang left to arrive at Ferry Point Park, where you can access the trail again and head toward the Oil Docks.

Section 9: Oil Docks to St George's

The oil docks are fenced off, so you'll need to cut over to Ferry Road and continue on to Mullet Bay Road to finish. Take a left on the small road across from Banjo Island to pick up the trail, which will take you all the way to St George's.

QUICK TOUR

You can easily break up the entire route into accessible sections ranging from 2.5km to 5.5km in length. The Evans Bay–Khyber Pass and Railway Museum–Coney Island sections are the longest, at 5.5km each, while the Somerset section and Oil Docks–St George's section are the shortest, coming in at about 2.5km.

TOP TIPS

- In order to cover the most ground on your trip, rent a bicycle from Oleander's or Pedego; Oleander's has multiple locations around Bermuda, and Pedego's main office is in St George's.
- In general, motorized vehicles are not allowed on the trail, though some small scooters are allowed on paved sections.
- The trail regularly intersects with busy roads, so keep an eye out for traffic, especially if you're with children.
- On windy days, the south-facing and west-facing sections of the island can get quite blustery. Bring a windproof jacket and keep your wits about you!

EXILE ISLAND

Bermuda became one of Britain's penal colonies in 1823, hosting thousands of prisoners for the next forty years.

Exile was considered a more humane sentence than capital punishment, but conditions were harsh, and all convicts were condemned to hard labor for their crimes.

The convicts were housed in large 'convict hulks,' which consisted of floating prisons constructed in old naval ships. Penal exile was abolished in 1863, but the islands in the Great Sound would later house prisoners from the Anglo-Boer War and both WWI and WWII.

WWING/GETTY IMAGES ©

Bermuda Botanical Gardens

The house itself is a shell that will thrill the urbex crowd, but head down the path to the coast for the real cherries on top – a lovely, somewhat private swimming hole, a cliff lookout and a coastal cave for the adventurous.

From here, head south back into town to make a pit stop at the small-but-mighty **Victoria Park**, which features a sculpture garden, a bandstand and a rather adorable tea shop steeping leaves and serving tonics from all over the world.

If you're looking for spaces that are a bit more interactive, first make your way to the **Arboretum**, a 22-acre expanse of meadow and forest that is just perfect for lazy picnics and (and for running around in general); you'll also find exercise stations strewn throughout the park if you fancy working up a sweat. Then head south to the **Bermuda Botanical Gardens** for more green space, curated flowers and shrubs, sculptures and a sensory garden for those who are vision impaired.

GETTING AROUND

Hamilton is a fairly walkable city, with all the major historical sites and museums sitting pretty close together – park your scooter down by the ferry port and you'll be well situated for exploration on foot. You'll need wheels, though, if you want to visit places slightly further afield, like Spanish Point.

ST GEORGE'S & EAST END

St George's & East End

HAMILTON

Interesting fact: Bermuda was settled by a shipwreck. The island was uninhabited until, in 1609, Admiral Sir George Somers wrecked his ship near what is now known as Discovery Bay, following an encounter with an Atlantic hurricane. Somers and his 150 passengers somehow made it ashore miraculously unscathed, and Bermuda was born.

St George's Island is home to Bermuda's oldest city and its first capital, a Unesco World Heritage Site that is home to a large proliferation of historic buildings which still stand as testaments to 400 years of English colonization. Built as a protective garrison, St George's also harbors several of the island's oldest forts and batteries.

The rest of East End – namely St David's Island and the top of Hamilton Parish – features spectacular nature reserves that are home to turtle nesting sites, mangrove forests and ecologically important wetlands.

TOP TIP

Much of Bermuda shuts down on Sundays, so if you want to take part in any historical tours and/or experience local fare in East End, plan to visit on literally any other day of the week.

FELIX LIPOV/SHUTTERSTOCK ©

Unfinished Church (p675)

WHERE TO EAT IN ST GEORGE'S & EAST END

Temptations
A cafe serving Bermuda-breakfast staples (such as cod and potatoes), and pastries and cupcakes. $

Munchies By The Sea
Known for made-from-scratch Bermudian specialties, as well as their signature 'Johnny Dog' and a lobster dinner. $$

Mama Angie's Coffee Shop
A local haunt serving up breakfast and lunch – try the codfish cakes and the spicy fries. $

Swizzle Inn, East End
Bermuda's oldest bar and the celebrated home of the island's national drink: the rum swizzle.

Bailey's Ice Cream, East End
An inviting ice cream parlor serving homemade ice creams in unique flavors like rum raisin, ginger, and nutty cumin.

Tom Moore's Tavern, East End
Bermuda's oldest restaurant, serving up French-continental cuisine in a 17th century home.

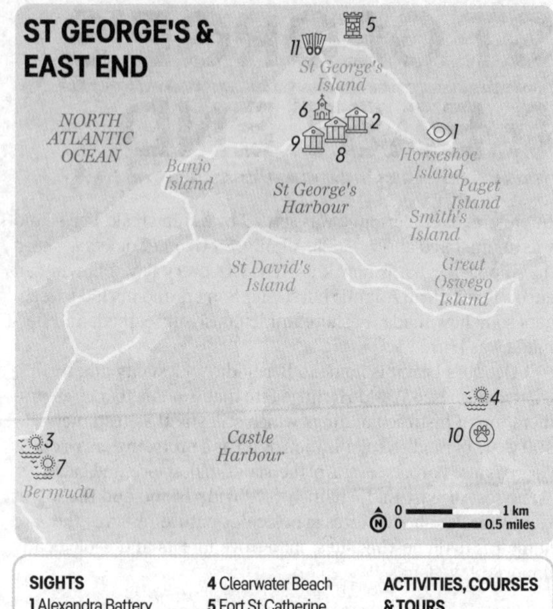

SIGHTS
1 Alexandra Battery
2 Bermuda Heritage Museum
3 Blue Hole Park
(see 1) Building Bay Beach
4 Clearwater Beach
5 Fort St Catherine
6 St Peter's Church
7 Tom Moore's Jungle
8 Town Hall
9 Tucker House Museum
(see 9) Water St

ACTIVITIES, COURSES & TOURS
10 Cooper's Island Nature Reserve
11 Tobacco Bay

Bermuda Goes Wild

ENJOY BERMUDA'S RESPLENDENT NATURE RESERVES

It's in St George's and St David's that Bermuda's signature beaches and craggy shores come together with delightful exuberance. A rocky inlet at the northeastern tip of the country, **Tobacco Bay** is widely regarded as one of Bermuda's best snorkeling spots; so grab a mask and head below to see parrot fish, sergeant majors and coral.

Once you've had your fill of underwater exploits, make your way to **Cooper's Island Nature Reserve**, an ambitious 'undevelopment' program focused on reintroducing and protecting endemic plant and animal species along a stretch of land that has worn many hats: an 18th-century fort, an agricultural hub, a WWII-era US military base, and finally, a NASA outpost. Today, the Bermudian government is in the process

WHERE TO SHOP IN ST GEORGE'S

Long Story Short
Boutique featuring the work of Black and female artisans and authors. Try their skincare line or book a history tour.

Dragon's Lair Gallery
An airy gallery that celebrates the work of local artists; buy prints, jewelry, carvings and more here.

Lili Bermuda Perfumery
A perfumery and tea house in a historic white cottage near the town center. Don't miss the scents created from island plants.

of demolishing old bunkers and buildings to make room for native ospreys, petrels, sea turtles and hermit crabs, all while encouraging the regrowth of fauna such as seaside morning glories and the national tree, the Bermuda cedar.

After you've hiked your way through the various sandpits and coastal forest of the reserve, make your way to the adjacent **Clearwater Beach** to put your feet up and enjoy the bites and drinks from the nearby restaurant.

Head south to Hamilton Parish to venture into Bermuda's tangled mangroves at the **Blue Hole Park** and **Tom Moore's Jungle**, where you can enjoy small beaches, spot giant anemones and their blue-striped companions in shallow pools, and peer into the depths of the namesake Blue Hole. This little oasis also gives visitors a glimpse of subterranean Bermuda: you can wander down to the park's photogenic cave, a towering recess decorated in salt-worn stalactites.

Unesco World Heritage on Display

WALKING THROUGH 17TH-CENTURY STREETS

Begin your tour of St George's at the **town hall**, located just across from the cruise terminal. Head down **Water St** – the historic front street that has since been turned into a shopping boulevard – to find the **Tucker House Museum**. Here you'll learn about two famous residents: Henry Tucker, President of the Governor's Council; and Joseph Rainey, who became the first Black US Senator.

Alternatively, a walk straight up to York St reveals more historic architecture, including **St Peter's Church**, which was built in the early 1700s. A couple of blocks northeast sits the dramatic **Unfinished Church**, the skeleton of a would-be-replacement St Peter's that began construction in 1874. The project was ultimately abandoned when the congregation couldn't agree on designs for the building.

Over on the corner of Water St and York St sits the **Bermuda Heritage Museum**, a museum dedicated to Black history in Bermuda. The museum is part of Bermuda's **African Diaspora Heritage Trail**, a cultural initiative that highlights locations around the island that speak to the history and impact of slavery, and the many accomplishments of Black Bermudians.

If military history is of interest and you have a set of wheels, take the loop around the easternmost tip of St George's (via Cut Rd and Barry Rd) to see **Fort St Catherine** – Bermuda's biggest fort – and the **Alexandra Battery**, built in 1864. Bonus: the battery sits adjacent to **Building Bay Beach**, a pretty little corner of beach covered with sea glass.

WHY I LOVE EAST END

Bailey Freeman, writer

Bermuda's East End combines so much of what makes Bermuda special, in one compact space. With its pastel buildings and collection of 17th-century forts, St George's delivers on the history front, while also catering to folks looking to wine and dine at establishments with a distinctly local feel.

This region of Bermuda also features some truly remarkable beaches and coves nestled away from the main hot spots, giving visitors the opportunity to take in the amazing natural world at their own pace.

I love standing on the rocks by Tobacco Bay and letting the Atlantic wind whip around me, or watching birds flit amongst the cedars in Cooper's Reserve.

GETTING AROUND

Navigating St George's and East End is pretty straightforward – Mullet Bay Road/York Street makes up the main thoroughfare, with Barry Road encircling the easternmost tip of the island. Parking in downtown St George's is limited, but once you find a spot, everything is walkable.

SOUTH SHORE & WEST END

Home to heavy hitters like the Royal Naval Dockyard and rosy beaches, Bermuda's South Shore and West End feature some of the destination's biggest bucket-list items. However, the region doesn't lose itself to an uncanny tourism sheen – it largely maintains a laid-back, local feel, particularly in its main town of Somerset.

South Shore tops every Bermuda must-see list – these beaches may just be some of the most beautiful in the western hemisphere. Long stretches of pristine sand gleam against shimmering water, while characterful coves welcome all manner of marine life.

Head further west, and the long beaches of Warwick Parish give way to the cozy bays of narrow Sandys Parish. Here you'll find nature preserves, historic ruins and pleasant Somerset, a buzzy hub in an otherwise quiet stretch. West End terminates in the Royal Naval Dockyard, the island's most celebrated historical site and a center for tours and activities.

TOP TIP

Make use of Bermuda's ferry system to get from the Royal Naval Dockyard to Hamilton – beats having to drive yourself! There are two other ferry ports in Sandys that also may be useful, depending on where you're based, but Rockaway is the only one that lets you bring a scooter.

Horseshoe Bay

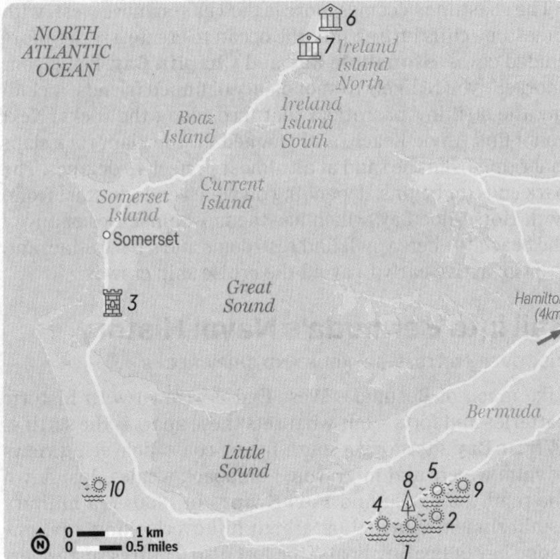

SIGHTS
1 Angle Beach
2 Chaplin Bay
3 Fort Scaur
4 Horseshoe Bay
5 Jobson's Cove
6 National Museum of Bermuda
7 Royal Naval Dockyard
8 South Shore Park
(see 2) Stonehole Bay
9 Warwick Long Bay
10 Whale Bay

LISTEN FOR THE BERMUDA KITE

The **Bermuda kite** is a geometric kite that you'll spot twirling skyward around Easter time. These colorful crafts were introduced to the island when British Army troops used them as tools to plan telephone lines, and they've since become closely tied to Easter, as symbols of Christ's resurrection.

In Somerset you'll find (or hear) a particular kite. These noisy kites 'scream' as they loop about in the wind thanks to a small piece of paper or plastic, called a hummer, attached to the kite's back. Kite makers try to make the loudest, strongest kites around, and these things will stay airborne even in heavy wind thanks to the strong fishing line used as an anchor.

Pink Beaches, Blue Bays & Sun Rays

BERMUDA'S BEST BEACHES

The beaches of South Shore are legendary swaths of pristine sand, salt-pummeled stone and cerulean waters perfect for snorkeling, fishing or splashing around. These jewels are linked together like a fine necklace by **South Shore Park**. As you head west from expansive Warwick Long Bay, you'll find the oft-photographed **Jobson's Cove**, **Angle Beach** and the famous **Horseshoe Bay**, a perfect arc of beach framing an inviting bit of ocean that's a local favorite. The park features a short trail that connects each beach, and this will be your primary path of exploration; it's not possible to walk the park from end to end on the beaches alone unless you're prepared to do some swimming and rock scrambling. **Warwick Long Bay**, the park's easternmost beach, is just that – long and flat with calm waters. This is a place for prime relaxation.

WHERE TO EAT IN SOUTH SHORE AND WEST END

Woody's
Serves up the best fried-fish sandwich – a combo of fish, coleslaw and cheese on raisin bread. $

Baxter's Pies
A hole-in-the-wall that keeps the Bermudian meat pie alive – choose from chicken, beef, or mussel. $

Lonestar
A food truck serving seafood dishes like fish cake on a bun, rockfish and chips, and oysters. $$

BERMUDA'S PORTUGUESE COMMUNITY

Did you know that Bermuda is home to a robust Portuguese community? Nearly a quarter of the island's population hails from this part of Europe.

The first Portuguese to arrive in Bermuda used the island as a stopover in the 16th century on their way to and from the Caribbean, some unwillingly due to shipwrecks. Later on, in the 1800s, Bermuda actively recruited Portuguese laborers – primarily from Madeira and the Azores – to work on farms, thus establishing an ongoing relationship between the two countries that continues to this day.

The coastline becomes more jagged as you move west, with limestone cliffs jutting into the ocean to create a series of secluded coves: **Stonehole Bay** and **Chaplin Bay**. Bring your snorkel – you're likely to spot plenty of finned friends, including the striking parrotfish that feed along the rocks. Next you'll find Angle Beach, aptly named for the giant rock slabs emerging from the sand at an almost perfect 45 degrees. The park ends (or begins, depending on which end you start from) with Horseshoe Bay, which has the most amenities of any of the beaches – here you'll find restrooms and a bar/restaurant. Pro tip: arrive early to avoid the cruise ship crowds.

Sail into Bermuda's Naval History

DISCOVER FORTS, SHIPYARDS AND SHIPWRECKS

Like much of Bermuda, West End is strewn with historic batteries and forts – but what sets these apart is the setting. **Whale Bay** sits along a south-facing coast, delivering views of calm waters and migrating humpback whales. Just down the road you'll also find **Fort Scaur**, an 1860s-era military establishment perched on a high hill overlooking a picturesque bay of floating boats; the fort also features some short trails that connect right to the ocean's edge and to the Railway Trail (p670). Learn about Bermuda's military history and take some food along for an epic alfresco lunch.

The jewel in Bermuda's historical crown is the **Royal Naval Dockyard**, a sprawling complex built in 1809 to house the royal fleet as it made its way to and from the Americas. While much of the site has been 'cruise-ified' with restaurants, shops and even escape rooms, the **National Museum of Bermuda** is a must-visit for anyone interested in the country's history. Housed in the Commissioner's Residence and its adjacent buildings, this treasure covers Bermuda's shipwrecked origins, its role as a penal colony, its involvement in the brutal institution of slavery, immigration patterns that have influenced its contemporary cultural melange, its boating and sailing legacy, and even the growth of the tourism industry. Leave yourself plenty of time to explore – there's a lot to learn.

One of the most fascinating wings explores the role that underwater archeology has played in uncovering Bermuda's history – peruse the exhibits featuring salvaged ship equipment, valuables and other clues left behind by the victims of the island's perilous reefs.

GETTING AROUND

South Road and Middle Road run parallel to each other through Warwick Parish and part of Southampton Parish, and they'll be your main route of travel through these areas. Just past Church Bay Park, South Road swings north to connect with Middle Road, which takes you all the way to Sandys Parish; once you cross the parish line, it becomes Somerset Road. From there it changes names several times, but it will take you all the way to the Royal Naval Dockyard.

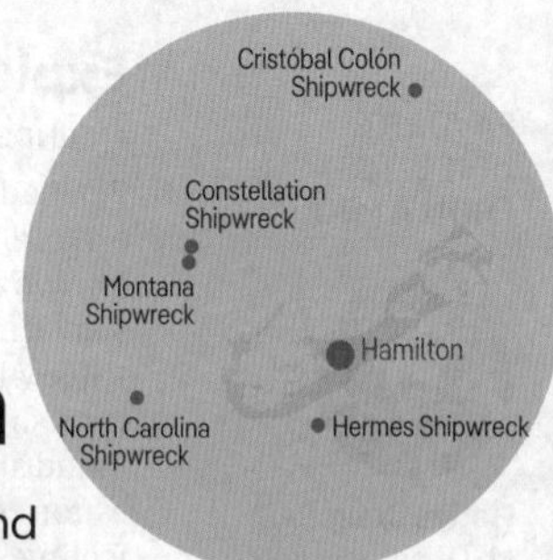

Beyond Bermuda

Submerge yourself in the natural beauty and nautical history that make Bermuda one of the world's most unique dive spots.

People will tell you that you've only seen half of Bermuda if you stay above water – and they'd be right.

Bermuda is home to some of the northernmost coral reefs in the Atlantic thanks to the warm waters brought in by the Gulf Stream. The subaquatic landscape features three different kinds of reef formations – rim, lagoon, and terrace reefs – making Bermuda a spectacularly diverse place to dive and snorkel.

As beautiful and ecologically essential as these reefs are, they've also greatly contributed to Bermuda's past reputation as a dangerous place – over the centuries, over 300 ships have struck them and sunk, resulting in underwater archaeology comprising a huge part of understanding Bermuda's history.

TOP TIP

You can dive in Bermuda year-round, but the best time is May–October, when the water is warm and calm.

DJANGOSUPERTRAMP/GETTY IMAGES ©

Shipwreck, Bermuda

FAVORITE DIVE SITES, FROM A PRO

Marlee Cram, PADI MSDT and manager of Dive Bermuda, shares her favorite underwater locations in Bermuda.

Mary Celestia
This shipwreck has a mysterious history, and some fascinating items were recovered here in 2011, including a perfume that has been meticulously remade by Lili Bermuda.

King George Dredger
An intact wreck unique from Bermuda's other shipwrecks, as it's an oasis in a huge, sandy, underwater desert. The marine life on this wreck is near impossible to locate anywhere else in Bermuda.

Virginia Merchant Reef Site
Imagine an underwater maze for divers – there are canyons, valleys, arches, swim-throughs, caverns, overhangs, pristine coral and pink sand.

Explore Bermuda's Shipwrecks

AN UNDERWATER TRIP THROUGH HISTORY

Bermuda's waters contain a profusion of fascinating sites to explore, both natural and human-made, and the area is known for above-average water clarity thanks to the Gulf Stream – sometimes visibility can reach a whopping 60m in depth!

But what really sets diving in Bermuda apart from the rest is its shipwrecks – while only 40 are named, over 300 can be found strewn about the reef. These hulls make excellent places for coral to grow, and divers delight in the otherworldly feeling of these abandoned vessels. Most wrecks only take a 20-minute boat ride to reach, making them an easily accessible trip from the shore.

The wrecks to the east and north of Bermuda are well-preserved, sitting between 12m and 24m in depth. Here you'll find the **Cristóbal Colón**, a Spanish cruise liner that sank in 1926. It's one of the island's biggest shipwrecks, at nearly 152m long.

The West End wrecks sit at a more shallow depth, and it's here you'll discover the **Constellation**, a World War II–era American schooner that sank carrying medical supplies and 700 cases of whisky to Venezuela. Adjacent to the Constellation sits the **Montana**, a Civil War blockade-runner that met its watery fate while attempting to evade Union gunboats.

To the south, divers will find the **North Carolina**, an English freighter that foundered here in 1880; and the **Hermes**, a WWII buoy-tender turned freighter that was intentionally scuttled in 1984 as part of an artificial reef project.

DIVE DEEPER INTO BERMUDA'S HISTORY

Learn about the work that underwater archaeologists have done around Bermuda's shipwrecks at the **National Museum of Bermuda** (p678). Over 1500 artifacts from Bermuda's earliest wrecks are on display in the Queen's Exhibition Hall.

GETTING AROUND

Bermuda's shipwrecks are not accessible from shore, and they require a short boat ride to get to them. Dive outfitters provide transportation to these sites.

Arriving

Unless you're on a cruise ship, all travelers to Bermuda arrive at the L. F. Wade International Airport (BDA), the island's only airport. Wade is small, with only a handful of flights arriving and departing each day, but you'll still want to show up early for your return flight to avoid any rushing.

By Air

Wade Airport is located on the East End, meaning you'll need transport to your accommodation since rentals aren't available. Taxis are available, expensive, and will need to be paid in cash. The ride to Hamilton is around $45.

By Boat

Cruisers dock at King's Wharf (pictured) in the Royal Naval Dockyard – use the ferry to cross the sound to Hamilton. Bermuda's ferry system is reliable and budget-friendly – boats depart from terminals in Paget, Warwick and Southampton Parishes.

Money

Currency: Bermudian Dollar (BM$); US dollar (US$) also accepted

US OR BERMUDIAN DOLLAR?

The Bermudian dollar is pegged to the US dollar at a rate of 1:1, and the two currencies are used interchangeably throughout Bermuda. Note that the majority of ATMs only dispense Bermudian dollars, and you'll likely get some back in your change from time to time. However, most businesses will try to match your currency of payment.

CASH & CARD

Cards are widely accepted across the island, except when it comes to transport – make sure you have cash to pay taxis, as well as ferries and buses, if you haven't purchased a pass ahead of time. The only exception to this is if you book a taxi using the Hitch taxi app – the payment will go to the card you have on file.

CREDIT CARDS

Major credit cards – Visa, Mastercard and American Express – are accepted across the island.

TOOLKIT

The chapters in this section cover the most important topics you'll need to know about in the Caribbean Islands. They're full of nuts-and-bolts information and valuable insights to help you understand and navigate the Caribbean Islands and get the most out of your trip.

Accommodations p684

Family Travel p685

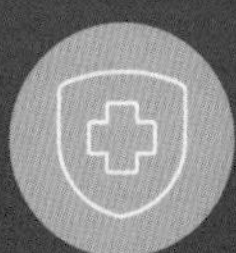

Health & Safe Travel p686

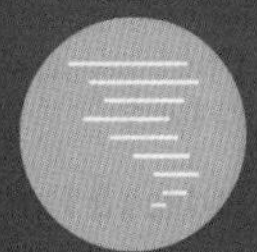

How to Travel during Hurricane Season p687

Food, Drink & Nightlife p688

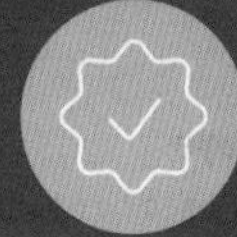

Responsible Travel p690

LGBTIQ+ Travelers p692

Accessible Travel p693

How to Dive in the Caribbean p694

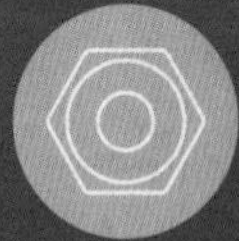

Nuts & Bolts p695

Charlestown, Nevis (p512)

Accommodations

Resorts

For better or worse, all-inclusive and luxury resorts are kind of the Caribbean's thing, but note the differences between the two. All-inclusive resorts tend to focus on convenience and generally go one of two ways: a family-oriented hot spot or an adults-only getaway. Luxury resorts cater to upscale tastes and frequently don't fall under the 'all-inclusive' umbrella.

Self-Catered Apartments

A popular option in many Caribbean destinations, self-catered apartments are great for those who don't mind DIYing meals and transport. These apartments range in size and style from studios to multi-bedroom units, and some have amenities such as pools and beach equipment. Many are booked by the week, so apartments are ideal for longer stays.

Ecolodges & Farm Stays

An excellent choice for budget travelers, ecolodges and farm stays provide unique, environmentally friendly accommodations in rural surrounds. Ecolodges vary in style (and price) from glamping set-ups to luxury digs; farm stays tend to be a bit more rustic, and often guests participate in daily farm activities and/or interact closely with hosts.

Boutique Hotels

As in many destinations, boutique hotels are experiencing a renaissance in the Caribbean, offering higher-end accommodation in a more intimate setting than the larger resorts offer. Options range from art hotels to revamped historic buildings to earthy cottages.

Dive Resorts

These resorts incorporate one of the Caribbean's most popular activities: bookings generally have a built-in number of dives per person. If the scuba shops aren't on the grounds, the hotels provide free transport. PADI has a bookable list of certified dive resorts.

Homestays

This Cuba-specific option is worth a call-out: homestays, or *casas particulares,* are the primary accommodations on the island. These are essentially mini-B&Bs where guests stay in their hosts' homes; *casas* often offer meals and other activities as part of the stay, and they're a great way to get to know Cuba from a local perspective.

BOOK RESPONSIBLY

While tourism is a fundamental part of many Caribbean economies, not all tourism is beneficial on the ground, and this is particularly evident in the accommodation sector. Look for hotels and resorts that are locally owned rather than owned by international conglomerates – the end goal is to keep money in the destination rather than export it to entities based abroad. Similarly, endeavour to support resorts that keep their beaches public rather than private, as local access is an important part of creating culturally sustainable tourism.

Family Travel

With so many islands – and experiences – to choose from, the Caribbean makes an excellent destination for families with kids of any age. Whether you want to splash an afternoon away on a calm beach with little ones or jump into swimming holes with teenagers, this region has something for everyone.

KID-FRIENDLY PICKS

Beach time

Seek out family-friendly beaches with calm water and helpful amenities, such as Curaçao's Grote Knip, Turks and Caicos' Taylor Bay, or Miami Beach in Barbados.

Zip lining

Great for teens: fly over the forests of Jamaica, the beachside towns of St-Martin, or the hills of St Lucia.

National parks

Hike the rainforests of Puerto Rico's El Yunque National Forest or dive into Tobago Cays Marine Park in St Vincent and the Grenadines.

Accommodations

Destinations with well-established tourism infrastructure have a healthy number of family-friendly accommodation options. Self-catered apartments are great options for families who need a bit more space or who want to operate on their own schedules, while some all-inclusive resorts have childcare facilities and child-specific attractions. Ask your accommodations about cots and other sleep-away amenities.

Getting Around

If you want to do some independent exploring and you've got more than one small kiddo in tow, it's best to rent a car. Public transit varies in availability and reliability across islands, so having your own wheels is the best bet for smooth transport. Ferry services normally offer discounted rates for kids, but they sometimes require adult accompaniment, so double-check before sending preteens/teens off solo.

Sights

Parents often have to pay entry to privately owned sights and activities for their kids, though discounted tickets are sometimes available (normally for kids under 12). Some state-funded museums and sights – national museums, aquariums, etc – offer free entry to kids.

Facilities

Changing stations aren't common outside of tourism hubs and large attractions. Groceries and pharmacies do tend to close early (and on Sundays) on smaller islands, so plan ahead if you have any kid-related errands to run.

SCUBA DIVING WITH KIDS

Believe it or not, scuba diving isn't just an activity for adults – kids over the age of eight can learn the fundamentals of diving at outfits throughout the Caribbean. Not sure where to start? PADI Bubblemaker and Seal Team courses are tailored to kids aged between eight and 12 and focus on learning in a controlled pool environment, while kids aged 10 and up can participate in Open Water diving courses. These youth-oriented programs provide kid-appropriate equipment and can be completed on-site (no at-home training required).

Health & Safe Travel

TAP WATER

While many islands have drinkable tap water, this is not a universal truth. Check with resources within your specific destination for more details. Resorts in destinations where drinking tap water is not recommended often provide filtered water for guests, and bottled water is available everywhere. For a more sustainable alternative, bring along a reusable water bottle with a filter.

Hurricane Season

Hurricanes are serious business in the Caribbean. The season runs from June to November, with August to October the period of highest concern. Some islands lie outside the main hurricane belt, but they are not immune to weather spiraling off major storms.

Heat & Sun

It's no secret that the Caribbean is a warm-weather destination, but special care is needed to avoid heat exhaustion and sun-related injuries. The UV index is often extremely high and ocean breezes may disguise the sun's intensity because it doesn't 'feel hot.' It's easy to get dehydrated, so always make sure you've got something to drink with you.

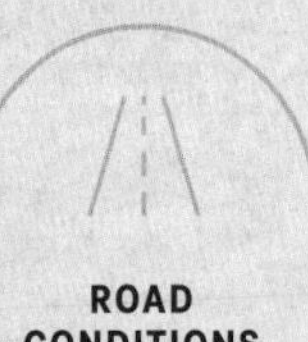

ROAD CONDITIONS

Roads throughout the Caribbean vary in quality: some are paved, some gravel (with potholes). If locals say a route requires a 4WD, listen.

Theft

Theft and pickpocketing aren't huge issues in the Caribbean, but it's always good to be vigilant. Most locals will tell you not to leave anything of value in your car overnight, and avoid leaving valuables on the beach unattended. If you're traveling solo, a waterproof waist pack is super handy – simply take your stuff with you whenever you fancy a dip.

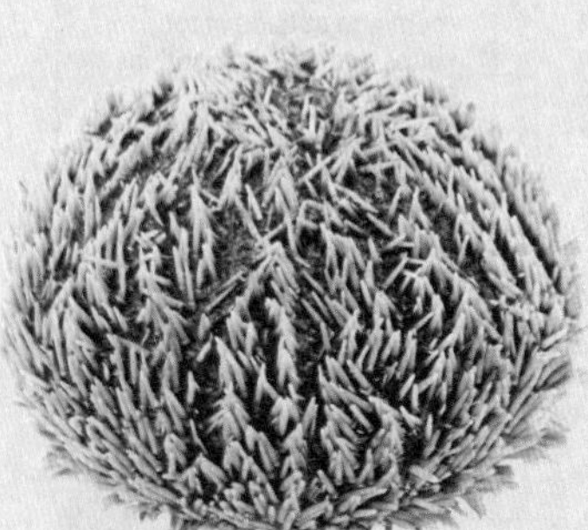

SWIMMING SAFELY

The Caribbean is a swimmer's paradise, but the ocean is powerful and not all coastlines are gentle. Pay attention to water-safety signs, and heed any official advice to steer clear of a particular beach.

And be careful where you put your feet: sea-urchin spines (pictured) are no joke, and rays are often camouflaged against the sand. Shuffle before stepping.

DERSON SANTANA/SHUTTERSTOCK ©

Shoal Bay East (p66)

HOW TO... Travel during Hurricane Season

Hurricane season is a fact of life in the Caribbean. While the potential dangers should definitely be heeded, they don't need to thwart all your late summer/early fall travel ambitions. With a little planning, you'll be able to enjoy the best of the Caribbean – and some of the lowest travel prices – during this time of year.

Remember the Dates

Hurricane season lasts from June through November; the most active months are August through October.

Get the Travel Insurance

Should your trip be interrupted by inclement weather, travel insurance can help cushion the blow and get you back in the Caribbean again at a later date. A range of companies cover trip interruptions and cancellations – just make sure that there's a 'cancel for any reason' clause that includes weather.

Stay Weather Aware

Thanks to sophisticated tracking systems and the slow-build nature of hurricanes, you know pretty well in advance if a storm is heading your way. Pay attention to forecasts in the time leading up to your vacation and avoid completely unplugging while you're on the road – you'll have to act quickly should an emergency arise. And if local authorities say to evacuate an area, listen.

Know What to Do

If you're in the storm's path and evacuation is not an option, take refuge by putting as much space between you and the outdoors as you can – shelter in interior rooms, and avoid glass and windows.

Watch for Weather Changes

Even if an island sits outside the hurricane belt, it's still possible to feel some effects from passing storms, such as wind, heavy rain, and rough seas. Pay attention to the forecast if you know a system is close by, and ask locals about the drivability of routes during and after rain.

Resources

US National Oceanic and Atmospheric Administration (nhc.noaa.gov) Tracks hurricane activity in the Gulf of Mexico and the Caribbean Sea.

Caribbean Hurricane Network (stormcarib.com) Blog with NASA-powered radar, and hurricane correspondents across the islands.

CHECK THE MAP

Determine whether your prospective destinations are located in the primary areas for hurricane landfall – you might be surprised to see that many islands lie largely outside of the action. For example, more southern islands such as Barbados, Trinidad and Tobago, St Vincent and the Grenadines, Grenada, and the ABCs rarely see major hurricanes, while the Greater Antilles and their neighbors tend to experience more activity. Nothing is guaranteed in the end, but you'll get a better sense of your chances by knowing where the main hurricane belt lies.

TOOLKIT

Food, Drink & Nightlife

Caribbean Do's & Don'ts

Dining culture in the Caribbean is relaxed – take your time and don't expect service to be snappy.

Avoid wearing beachwear to non-beachy establishments, and cover up if you're headed into the grocery store.

Tipping is welcomed throughout the Caribbean, usually to North American norms (20% or higher for good service). Gratuity is sometimes included in the bill, so check before paying.

MENU DECODER

Caribbean cocktails are an art form, with tons of regional specialties – some are simple-but-effective two-ingredient staples, while others are sophisticated combinations of liquor, fruit juice, and other add-ins. Some staple drinks:

Bahama Mama (Bahamas) Coconut rum, dark rum, pineapple, orange juice, lime, grenadine

Bushwacker (USVI) Dark rum, coffee liqueur, creme de cacao, coconut

El Presidente (Cuba) White rum, dry vermouth, orange curaçao, grenadine

Daiquiri (Cuba) Light rum, citrus, simple syrup; often flavored with other fruits

Dark 'n' Stormy (Bermuda) Dark rum, ginger beer, lime

Painkiller (BVI) Dark rum, pineapple, orange, coconut cream

Planter's Punch (Jamaica) Dark rum, lime, simple syrup, bitters; sometimes includes pineapple and orange

Rum Swizzle (Bermuda) Dark rum, light rum, orange, pineapple, grenadine, bitters

Ti' Punch (Martinique, Guadeloupe) Rhum agricole, cane syrup, lime

Where to Eat & Drink

Beach bars Casual restaurants right on the sand – or beach-adjacent – serving US cuisine with some local favorites mixed in. Some become nightlife spots when the sun goes down.

High-end dining Top-tier eateries that vary in cuisine type. Elevated Caribbean food is common.

Rum shops Casual, locally run watering holes that serve beer and liquor at affordable prices.

Food trucks Popular options for small businesses. The type of food varies, and some may even skew high-end.

HOW TO... Find Your Favorite Seafood

Some seafood staples are available pretty much year-round, but others have a 'closed' season to allow them to breed and maintain stock levels. Where you can, try to order dishes that use sustainable catches – preferably wild-caught from managed stocks of local fish, rather than imported, farmed fish; don't be afraid to ask questions about where your seafood is coming from.

Lobster This season varies from island to island, but lobster is generally available from late summer (July and August) through the winter (February and March).

Conch The season for this tasty mollusk runs from October to June, though some destinations prohibit harvest at any time. Look for farm-raised versions, as conch in the wild are endangered.

HOW TO... Make a Good First Impression

It's understandable: you're on vacation in a tropical paradise and you want to have fun. That said, tourists behaving badly while under the influence can be an issue, so be careful not to let that rum sneak up on you. Behave as you would at home and keep your partying contained to appropriate locations.

HOW TO... Enjoy Caribbean Street Parties

From Jamaica's dancehall scene to St Croix's jump-ups to St Lucia's Friday-night festivities, Caribbean street parties are the stuff of legend. Here are some hacks to help you do as the locals do:

- Street parties are usually free to attend, but it's expected that revelers will show support by buying drinks and food, and tipping the DJ (when appropriate).
- If you're at a dancehall party, let the pros take center stage. Keep in mind that you're a visitor – follow appropriate etiquette and don't try to steal the spotlight from veterans of the scene.
- Remember: this is a marathon, not a sprint. Parties can last until the wee hours of the morning and some folks even continue on to nearby beaches for sunrise.
- Street parties are generally casual affairs, but some folks do seize the opportunity to make fashion statements – dress in whatever makes you feel good. But don't bother wearing make-up – it's very likely you'll sweat it off with all that dancing!
- The heart of a street party is the sound system, and the louder the better. If you've got sensitive ears, consider bringing earplugs.
- Dancing with lots of people is normal, and it's not unusual for partners to swap around. While dancing is always encouraged, it's totally fine to decline an invitation if you'd rather groove solo.

Dancehall

Emerging in Jamaica in the 1970s, dancehall was the creation of working-class musicians and dancers. The genre took off in the 1980s with the advent of digital music technology, and today it's a huge influence on popular music worldwide.

WHAT IS A FISH FRY?

Virtually every Caribbean island has had a fishing industry, and local fisherman have been hawking their catches at ports and piers for centuries. The fish was sold fresh, of course, but enterprising individuals with a flair for the culinary began frying fish to sell to sailors and other visitors. This tradition has really taken off in a few countries, and today a fish fry is a must-do for anyone interested in local Caribbean cuisine.

The event centers on a food fair – vendor stalls (and sometimes full bricks-and-mortar restaurants) sell everything from whole fried fish to conch fritters to sides such as peas and rice. Locals and visitors settle in for a good plate and cold drinks, and it's not uncommon for musicians to take the stage.

At the Arawak Cay Fish Fry in The Bahamas, stalls named for different Bahamian islands serve dishes unique to their namesakes, while others serve proprietary family recipes. Sunday is the favorite day for locals, but the fish fry happens every day of the week.

Oistins Fish Fry in Barbados happens every Friday night, with vendors preparing dishes such as flying fish, mahi mahi, lobster, and more. Here, sound systems blare everything from vintage calypso classics to contemporary hits, and some nights live bands entertain while revelers dance.

On Thursdays, Stubbs Diamond Plaza in Turks and Caicos sees local chefs serving fish, conch, lobster, and crab. Bands play traditional and pop tunes, stalls sell local and imported crafts, and sometimes dancers take the stage for cultural performances.

Responsible Travel

Climate Change & Travel

It's impossible to ignore the impact we have when travelling, and the importance of making changes where we can. Lonely Planet urges all travellers to engage with their travel carbon footprint. There are many carbon calculators online that allow travellers to estimate the carbon emissions generated by their journey; try resurgence.org/resources/carbon-calculator.html. Many airlines and booking sites offer travellers the option of offsetting the impact of greenhouse gas emissions by contributing to climate-friendly initiatives around the world. We continue to offset the carbon footprint of all Lonely Planet staff travel, while recognising this is a mitigation more than a solution.

Support Caribbean Owned

Foreign interests have had their hands in the Caribbean economy for centuries, and this continues today in the tourism industry. Seek out locally owned restaurants, hotels, and outfitters to keep your dollars in your destination.

Steer Clear of Wildlife

The Caribbean teems with animals, but it's important to give them a wide berth, for your safety and theirs. Don't chase or touch turtles, and be extra careful to avoid physical contact with corals.

Many islands have prohibited plastic bags in grocery stores – plan ahead and bring your own bags.

Lonely Planet doesn't condone the keeping of cetaceans in captivity – instead, opt for a dolphin-viewing cruise, where you can see the animals in the wild.

USE REEF-SAFE SUNSCREEN

Many common sunscreens contain ingredients that can be harmful to ocean life, specifically corals. Always opt for reef-safe options; if you have concerns about efficacy, a swim shirt will do wonders!

Caribbean countries are minor contributors to climate change but will suffer some of its most severe consequences.

Pick Up Beach Plastic

Being plastic conscious is extra relevant in the Caribbean, where litter from other countries washes ashore. Every bit helps – take five minutes to help clean up before you enjoy your day on the sand.

Leave Big Seashells Behind

Shelling is a popular Caribbean pastime, but it's important to check the rules of your destination for taking shells from the beach. In most countries it's prohibited to take conch shells.

Quick Showers, Please!

Water is expensive in the Caribbean, and the supply varies depending on where it comes from – some islands rely on rainwater systems, while others draw from desalination plants. Either way, be water conscious and minimise waste.

Enter with Respect

History can be pretty heavy in the Caribbean and visitors should act accordingly. If you're visiting a plantation, an Indigenous sacred space, or anywhere else tied to significant cultural history, enter respectfully.

Bonaire as a Sustainability Leader

In 2022, Bonaire instituted a US$75 tourist tax to support infrastructure, community development, and sustainability initiatives. Visitors also pay a US$40 nature fee to access Bonaire's legendary marine park and other natural attractions.

Socially oriented voluntourism can be detrimental to local communities when done incorrectly (eg orphanage/school 'visits'). If you want to participate in a voluntourism experience, be judicious – it's safest to stick with environmental opportunities.

Stony coral tissue loss disease was discovered in Florida in 2014 and has spread to many Caribbean reefs; to help keep it contained, disinfect your dive/snorkel gear each day and avoid diving in infected areas.

10%

The Caribbean is home to the second-largest reef in the world – the Mesoamerican Barrier Reef – and it harbors 10% of the world's reefs.

RESOURCES

onecaribbean.org

The Caribbean's tourism development agency.

sustainabletravel.org

Global organization dedicated to helping reduce the travel industry's carbon footprint.

LGBTIQ+ Travelers

The Caribbean varies widely in its acceptance of the LGBTIQ+ community – some destinations welcome folks with enthusiasm, some adopt an attitude of sober tolerance, and others have anti-LGBTIQ laws that carry jail time. Many of the islands' more conservative attitudes remain in place thanks to legacy colonial laws and religious influence, but attitudes are changing as progressive groups work for equality.

Destinations with LGBTIQ+ Scenes

When it comes to safety and community, several islands are good bets. The Dutch Caribbean – particularly Aruba and Curaçao – welcomes LGBTIQ+ travelers and offers great accommodation and nightlife options. St-Barthélemy also has a good reputation for being welcoming. Puerto Rico is known for a thriving LGBTIQ+ scene, particularly in San Juan, and it hosts queer-oriented events throughout the year, though discretion is suggested in more rural areas. The same goes for the US Virgin Islands – St Croix functions as the LGBTIQ+ hub, but other areas can lean more conservative.

PRIDE PARADES

Several islands host Pride events of varying size, though festivities are still getting back on their feet following the impact of the Covid-19 pandemic. Three of the most recognized are Pride Puerto Rico and Orgullo Boquerón – which both take place in June – and Curaçao Pride in September.

Trans Travelers

While policies and attitudes about homosexuality have progressed in most Caribbean destinations in recent years, protections for transgender people lag behind. Travel in a group, avoid security checkpoints when possible, and know where your embassy is in case of emergency.

THE FIGHT FOR EQUALITY

Former English colonies tend to have a tougher reputation when it comes to LGBTIQ+ travel. Jamaica has laws prohibiting same-sex intimacy for men, and public opinion is quite conservative; assaults on the local community are common. Barbados, Antigua and Barbuda, and St Kitts and Nevis recently ruled their anti-homosexuality laws unconstitutional, but LGBTIQ+ rights in these places are nascent and conservative attitudes remain.

Bars

San Juan, Puerto Rico, has one of the highest concentrations of gay-oriented establishments in the Caribbean, ranging from LGBTIQ+-owned hotels to drag bars to dance clubs. You'll find the most places in Santurce and along Calle Loiza.

RESOURCES

Local equal rights groups work throughout the islands – check your destination for resources. The Eastern Caribbean Alliance for Diversity and Equality (ECADE) is a regional organization that operates in the eastern islands from the Virgin Islands to Grenada. International database Equaldex partners with on-the-ground rights groups to summarize laws and attitudes around the world.

Accessible Travel

Accessibility varies widely across islands – and even within them – so disabled travelers will have to do some extra planning. That said, accessible infrastructure is improving across the region, and travelers are sure to find a destination that suits their needs.

Town vs Country

Most islands have a developed town center that frequently overlaps with the cruise port; these areas have the best sidewalks and accessible amenities. Further afield, infrastructure can be less robust.

Airport

Airports across the region vary in size and amenities, but all that host major airlines will have standard accessibility protocols in place. Smaller airlines may not be wheelchair accessible – call ahead to confirm.

Accommodations

Many resorts across the Caribbean do a good job of welcoming guests with disabilities, and providing accessible transport and amenities such as beach wheelchairs. Boutique hotels are hit-or-miss, especially those housed in historic buildings.

Fully Accessible Barbados

Barbados participates in one of the most developed accessibility programs in the Caribbean. Fully Accessible Barbados, run by the Barbados Council for the Disabled, offers accreditation for organizations that make their businesses more accessible. It also has an excellent online resource for navigating the island – find accessible beaches, restaurants, hotels, attractions, and more.

MUSEUMS

Accessibility in museums varies across the Caribbean – always call ahead. Larger museums may have audio accessibility for vision-impaired visitors, but this is not a given at most places.

Cruises

Cruising is one of the most accessible ways to see the Caribbean, offering a more streamlined point of entry. Be alert for tender-only ports, as these are generally not accessible for non-manual-wheelchair users.

Activities

Some dive outfits offer adaptive scuba and snorkel trips for those with limited mobility, and many large cruise ships organize accessible shore excursions tailored to avoid transport issues.

Americans with Disabilities Act

Many sights and hotels in Puerto Rico and the US Virgin Islands have wheelchair accessibility due to compliance with the Americans with Disabilities Act (ADA).

PUBLIC TRANSPORT

Public transport can be patchy across islands and even the more consistent services may not be wheelchair accessible. Travelers with disabilities will have more luck booking a taxi or car service independently.

BLUE-SEA.CZ/SHUTTERSTOCK ©

Diving, Aruba (p100)

HOW TO... Dive in the Caribbean

The Caribbean is one of the world's best places to scuba dive, and the number of dive sites and outfitters at your fingertips is almost unfathomable. Whether you're a beginner or an advanced diver, this spectacular region will enchant you with its incredible undersea life.

PADI vs SSI

PADI (Professional Association of Diving Instructors) and SSI (Scuba Schools International) are the two main certification companies you'll see in the Caribbean. Their course content is broadly the same, with the main difference being that PADI requires students to learn skills in a specific order while SSI incorporates a bit more flexibility in its curriculum. You'll likely see more PADI-affiliated shops, but the certifications are interchangeable (ie you'll be able to dive no matter which one you have). SSI courses tend to be a bit more budget friendly.

Shore Diving & Boat Diving

Shore diving is the most DIY way for divers to get to their sites – all you need to do is find the entry point on the shore and swim out. The Bahamas, Cayman Islands, Bonaire and Curaçao all have amazing shore-dive sites. However, shore sites can see more damage than deeper offshore sites due to factors such as weather and human impact, so boat diving may allow you to see more untouched reefs. In general, boat-diving excursions are more common across the islands.

Liveaboards

Sometimes called dive safaris, liveaboard dives are multi-day trips on larger boats that visit deeper water; they're also a good way to see sites that may not be accessible on a day-long boat trip. While liveaboards are mostly geared towards more advanced divers, some cater to beginners. If you want to see shipwrecks, sharks and other large animals, this is a good option.

Resources

PADI (padi.com/diving-in/caribbean) Provides a complete list of PADI-certified shops, resorts, and liveaboards across the Caribbean.

Undercurrent (undercurrent.org) A subscription-based guide that features every Caribbean island, providing seasonal planners, dive reports, articles and more.

GET CERTIFIED

Most courses consist of pre-study where students learn the basics online or in a classroom, a confined dive in a controlled space (like a pool) to get to know the equipment, and an open-water dive to explore skills acquired in the course. Most shops will recommend completing your independent study before arriving in the destination and then doing the confined and open-water course when you get there. The in-destination training takes about three or four days.

Some outfitters offer monitored half-day 'taster dives' for non-certified folks to see how they like the diving experience.

Nuts & Bolts

OPENING HOURS

Opening hours vary between rural and urban destinations, and often change due to weather and other temporary factors. Smaller islands tend to close down on Sundays – even businesses such as pharmacies and small groceries. Restaurants tend to close between lunch and dinner service. Call ahead when booking activities – many bricks-and-mortar businesses only open if they have preexisting bookings (ie no walk-ins).

Internet Access & Cell Service

Internet access is readily available in most locations. Cell service can be spotty in rural areas, so always download driving directions.

GOOD TO KNOW

Time zone
GMT -5, GMT -4

Country code
Varies

Emergency number
Varies

Population
44 million

Weights & Measures

Some Caribbean countries use the metric system, others use the imperial system, and a few use a confusing combination of both.

Smoking

Smoking is pretty tightly controlled in the Caribbean – there's generally no smoking inside or close to building entrances.

Restrooms

Except in major tourist areas, there are usually few public toilets, and those that do exist are often best avoided. Most restaurants have restrooms, but may require you to make a purchase before you can use them.

Insurance

It's extremely foolhardy to travel without insurance to cover theft, loss and medical problems. Check that your policy includes emergency medical-evacuation costs, and any activities deemed risky by insurers, such as scuba diving or other adventure sports.

PUBLIC HOLIDAYS

Public holidays differ across islands, but a few are pretty consistently celebrated and can cause closures and/or travel challenges. Keep the following dates in mind while you're planning your trip.

New Year's Day
January 1

Three Kings Day
January 6

Carnival February

Easter March/April

Christmas Day
December 25

Boxing Day
December 26

Other common holidays include Independence Day, Emancipation Day, Heroes' Day and Labor Day. The dates for these vary from island to island.

THE CARIBBEAN ISLANDS

STORYBOOK

Our writers delve deep into different aspects of life on the Caribbean Islands.

A History of the Caribbean Islands in 15 Places

Though still healing from an often tragic past, the Caribbean Islands embraces its unique history.

Bailey Freeman

p698

Music: Pride & Purpose

The melodic notes of this diverse region provide deeper insight into its history and heritage.

Tenille Clarke

p702

Sustainability in the Caribbean

The Caribbean Islands bring sustainability issues into sharp focus.

Wendy Yanagihara

p704

Saltwater Bliss: The Caribbean's Best Beaches

These world-class beachfronts are every vacationer's dream.

Tenille Clarke

p706

Caribbean Wildlife

On this chain of islands, biodiversity hot spots abound; immerse yourself in the most vibrant underwater wilderness.

Wendy Yanagihara

p710

Spend Wisely, Travel Fully

How to create beautiful memories without burdening your wallet.

Tenille Clarke

p712

Fort Amsterdam, Philipsburg (p550)

A HISTORY OF THE CARIBBEAN ISLANDS IN 15 PLACES

The Caribbean is a multifaceted patchwork of cultures from around the world, due largely to the mechanizations of large-scale colonization and slavery. Though still healing from an often tragic past, it has embraced its unique melange of indigenous, African, European and Asian history to become one of the world's most culturally vibrant destinations. By Bailey Freeman.

THE CARIBBEAN ISLANDS were first populated around 6000 years ago by Archaic-Age groups migrating from the mainland Americas. Indigenous people arrived in waves – first the Arawak-speaking Igneri and Taíno, and then the Kalinago (Carib).

With the arrival of the Spanish at the end of the 15th century, the world entered a new era as the rest of Europe's superpowers followed suit, establishing what would be some of their wealthiest colonies in the Caribbean. The money gleaned from these outposts fed the colonial machines, building some of the world's richest nations and helping them extend the tentacles of empire across the globe. These riches came at the expense of others: industrialized slavery defined the region, churning millions through its system over the course of three centuries.

After slavery was abolished via a series of laws throughout the 19th century, the European empires began to crumble and the Caribbean entered a more (though not entirely) independent existence. The 20th century brought global challenges to the Caribbean Sea – the islands experienced world wars, US neocolonialism driven by communism anxiety, new governments and new alliances.

Today the Caribbean exists as a unique cultural bastion, churning out music, art, literature and scientific work of worldwide importance.

1. Centro Ceremonial Indígena de Tibes

INDIGENOUS CEREMONIAL GROUNDS

One of Puerto Rico's most enthralling archaeological sites wasn't uncovered until 1975, when receding flood waters from a tropical storm unearthed ruins of an ancient ceremonial ground north of Ponce. Now known as the Centro Ceremonial Indígena de Tibes, this site prospered from roughly 400 CE to 1000 CE, starting with the Igneri (the area's oldest-recorded inhabitants) and followed by the Taíno.

The attached museum is filled with artifacts like *cemíes* (deities) and a skeleton found buried in the fetal position, a pre-Taíno tradition. The highlight is an outdoor exhibit exploring indigenous heritage in the Caribbean, which serves a searing critique of European colonization.

For more on Centro Ceremonial Indígena de Tibes, see p479.

2. Cueva de las Maravillas

UNDERGROUND PICTOGRAPH GALLERIES

Before the Spanish anchored their ships off Hispaniola's shores, the indigenous Taíno populated the region, establishing a rich culture that focused on farming and fishing. While most of this group was destroyed as a result of colonialism, the Taínos left behind a network of tunnels and underground galleries on the southeastern coast of the island, now known as Cueva de las Maravillas (Cave of Wonders). Discovered in 1926, paintings inside the cave depict funeral rituals, plants, animals and abstract designs that offer a glimpse into the life of Hispaniola's first inhabitants.

For more on Cueva de las Maravillas, see p318.

3. Bermuda's Shipwrecks

UNDER THE SEA

Bermuda's mythical status as the 'Devil's Isle' is largely attributed to the extremely dangerous (but spectacularly beautiful) reef encircling the mid-Atlantic archipelago. Today more than 300 ships lie beneath the surface of the waves – the world's highest concentration of shipwrecks – dating all the way back to the 17th century. Bermuda was actually first settled by Sir George Somers and his 150 crew and passengers after wrecking their ship on the reef following an encounter with an Atlantic hurricane. With a scuba certification you can explore many of these shipwrecks yourself, including colonial supply ships, Civil War–era blockade runners, and Spanish cruise liners.

For more about Bermuda's shipwrecks, see p678.

Centro Ceremonial Indígena de Tibes (p318)

4. Villa Santana

A PRESIDENTIAL EXILE'S HIDEOUT

Dueling lookout towers at Blackbeard's Castle and Bluebeard's Castle along with a 17th-century Dutch fort dominate the green hills above Charlotte Amalie, but St Thomas' signature city has a lesser-known story – visitors can walk in the footsteps of a historical legend.

Decades after his victory at the Alamo, Mexican general turned president Antonio López de Santa Anna found himself living in exile on St Thomas. He set up shop on a hill beneath the governor's mansion, directly above the harbor, and built a grand estate – the room where Santa Anna penned his memoirs is now part of the Villa Santana.

For more about Villa Santana, see p656.

5. Nelson's Dockyard

MARITIME HISTORY

Nelson's Dockyard in English Harbour is a Unesco World Heritage site that still functions as a working marina. The dockyard was originally constructed here to take advantage of the protection the harbor afforded when it came to hurricanes, and it assumed a position of importance as one of the only harbors big enough for ship repairs. Within the restored 18th-century buildings – which include an inn, restaurants and typical boatyard service/repair shops – is a museum detailing the history of the dockyard, maritime life and the role of slavery as the foundation on which it was all built.

For more about Nelson's Dockyard, see p79.

6. Wingfield Estate

A TIME CAPSULE OF ST KITTS' HISTORY

Local lore purports that the powerful Carib Chief Tegreman ruled over several islands from his home base on St Kitts, near the property now known as Wingfield Estate – petroglyphs recall the Amerindian presence here. In 1625, Samuel Jefferson II (forerunner of the US President) purchased this property, eventually growing sugarcane and prospering on the backs of slave labor. But in 1834, then-owner Lord Romney freed the enslaved Africans working here, defying instructions from the British Parliament.

Wingfield Estate continued to produce sugarcane into the 21st century. Nowadays, Old Road Rum Company has brought the rum distillery back to life.

For more about Wingfield Estate, see p509.

7. Kura Hulanda Museum

NEXUS OF CARIBBEAN SLAVERY

The Dutch West India Company used Curaçao as the main transit point for its slave ships throughout the 17th and 18th centuries, funneling thousands of enslaved people through Willemstad's port on their way to other islands in the Caribbean.

The Kura Hulanda Museum in Otrobanda explores the painful legacy that slavery created on the island and abroad, shedding light on the machinations of the trade itself and amplifying the voices of those who experienced the horror firsthand. The Kura Hulanda Museum also explores the history of precolonial African kingdoms and their effect on the cultural heritage of the Caribbean.

For more about Kura Hulanda Museum, see p118.

8. Educulture Junkanoo Museum

CULTURE, YESTERDAY AND TODAY

A retention of African heritage, Junkanoo began as a masquerade in the 17th century and it continues to be the heart and soul of Bahamian culture. The event takes place every Christmas and New Year in the form of a competitive parade. More than just a Christmas festival, Junkanoo is a painstaking creative lifestyle that is anchored in community and ritual traditions. Take an immersive tour of the Educulture Junkanoo Museum in Nassau to learn all about the history of this celebration and how it connects to the contemporary Bahamas.

For more about Educulture Junkanoo Museum, see p140.

9. Cap-Haïtien

HAITI'S REVOLUTIONARY HISTORY

The first successful slave revolt was born in the city of Cap-Haïtien; in 1791, Boukman, an enslaved revolutionary, presided over the now famous ceremony of Bois Caïman, alongside Cécile Fatiman. This ceremony would be the catalyst for the Haitian revolution, which would go on to inspire and influence revolutions all over Latin America and beyond. A curated tour starting from just outside the city at the Bois Caïman monument can provide a more in-depth understanding of the significance of this event – both for Haiti and Latin America. Cap-Haïtien is also a convenient jumping-off point for visiting Haiti's Unesco World Heritage site, Citadelle Laferrière and Sans Souci.

For more about Cap-Haïtien, see p376.

10. Pigeon Island National Park

NATURE AND NATIONAL HISTORY

Pigeon Island National Park is one of St Lucia's most-visited destinations, thanks to its natural beauty and lengthy history. French pirate François 'Jambe de Bois' Le Clerc (jambe de bois translates as 'peg-leg') was the first European to arrive in St Lucia, using Pigeon Island as a vantage point for targeting passing Spanish ships. The Dutch, the English and the French all followed, their efforts at colonization largely thwarted by fierce resistance from the Kalinago (Caribs). The English eventually gained control over the area in the late 1700s, building Fort Rodney on Pigeon Island – today, visitors can explore these ruins.

For more about Pigeon Island National Park, see p538.

11. Memorial ACTe

A MEMORIAL TO A PAINFUL HISTORY

Built on the site of the Darboussier sugar factory along the waterfront of Pointe-à-Pitre, the Memorial ACTe cultural center tells the history of Guadeloupe and slavery in the Caribbean at large. More than a museum, the building itself is a sculptural shrine dedicated to the history it explores. It features silvery, mesh-like walls – designed to evoke local fig trees – that encase a black box built to represent the Black people of the Caribbean. The facades feature pieces of quartz that symbolize the souls who were victims of slavery. In addition to its permanent exhibitions, the Memorial ACTe is also an arts center and congress hall.

For more about Memorial ACTe, see p349.

12. Magnificent Seven

ARCHITECTURE IN POLITICS

Architecture and history buffs will discover a double whammy of delight at Queen's Park Savannah in Port of Spain; here stand the Magnificent Seven, a collection of early 20th-century mansions that represent a tour through Trinidad and Tobago's political history. Built in a variety of unique styles – French Colonial, Indian Empire and Scottish Baronial, to name a few – these mansions have served several roles of international importance. The homes were commandeered by US military forces during WWII, White Hall was the office of the Prime Minister, and Stollmeyer's Castle was used to host foreign dignitaries.

For more about the Magnificent Seven, see p598.

13. Cuartel Moncada

CASTRO'S FIRST MOVE

Santiago de Cuba is where the Cuban revolution began – in 1953, Fidel Castro led 150 revolutionaries in an attack on the Cuartel Moncada, Fulgencio Batista's second-most important military garrison. The attack was quelled and many of the guerrilla fighters killed or imprisoned, but it put Castro and his movement on the map and set in motion the series of events that would lead to the eventual overthrow of Batista's government.

Today the barracks contain a museum dedicated to the events of that July day in 1953 – it features military artifacts, attack plans and photos of the fallen.

For more about Cuartel Moncada, see p248.

14. Bob Marley Museum

HOME OF A LEGEND

On Hope Rd in Uptown Kingston, Jamaica, the Bob Marley Museum is a fitting memorial to one of Jamaica's most famous sons. Marley lived and recorded in this large, creaky wooden house from 1975 until his death in 1981. Tours give an intimate window into his life, the house left as it was, from the simple bedroom and Marley's favorite denim stage shirt to the kitchen where he used to cook. The recording studio turned exhibition hall out back features some wonderful photographs of Marley performing live, while the bullet holes at the rear of the house from a failed assassination attempt add a sobering note.

For more on the Bob Marley Museum, see p389.

Cuartel Moncada (p389)

15. Fort George

FROM COLONIALISM TO THE COLD WAR

Perched high above the capital, Fort George has borne witness to much of Grenada's tumultuous history. Built by the French in 1705 to defend the colony from the British, it hosted troops from both nations over the years, as control of the island repeatedly changed hands.

But it was in 1983 that the fort became the scene of one of the most shocking events in modern Caribbean history. Prime Minister Maurice Bishop and 10 of his colleagues were shot in the interior courtyard by radical elements within the revolutionary government, leading to the infamous US invasion less than a week later.

For more about Fort George, see p330.

MUSIC: PRIDE & PURPOSE

The melodic notes and sounds of this diverse region provide deeper insight into its reverence for history and heritage. By Tenille Clarke.

THE PASSION OF Caribbean people is often characterized by a symphony of sights, smells, tastes and, most notably, sounds. From every car, at every bar, during every fete – where strangers meet, greet, dance and smile – the soundtrack of our dynamic music scene permeates every aspect of the lives we live. But rhythm and groove aside, the Caribbean is much more than the party atmosphere.

Caribbean music is inherently purposeful; singers, songwriters and musicians form a social bedrock that helps to tell the stories of a region that has weathered many historical, ancestral and cultural storms over time. Physiographically, many would argue that we are made up of the island chain that excludes European dependents. However, the music paints a more in-depth picture. It is a source of pride, pain, play and promise.

With dozens of derivatives to satisfy your listening pleasures, familiarize yourself with these genres of Caribbean music, and intimately experience the power of sound and song.

In a class of its own when it comes to caustic public commentary, the birth of

Steel-pan band, Philipsburg (p550)

calypso music can be traced back to African heritage in the 1700s as an act of resistance. Calypsonians – who were formerly known as chantuelles, the French patois term for 'storytellers' – frequently used their melodious compositions to challenge authority, the status quo and to speak out against daily social injustices faced by the masses. Legendary calypsonians such as Lord Kitchener, The Mighty Sparrow and Calypso Rose routinely used double entendre, or double meaning, to covertly convey messages in calypso songs often seen to be socially unacceptable, politically offensive or salacious. Today, calypso can be heard in Trinidad and Tobago, Dominica and other islands.

THE SOUNDS OF THE GWO KA – OR 'LARGE DRUM' – ARE TIED INTO GENERATIONS OF AFROCENTRIC HERITAGE AND TRADITIONS IN THE REGION.

A direct evolutionary product of calypso, soca's genesis – originally spelled sokah - was created to bridge the gap between African and Indian culture, which predates the 1970s. Cultural icon Garfield 'Ras Shorty I' Blackman is heavily credited as a pioneer of the genre, and with its fusion of percussive indentations and an abundance of drums, the crossover effect has been undeniable. With Carnival as the vehicle for this new-age sound, soca birthed subgenres such as chutney soca, dennery in St Lucia, bashment soca in Barbados, bouyon in Dominica and 'jab' in Grenada.

With a blended use of African folk songs, rhythm and blues, jazz, mento, rocksteady and ska, reggae music is connected to the Rastafari movement, where artists are seen as vessels of truth and messengers of peace and unity. Global icon Bob Marley was one such example; he popularized reggae music in the 1960s with his band, The Wailers. Today, reggae music holds an undeniable reign in modern popular music for Jamaica and the Caribbean diaspora.

Stylistically connected to merengue, kompa was introduced in the 1950s by maestro pioneer Nemours Jean-Baptiste. This form of dance music often sings about love and romance, and incorporates a big brass sound to its celebrated homegrown style. However, it's the tanbou beat and brass accompaniment from stars such as Alan Cavé, Sweet Micky and Nu-Look that make this music truly special.

Formed in the 1960s, salsa music's distinct sound features a wide array of Afro-Cuban and Afro-Caribbean rhythms and sounds – most notably, bell patterns, maracas, bass strings and impassioned Spanish lyrics. This high-energy music is popular throughout Latin America and the Spanish-speaking Caribbean, including Puerto Rico and Cuba.

Loosely meaning 'to party' in French Antillean Creole, zouk's success began in the 1980s, thanks to global band sensation Kassav'. The sounds of the *gwo ka* – or 'large drum' – are tied into generations of Afrocentric heritage and traditions in the region. Caribbean countries such as Martinique, Guadeloupe, St Lucia and other islands with a heavy French influence continue to hold this style of music close – the indigenous pride and joy of a region that doubles as a sonic testament to the region's innovative approach to music.

Street musicians, Havana (p220)

SUSTAINABILITY IN THE CARIBBEAN

Microcosms of the planet, the Caribbean Islands bring sustainability issues into sharply relevant focus as some of the planet's most vulnerable places to short- and long-term effects of climate change. By Wendy Yanagihara.

SURROUNDED BY THE clear waters of the Caribbean Sea, this island chain's overarching allure comes from its pristine waves washing up on peaceful sunny beaches. Most Caribbean island economies rely nearly exclusively on tourism based on this archetypal vision of an island paradise. At the same time, that very tourist traffic increases the need for sustainable practices to preserve the thriving coral reefs, colorful communities and clean beaches that make it paradisiacal.

While islands like Jamaica and Dominica do receive adequate rainfall, with aquifers and surface water resources that support the population, many other Caribbean islands do not. Islands less blessed by precipitation depend on desalination plants to provide fresh water for residents and the tourist populations.

On its face, desalinating seawater on Caribbean islands appears to be the simplest solution to sourcing fresh water. In actuality, the process of removing salt from seawater results in a concentrated brine that must be pumped back into the sea or otherwise distributed on land. When discharged into the sea, the excessive salinity of this brine is toxic to marine ecology, and over time can

Angelfish and coral reef, Jamaica (p382)

damage or kill reefs near desalination sites.

Local communities may use a combination of groundwater infrastructure, individual water catchment systems, and desalinated and imported bottled water; large resorts often build their own desalination plants to run their operations. Cruise ships also use onboard desalination systems to support their floating cities. As a visitor, consciously minimizing your water use is a key and easy way to tread more lightly.

As with limited water, local resources like queen conch populations are under pressure. Conch traditionally provided an inexpensive, readily available source of protein on many islands and remains a favorite – conch fritters, conch curries and spicy conch salads embody the taste of the Caribbean. Sustaining these food sources for an ever-increasing human population has meant that governments like the US Virgin Islands have closed conch fishing during their spawning season and enforced minimum size regulations to allow them to grow to maturity and support reproduction.

ON THE ENERGY FRONT, THE CARIBBEAN REGION POSSESSES A NATURAL WEALTH OF SUNSHINE, TRADE WINDS AND TECTONIC ACTIVITY THAT IS ALREADY IN PLAY, PROVIDING RENEWABLE ENERGY FOR SOME CARIBBEAN ISLES.

The warming climate – resulting in unpredictable weather and warming waters changing the marine ecosystem – has also affected conch reproduction and migration in such a way that finding mature conch has meant moving to deeper waters. Sustaining the conch population in The Bahamas, where the conch is emblematic of the Bahamian identity, also sustains the fishers and their traditional industry. Placing limits on a way of life in order to sustain it has proven more challenging here, illustrating the complexity of balancing cultural values with ecology management and unpredictable climate change variables.

But small changes to old ways have happened throughout the islands. Antigua and Barbuda was the first Caribbean island nation to ban plastic bags in 2016, and since then, single-use plastic bans have been adopted in around a dozen Caribbean nations, including Aruba, Barbados, Dominican Republic, and Trinidad and Tobago.

Conch shell

And on the energy front, the Caribbean island region possesses a natural wealth of sunshine, trade winds and tectonic activity that is already in play, providing renewable energy for some Caribbean isles. The volcanic islands of the Caribbean chain certainly have potential to harness geothermal power, but thus far Guadeloupe is the only one with a geothermal plant, which generates about 11% of the island's electricity. Wind farms have been established on Aruba, Jamaica, Cuba and Curaçao, among other islands, and it's within the realm of possibility that some nations could achieve 100% renewable energy within the next decade. Solar microgrids have popped up in Puerto Rico and The Bahamas, while in Barbados solar accounts for over 10% of energy.

With visitors flying or cruising in from all over the world to enjoy the islands' thriving seas, dreamy beaches and sunny weather, their human impact might be mitigated by using those very resources. The beauty of the Caribbean islands' breezes, sun and sea may also sustain their salvation.

Parlatuvier Bay (p610)

PHBCZ/GETTY IMAGES ©

SALTWATER BLISS
THE CARIBBEAN'S BEST BEACHES

Offering a vast tropical biodiverse paradise, these world-class beachfronts are every vacationer's festival dream. By Tenille Clarke.

THE WARMTH OF the Caribbean region isn't just found in perennially brilliant, sun-soaked weather. It's in the way locals unapologetically live: the innate sense of hospitality towards visiting guests as a sumptuous home-cooked meal is lovingly served; the way bodies hypnotically twist and waistlines turn to the first bassline beat of a classic dancehall song; when smiles are welcomed forms of currency, whether exchanged for a hug at a church or a bar; and where diversity of culture, race and history is not separated but harmoniously honored and celebrated.

Caribbean beaches are perfect. Throughout this archipelago of ecological wonders – with powdery sands and crystal-clear saltwater that stretches as far as the eye can see – these beaches are a source of food, joy and freedom. This is bliss.

With some of the most mesmerizing beaches in the world, choosing the Caribbean's best in show is no easy feat. However, if you're a seasoned traveler, your curiosity may be piqued for your next getaway by some of these hidden coastal treasures. And if you're a first-time visitor to the Caribbean desperately seeking serenity in a world laden with bustle and noise: welcome to your next island paradise.

Seven Mile Beach, Jamaica

There's no shortage of beaches on the pristine west coast of Jamaica. However, Negril holds one natural gem that showcases the best of what the home of reggae music has to offer – Seven Mile Beach, which was once under the rule of pirates according to the island's history. If you're looking for marine sightings such as seahorses, stingrays and a variety of fish, then look no further than this beach surrounded by precipitous cliffs and swaying palm trees.

With bars and eating options nearby, amenities are a stone's throw away from the beach – but if walking isn't your pleasure, consider taking a horseback ride. Seven Mile Beach is also perfect for scuba diving and snorkeling. Make sure you plan your trip here early: it's a 90-minute drive from Sangster International Airport.

Parlatuvier Bay, Tobago

If you're willing to make the trek past the southwest peninsula of Trinidad's sister isle – which is home to popular beaches such as Crown Point, Pigeon Point and Mt Irvine – you won't be disappointed with the serenity and near-untouched beauty of Parlatuvier Bay. The winding Northside Rd leads you to this beach, located an hour's drive from Tobago's ANR Robinson International Airport. It's known for its warm

seawater, distinctly clean air and active fishing industry. Make a quick pit stop on the paved area before descending the hillside for an incredible panoramic view. If you're an adventurous nature-seeker, the Parlatuvier Waterfall is also nearby for a two-in-one ecological special.

Maho Beach, Sint Maarten

Maho Beach is truly the ideal Caribbean trifecta of land, sea and air: in addition to the picture-perfect views, there's one daily ritual that may interrupt your jaunt in the sun. Visitors and aviation enthusiasts often flock to this beach to marvel at the high-decibel thrill of landing and departing flights from nearby Princess Juliana Airport. Located on the Dutch side of the island, there's also a stunning coral reef nearby that's perfect for snorkeling. In addition to zooming aircraft above, Sunset Bar and Grill is close to the shoreline – not just for your dining pleasure, but also for the brilliant views at the close of day.

Horseshoe Bay Beach, Bermuda

In the heart of South Shore Park, a bike ride or a brisk walk will lead you to this iconic crescent of rose-gold-tinted sand. As one of the most popular beaches in this British territory, Horseshoe is named for its shape, where a coastal trail connects a number of other beaches. There is snorkeling and boogie boarding in abundance here, and the Horseshoe Beach Cove has a natural pool that's suitable for groups with small children who are seeking shallower water action. This Southampton parish favorite also hosts a few land-based activities, including weekly volleyball showdowns and the Bermuda Sandcastle Competition held every year in the month of September.

Magazine Beach, Grenada

Grenada has consistently been the center of global adulation for its award-winning variety of spices – and equally as impressive are the Spice Isle's spectacular beaches that can be found in abundance on this small island that's only 21 miles long. It should be no wonder, therefore, that the Magazine Beach is your seaside 'aloha': say hello and hop over to this spot on the southern coastline as soon as you land at Maurice Bishop International Airport, or bid goodbye by taking a last-minute dip in its warm waters just before you depart. Snorkeling and kayaking are regular activities here, and this Point Saline spot is as convenient as it is beautiful, making it a postcard-perfect way to experience the island.

Brandon's Beach, Barbados

Walking distance from the cruise-ship terminal and close to the Mighty Grynner Hwy, Brandon's Beach is both ideal and idyllic for the tourist seeking fun in the sun. It shares its white sandy borders with

Sugar Beach, St Lucia (p524)

Brighton Beach, and visitors have the option of renting an umbrella and lounge chairs to maximize a full day of rest and relaxation. If water sports are your thing, Jet Skis and snorkeling are readily available – and for the kids, there is a water park conveniently located just off the coastline. Finish your day with a spectacular view of the sunset from Rascals Bar at this calm and easily accessible landmark treasure located in St Michael's parish.

Playa Paraíso, Cuba

As the largest island in the Caribbean region, Cuba certainly does not lack options in the beach department. However, venturing away from the southern mainland will lead you to Cayo Largo del Sur – the home of this tourist attraction that loosely translates to 'Paradise Beach.' The name here is intentional and self-explanatory: a summation of powdery white sands, turquoise-blue waters and a host of marine life, including starfish, shellfish, sea turtles and iguanas that can also be spotted throughout the island. Although Playa Paraíso is off-limits to US visitors, the world-class seaside location is simply peace personified for the traveler agog with curiosity.

Sugar Beach, St Lucia

If you're looking for a bit of ecological charm with your beach run, then Sugar Beach – also known as Jalousie Beach – is the perfect spot for you. With an inimitable view of the World Heritage–listed Pitons – two dormant volcanic plugs located on the southwestern coast – and shrouded by acres of lush tropical rainforest, this majestic location holds the best of what the 'Helen of the West Indies' has to offer. You don't have to be a guest at the nearby resort of the same name to access this dreamy stretch, and snorkeling is also readily available at the nearby Anse des Pitons Marine Reserve.

Horsehoe Bay, Bermuda (p677)

LES ANSES D'ARLET IS AN ACTIVE FISHING VILLAGE, SO DELICIOUS FRESH SEAFOOD DAILY IS THE NORM AND NOT THE EXCEPTION.

Pink Sands Beach, The Bahamas

Timeless, magical elegance. Located on the lightly populated Harbour Island – with less than 2000 residents – here the unusual sand color is only rivaled by its aquamarine-blue water stretching out for 3 miles. The pastel prettiness is caused by foraminifera, red-shelled marine animals whose exteriors crush and blend with the formerly white sand. The beach is relatively private and serene, making it perfect for a meditative day of swimming, snorkeling and sunbathing.

Grande Anse d'Arlet, Martinique

Take a scenic 45-minute drive from the Aimé Césaire International Airport in Fort-de-France to the rural community of Les Anses d'Arlet, and you will find this hidden coastal jewel of Martinique. The view from the pier of Église St-Henri des Anses-d'Arlet – known among English speakers as St Henry's Catholic church – is as picturesque as they come. Les Anses d'Arlet is an active fishing village, so delicious fresh seafood daily is the norm and not the exception. Have lunch courtesy of the catch of the day under the shade of palm trees on the sand and mingle with friendly residents for an authentic, charming Caribbean experience.

Darkwood Beach, Antigua & Barbuda

Take a photo in front of the wooden, colloquial 'Wadadli' sign, in Antigua and Barbuda's national colors, and prepare to make your friends jealous in an instant. The hillside landscape makes for the perfect backdrop for this popular west-coast spot, one of 365 beaches across the islands. On a clear, sunny day, you can glimpse a view of neighboring Montserrat island from Darkwood Beach – it's only about an hour away via ferry and 20 minutes by plane. The most enchanting feature at Darkwood is the dazzling sunset – the best kind of Caribbean gold that can never be bought.

CARIBBEAN WILDLIFE

Biodiversity hot spots abound. By Wendy Yanagihara.

MILLENNIA-OLD RHYTHMS SILENTLY persist in the Caribbean as some of the most real magic that can be experienced. You can find it just by lowering your masked face beneath the surface of the water, when this simultaneously otherwordly and firmly earthbound marine environment comes into focus. Tiny reef fish dart away on your approach, and as you ease into the flow of moving like a marine mammal through the water, you might notice a parrotfish audibly crunching coral, a spiny lobster trundling beneath, or the swish of a hawksbill turtle cruising placidly into your peripheral vision.

Marine Life

Hawksbill, olive ridley, green leatherback and loggerhead turtles return to their natal beaches around the Caribbean islands to lay their eggs. It's possible to see nesting or hatching turtles from Cuba to Trinidad and Tobago between roughly March and October, depending on the species. On many islands, conservation programs welcome volunteers to observe and safeguard hatchlings on their first vulnerable journeys to the sea. Encounters with freely swimming sea turtles can happen year-round.

Similarly, some whale species can be spotted in the Caribbean islands throughout the year, but the most spectacular

Pictured clockwise from top left: Lizard; Loggerhead turtle; Frigate birds, Codrington (p89); Angelfish

whale-watching experiences come during the humpback-whale migration season. As the pods move through warmer waters, it's possible to see humpbacks lingering in places like Turks Island Passage in Turks and Caicos or Samana Bay in the Dominican Republic. The humpback migration season runs from mid-January to April.

Rarer aquatic mammals include the West Indian manatee and its subspecies the Antillean manatee, whose small populations reside in rivers and estuaries of The Bahamas, Curaçao, Cuba, the Dominican Republic, Jamaica and Puerto Rico. These charismatic mammals represent the biggest fauna in the marine environment, but the wilderness beneath the waves is where the Caribbean islands' greatest biodiversity is found.

Caribbean reefs make up 9% to 10% of the planet's coral reefs, harboring around 65 species of hard corals and 500 to 700 fish species. Off Cuba's southern coast Cuba, the archipelago Jardines de la Reina, for example, is one of the Caribbean's major marine protected areas (MPAs). As no fishing is allowed, its reefs thrive with corals like elkhorn coral and sea fans, and with the abundant diversity supported by a healthy reef. A rainbow of wrasses, parrotfish, tangs and sergeant majors populate these 'Queen's Gardens.'

Meanwhile the entirety of Bonaire's coast makes up the Bonaire National Marine Park, protecting the pristine fringing reefs that contain around 50 species of corals and over 350 species of reef fish, like green morays, queen triggerfish, goliath groupers, angelfish and trumpet fish. Bimini in The Bahamas is known for its healthy population of hammerhead sharks, while various shark species like Caribbean reef sharks, nurse sharks and blacktip reef sharks are commonly seen throughout the region. Eagle rays and southern stingrays are among the most frequently spotted rays.

Free-Flying Caribbean Color

Above the surface of the sea, on Barbuda, the largest breeding and nesting colony of frigate birds wheels above a lagoon of protected mangroves. With the largest wingspan-to-body-weight ratio of any bird, they can soar for hours for great distances, returning to roost at sunset without having landed anywhere since leaving their nesting sites in the morning. Protected salt flats in southwestern Bonaire provide breeding and nesting grounds for flamingos, creating a showy pink profusion of these unique wading birds. In Puerto Rico, witness the winter migration of 40,000 birds at the salt flats of Cabo Rojo.

The smallest bird in the world, the diminutive bee hummingbird, is endemic to Cuba. Weighing in at around 0.09oz (2.5g; males are even smaller), the female bee hummingbird lays eggs the size of a coffee bean. Much like this tiny gem, over 100 of the Caribbean's 700 bird species are endemic to one particular island. The birdsong of tanagers, trogons and bullfinches fills the soundscape, with pelicans and ibis among the islands' shorebirds. Other rarities include the critically endangered Puerto Rican parrot and St Vincent parrot, endemic to their respective islands.

Terrestrial Island Dwellers

Larger terrestrial mammals in the Caribbean have generally been eradicated over the centuries by human occupation. Feral donkeys and goats roam the rural areas of various islands. Some larger rodent species that remain include the rabbit-sized hutia in Cuba and The Bahamas, various species of fruit bats and the introduced Indian mongoose, which has wiped out some endemic species.

The Antiguan racer represents one wildlife success story, despite its population being hunted to extinction by mongoose – or so it was believed. Though now one of the rarest snakes in the world, this non-poisonous little gray snake is no longer the rarest, as a tiny population survived on Antigua's offshore islands and continues to grow. Various species of anoles, geckos and iguanas are common through the islands, while rare species of skink and ground dragon remain endemic to their tiny island outposts.

Measures to protect many of the Caribbean's uninhabited islands have been the saving grace of many species dwindling in numbers. Conservation efforts, including reintroducing native flora and fauna in protected isolation, have effectively reversed population declines in targeted species.

On the inhabited islands, seasonal and dedicated whale-watching cruises, birdwatching hikes and dive trips showcase Caribbean wildlife at its most dramatic. But wildlife watching can be as easy as tuning in to the local birdsong or donning a mask and snorkel to commune with the corals.

SPEND WISELY, TRAVEL FULLY

Seizing Caribbean moments doesn't have to be a big burden on your wallet – here's how to create beautiful memories on a budget. By Tenille Clarke.

WITH LUSH MOUNTAIN ranges, jewel-toned beaches and mouthwatering delicacies at your fingertips and tastebuds, there's a silver lining to be revealed in every sandy crevice of the Caribbean. This region is more than just a cluster of nondescript islands and cays: it's also an amalgamation of vibrant cultures, fusional dialects, a layered history of many faces and spaces and, most impressively, it can be as laid-back or action-packed as your vacationing heart desires.

While the easygoing environment is perfect for relaxation, reflection and rejuvenation, many travelers are often roadblocked by the sometimes-steep price tags. The COVID-19 pandemic has created unexpected economic pitfalls for the average wanderlust, and reality hits quickly when faced with constrained financial resources and increasingly high expenses. However, there's no reason to disrupt your peace of mind when mapping out a financial blueprint for your next trip to this island haven.

From The Bahamas in the north, meandering downwards to the twin-island Republic of Trinidad and Tobago in the south,

Pictured clockwise from top left: Nevis Peak (p515); Trinidadian doubles (two fried flatbreads); Hunte's Gardens (p168); Great Bay, Philipsburg (p550)

the options are vast. Whether you're a solo traveler or a family-focused group, here are some key tips and tricks to live your best life on a budget as you plan your next Caribbean getaway – both your mind and purse will be left in a perfect state of happiness.

Travel Outside of Peak Season

For many travelers, the clarion call for Caribbean living usually peaks in the blisteringly cold winter period – for many, the glacial gloom that blankets North America and Europe from December to February. While the allure of warmer weather beats all for some, the caveat on the cost of travel has always been the seasonality of the Caribbean. So, if you're looking for a break from the monotony of 'winter wonderlands,' keep in mind that high-season periods in the Caribbean – such as Easter, Christmas and New Year's – will always translate to higher prices for flights, accommodations, car rentals and other activities.

This is especially the case for islands such as Jamaica, The Bahamas and St Kitts and Nevis, where civic holidays and festivals that close out the year can result in increased traffic of returning citizens. Since demand drives cost, consider planning your next Caribbean getaway during more affordable times of year such as May to June, or October. Although these months are technically during the hurricane season, hurricanes are statistically rare events that aren't likely to affect your travel plans. Most fortunately, the Caribbean only experiences two seasons perennially – rainy season, from May to October, and dry season, from November to April. This means that you won't pay too much of an opportunity cost if you decide to opt out of travelling during periods of low humidity and less rain. You can also put your credit-card points to good use – planning early is the major key.

Island-Hopping

Globally, it's no secret that the travel industry has been adversely impacted by the rising cost of flights, which have increased exponentially since the onset of the COVID-19 pandemic. In addition to choosing vacation packages with a Caribbean cruise line, here's the ultimate cheat code when it comes to visiting the Caribbean: island-hopping.

Many nations are geographically near each other, which, at the right time of year, can make multicity travel an attractive bonus when scoping out the region's island options. For example, from Trinidad, you can fly to Tobago in 20 minutes, Grenada in 40 minutes and Barbados in one hour. In the case of the French and Dutch territories that make up Sint Maarten, you can consider a day trip with a ferry ride to St-Barthélemy, Anguilla or Saba in less than an hour. For less than a cross-continental flight to Europe, if you plan smartly, you can make multiple Caribbean stops. Pack your swimwear and sunscreen – beaches in abundance are calling.

Street-Food Delights

The heart and soul of any destination is the food. At the table, it acts as the ultimate communicator where words and language barriers may fail. The Caribbean region is no different – and consisting of African, Indian, Chinese, British, French, Spanish and Dutch influences on the gastronomy landscape, there's no shortage of palate-pleasing excellence. Although exquisite fine-dining restaurant experiences are always a winner in any food-lover's book, they can be a drain on the average tourist's budget, especially for longer travel stints. The solution? Exploring the off-beaten path into the world of street food, which can lead you to unexpected five-star experiences.

Discover succulent jerk chicken served on a bed of rice and peas with a side of freshly fried plantains out of an unlikely van from a neighborhood vendor in the heart of Kingston, Jamaica. Head to the seaside village of Oistins in southside Barbados for the Friday night fish fry featuring the catch of the day. Or take a sunrise joyride for Trinidadian doubles – a sloppy sandwich made with pillowy-soft flat fried doughs, laced with curried chickpeas and its trusty sidekicks: tamarind sauce, cucumber and mango chutney. Whether you're in search of breakfast, lunch, dinner or snacks, Caribbean street food is an incredibly affordable alternative and can satisfy almost any craving – and at less than US$10 per day, this option will be less pressure on the wallet while also giving you the ultimate lesson on the diversity of a unique region's culture and people.

INDEX

4WD 647

Abacos 134-5
accessible travel 693
accommodations 42, 684, 685
Accompong 403
Acklins 150
activities 42-3, 50-1, 52-3, **52-3**, *see also individual activities*
adventure parks 316, 450, 469, 535, 551
Alligator Pond 399
Altos de Chavón 318
amber 300, 303
Anegada 188-9
Anguilla 57-71, **58-9**
  festivals & events 60-1
  itineraries 60-1
  planning 60-1, 71
animals 21, 710-11, *see also individual species*
Annie Palmer 415
Anse Bertrand 351
Antigua & Barbuda 72-93, **74-5**
  festivals & events 76-7
  itineraries 76-7
  planning 76-7, 93
architecture 13, 478, 675, 699, **478**
Arikok National Park 104-5
art festivals 107, 118
art galleries, *see also* museums, street art
  81C 657-8
  ArtCafe 92
  Artisa Gallery 107
  Aruba Atelier 102
  Basseterre Gallery & Restaurant 507
  Bermuda National Gallery 669
  Cathedral Labyrinth of Thorns 118
  Cayman National Gallery 203
  Creative Native 657-8
  Fig Tree Studio Art Gallery 82
  Jamaica Giants Park 409
  Masterworks Museum of Bermuda Art 669
  Musée des Beaux Arts 377
  My Gallery 102
  National Gallery of Jamaica 390
  National Gallery West 413
  Papèl Craft Centre 529
  Puerto Rico 461
  Space21.art 106
  Terrafuse 102
Aruba 38, 95-107, **96-7**, **101**
  festivals & events 98-9
  itineraries 38-9, 98-9, **38-9**
  planning 98-9, 107, 125

Bahamas 126-51, **128-9**
  festivals & events 130-1
  itineraries 130-1
  planning 130-1, 151
Bahía de Las Calderas 287
Bahía de Samaná 308
Bahía Fosforescente 482
Bankie Banx's Dune Preserve 70
Barahona 290
Barbados 153-71, **154-5**
  festivals & events 156-7
  itineraries 156-7
  planning 156-7, 171
barbecue 63-4
Barbuda, *see* Antigua & Barbuda
baseball 43, 281, 285
Basse-Terre (Guadeloupe) 344-8, **344**
Basseterre (St Kitts) 506-11, **506**
Bassin Bleu 369
Bath 425
bathrooms 695
Bathsheba 170
bats 207, 379, 402, 421, 711
beaches 10-11, 706-9, *see also* lagoons
  Alleyne's Bay 165
  Anse de Mays 355
  Anse du Belle 353
  Anse du Château 350
  Anse Dufour 448
  Anse La Roche 336
  Anse Mamin 527
  Anse Mitan 450
  Anse Noire 448
  Baby Beach 102
  Bachelor's Beach 115
  Bahía de las Águilas 291
  Balneario de Carolina 463
  Balneario de Rincón 494
  Balneario El Escambrón 460
  Bath Beach 170
  Bathsheba Beach 170
  Bathway Beach 331
  Batibou Beach 266
  Batts Rock Beach 165
  Bermuda 677
  Boka Kokolishi 113
  Bottom Bay 163
  Brandon's Beach 707-8
  Brownes Beach 160
  Cable Beach 141
  Cas Abao 123
  Cayo Jutías 230-1
  Cayo Levisa 230
  Cove Bay 70
  Crane Beach 163
  Crocus Bay 64
  Cyvadier 372-3
  Darkwood Beach 709
  Dead End Beach 413
  Dickenson Bay 88
  Doctor's Cave Beach 413
  Dos Playa 105
  Dover Beach 160
  Eagle Beach 103
  El Alambique 463
  English Harbour 80
  Exumas, The 148-9
  Fisherman's Beach 398
  Fort James Beach 88
  Frenchman's Beach 398
  Frenchman's Cove 423
  Gaulding Cay 142
  Gilligan's Island 482
  Gold Rock Beach 137
  Governor's Beach 205
  Grand Anse 330
  Grand Case 561
  Grand Turk 636, 638
  Grande Anse (Martinique) 448
  Grande Anse d'Arlet 709
  Grande Anse des Salines 350, 352, 448-9
  Grooms Beach 333
  Grote Knip 122
  Half Moon Bay 86
  Hellshire Beach 396
  Horseshoe Bay Beach 708
  Isla Verde 463
  Island Harbor 67
  Jabberwock Beach 88
  Jan Thiel Beach 124
  Kingstown 572
  Kite Beach 304
  Klein Knip 122
  La Caravelle 353
  La Jungla 482
  La Monserrate 469
  La Pared 469
  La Plage à Fifi 358
  La Plage de Grande Anse 347
  La Plage de Sinaï 445
  La Plage du Souffleur 358
  La Playita 312
  La Playuela 497
  Lac Bay 115
  Langley Resort Fort Royal 348
  Levera Beach 331
  Little Bay 64
  Long Bay Beach 406
  Magazine Beach 331, 708
  Maho Beach 708
  Mahogany Beach 418
  Mambo Beach 124
  Mangel Halto 101-102
  María La Gorda Beach 231
  Mayreau & Tobago Cays 577
  Miami Beach 160
  Morne Rouge 331
  Nevis 515
  Northeast Coast (Trinidad) 604
  Ocho Rios Bay Beach 418
  Palm Beach 103
  Paradise Cove Beach 137
  Parlatuvier Bay 706
  Paynes Bay Beach 165
  Pebbles Beach 160
  Petit Carenage Beach 336
  Pine Grove Beach 463
  Pink Beach 114
  Pink Sands Beach (The Bahamas) 146, 709
  pink-sand beach (Barbuda) 90
  Piñones 463
  Plage de Chapelle 353

Map Pages **000**

Plage de Grande Anse 348
Plage de La Datcha 353
Plage de la Feuillère 355
Plage de la Perle 348
Plage de Madiana 442
Plage de Malendure 346-7
Plage de Pain de Sucre 357
Plage de Petit Havre 353
Plage de Pompierre 357
Plage de Souffleur 353
Plage du Bourg 352-3
Playa Ancón 236
Playa Cabarete 304
Playa Caracas 473
Playa Carlos Rosario 475
Playa Encuentro 304
Playa Flamenco 475
Playa Fortuna 469
Playa Lagún 123
Playa Isla Verde 463
Playa María Aguilar 236
Playa Negra 473
Playa Ocean Park 460
Playa Paraiso 709
Playa Pilar 238
Playa Porto Mari 123
Playa San Miguel 469
Playa San Rafael 291
Playa Santa 482
Playa Sosúa 304
Playa Tamarindo 475
Playa Vacía Talega 463
Point of Sand 212
Prickly Pear Cays 66
Princess Diana Beach 92
Providenciales 624
Punta Bandera 469
Queen's Bath 142-3
Reduit Beach 535
Reggae Beach 418
Rendezvous Bay 70
Río San Juan 304
Rockley Beach 160
Runaway Bay 88
San San Beach 423
Savaneta Beach 102
Savannah Bay Beach 185
Scilly Cay 66
Seven Mile Beach (Cayman Islands) 205
Seven Mile Beach (Jamaica) 406, 706
Shark Hole 163
Shoal Bay East 66
Sint Maarten 553
Smith's Point 137
St Croix 650
St John 654
St Kitts 507, 511
St Thomas 659-60
St-Felix 353
Sugar Beach 709
Taino Beach 137
Te Amo Beach 115
Turners Beach 82
Turtle Beach 418
Varadero 224
Westpunt Beach 106
Winnifred Beach 423
Worthing Beach 160
Beauséjour 358
Beef Island 182
beignets 368
Belmont 410
Bequia 576-8, **577**
Bermuda 662-79, **664-5**
festivals 666-7, 669
itineraries 666-7
planning 666-7, 680-1
Berry Islands 136
bioluminescence 472, 481
bird-watching
Aruba 104, 106
Barbuda 90
Bonaire 113
British Virgin Islands 187
Cayman Islands 212
Cuba 225
Curaçao 121
Jamaica 403, 410
Puerto Rico 472
St Vincent 574
Tobago 614
Trinidad 593, 600
Bloody Bay (Cayman Islands) 210
Bloody Bay (Jamaica) 406
Blue Hole (Negril) 409-10
Blue Hole (Ocho Rios) 418
Blue Mountains 394
boat trips 20, 583, 637
Bahamas 141, 146
Barbados 165-6
Dominica 274
Dominican Republic 310
Guadeloupe 348
Jamaica 403, 406
Kingston 396
Puerto Rico 497
Trinidad & Tobago 593
Boeri Lake 270
Bogles 336
Boiling Lake 270
Boiling Nuclear Superheater Plant 494
Bonaire 39, 95-9, 108-15, **96-7**, **109**
festivals & events 98-9
itineraries 38-9, 98-9, **38-9**
planning 98-9, 115, 125
books 45, 374, 513
Boston Bay 424
Bouillante 347
Bowden Pen 427
breweries 137, 300
Bridgetown 158-63, **159**
British Virgin Islands 172-95, **174-5**
festivals & events 176-7
itineraries 176-7
planning 176-7, 194
Buccoo 609

Cabo San Antonio 231
Cachita 250
Calibishie 266
Callwood, 'Foxy' 193
*canchánchara*s 234
Cañón Blanco 490
Cañón de San Cristóbal 483
Cañonazo 222
canyoning 51, 345
Cap-Haïtien 376-7, **376**
car travel 686, *see also* driving tours
Route de la Trace 440
Ruta Panorámica 492
Carenage 330
Carnival 12, 43
Antigua & Barbuda 77
Bermuda 667
Carriacou 326, 336
Cuba 248
Dominican Republic 280
Guadeloupe 342
Haiti 364, 367-8
Martinique 437
Mas Dominik 262
Ponceño 456
Santiago 219
Sint Maarten 548
St John's Carnival 645
St Lucia's Carnival 523
St-Martin Carnival 548
Trinidad Carnival 590
Virgin Islands 645
Carriacou 334-6, **335**
cascading 51
Castara 610-14, **610**
Castries 530-3, **530**
Cat Island 144
caves
Arikok National Park 105
Bat Cave 207
Cueva de las Maravillas 318, 699
Darby Cave 92
Discoteca Ayala 234
Dondon 379
Exumas, the 149
Green Grotto Caves 421
Hamilton's Cave 150
Little Bay 64
Negril 406
Parque de las Cavernas del Río Camuy 490
Printed Circuit Cave 402
Rebecca's Cave 207
Tres Ojos 288
Windsor Great Cave 402
Cayes Jacmel 374
Cayey 464
Cayman Brac 41, 206-8, **206**
Cayman Islands 197-213, **198-9**
festivals & events 200-1
itineraries 40-1, 200-1, **41**
planning 200-1
caymanite 207
Cayo Coco 238
Cayo Guillermo 237-8
cell phones 695
chairlifts 551
Charlestown 512-16, **512**
charter boats 66
cheese 291
chocolate 266, 303, 332, 526, 533
chupacabras 489
churches & cathedrals
Aruba 106
Bermuda 675, 675
Cuba 233, 246, 250
Dominica 268
Dominican Republic 284, 319
Grenada 330
Guadeloupe 358
Haiti 377
Jamaica 392, 416
Martinique 438, 439
St Lucia 531
Ciénaga de Zapata 225
cigars 218
classic cars 224
climate 42-3, 690, 704-5
climbing 208, 442
Codrington 89-90, **89**
coffee 298, 394-5, 459, 487
Colonia Juancho 291
Columbus, Christopher 150
Compartición 299
Conch Island 191
Congo Plage 369
Coward, Noël 421
crabbing 145
crafts 369, 440
cricket 43, 76, 88, 538, 667
crocodiles 403
Crooked Island 150
Crown Point 605-9, **605**
Cuba 214-53, **216-17**
festivals & events 218-19, 240, 245
itineraries 218-19
planning 218-19, 252-3
cultural centers
Centro Ceremonial Indígena de Tibes 477, 698-9
Centro Cultural Polo Moñtanez 227
Centro León 300
Kalinago Barana Auté 268
Maroon 427
Memorial ACTe 700-701
Montego Bay 413
Curaçao 38, 95-9, 116-25, **96-7**, **117**
festivals & events 98-9
itineraries 38-9, 98-9, **38-9**
planning 98-9, 124-5
cycling 435, 515, 630

dancehall 392, 689
dancing 234, 392, 407, *see* dancehall, music, street parties
Darkwood Beach 82-3
Dean's Blue Hole 150
Death in Paradise 348
Deshaies 348
Désiles 444
Dickenson Bay 88
disabilities, travelers with 693
distilleries, *see also* rum
- Bahamas, The 141
- Bonaire 111
- Cuba 248
- Dominica 270
- Dominican Republic 303
- Grenada 331
- Guadeloupe 358
- Jamaica 402, 416
- Martinique 439, 445-6
- Puerto Rico 460, 471

diving & snorkeling 14-15, 50-1, 685, 694
- Anguilla 64, 67
- Antigua & Barbuda 83-4
- Aruba 103
- Bahamas 134-5
- Barbados 160, 165
- Bermuda 674, 680
- Bonaire 113, 114-15
- British Virgin Islands 189
- Cayman Islands 203, 205, 208, 210-11
- Cuba 231, 236
- Curaçao 121, 124
- Dominica 272
- Grenada 332-3
- Grenadines 580
- Guadeloupe 346-7, 348, 357
- Jamaica 406, 423
- Martinique 448
- Prickly Pear Island 187
- Puerto Rico 472-3, 475, 497
- Sint Maarten 551
- St Kitts 510
- St Thomas 656
- Union Island 584
- Turks & Caicos 624
- US Virgin Islands 650

Dominica 36, 255-75, **256-7**
- festivals & events 258-9
- itineraries 258-9
- planning 258-9, 275

Map Pages **000**

Dominican Republic 276-321, **278-9**
- festivals & events 280-1
- itineraries 280-1
- planning 280-1, 320-1

dominoes 373
donkeys 86, 110, 316, 396, 638
drinks 47, 288, 438, 459, 688, *see also* rum
driving tours
- Eleuthera 142-143, **143**
- Barbados 168, **168**
- Caicos 631-2, **633**
- Cayman Islands 204, **204**
- Dominican Republic 290-1, **291**
- Guadeloupe 351, **351**
- Jamaica 424-5, **425**
- St Kitts 509, **509**
- St Vincent 575, **575**

Duarte, Juan Pablo 285
Dunas de Baní 287
Dunmore Town 146
Dunn's River Falls 418

Eagle Beach 103
El Cobre 250-1
Elbow Cay 135
El Yunque National Rainforest 466-7
Eleuthera 146
Elizabeth Harbour 149
Embalse Hanabanilla 245
English Harbour 78-80, **78**
etiquette 44, 688, 689, 691
events, *see* festivals & events

Falmouth 415-16
family travel 51, 685
farm stays 684
festivals & events 12, 43, *see also* art festivals, food festivals, music festivals, Carnival, sailing festivals, street parties, *individual locations*
- Bermuda Kite Festival 666
- Fèt a Kabrit 358
- Goat Races 609
- Jounen Kwéyòl (Creole Day) 523
- *J'ouvert* 63, 505
- Junkanoo 131, 140, 700
- Maroon Festival 403
- Tobago Heritage Festival 591, 609
- Vincy Mas 569, 574

Ffryes Beach 83
Fidel Castro 699
films 45
fish frys 689
- Bahamas, The 137, 144
- Barbados 162-3
- St Lucia 533
- Trinidad & Tobago 600
- Turks & Caicos 626, 636

fishing
- Bahamas, The 136, 137, 150
- Caicos 621, 630
- Cuba 241, 245
- Dominican Republic 305
- Puerto Rico 497
- Tobago 611
- US Virgin Islands 648

Flamingo Bay 333
flamingos 114, 141, 189, 290
Fleming, Ian 421
food 26-7, 46-9, 688-9, *see also individual locations*
- cooking courses 262, 442

food festivals 47
- Bahamas Culinary & Arts Festival 131
- Barbados Food & Rum Festival 157
- Chocolate Heritage Month 523
- Fête des Cuisinières 343
- Mango Melee 645
- Nassau Paradise Island Wine & Food Festival 130
- Stush in the Bush 420
- Tropical Fruit Festival 645
- Union Island Conch Festival 568, 577
- Urlings Seafood Festival 77

food trucks 507, 538
Fort-de-France 436-40
forts
- Alexandra Battery 675
- Betsey's Hope 614
- Campbleton Battery 614
- Castillo San Felipe del Morro 459
- Christiansted National Historic Site 650
- Citadelle Laferrière 380
- Fort Hamilton 669
- Fort Charles 396
- Fort Delgrès 347
- Fort George 330, 699
- Fort James 88
- Fort Joséphine 356
- Fort King George 614
- Fort Napoléon des Saintes 356
- Fort Ogé 373
- Fort Oranje 109
- Fort Rodney 538
- Fort Segarra 659
- Fort Shirley 274
- Fort St Catherine 675
- Fort St-Louis 438
- Fortaleza de San Carlos de La Cabaña 222
- Fortaleza Ozama 285
- Fortaleza San Felipe 302
- Fortín Conde de Mirasol 472
- Fuerte Caprón 481-2

free-diving 636
Freeport 136
Freshwater Lake 270
Frigate Bay 506-11

gardens, *see* parks & gardens
gay travelers 692
George Town 41
Goldeneye 421
Grand Case 555-60, **555**
Grand Cayman 202-5, **202**
Grand Turk 635-8, **635**
Grande-Terre 349-53, **349**
Great Bird Island 83
great houses 205, 394, 403, 415, 416, 420, 516
Great Morass 403
Green Island 83
Green Turtle Cay 135
Grenada 37, 323-37, **324-5**
- festivals & events 326-7
- itineraries 325-6
- planning 326-7, 337

Grenada Island 328-33, **329**
Grenadines 564-9, 578-86, **566-7**
- festivals 568-9, 577
- itineraries 568-9
- planning 568-9, 585

Grenville 331
Guadeloupe 338-59, **340-1**
- festivals & events 342-3, 358
- itineraries 342-3
- planning 342-3, 359

Guánica 481
Guavate 464
Guayacán Centenario 481
Guevara, Ernesto 'Che' 243

Haiti 361-81, **362-3**
- festivals & events 364-5, 367-8, 375, 379
- itineraries 364-5
- planning 364-5, 381

Half Moon Bay 86
Hamilton 668-70, **668**
Hamilton, Alexander 513
Havana 220-2, **220**
health 686
heat exhuastion 686
helicopter ride 540
Hells Gate Island 83
Hemingway, Ernest 230, 237, 238
highlights 10-27

hiking 22-3, 43, 51
Antigua 80, 82
Aruba 105, 106
Bahamas 148
Bonaire 112-13
British Virgin Islands 180, 185, 187
Caicos 630
Cayman Islands 208
Cuba 245, 251
Curaçao 122
Dominica 268, 272
Dominican Republic 298-9
Grenada 333, 336
Guadeloupe 346, 348, 357
Haiti 369
Jamaica 394, 403, 410, 427
Martinique 444-5, 446
Nevis 515
Puerto Rico 467, 481, 483, 487, 489-90, 492
St Kitts 510
St Lucia 525, 529
St Vincent 574
St-Martin 560
Trinidad 599, 604
Union Island 583
US Virgin Islands 648, 652
historical sites, *see also* forts, great houses
Anally Sugar Mill Ruins 647
Balashi Gold Mills 101
Betty's Hope 86
Bibliothèque Schoelcher 438
Big Spring Heritage Site 67
Blackwoods Screw Dock 161
Cargill Salt Flats 115
Casa de Diego Velazquez 248
Central Azucarero Patria 241
Cultural Park Mangazina di Rei 111
Devon House 392
Garrison Savannah 161
George Washington House 161
Highland House 92
Houses of Parliament 161
Landhuis Bloemhof 118
L'Habitation Murat 355
Magnificent Seven 699
Nanny's Grave 427
Nelson's Dockyard 79-80
Nelson's Dockyard 79, 699
Old Gaol House 396
Pearls Airport 331
Wade's Green Plantation 634
Wingfield Estate 700
history 698-701
African Diaspora Heritage Trail 675
Antigua 699
Bahamas 698
Bermuda 672, 678, 699
Cuba 699
Curaçao 123, 700
Grenada 699
Guadeloupe 700-1
Haiti 700
Jamaica 412-13, 699
Lopinot 604
Nelson Island 600
Nevis 516
petroglyphs 92, 104, 266, 485, 490, 604, 699
Puerto Rico 485
Santa Rosa 604
Santiago de Cuba 699
slavery 634, 647, 634
St Croix 647
St Kitts 509, 700, **509**
St Lucia 700
Taíno people 67, 305, 318, 379, 420, 477, 485, 698
Trinidad & Tobago 614, 699
US Virgin Islands 699
WWII 659
Holetown 165, 168-9
homestays 684
Hope Town 135
Horatio Nelson 396
horseback riding 70, 170, 296, 469, 554, 647
hot springs & spas 264, 295, 347, 348, 425, 513, 527
hurricanes 43, 686, 687

Îlet à Cabrit 356
Îlet du Gosier 352
Indian River 274
insurance 695
internet 695
Isabela de Sagua 246
Isla Desecheo 497
islands 24
itineraries, *see also individual places*

Jacmel 366-9, **366**
Jamaica 382-429
festivals & events 386-7, 403
itineraries 40, 386-7, **41**
planning 386-7, 428-9
Jarabacoa 294-6
Jayuya 484-5
jazz music 106, 141, 218, 435
Jeans Bay 142
jewelry 207, 293, 300
Josiah's Bay 179-80
Jost Van Dyke 192-3
Junkanoo 131, 140, 700
Jurassic Park 310

kayaking 562
Anguilla 64, 67
Bahamas, The 142
Bonaire 115
British Virgin Islands 182, 187
Cayman Islands 211-12
Dominican Republic 304
Guadeloupe 347, 353, 355, 356
Jamaica 423
Puerto Rico 469, 472, 483
Turks & Caicos 624
US Virgin Islands 652
Kingston 388-92, **389**
kiteboarding 50, 51, 561
kites 364, 375, 666, 677
kitesurfing 83, 88, 189-90, 304, 353, 584
Klein Bonaire 115
Klein Curaçao 120-1
Kralendijk 39, 109-10
krioyo music 111

La Bajada 231
La Désirade 358
La Gran Piedra 251
La Parguera 481
La Perla 461
La Savane 438
La Soufrière volcano 572
La Vallée de Jacmel 375
Lac Bay 115
lagoons, *see also* beaches
Arroyo Salado 291
Blue Lagoon 318
Codrington Lagoon 90
Dudu Lagoon 313
Laguna de la Leche 241
Laguna Redonda 241
Le Grand Cul-de-Sac Marin 348
Port D'Enfer 351
Spanish Lagoon 101-2
Lake Enriquillo 290
Lakou Nouyòk 369
language 45
larimar 292-3
Las Galeras 312
Las Terrenas 312
Le Gosier 352
Le Moule 351
Le Rocher du Diamant 448
lechoneras 464
Les Anses d'Arlet 448
Les Saintes 356-7
lesbian travelers 692
Lewis, Sir Arthur 522-3
LGBTIQ+ travelers 692
lighthouses 106, 121, 208, 347, 425, 494, 540, 604
Lime Cay 396
Little Bay 64
Little Cayman 41, 209-12
Long Bay 86, 424
Long Cay 150
Los Acuáticos 228
Lost City of Atlantis 208
Luquillo 469

mamajuana 288
Manabao 298
mangroves 107, 182
Marie-Galante 355, 358
markets 507, 531, 657
Marley, Bob 389, 420, 699, 701
Maroon Festival 403
Marsh Harbour 135
Martinique 431-51, **432-3**
festivals & events 434-5, 437
itineraries 434-5
planning 434-5, 451
Mayreau & Tobago Cays 579-80, **579**
McBean, Mathilda 647
mobile phones 695
monkeys 21, 165, 168, 170, 511, 600
Mont Pelée 444
Montaña Redonda 316
Montego Bay 40, 411-12, **411**
Moore Town 427
Morne Pavillon 350
Morne Trois Pitons National Park 269-70
Morne-à-l'Eau 351
Morón 240-1
Mosquito Bay 472
Mount Gay Rum Distillery 161-2
mountain climbing 526
Mt Alvernia 144
Mt Obama 82
museums, *see also* art galleries, cultural centers, forts, great houses
African Caribbean Institute 391
African Diaspora Heritage Trail 675
Aloe Museum 102
Anguilla National Museum 64
Barbados Museum 161
Bermuda Heritage Museum 675
Bermuda Historical Society Museum 669
Betty's Hope 86
Bob Marley Centre & Mausoleum 420
Bob Marley Museum 389-90, 699

museums *continued*
- Cayman National Museum 203
- Dockyard Museum 79
- Dominica Museum 261-2
- Educulture Junkanoo Museum 140, 700
- Frank Perret Museum 446
- Instituto Duartiano 285
- Jewish Cultural Historic Museum 118
- Kura Hulanda Museum 118, 700
- La Savane des Esclaves 449
- L'Habitation Murat 355
- Little Cayman Museum 210
- Maritime History Museum 118
- Maritime Museum 396
- Money Museum 391
- Musée de la Pagerie 449-50
- Museo Caonabo 240-1
- Museo Castillo Serrallés 479
- Museo Chich'i Tan 111
- Museo de Archeología 233
- Museo de Historia de Trinidad 233
- Museo de la Historia de Ponce 478
- Museo de la Lucha Clandestina 248
- Museo de la Música Puertorriqueña 479
- Museo del Ámbar Dominicano 303
- Museo del Café de Puerto Ric 487
- Museo del Carnaval 248
- Museo del Cemí 485
- Museo del Ron y la Caña 285
- Museo de Naipes 221
- Museo Gregorio Luperón 303
- Museo Histórico de Culebra 475
- Museo Nacional de la Lucha Contra Bandidos 233
- Museo Romántico 233
- Museum of Antigua & Barbuda 88
- Museum of Nevis History 513
- Music Museum 391
- National Archeological Museum 102
- National Museum (Jamaica) 391
- National Museum of Bermuda 678
- Ron Santiago de Cuba Distillery 248
- Royal Naval Dockyard 678
- St Kitts National Museum 507
- Terramar Museum 110
- Tucker House Museum 675
- Turks & Caicos National Museum 638

music 111, 16, 45, 702-3, *see also* jazz music, reggae

music festivals
- Bequia Music Fest 568, 577
- Big In Jazz Festival 435
- Crop-Over Festival 157, 163
- Festival de Merengue 281
- Festival Internacional de Ballet 219
- Fête de la Musique 434
- International Gombey Festival 667
- Jazz Artists on the Greens 590
- Jazz Festival 218
- Maroon & String Band Festival 327
- Moonsplash Music Festival 69
- Rake & Scrape Festival 130
- Rebel Salute 420
- Reggae Sumfest 412
- Saint Lucia Jazz & Arts Festival 522
- St Kitts Music Festival 504
- SXM Music Festival 548
- Terre de Blues Festival 343
- Tobago Jazz Experience 590
- World Creole Music Festival 262

N

Nassau 140-1

national parks & reserves
- Antigua & Barbuda National Park 79-80
- Arikok National Park 104-5
- Armando Bermudez National Park 298
- Asa Wright Nature Centre 602
- Bacanao Biosphere Reserve 251
- Baths National Park 184-5
- Blue Holes National Park 144
- Booby Pond Nature Reserve 212
- Cabrits National Park 274
- Christoffel National Park 119, 122
- Clifton Heritage National Park 141
- Columbus Landfall National Park 637
- Cooper's Island Nature Reserve 674
- Devil's Bridge 86
- El Yunque National Rainforest 466-7
- Gorda Peak National Park 185
- Grand Etang National Park 333
- Guanahacabibes Biosphere Reserve 231
- Le Domaine d'Émeraude 446
- Lucayan National Park 137
- Maria Islands Nature Reserve 540
- Morne Trois Pitons National Park 269-70
- Parque Nacional Jaragua 291
- Parque Nacional Los Haitises 310
- Parque Nacional Los Tres Ojos 288
- Petite-Terre 350
- Pigeon Island National Park 538, 700
- Refugio Nacional Cabo Rojo 497
- Sage Mountain National Park 180
- Salt River Bay National Historical Park & Biological Preserve 650
- Seaside Nature Park 554
- Shete Boka National Park 122
- Tobago Main Ridge Forest Reserve 614
- Wallings Forest 82
- Washington Slagbaai National Park 112-13
- West Side National Park 144-5

Negril 40, 404-7, **405**

Nelson's Dockyard 79-80

New Providence 140-1

Nonsuch Bay 83

nutmeg 332

Ocho Rios 40, 417-18

opening hours 695

Oranjestad 102

Owen Island 211

palaces 285, 380

Paradise Island 141

paragliding 50

parasailing 648

parks & gardens
- Bermuda 669, 672
- Barbados 170
- Dominica 261
- Jamaica 409
- Cuba 228, 233-4, 251
- Dominican Republic 300
- Guadeloupe 358
- Martinique 439
- Trinidad 596, 598
- St Lucia 542
- Puerto Rico 472, 478

Pedernales 291

Pelican Bar 400

Península de Samaná 307-10, **308**

Petit Canal 351

Philipsburg 550-4, **550**

Pico Duarte 298

pigs 149

pirates 161, 231, 395, 654

Pirates of the Caribbean 192, 255, 266, 273, 274

planning 44-5, 712-13

Plantation Cove 419

plastic 691

podcasts 45

Ponce 476-9, **477**, **478**

popcorn 137

Port Antonio 422-3

Port Louis 351

Port of Spain 597-600, **597**

Port Royal 395-6

Portsmouth 273-4, **273**

Prickly Pear Cays 66

Prickly Pear Island 187

Providenciales 622-7, **623-8**

public holidays 695

Puerto Esperanza 230

Puerto Plata 302-3

Puerto Rico 452-99, **454-5**
- festivals & events 456-7, 494
- itineraries 456-7
- planning 454-7, 498-9

Punta Cana 314-16, **315**

Qua Qua 333

Queen Nanny 427

Queen's Bath 142-3

radio 45

Rafter's Village 427

rafting 50, 296, 427

railways 596, 670-1

rainforests 510, 612, 648

Map Pages **000**